# Adventuring with Books

Bibliography Series

# Adventuring with Books

**A Booklist for Pre-K–Grade 6**

**13th Edition**

**Amy A. McClure and Janice V. Kristo, Editors,**
and the Committee to Revise the Elementary School Booklist

With a Foreword by
**Rudine Sims Bishop**

National Council of Teachers of English
1111 W. Kenyon Road, Urbana, IL 61801-1096

Staff Editor: Bonny Graham
Interior Design: Doug Burnett
Cover Design: Joellen Bryant
Series Cover Design: R. Maul

NCTE Stock Number: 00732-3050

ISSN 1051-4740

ISBN 0-8141-0073-2

# About the NCTE Bibliography Series

The National Council of Teachers of English is proud to be part of a tradition that we want to share with you. In our bibliography series are four different booklists, each focused on a particular audience, each updated regularly. These are *Adventuring with Books* (pre-K through grade 6), *Kaleidoscope* (multicultural literature, grades K through 8), *Your Reading* (middle school/junior high), and *Books for You* (senior high). Together, these volumes list thousands of recent children's and young adult trade books. Although the works included cover a wide range of topics, they all have one thing in common: they're good books that students and teachers alike enjoy.

How are these volumes put together? The process begins when an educator who knows literature and its importance in the lives of students and teachers is chosen by the NCTE Executive Committee to serve as booklist editor. That editor then works with teachers and librarians who review, select, and annotate hundreds of new trade books sent to them by publishers. It's a complicated process, one that can last three or four years. But because of their dedication and strong belief in the need to let others know about the good literature that's available, these professionals volunteer their time in a way that is commendable and serves as an inspiration to all of us. The members of the committee that compiled this volume are listed in the front of the book, and we are truly grateful for their hard work.

As educators know, no single book is right for every reader or every purpose, so inclusion in this booklist is not necessarily an endorsement from NCTE. But it does indicate that the professionals who make up the booklist committee feel that the work in question is worthy of teachers' and students' attention, whether for its informative or aesthetic qualities. Similarly, exclusion from an NCTE booklist is not necessarily a judgment on the quality of a given book or publisher. Many factors—space, time, availability of certain books, publisher participation—may influence the final shape of the list.

We hope that you'll find this booklist a useful resource in discovering new titles and authors, and we hope that you will want to collect other booklists in the series. Our mission is to help improve the teaching and learning of English and the language arts, and we hope you'll agree that the quality of our booklists contributes substantially toward that goal.

Zarina M. Hock
Senior Editor

# Contents

# Foreword

The tradition of NCTE booklists is almost as old as the National Council of Teachers of English itself. According to J. N. Hook's 1979 history of the Council, *A Long Way Together,* the first such booklist, titled *A List of Books for Home Reading,* was published in 1912, one year after the founding of the Council. The main catalyst for the founding of the Council had been a protest against what amounted to a prescribed list of required readings for high school students, dictated by entrance requirements for prestigious schools and colleges such as Harvard. That mandatory reading list in turn had a major influence on the high school English curriculum of the time. That first NCTE reading list was simultaneously a recognition of the importance of appealing to the interests of a variety of students and a tacit criticism of one-size-fits-all English curricula. In addition, it recognized that reading and literature were not only school subjects but also important contributions to the quality of students' lives.

*Adventuring with Books* is the Elementary Section and elementary school–level successor to that first NCTE reading list. I first became aware of it in the early 1970s when I joined the Council. The first new *Adventuring* published during my membership years was the 1973 edition, edited by the late Shelton Root, and it contained annotations of 2,400 titles for children up to grade 8. This impressive number, culled from books published since the 1966 edition, reflected the dramatic increase in the number of books put out each year by the major publishers of children's books. Given the impossibility of keeping up with thousands of books every year, I eagerly looked forward to each new edition of *Adventuring* for reliable recommendations of a wide variety of good new and recent books, and for evidence of trends in the field. Compiled by dedicated and hard-working committees under the leadership of outstanding language arts educators, *Adventuring* has always been a useful resource for busy teachers, both preservice and inservice, who recognize the value of good literature.

It is perhaps paradoxical that, ninety years after the first NCTE booklist, we have virtually come full circle, and this last edition of *Adventuring with Books* appears in an environment in which school curricula are once again being highly influenced by national trends and issues. The benefits of reading literature can be easily forgotten in an atmosphere in which standardized test results are vested with political and financial power. In such an environment, *Adventuring with Books* stands as a reminder that books and literature can be far more than merely instruments for instruction; their real and lasting value is that they nurture imaginations, widen horizons, and illuminate life experiences. Helping teachers and parents open the doors to such adventures of the mind is the enduring contribution of *Adventuring with Books.*

Rudine Sims Bishop

# Acknowledgments

The 13th edition of *Adventuring with Books* is a project that represents the hard work and dedicated efforts of many educators—from university faculty to classroom teachers, librarians, and other educators around the country. We'd like to thank our chapter editors and their groups of reviewers for their efforts over the last three years and for their hard work and unrelenting desire to find the best books for each chapter. Each group read and reviewed a mountain of books and spent hours sharing, discussing, and negotiating which titles would make the final cut. This was a true labor of love, an exciting professional development project, and, at the same time, an incredible commitment from each satellite group. We also thank them for their patience and support, as every new memo we sent about the project added yet another detail or task to their already full plates.

We also acknowledge and give a huge round of applause to the many publishers who contributed books for this project. Without them our task would have been nearly impossible. Our publishers were more than willing to send books upon special request and regularly sent additional books for our inspection. We are truly grateful for their kind generosity over the years.

Our deep appreciation and thanks go to Nancy Groome of Ohio Wesleyan University and Theresa McMannus and Casey Scott from the University of Maine for their efforts throughout the project that encompassed everything from sending out requests for books to shipping them to our satellite groups around the country. We are indebted to them for the creation of our massive database and the meticulous final preparation of the manuscript.

We'd also like to thank the staff of NCTE, particularly Pete Feely, who never seemed to tire over our endless stream of e-mail messages, and Kurt Austin, who assisted us in the final stages of the project.

# Introduction

Welcome to the 13th edition of *Adventuring with Books: A Booklist for Pre-K–Grade 6.* This edition represents a curriculum project of the grandest magnitude and, at the same time, a labor of love. Building on the strong, proud heritage of past volumes, we hope that this edition will bring new titles into your classroom, inspire your teaching, and invite you to explore the wonders of bringing children and books together.

## Our Goal

First and foremost, our goal is to offer all our prospective readers—teachers, librarians, parents, curriculum coordinators, students of children's literature, and other educators—the best books for prekindergarten through grade 6 children. We believe these titles meet the highest literary standards and are excellent examples of books for the topic of each chapter for the years 1999–2001.

## Our Process

As with the last edition of *Adventuring with Books,* we believed it was important to invite both university teacher educators and classroom teachers from across the country to be contributors to this edition. We invited each chapter editor to bring together a group of educators whose purpose was to read and review children's books on a specific topic or genre published from 1999 to 2001. What an awesome task was before each of our satellite groups for the last couple of years! Their charge was to select around thirty to forty titles—the best of the best—on a specific topic or genre and representing a range of grade levels. In addition, the books needed to meet the rigorous criteria that each group developed for their chapter.

The books started to pour in, and off we went to read, ponder, and reflect on each new title. Groups met repeatedly to talk, argue, and discuss the merits of each book. This NCTE project was truly a gift for all of us; the professional development and collegiality we all enjoyed wouldn't be easy to duplicate. Reading, discussing, and selecting texts was a monumental task, as our chapter editors and groups would attest, but it was truly one that asked the best of each of us and represented professional development at its finest. Most of us felt keen regret when the task was over and were reluctant to stop. Some of us are still meeting! The opportunity to discuss wonderful books with like-minded colleagues has been so energizing that we felt compelled to stay together.

## Organization

For ease and familiarity, our chapter topics are fairly consistent with those of the previous edition. We've added a chapter on animals in fiction and also offer separate chapters on mysteries, traditional literature, and international literature. For ease in finding titles about specific cultural groups, we included full chapters on Asian and Pacific Island literature, African American literature, and Hispanic literature, as well as a chapter focusing on indigenous peoples.

You'll notice a new feature in this edition. At the beginning of each chapter, we've added a summary page listing the criteria used to determine the book selections, as well as a categorized list of all books in the chapter. This will be a handy and quick reference for the specific books chosen for each chapter. Certain books are starred on each summary list and again within the chapters, noting titles not to be missed.

Each chapter begins with a brief introduction to launch readers into the topic and book annotations. Criteria for choosing the books are discussed as well as the categories used to organize the titles. Annotations follow the chapter introduction and include all necessary bibliographic information plus an indication of interest level—(P) for primary-aged children, kindergarten through grade 3; (I) for the intermediate grades 4–6; and (ALL), indicating that the title will interest children across age levels. Many of the annotations include response suggestions as well as titles of related books.

Some titles within chapters contain only bibliographic information and not an annotation. This indicates that it is a duplicate title and will be found as an annotated book in another chapter. We found that many titles fit nicely in one, two, or more chapters, so we had to make some difficult decisions about where the book would find a primary home. All titles except those with full annotations elsewhere are numbered within each chapter. As in previous editions, readers can peruse the subject index to help locate specific titles on topics, or use the author, illustrator, or title indexes. A complete list of contributors is located at the end of the book.

## Conclusions and New Beginnings

We understand that this is the last edition of *Adventuring with Books.* We are honored to know that so many educators from across the country will see the results of their labor on this project. Now we ask you to enter the wonderfully exciting world of books presented in this volume. In the spirit of *Adventuring with Books,* we invite you to form your own circle of readers who will read the books recommended in this edition, study them, talk about them, question the author, examine illustrations, and enjoy some lively book talk. Then share the joy with children. Happy reading!

# 1 Science Nonfiction

**Janice V. Kristo and Rosemary A. Bamford**

*Contributing reviewers included Jan Elie, Mary Fusaro Evans, Candis M. Penley, Susan J. Pidhurney, Andrew W. Stephenson, Peg Welch, and Sandip L. Wilson.*

---

### Criteria for Excellence

- Accurate, interesting, and engaging format, layout, and illustrative materials
- Indications of author credibility and integrity
- Accurate and up-to-date scientific information presented in an understandable style
- Clear organizational flow and appropriate access features (e.g., table of contents, index, glossary, and appended materials)

---

## Botany

Gibbons, Gail. **The Pumpkin Book.** Holiday House, 1999.

Goodman, Susan E. **Seeds, Stems, and Stamens: The Ways Plants Fit into Their World.** Photographs by Michael I. Doolittle. Millbrook, 2001.

## Earth Science

Bortz, Fred. **Collision Course! Cosmic Impacts and Life on Earth.** Millbrook, 2001.

Ross, Michael Elsohn. **Earth Cycles.** Illustrated by Gustav Moore. Millbrook, 2001.

Sutherland, Lin. **Earthquakes and Volcanoes.** Reader's Digest, 2000.

★ Vogel, Carole Garbuny. **Nature's Fury: Eyewitness Reports of Natural Disasters.** Scholastic, 2000.

## Ecology

Arnosky, Jim. **Wild and Swampy: Exploring with Jim Arnosky.** HarperCollins, 2000.

Bial, Raymond. **A Handful of Dirt.** Walker, 2000.

Miller, Debbie S. **River of Life.** Illustrated by Jon Van Zyle. Clarion, 2000.

## Human Body

Darling, Kathy. **There's a Zoo on You!** Millbrook, 2000.

Nicolson, Cynthia. **Baa! The Most Interesting Book You'll Ever Read about Genes and Cloning.** Illustrated by Rose Cowles. Kids Can Press, 2001.

## Hydrology

Seuling, Barbara. **Drip! Drop! How Water Gets to Your Tap.** Illustrated by Nancy Tobin. Holiday House, 2000.

## Marine Life

Batten, Mary. **The Winking Blinking Sea: All about Bioluminescence.** Millbrook, 2000.

Cerullo, Mary M. **The Truth about Great White Sharks.** Photographs by Jeffrey L. Rotman. Illustrations by Michael Wertz. Chronicle, 2000.

George, Twig C. **Jellies: The Life of Jellyfish.** Millbrook, 2000.

## Paleontology

Chorlton, Windsor. **Woolly Mammoth: Life, Death, and Rediscovery.** Scholastic, 2001.

Dixon, Dougal. **Dougal Dixon's Amazing Dinosaurs: The Fiercest, the Tallest, the Toughest, the Smallest.** Boyds Mills, 2000.

Lessem, Don. **Dinosaurs to Dodos: An Encyclopedia of Extinct Animals.** Illustrated by Jan Sovak. Scholastic, 1999.

★ Relf, Pat (with the SUE Science Team of the Field Museum). **A Dinosaur Named SUE: The Story of the Colossal Fossil, the World's Most Complete T. rex.** Scholastic, 2000.

## Physical Science

Pipe, Jim, and Mark Jackson, editors. **How Science Works: Discover the Science behind Planes, Boats, Rockets, Cars, Trucks.** Copper Beech, 2001.

## Space

Branley, Franklyn M. **The International Space Station (Let's-Read-and-Find-Out Science).** Illustrated by True Kelley. HarperCollins, 2000.

Couper, Heather, and Nigel Henbest. **Space Encyclopedia.** DK, 1999.

★ Croswell, Ken. **See the Stars: Your First Guide to the Night Sky.** Boyds Mills, 2000.

★ Dyson, Marianne J. **Space Station Science: Life in Free Fall.** Scholastic, 1999.

## Technology

Baker, Christopher W. **Scientific Visualization: The New Eyes of Science.** Millbrook, 2000.

## Zoology

George, Jean Craighead. **How to Talk to Your Cat.** Illustrated by Paul Meisel. HarperCollins, 2000.

★ Goodall, Jane. **The Chimpanzees I Love: Saving Their World and Ours.** Scholastic, 2001.

Lewin, Ted, and Betsy Lewin. **Gorilla Walk.** Lothrop, Lee & Shepard, 1999.

★ Markle, Sandra. **Growing Up Wild: Wolves.** Atheneum, 2001.

Mattison, Chris. **Snake: The Essential Visual Guide to the World of Snakes.** DK, 1999.

★ Pringle, Laurence. **A Dragon in the Sky: The Story of a Green Darner Dragonfly.** Illustrated by Bob Marstall. Scholastic, 2001.

Ryder, Joanne. **Little Panda: The World Welcomes Hua Mei at the San Diego Zoo.** Simon & Schuster, 2001.

Swinburne, Stephen R. **Bobcat: North America's Cat.** Boyds Mills, 2001.

★ Webb, Sophie. **My Season with Penguins: An Antarctic Journal.** Houghton Mifflin, 2000.

Wechsler, Doug. **Bizarre Birds.** Photographs by Doug Wechsler and VIREO. Boyds Mills, 1999.

## Science Series

### *Experiments in Science Series*

Glover, David. **How Does It Work?** Dorling Kindersley, 2001.

Glover, David. **How Do Things Grow?** Dorling Kindersley, 2001.

Glover, David. **What Is It Made Of?** Dorling Kindersley, 2001.

### *My First Look At Series*

Hickman, Pamela. **A New Duck: My First Look at the Life Cycle of a Bird.** Illustrated by Heather Collins. Kids Can Press, 1999.

Hickman, Pamela. **A New Frog: My First Look at the Life Cycle of an Amphibian.** Illustrated by Heather Collins. Kids Can Press, 1999.

### ★ *Scientists in the Field Series*

Bishop, Nic. **Digging for Bird-Dinosaurs: An Expedition to Madagascar.** Houghton Mifflin, 2000.

Jackson, Donna M. **The Wildlife Detectives: How Forensic Scientists Fight Crimes against Nature.** Photographs by Wendy Shattil and Bob Rozinski. Houghton Mifflin, 2000.

Kramer, Stephen. **Hidden Worlds: Looking through a Scientist's Microscope.** Photographs by Dennis Kunkel. Houghton Mifflin, 2001.

Mallory, Kenneth. **Swimming with Hammerhead Sharks.** Houghton Mifflin, 2001.

Montgomery, Sy. **The Snake Scientist.** Photographs by Nic Bishop. Houghton Mifflin, 1999.

Swinburne, Stephen R. **Once a Wolf: How Wildlife Biologists Fought to Bring Back the Gray Wolf.** Photographs by Jim Brandenburg. Houghton Mifflin, 1999.

*Young Naturalist's Pop-Up Handbook Series*

Sabuda, Robert, and Matthew Reinhart. **Beetles.** Hyperion, 2001.

Sabuda, Robert, and Matthew Reinhart. **Butterflies.** Hyperion, 2001.

---

This is a halcyon age for children's literature, especially in the areas of nonfiction or informational trade books," says Susan Hepler in Bamford and Kristo's *Making Facts Come Alive: Choosing Quality Nonfiction Literature K–8* (1998, p. 3). Yes, more nonfiction is being published than ever before for children of all ages—from young readers mesmerized by a concept book such as *A New Frog: My First Look at the Cycle of an Amphibian* (Hickman, 1999) to a middle level student engrossed with *The Wildlife Detectives: How Forensic Scientists Fight Crimes against Nature* (Jackson, 2000), a survey book that details the intricate work of scientists who specialize in detective work. Our top selections of science nonfiction run the gamut from serious studies of a topic to lighthearted but fact-filled texts such as Jean Craighead George's (2000) *How to Talk to Your Cat*, a humorous look at why the cat in your life acts the way it does.

Although Hepler was commenting on the abundance of nonfiction for children in general, more specifically, the world of science nonfiction has burgeoned as well. Teachers wishing to include more science nonfiction trade books as part of the curriculum will be pleasantly surprised to find a variety of titles across several kinds of science, most notably zoology, space, earth science, ecology, and paleontology. Too few books, however, are published in such areas as technology, the physical sciences, and the processes of doing science.

Science information is readily available through other venues as well, particularly on the Internet. Internet usage indicates that well over 70 percent of Internet users are searching for information (O'Toole, 2000). Reading researcher Richard Allington (2001) cautions us that

> the Internet imposes virtually no controls on information quality and reliability. Type the word *Holocaust* into an Internet search engine and you will find more web pages exist denying the Holocaust ever took place than pages offering reliable historical data.

While materials denying the Holocaust have been around since the 1950's, never have they been so widely accessible to so many people. Never have they appeared so "official." (p. 7)

Although Allington's caveat speaks to historical nonfiction, we believe that the same cautions should extend when searching for any kind of information on the Internet. Science information, for example, can quickly become outdated; think of all the articles in the newspaper about the latest dinosaur findings or the newest space technology. Also, readers need to question the author. Who is the author? What are the author's qualifications and credentials to write about the topic? What bias or perspective does the author bring to the writing?

Because we agree that the Internet is a seductive tool for inquiring minds, we echo Allington's strong recommendation that we teach students how to sort through, analyze, and evaluate the information they find, whether they are using the Internet or traditional print resources. These literacy strategies also need to be applied when teachers and students are selecting the best science nonfiction books to read. With the increase in titles available across a host of science topics, teachers and students can opt for nothing but the best and highest quality nonfiction.

Our science nonfiction reviewers for this chapter used guidelines described in *Checking Out Nonfiction K–8: Good Choices for Best Learning* (Bamford & Kristo, 2000, pp. 134–35). The four basic questions we used in evaluating each book are:

- How does the book look visually inside and out?
- How do readers find out what the author knows?
- How does the writing hold the reader's attention?
- How does the author organize the content and help readers navigate the information?

We also asked specific questions about whether the science was accurate and presented in a way that readers of a particular age could understand. At times we needed to consult university experts to help us make that judgment because there wasn't enough information about the author's credentials or because some of the information just didn't ring true. We looked critically at the format and the visual information in each book. It was important that this information be presented not only in a clear and uncluttered manner, but also in a way that facilitated the understanding of the material.

Our top selections are categorized alphabetically by field of science for ease of locating titles: botany, earth science, ecology, human body, hydrology, marine life, paleontology, physical science, space, technology, and zoology. We also included four excellent science series.

## References

Allington, R. L. (2001). *What really matters for struggling readers: Designing research-based programs.* New York: Longman.

Bamford, R. A., & Kristo, J. V. ( 2000). *Checking out nonfiction k–8: Good choices for best learning.* Norwood, MA: Christopher-Gordon.

Hepler, S. (1998). Nonfiction books for children: New directions, new challenges. In R. A. Bamford & J. V. Kristo (Eds.), *Making facts come alive: Choosing quality nonfiction literature k–8* (pp. 3–17). Norwood, MA: Christopher-Gordon.

O'Toole, K. (2000, February 16). Study offers early look at how Internet is changing daily life [Online press release]. Stanford Institute for the Quantitative Study of Society. Available: http://www.stanford.edu/group/siqss/Press_Release/press_release.html.

## Botany

**1.1**  Gibbons, Gail. **The Pumpkin Book.** Holiday House, 1999. ISBN 0-8234-1465-5. Unpaged. (P).

With simple, easy-to-understand text and bright, colorful illustrations, the life cycle of pumpkins is made clear and accessible for primary students. The illustrations, many with labels, diagrams, and cross sections, work well with the text. A helpful feature for young readers is the predictable placement of the text at the bottom of each page. Although there is no glossary, words are defined within the text, eliminating the need to flip pages when the book is read aloud. Approximately half the book is devoted to what happens after pumpkins are full grown and ready to be harvested. Two pages focus on the importance of pumpkins to the Pilgrims. Activities for carving pumpkins and drying pumpkin seeds, as well as interesting facts about pumpkins, are included. This book would also be a valuable addition to the classroom library because of its connections to thematic units on fall celebrations, plants, and Native Americans. (SJP)

**1.2**  Goodman, Susan E. **Seeds, Stems, and Stamens: The Ways Plants Fit into Their World.** Photographs by Michael I. Doolittle. Millbrook, 2001. ISBN 0-7613-1874-7. 48 pp. (ALL).

The many ways plants adapt are described through the effective presentation and complementary efforts of succinct text and clear, sharp photography. Each chapter focuses on a specific condition for survival, such as "Getting Sun" and "Making New Plants." Page design is user-friendly and attractive. The first page of each new chapter presents a photograph and a brief description followed by the text's recurring question asking readers about the plant's adaptation. The next page answers the question using photographs and brief but informative captions. This book is a perfect addition to a unit study on plants. It includes a table of contents, an easy-to-use index, and humorous information about how both the author and photographer adapt to each other and to their environment. (MFE)

## Earth Science

**1.3**  Bortz, Fred. **Collision Course! Cosmic Impacts and Life on Earth.** Millbrook, 2001. ISBN 0-7613-1403-2. 72 pp. (I).

*Collision Course* provides essential background for understanding impact theory, including the creation of our solar system and evidence of the impacts of asteroids on Earth and their relationship to mass extinctions throughout Earth's geologic history. In the book's final two chapters, Bortz clarifies fundamental concepts for identifying potentially dangerous asteroids and techniques for preventing another impact. Photographs, diagrams, and computer-generated models complement all this rich material. The book also lists print and Internet resources for additional information. Focusing on the recently accepted impact theory in an appropriate and accessible fashion for older intermediate students, *Collision Course* is bursting with outstanding information. Readers shouldn't miss the author's note at the end of the book in which Bortz describes his passion for the topic of asteroids and those individuals who have influenced his work. Douglas Henderson's *Asteroid Impact* (Dial, 2000) is an excellent companion book to *Collision Course*. (AWS)

**1.4**  Ross, Michael Elsohn. **Earth Cycles.** Illustrated by Gustav Moore. Millbrook, 2001. ISBN 0-7613-1815-1. Unpaged. (P).

Did you ever think of the Earth as turning "like the wheels on a bike" or being "like a giant orange"? Ross makes the shape and movement of the Earth simple for young children to understand. He uses clear poetic language to explain three of the Earth's cycles: day to night to day again, the seasons of the year, and the cycles of the moon. Throughout, Moore uses simple sequential diagrams and time-lapse drawings to accompany the text and further explain these concepts. Teachers will find Ross's book useful for teaching the scientific reasons behind the Earth's cycles and the effect they have on us. (PW)

**1.5**    Sutherland, Lin. **Earthquakes and Volcanoes.** Reader's Digest, 2000. ISBN 1-57584-374-9. 64 pp. (ALL).

*Earthquakes and Volcanoes* will rock readers with engaging information about the effects of heat within our planet—pun intended. Principal research scientist Lin Sutherland and consultant Thomas L. Wright have produced an informative and engaging book that is divided into three sections: Dynamic Earth, Earthquakes, and Volcanoes. Double-page spreads are full of detailed illustrations and photographs of scientists at work and the disastrous effects of geological phenomenon. Part of the Reader's Digest Pathfinders series, *Earthquakes and Volcanoes* boasts many unique access features: information is cross-referenced so that readers can become pathfinders themselves by navigating from concept to related concept. Pathfinder instructions, a glossary, and an index help readers take advantage of all this book has to offer. (MFE)

**1.6**    ★ Vogel, Carole Garbuny. **Nature's Fury: Eyewitness Reports of Natural Disasters.** Scholastic, 2000. ISBN 0-590-11502-2. 126 pp. (I).

Survivors' reports of devastating natural events are integrated with the author's background information, summaries, and generalizations about the events. In sharing this book with readers, teachers can show students how writers integrate primary sources when writing informational texts, how they use figurative language, explain vocabulary, make transitions from one topic to another, and how they discuss their process of research and their perspective on a topic. Each disaster presented begins with background information that creates a context for the reports. Sidebars capture moments using quotes from eyewitnesses. Each chapter is filled with many photographs. The table of contents and the double-page map pinpointing disaster locations provide a detailed overview of the book's contents. A connecting book is Pat Lauber's *Hurricanes: The World's Mightiest Storms* (Scholastic, 1996). Laurence Pringle's *Fire in the Forest: A Cycle of Growth and Renewal* (Atheneum, 1995) provides a different perspective on a forest fire. (SLW)

## Ecology

**1.7**     Arnosky, Jim. **Wild and Swampy: Exploring with Jim Arnosky.** HarperCollins, 2000. ISBN 0-688-17119-2. Unpaged. (ALL).

Jim Arnosky takes readers along on an exploration of southern swamps. A yellow-crowned heron perched on a fallen cypress trunk, an alligator lurking in a bayou, and a venomous cottonmouth coiled on the edge of a swamp are just a few of the creatures he brings to life with his descriptions, paintings, and pen-and-ink sketches. Readers are encouraged to make their own wildlife sketches. The combination of nature journal and large, colorful illustrations makes this book an excellent read-aloud. Teachers will find it useful for a study of wetland habitats and as a model for young naturalists learning to record their own observations. A spelling error in the introduction ("fur" tree) does not negate the value of this extraordinary book. (CMP)

**1.8**     Bial, Raymond. **A Handful of Dirt.** Walker, 2000. ISBN 0-8027-8699-5. 32 pp. (ALL).

Get down to the "nitty-gritty" with this excellent book on an unusual topic—soil ecology. Included are large, attractive photographs and clear, down-to-earth information about inorganic and organic matter in soil. From microscopic bacteria to earthworms to prairie dogs, the author describes how organisms that live in the soil break down organic materials such as leaves, grass, and dead animals. As a read-aloud for grades 2 and 3 and as independent reading for older students, this book is full of interesting facts such as "a single acre of land may provide food and shelter for a million ants, two hundred thousand mites, and four thousand worms." Access features include an index and suggested book list. (CMP)

**1.9**     Miller, Debbie S. **River of Life.** Illustrated by Jon Van Zyle. Clarion, 2000. ISBN 0-395-96790-2. 32 pp. (P).

Miller describes an Alaskan river and the diverse plants and animals that live in it and along its shore. Rich language, such as "Old spruce trees bow to the river," evokes vivid images of the river and its wildlife throughout the seasons. A harlequin duck diving for caddis fly larvae, a brown bear eating salmon, a robin swallowing a fat worm, and dragonflies catching mosquitoes are just a few of the many images that reveal the web of life along the river, and Van Zyle's richly colored oil paintings enhance the descriptive text. A helpful glossary provides further information about each animal. Children of all ages will enjoy hearing this book read aloud, but it also may be used as a springboard for discussing many topics, including the changing seasons, animal groups, habitats, food webs, and the cycle of life. Another good book for investigating biomes is Linda Sonntag's *The Atlas of Animals* (Copper Beech, 2000). (CMP)

## Human Body

1.10    Darling, Kathy. **There's a Zoo on You!** Millbrook, 2000. ISBN 0-7613-1357-5. 48 pp. (I).

This beautifully designed book about microbiology combines reader-friendly text with sharp, colorful images of the multitude of microorganisms with which we coexist. Boldfaced captions describe each image in simple language and provide elaboration of the fascinating text. Even more impressive, however, are this book's access features. Vocabulary is highlighted within the text, and corresponding definitions are color-coded in the margins, providing easy transitions between the main text and the marginalia. A pronunciation guide for all the scientific names and an index also help the reader negotiate the text and new concepts. Corrine Naden's biography *Jonas Salk: Polio Pioneer* (Millbrook, 2001) also complements units on microbiology, exploring the arduous and political work of disease research. (AWS) (MFE)

1.11    Nicolson, Cynthia Pratt. **Baa! The Most Interesting Book You'll Ever Read about Genes and Cloning.** Illustrated by Rose Cowles. Kids Can Press, 2001. ISBN 1-55074-856-4. 40 pp. (I).

Baffled by genetics? Then this brief but informative work on genetics and cloning is for you. Nicolson effectively uses true stories, interesting comparisons, and an engaging, imaginative style in this introduction to genetics. Feeling special as a human? How does the fact that 90 percent of a human genome is identical to that of a mouse grab you? Fascinating information about Gregor Mendel as well as the DNA duo, Francis Crick and James Watson, provides the reader with a historical base for understanding genetics. In the section on cloning and DNA manipulation, the author presents readers with many opportunities to challenge opinions about the future applications of genetics research. The cartoonlike illustrations are both informative and entertaining, and a table of contents, glossary, and index are effective access features. You Try It insets offer activities to supplement the text, making it a useful companion text for a unit on the human body. (MFE)

## Hydrology

**1.12**   Seuling, Barbara. **Drip! Drop! How Water Gets to Your Tap.** Illustrated by Nancy Tobin. Holiday House, 2000. ISBN 0-8234-1459-0. Unpaged. (P).

Through clear, age-appropriate humorous writing, colorful illustrations, and the observations of Jojo and her dog, Willy, young readers explore the water cycle. The information begins and ends with turning on the tap. Readers learn about evaporation, filtration, and condensation. Simple, labeled flow diagrams show how water gets from the reservoir through the filtration system, mixing basins, and water treatment plant to the main water lines, where it gradually flows to smaller and smaller pipes until it reaches individual homes. The concept of water pressure is described, helping readers understand the necessity for water pressure that is just right. *Drip! Drop!*, a great read-aloud for young students as well as an independent read for older students, tackles a subject not often found on primary book lists. Included are several hands-on activities sure to spark exploration and discovery. (SJP)

## Marine Life

**1.13**   Batten, Mary. **The Winking Blinking Sea: All about Bioluminescence.** Millbrook, 2000. ISBN 0-7613-1550-0. Unpaged. (ALL).

Batten takes the reader deep into the oceans of the world and offers her readers an overview of bioluminescent sea life. She has made the study of bioluminescence easily accessible to young readers through colorful photographs and descriptions of selected sea animals. The pronunciation of each new animal name is provided in the text for easy reading. Batten assists readers in making connections to everyday life by comparing some of these sea animals to common objects such as burglar alarms, Christmas tree lights, tiny spaceships, fireworks, fireflies, and stars in the galaxy—all easily understood by children. This is a great read-aloud for younger children or personal reading for older students. Another aspect of ocean life is found in Mary M. Cerullo's *Sea Soup: Phytoplankton* (Tilbury House, 1999). (PW)

**1.14** Cerullo, Mary M. **The Truth about Great White Sharks.** Photographs by Jeffrey L. Rotman. Illustrations by Michael Wertz. Chronicle, 2000. ISBN 0-8118-2467-5. 48 pp. (ALL).

"Gleaming white teeth and coal black eyes: This is what people who have come face-to-face with a great white shark remember most" (pp. 3–4). From the first line of this captivating book, the reader is drawn into the underwater world of great white sharks. Through inviting, understandable language, interesting photographs, diagrams, and sidebars, many misconceptions about great white sharks are clarified. Surprisingly, great whites are good mothers, don't attack in a feeding frenzy, and can leap out of the water to search for their prey. In a captivating foldout page, the size of a human is compared to the great white shark. Access features included are sidebars, glossary, bibliography, and index. An excellent companion book that presents information on a wide variety of sharks, and with the same across-grade appeal, is Laurence Pringle's *Sharks! Strange and Wonderful* (Boyds Mills, 2001). (CMP)

**1.15** George, Twig C. **Jellies: The Life of Jellyfish.** Millbrook, 2000. ISBN 0-7613-1659-0. Unpaged. (P).

Did you know that a Portuguese man-of-war is not a jellyfish, or that there is a jellyfish as long as a blue whale? Using simple text and colorful underwater photographs, George presents a fascinating introduction to the life of jellyfish. She even describes a jellyfish that has yet to be named, a reminder that scientific discoveries are still being made every day. In her dedication, George provides a great incentive for children to read: "Maybe you will be the scientist who discovers the next new jellyfish!" Teachers will love this book as a read-aloud, and older children can use it as a stepping-stone to further research on a particular jellyfish. A companion book with wide appeal is *Meet My Grandmother: She's a Deep-Sea Explorer* by Lisa Tucker McElroy (with help from Russell T. Mead) (Millbrook, 2000). (PW)

## Paleontology

**1.16** Chorlton, Windsor. **Woolly Mammoth: Life, Death, and Rediscovery.** Scholastic, 2001. ISBN 0-439-24134-0. 40 pp. (I).

This engaging two-part book recounts the discovery and excavation in 1997 of a woolly mammoth buried in the permafrost of the far northern reaches of Siberia. In the first part, Chorlton explains and describes the paleontological history of the mammoth and mammoth findings since the eighteenth century. In the second part, the explorer's diary, he recounts the removal of the mammoth and provides details of how scientists work. With the table of contents, chapter and section headings, inserted maps, sidebars of quotations, and captions that elaborate on the abundant photographs, the book's organization is accessible to many young readers and makes for an exciting, captivating, and instructional read-aloud. It provides middle grade children with an example of how the use of primary sources and a diary format can structure scientific information and inquiry. An excellent companion book is *Ice Age Mammoth* by Barbara Hehner (Crown, 2001). (SLW)

1.17    Dixon, Dougal. **Dougal Dixon's Amazing Dinosaurs: The Fiercest, the Tallest, the Toughest, the Smallest.** Boyds Mills, 2000. ISBN 1-56397-773-7. 128 pp. (ALL).

This up-to-date dinosaur reference book for children is organized into four color-coded sections: Meat-Eaters, Long-Necked Plant-Eaters, Armored Dinosaurs, and Two-Footed Plant-Eaters. Dinosaur facts and theories are presented in a clear, uncluttered format with a full-page spread for each dinosaur. Full-color illustrations and diagrams are attractive, informative, and include detailed captions. In Facts and Figures sidebars, basic facts are presented for each dinosaur, including size, weight, classification, and the pronunciation of its name. In addition, size comparison drawings depict each dinosaur with an adult man. A table of contents, glossary, suggested book list, and index are included, making this an easy-to-use resource for children who are looking for specific information, as well as a valuable compendium for teachers. For younger readers, Elizabeth MacLeod's *What Did Dinosaurs Eat? And Other Things You Want to Know about Dinosaurs* (Kids Can Press, 2001) also presents facts in a clearly organized and engaging question-and-answer format. (CMP)

1.18    Lessem, Don. **Dinosaurs to Dodos: An Encyclopedia of Extinct Animals.** Illustrated by Jan Sovak. Scholastic, 1999. ISBN 0-590-31684-2. 112 pp. (ALL).

In *Dinosaurs to Dodos,* readers take a tour through millions of years of life on Earth. The collection of illustrations for each evolutionary period corresponds to a color-coded time line at the beginning of each chapter that situates readers in the time period.

Full-page illustrations, inserted boxes, and illustrated double-page discussions of particular questions about the history of life are organized to help readers consider big ideas. The author points out that scientists don't know everything as he discusses how they construct tentative conclusions from their research. Excellent access features include a table of contents with summarizing statements about each period and chapter headings with bulleted key points that draw readers into the text. The organization of the book includes descriptive facts about animals in each period along with pronunciation guides for their names. (SLW)

1.19    ★ Relf, Pat (with the SUE Science Team of the Field Museum). **A Dinosaur Named SUE: The Story of the Colossal Fossil, the World's Most Complete T. rex.** Scholastic, 2000. ISBN 0-439-09985-4. 64 pp. (ALL).

This book not only has great leads, but the engaging text also gives an in-depth account of the recovery and reconstruction of SUE, a Tyrannosaurus rex named after the woman who made the discovery in the hills of Montana. The author carefully explains in detail the processes the SUE Science Team of technicians and scientists used to reconstruct the dinosaur at the Field Museum in Chicago. She also shows how the painstaking scientific research became detective work, explaining what we knew about dinosaurs, what we didn't know but hypothesized until SUE came along, and what we have yet to learn. The abundant photographs first trace the paleontological history of dinosaurs and then show the process of cleaning the rock from SUE's bones, making the archaeological process accessible to many readers. (SLW)

## Physical Science

1.20    Pipe, Jim, and Mark Jackson, editors. **How Science Works: Discover the Science behind Planes, Boats, Rockets, Cars, Trucks.** Copper Beech, 2001. ISBN 0-7613-2278-7. 128 pp. (I).

Students are exposed to real science in the How Science Works series (see John Farndon's *Rockets and Other Spacecraft* [Copper Beech, 2000] and Bryson Gore's *Trucks, Tractors and Cranes* [Copper Beech, 2000]). *How Science Works* is a compilation of both books and others. Farndon's *Rockets and Other Spacecraft* unveils Newton's Three Laws of Motion and the concepts of gravity and radiation. In *Trucks, Tractors and Cranes*, Gore explains concepts of force, work, and the five kinds of simple machines (wheels and axles, levers, pulleys, screws, and ramps). The individual books are attractive with well-organized pages that combine diagrams, photographs, and text into easily managed chapters. Information is accessed through a table of contents, index, bold headings, and insets. The integration of hands-on activities with the formal laws of motion, force, and work, as well as other science concepts, results in a powerful learning tool. (AWS)

## Space

**1.21**   Branley, Franklyn M. **The International Space Station (Let's-Read-and-Find-Out Science).** Illustrated by True Kelley. HarperCollins, 2000. ISBN 0-06-028702-0. 32 pp. (ALL).

Fascinating information about the International Space Station, written in understandable language for young children, makes this book a high-quality resource for primary classrooms. Included are descriptions of the structure and size of the station as well as the purpose of each component. Children will be interested in the specifics of how astronauts live in space, including how spacewalkers work, the purpose and design of space suits, and day-to-day activities on the space station. True Kelley's detailed drawings, along with helpful labels and captions, add clarity to the text. An introduction by Mercury astronaut Scott Carpenter and an invitation to look for the International Space Station in the sky will spark the enthusiasm of many young scientists. This book can be enjoyed as a read-aloud for younger children, while older students might prefer to read it themselves to get a closer look at the illustrations. (CMP)

**1.22**   Couper, Heather, and Nigel Henbest. **Space Encyclopedia.** DK, 1999. ISBN 0-7894-4708-8. 304 pp. (A).

Are you searching for one book to cover a vast selection of topics about space? Couper and Henbest include such topics as observing the universe, space travel, our solar system, stars, galaxies, and much more. All this is supplemented with a How to Use This Book section, a time line, and a "who's who" of astronomical history. As is typical with DK publications, the printed page combines graphics, text, sidebars, and insets to create an attractive and coordinated set of information. Young and old alike will delight in the visual appeal of this book, while more sophisticated readers will also appreciate the clean, well-written text. If you're dealing exclusively with younger readers, consider Jack Challoner's *The Atlas of Space* (Copper Beech, 2001); the focus is the same, but the effect is less powerful. As a result, the book is less intimidating than Couper and Henbest's *Space Encyclopedia*. (AWS)

1.23    ★ Croswell, Ken. **See the Stars: Your First Guide to the Night Sky.** Boyds Mills, 2000. ISBN 1-56397-757-5. 32 pp. (I).

For each month of the year, *See the Stars* details one or two constellations with a diagram of each, including a location guide and, most important, a photograph of the night sky with relevant stars labeled. Croswell also discusses concepts such as where new stars are born, use of the Big Dipper as a star locator, aging stars, black holes, and finding the center of the galaxy. This content is presented in readable text that provides a rich and accessible study of what can be an often intimidating unit. Further support is provided by the introductory How to Use This Book section, which describes how to read the Where and When to Look charts found in each monthly section. Science teachers looking for a good first book on astronomy will find that this text hits the mark. (AWS)

1.24    ★ Dyson, Marianne J. **Space Station Science: Life in Free Fall.** Scholastic, 1999. ISBN 0-590-05889-4. 128 pp. (I).

Not only does Dyson explain how scientists and astronauts train for the basics of living on a space station, but she also describes science experiments that have been conducted on one. Simple activities that demonstrate major concepts of living in space are included. Dyson acknowledges scientists and technicians who have contributed information, answered her questions, and reviewed the written text for accuracy and completeness. The author has made the science and problem solving of working on a space station accessible to readers by including information about such things as how the space suits work, how astronauts exercise, and how they eat and sleep. In each section, dialogue and narrative precede the information, and captions provide additional commentary. The foreword is written by astronaut Buzz Aldrin. (SLW)

## Technology

1.25    Baker, Christopher W. **Scientific Visualization: The New Eyes of Science.** Millbrook, 2000. ISBN 0-7613-1351-6. 48 pp. (I).

In *Scientific Visualization,* readers learn how scientists observe what people have thought to be unobservable. Baker writes, "Simply said, scientific visualization is a fancy term for making pictures on the computer from scientific data or scientific theory" (p. 7). The book's organization follows this dual definition: the first part explains how scientists visualize data, and the second part describes visualizations of theory. Color photographs show how scientists visualize data in a three-dimensional picture of the human torso, a cross section of a brain tumor, and ordinary events such as the mixing of oil and water. The photographs also show theoretical visualizations such as the formation of stars. Baker explains the importance of the research and uses metaphors that help readers visualize things both incredibly small and immense. This book demonstrates to students that science is as much about visualizing phenomena as it is about observation. (SLW)

## Zoology

**1.26**    George, Jean Craighead. **How to Talk to Your Cat.** Illustrated by Paul Meisel. HarperCollins, 2000. ISBN 0-06-027968-0. 28 pp. (ALL).

"Can I take this book for the weekend? Please? Please?" This was the effect George's book had on third graders. Enchant your students and learn why your cat acts the way he or she does. Learn why you act the way you do around your cat! Jean Craighead George presents a fact-filled, tongue-in-cheek book on how cats interact with their owners and why they do the things they do. Learn how to distinguish one meow from another, how moving whiskers communicate, and what your cat's tail is really saying. Meisel's whimsical illustrations complement the text, and children will love the photographs of Jean Craighead George that appear throughout the book. This is an ideal read-aloud for all children and a good independent or shared reading book for third graders. (PW)

**1.27**    ★ Goodall, Jane. **The Chimpanzees I Love: Saving Their World and Ours.** Scholastic, 2001. ISBN 0-439-21310-X. 80 pp. (ALL).

Reading this first-rate photo essay is like being on tour in the Gombe National Park in Tanzania with Jane Goodall as your guide. Her fascinating account of studying chimpanzee behaviors for forty years flows with beauty and clarity in tandem with remarkable photographs of the chimpanzees, many filling entire pages. She describes her curiosity and love for animals as a child and her later work with Louis Leakey leading to her study of chimpanzees. The final chapter of the book discusses action being taken to protect these fascinating creatures. The book also has an impressive fact and resource section, including a diagram of the primate family, chimpanzee facts, information about habitats, a map, and related sources. The proceeds from the sales of the book will support Roots and Shoots, an educational program of the Jane Goodall Institute. (JVK)

1.28     Lewin, Ted, and Betsy Lewin. **Gorilla Walk.** Lothrop, Lee & Shepard, 1999. ISBN 0-688-16509-5. 48 pp. (ALL).

In their first collaboration, Ted and Betsy Lewin enthusiastically recount the story of their real-life adventure into the Bwindi Impenetrable Forest in southern Uganda to visit the habitats of mountain gorillas. Through vivid descriptions of their expedition and exquisite watercolor illustrations, they share their own wonder as they track and observe two groups of endangered mountain gorillas. Their observations of behaviors and social interactions are specific and detailed. Through the authors' eyes, we are even able to glimpse intimate gorilla family scenes. A two-page spread of Mountain Gorilla Facts and a comprehensive index are helpful access features. The history of the relationship between mountain gorillas and humans is conveyed in the introduction, along with the pros and cons of tourist visits to wild gorilla habitats. Readers who enjoy *Gorilla Walk* may also be interested in the Lewins' *Elephant Quest* (HarperCollins, 2000). (CMP)

1.29     ★ Markle, Sandra. **Growing Up Wild: Wolves.** Atheneum, 2001. ISBN 0-689-81886-6. 31 pp. (ALL).

Accessible text and large, striking, colorful photographs make this book on wolves an exciting read-aloud for young children. Older children will prefer to read Markle's book themselves to get a closer look at the exquisite photographs and to engage with the text. The author takes the reader from the birth of a wolf pack through their first year. Children will feel as though they are present in the den and alongside the young wolves as they grow and learn how to contribute to the pack. A glossary and a pronunciation guide facilitate students' independent access to the text. Part of the Growing Up Wild series (also see *Growing Up with Bears* [Atheneum, 2000]), this book is a "must have" in any teacher's library on wolves. Children can use this book to compare and contrast information on wolves by Jim Brandenburg and others. (PW)

1.30    Mattison, Chris. **Snake: The Essential Visual Guide to the World of Snakes.** DK, 1999. ISBN 0-7894-4660-X. 192 pp. (ALL).

Clearly divided into three sections, The Essential Snake, Snake Gallery, and Snake Directory, this book will delight readers. The Essential Snake section provides important information through text, detailed illustrations, and stunning close-up photographs that help readers gain the scientific understanding needed to appreciate these fascinating animals. The Snake Gallery showcases sixty-one snakes from around the world, beautifully photographed and explained. Each snake entry includes a Fact File and an illustration that depicts the average length of the snake. Finally, the Snake Directory lists snakes by scientific classification. Mattison cites this as the most complete listing of snake species to date. Information about Mattison, a well-known herpetologist and world-class photographer, is given on the attractive dust jacket. A table of contents, a glossary, and an index are included to assist readers in finding information. (MFE)

1.31    ★ Pringle, Laurence. **A Dragon in the Sky: The Story of a Green Darner Dragonfly.** Illustrated by Bob Marstall. Scholastic, 2001. ISBN 0-531-30315-2. 64 pp. (ALL).

The creators of the Orbis Pictus Award–winning book *An Extraordinary Life: The Story of a Monarch Butterfly* (Orchard, 1997) have collaborated on this companion book, another fascinating account of an insect's life. Through the life story of Anax, a green darner dragonfly, Pringle reveals the details of the dragonfly's life in a western New York swamp, where Anax emerges as a nymph from a tiny egg. The story of Anax's amazing development from nymph to mature dragonfly and its eventual migration to a Florida pond will captivate readers. Thrilling accounts of narrow escapes from predators remind one of the fragility of life in the wild. Captions and sidebars contain additional information about green darners and other species encountered by Anax. Young researchers will also find the table of contents and the index helpful for locating specific information. Also included is a list of books, articles, and Web sites for further reading. (CMP)

**1.32**    Ryder, Joanne. **Little Panda: The World Welcomes Hua Mei at the San Diego Zoo.** Simon & Schuster, 2001. ISBN 0-689-84310-0. Unpaged. (P).

Captivating photographs and minimal descriptive text chronicle a panda cub's first year of life at the San Diego Zoo. During this year, Hua Mei grows and develops from a tiny, helpless creature into a curious, playful baby panda. She learns about her world by exploring, climbing trees, and playing with her mother. Throughout the book, small panda icons and italicized print indicate additional facts about Hua Mei, her mother, and pandas in general. This book can be used to help primary children compare and contrast their own development with that of the panda. Children might also enjoy gathering and sharing photographs of themselves at various ages and writing or dictating text to accompany the photographs. *Little Panda* would also be useful in a study of endangered animals. Students will find basic information about pandas that could become the foundation for a more in-depth research project. (CMP)

**1.33**    Swinburne, Stephen R. **Bobcat: North America's Cat.** Boyds Mills, 2001. ISBN 1-56397-843-1. 32 pp. (ALL).

Beginning with a prologue, Swinburne takes us on the trail of the bobcats of North America through chapters with titles such as "A Cat Is Not a Dog" and "Bobcats Don't Eat Pizza," and the conversational language draws the reader into the life of this elusive and much hunted cat. The author describes general information about bobcats, a winter expedition with naturalists who are studying this animal, and a sixth-grade class's early spring outing to a nature preserve in Pawlet, Vermont, to learn about the bobcat and its habitat. Full-color photographs, some with captions, and sidebars of Bobcat Facts complement the narrative. Features such as maps, comparative drawings, glossary, and index are included. Although there's a lot of text on the page, the writing is inviting and clear, making this book suitable as a read-aloud for young students. (SJP)

**1.34**    ★ Webb, Sophie. **My Season with Penguins: An Antarctic Journal.** Houghton Mifflin, 2000. ISBN 0-395-92291-7. 48 pp. (ALL).

Webb's two-month adventure studying and drawing Adelie Penguins in the Antarctic is chronicled in this fascinating journal. Written in clear language and with a touch of humor, the narrative follows the research group as they depart from San Francisco for New Zealand and on to the Antarctic. Information such as selecting clothing, attending survival school at McMurdo, and the daily activities of the research team as they study the penguins is described in detail. Maps, well-captioned scientific drawings, and a glossary help make the information highly accessible. This book is an excellent model for learning about writing using the journal format and is a great read-aloud for young readers. An ideal companion book is Jennifer Dewey's *Antarctic Journal: Four Months at the Bottom of the World* (HarperCollins, 2001), which also chronicles the author's trip. Dewey's focus, however, is broader and less in-depth regarding the Adelie Penguins. (SJP)

**1.35** Wechsler, Doug. **Bizarre Birds.** Photographs by Doug Wechsler and VIREO. Boyds Mills, 1999. ISBN 1-56397-760-5. 48 pp. (ALL).

*Bizarre Birds* is filled with intriguing facts about unusual birds for interested readers and amateur ornithologists. Beginning with a description of the origin of birds as pterodactyls, the author convincingly describes the uniqueness of their descendants. Children will be amazed, for example, at the things a bird will eat, such as wax, clay, or seal droppings. Wechsler effectively invites readers into the interesting world of birds' lifestyles while simultaneously helping readers understand the scientific concepts of avian adaptations and survival techniques. Birds are complex—they must be in order to survive. The book ends with a plea to leave a dead tree standing for our feathered friends. A table of contents, glossary (of words boldfaced in the text), index, and well-labeled, brilliant photographs make this book an indispensable resource. (MFE)

## Science Series

**1.36** **Experiments in Science Series:**

Glover, David. **How Does It Work?** Dorling Kindersley, 2001. ISBN 0-7894-1252-5. 125 pp. (P).

Glover, David. **How Do Things Grow?** Dorling Kindersley, 2001. ISBN 0-7894-7848-X. 125 pp. (P).

Glover, David. **What Is It Made Of?** Dorling Kindersley, 2001. ISBN 0-7894-1251-7. 125 pp. (P).

DK's Experiments in Science series for ages five through seven is a hands-on guide to help young scientists answer questions about the world around them through step-by-step explorations and full-color illustrations. The introduction clearly organizes the text for adult readers, including what young experimenters need to do before they begin, cautions about experimentation, science safety, explanations about the science (a sidebar that helps readers understand the results of each experiment), and how to quiz themselves after completing each section. For use at home or in the classroom, these books provide basic information on the natural world, such as how things grow, electricity, forces and movement, sound, color, light, music, and materials and their properties. Although some activities may be "crafty," over-all these books are valuable resources and can complement most early elementary science curriculums. (SJP)

**1.37**    **My First Look At Series:**

Hickman, Pamela. **A New Duck: My First Look at the Life Cycle of a Bird.** Illustrated by Heather Collins. Kids Can Press, 1999. ISBN 1-55074-613-8. Unpaged. (P).

Hickman, Pamela. **A New Frog: My First Look at the Life Cycle of an Amphibian.** Illustrated by Heather Collins. Kids Can Press, 1999. ISBN 1-55074-615-4. Unpaged. (P).

These books from the My First Look At series introduce young students to the life cycles of a duck and a frog. Shared as a read-aloud for young students, the repetitive, cumulative text invites participation. Each page includes a flap uncovering additional scientific information suitable for independent readers. In *A New Frog,* the reader learns how to make a water scope for viewing plants and animals underwater. In *A New Duck,* the reader discovers how to attract birds to backyards with birdbaths, feeders, and simple birdhouses. In both books, endnotes offer parents activities to do with children. A companion book that also addresses environmental issues is Bruce McMillan's *Days of the Ducklings* (Houghton Mifflin, 2001), a photochronicle of a family raising over two hundred wild eider ducklings to reestablish a colony on an island off the coast of Iceland. (SJP)

**1.38**    ★ **Scientists in the Field Series:**

Bishop, Nic. **Digging for Bird-Dinosaurs: An Expedition to Madagascar.** Houghton Mifflin, 2000. ISBN 0-395-96056-8. 48 pp. (I).

Jackson, Donna M. **The Wildlife Detectives: How Forensic Scientists Fight Crimes against Nature.** Photographs by Wendy Shattil and Bob Rozinski. Houghton Mifflin, 2000. ISBN 0-395-86976-5. 48 pp. (I).

Kramer, Stephen. **Hidden Worlds: Looking through a Scientist's Microscope.** Photographs by Dennis Kunkel. Houghton Mifflin, 2001. ISBN 0-618-05546-0. 57 pp. (I).

Mallory, Kenneth. **Swimming with Hammerhead Sharks.** Houghton Mifflin, 2001. ISBN 0-618-05543-6. 48 pp. (ALL).

Montgomery, Sy. **The Snake Scientist.** Photographs by Nic Bishop. Houghton Mifflin, 1999. ISBN 0-395-87169-7. 44 pp. (ALL).

Swinburne, Stephen R. **Once a Wolf: How Wildlife Biologists Fought to Bring Back the Gray Wolf.** Photographs by Jim Brandenburg. Houghton Mifflin, 1999. ISBN 0-395-89827-7. 49 pp. (I).

Each book in the Scientists in the Field series launches readers into the exciting world of a field scientist and provides testimony to the challenge, excitement, and meticulous thinking involved in doing field science. What events lead scientists to want to protect wolves, sharks, or snakes? How do forensic scientists systematically use clues to locate poachers and bring them to justice? What life experiences mold one scientist to want to look for dinosaur bird bones, and what did she learn along the way about another country and culture? How was Dennis Kunkel to know that the microscope he received one Christmas would provide us with a peek into the awesome world of the unseen? Written in an inviting and clear style, these books educate readers about scientific and environmental research, and the historical and ethical implications of scientists' decisions. Stunning close-up photographs, informative maps, and charts are included. (MFE)

**1.39    Young Naturalist's Pop-up Handbook Series:**

Sabuda, Robert, and Matthew Reinhart. **Young Naturalist's Pop-up Handbook: Beetles.** Hyperion, 2001. ISBN 0-78680-557-9. Unpaged. (ALL).

Sabuda, Robert, and Matthew Reinhart. **Young Naturalist's Pop-up Handbook: Butterflies.** Hyperion, 2001. ISBN 0-78680-558-7. Unpaged. (ALL).

Robert Sabuda's paper engineering reaches new heights with these two superbly crafted five-by-seven-inch, twelve-page insect handbooks. Each book is attractively packaged in a plastic case along with a separately boxed paper replica of either a butterfly or a beetle. These boxes are similar to actual insect collections, complete with a label including the scientific name of the particular butterfly or beetle. Each book is packed with exquisite pop-ups and pull tabs, effectively complementing the written text without overpowering it. Sophisticated scientific information is balanced with illustrations and brief conversational pieces of text. *Beetles* and *Butterflies* are terrific choices with which to captivate the most reluctant learner as well as whet the appetite of students beginning a study of insects. (JVK)

# 2 Historical Nonfiction and Biography

**Myra Zarnowski**

*Contributing reviewers included Deborah Aizenstain, Marianne Fuscaldo, Sabrina Gioieni, Mary Ann Jordan, Deise Kenny, Evelyn Lolis, Erika Padilla, Laurie Robilotto, Kathy Tomasino, and Maria Tsahalis.*

---

**Criteria for Excellence**

- Accuracy of information
- Clear organization
- Illustrations that support the written text and maps that orient the reader
- Writing style that engages the reader through the use of interesting descriptions, details, and anecdotes
- Evidence of the writer's enthusiasm for the subject
- Use of primary sources
- "Visible" author who speaks directly to the reader about the process of "doing history"
- Connection to the social studies curriculum

---

## Biography

Adler, David A. **America's Champion Swimmer: Gertrude Ederle.** Illustrated by Terry Widener. Harcourt, 2000.

Andronik, Catherine M. **Hatshepsut: His Majesty, Herself.** Illustrated by Joseph D. Fiedler. Atheneum, 2001.

Bausum, Ann. **Dragon Bones and Dinosaur Eggs: A Photobiography of Explorer Roy Chapman Andrews.** Illustrated with photographs from the American Museum of Natural History. National Geographic Society, 2000.

★ Bridges, Ruby. **Through My Eyes.** Scholastic, 1999.

Corey, Shana. **You Forgot Your Skirt, Amelia Bloomer! A Very Improper Story.** Illustrated by Chesley McLaren. Scholastic, 2000.

Dash, Joan. **The World at Her Fingertips: The Story of Helen Keller.** Scholastic, 2001.

★ Giblin, James Cross. **The Amazing Life of Benjamin Franklin.** Illustrated by Michael Dooling. Scholastic, 2000.

Gold, Alison Leslie. **A Special Fate: Chiune Sugihara, Hero of the Holocaust.** Scholastic, 2000.

Kostyal, K. M. **Trial by Ice: A Photobiography of Sir Ernest Shackleton.** National Geographic Society, 1999.

Krull, Kathleen. **Lives of Extraordinary Women: Rulers, Rebels (and What the Neighbors Thought).** Illustrated by Kathryn Hewitt. Harcourt, 2000.

Lowery, Linda. **Aunt Clara Brown: Official Pioneer.** Illustrated by Janice Lee Porter. Carolrhoda, 1999.

Murphy, Jim. **Pick & Shovel Poet: The Journeys of Pascal D'Angelo.** Clarion, 2000.

Myers, Walter Dean. **At Her Majesty's Request: An African Princess in Victorian England.** Scholastic, 1999.

Myers, Walter Dean. **Malcolm X: A Fire Burning Brightly.** Illustrated by Leonard Jenkins. HarperCollins, 2000.

Pinkney, Andrea Davis. **Let It Shine: Stories of Black Women Freedom Fighters.** Illustrated by Stephen Alcorn. Harcourt, 2000.

Reich, Susanna. **Clara Schumann: Piano Virtuoso.** Clarion, 1999.

Rockwell, Anne. **Only Passing Through: The Story of Sojourner Truth.** Illustrated by R. Gregory Christie. Knopf, 2000.

Severance, John B. **Einstein: Visionary Scientist.** Clarion, 1999.

★ Stanley, Diane. **Michelangelo.** HarperCollins, 2000.

## U.S. History and Culture

Bial, Raymond. **One-Room School.** Houghton Mifflin, 1999.

Curlee, Lynn. **Liberty.** Simon & Schuster, 2000.

Freedman, Russell. **Give Me Liberty! The Story of the Declaration of Independence.** Holiday House, 2000.

Freedman, Russell. **In the Days of the Vaqueros: America's First True Cowboys.** Clarion, 2001.

Govenar, Alan, collector and editor. **Osceola: Memories of a Sharecropper's Daughter.** Illustrated by Shane W. Evans. Jump at the Sun/Hyperion, 2000.

Haskins, James, and Kathleen Benson. **Bound for America: The Forced Migration of Africans to the New World.** Illustrated by Floyd Cooper. Lothrop, Lee & Shepard. 1999.

Maestro, Betsy, and Giulio Maestro. **Struggle for a Continent: The French and Indian Wars, 1689–1763.** Illustrated by Giulio Maestro. HarperCollins, 2000.

Peterson, Cris. **Century Farm: One Hundred Years on a Family Farm.** Photographs by Alvis Upitis. Boyds Mills, 1999.

★ Stanley, Jerry. **Hurry Freedom: African Americans in Gold Rush California.** Crown, 2000.

Sullivan, George. **Picturing Lincoln: Famous Photographs That Popularized the President.** Clarion, 2000.

## World History and Culture

Ancona, George. **Carnaval.** Harcourt Brace, 1999.

★ Blumberg, Rhoda. **Shipwrecked! The True Adventures of a Japanese Boy.** HarperCollins, 2001.

Cooper, Michael L. **Fighting for Honor: Japanese Americans and World War II.** Clarion, 2000.

Donoughue, Carol. **The Mystery of the Hieroglyphs: The Story of the Rosetta Stone and the Race to Decipher Egyptian Hieroglyphs.** Oxford, 1999.

Gottfried, Ted. **Nazi Germany: The Face of Tyranny.** Illustrated by Stephen Alcorn. Twenty-First Century Books, 2000.

★ Kurlansky, Mark. **The Cod's Tale.** Illustrated by S. D. Schindler. Putnam, 2001.

Levine, Ellen. **Darkness over Denmark: The Danish Resistance and the Rescue of the Jews.** Holiday House, 2000.

Martin, Jacqueline Briggs. **The Lamp, the Ice, and the Boat Called *Fish*.** Illustrated by Beth Krommes. Houghton Mifflin, 2001.

McMahon, Patricia. **One Belfast Boy.** Photographs by Alan O'Connor. Houghton Mifflin, 1999.

---

Writers of nonfiction history and biography for children face the stiff challenge of making the past knowable and understandable. This may explain why author Russell Freedman has commented that it is his job to "bring 'em back alive" (Freedman, 1993, 1994). While many nonfiction writers can point concretely to what they are writing about—a building, a painting, a forest, or an animal—history writers must contend with "reassembling the dust" (Mariani, 1983). They comb archives, look at documents, gather photographs, interview observers, and read books in order to piece together narratives from evidence left behind.

As if that weren't challenging enough, writers of history and biography must decide what information to put in and what to leave out. Young readers need background information, but how much? A skillful writer such as Diane Stanley takes the time to set the stage for her biography *Michelangelo* (2000) by providing an author's note with a description of the artistic revival of the Renaissance into which Michelangelo was born and a map of Italy during his time. This introductory material gives young readers a sense of time and place before plunging into Michelangelo's life story. But it is important to find the right balance of background information. Giving too much information is likely to annoy readers who then complain that the author just "goes on and on," piling fact on fact and example on example.

Writers of history and biography also face the ticklish problem of what to do with negative information about their subjects—the bad and malicious deeds, the slander, the senseless violence, the denials of freedom and equality. Author Milton Meltzer insists that "biographers owe readers the historical truth. And that truth must include the negative as well as the positive" (1998, p. 102). Yet picture book histories and biographies, limited to thirty-two or forty-eight pages, are bound to be incomplete. In fact, some authors take pains to point out what they have left out. In *Only Passing Through* (2000), author Anne Rockwell tells readers, "I've told her story only up to when her transformation took place, for that part of the story moves me most. But there is more to tell of Sojourner Truth's life." In the end, it's up to the reader to look for the gaps in historical narratives and think about the effects of the missing information.

When history and biography succeed in drawing us in, it is because writers have met the unique challenges they face with artistry and accuracy. They introduce people from the past in settings we cannot experience, but they show us that these people had the same feelings we do. We can share Ruby Bridges's bewilderment (see *Through My Eyes*), Mifflin Gibbs's frustration (see *Hurry Freedom* by Jerry Stanley), and Gertrude Ederle's pride in accomplishment (see *America's Champion Swimmer* by David A. Adler) because we know what it means to feel bewildered, frustrated, and proud. When artistry and accuracy come together, biography and history become page-turners that hold readers' attention.

When selecting books to include in this chapter, our review committee began by using the general criteria adopted by NCTE's Orbis Pictus Award Committee to select outstanding nonfiction for children. We looked at the following criteria:

- *Accuracy.* We were particularly interested in books in which authors documented their research. A book such as *The Amazing Life of Benjamin Franklin* (Giblin, 2000) stands out because of its excellent bibliography and source notes and its informative artist's note detailing the research done by the artist.

- *Organization.* We selected books in which information was clearly presented. Usually this meant a chronological narrative, but other organizational patterns such as cause and effect, comparison and contrast, and description were embedded within the narrative. *Kids on Strike!* (Bartoletti, 1999), for example, vividly describes the conditions under which children labored during the mid-1800s and early 1900s.

- *Illustration.* We selected books with powerful photographs, drawings, and paintings that support the written text and maps that orient the reader to the setting of a book. *Picturing Lincoln* (Sullivan, 2000) is notable for its in-depth discussion of five widely distributed photographs of Lincoln and the impact of these photos on Lincoln's career and our national memory.

- *Writing Style.* The group selected books that draw the reader in because of their interesting descriptions, details, and anecdotes. We also looked for evidence of the writer's enthusiasm for digging into the subject. In *Let It Shine* (2000), Andrea Davis Pinkney explains why she was interested in writing about black women freedom fighters. Her reasons are deeply rooted in her family's history of participation in the civil rights movement.

In addition, we also used more specific criteria relevant to teaching and learning history and biography:

- *Primary Sources.* We searched for books that introduce young readers to primary sources—posters, letters, diary entries, newspaper articles, and photographs. These items bring us closer to the past and give us a sense of the "raw" material the author worked with. *Pick & Shovel Poet* (2000) and *Blizzard* (2000) by Jim Murphy are notable for their extensive use of photographs, newspaper clippings, and prints.

- *Visible Authors.* Authors who speak directly to their readers about sifting and shaping their material provide valuable insight into the process of "doing" history. The epilogue to *Clara Schumann* (Reich, 1999) deals specifically with how the author pieced together all her different sources of information.

- *Curriculum Connection.* We considered it a plus if a book was not only an outstanding choice, but it also supported the social studies curriculum. While topics covered in social studies classes vary somewhat across the country, a book such as *The Mystery of the Hieroglyphs* (Donoughue, 1999) was a favorite of sixth-grade teachers who teach about ancient civilizations. *One-*

*Room School* (Bial, 1999) provided primary grade teachers with
an interesting historical contrast to current community schools.

The books reviewed in this chapter are divided into three sections. The first section, Biography, includes both picture book biographies and lengthier chapter books about the well known and the not so
famous. A number of collective biographies are also included. The second section, U.S. History and Culture, ranges from books about early
American history to more recent accounts of cultural practices rooted in
history. In addition, a number of books provide insight into how children lived in the past. The last section, World History and Culture,
includes accounts of life in other times and places, introducing young
U.S. readers to the world beyond our borders. Books in this section
bring readers to Africa, Asia, Latin America, and even the Antarctic.

Books in this chapter introduce people from the past and "bring
'em back alive" so that today's readers can see them in their complexity.
These books provide an appealing introduction to the discipline of
history.

### References

Freedman, R. (1993). Bring 'em back alive. In M.O. Tunnell & R. Ammon (Eds.),
    *The story of ourselves: Teaching history through children's literature* (pp.
    41–47). Portsmouth, NH: Heinemann.

Freedman, R. (1994). Bring 'em back alive. *School Library Journal, 40,* 138–41.

Mariani, P. (1983). Reasssembling the dust: Notes on the art of the biographer.
    *New England Review and Bread Loaf Quarterly, 5,* 276–96.

Meltzer, M. (1998). If the fish stinks . . . *The New Advocate, 11,* 97–105.

## Biography

2.1     Adler, David A. **America's Champion Swimmer: Gertrude
        Ederle.** Illustrated by Terry Widener. Harcourt, 2000. ISBN 0-15-
        201969-3. Unpaged. (P).

        Gertrude Ederle, the first woman to successfully swim the
        English Channel, helped shatter the stereotype of women as the
        "weaker sex." Through her courage, grace, and athleticism, she
        became a symbol of strength for girls and women everywhere.
        Adler begins by setting the scene: "In 1906 women were kept out
        of many clubs and restaurants. In most states they were not
        allowed to vote. Many people felt a woman's place was in the
        home." Within this context, Ederle's accomplishments become
        even more significant. Widener's full-color illustrations give

readers an up close view of Ederle's engrossing and sometimes humorous story. An author's note provides further information about Ederle's accomplishments, and a final paragraph tells readers that periodicals of the time were used as sources. This is a winning introduction to an American winner. (MF)

2.2    Andronik, Catherine M. **Hatshepsut: His Majesty, Herself.** Illustrated by Joseph D. Fiedler. Atheneum, 2001. ISBN 0-689-86562-5. 40 pp. (I).

The intriguing story of Egypt's only successful female pharaoh is still being uncovered by archaeologists. Despite the attempts of Hatshepsut's successor to erase the evidence of her existence by erasing her name from records and destroying monuments to her, this is a story that was not completely lost. Instead, this biography makes use of evidence compiled from hieroglyphs and artifacts that date back five thousand years. In a male-dominated society, Hatshepsut ascended to the throne of Egypt and gave her country a peaceful and prosperous reign. The author describes Hatshepsut's royal genealogical background to help readers understand why Hatshepsut felt compelled to rule and why it took so long for archaeologists to recognize her existence. Vivid illustrations using papyruslike textures and earthen hues help readers envision the setting. This biography invites comparison with another strong Egyptian ruler: Cleopatra. (EL)

2.3    Bausum, Ann. **Dragon Bones and Dinosaur Eggs: A Photobiography of Explorer Roy Chapman Andrews.** Illustrated with photographs from the American Museum of Natural History. National Geographic Society, 2000. ISBN 0-7922-7123-8. 64 pp. (I).

From a very young age, Roy Chapman Andrews loved animals, not only as pets, but also as subjects to study—inside and out. He taught himself taxidermy from a book, worked at odd jobs to pay for his education, and was eventually offered a job at the American Museum of Natural History, assigned to the taxidermy department. This was the start of his adventurous life. Bausum's photobiography highlights Andrews's five fossil-hunting expeditions to the Gobi Desert in Mongolia where his team of scientists found the bones of a new species of dinosaur, unearthed prehistoric dinosaur eggs, and identified more than 380 new species of living and fossilized animals and plants.

Large, well-captioned photographs drawn from the collections of the American Museum of Natural History bring this story to life and provide a fascinating glimpse of a scientist at work. The book includes numerous quotes from Andrews's books and letters, a foreword by Andrews's son, and an afterword that describes current expeditions to the Gobi. (DK)

2.4    ★ Bridges, Ruby. **Through My Eyes.** Scholastic, 1999. ISBN 0-590-18923-9. 64 pp. (I).

*Through My Eyes* chronicles a critical year in the civil rights movement in the United States and in the life of stoic six-year-old Ruby Bridges. She was called on to be one of the nation's first black children to integrate a school in the resistant Deep South. The understated prose pounds at the heart: "Still, I sometimes feel I lost something that year. I feel as if I lost my childhood" (p. 56). The small girl, sprightly dressed, carrying a tiny purse, and surrounded by huge federal marshals as she scales the steps to school, faces mobs of angry protesters. It is an ugly story, beautifully told. *Through My Eyes* includes poignant reflections by Ruby's mother and her valiant teacher, as well as excerpts from 1960 *New York Times* and *U.S. News & World Report* articles. Bridges tells us what she thought was happening then and how she sees the events now. Students can compare this book to Robert Coles's simpler version, *The Story of Ruby Bridges* (Scholastic, 1995). (KT)

★ Cline-Ransome, Lesa. **Satchel Paige.** Illustrated by James E. Ransome. Simon & Schuster, 2000. ISBN 0-689-81151-9. Unpaged. (ALL). (See **12.2.**)

2.5    Corey, Shana. **You Forgot Your Skirt, Amelia Bloomer! A Very Improper Story.** Illustrated by Chesley McLaren. Scholastic, 2000. ISBN 0-439-07819-9. Unpaged. (P).

"Who wants to be a proper lady?" Amelia Bloomer asked herself. Especially since being a proper lady meant you could not vote or work, and you had to wear heavy, restrictive clothing that made it hard to move, breathe, or even fit through a doorway. Instead of becoming a proper lady, the feisty Amelia Bloomer began her own newspaper and, in a daring move, adopted the looser, freer style of clothing that came to be known as bloomers. Hand-lettered print with swirls and curls and humorous, vibrant illustrations add tremendous life to this historical account and support the author's amused stance. This is an entertaining introduction to biography and women's history. (EP)

**2.6**   Dash, Joan. **The World at Her Fingertips: The Story of Helen Keller.** Scholastic, 2001. ISBN 0-590-90715-8. 235 pp. (I).

This account of Helen Keller's life emphasizes the astonishing will to excel of both Helen and her teacher, Anne Sullivan Macy. Helen, though deaf and blind, manages with Anne's help to master written language and oral speech, prepare for and graduate from Radcliffe College, and launch an extensive writing career. Persistently energetic, Helen becomes a world-famous figure, traveling all over to promote world peace and the cause of people with disabilities. Author Joan Dash provides a textured portrait by exploring the various facets of Helen's life: she explains Helen's socialist leanings and her outspoken support of workers' rights, details Helen's vaudeville and movie appearances, and describes her friendships with Eleanor Roosevelt, Alexander Graham Bell, and Mark Twain. What emerges is an understanding of a remarkable life—a triumph of intelligence and persistence over enormously challenging physical disability. For additional insights, see Laurie Lawlor's *Helen Keller: Rebellious Spirit* (Holiday House, 2001). (MZ)

**2.7**   ★ Giblin, James Cross. **The Amazing Life of Benjamin Franklin.** Illustrated by Michael Dooling. Scholastic, 2000. ISBN 0-590-48534-2. 48 pp. (I).

This biography emphasizes the "amazing" aspects of Franklin's life—from his early years as a printer, to his civic projects, his experiments with electricity, his diplomatic missions to England and France, and his role in writing the Constitution. An unusual aspect of this book is its discussion of Franklin's strained relationship with his son William, who was a royal governor and British loyalist. In this balanced portrait, Giblin concludes that Franklin "had proved himself a true patriot—even though it meant losing the love and respect of his only living son" (p. 40). Useful material at the end of the book includes a list of important dates in Franklin's life, a description of several of his inventions, and a collection of sayings from *Poor Richard's Almanack*. Most interesting are the author's source notes and the illustrator's notes dealing with their extensive research. Readers learn why Franklin is known as the "wisest American." (MF)

**2.8**     Gold, Alison Leslie. **A Special Fate: Chiune Sugihara, Hero of the Holocaust.** Scholastic, 2000. ISBN 0-590-395254. 176 pp. (I).

Chiune Sugihara was a Japanese diplomat whose courage helped save the lives of many Jews in Kaunas, Lithuania, who were at the mercy of Hitler's vicious agenda during World War II. When Hitler invaded Lithuania, Sugihara disobeyed the instructions given to him by his government and instead issued approximately six thousand visas to Jews so that they could escape the Nazis. He was so determined to help his fellow man that he defied orders to close down the Japanese consulate. Sugihara's courageous actions resulted in one of the largest rescues of Jews during the Holocaust. To tell this heroic story, the author was able to draw on interviews with Sugihara's widow and with two Holocaust survivors, who as children in 1940 were Sugihara visa recipients. *A Special Fate* is a dramatic and inspiring story about how one person's decision to do what was morally right saved the lives of thousands. (EP)

**2.9**     Kostyal, K. M. **Trial by Ice: A Photobiography of Sir Ernest Shackleton.** National Geographic Society, 1999. ISBN 0-7922-7393-1. 64 pp. (I).

The idea of exploring the frigid continent of ice that is Antarctica appealed to Ernest Shackleton, an Irishman with a sense of adventure. Shackleton's first experience with Antarctica was on an expedition with Robert Scott, commander of the *Discovery.* Shackleton learned much from Scott, including the fact that he himself was a natural leader. In 1908 a determined Shackleton led his own expedition on an unsuccessful attempt to reach the South Pole. Shackleton's third expedition to Antarctica in 1914 had a new goal: to be the first to cross the entire continent. Only months after the ship and its crew started out, the *Endurance* was locked in place by ice and eventually crushed by its enormous pressure. The crew members were now stranded on the frozen sea. Shackleton's new goal was a difficult but basic one: survival! This engrossing tale is complemented by a fascinating collection of photographs. (DK)

**2.10**    Krull, Kathleen. **Lives of Extraordinary Women: Rulers, Rebels (and What the Neighbors Thought).** Illustrated by Kathryn Hewitt. Harcourt, 2000. ISBN 0-15-200807-1. 95 pp. (I).

Short descriptions of the daring deeds of extraordinary women throughout history whet the reader's appetite to find out even more. Not only does the author entice the reader with a general biographical overview of politically powerful women such as Cleopatra, Queen Victoria, Golda Meir, and Rigoberta Menchú, but she also adds little-known tidbits of information that add interest. To learn that Isabella I crowned herself queen when Ferdinand was out of town, or that Catherine the Great "wrote operas, essays on history, and the first stories for children ever published in Russia" (p. 38), adds to the humanity of these great female personalities. A caricature of each woman along with objects associated with her exploits accompanies each biographical piece. These caricatures are a perfect visual complement to writing that seeks to answer what the author refers to as "unusually nosy questions" (p. 9). (DA)

2.11 Lowery, Linda. **Aunt Clara Brown: Official Pioneer.** Illustrated by Janice Lee Porter. Carolrhoda, 1999. ISBN 1-57505-045-5. 48 pp. (P).

Combining simple text with dramatic illustrations, this biography tells the remarkable story of Clara Brown (1800–1885), a former slave who traveled to Colorado to seek a better life. Above all, she hoped that this life would include finding her daughter, who had been sold as a slave when just a little girl. Clara worked hard to become rich and ultimately became the first official Colorado pioneer who was not both white and male. She became known as "Aunt Clara" to the many freed slaves she helped get on their feet. This new family would help ease her loneliness until the day she was reunited with her precious Eliza Jane. This book includes an afterword and a chronology of important dates, both of which include extra details of Clara's distinguished life. This is an inspiring story of courage, generosity, and overwhelming determination. (SG)

2.12 Murphy, Jim. **Pick & Shovel Poet: The Journeys of Pascal D'Angelo.** Clarion, 2000. ISBN 0-395-77610-4. 162 pp. (I).

An amazing source of inspiration, Pascal D'Angelo came to America in 1910 with a dream. Like many other immigrants of the time, he found that work was scarce. D'Angelo became a pick-and-shovel man and helped build the country he eventually came to love. Though construction work was extraordinarily difficult, his determination to do more with his life never vanished. This narrative follows D'Angelo as he encounters con artists, endures endless hard work, and experiences prejudice and stereotyping. Readers will feel his isolation from the English-speaking world around him. Ultimately, D'Angelo learns to speak and read English and begins to express himself through writing. He becomes known as a poet with a remarkable ability to share his feelings with force and passion. Readers of this fascinating biography will not only learn about Pascal D'Angelo, but also about the larger story of Italian immigration in the early 1900s. (SG)

2.13    Myers, Walter Dean. **At Her Majesty's Request: An African Princess in Victorian England.** Scholastic, 1999. ISBN 0-590-48669-1. 146 pp. (I).

Beginning with an introduction that tells readers how he received a catalog from a book dealer in London showing a group of letters concerning an African princess who had been rescued from certain death in Africa, author Walter Dean Myers lets readers in on the process of pulling this unique story together. The woman who later became known as Sarah Forbes Bonetta was born a princess, captured by Dahomian women warriors, and about to be sacrificed when she was rescued by an Englishman, Commander Frederick Forbes. Forbes convinced Sarah's captors to release her, and she became instead Forbes's "gift" to Queen Victoria. This book follows Sarah's unique experiences in Victorian England, contrasting Sarah's lavish lifestyle with the lives of poor English children during the 1850s. In an intriguing epilogue filled with wonderings about Sarah, Myers reminds his readers that many questions about Sarah's life remain unanswered. (LR)

2.14    Myers, Walter Dean. **Malcolm X: A Fire Burning Brightly.** Illustrated by Leonard Jenkins. HarperCollins, 2000. ISBN 0-06-027707-6. Unpaged. (P).

Faced with the challenge of bringing to life for a young audience a powerful and controversial figure such as Malcolm X, Myers and Jenkins used an innovative format. The author gives a brief account, unencumbered by dates or citations, of Malcolm X's life from the time he was born in Omaha to his early upbringing in Detroit, his move east, his imprisonment at the age of twenty-one, his conversion to Islam, his split from that group, and finally his assassination. Quotations from Malcolm X's autobiography and speeches serve as a counterpoint to the biography.

Setting the scene and creating the mood are Jenkins's powerful, and very urban, illustrations. A chronology in the back of the book fills in the missing dates and makes use of quotes (one and often more) to support and amplify each date listed. This innovative format can serve as a model for student writing. (KT)

**2.15** Pinkney, Andrea Davis. **Let It Shine: Stories of Black Women Freedom Fighters.** Illustrated by Stephen Alcorn. Harcourt, 2000. ISBN 0-15-201005-X. 107 pp. (I).

Following a brief introduction by the author that connects her life to the topic of civil rights, this handsome book offers ten brief chapter-length biographies of "women [who] fought for many freedoms—freedom from sexism, oppression, and the fear of being silenced. Freedom to choose housing, ride public transportation, and express themselves both in newspapers and on television" (p. xi). The ten women featured are Sojourner Truth, Biddy Mason, Harriet Tubman, Ida B. Wells-Barnett, Mary McLeod Bethune, Ella Josephine Baker, Dorothy Irene Height, Rose Parks, Fannie Lou Hamer, and Shirley Chisolm. A notable feature of this book is Pinkney's spunky, conversational language, which makes for enjoyable reading. Full-page illustrations by Stephen Alcorn emphasize the activism of these women and should stimulate much discussion. (DA)

**2.16** Reich, Susanna. **Clara Schumann: Piano Virtuoso.** Clarion, 1999. ISBN 0-395-89119-1. 118 pp. (I).

Using many illustrations and excerpts from primary sources, this well-crafted biography portrays the life of Clara Schumann, whose exceptional musical talent is inspirational. At the age of twelve, Clara dazzled audiences with her first concert tour. From that time on, she dedicated herself to her music, which became a source of comfort throughout her life. This biography emphasizes the context of Clara's growing up under the strict guidance of her father, which was the beginning of a difficult life—a life that included supporting her eight children when her husband, Robert Schumann, was committed to a mental hospital. Reich asks readers to consider the meaning of such a life, suggesting that "to Clara Schumann, music was not only a gift that enabled her to bear the misfortunes of a difficult life, but a voice with which she could share her deepest experiences of that life" (p. 100). (SG)

**2.17** Rockwell, Anne. **Only Passing Through: The Story of Sojourner Truth.** Illustrated by R. Gregory Christie. Knopf, 2000. ISBN 0-679-89186-2. Unpaged. (P).

This powerfully illustrated biography of Sojourner Truth emphasizes the formative influences in her life. Beginning in 1806, when Sojourner was auctioned off with a flock of sheep, this book chronicles the legacy of deception that surrounded her life: her brother and sister had been kidnapped; she had been promised her freedom and then betrayed; and her son was sold down South. Inspired by Bible stories—especially the story of Moses—Sojourner Truth took her promised freedom and transformed herself into a sojourner, a traveler with an important tale to tell about freedom and bondage. An amazing element of this story is that she—a black woman—sued in court to bring her son back when he was illegally sold out of the state of New York. The combination of a convincing authorial voice and dramatic illustrations make this biography a powerful reading experience. (MZ)

**2.18** Severance, John B. **Einstein: Visionary Scientist.** Clarion, 1999. ISBN 0-395-93100-2. 144 pp. (I).

In some ways, Albert Einstein the man remains as much of an enigma as his theory of relativity does to the average nonscientist. In this biography, Severance reveals the many facets of Einstein's life, depicting him as a study in contradictions: Einstein was a genius who was slow to begin speaking and whose speech throughout his childhood remained so hesitant that his early teachers thought him dull. A less than dedicated student, in later life he published ten scientific papers and one book in a very short time, causing his physical and mental health to decline. Einstein was a nonreligious Jew whose name became associated with Zionism. And he was a pacifist who did the mathematics that enabled U.S. scientists to use uranium to build the atomic bomb. Severance does a masterful job of explaining Einstein's complex theory of relativity in terms that children will comprehend. (MAJ)

**2.19** ★ Stanley, Diane. **Michelangelo.** HarperCollins, 2000. ISBN 0-688-15085-3. Unpaged. (I).

This book describes the magnificent career of Michelangelo, whose artistic creations in sculpture, painting, and architecture include the *Pietà*, the *David*, the ceiling paintings in the Sistine

Chapel, the marble statue *Moses,* and the architectural planning of St. Peter's Cathedral. The book begins with a map of the Italian city-states as they were during Michelangelo's time and an author's note describing the Renaissance era in which he lived. This background information gives young readers a sense of both time and place. The remainder of the book follows Michelangelo's eventful career, from his apprenticeship to his work for the famous Medici family in Florence as well as work for Pope Julius II and Pope Leo X. Large, detailed illustrations show the artist in the process of creating his well-known masterpieces and provide an excellent introduction to the career of an extraordinary Renaissance artist. (MAJ)

★ Tallchief, Maria, with Rosemary Wells. **Tallchief: America's Prima Ballerina.** Illustrated by Gary Kelley. Viking, 1999. ISBN 0-670-88756-0. 28 pp. (ALL). (See **11.26.**)

## U.S. History and Culture

Bartoletti, Susan Campbell. **Kids on Strike!** Illustrated with photographs. Houghton Mifflin, 1999. ISBN 0-395-88892-1. 208 pp. (I). (See **24.14.**)

2.20    Bial, Raymond. **One-Room School.** Houghton Mifflin, 1999. ISBN 0-395-90514-1. 48 pp. (ALL).

An exquisitely photographed journey through the 250-year history of one-room schools in the United States, the text is flavored with interesting details. Abraham Lincoln "ciphered, or solved math problems, on a wooden board, then shaved the numbers off with a knife for the next lesson" (p. 7). While Bial's focus is one-room schools, he also makes important connections between education and democracy and between history and geography. He details the formidable job of the one-room schoolteacher, and infers that the success of strategies such as memorization and repetition may have implications for schools today. But the heart of this book is the extraordinary art of the photography. From the golden sun shining on the worn wooden floors to the illuminating close-ups of the potbelly stove and *The Eclectic First Reader,* Bial's photographs are rich in historical detail. *One-Room School* is a valuable contribution to the literature of U.S. history. (KT)

**2.21**    Curlee, Lynn. **Liberty.** Simon & Schuster, 2000. ISBN 0-689-82823-3. 44 pp. (I).

This handsome picture book describes the origin of the idea for the Statue of Liberty, the major players in the project—including Édouard de Laboulaye, the French law professor and expert on U.S. history; Frédéric-Auguste Bartholdi, the sculptor; and Gustave Eiffel, the engineer—and the process by which the statue was constructed. The illustrations—full-page acrylic paintings—bring the story to life: a map identifies the location of the statue in New York harbor, and paintings show the original design and later modifications. Views of the partially constructed statue give a sense of its scale. In addition, readers learn how and why this statue has become a symbol of hope and freedom for immigrants throughout the world. This book is a fine introduction to Lady Liberty. Also of interest is Curlee's recent book, *Brooklyn Bridge* (Atheneum, 2001), which describes another of New York's "greatest landmarks and grandest sights" (p. 30). (MF)

**2.22**    Freedman, Russell. **Give Me Liberty! The Story of the Declaration of Independence.** Holiday House, 2000. ISBN 0-8234-1448-5. 90 pp. (I).

Russell Freedman chronicles the events leading up to the writing and signing of the Declaration of Independence, events made more immediate through the use of exact quotes from militiamen and ordinary citizens of the time. Included is a detailed description of the ragtag group of colonists and how they were molded into organized troops to fight for their independence. One of the many interesting points Freedman makes is that free black men were able to serve in integrated units—something that didn't happen again until the Korean War. The appendix includes a replica and a typed copy of the Declaration of Independence, a chronology of events, and a short passage about the history of housing this important document. This historical narrative provides a rich context for understanding why the Declaration was written and why it continues to have significance as a timeless affirmation of human rights. (DA)

**2.23**    Freedman, Russell. **In the Days of the Vaqueros: America's First True Cowboys.** Clarion, 2001. ISBN 0-395-96788-0. 70 pp. (I).

As Freedman informs us, "Today, wherever a man chooses to call himself a cowboy, . . . he is paying tribute to those barefoot Indian cowherders who started it all nearly five hundred years ago" (p. 59). The first cowboys, Mexican laborers who called themselves *vaqueros*, developed the tools of the trade such as the lariat, chaps, and saddle with a large saddle horn and stirrups; they introduced distinctive clothing such as the sombrero, the serape (poncho), and the *chaqueta* (short jacket). They also developed new contests and games that required them to apply their skills as horsemen. Using photographs, drawings, and color reproductions of paintings, Freedman explains how these men developed the role of cowboy, yet because they were poor, landless, and often in debt, they never received the cultural status of the U.S. cowboy. This book sets the record straight. Pair this book with Martin Sandler's *Vaqueros* (Holt, 2001) for additional information. (MZ)

**2.24**  Govenar, Alan, collector and editor. **Osceola: Memories of a Sharecropper's Daughter.** Illustrated by Shane W. Evans. Jump at the Sun/Hyperion, 2000. ISBN 0-7868-0407-6. 64 pp. (I).

*Osceola* is an excellent example of an oral account that allows us to look at historical events from a different perspective: the perspective of the common person. Osceola Mays, the daughter of a sharecropper and the granddaughter of a slave, describes her life as a poor African American girl who endured fear, poverty, hardship, and loss. Her childhood memories are recounted through a collection of poems, songs, and stories she heard from her mother and grandmother. As Osceola remembers her childhood, she gives us a glimpse of the past through the eyes of a child. Slavery, freedom, segregation, war, and faith are some familiar topics discussed in an unusual way, and the stories, songs, and poems show us the importance of passing on history to our children. The combination of beautiful illustrations and a powerful, well-written text makes this book an excellent biography. (MT)

**2.25**  Haskins, James, and Kathleen Benson. **Bound for America: The Forced Migration of Africans to the New World.** Illustrated by Floyd Cooper. Lothrop, Lee & Shepard, 1999. ISBN 0-688-10258-1. 48 pp. (I).

A clearly presented history of forced migration of Africans to the New World, this book details the cruel treatment slaves endured from their capture and march to the coast to time spent in holding pens, branding, brutal conditions on ships, and more.

Haskins and Benson's powerful writing style allows young readers to understand history and respond emotionally to the events and conditions described in the book. Floyd Cooper's illustrations detail the emotions and pain endured by the slaves, while photographs and prints help readers envision the historical context. A detailed time line of "Milestones in the History of Slavery" and a bibliography of books "especially for young readers" provide additional information. (MF)

2.26    Maestro, Betsy, and Giulio Maestro. **Struggle for a Continent: The French and Indian Wars, 1689–1763.** Illustrated by Giulio Maestro. HarperCollins, 2000. ISBN 0-688-13450-5. 48 pp. (I).

The French and Indian Wars were a series of wars fought in the colonies to align loyalty to either England or France. From King William's War in 1689 to the French and Indian War in 1756, strong alliances between the French and the Algonquians and between the English and the Iroquois were forged. Because the Indians had developed a great dependence on the Europeans for goods and weapons, each group of colonists sought to use this dependence to their advantage. Throughout this seventy-year period, whenever France and England were at war, their counterparts in the colonies saw fit to do the same. Betsy Maestro's informative writing allows students to understand the relationships between these various groups, while Giulio Maestro's illustrations give a clear sense of the setting by providing an abundance of maps, scenes of conflict, and portraits of the people involved. (DA)

★ Murphy, Jim. **Blizzard!** Scholastic, 2000. ISBN 0-590-67309-2. 136 pp. (I). (See **5.26**.)

2.27    Peterson, Cris. **Century Farm: One Hundred Years on a Family Farm.** Photographs by Alvis Upitis. Boyds Mills, 1999. ISBN 1-56397-710-9. Unpaged. (P).

*Century Farm* tells the history of the Peterson family farm. The concise text compares the processes of milking, haying, planting, and harvesting at the beginning and at the end of the twentieth century. "Grandma milked a dozen cows by hand" stands in extraordinary contrast to "Today we milk two hundred cows in a milking parlor." The muted black-and-white photographs, dating back to 1910, contrast starkly with the crisp, colorful photographs taken by Alvis Upitis at the end of the century. The photographs also show Peterson children growing into young adults. By reaching back to the early days of the century and looking ahead to the future, when these children will farm the same land, *Century Farm* reflects the change and continuity that are always part of history. This is a valuable contribution to the small but growing number of books that invite young students to contemplate important historical ideas. (KT)

**2.28**  ★ Stanley, Jerry. **Hurry Freedom: African Americans in Gold Rush California.** Crown, 2000. ISBN 0-517-80094-2. 86 pp. (I).

Through the story of a black man named Mifflin Gibbs, readers learn about the impact of the gold rush on African Americans. Mifflin Gibbs headed west for a better life. What he found was discrimination against blacks as a group and acceptance by a few individual whites. Gibbs also found economic advancement but no rights as a citizen. This compelling narrative describes how Gibbs and fellow African Americans finally won their right to testify in court. Although this is one man's story, in a larger sense it is the story of how we came together as a nation. As Stanley notes at the end of the book, "It was a long road traveled to a fitting end and a lesson well learned: history has a knack for justice" (p. 80). This gripping historical narrative is sure to provoke conversations about social justice. (MZ)

**2.29**  Sullivan, George. **Picturing Lincoln: Famous Photographs That Popularized the President.** Clarion, 2000. ISBN 0-395-91682-8. 88 pp. (I).

*Picturing Lincoln* is a welcome addition to the literature about our sixteenth president. It briefly describes the emerging photographic technology of the times and makes interesting connections between five famous photographs of Lincoln and his political career. The book is chronologically divided into five chapters, each of which focuses on one photograph. Chapter 1 addresses "The Tousled-Hair Photograph," which was taken to give many Americans their first image of the eloquent Republican speaking out against the expansion of slavery. Chapter 2 relates how the dignified "Cooper Union" photograph was widely copied and circulated to support Lincoln's presidential candidacy. The other three photographs—"The Penny Profile," "Lincoln and Tad," and "The Five-Dollar-Bill Portrait"—all contribute to the moving story of Lincoln and his time. Sullivan's artful arrangement of text and photographs make *Picturing Lincoln* an informative and memorable book. (KT)

## World History and Culture

**2.30**    Ancona, George. **Carnaval.** Harcourt Brace, 1999. ISBN 0-15-201793-3. Unpaged. (ALL).

George Ancona takes the reader to Olidna, Brazil, to view the preparations for the festivities that take place during *carnaval*, the five-day festival that comes before Lent. Ancona's many vibrant photographs bring the preparations and the actual celebration to life, while the text details the preparations and explains the traditions and folklore behind many of the giant puppets, dances, and costumes seen on the streets. The photographs successfully capture the lavish excitement of *carnaval*. Through both photographs and text, students can look for examples of how "*Carnaval* celebrates the three main cultures of Brazil—indigenous, European, and African" through song, story, and dance. They can also examine how Ancona's photographs provide information that goes well beyond the words. (LR)

**2.31**    ★ Blumberg, Rhoda. **Shipwrecked! The True Adventures of a Japanese Boy.** HarperCollins, 2001. ISBN 0-688-17484-1. 80 pp. (I).

The amazing adventures of a Japanese fisherman named Manjiro begin when he is shipwrecked for five months on an island three hundred miles from Japan. At that time, the early nineteenth century, Japanese ports were closed to the outside world and foreigners prohibited from entering. Rescued by an American whaler, Manjiro is adopted by the ship's captain who takes him to New Bedford, Massachusetts, where he becomes the first Japanese person to set foot in the United States. In 1848 he joins in the California gold rush in an effort to raise money to finance his return home. On his return to Japan, he is elevated to the rank of samurai, assists Japanese officials in dealing with Commodore Perry's demands to open Japan to U.S. ships, and becomes a diplomat and government consultant. Readers will not only enjoy a page-turning adventure story, but they will also learn about the history of Japanese-American relations. (MZ)

**2.32**    Cooper, Michael L. **Fighting for Honor: Japanese Americans and World War II.** Clarion, 2000. ISBN 0-395-91375-6. 118 pp. (I).

When the bombing of Pearl Harbor drew the United States into World War II, the prejudice against Japanese Americans dramatically increased. While Japanese immigrants had been mistreated before the war—even denied citizenship—during the war these hardworking, loyal people were evacuated from their homes and placed in internment camps. At the same time, Japanese American males were expected to join the army and fight in Europe. Cooper details the patriotism and valiant fighting of the 100th and 442nd battalions of Japanese Americans—"fighting for honor"—while their families at home endured suspicion, racism, and denial of freedom. Photographs from the National Archives add dimension to this well-documented text. The story underscores the importance of vigilantly guarding the rights and freedoms of citizens against unfounded prejudice, for despite our constitutional guarantee of equal protection under the law, this was a promise betrayed. (DA)

2.33    Donoughue, Carol. **The Mystery of the Hieroglyphs: The Story of the Rosetta Stone and the Race to Decipher Egyptian Hieroglyphs.** Oxford, 1999. ISBN 0-19-521553-2. 48 pp. (I).

The difficulties and ingenuity of those who wanted to break the code and decipher the ancient Egyptian hieroglyphs are recounted in a colorful and captivating manner. The author not only tells the story of the Rosetta stone, but also fully explains the process by which scribes learned and practiced hieroglyphs and documented history using the pictures and symbols of the hieroglyphic alphabet. Beautiful illustrations are a true complement to the text. A chapter explaining how to read hieroglyphs, a detailed glossary, a further reading list, and an index all serve to fully engage the reader. Another notable book on the topic is James Rumford's *Seeker of Knowledge* (Houghton, 2000), which tells the story of Jean-François Champollion, the man who was ultimately responsible for decoding Egyptian hieroglyphs. (DK)

2.34    Gottfried, Ted. **Nazi Germany: The Face of Tyranny.** Illustrated by Stephen Alcorn. Twenty-First Century Books, 2000. ISBN 0-7613-1714-7. 128 pp. (I).

Unlike other Holocaust books written for elementary school students, this one describes the historical background of Germany from the late nineteenth century up to and including World War II. Gottfried's discussion of historical events includes Prussian Chancellor Otto von Bismarck's forming the German states into a nation, World War I, the Treaty of Versailles, and the formation of the Nazi Party. He also discusses how and why many neighboring

European nations were so easily influenced by the Nazi philosophy of anti-Semitism. Quotes from Hitler's *Mein Kampf*—"Propaganda must present only that aspect of truth which is favorable to one's own side. The people must be misled"—offer some explanation. The book includes a time line, glossary, chronology, bibliography with Internet sites, and source notes. (DA)

2.35    ★ Kurlansky, Mark. **The Cod's Tale.** Illustrated by S. D. Schindler. Putnam, 2001. ISBN 0-399-23476-4. 48 pp. (I).

This book explains the huge impact of the Atlantic cod on the history of North America and Europe—how it fed the Viking explorers, brought Basques fishermen to North America, fed the men who sailed with Columbus in 1492, lured the Pilgrims to Plymouth, made New England into a commercial center, helped sustain the slave trade, and was an issue in the settlement of the American Revolution. The book challenges readers to consider the impact of commercial fishing on today's shrinking cod population. Handsome watercolor-and-ink illustrations add information and humor. Time lines, sidebars, and selected excerpts from related books both entertain and inform. Pair this book with Milton Meltzer's *The Amazing Potato* (HarperCollins, 1992) for another look at how a seemingly ordinary food has made an extraordinary impact on people's lives. (MZ)

2.36    Levine, Ellen. **Darkness over Denmark: The Danish Resistance and the Rescue of the Jews.** Holiday House, 2000. ISBN 0-8234-1447-7. 164 pp. (I).

This book raises the question of why Denmark chose to protect its Jews during World War II while other countries did not. After citing many explanations given by historians, Levine suggests that in Denmark Jews were not defined as "the other." *Darkness over Denmark* is based on interviews with more than twenty Danish survivors, rescuers, and resistance fighters. The collection of memories and actual historical events clearly depict how an entire country fought a war with the enemy through individual acts of defiance. As Levine notes, "Thousands of Danes had fought to save the Jews of their nation, and they had largely succeeded" (p. 145). This makes for engaging reading, not only because of the thrilling acts of heroism, but also because of the author's willingness to put to rest well-known but untrue stories of Danish resistance. This is an excellent book to include during studies of the Holocaust. (EL)

Maestro, Betsy. **The Story of Clocks and Calendars: Marking a Millennium.** Illustrated by Giulio Maestro. Lothrop, Lee & Shepard, 1999. ISBN 0-688-14548-5. 48 pp. (I). (See **9.21.**)

2.37    Martin, Jacqueline Briggs. **The Lamp, the Ice, and the Boat Called** *Fish.* Illustrated by Beth Krommes. Houghton Mifflin, 2001. ISBN 0-618-00341-X. Unpaged. (I).

In six separate sections, this poetic account tells how the Canadian Arctic Expedition of 1913 set off from the coast of Alaska to study plants and people. The travelers included a captain and crew as well as an Inupiaq family with two daughters and a friend of the father; the family and friend would help provide food, clothing, and survival knowledge. This fascinating story describes how the boat became locked in the ice, was abandoned, and ultimately sank. The family and some of the crew survived on what they called Shipwreck Camp, but this refuge too was later abandoned for Wrangel Island, where the group spent a hungry summer. Ultimately, the survivors were rescued and taken to Nome, where they began their journey home. Beautiful scratchboard-and-watercolor illustrations enhance this exciting and informative tale of endurance in the Arctic. Photographs of the Inupiaq family are also included. (MZ)

2.38    McMahon, Patricia. **One Belfast Boy.** Photographs by Alan O'Connor. Houghton Mifflin, 1999. ISBN 0-395-68620-2. 54 pp. (I).

This well-illustrated book follows the daily life of a young boy named Liam Leathem who lives in Belfast and is interested in boxing. His seemingly ordinary life is affected by the turmoil in Ireland, which is evident at every turn: from the graffiti on the walls with slogans about the IRA and statements proclaiming "We shall never be defeated," to news and rumors about bombs, to the endless hatreds between Catholics and Protestants, to the impossibility of going to a new movie theater in a Protestant neighborhood. An introduction to the book gives background on the struggles in Ireland and provides a useful map. This book should open up discussions of how even ordinary activities are affected by political and social realities. One boy's true story provides insight into an enduring conflict. (DK)

Warren, Andrea. **Surviving Hitler: A Boy in the Nazi Death Camps.** HarperCollins, 2001. ISBN 0-688-17497-3. 146 pp. (I). (See **5.6.**)

# 3 Historical Fiction

**Linda Leonard Lamme and Roseanne Russo**

*Contributing reviewers included Be Astengo, Ruth Lowery, Diane Masla, Nancy Rankie Shelton, and Debbie Savage.*

---

### Criteria for Excellence

- The novel must be well written and engaging.
- The novel must contain historically accurate information and authentic depictions of historical events and places.
- The novel must contain a strong underlying theme that is relevant to today's reader.
- As a group, the novels must cover a historical spectrum of events, peoples, and places.
- As a group, the novels must cover a wide range of reading levels.

---

## Twelfth- to Sixteenth-Century History

★ Barrett, Tracy. **Anna of Byzantium.** Dell, 1999.

Casanova, Mary. **Curse of a Winter Moon.** Hyperion, 2000.

★ Meyer, Carolyn. **Mary, Bloody Mary.** Harcourt, 1999.

Platt, Richard. **Castle Diary: The Journal of Tobias Burgess.** Illustrated by Chris Riddell. Candlewick, 1999.

Williams, Laura E. **The Executioner's Daughter.** Holt, 2000.

## Nineteenth Century

*Slavery and the Civil War*

★ Ayres, Katherine. **Stealing South: A Story of the Underground Railroad.** Delacorte, 2001.

Pinkney, Andrea Davis. **Silent Thunder: A Civil War Story.** Hyperion, 1999.

★ Ransom, Candice F. **The Promise Quilt.** Illustrated by Ellen Beier. Walker, 1999.

★ Schwartz, Virginia Frances. **Send One Angel Down.** Holiday House, 2000.

Stowe, Cynthia M. **The Second Escape of Arthur Cooper.** Marshall Cavendish, 2000.

*Westward Movement in North America*

Avi. **Prairie School.** Illustrated by Bill Farnsworth. HarperCollins, 2001.

★ Holm, Jennifer. **Our Only May Amelia.** HarperCollins, 1999.

★ Lawson, Julie. **Destination Gold!** Orca, 2000.

★ Spooner, Michael. **Daniel's Walk.** Holt, 2001.

*Industrial Revolution/Railroads/Factories*

★ Howard, Ellen. **The Gate in the Wall.** Atheneum, 2000.

Karr, Kathleen. **Skullduggery.** Hyperion, 2000.

Williams, Barbara. **Making Waves.** Dial, 2000.

## Late Nineteenth Century and Twentieth Century

*Women's History*

Moss, Marissa. **True Heart.** Illustrated by C. F. Payne. Harcourt, 1999.

★ Namioka, Lensey. **Ties That Bind, Ties That Break.** Dell, 1999.

Ryan, Pam Muñoz. **Amelia and Eleanor Go for a Ride.** Illustrated by Bryan Selznick. Scholastic, 1999.

*Economic Migration/Immigration/The Great Depression*

Brooke, Peggy. **Jake's Orphan.** DK Inc., 2000.

Harris, Carol Flynn. **A Place for Joey.** Boyds Mills, 2001.

Lee, Milly. **Earthquake.** Illustrated by Yangsook Choi. Farrar, Straus & Giroux, 2001.

Littlesugar, Amy. **Tree of Hope.** Illustrated by Floyd Cooper. Philomel, 1999.

McKissack, Patricia C. **Color Me Dark: The Diary of Nellie Lee Love, the Great Migration North.** Scholastic, 2000

Recorvits, Helen. **Goodbye, Walter Malinski.** Illustrated by Lloyd Bloom. Farrar, Straus & Giroux, 1999.

## Wars

*World War I*

Lawrence, Iain. **Lord of the Nutcracker Men.** Delacorte, 2001.

Lindquist, Susan Hart. **Summer Soldiers.** Dell, 1999.

*World War II*

Denenberg, Barry. **The Journal of Ben Uchida: Citizen 13559, Mirror Lake Internment Camp.** Scholastic, 1999.

Lisle, Janet Taylor. **The Art of Keeping Cool.** Atheneum, 2000.

★ Mazer, Norma. **Good Night, Maman.** Harcourt, 1999.

*Recent Conflicts*

    Ellis, Deborah. **The Breadwinner.** Douglas & McIntyre, 2000.

    Mead, Alice. **Girl of Kosovo.** Farrar, Straus & Giroux, 2001.

*Desegregation and Prejudice*

★ Armistead, John. **The $66 Summer.** Milkweed, 2000.

    Carbone, Elisa. **Storm Warriors.** Knopf, 2001.

    Holt, Kimberly Willis. **Dancing in Cadillac Light.** Putnam, 2001.

---

Contemporary historical fiction presents children with a passage into another time, a glimpse into the ordinary lives of ordinary people under duress. Good historical fiction transports readers into the pain of war, the despair of depression, and the injustice of racial discrimination. Today's historical fiction includes authentic depictions of ordinary people as well as those who are famous, girls as well as boys, and minorities as well as whites. Stories describe life on the home front as well as on the battleground, and in the world arena as well as in North America. Because four chapters of this book focus on cultural/racial groups (Hispanics, African Americans, Asian and Pacific Islanders, indigenous peoples), this chapter contains fewer works of historical fiction from these cultures than books from Western cultures.

We chose a broad range of histories involving art, music, disease, and travel by ship, train, plane, canal boat, car, and foot. Illustrators have created elegant and historically accurate pictures to accompany historical texts, and the novels are intricately researched and crafted. Our collection is organized around historical periods, topics, and locales so that teachers can easily access the books for a social studies curriculum.

We discussed many issues when making decisions about which books to include in this chapter. Many of the stories take place in eras in which violence against women and violence in general was common. While we don't condone sensationalized violence, we do believe that children have a right to historical accuracy in the stories they read. Authors of the books we selected do not sugarcoat the events of the time, nor do they overemphasize the violence that did exist.

Another issue that repeatedly arose was how to balance our collection with regard to age-appropriate material for younger children. One of the earmarks of a successful piece of historical fiction is that the story and characters are well developed. Many of the truly exemplary books, therefore, are written for older children. We challenged ourselves to find quality picture books and short novels for younger and less skilled readers.

Because the world is becoming a more global society, we sought out books that went beyond U.S. history. We noticed that most historical novels set outside our country are about ancient times, whereas most of those set at home are about more recent events. Among books set in the United States, we sought stories about immigrant people, American Indians, and people of minority cultures, since most historical fiction of the past is about middle- or upper-class white Americans. While there has been an increase in the number of books about African American and immigrant experiences, some cultures, such as Caribbean, Middle Eastern, and South American, are underrepresented in the literature. There are still remarkably few good books about the many Native American nations that are the longest residents of our land.

Historical fiction about the earliest times is usually set in Asia or Europe. Most of the stories feature women who overcome oppression, such as *Anna of Byzantium* (Barrett, 1999), *Mary, Bloody Mary* (Meyer, 1999), and *The Executioner's Daughter* (Williams, 2000), or religious persecution, as in *Curse of a Winter Moon* (Casanova, 2000). The adventures of a page in a medieval castle are chronicled in *Castle Diary: The Journal of Tobias Burgess* (Platt, 1999) for readers interested in the medieval life of the ruling class. For variety and excitement, readers won't find better books than these.

Moving to the nineteenth century, historical topics include slavery and the Civil War, the westward movement and stories linked to the industrial revolution and immigration, all set in North America. *Silent Thunder: A Civil War Story* (Pinkney, 1999) shares dual stories of a brother and sister, each with distinctively different roles on the plantation, but both of whom have a "silent thunder," an inner desire for literacy and freedom. A similar slave story is told in *Send One Angel Down* (Schwartz, 2000), but with the added dimension of slave songs and chants sung to endure the oppression and nurture the dream of freedom. *Stealing South* (Ayers, 2001) is an Underground Railroad story that contains details of slave life. *The Second Escape of Arthur Cooper* (Stowe, 2000) involves an escaped slave living in the North. When slave catchers arrive on Nantucket Island to recapture him, the Quakers rally to his defense. The support of allies such as the Quakers is an important element in the history of slavery. *The Promise Quilt* (Ransom, 1999) is a picture book about a child who loses her father and her opportunity for an education during the Civil War. These five new slavery and Civil War stories are meticulously researched and often contain details not previously available in books for children.

Westward movement stories used to be mostly about male gun-slingers or hardships for women on the prairie. The books we discovered reveal the harsh realities of living on the frontier and the eventual triumph of surviving difficult conditions. *Prairie School* (Avi, 2001) reveals what school was like for children on the frontier. Three great adventure stories include *Our Own May Amelia* (Holm, 1999), about life in a Finnish Washington community, *Destination Gold!* (Lawson, 2000), about the Klondike gold rush, and *Daniel's Walk* (Spooner, 2001), about life on the Oregon Trail. These westward movement stories also contain lively action and sensitive portrayals of Native Americans.

The onset of the industrial revolution brought with it deplorable conditions in factories and people who immigrated to the United States to find work. Several books focus on forms of transportation. *The Gate in the Wall* (Howard, 2000) shares the adventures of a girl who first labors in a factory as the sole support for her family, then finds work on a canal boat in England. *Skullduggery* (Karr, 2000) is a mystery about a boy who works for a phrenologist in New York. In *Making Waves* (Williams, 2000), we learn of the deplorable working conditions in Baltimore factories. These are honest, detailed stories of conditions people suffered due to poverty, race, and gender.

The women's rights movement of the late nineteenth and early twentieth centuries sparked several novels and picture books. Half of the books in our collection feature female protagonists, many of whom encounter prejudice because of their gender, but in two cases, gender issues are the primary focus of the stories. In the picture book *True Heart* (Moss, 1999), Bee is the sole support for her eight brothers after their parents die, and she is determined to get a better-paying job as a railroad worker. She succeeds and eventually becomes an engineer. Ailin protests the ancient Chinese tradition of feet binding in *Ties That Bind, Ties That Break* (Namioka, 1999), suffering dire consequences for her actions. In each case, these women become pioneers in defense of women's rights. In *Amelia and Eleanor Go for a Ride* (Ryan, 1999), readers learn about the time Amelia Earhart took Eleanor Roosevelt for a plane ride. Teachers should share the author's note at the end of this book with students because it contains important information about what is fact and what is fictionalized in this story.

As a result of the industrial revolution, people immigrated to the United States and migrated to cities to find jobs. Two of the novels we chose involve children from Italian and Polish immigrant families, respectively; all are based on actual historical events. In *A Place for Joey* (Harris, 2001), Joey, from north Boston, deals with prejudice from Irish immigrant children as he seeks work at the docks and witnesses the explosion of a tanker full of molasses. Walter endures extreme embarrassment and prejudice in a desperately poor Polish family in *Goodbye, Walter Malinski* (Recorvits, 1999). These immigrant children all seek to fit in and are embarrassed by their families' traditional language and culture.

Depression-era stories are survival stories. Tree is adopted, but his brother remains in the orphanage in *Jake's Orphan* (Brooke, 2000). In *Tree of Hope* (Littlesugar, 1999), Florie and her father visit the Tree of Hope outside the Lafayette Theater where he once worked and now desperately needs a job. *Color Me Dark: The Diary of Nellie Lee Love, the Great Migration North* (McKissack, 2000) shares a family's attempt to escape racism and poverty in the South and to find employment in the big city of Chicago. Hard times were had by all during the Great Depression. These books tell three very different stories of the impact of the Depression on children from the North, the South, and the Midwest.

War has always been a major topic of historical fiction for children, but usually the stories have been about children fighting in battles. The war stories in this chapter chronicle the impact of war on people who are not at the forefront of the battles. Two are World War I stories: In *Lord of the Nutcracker Men* (Lawrence, 2001), a young boy is sent to live with his aunt in the country north of London while his dad goes to war and his mother works in a munitions factory. *Summer Soldiers* (Lindquist, 1999) describes the discrimination faced by a boy whose father chooses not to fight in the war. Two stories depict conditions in internment camps where families are incarcerated "for their own protection" during World War II: *The Journal of Ben Uchida: Citizen 13559, Mirror Lake Internment Camp* (Denenberg, 1999) takes place in a Japanese internment camp and *Good Night, Maman* (Mazer, 1999) in a Jewish camp in upstate New York. Although treatment of the Japanese was worse than treatment of the Jewish children, both are heart-wrenching stories of the impact of war on minority peoples. *The Art of Keeping Cool* (Lisle, 2000) depicts tense conditions on the home front during World War II. Only *Girl of Kosovo* (Mead, 2001) and *The Breadwinner* (Ellis, 2000) take place in the heart of the battle in the more recent conflicts in Kosovo and Afghanistan, respectively.

The civil rights movement chronicles the impact of segregation and attempts at desegregation on African American people. Few people have heard of the surfmen who patrolled lifeguard stations on islands off the eastern coast of the United States, but an engaging tale of the only black coast guard station is told in *Storm Warriors* (Carbone, 2001). Several stories are about black children and white children who become friends and lead the way toward integration in schools and neighborhoods. *The $66 Summer* (Armistead, 2000) examines racial prejudice from the point of view of northern white children who live for a summer in the South. *Dancing in Cadillac Light* (Holt, 2001) unravels the mystery of a grandfather's kindness to "white trash" in Texas during the 1960s.

All of the books included in this chapter are historically accurate, highly entertaining stories full of worthwhile themes. They present perspectives of minorities and women more frequently than did older historical fiction. Our collection portrays a balance of male and female characters, including those that counter stereotypical gender roles. The characters stand up to injustice in many different forms.

Our collection is still dominated by U.S. history, though more than ten books focus on some aspect of African American history. The locales of stories include plantations in the South, a logging village in the state of Washington, a Klondike village in Alaska, a Japanese internment camp in California, a home on Nantucket Island, and farms in the Midwest. Overseas settings include China, Korea, Afghanistan, Kosovo, England, France, and Byzantium. Stories take place in ancient and modern times. Some stories are about familiar historical events such as the Underground Railroad, westward movement, and the gold rush, while others involve less common topics such as the surfmen on the Outer Banks of North Carolina.

There are books in this collection for everyone. We are pleased to be able to include several easy-to-read novels for older children who are struggling readers; in many cases, however, the best books tend to be for more mature readers.

## Twelfth- to Sixteenth-Century History

**3.1**    ★ Barrett, Tracy. **Anna of Byzantium.** Dell, 1999. ISBN 0-385-32626-2. 209 pp. (I).

Written from the convent where she lives in exile, Princess Anna Comnena recounts, through her memoirs, life in the palace of the Byzantine Empire of the 1100s. Anna is the firstborn child of Emperor Alexius I of Byzantium and the heir apparent to the throne. She is arrogant and proud of her position, never disguising her ambitions to be empress. She is eager and quick in her studies at a time when the scholarship of girls is uncommon. When her brother, John, is born, Anna fears that her father will be convinced by his counselors to make John his heir instead of her. But it is Anna's own jealousy of her sibling and insolence toward her powerful grandmother that ultimately lead to her undoing. In her author's note, Barrett clarifies details of Anna Comnena's life and dedicates the book to forgotten women writers of the Middle Ages. (BA/RR)

**3.2**    Casanova, Mary. **Curse of a Winter Moon.** Hyperion, 2000. ISBN 0-7868-0547-1. 135 pp. (I).

In mid-sixteenth-century France, when the power and corruption of the Catholic Church was at its peak and reading was considered heresy, religious turbulence ravaged Europe. When Marius is six years old, his mother dies giving birth to his younger brother, John-Pierre. Her last words are, "Tell Marius to take good care of his brother" (p. 4). We soon learn the burden of these last words. Jean-Pierre is considered a werewolf because of his Christmas Eve birth, and Marius lives in fear, caring for his brother. The day soldiers march through town dragging heretics who are to be burned at the stake, Marius confirms his knowledge that he must keep a close watch on Jean-Pierre. Marius then learns that his father is a heretic because he can read! Life as he knows it changes forever. (BA)

**3.3**    ★ Meyer, Carolyn. **Mary, Bloody Mary.** Harcourt, 1999. ISBN 0-15-201906-5. 227 pp. (I).

Mary Tudor, who reigned briefly as queen of England during the sixteenth century, tells the story of her troubled childhood as the eldest daughter of King Henry VIII. Mary vividly describes how her father, in his desperate desire to have a son, declared her an illegitimate child so she would not be eligible to reign as queen. Mary is banished from the royal home, only to be brought back as her younger sister's babysitter. Meyer's compelling story portrays the complexities of court life in the sixteenth century as Mary struggles to come to terms with her powerful father's irrational behavior and decisions. Mary's character is so compassionately portrayed that the reader develops a deeper insight into the reasons for the actions of the woman historically known as Bloody Mary. The companion book, *Beware, Princess Elizabeth* (Harcourt, 2001), chronicling the life of Mary's younger sister, is equally compelling. (RL/RR)

★ Park, Linda Sue. **A Single Shard.** Clarion, 2001. ISBN 0-395-97827-0. 152 pp. (I). (See **16.31.**)

**3.4**  Platt, Richard. **Castle Diary: The Journal of Tobias Burgess.**
Illustrated by Chris Riddell. Candlewick, 1999. ISBN 0-7636-
0489-5. 64 pp. (I).

Just before his eleventh birthday, in the year 1285, Tobias Burgess
begins life as a page in his uncle's castle. There is much to learn,
and Tobias records it all in his diary with good humor, determination, and language tinged with medieval dialect. Detailed
illustrations liberally spiced with whimsy accompany Tobias's
account of the excitement and danger of tournaments, the elaborate preparation of feasts, and the stalwart skills needed by a
true knight. He also receives instructions from his cousin on
table manners: "When I sniffed, she reminded me that if I should
wipe my nose, it is only seemly to clean my hand on my clothes
before touching food" (p. 72). Fun, combined with generous historical detail, makes this an excellent book for students interested in the medieval period. (DM)

**3.5**  Williams, Laura E. **The Executioner's Daughter.** Holt, 2000.
ISBN 0-8050-6234-3. 134 pp. (I).

Life in fifteenth-century England is fraught with turmoil for
thirteen-year-old Lily, who lives with her parents on the out-
skirts of town. The town folk and children torment her because
her father is the local executioner, administering beheadings and
maimings prescribed by the authorities. Lily tolerates life as an
outcast, believing that her father is carrying out justice by pun-
ishing people who have committed criminal acts. But after she
learns that her own mother was once slated for execution, she
realizes that the line between bad and good is not always clear.
Knowing this, she can no longer bear to live with her father or to
live out her destiny as his assistant. Through superb writing,
Williams adeptly conveys how the young and gentle survived in
the harsh realities of medieval England. (BA)

## Nineteenth Century

### Slavery and the Civil War

**3.6**  ★ Ayres, Katherine. **Stealing South: A Story of the Underground Railroad.** Delacorte, 2001. ISBN 0-385-72912-X. 201 pp.
(I).

Will Spencer has been a driver for the Underground Railroad
since he was twelve years old. Now, at sixteen, he is ready to set

out on his own to become a peddler. On his last trip, he is to train his brother, Tom, to take his place. But when they deliver their passenger, Noah, to the next station, Noah has one request. He wants Will to steal his siblings from the farm where they are slaves. Will's strong opposition to slavery convinces him to make one more trip. Ayers has created a fast-paced adventure story sure to grasp the attention of even the most reluctant readers, who vicariously experience the horrors of slave breeding and "soul dealing"—the selling of children to work on the cotton plantations of the Deep South. For more child-driven adventure, try Ayers's *Silver Dollar Girl* (Dell, 2000), which provides a glimpse into mining life in the Old West. (BA)

McGill, Alice. **Molly Bannaky.** Illustrated by Chris K. Soentpiet. Houghton Mifflin, 1999. ISBN 0-395-72287-X. Unpaged. (I). (See **19.22.**)

**3.7**    Pinkney, Andrea Davis. **Silent Thunder: A Civil War Story.** Hyperion, 1999. ISBN 0-786-80439-4. 216 pp. (I).

Thirteen-year-old Roscoe and his eleven-year-old sister Summer alternate chapters to weave the story of their lives as slaves on a Virginia plantation. Roscoe seeks to increase his knowledge through reading. His learning is an unusual accomplishment for an enslaved child and, accordingly, he does not take it for granted. He becomes the teacher, teaching his sister to read, and the news bearer, informing his friend Clem about the Emancipation Proclamation and about blacks fighting for the Union Army. Summer seeks to discover the unspoken truth about her birth, held by her master—a truth she intuitively knows: "But truth, now that was another story." Pinkney's research, coupled with her ability to write for young people using two distinct voices, exposes the breeding, branding, and beating of slaves in this gripping story that reveals more facts about slavery than are usually found in children's books. (NRS)

**3.8**    ★ Ransom, Candice F. **The Promise Quilt.** Illustrated by Ellen Beier. Walker, 1999. ISBN 0-8027-8694-4. Unpaged. (ALL).

Before leaving to serve in the Civil War, Addie's father promises that she will someday go to school and learn to read and write so that she can make her mark in the world. But Addie's life changes as Union and Rebel soldiers repeatedly trample and burn all that is dear to her family—including the school. When the war is over, all that is left of Papa is his red shirt, returned to Addie and her mother by a woman from Pennsylvania. Addie cherishes her memories of Papa and that red shirt, rarely taking it off. But when a sacrifice proves necessary for the good of all, Addie willingly contributes her Papa's red shirt, knowing that now Papa has made *his* mark in the world. An author's note explains that the checkerboard pattern on the shirt became a coverlet design after the war. (LLL/RR)

**3.9**    ★ Schwartz, Virginia Frances. **Send One Angel Down.** Holiday House, 2000. ISBN 0-8234-1484-1. 163 pp. (I).

Abram, a slave boy, raises and protects his cousin Eliza, daughter of Abram's Aunt Charity and Master Turner, the plantation owner. Eliza, with her blue eyes and fair skin, is "a precious jewel born to trouble." Abram shares stories of cotton fields, breeding cabins, and the Saturday night parties in the bottoms. He expresses his frustration about being enslaved: "Out in the fields, I felt just like the cotton. Trapped in a cage." And later, "I was chained to that overseer. . . . He rode up and down the rows. . . . He was thirsty for blood from a slave's back." (p. 94). Yet despite all the difficulties, there is hope, an unending hope of freedom, often expressed in song. Using original documents and audio histories as background, Schwartz's vivid representation of slave life will appeal to older children appreciative of historical accuracy. Her story was inspired by Julius Lester's Eliza in *To Be a Slave* (Dial, 1969, 1998). (LLL)

**3.10**    Stowe, Cynthia M. **The Second Escape of Arthur Cooper.** Marshall Cavendish, 2000. ISBN 0-7614-5069-6. 112 pp. (I).

Arthur Cooper was born into slavery in Virginia in 1789. He escaped at the age of nineteen, married Mary, a freeborn person, and lived with her and their four children in a Quaker community on Nantucket Island. Ten-year-old Phebe Folger tells how Mary is hired to help her mother, bedridden from being thrown off a horse. Phebe and Mary strike up a friendship, sharing confidences. Phebe shares her struggles with reading and writing, and Mary relates how Arthur escaped slavery. When slave catchers arrive to recapture Arthur, the entire Quaker community rallies to keep Arthur and his family free. Phebe, a feisty, determined, honorable girl, is instrumental in helping Arthur's family hide. Stowe presents a moving tale of courage and conviction written in an easily understandable style for younger readers. (LLL)

**Westward Movement in North America**

**3.11**   Avi. **Prairie School.** Illustrated by Bill Farnsworth. Harper-Collins, 2001. ISBN 0-06-027664-9. 48 pp. (P).

It is 1880. Nine-year-old Noah is happy to build a new life on the prairie of Colorado until his parents decide he needs better "schooling." Stubbornly, Noah refuses to learn, until his clever Aunt Dora compares the act of reading to his love of nature and his curiosity about the world. Avi's touching story of determination includes depictions of life on the prairie and the gloominess of sod houses. Farnsworth's paintings are muted in tone, reflecting the browns, yellows, and blues of the prairie. Third-grade students commented on the tone of the pictures, noting, "how different it is inside the little school and outside. No wonder Noah loves the prairie!" Similar to Avi's *The Secret School* (2001; **19.34**), in which the oldest student teaches the others when their schoolmarm must leave, these stories testify to the difficulty of western life and the importance of education as a route out of poverty. (NRS)

★ Erdrich, Louise. **The Birchbark House.** Hyperion, 1999. ISBN 0-7868-0300-2. 244 pp. (I). (See **18.5**.)

★ Hill, Kirkpatrick. **The Year of Miss Agnes.** Margaret K. McElderry Books, 2000. ISBN 0-689-82933-7. 115 pp. (I). (See **6.24**.)

**3.12**   ★ Holm, Jennifer. **Our Only May Amelia.** HarperCollins, 1999. ISBN 0-06-028354-8. 253 pp. (I).

Twelve-year-old May Amelia is the only girl in the Nasel River settlement in Washington in 1899. She has seven brothers and works alongside them, mucking out barns and doing farm chores, but she has learned the hard way that there are double standards for girls and boys. Nevertheless, her adventurous spirit refuses to be confined by unfair rules. This attitude leads her on all sorts of escapades as she cuts off her hair to become a runner for the logging camp and gets trapped up a tree by a bear. May Amelia's voice is fresh, bold, and curious. Her chatty stories reveal aspects of Finnish pioneer life and of Chinook Indians and Chinese immigrants who lived in the area. Inspired by the diary of her great-aunt Alice Amelia, Holm has created a story that will hearten any spirit confined by the conventions of sex roles. (BA)

**3.13**    ★ Lawson, Julie. **Destination Gold!** Orca, 2000. ISBN 1-55143-155-6. 210 pp. (I).

It's 1897 and the gold rush is on! With hopes of adventure and fortune, sixteen-year-old Ned Turner, believing that the Klondike holds the key to his widowed mother's debt, sets off from Victoria, British Columbia, to strike it rich. Naive about his surroundings, Ned trusts and is duped by Montana, a ruthless and vicious man. Despite all odds, however, Ned and his adopted mutt, Nugget, reach the Yukon and survive the winter. His younger sister, Sarah, a weakling in her mother's eyes, travels alone the next summer to find her brother and discover herself. Then there is Catherine, abused for two years by Montana; Catherine befriends Sarah on the trip north. Danger lurks at every corner for this trio of likable and determined young adventurers. Lawson has provided a valuable tale for older readers, complete with maps and archival photographs. (LLL/RR)

**3.14**    ★ Spooner, Michael. **Daniel's Walk.** Holt, 2001. ISBN 0-8050-6750-7. 214 pp. (I).

Fourteen-year-old Daniel is awakened by a harsh voice telling him that his father is in trouble. It's 1844 and Daniel's father has been hunting in the Rockies for many months. Daniel, who lives in Missouri, begins walking along the Oregon Trail, determined to find his father. Daniel joins up with a wagon train led by James Clyman and finds help in the form of a free black man and a feisty orphan girl. As the story unfolds, Daniel learns that the wide-open West is in fact already well populated by native peoples. Daniel's father, deeply transformed by his connection with Native Americans, is both saint and criminal when Daniel finally finds him. Daniel realizes he could never have truly understood his father without having made his own long journey. Spooner combines good historical detail, exciting adventure, and a sensitivity to the thriving peoples displaced by European intrusion in this engrossing story. (DM)

### Industrial Revolution/Railroads/Factories

★ Giff, Patricia Reilly. **Nory Ryan's Song.** Delacorte, 2000. ISBN 0-385-32141-4. 148 pp. (I). (See **5.14.**)

**3.15**    ★ Howard, Ellen. **The Gate in the Wall.** Atheneum, 2000. ISBN 0-689-82295-2. (I).

Ten-year-old Emma lives with her older sister, abusive brother-in-law, and their infant in late-eighteenth-century England. She slaves away in a silk mill ten hours a day to provide food for her family. One day she is a minute late for work and is locked out of the mill. Knowing she will be docked a day's wages, Emma searches for a way to earn some money, when she discovers a gate that opens into a whole new world. An elderly woman hires her as a huffler (crew member) on a narrow boat that travels the canals carting goods from one place to another. Emma learns that with hard work she can live a successful life, but first she must deal with her sense of obligation to her sister. Full of interesting details about life on canals, this unforgettable story is action-packed with strong, smart, hard-working female characters. (LLL)

**3.16** Karr, Kathleen. **Skullduggery.** Hyperion, 2000. ISBN 0-7868-0506-4. 160 pp. (I).

Life on the streets of New York in 1839 isn't easy for twelve-year-old Matthew, recently orphaned after a cholera epidemic wipes out his entire family. He believes himself fortunate to find lodging and work with Dr. ABC—Asa B. Cornwall—because he is eager to find a cure for cholera. To his disappointment, Matthew discovers that the doctor is a phrenologist, a scientist who judges character by interpreting the bumps on the cranium. Being an apprentice to Dr. ABC means working with skulls, not researching medical cures. As his apprenticeship intensifies, Matthew is horrified to learn that he must participate in the dangerous and illegal act of grave robbing in order to obtain new specimens. Karr skillfully presents a suspenseful and intense look at one of the more covert elements of the nineteenth century, perfect for older readers who like their history tinged with mystery. (RL/RR)

**3.17** Williams, Barbara. **Making Waves.** Dial, 2000. ISBN 0-8037-2515-9. 215 pp. (I).

After surviving the sinking of the *Titanic* in *Titanic Crossing* (Dial, 1995), Emily Brewer and Albert Trask continue their friendship by writing to each other, finally arranging a visit. Emily, who lives in Baltimore, struggles with the deplorable and dangerous working conditions in the factories, especially for women and children. She becomes an activist, exposing and fighting for improved conditions. Meanwhile, Albert, living with his grand-mother in Virginia, focuses his attention on informing politicians of the serious but preventable problems aboard the *Titanic*. Williams's gripping story of friendship accurately reveals the inequities in our country based on gender and social class. Inspired by the life and works of Dorothy Jacobs Bellanca, the story allows the young reader to view life in the United States at the turn of the twentieth century. For the older reader, Katherine Paterson's *Lyddie* (Lodestar, 1991) presents an even bleaker side of this period. (NRS)

★ Yin. **Coolies**. Illustrated by Chris Soentpiet. Philomel, 2001. ISBN 0-399-23227-3. Unpaged. (ALL). (See **16.33.**)

## Late Nineteenth Century and Twentieth Century

### Women's History

Corey, Shana. **You Forgot Your Skirt, Amelia Bloomer! A Very Improper Story.** Illustrated by Chesley McLaren. Scholastic, 2000. ISBN 0-439-07819-9. Unpaged. (P). (See **2.5.**)

★ Howard, Elizabeth Fitzgerald. **Virgie Goes to School with Us Boys.** Illustrated by E. B. Lewis. Simon & Schuster, 2000. ISBN 0-689-80076-2. Unpaged. (ALL). (See **6.9.**)

3.18    Moss, Marissa. **True Heart.** Illustrated by C. F. Payne. Harcourt, 1999. ISBN 0-15-201344-X. Unpaged. (ALL).

Bee wants more than anything to become a railroad engineer. In 1893, after her parents die from the typhus, she is left to raise eight brothers and sisters. Because the pay is good, Bee signs on to load freight for the Union Pacific Railroad. Soon nine other girls are hired. Bee rides in the cab whenever she can, studying the way the engineer drives the train. Her dream comes true after bandits hold up the *True Heart*, leaving the engineer wounded. Bee quickly volunteers herself as engineer and two of her cohorts as coal shovelers. After much hesitation (and insistent urging by the already delayed passengers), the stationmaster decides that Bee can run the train. An old photograph of female freight loaders in the California State Railroad Museum inspired Moss to write this story. Payne's realistic illustrations capture the vigor of the pioneer women of the railroad. (LLL)

**3.19**    ★ Namioka, Lensey. **Ties That Bind, Ties That Break.** Dell, 1999. ISBN 0-385-32666-1. 154 pp. (I).

In the early 1900s, China begins a movement toward modernization, discarding many archaic practices. In 1911 Ailin is the third daughter born into an upper-class Chinese family. Following tradition, Ailin will have her feet bound when she is four years old. But her progressive-minded father listens to her protests and decides against such deformation. Ailin's feet are left unbound. Unfortunately, progressive thinking is not always accepted by society at large. When Ailin's future in-laws find out that she has not had her feet bound, they cancel the arranged marriage. At age nine, Ailin is enrolled in the MacIntosh School run by U.S. missionaries and enjoys the happiest days of her life. When she is twelve, however, her family refuses to support her, deciding to sell her as a concubine. In an era when women are bound by tradition, Ailin takes her life into her own hands to change her destiny. (BA)

★ Rappaport, Doreen, and Lyndall Callan. **Dirt on Their Skirts: The Story of the Young Women Who Won the World Championship.** Illustrated by E. B. Lewis. Dial, 2000. ISBN 0-8037-2042-4. Unpaged. (ALL). (See **12.27.**)

**3.20**    Ryan, Pam Muñoz. **Amelia and Eleanor Go for a Ride.** Illustrated by Bryan Selznick. Scholastic, 1999. ISBN 0-590-96075-X. Unpaged. (ALL).

Amelia Earhart is one of the most famous women in the world. Daring, bold, and determined, she is the first woman to fly solo across the Atlantic Ocean. Eleanor Roosevelt is also famous, outspoken, and bold. As a political mover and shaker in her own right, she is a new breed of first lady. One evening Eleanor invites Amelia to the White House for dinner. The dinner is elegant, and the guests are mesmerized by Amelia's description of flying through the night sky. After dinner the daring duo impulsively leave the White House and fly off in an airplane to experience the night sky over Washington D.C. Selznick's black-and-white illustrations resemble early issues of *LIFE* magazine, providing an enthralling glimpse into the past and making Ryan's fictionalized account of a true story seem more real. Author notes verify that this event actually happened, although the details have been fictionalized. (BA)

**Economic Migration/Immigration/The Great Depression**

3.21    Brooke, Peggy. **Jake's Orphan.** DK Inc., 2000. ISBN 0-7894-2628-5. 261 pp. (I).

Tree and his adventurous little brother Acorn have been living in the St. Paul Orphanage so long that Tree has nearly given up hope of escape. But in 1926, laborers are needed on farms in the Midwest, and twelve-year-old Tree is adopted by the Gundersons to work on their North Dakota farm. Tree decides that he must leave Acorn behind because it is necessary to earn money for the brothers' future together. Mr. Gunderson is a hard man, but his brother Jake takes a special interest in Tree, and the two become close. When Acorn, wild as ever, runs away from the orphanage and joins Tree, Tree must choose between his accustomed role as Acorn's protector or remain under the newfound care of Jake Gunderson. A story that tests the obligations of loyalty, this book will captivate intermediate readers. (DM)

3.22    Harris, Carol Flynn. **A Place for Joey.** Boyds Mills, 2001. ISBN 1-56397-108-9. 90 pp. (ALL).

*A Place for Joey* is based on an actual event in Boston in 1919. Joey's Italian immigrant family has plans to move from the north end in Boston. Joey dreads the move and begins "hooking" school to find a job so that he can remain in his neighborhood with his friends. At the docks, he encounters Irish lads and a police officer who scorn him, but he persists, certain that even though he is only fourteen he will be able to find a job. One day a tanker full of molasses explodes and Joey helps rescue the police officer. This event changes his perspective on life and gives him dreams for the future. Like many immigrant children today, Joey wishes his mom would speak English and helps her learn the language, faces ridicule because he is an immigrant, and along with his family has to work hard in order to make it in this new land. (LLL)

3.23    Lee, Milly. **Earthquake.** Illustrated by Yangsook Choi. Farrar, Straus & Giroux, 2001. ISBN 0-374-39964-6. Unpaged. (ALL).

A Chinese American family flees their home in Chinatown during the San Francisco earthquake of 1906. They load their belongings into a cart, including their most treasured Buddhist statue of Kwan Yin, goddess of mercy. As fires threaten their lives, they join many other Chinese families who are pushing and pulling overloaded carts all the way to Golden Gate Park, where the army has set up tents for people displaced during the earthquake. The trip is especially hard on the grandmother and mother, whose feet were bound as children in China. Lee shares historical information in an author's note to complete the story of what happened to her family—her grandmother, father, mother, and two brothers—who experienced the earthquake. Choi's illustrations graphically depict the catastrophic nature of the earthquake. (LLL)

3.24    Littlesugar, Amy. **Tree of Hope.** Illustrated by Floyd Cooper. Philomel, 1999. ISBN 0-399-23300-8. Unpaged. (ALL).

Young Florie loves listening to her dad reminisce about his days as an actor during the golden era of the Lafayette Theater in Harlem. Memories are all that remain of this once "glittering palace" since the Lafayette dimmed the stage lights and closed its doors during the Great Depression. Florie and her dad still visit an old tree, called the Tree of Hope, outside the boarded up theater, because folks believe the tree can bring good luck to those who dream. Florie's dream is for her dad to be an actor again. When Director Orson Welles comes to town for auditions, promising a Harlem version of a Shakespeare classic, some white folks object to blacks performing a "white" play. Illustrator Floyd Cooper's oil wash paintings provide a compelling look at Harlem during the 1930s in this story about holding on to dreams even in the hardest of times. (DS)

3.25    McKissack, Patricia C. **Color Me Dark: The Diary of Nellie Lee Love, the Great Migration North.** Scholastic, 2000. ISBN 0-590-51159-9. 211 pp. (I).

Growing up in the South, young Nellie Lee Love is all too aware of the heavy emphasis placed on skin color. When told that she could "pass for white," Nellie Lee, like her grandmother, insists that people should just "color me dark." In 1919, Nellie Lee's family moves north to Chicago in search of a better life. Like many African Americans before them, they hope to escape the racism of the rural South and find employment in the North. Mr. Love wants to take advantage of the opportunities in the city and dreams of opening his own funeral parlor. Nellie Lee and her family quickly learn that prejudice still exists in various forms in the big city. Through this story in the Dear America series, McKissack presents a positive portrayal of middle-class African American life after World War I. (RL)

**3.26**    Recorvits, Helen. **Goodbye, Walter Malinski.** Illustrated by Lloyd Bloom. Farrar, Straus & Giroux, 1999. ISBN 0-374-32747-5. 85 pp. (I)

The Great Depression was a difficult and emotional time for many families across the United States. Fifteen-year-old Walter, who has trouble reading and writing, is the target of all his father's frustration and criticism. Although his sisters and mother try to help, it is his father's approval that Walter seeks. Seen through the eyes of Walter's little sister Wanda, events pull the reader through poverty-driven embarrassment, violent attacks both in school and at home, atrocious living conditions for immigrants, death, despair, and eventual healing. The mature content of this book is written at a relatively easy reading level. (NRS)

Ryan, Pam Muñoz. **Esperanza Rising.** Scholastic, 2000. ISBN 0-439-12041-1. 262 pp. (I). (See **17.38**.)

★ Yep, Laurence. **Dream Soul.** HarperCollins, 2000. ISBN 0-06-028390-4. 245 pp. (I). (See **16.36**.)

## Wars

### World War I

**3.27**    Lawrence, Iain. **Lord of the Nutcracker Men.** Delacorte, 2001. ISBN 0-385-72924-3. 212 pp. (I).

Ten-year-old Johnny is sent from London to stay with his Auntie Ivy in Cliffe after his father enlists in the Great War. The year is 1914 and enthusiasm for the war is high. Johnny's father, a toy maker, has made Johnny an army of toy soldiers. As a way to feel closer to his father, Johnny immerses himself daily in imaginary battles between the "Tommies" and the "Fritz." These imaginary battles seem to prophesy events in the real war. Every week, Johnny receives a letter from his father describing the realities of trench warfare on the Western Front. Each letter includes another carved miniature war figure. At first the letters are graphic and disturbing. Later Johnny's father attempts reassurance by creating a fantasy leisure life on the battlefront. Through Johnny we see a transition from glorification of war to the heartbreak of its consequences, an important message for today's world. (BA)

**3.28**  Lindquist, Susan Hart. **Summer Soldiers.** Dell, 1999. ISBN 0-385-32641-6. 178 pp. (I).

Is Mr. Morgan a coward because he doesn't enlist to fight in World War I, or is he a gentle man with a knack for caring for horses? Most people in his California town believe the former and therefore shun Mr. Morgan and his son, Jim. Eleven-year-old Joe Farrington describes the summer of 1918 when he and Jim and their buddies take over for the fathers who have left to serve in the war. They unite against the merciless bullying of the local Thornton brothers in the same way their fathers unite in their fight against the Germans. When Joe's dad is reported as missing in action and Jim's father rescues shipwrecked horses, Joe acquires a different perspective on bravery. This "boy" book mirrors today's culture in which boys are taunted for being gentle and kind and not "manly" enough to fit the mainstream. (LLL)

**World War II**

**3.29**  Denenberg, Barry. **The Journal of Ben Uchida, Citizen 13559, Mirror Lake Internment Camp.** Scholastic, 1999. ISBN 0-590-48531-8. 157 pp. (I).

After the Japanese attacked Pearl Harbor in 1941, the U.S. government sought to "protect" our citizens of Japanese ancestry by placing them in guarded camps. Ben, a twelve-year-old Japanese American boy, is sent with his family to an internment camp in Mirror Lake, California—all except his father, who is fighting with the Allied forces. Ben maintains a journal of his experiences, describing in harsh detail his family's poor living conditions. Ben's participation on the camp's baseball league helps to pass the time as he and his family wait anxiously to find out if his father is safe. Through Ben's diary, Denenberg shares the injustices faced by many Japanese Americans and their struggles to come to terms with the reason for their imprisonment. *The Journal of Ben Uchida* is part of the My Name Is America series. For older readers, supplement this novel with Eric Walters's *Caged Eagles* (Orca, 2000), which looks at a similar situation involving our Canadian neighbors. (RL)

**3.30**  Lisle, Janet Taylor. **The Art of Keeping Cool.** Atheneum, 2000. ISBN 0-689-83787-9. 207 pp. (I).

In February 1942, the United States has just entered World War II, and tension can be felt everywhere. Certainly thirteen-year-old Robert can feel it tightening around him, as his father leaves to fly fighter planes and the rest of the family moves to live with Robert's paternal grandparents in Rhode Island. There, mysterious rules hide secrets that no one will reveal to Robert. Robert's cousin Elliot is a strange boy with an incredible talent for drawing. When Elliot begins visiting a German artist living as a refugee in the woods, a man who everyone angrily suspects is a spy, Robert's anxiety heightens. Robert learns that the only way to cut through the bonds of tension is through understanding, and he courageously works to uncover the truth. This historically accurate novel brims with both excitement and compassion. (DM)

**3.31**      ★ Mazer, Norma. **Good Night, Maman.** Harcourt, 1999. ISBN 0-15-201468-3. 185 pp. (I).

Ten-year-old Karin Levi lives with her mother and brother Marc in an attic closet in Paris. The previous year German soldiers captured their city and arrested Karin's father. Karin, her brother, and mother must figure out a way to escape the Germans, eventually journeying to a basement in the south of France. When their mother becomes ill, the children continue on without her to Italy, where they are two of the very few war refugees shipped on to a camp in Oswego, New York. Mazer details a little known chapter of U.S. history in this poignant tale of the travails of a young girl as she undergoes many personal changes, from leaving her mother to accepting a new life in the United States. Combine this book with Vera Propp's *When the Soldiers Were Gone* (Putnam, 1999) and Patricia Polacco's *The Butterfly* (Philomel, 2000; **5.28**), which are also about harboring Jewish children during the war. (BA)

**Recent Conflicts**

**3.32**      Ellis, Deborah. **The Breadwinner.** Douglas & McIntyre, 2000. ISBN 0-88899-419-2. 170 pp. (I).

One and a half years after the Taliban has taken over Afghanistan, the women of Kabul, who formerly led vigorous, productive lives, are still in a state of disbelief. Under Taliban law, women are not allowed out without a male escort. When eleven-year-old Parvana's father is imprisoned for his English education, the family is left without any means of support. The only solution is for Parvana to cut her hair, dress like a boy, and earn money to support the family. Frightened at first, she quickly learns her role. She reads letters, sells her family's last possessions, and then works as a tea boy and a bone digger to earn money. This moving novel sheds light on the oppression and enduring strength of the Afghani people under siege. (BA)

**3.33**   Mead, Alice. **Girl of Kosovo.** Farrar, Straus & Giroux, 2001. ISBN 0-374-32620-7. 113 pp. (I).

"Don't let them fill your heart with hate. Whatever happens." Eleven-year-old Zana often recalls her father's advice as tensions mount between the Kosovo Albanians and Serbians. The Albanians see the Serbs as murderers and seek to defend themselves. The Serbs perceive the Albanians as terrorists. Zana lives in growing fear and confusion. How can the Serbs be bad when Lena, a Serbian, is her best friend? Zana's world is torn apart by a blast that kills her father and brothers and leaves her with a devastating injury. Hate fills her, nearly killing her. But, guided by her father's words and Lena's friendship, Zana conquers the malevolence in her village and frees her spirit from bitterness. Mead's many visits to war-torn Kosovo and her friendship with an Albanian child provided her with the compassion, sensitivity, and background needed to present this war as it affected people rather than governments. (RR)

### Desegregation and Prejudice

**3.34**   ★ Armistead, John. **The $66 Summer.** Milkweed, 2000. ISBN 1-57131-626-4. 213 pp. (I).

As a white boy growing up in the South in the 1950s, thirteen-year-old George thinks he knows something about prejudice. But he is shocked when his own father brags about the death of a black man, killed by one of Daddy's friends. It is with relief that George leaves his racist father to spend the summer working in his grandmother's store, reviving his friendship with two black children, Bennett and Esther. As the summer progresses, George becomes aware of the bigotry inherent in southern tradition by observing the social injustices constantly inflicted on his friends. The children's friendship is strained by the differences in their lives but holds fast, leading to a triumphant conclusion. The novel reads easily, allowing the characters to reveal the story. This is an excellent choice for fifth and sixth graders, demonstrating that racism can be fought one friendship at a time. (DM)

**3.35**  Carbone, Elisa. **Storm Warriors.** Knopf, 2001. ISBN 0-375-80664-4. 168 pp. (I).

At the turn of the century, the treacherous coast of the Outer Banks of North Carolina were patrolled by surfmen who kept watch for shipwrecks, risking their own lives to rescue passengers and crew. Only one group, the men of the Pea Island Life-Saving Station, was composed of African Americans. More than anything in the world, twelve-year-old Nathan wants to grow up to join these brave surfmen. Despite his father's opposition, Nathan begins secretly learning about anatomy and life-saving techniques so that he will be prepared for a rescue. During a violent hurricane, Nathan gets his chance to find out if he is truly able to serve with the heroic surfmen. The story reveals much about the segregation of the times and the limited opportunities offered to black men. It is also a thrilling account of a historical ship rescue. (DM)

Curtis, Christopher Paul. **Bud, Not Buddy.** Delacorte, 1999. ISBN 0-385-32306-9. 245 pp. (I). (See **19.37.**)

**3.36**  Holt, Kimberly Willis. **Dancing in Cadillac Light.** Putnam, 2001. ISBN 0-399-23402-0. 167 pp. (I).

After Grandma dies, Jaynell worries with the rest of her family that Grandpap has lost his marbles. For one thing, he buys himself a gorgeous white Cadillac, an amazing sight in rural Texas in 1968. Stranger still is his sudden attachment to the Pickens family, when everyone knows that the yellow-haired Pickenses are just "white trash." Grandpap allows the family to move into his home place but then dies, leaving his own family bewildered and angry. Jaynell can't understand why Grandpap should exhibit such kindness to people she has been taught to despise. This is her story, simply and eloquently told in the language of her time and people, appropriate for older readers. As the story evolves, Jaynell learns of her grandfather's hidden shame, a secret that ultimately binds her closer to the Pickenses than she had ever imagined possible. (DM)

★ Littlesugar, Amy. **Freedom School, Yes!** Illustrated by Floyd Cooper. Philomel, 2001. ISBN 0-399-23006-8. Unpaged. (I). (See **15.3.**)

Miller, William. **Night Golf.** Illustrated by Cedric Lucas. Lee & Low, 1999. ISBN 1-880000-79-2. Unpaged. (ALL). (See **12.26.**)

★ Nelson, Vaunda Micheaux. **Beyond Mayfield.** Putnam, 1999. ISBN 0-399-23355-5. 138 pp. (I). (See **6.10.**)

Robinet, Harriette Gillem. **Walking to the Bus-Rider Blues.** Atheneum, 2000. ISBN 0-689-83191-9. 146 pp. (I). (See **15.7.**)

Wiles, Deborah. **Freedom Summer.** Illustrated by Jerome Lagarrigue. Atheneum, 2001. ISBN 0-689-83016-5. Unpaged. (ALL). (See **24.13.**)

★ Woodson, Jacqueline. **The Other Side**. Illustrated by E. B. Lewis. Putnam, 2001. ISBN 0-399-23116-1. Unpaged. (ALL). (See **15.8.**)

# 4 Families

**Evelyn B. Freeman, Barbara A. Lehman, and Patricia L. Scharer**

*Contributing reviewers included Jan Johnson, Sue Kennedy, Susan Matthews, Carol McKinley, Donna Peters, Becky Reid, Susie Semer, Anne Sylvan, Lori Thompson, W. Quinn White, and Linda Woolard.*

---

**Criteria for Excellence**
- Appropriateness for the topic of families
- Literary merit
- Variety of genres
- Child appeal
- Appropriateness for different audience levels
- Representations of diverse cultures
- Potential for curricular links

---

## Family Relationships

Bernier-Grand, Carmen T. **In the Shade of the Níspero Tree.** Orchard, 1999.

Browne, Anthony. **My Dad.** Farrar, Straus & Giroux, 2001.

Ehrlich, Amy. **Joyride.** Candlewick, 2001.

Fletcher, Ralph. **Relatively Speaking: Poems about Family.** Illustrated by Walter Lyon Krudop. Orchard, 1999.

Gantos, Jack. **Joey Pigza Loses Control.** Farrar, Straus & Giroux, 2000.

Micklos, John Jr., selector. **Daddy Poems.** Illustrated by Robert Casilla. Boyds Mills, 2000.

Micklos, John Jr., selector. **Mommy Poems.** Illustrated by Lori McElrath-Eslick. Boyds Mills, 2001.

Nolen Jerdine. **In My Momma's Kitchen.** Illustrated by Colin Bootman. Lothrop, Lee & Shepard, 1999.

Wong, Janet S. **The Rainbow Hand: Poems about Mothers and Children.** Illustrated by Jennifer Hewitson. Simon & Schuster, 1999.

## Changing Family Roles

★ Almond, David. **Heaven Eyes.** Delacorte, 2000.

Bond, Rebecca. **Bravo, Maurice!** Little, Brown, 2000.

★ Bunting, Eve. **The Memory String.** Illustrated by Ted Rand. Clarion, 2000.

Horvath, Polly. **Everything on a Waffle.** Farrar, Straus & Giroux, 2001.

Johnston, Tony. **Uncle Rain Cloud.** Illustrated by Fabricio Vanden Broeck. Charlesbridge, 2001.

Jones, Jennifer B. **Dear Mrs. Ryan, You're Ruining My Life.** Walker, 2000.

Smalls, Irene. **Kevin and His Dad.** Illustrated by Michael Hays. Little, Brown, 1999.

★ Stuve-Bodeen, Stephanie. **Mama Elizabeti.** Illustrated by Christy Hale. Lee & Low, 2000.

## Wisdom and Heritage of Family Elders

Bunting, Eve. **The Days of Summer.** Illustrated by William Low. Harcourt, 2001.

Grimes, Nikki. **Stepping Out with Grandma Mac.** Illustrated by Angelo. Orchard, 2001.

Michelson, Richard. **Grandpa's Gamble.** Illustrated by Barry Moser. Marshall Cavendish, 1999.

Monk, Isabell. **Hope.** Illustrated by Janice Lee Porter. Lerner, 2000.

Rosenberg, Liz. **The Silence in the Mountains.** Illustrated by Chris K. Soentpiet. Orchard, 1999.

★ Wood, Douglas. **Grandad's Prayers of the Earth.** Illustrated by P. J. Lynch. Candlewick, 1999.

## Family Roots and Childhood Memories

★ Delacre, Lulu. **Salsa Stories.** Scholastic, 2000.

dePaola, Tomie. **26 Fairmount Avenue.** Putnam, 1999.

Lanier, Shannon, and Jane Feldman. **Jefferson's Children: The Story of One American Family.** Random House, 2000.

Philip, Neil, selector. **Weave Little Stars into My Sleep: Native American Lullabies.** Photographs by Edward S. Curtis. Clarion, 2001.

Rocklin, Joanne. **Strudel Stories.** Delacorte, 1999.

Rohmer, Harriet, editor. **Honoring Our Ancestors.** Children's Book Press, 1999.

Strand, Keith. **Grandfather's Christmas Tree.** Illustrated by Thomas Locker. Harcourt Brace, 1999.

★ Wong, Janet S. **The Trip Back Home.** Illustrated by Bo Jia. Harcourt Brace, 2000.

## The Sustaining Power of Family

Barron, T. A. **Where Is Grandpa?** Illustrated by Chris K. Soentpiet. Philomel, 2000.

Brisson, Pat. **Sky Memories.** Illustrated by Wendell Minor. Delacorte, 1999.

★ Joseph, Lynn. **The Color of My Words.** HarperCollins, 2000.

Madrigal, Antonio Hernández. **Erandi's Braids.** Illustrated by Tomie dePaola. Putnam, 1999.

O'Connor, Barbara. **Moonpie and Ivy.** Farrar, Straus & Giroux, 2001.

★ Park, Barbara. **The Graduation of Jake Moon.** Atheneum, 2000.

★ Paulsen, Gary. **Alida's Song.** Delacorte, 1999.

Theorists and researchers have long recognized the importance of families in child development (Schickedanz, Schickedanz, Forsyth, & Forsyth, 2001). Parents provide attachment for their infants, the emotional security that is the basis for healthy human relationships, and moral development. Parenting styles and disciplinary practices can promote preschool children's developing sense of competence. Security and competence in turn enhance positive socialization, allowing school-aged children to become more outwardly directed toward their peers. Finally, in adolescence children engage in individuation, "the process of achieving an identity, independent of one's parents" (p. 628). This can create tension, as young people realize their parents' imperfections.

Siblings and grandparents add their own variables in the growing child's development: the former may provide both rivalry and companionship, the latter a sense of unconditional love, unhurried attention, connection to the past, and wisdom. Extended relatives and even distant ancestors can also make important contributions in the progression from infancy to young adulthood, allowing children to see themselves and their place in a larger context. Children's literature reflects all of these themes in books that portray families.

But other issues also arise in many of these books: changing family structures and roles within families; how families cut across racial, ethnic, and religious lines; rediscovering lost heritage; dealing with family conflict, expectations, and pressures; the power of love to sustain families facing pain or hardship together; working out new family relationships; children having to assume responsibilities usually held by their elders; and even rejection, abuse, and neglect within families. Not all books are serious or depressing, of course. Many depict the lighter side of family life: the humor that can develop from knowing one another's quirks well, shared experiences that seem funny only later, or pranks remembered. Families are also a great source of joy: celebrations, special intimate moments, thoughtful deeds performed for one another, and common, often unspoken understandings.

With these ideas in mind, we selected books for this chapter on the basis of the following criteria:

1. *Appropriateness for the topic of families.* Books included have as their primary focus themes related to families and family relationships.

2. *Literary merit.* We have included titles of fiction, nonfiction, picture books, and poetry. Each met the criteria appropriate for quality writing in its genre. For fiction these include a well-developed plot; important themes; intriguing characters; appropriate, original style; and defined, believable setting. Poetry needs to show fresh, appealing use of language and imagery. Informational books need to be factually accurate; identify sources; have appealing layout and design; and demonstrate clear, understandable writing. In addition to the qualities for these specific genres, picture books in every genre need to have high quality artwork that complements and enhances the text it accompanies.

3. *Varied genres.* Although not perfectly balanced, we purposely tried to achieve some representation across the genres identified in criterion 2.

4. *Child appeal.* The books we reviewed were tested with children—read to or by them, discussed with them, and responded to by them. Books that received positive reactions from children were more likely to be included in this selection.

5. *Appropriateness for different audience levels.* We attempted to select a balance of titles across the kindergarten through sixth-grade range.

6. *Representations of diverse cultures.* An important consideration was the inclusion of books that portray a variety of contemporary cultures and ethnicities that reflect our multicultural world.

7. *Potential for curricular links.* We worked with a group of eleven teachers who shared the books we were reviewing with their students. These teachers indicated how and which books worked best within their courses of study and curricular topics.

These were the factors we considered overall; not every book necessarily meets all criteria equally well. We believe, however, that the collection as a whole demonstrates these qualities.

Once selected, books were grouped into five categories that emerged from their themes. At the same time, we recognized that many books did not fit tidily within a single category; that is, often a particular book would be appropriate in more than one of these groups.

*Family relationships* includes books about the interactions in nuclear and extended families, between mothers or fathers and children, and with siblings and grandparents. Most relationships depicted are positive, some are more challenging, and a few show yearning for closer ties.

*Changing family roles* builds on the previous theme to portray how these roles evolve in relationships: dads or other male relatives who are caregivers, children adjusting to a new sibling or stepparent, a character finding personal identity in the midst of family expectations, or families that do not fit the traditional definition.

*Wisdom and heritage of family elders* naturally relates to the traditional role of older family members—often grandparents—in passing on insights about life and helping children better understand or deal with their experiences.

*Family roots and childhood memories,* many of which are provided by the elders, includes tracing family lineage, recording family stories, paying tribute to ancestors, remembering childhood events, and revisiting family homes.

*The sustaining power of family* refers to difficulties made more bearable through the strength of family members' love for one another. These challenges range from making hard choices, being rescued from an abusive environment, understanding and accepting serious illness, coping with death, and facing outside crises.

Literature both reflects and shapes life. In these selections, child readers should find characters and situations with which they can identify and themes and content that offer insight and catharsis, along with topics that appeal to their interests and satisfy their curiosity as they seek to understand their families and their own place in them. This kind of knowledge can in turn support young people's personal development into the kind of adults who make a positive contribution to their own children's development. Thus, the cycle of life continues from one generation to the next.

### Reference

Schickedanz, J. A., Schickedanz, D. I., Forsyth, P. D., & Forsyth, G. A. (2001). *Understanding children and adolescents* (4th ed.). Boston: Allyn and Bacon.

## Family Relationships

**4.1** Bernier-Grand, Carmen T. **In the Shade of the Níspero Tree.** Orchard, 1999. ISBN 0-531-30154-0. 186 pp. (I).

Best friends Teresa and Ana happily attend fourth grade at their neighborhood school in Puerto Rico. Teresa's ambitious mother, however, wants her daughter to transfer to La Academia, an upscale private girls' school the family cannot afford. At first Teresa does not accept her mother's plan, and Papi grumbles about sacrifices the family must make if she switches schools. Then Teresa denies instigating a school prank, calls Ana a liar, and decides to try La Academia. There she makes a new friend but also discovers that she is not accepted by other popular girls, eventually realizing the value of true friendship. This novel highlights tensions over skin color as a status symbol and contains many details, names, and Spanish words that particularize its 1960s setting. At the same time, the themes of dealing with parental expectations and the meaning of friendship make the story one with which many children can identify. (BAL)

**4.2** Browne, Anthony. **My Dad.** Farrar, Straus & Giroux, 2001. ISBN 0-374-35101-5. Unpaged. (P).

In this delightful picture book, originally published in Great Britain, a young boy offers accolades to his dad who "isn't afraid of ANYTHING, even the Big Bad Wolf." Internationally honored British author-illustrator Anthony Browne presents a slightly overweight dad wearing a brown plaid bathrobe. The plaid design pervades the entire book, including the endpapers and other illustrations, such as the toast as it pops up from the toaster and the body of a fish. From the son's perspective, his dad is indeed special, but most important, "HE LOVES ME!" Each page contains a large illustration rendered in chalk and gouache with one line of text. This humorous and joyful treatment of a young boy's love for his father pairs well with the poetry anthology *In Daddy's Arms I Am Tall: African Americans Celebrating Fathers* edited by Javaka Steptoe (Lee & Low, 1997). (EBF)

**4.3** Ehrlich, Amy. **Joyride.** Candlewick, 2001. ISBN 0-7636-1346-0. 241 pp. (I).

Family life for Nina Lewis and her mother, Joyce, has always centered on moving from one small town to another, sometimes living in their van between apartments. Despite the constant upheaval, the two approach each new location and job with a sense of adventure, celebrating each other's unique characteristics and their new environment. Nina begins to notice, however, that Joyce is becoming increasingly protective, often forbidding Nina to make new friends or talk with neighbors. Further complicating matters, the moves have become more frequent at a time in her life when Nina's desire for a permanent home, school-age friends, and a stable family life is growing. The novel's surprising conclusion explains the mystery behind their mobility, which forces both Nina and Joyce to redefine their family relationships. (PLS)

**4.4**　Fletcher, Ralph. **Relatively Speaking: Poems about Family.** Illustrated by Walter Lyon Krudop. Orchard, 1999. ISBN 0-531-30141-9. 42 pp. (I).

Forty-two short, snappy free-verse poems about family fill this slim volume. Written from the perspective of the youngest child, who subsequently becomes the middle child when Mom has a baby girl, they reflect a typical eleven-year-old boy's concerns: observing an older brother who seems more preoccupied with his girlfriend than with the narrator, comparing what and how his family eats to the practices of other families, spending time with and collecting wisdom from grandparents, visiting relatives, doing chores together, weathering family crises and reunions, and adjusting to a new sibling. Humor abounds, as on the subject of inheritance: "You can have my warped big toes / or my hairy ears" (p. 4); and poignancy emerges, as in the comparison of a disinherited cousin to a missing jigsaw puzzle piece. Black-and-white line drawings accompany these highly accessible verses that may prompt young poets to pen their own lines about everyday family topics. (BAL)

**4.5**　Gantos, Jack. **Joey Pigza Loses Control.** Farrar, Straus & Giroux, 2000. ISBN 0-374-39989-1. 196 pp. (I).

In this 2001 Newbery honor book, Gantos writes a sequel to the popular *Joey Pigza Swallowed the Key* (1998). Joey, a lovable character with attention deficit hyperactivity disorder, desires more than anything to be a normal kid. Since he began wearing a medicated patch, Joey has renewed confidence in himself and plans a summer visit to the father who walked out on him and his mother. Joey soon learns that Dad is as hyper as he is, and when his dad decides Joey no longer needs his medication, disaster ensues. Serious issues of parent/grandparent-child relationships, children dealing with medical conditions, and the importance of self-esteem are presented with humor and pathos. Students will identify with Joey and his need for family love, security, and acceptance. (EBF)

**4.6**  Micklos, John Jr., selector. **Daddy Poems.** Illustrated by Robert Casilla. Boyds Mills, 2000. ISBN 1-56397-735-4. 32 pp. (ALL).

Twenty-two poems celebrate the interactions and relationships of fathers and children. Piggyback rides, shaving, waltzing in the kitchen, enjoying nature, buying a ball glove, hugging, coming home from work, praying before dinner, and bath and bedtime rituals are some of the everyday occurrences targeted. Also included are poems about absent fathers whose visits are anticipated and stepfathers whom children don't know what to call. The poets' credentials are diverse, from those widely published, such as Mary Ann Hoberman and X. J. Kennedy, to others better known for their academic writing, such as Donald Graves. Realistic illustrations reflect the cultural diversity of the poets' backgrounds and the poems' subjects. A foreword by Jim Trelease encourages fathers to read these poems aloud to their children. A table of contents, indexes of authors and first lines, and biographical notes about the poets complete this collection. (BAL)

**4.7**  Micklos, John Jr., selector. **Mommy Poems.** Illustrated by Lori McElrath-Eslick. Boyds Mills, 2001. ISBN 1-56397-849-0. 32 pp. (ALL).

The many roles of motherhood are represented in this companion volume to Micklos's earlier collection, *Daddy Poems.* Each two-page spread offers one or two of the nineteen poems matched with full-page, colorful oil paintings about topics such as naptime, feelings, cuddle time, family meals, and the arrival of a new stepmother. Poets such as Lee Bennett Hopkins, Janet S. Wong, Arnold Adoff, Mary Ann Hoberman, Aileen Fisher, and Nikki Giovanni pay tribute to mothers who save every scrap of their child's writing, play games with delight, nurse the sick with skill and patience, and take care of their loved ones from morning until night. A table of contents in the beginning and brief biographies of each poet at the end frame this collection and provide helpful information for readers. (PLS)

**4.8**    Nolen, Jerdine. **In My Momma's Kitchen.** Illustrated by Colin Bootman. Lothrop, Lee & Shepard, 1999. ISBN 0-688-12760-6. Unpaged. (P).

Short vignettes describe, from a young girl's first-person perspective, all the good things that happen "in my momma's kitchen": an older sister receiving her college acceptance letter, a doll and cat's wedding, Momma and her three sisters cooking together on Talking Pots Day, a visit by Great-Aunt Caroline, the cat's disastrous playing with apples, Daddy making corn pudding, the workings of the third-generation stove known as Gran Lee, and middle-of-the-night family snacks. The kitchen's importance in all these events highlights the warmth and closeness of family ties, and realistic full-page oil paintings edged with dark lines and generous white borders resemble a photo album. Golden tones in many illustrations enhance the cheery mood associated with these cherished memories. This picture book celebrates an African American family and their particular traditions but will resonate with families universally. (BAL)

**4.9**    Wong, Janet S. **The Rainbow Hand: Poems about Mothers and Children.** Illustrated by Jennifer Hewitson. Simon & Schuster, 1999. ISBN 0-689-82148-4. Unpaged. (ALL).

Vibrant, rainbow-colored illustrations by Jennifer Hewitson, rendered in scratchboard and watercolor dyes, accompany this collection of poems about mothers and their children. Janet Wong's poems cover an emotional range from loving and tender to humorous and sarcastic while exploring the unique relationships and perspectives of mothers and children. Mother is compared to an onion, "her golden skin / smooth and soft" with a sweetness "so you forget / how she makes you cry / each time you cut her / with your words." The mother working in the school library "reading poems and stories / in a voice that soars up to the ceiling, / flapping her arms in the air, / flying us around the world / and leaving us there" will resonate with teachers. Although the poems were inspired by Wong's relationship with her own mother, all mothers and children will recognize the universality of these bonds. (PLS)

## Changing Family Roles

**4.10**    ★ Almond, David. **Heaven Eyes.** Delacorte, 2000. ISBN 0-385-32770-6. 233 pp. (I).

The children in this novel by one of Great Britain's most respected authors are orphans living in a home called Whitegates. Erin and her friend January are joined by another resident, Mouse, when they decide to escape by floating on a homemade raft downriver toward the sea. Their journey is aborted, however, when they get stuck in the Black Middens and are rescued by a strange girl named Heaven Eyes and a sinister old man she calls Grampa. Unwillingly at first, the three companions solve the mystery of Heaven Eyes's origins and Grampa's secrets. In the process, Heaven Eyes becomes their friend and shows them the beauty of life and love that these three hardened outcasts have never known. Through a skillful blend of realism and magic in the manner of Almond's award-winning *Skellig* (Delacorte, 1999; **14.25**), the narrative portrays family as much more than a group of related individuals. (BAL)

**4.11**    Bond, Rebecca. **Bravo, Maurice!** Little, Brown, 2000. ISBN 0-316-10545-7. Unpaged. (P).

When Maurice Duncan Marcel is born, each member of his extended family has an idea regarding Maurice's future occupation. Uncle Eddie wants him to be a taxi driver like he is; Papa plans for Maurice to work with him in his bakery; Mama hopes he will follow in her footsteps and become a writer. Although Maurice enjoys accompanying his family members to work, he especially enjoys listening to the sounds wherever he goes. One day, while taking his bath, Maurice bursts into song; he has found his own interest—singing. His family cheers that he will be the first singer in the family: "Bravo, Maurice!" Bond's acrylic illustrations are quite detailed and portray each occupation and the urban setting described in the text. This joyful family story shows that each of us has a special gift. (EBF)

**4.12**    ★ Bunting, Eve. **The Memory String.** Illustrated by Ted Rand. Clarion, 2000. ISBN 0-395-86146-2. 32 pp. (P).

Laura's memory string holds buttons from her great-grandmother's first "grown-up dress," Laura's christening gown, Dad's uniform from the Gulf War, and the nightgown Mom was wearing when she died. The buttons and their memorable stories comfort Laura as she struggles to define her relationship with her new stepmother, Jane. Unfortunately, Whiskers the cat strikes and breaks the string, scattering the forty-three buttons in the grass. Dad and Jane join Laura's recovery efforts and manage to find all but one: Mom's favorite from Dad's military uniform. Late that night, Laura sees Jane and Dad out in the yard armed with flashlights and shares Jane's delight when she finds the missing button, an act that marks the beginning of a new relationship between the two of them. Ted Rand's watercolor illustrations on every two-page spread further develop the three characters, yet leave readers with much room for personal response and reflection. (PLS)

**4.13**   Horvath, Polly. **Everything on a Waffle.** Farrar, Straus & Giroux, 2001. ISBN 0-374-32236-8. 150 pp. (I).

Primrose Squarp's parents are missing and presumed dead after a storm off the coast of Coal Harbour, British Columbia, but Primrose never loses faith in their return. Meanwhile, she stays with Miss Perfidy, her babysitter, until her uncle Jack, a navy officer, can be located to care for her. Not a family man, Jack surprisingly rises to the occasion, much to the disbelief of Miss Honeycut, the school guidance counselor. After a series of misadventures, however, he then loses custody of Primrose to a kindly childless couple, Evie and Bert. Each chapter ends with a recipe of a food mentioned in that chapter. Many of these dishes are developed by Primrose's ally, Miss Bowzer, owner of The Girl on the Red Swing, a restaurant in which everything is served on a waffle. This rollicking, tongue-in-cheek adventure, a *Boston Globe* Horn Book and Newbery honor book, finally leads to a happy, if predictable, resolution. (BAL)

**4.14**   Johnston, Tony. **Uncle Rain Cloud.** Illustrated by Fabricio Vanden Broeck. Charlesbridge, 2001. ISBN 0-88106-371-1. Unpaged. (P).

Carlos secretly refers to his Uncle Tomás as Uncle Rain Cloud because he is always gloomy since leaving his Mexican home and moving to Los Angeles. Because Carlos's parents work late, his uncle helps to care for him at night and tells Carlos wonderful stories of Mexico and the tongue-twister gods. When Uncle Tomás attends parent-teacher conferences, Carlos must translate because his uncle doesn't speak English. After his uncle admits to Carlos that he is afraid to speak English, Carlos begins to teach him. The changing family role of the young nephew who helps his uncle is poignantly and realistically portrayed and can be readily compared to the role reversal of grandmother and granddaughter in Eve Bunting's *The Wednesday Surprise* (Clarion, 1989). Mexican illustrator Fabricio Vanden Broeck depicts the special relationship between the boy and his uncle in acrylic and colored pencil illustrations that extend across each double-page spread. (EBF)

**4.15** Jones, Jennifer B. **Dear Mrs. Ryan, You're Ruining My Life.** Walker, 2000. ISBN 0-8027-8728-2. 122 pp. (I).

Fifth grader Harvey Ryan loves to play baseball and has a famous mom who writes children's books. Much to Harvey's chagrin, many of these books are based on his life and the funny things he has done. To divert his mom's attention from writing books about him, Harvey and his best friend Seal decide to play matchmaker for his divorced mom and the school principal. But Harvey learns that his mom actually *is* dating the school principal, which complicates his life even more than her writing books about him. In this humorous, realistic story, several subplots are developed, including Harvey's relationship with his dad and stepmom and his baseball rivalry with Bart. A school librarian read this book aloud to students and received responses such as, "It's a really funny book," and "On a scale of one to ten, I would rate it a 9.99." (EBF)

**4.16** Smalls, Irene. **Kevin and His Dad.** Illustrated by Michael Hays. Little, Brown, 1999. ISBN 0-316-79899-1. Unpaged. (P).

Kevin and his dad spend Saturday together while Mom is away. First they "work—then we play," but even work seems more like play with Dad. The vacuum cleaner becomes a train, the dog gets dusted, and the dishes are dunked. After chores are finished, the pair sets out for even more fun: playing ball, an action movie, and a snack on the way home. The important theme of parent and child working and playing together in a familiar home setting has the added bonus here of a father portrayed as cheerfully and competently managing housework and child care. Told in first person, the narration bounces with rhyme, rhythm, repetition, and alliteration that evoked positive responses from primary-aged children. Double-spread acrylic illustrations incorporate the text within the pictures, and the linen canvas on which they are painted adds texture to muted, predominantly primary colors. (BAL)

**4.17**    ★ Stuve-Bodeen, Stephanie. **Mama Elizabeti.** Illustrated by Christy Hale. Lee & Low, 2000. ISBN 1-58430-002-7. Unpaged. (P).

Elizabeti, the beloved character from award-winning *Elizabeti's Doll* by the same author (Lee & Low, 1998), returns in this picture book set in contemporary Tanzania. When Elizabeti's baby sister is born, Elizabeti becomes responsible for taking care of her younger brother, Obedi. Elizabeti finds that caring for her brother is more challenging and requires more attention than caring for her rock doll, Eva. When Elizabeti sweeps the floor, Obedi pulls her hair; when she sifts rice, he hits the basket, spilling the rice; and when she leaves him for a few minutes to fill the water jug, he wanders away. This is a realistic and touching story of a loving sibling relationship. Hale's illustrations, rendered in mixed media, capture Elizabeti's emotions and the African village setting. (EBF)

## Wisdom and Heritage of Family Elders

**4.18**    Bunting, Eve. **The Days of Summer.** Illustrated by William Low. Harcourt, 2001. ISBN 0-15-201840-9. Unpaged. (P).

The endpapers in this book, illustrated in deep, rich colors, depict a close-up of a photograph collection on a fireplace mantle, symbolizing a loving family with a history of memories. The same mantle in the opening two-page spread, however, is obscured in darkness, foreshadowing the first sentence of the text: "Grandma and Grandpa are getting a divorce." The news shakes all family members as they move between disbelief, anger, problem solving, and worry while trying to anticipate what life will be like after the divorce. Through the eyes of one grandchild, readers learn about the new lives Grandma and Grandpa are planning that will create new memories with their children and grandchildren and help each to find comfort in the possibility that he or she will be able to cope with this news. (PLS)

**4.19**    Grimes, Nikki. **Stepping Out with Grandma Mac.** Illustrated by Angelo. Orchard, 2001. ISBN 0-531-30320-9. 39 pp. (I).

Twenty free-verse poems, accompanied by realistic pencil drawings, create the character of an atypical grandmother and her relationship with her equally unique granddaughter. Grandma Mac is direct, fashion conscious, and highly particular, but she shows her love by sharing her considerable wisdom about such things as using perfume, setting a proper table, picking quality clothing, getting an education, learning new foods, and wearing appropriate seasonal colors. Other clues, such as an unexpected gift, the light in Grandma Mac's eyes when she sees her granddaughter, sharing a secret, or her use of the granddaughter's picture as a bookmark, also demonstrate the caring that her sharp words do not convey. Readers who have untraditional grandparents may identify with the vignettes these poems offer as a counterbalance to more stereotypical images. (BAL)

Look, Lenore. **Love as Strong as Ginger.** Illustrated by Stephen T. Johnson. Atheneum, 1999. ISBN 0-689-81248-5. Unpaged. (ALL). (See **16.9.**)

**4.20** Michelson, Richard. **Grandpa's Gamble.** Illustrated by Barry Moser. Marshall Cavendish, 1999. ISBN 0-7614-5034-3. Unpaged. (I).

Grandpa is constantly praying, and the children are bored with being quiet. To amuse themselves, a brother and sister pretend to play baseball, knock into an old credenza, and cause old photographs to fly "like a swarm of locusts." The children are amazed to find a photograph of Grandpa as a young, handsome man holding a little girl; Grandpa's stories of his youth are even more amazing. Grandpa's parents had sent him to the United States from Poland to escape hunger, beatings, and life in the ghetto. In the United States, he learned to cheat at cards and gamble to support his wife and young daughter. One Passover evening, however, Grandpa placed his last bet on God's mercy to save the life of his critically ill daughter, forever substituting praying for cheating. Illustrations in sepia tones framed in white complement the theme of remembering the past through stories and images. (PLS)

★ Mills, Claudia. **Gus and Grandpa and Show-and-Tell.** Illustrated by Catherine Stock. Farrar, Straus & Giroux, 2000. ISBN 0-374-32819-6. 47 pp. (P). (See **6.27.**)

**4.21** Monk, Isabell. **Hope.** Illustrated by Janice Lee Porter. Lerner, 2000. 1-57505-230-X. 32 pp. (ALL).

Hope loves to visit her Aunt Prudence (affectionately called Aunt Poogee) every summer. When first introduced to Miss Violet, a family friend, Hope is confused and disturbed when Miss Violet asks, "My goodness, Prudence, is the child mixed?" Their special evening story time becomes the opportunity for Aunt Poogee to tell stories of Hope's grandparents on her father's side of the family who emigrated from Europe and the generations on her mother's side who slaved in the cotton fields. Aunt Poogee wisely advises Hope that if anyone ever again asks if she is mixed, to reply, "Yes, I am generations of faith 'mixed' with lots of love! I AM HOPE!" Oil paintings in bright, vibrant colors appropriately set the mood for this story of faith, hope, and love. (PLS)

4.22    Rosenberg, Liz. **The Silence in the Mountains.** Illustrated by Chris K. Soentpiet. Orchard, 1999. ISBN 0-531-30084-6. Unpaged. (P).

Iskander and his family live in "a land so sweet, so beautiful, some people call it paradise." When his country becomes plagued by war, Iskander and his family relocate to the United States. Although they live in a rural area, Iskander is still homesick and yearns for his native land. Through Grandfather's wisdom and understanding, Iskander finds a reminder of home in his new country, "silence spreading over the mountains." Although Iskander's native country is not named in the text, Rosenberg dedicates the book to "Dr. Iskander Kassis and his family, to the people of Lebanon, and to all exiles everywhere." Soentpiet's realistic watercolor paintings establish an initial Middle Eastern setting and then the family's new surroundings in the United States. (EBF)

4.23    ★ Wood, Douglas. **Grandad's Prayers of the Earth.** Illustrated by P. J. Lynch. Candlewick, 1999. ISBN 0-7636-0660-X. Unpaged. (ALL).

A young boy asks questions about life of his beloved grandfather on their walks together in the woods. When the boy asks about prayers, Grandad tells him that each tree and everything on the earth prays in its own way by giving "its life to the beauty of all life, and that gift is its prayer." He goes on to describe how people pray in the smallest happenings of everyday living. When the boy asks if prayers are answered, Grandad does not respond directly. Only long after Grandad has died does the boy find the answer to this question and healing for his sense of loss. Double-spread watercolor representational paintings in warm nature tones depict the loving relationship of grandson and grandfather in the landscapes they enjoyed most. The text, in bordered insets on each page, blends unobtrusively with the lovely surrounding illustrations in this oversized book. (BAL)

## Family Roots and Childhood Memories

**4.24**  ★ Delacre, Lulu. **Salsa Stories.** Scholastic, 2000. ISBN 0-590-63118-7. 103 pp. (I).

When Carmen Teresa receives a journal as a New Year's gift, she is surrounded by family and friends who encourage her to collect stories from each of them for her journal. One by one, they share their stories of creating a carpet for Holy Week, adventures at the beach, a mother's risks as she crosses the border each day to support her family in Mexico, and a birthday piñata. In the final chapter, Carmen Teresa decides to use her journal to record family recipes, each with a story to remember. Settings of the seven stories vary and include locations such as Puerto Rico, Mexico, and Peru. Love of family and friends, however, links each story together. Black-and-white woodcuts by Delacre illustrate each chapter. Readers will find many similarities with the short stories of a Jewish family in Joanne Rocklin's *Strudel Stories* (Delacorte, 1999; **4.28**). (PLS)

**4.25**  dePaola, Tomie. **26 Fairmount Avenue.** Putnam, 1999. ISBN 0-399-23246-X. 56 pp. (ALL).

Tomie dePaola's voice is particularly strong as he shares family stories about his childhood home at 26 Fairmount Avenue. In brief chapters illustrated with dePaola's black-and-white self-portraits, readers learn about both natural and man-made disasters surrounding the building of the family home and also gain insight into dePaola's childhood experiences. In 1938, for example, Tomie was thrilled to watch Disney's version of "Snow White and the Seven Dwarfs" but was so distressed at the departures from the story his mother had read to him that he shouted, "Mr. Walt Disney didn't read the story right!" as his mother pulled him out of the theater. Later, when his kindergarten teacher told him that he would not learn to read that year, he walked out of school and went home to teach himself to read. Readers of all ages will easily find connections between this brief biography and dePaola's numerous, beloved picture books. (PLS)

**4.26**     Lanier, Shannon, and Jane Feldman. **Jefferson's Children: The Story of One American Family.** Random House, 2000. ISBN 0-375-80597-4. 144 pp. (I).

Shannon Lanier, a ninth-generation descendant of Thomas Jefferson and Sally Hemings, grew up knowing the family oral history that linked his ancestry to the third U.S. president, a claim supported by DNA evidence in 1998. Inspired by a reunion of the Martha Jefferson and Sally Hemings families at Monticello, Lanier journeyed with photographer Jane Feldman across the United States interviewing family members for what evolved into this meticulously researched but highly personal account of his extended relations. In the process, Lanier came to view his odyssey as symbolic of the larger American family and the importance of ties that transcend racial and cultural barriers to unite us. Numerous photographs, graphics of family trees, and other illustrations accompany the more than thirty profiles of progeny from various branches of families descended from Jefferson in this complex, fascinating family portrait. An index and bibliography of related readings provide informational aids. (BAL)

**4.27**     Philip, Neil, selector. **Weave Little Stars into My Sleep: Native American Lullabies.** Photographs by Edward S. Curtis. Clarion, 2001. ISBN 0-618-08856-3. Unpaged. (P).

Traditional Native American lullabies in this collection have been translated into English in a manner that preserves the loving sentiment of mothers all over the world as they sing their babies to sleep. Some are brief with repetitive refrains; others are longer and nearly storylike lessons on the wisdom of obedience, resting at night, and waking early to fulfill the day. Duotone photographs opposite each page of poetry depict parents and children from Eskimo villages to the pueblos of the Southwest. The tribal origin of each poem and photograph is clearly identified in gold-tone and more fully explained in the author's note at the end. (PLS)

**4.28**     Rocklin, Joanne. **Strudel Stories.** Delacorte, 1999. ISBN 0-385-32602-5. 131 pp. (I).

This novel traces seven generations of a Jewish family as members tell stories while preparing apple strudel. The book is organized into short stories organized by generation, each represented by a different narrator. The first story is set in Odessa, Russia, and then the location moves to Brooklyn, New York, after some family members immigrate to the United States; the final segment takes place in Los Angeles. Some stories are humorous, others are poignant, but all reflect the joys and sorrows of family life. A family tree of the fictional strudel makers and apple strudel recipes are included. The author's note provides historical background on the eastern European Jewish experience. This book demonstrates how family heritage is passed down through the generations and how stories can bind families together. Readers may enjoy comparing these stories with those in *Salsa Stories* by Lulu Delacre (Scholastic, 2000; **4.24**). (EBF)

**4.29**   Rohmer, Harriet, editor. **Honoring Our Ancestors.** Children's Book Press, 1999. ISBN 0-89239-158-8. 31 pp. (ALL).

Fourteen acclaimed artists have created paintings and written tributes to honor one or more of their ancestors, both biological and spiritual, in this edited collection. These ancestors' diverse cultural backgrounds range from Pacific Islander, Latino, African American, Chinese, and Native American to Jewish, West Indian, and Arab American. Each double-page spread contains a full-page painting, a photograph with artist's biographical statement, another photograph of his or her ancestor(s), and the author's tribute. The illustration media are diverse as well: acrylics, oil, pencil, gouache, mixed media, and ink on paper, canvas, burlap, and rag paper. Teachers have used this well-conceived work to inspire students to describe and illustrate their relatives for pages in a class book. Two companion books are Dinah Johnson's picture book *Quinnie Blue* (Holt, 2000; **8.3**) and Nikki Giovanni's *Grand Fathers* (Holt, 1999), a volume of stories, poems, recipes, and photographs from forty-eight contributors. (BAL)

**4.30**   Strand, Keith. **Grandfather's Christmas Tree.** Illustrated by Thomas Locker. Harcourt Brace, 1999. ISBN 0-15-201821-2. Unpaged. (ALL).

A young child asks why the single tall spruce on Grandfather's ranch is decorated each Christmas by a wooden nest with two carved geese and five tiny goslings; the parent responds with a story of long ago. In 1886, Grandma and Grandpa built a cabin in a valley near Denver, Colorado. Just before Christmas, blizzards struck, making it impossible to move beyond the cabin to gather firewood. Nearby blue spruce trees, while offering hope for warmth, also shelter a family of geese who would die if the trees were cut for firewood. Hoping to save the geese, Grandma begged Grandpa to wait until after Christmas Day to cut the trees. A thaw that morning brought new life to the valley and its inhabitants, including five new baby geese. Strand's text is placed on white and framed in gold opposite full-page oil paintings by Locker, revealing the warmth of the human spirit in frigid conditions. (PLS)

**4.31**    ★ Wong, Janet S. **The Trip Back Home.** Illustrated by Bo Jia. Harcourt Brace, 2000. ISBN 0-15-200784-9. Unpaged. (P).

Dedicated to her Korean mother, grandparents, and aunt, Janet Wong poetically describes a young girl's trip back to "the village where Mother grew up." Written from the young girl's first-person perspective, this picture book reveals the rhythm of everyday family life. Korean words in the text introduce young readers to *haraboji* (grandfather), *halmoni* (grandmother), and *changpan* (oiled paper floor). Jia's realistic watercolor illustrations depict the setting and the young girl feeding pigs, accompanying her grandmother to the outdoor market, and playing cards with her family. The book is a tribute to the strong bonds of family and the joys of spending time together. Children can chart the similarities and differences between their daily life in the United States and the young girl's experiences during her visit to Korea. They also may compare the similar plots and themes in *Going Home* by Eve Bunting (HarperCollins, 1996) and *Halmoni's Day* by Edna Coe Bercaw (Dial, 2000; **16.1**). (EBF)

## The Sustaining Power of Family

**4.32**    Barron, T. A. **Where Is Grandpa?** Illustrated by Chris K. Soentpiet. Philomel, 2000. ISBN 0-399-23037-8. Unpaged. (ALL)

In his first picture book, T. A. Barron presents a fictionalized autobiography about a young boy trying to understand his grandfather's death. After family members recall their special, shared times with Grandpa, the young boy asks his father, "Where is Grandpa now?" The father's sensitive response, "Heaven is any place where people who love each other have shared some time together," is spiritual yet respectful of various religious beliefs. For the young boy, this means Grandpa is in the waterfall, the pine tree, and the tree house. Soentpiet's vibrant watercolor illustrations portray natural scenes and landscapes, and photo-realistic people are painted against the backdrop of mountains. This touching story may help young children deal with the death of a loved one. (EBF)

**4.33**   Brisson, Pat. **Sky Memories.** Illustrated by Wendell Minor. Delacorte, 1999. ISBN 0-385-32606-8. 71 pp. (I).

At age ten, Emily learns that her mother has cancer, and they spend the last year of her mother's life gathering sky memories. They learn to take the time to snap mental pictures of the sky's various, wonderful states—ordinary cloudy sky with a patch of blue, night sky with fat snowflakes falling, November sunset sky behind skeleton trees, or the gloaming twilight sky. Like the sky, which Emily seldom noticed until Mom shows her its beauty, loved ones can be taken for granted until loss sharpens one's appreciation for them. After Mom's death, memories of their shared sky snapshots comfort Emily and remind her of their special relationship. Delicate but vibrant watercolor paintings provide visual images of the sky descriptions so lyrically portrayed in this moving novella about a sad, sensitive subject. A related picture book about a mother's battle with cancer and a more hopeful outcome is Elizabeth Winthrop's *Promises* (Clarion, 2000). (BAL)

**4.34**   ★ Joseph, Lynn. **The Color of My Words.** HarperCollins, 2000. ISBN 0-06-028232-0. 138 pp. (I).

Twelve-year-old Ana Rosa describes the pain of change in a poor coastal Dominican Republic village. She has a fierce, passionate need to write, and her talent becomes the primary tool in her village's fight to maintain their homes when the government sells the land to a developer planning to build a hotel and casino. Ana Rosa's words capture the community's protests in a newspaper article. Sadly, however, bulldozers invade the village, claiming the life of Ana Rosa's brother. She blames herself until she decides to write about her brother, his death, and his cause. The power of words permeates this novel beyond the plot through poems that introduce each chapter and the effective use of first-person narration. A related novel that also portrays a family's struggle in the face of adversity is Patricia Reilly Giff's *Nory Ryan's Song* (Delacorte, 2000; **5.14**). (PLS)

**4.35**   Madrigal, Antonio Hernández. **Erandi's Braids.** Illustrated by Tomie dePaola. Putnam, 1999. ISBN 0-399-23212-5. Unpaged. (ALL).

Throughout history families have faced hardships and difficult choices. In the 1940s and 1950s, the women of Pátzcuaro, Mexico, sold their attractive black braids to hair buyers from the city, providing some relief from their financial woes despite the beliefs of some that the barber's scissors cast an evil spell. When her mother's braids are too short to sell, young Erandi climbs into the barber's chair so he can cut off her own beautiful braids, despite her mother's protests. Erandi's painful decision provides money for a much-needed fishing net for Mamá and a doll for Erandi's birthday. Tomie dePaola's vibrant illustrations in deep hues portray village life and the loving relationship between Erandi and Mamá. The author's note at the end assures readers that buyers no longer purchase women's hair in the village of Pátzcuaro. (PLS)

Mead, Alice. **Girl of Kosovo.** Farrar, Straus & Giroux, 2001. ISBN 0-374-32620-7. 113 pp. (I). (See **3.33.**)

**4.36**   O'Connor, Barbara. **Moonpie and Ivy.** Farrar, Straus & Giroux, 2001. ISBN 0-374-35059-0. 152 pp. (I).

Although Pearl's mother Ruby abandons her at Aunt Ivy's house in rural Georgia, unpredictable, irresponsible Ruby and their life on the road are the only family and lifestyle that Pearl has known. Anger toward and loneliness for her mother and uncertainty about her place in Aunt Ivy's home cause considerable confusion for Pearl. A neighbor boy called Moonpie, also abandoned by his mother but lovingly cared for by old Mama Nell, seems to be more important to Aunt Ivy and her boyfriend John Dee than Pearl is. Pearl acts out her insecurities rebelliously, but her discovery of Aunt Ivy's infant daughters' graves and a cathartic encounter between the aunt and niece bring them together. Resisting a neat resolution in which Pearl remains with Aunt Ivy happily ever after, the narrative realistically concludes with Ruby's return; she takes Pearl away with her to yet another new city. (BAL)

**4.37**   ★ Park, Barbara. **The Graduation of Jake Moon.** Atheneum, 2000. ISBN 0-689-83912-X. 115 pp. (I).

In this poignant, realistic novel about Alzheimer's disease and its devastating effect on families, eighth grader Jake Moon recounts the changes in his beloved grandfather due to this ravaging illness. Jake, who never knew his father, lives with and was raised by Skelly (his grandfather) and his mother. When Skelly is diagnosed with Alzheimer's, Jake's life is irrevocably changed. Jake experiences many conflicting emotions—love and guilt, loyalty and shame, a sense of responsibility and resentment. At Jake's eighth-grade graduation, an incident with Skelly reveals Jake's growth in accepting his grandfather's illness and understanding its effects on other family members. In response to the book, one teacher commented that Jake offers a wonderful example of a character study, and the story's personal relationships will prompt discussion. Students may consult the informational book *Alzheimer's Disease* by Elaine Landau (Franklin Watts, 1996) to learn more about this illness. (EBF)

**4.38**  ★ Paulsen, Gary. **Alida's Song.** Delacorte, 1999. ISBN 0-385-32586-X. 88 pp. (I).

An unnamed fourteen-year-old boy narrates this novel about the summer his grandmother, Alida, rescues him from an abusive family to be a hired hand on the Nelson farm where she is the cook. Work days with bachelor brothers Gunnar and Olaf are long, but good food is abundant; long evenings are filled with telling stories, playing games, and making music; and dances are held in town the first Saturday of every month. In this sequel to *The Cookcamp* (Orchard, 1991), the boy learns that life doesn't have to be an ugly struggle to survive when his grandmother shows him love and a more tender, beautiful side to the world. Written in a style that sounds like oral reminiscing, this story is good for reading aloud to students who have enjoyed other books by this well-known author. (BAL)

# 5 Struggle and Survival

Nancy J. Johnson

*Contributing reviewers included Abby Franklin, Cyndi Giorgis, Janine A. King, and Sylvia Tag.*

---

### Criteria for Excellence

- Each book meets the expectations of quality for its genre.
- Each book presents themes of realistic challenge and hope.
- Characters (real and fictional) are fully developed, reveal believable traits, and reflect bravery and courage in realistic ways.
- Content is compelling and written with voice and life.
- Writing is accompanied by strong, colorful illustrations and/or images that support and extend the text.

---

## Larger Than Life Heroes, Heroines, and Events

Appelt, Kathi, and Jeanne Cannella Schmitzer. **Down Cut Shin Creek: The Pack Horse Librarians of Kentucky.** HarperCollins, 2001.

★ Armstrong, Jennifer. **Spirit of Endurance: The True Story of the Shackleton Expedition to the Antarctic.** Illustrated by William Maughan. Crown, 2000.

Krensky, Stephen. **Shooting for the Moon: The Amazing Life and Times of Annie Oakley.** Illustrated by Bernie Fuchs. Farrar, Straus & Giroux, 2001.

Nobisso, Josephine. **John Blair and the Great Hinkley Fire.** Illustrated by Ted Rose. Houghton Mifflin, 2000.

★ Talbott, Hudson. **Forging Freedom: A True Story of Heroism during the Holocaust.** Putnam, 2000.

Warren, Andrea. **Surviving Hitler: A Boy in the Nazi Death Camps.** HarperCollins, 2001.

## Finding One's Own Identity

Buchanan, Jane. **Hank's Story.** Farrar, Straus & Giroux, 2001.

★ Creech, Sharon. **The Wanderer.** Illustrated by David Diaz. HarperCollins, 2000.

★ Medina, Jane. **My Name Is Jorge on Both Sides of the River: Poems.**
   Illustrated by Fabricio Vanden Broeck. Boyds Mills, 1999.

Osborne, Mary Pope. **Adaline Falling Star.** Scholastic, 2000.

Warren, Andrea. **We Rode the Orphan Trains.** Houghton Mifflin, 2001.

## Family Hardships

Arrington, Frances. **Bluestem.** Philomel, 2000.

DeFelice, Cynthia. **Nowhere to Call Home.** Farrar, Straus & Giroux, 1999.

★ Giff, Patricia Reilly. **Nory Ryan's Song.** Delacorte, 2000.

Grove, Vicki. **Destiny.** Putnam, 2000.

Vaughan, Marcia. **The Secret to Freedom.** Illustrated by Larry Johnson. Lee
   & Low, 2001.

## Meeting Life Challenges: Physical, Mental, and Emotional

Cummings, Priscilla. **A Face First.** Dutton, 2001.

Hobbs, Will. **Jason's Gold.** Morrow, 1999.

Martin, Ann M. **Belle Teal.** Scholastic, 2001.

★ Paulsen, Gary. **Guts: The True Stories Behind** *Hatchet* **and the Brian Books.**
   Delacorte, 2001.

★ White, Ruth. **Memories of Summer.** Farrar, Straus & Giroux, 2000.

Woodruff, Elvira. **The Memory Coat.** Illustrated by Michael Dooling.
   Scholastic, 1999.

## Catastrophe, Tragedy, and Hardship

Beard, Darleen Bailey. **Twister.** Illustrated by Nancy Carpenter. Farrar,
   Straus & Giroux, 1999.

Calabro, Marian. **The Perilous Journey of the Donner Party.** Clarion, 1999.

★ Kurtz, Jane. **River Friendly, River Wild.** Illustrated by Neil Brennan. Simon
   & Schuster, 2000.

★ Murphy, Jim. **Blizzard!** Scholastic, 2000.

O'Brien, Patrick. **The Hindenburg.** Holt, 2000.

Polacco, Patricia. **The Butterfly.** Philomel, 2000.

## Death and Despair

Atkins, Jeannine. **A Name on the Quilt: A Story of Remembrance.**
   Illustrated by Tad Hills. Atheneum, 1999.

Bunting, Eve. **Rudi's Pond.** Illustrated by Ronald Himler. Clarion, 1999.

★ Couloumbis, Audrey. **Getting Near to Baby.** Putnam, 1999.

Gray, Dianne E. **Holding Up the Earth.** Houghton Mifflin, 2000.

### Considering the Future

Kessler, Christine. **Jubela.** Illustrated by JoEllen McAllister Stammen. Simon & Schuster, 2001.

★ Lasky, Kathryn. **Interrupted Journey: Saving Endangered Sea Turtles.** Photographs by Christopher G. Knight. Candlewick, 2001.

Philbrick, Rodman. **The Last Book in the Universe.** Scholastic, 2000.

Robbins, Ken. **Thunder on the Plains: The Story of the American Buffalo.** Atheneum, 2001.

Sedwick, Marcus. **Floodland.** Delacorte, 200l.

Singer, Marilyn. **Tough Beginnings: How Baby Animals Survive.** Illustrated by Anna Vojtech. Holt, 2001.

---

Literature that focuses on the topic of struggle and survival initially brings to mind life-threatening events and cataclysmic situations that call on a character's courage and energy, often ending with exhausted relief. In recent years, television and other media have shaped our idea of what it means to be a survivor. Literature, however, has a long history of interest in survival and characters who struggle. Books published in the last few years are no exception. What may differ is the complexity of the represented struggles and the truthfulness of the authors, who go to great lengths to research and to write honestly and in compelling ways for readers whose views of survival are influenced by televised portrayals.

It might be surprising, but very few books selected for this chapter present stories—real or imagined—featuring blood-and-guts scenarios. Not all reflect struggle as a life or death situation. And none portrays survivors as movie star hopefuls involved in a series of episodes that ends tidily when the last obstacle has been overcome. Instead, the books presented in this chapter look at struggle and survival from a more realistic perspective. They don't all end happily ever after, with characters cheering wildly because they've been declared winners. Most of the books offer hopeful endings, yet they also reveal the complexity of the emotions involved and the variety of consequences that are possible.

The books selected for this chapter exhibit variety in genre and format, setting and character, topic and theme. Some present imaginary situations and place characters in challenging roles that have never existed in real life. Others recall real events, presenting true stories that exhibit characters performing heroic feats or facing difficult struggles. In addition, this chapter includes a few books that portray issues of survival in nontraditional formats, such as Jane Kurtz's *River Friendly, River Wild* (2000), a collection of poetry that chronicles Kurtz's family's and community's experience before, during, and after the devastating floods in Grand Rapids, North Dakota, in 1997.

As is often the case with survival literature, the books in this chapter represent the traditional themes of human against human, human against nature, and human against society. We have selected seven categories that showcase these themes: literature that presents bigger-than-life heroes, heroines, and events; literature portraying characters who discover their own identity; literature revealing family hardship; literature that demonstrates the physical, mental, and emotional challenges in characters' lives; literature about catastrophe, tragedy, and hardship; literature acknowledging death and despair; and literature that considers the future.

Books reflecting the struggle of humans challenged by other humans include tensions within families when circumstances such as poverty, alcohol, death, or betrayal influence how they treat one another, as in Vicky Grove's novel *Destiny* (2000). Similarly, literature can address how humans accept or reject the limitations imposed by others whose expectations are either honorable or selfish. Since not all human-against-human struggles exist within family or close friendships, we have included books in which characters endure challenges from mere acquaintances, such as influential members in their school or community, or from unknown but powerful personalities such as political figures. Several books, such as Ruth White's *Memories of Summer* (2000), introduce characters whose biggest challenge is overcoming their own demons, whether physical, mental, or emotional.

Literature focused on the struggles of humans against nature is plentiful and, once again, features situations that are both real and imagined. Some of these books showcase the frightening and powerful results when human beings are pitted against the elements, as Jim Murphy captures in *Blizzard!* (2000), or when they are caught up in natural phenomena that wreak havoc and disaster in their path. Not surprisingly, some of the most riveting survival stories are based on journal and diary accounts written by those who offer specific details of the situations and capture their emotional state of mind in the midst of a life-or-death struggle. Numerous books also feature the struggles of humans (and animals) as they face survival or extinction due to environmental changes in our world.

Books centered on the theme of people against society include historical portrayals of characters and events. In a few books, the characters are children who are taken in by adults who aid in their survival, as in Andrea Warren's *We Rode the Orphan Trains* (2001). Some of the literature introduces young people who take a stand against values and political systems they don't believe in. Readers will also discover compelling literature in which society's mores define some humans as valuable and others as insignificant, resulting in topics ripe for debate and thought-provoking responses.

When readers select a book featured in this chapter, they can expect to meet characters who exhibit the attributes of courage, bravery, fortitude, and perseverance. But these characters will also reveal contradictory, but just as realistic, behaviors such as fear, worry, and doubt. Readers will meet children whose actions and behaviors appear more adultlike than their age but who find the wherewithal to cope, deal with adversity, and endure against all odds. Whether the book's characters are real or fictional, whether they lived years ago or during contemporary times, they offer many ways to think about hardship. Reading about characters deep in the midst of struggle may even stimulate readers to raise provocative questions about their own lives, the lives of others, and the future of their environment. In addition, characters in situations of struggle indirectly model for readers some possibilities for taking action rather than waiting for someone else to resolve their dilemmas.

Images of what survivors look like and ideas of what it means to struggle will vary greatly from reader to reader. Books with clear and compelling text, accompanied by visually engaging illustrations, riveting photographs, and/or eye-opening author's notes, offer readers more extensive and realistic perspectives on what it means to struggle and survive in the past, today, and in the world to come.

## Larger Than Life Heroes, Heroines, and Events

5.1     Appelt, Kathi, and Jeanne Cannella Schmitzer. **Down Cut Shin Creek: The Pack Horse Librarians of Kentucky.** HarperCollins, 2001. ISBN 0-06-029135-4. 58 pp. (I).

This well-researched true story tells about a little-known program created by Franklin D. Roosevelt's Works Progress Administration in 1935 that was designed to bring library materials "neighbor to neighbor" to people living in the crooks and hollows of the Cumberland Mountains. An ordinary day for a pack-horse librarian started at 4:30 A.M., and often the material in their saddlebags consisted of tattered books and magazines, bulletins, and homemade scrapbooks. The majority of librarians were women who traveled year-round to reach isolated homes and schoolhouses. "Book women" had to know their "customers," making sure not to offer materials that might offend an individual. Paid $28 a month, these librarians were determined to open up the world to those in need of fuel for the mind. Black-and-white photographs and a rich bibliography breathe life into this interesting piece of history. (CG)

5.2     ★ Armstrong, Jennifer. **Spirit of Endurance: The True Story of the Shackleton Expedition to the Antarctic.** Illustrated by William Maughan. Crown, 2000. ISBN 0-517-80091-8. 32 pp. (I).

Readers will experience vicariously a remarkable expedition in this spellbinding true story. William Maughan's paintings accompany original photographs and bring to life the extraordinary survival story of Sir Ernest Shackleton's Antarctic adventure. His ship, *Endurance,* was trapped and ripped apart by freezing ice, marooning the crew on a constantly shifting ice pack and forcing the men to pull lifeboats across miles of ice to set sail for an uninhabited island. Leaving most of his men on that island, Shackleton and a small crew endured a daring open boat journey across a violent ocean and trekked over unmapped mountains to reach supplies and a rescue team. After months of waiting for the weather to subside, Shackleton kept his word and returned to rescue the men; every crew member eventually made it to safety. This oversized book offers a richly visual sense of Shackleton's spirit to survive and serves as a valuable companion to Armstrong's Orbis Pictus Award–winning *Shipwreck at the Bottom of the World* (Crown, 1998). (NJJ)

5.3     Krensky, Stephen. **Shooting for the Moon: The Amazing Life and Times of Annie Oakley.** Illustrated by Bernie Fuchs. Farrar, Straus & Giroux, 2001. ISBN 0-374-36843-0. Unpaged. (ALL).

"Aim at a high mark and you will hit it" was the belief of legendary sharpshooter Annie Oakley. Stephen Krensky's picture book biography details the events in this talented woman's life from her childhood spent in poverty in Ohio to her celebrity status as the star of Buffalo Bill's Wild West Show, where she became known worldwide for her daring stunts and incredible marksmanship. During her long and remarkable life, Oakley was tested by the social forces that limited women's roles, but her fortitude and skill resulted in recognition as one of the first great female sports figures. Bernie Fuchs's expressive oil paintings dramatize the life events of the incomparable Annie Oakley. (CG)

**5.4** Nobisso, Josephine. **John Blair and the Great Hinkley Fire.** Illustrated by Ted Rose. Houghton Mifflin, 2000. ISBN 0-618-01560-4. Unpaged. (ALL).

Passengers boarding *The Limited*, Train No. 4 in Duluth, Minnesota, on September 1, 1894, had no idea of the dangers they would encounter a few hours into their journey. When the sky turned black in the middle of the afternoon and the trees blazed on both sides of the train, they expected the worst. But conductor John Blair maintained his calm, easy manner, consoling passengers as he reached out to load the people of Hinkley onto his train when it was discovered that their town and train depot had burned. Retreating to avoid the fires ahead, the train was engulfed in flames. Blair risked his own life to lead passengers from the train before it exploded. He then tended to the injured, earning him accolades from the community. Ted Rose's watercolor illustrations capture the urgency and courage in this true story of an unknown hero. (NJJ)

**5.5** ★ Talbott, Hudson. **Forging Freedom: A True Story of Heroism during the Holocaust.** Putnam, 2000. ISBN 0-399-23434-9. 64 pp. (I).

This dramatic account of one person's efforts to protect his Jewish friends and neighbors in Amsterdam during World War II is echoed in the ancient proverb gracing his medal: "He who saves a single human life saves the entire universe." Jaap Penraat, a young Dutch architectural student, began his heroic actions by making fake ID cards and then progressed to more drastic schemes in an effort to outsmart the Nazis. Penraat risked his own life with each action, but he also had to risk his friends' lives in order to save them. This riveting true story, demonstrating bravery in the face of horrific odds, comes alive with Talbott's watercolor illustrations. Other intriguing looks at unsung heroes of the Holocaust are Carmen Agra Deedy's picture book *The Yellow Star: The Legend of King Christian X of Denmark* (Peachtree, 2000) and Susan G. Rubin's biography *Fireflies in the Dark: The Story of Freidl Dicker-Brandeis and the Children of Terezin* (Holiday House, 2000). (NJJ)

**5.6** Warren, Andrea. **Surviving Hitler: A Boy in the Nazi Death Camps.** HarperCollins, 2001. ISBN 0-688-17497-3. 146 pp. (I).

Andrea Warren tells the unforgettable true story of a Polish boy and his three-year struggle to survive intolerable conditions in Nazi concentration camps. As the narrative begins, readers meet happy twelve-year-old Jack Mandelbaum, who is hardly aware that he is Jewish. When Hitler comes to power, Jack is torn from his family as they are herded to a concentration camp and forced to work for the Nazis. In Jack's struggle to survive, he makes a silent vow to see his family again. Moved from camp to camp, Jack resolves not to hate his captors; instead, he befriends other prisoners, and together they endure one hour, one day, one week at a time. Black-and-white photographs and recommendations for further reading and viewing help make this story of an everyday hero a compelling read. Pair this book with Ruth Yaffe Radin's *Escape to the Forest* (HarperCollins, 2000), a fictional account of a young girl's life in a Jewish ghetto. Other books recommended for this category are Rhonda Blumberg's *Shipwrecked! The True Adventure of a Japanese Boy* (HarperCollins, 2001), Frederick Lipp's *The Caged Birds of Phnom Penh* (Holiday House, 2001), and Jacqueline Briggs Martin's *The Lamp, the Ice, and the Boat Called* Fish (Houghton Mifflin, 2001; **2.37**). (NJJ)

## Finding One's Own Identity

5.7   Buchanan, Jane. **Hank's Story.** Farrar, Straus & Giroux, 2001. ISBN 0-374-32836-6. 136 pp. (I).

Twelve-year-old Hank Donohue and his brother Peter have been living in Nebraska with Mr. and Mrs. Olson, a bitter childless couple, after leaving a New York City orphanage and boarding the Orphan Train. This historical novel is set during the time when homeless children were often placed in uncaring and abusive homes in rural communities throughout the Midwest. When Peter can no longer bear Mr. Olson's wrath, he leaves his younger brother to fend for himself. Hank must now do the work of both boys while also attempting to fit in with his classmates, who frequently tease the orphan children who attend school. When Hank meets Molly McIntire, the local "witch," he learns to look beyond his anger and to defend his rights as a human being. (CG)

5.8   ★ Creech, Sharon. **The Wanderer.** Illustrated by David Diaz. HarperCollins, 2000. ISBN 0-060-27730-0. 303 pp. (I).

When thirteen-year-old Sophie commits to sailing across the Atlantic Ocean to England on a forty-five-foot sailboat, she sets out to face her inner demons. Sophie feels called to the sea, joining an all-male crew of three uncles and two teenage cousins headed for the homeland of Bompie, her beloved grandfather. She is also called to take a personal journey that is in many ways as perilous as the adventure-filled challenges faced by the unseasoned crew on the *Wanderer.* Creech's precise descriptions, the edge-of-the-seat adventures, and her storytelling style, which intersperses Sophie's daily journal with cousin Cody's log entries, will captivate readers and keep them holding their breath as Sophie endures nature's harrowing mysteries in order to find her heart's desire. This novel was a deserving Newbery Medal honor book. (NJJ)

5.9     ★ Medina, Jane. **My Name Is Jorge on Both Sides of the River: Poems.** Illustrated by Fabricio Vanden Broeck. Boyds Mills, 1999. ISBN 1-563-97811-3. 48 pp. (ALL).

This collection of bilingual poems chronicles the struggle of a young Mexican boy as he learns the ways of his new country, the United States. "My name is Jorge / I know that my name is Jorge. / But everyone calls me George. / George. / What an ugly sound! Like a sneeze! / GEORGE!" (p. 7). Jorge is teased because of his language, experiences humiliation at the public library, earns low grades at his new school (while in Mexico he was a strong student), and hopes to make new friends. Medina's poignant verses provide opportunities for children to discuss what it feels like to seek acceptance for who they are and the strengths they bring to the classroom. Black-and-white illustrations add an emotional quality to the poetry. (CG)

5.10    Osborne, Mary Pope. **Adaline Falling Star.** Scholastic, 2000. ISBN 0-439-05947-X. 169 pp. (I).

This book took root when Mary Pope Osborne was researching legendary scout Kit Carson for another book. At that time, Osborne read that Carson married an Arapaho woman and had a daughter named Adaline, who was described by a relative of Carson as "a wild child." These few facts lingered for Osborne, eventually taking shape as the fictionalized story of Carson's little-known daughter. When Adaline Falling Star's mother dies, her father sets out on an expedition through the Rockies and sends eleven-year-old Adaline to live with cousins in St. Louis. Mistreated and misunderstood, she flees in search of her father.

When she acquires an abandoned dog on the trail, the two forge a bond that results in a dramatic tale of survival and personal identity. An author's note provides informational sources for this fictionalized account of a historical figure. (NJJ)

**5.11**    Warren, Andrea. **We Rode the Orphan Trains.** Houghton Mifflin, 2001. ISBN 0-618-11712-1. 132 pp. (I).

Andrea Warren tells the incredible stories of remarkable children whose common link is that they all rode orphan trains, or "baby trains," in the late 1800s and the early 1900s in the United States. While each of the children (now adults) interviewed for this book struggled with feelings of abandonment and inferiority, they grew into adults committed to telling the story of their experiences and how they overcame homelessness and persisted in the search for familial identity. This informational book includes a chapter about Clara Comstock, one of the many agents who worked for the Children's Aid Society, which helped place children with good families. Black-and-white archival photographs and a list of recommended readings and Web sites accompany these compelling stories of children searching for someone to care for them. Another useful nonfiction book to pair with this one is Holly Littlefield's *Children of the Orphan Trains* (Carolrhoda, 2001). Other recommended books include Christopher Paul Curtis's *Bud, Not Buddy* (Delacorte, 1999; **19.37**), Polly Horvath's *Everything on a Waffle* (Farrar, Straus & Giroux, 2001; **4.13**), and Vera W. Propp's *When the Soldiers Were Gone* (Putnam, 1999). (NJJ)

## Family Hardships

**5.12**    Arrington, Frances. **Bluestem.** Philomel, 2000. ISBN 0-399-23564-7. 140 pp. (I).

Frances Arrington's first novel sketches the harsh life on the American prairie in the 1870s and tells the story of two sisters forced to fend for themselves on their family's homestead. One day, eleven-year-old Polly and nineteen-year-old Jessie discover their mama sitting and rocking in front of their soddy, saying nothing. Certain that her behavior is due to the loss of another baby, the girls resolve to keep the farm going while they await their father's return from his brother's farm. Meddling neighbors from the closest farm promise to help, but they also threaten to send the girls away on an orphan train if their father does not return. Despite growing difficulties, Polly and Jessie survive, armed with newfound courage. An interesting book to pair with *Bluestem* is Maryanne Caswell's *Pioneer Girl* (Tundra, 2001), set on the prairies of Canada in the 1880s. (NJJ)

5.13    DeFelice, Cynthia. **Nowhere to Call Home.** Farrar, Straus & Giroux, 1999. ISBN 0-374-35552-5. 208 pp. (I).

Left penniless and without immediate family by her father's bankruptcy and subsequent suicide, twelve-year-old Frances Elizabeth Barrow decides that life as a hobo is sure to be better than living in Chicago with an unfamiliar aunt. This novel captures the despair of the Great Depression as readers meet a spirited heroine who disguises herself as Frankie in order to ride the rails, and Stewpot, an older boy who teaches Frankie the hobo life. Both children struggle with loneliness as they search for a place to call home during a period in history when individuals and families were challenged to endure drastic changes in lifestyle. (NJJ)

5.14    ★ Giff, Patricia Reilly. **Nory Ryan's Song.** Delacorte, 2000. ISBN 0-385-32141-4. 148 pp. (I).

Giff tells a gripping story of survival and compassion during the Irish potato famine of 1845. Every year, Nory's father spends months on a fishing boat to pay rent that has been unfairly imposed by an English lord. When a potato blight sweeps down the coast of Ireland, the rotting smell of potatoes is overwhelming. As the quest for food occupies starving villagers, the threat of eviction becomes a constant fear for those without money. Forced to work for a neighbor who is feared because of her strange behavior, Nory discovers that tragedy and connections draw them together in friendship. The struggle for survival against overwhelming circumstances that Giff's spirited and resourceful characters engage in will make this historical context come alive for young readers. Suggested companion books are Laura Wilson's *How I Survived the Irish Famine* (HarperCollins, 2001), Susan Campbell Bartoletti's *Black Potatoes: The Story of the Great Irish Famine 1845–1850* (Houghton Mifflin, 2001), and Mary E. Lyons's *Knockabeg: A Famine Tale* (Houghton Mifflin, 2001). (NJJ)

5.15    Grove, Vicki. **Destiny.** Putnam, 2000. ISBN 0-399-23449-7. 169 pp. (I).

While twelve-year-old Destiny Louise Capperson dreams of becoming an artist, her reality is selling not-so-fresh potatoes for extra money and serving as the main caregiver for her impoverished family. Destiny's mother spends her days watching television, believing that someday soon she will win the lottery with food stamp money. Destiny's half-siblings include little sisters and a brother whose legs were "scrunched" in a mysterious car accident. When she is encouraged by a favorite teacher to apply for a job reading to Mrs. Peck, an elderly retired Latin teacher, Destiny discovers a world in stark contrast to her home life. With Mrs. Peck, she enters an intellectually invigorating world of mythology and kindness and discovers hope for her own imperfect existence—until she is faced with her new friend's imperfection. (NJJ)

5.16    Vaughan, Marcia. **The Secret to Freedom.** Illustrated by Larry Johnson. Lee & Low, 2001. ISBN 1-58430-021-3. Unpaged. (ALL).

*The Secret to Freedom* challenges readers never to forget the adversity and triumph that are part of our history. The story begins with Aunt Lucy telling her great niece the story of Lucy's childhood as a slave in South Carolina. After her parents are sold, she and her brother Albert are left to care for one another on the plantation. When Albert brings home a sack of quilts with patterns representing codes used by the Underground Railroad, Lucy hangs them on the clothesline to assist runaway slaves. Unfortunately, Lucy must stay behind when Albert flees after he is caught helping the runaways. Years later a scrap of fabric received in the mail lets Lucy know that her brother is still alive, leading to a joyful reunion. Larry Johnson's vibrant acrylic paintings reflect the story's emotional quality, and an author's note reveals information about the quilt pattern codes. Pair this with *Stealing South: A Story of the Underground Railroad*, an adventure novel by Katherine Ayers (Delacorte, 2001). Other books recommended are Deborah Ellis's *The Breadwinner* (Douglas & McIntyre, 2001; **3.32**), Francisco Jiménez's *The Circuit: Stories from the Life of a Migrant Child* (Houghton Mifflin, 1999), Barbara O'Conner's *Moonpie and Ivy* (Farrar, Straus & Giroux, 2001; **4.36**), Barbara Park's *The Graduation of Jake Moon* (Atheneum, 2000; **4.37**), and Pam Muñoz Ryan's *Esperanza Rising* (Scholastic, 2000; **17.38**). (ST)

## Meeting Life Challenges: Physical, Mental, and Emotional

5.17    Cummings, Priscilla. **A Face First.** Dutton, 2001. ISBN 0-525-46522-7. 157 pp. (I).

When twelve-year-old Kelly awakens in the hospital, she has no recollection of the terrible car accident that has left her face, leg, and hand badly burned. As details of her lengthy and painful recovery become clear—including the fact that she will have to wear a face mask for at least a year—Kelly struggles to figure out how to face her friends and the world again. With the support of a caring community, including other burn victims, Kelly discovers many things about herself and her abilities that allow her to accept the arduous journey to recovery. (NJJ)

5.18    Hobbs, Will. **Jason's Gold.** Morrow, 1999. ISBN 0-688-15093-4. 221 pp. (I).

When gold is discovered in Alaska, fifteen-year-old Jason Hawthorn decides to leave his home in New York and begin the perilous 5,000-mile journey to the Klondike gold fields. This fictional novel takes readers across hazardous Chilkoot Pass to the Yukon River, encountering along with Jason individuals such as the not-yet-famous Jack London and an adventurous girl named Jamie. Jason also befriends an Alaskan husky he names King, who becomes his traveling companion and eventual savior. Hobbs's suspenseful novel, based on historical accounts of the Klondike gold rush, will keep readers enthralled through the entire journey. A map of the region and an author's note provide authentic background for the thrills and chills of this survival story and its adventure-filled sequel, *Down the Yukon* (Harper-Collins, 2001). Another fascinating companion book is Barbara Greenwood's *Gold Rush Fever: A Story of the Klondike, 1898* (Kids Can Press, 2001). (NJJ)

5.19    Martin, Ann M. **Belle Teal.** Scholastic, 2001. ISBN 0-439-09823-8-6. 216 pp. (I).

Fifth grader Belle begins a new school year against the backdrop of school integration in the early 1960s. She lives in a small rural town in the South with her mother, who is struggling financially, and her Gran, who is in the early stages of Alzheimer's disease. The family is poor in material wealth but rich in humanity. When Belle befriends Darryl, a new classmate who is African American, she discovers they share a love of writing. Unfortunately, most of the other students are not nice to Darryl and believe "his kind" do not belong in their school. When Darryl is falsely accused of shooting a fellow classmate, the struggles of other students are revealed, and new friendships form when the children realize they share common feelings. Even Belle Teal admits that the assumptions she made about her white class-mates are false, noting: "There's a lot we don't know about what goes on underneath people's skin" (p. 214). (NJJ)

5.20    ★ Paulsen, Gary. **Guts: The True Stories Behind *Hatchet* and the Brian Books.** Delacorte, 2001. ISBN 0-385-32650-5. 148 pp. (I).

This collection of autobiographical anecdotes concentrates on Paulsen's real-life experiences that inspired *Hatchet* and the other Brian books. The title *Guts* takes on multiple meanings as the author relives surviving in the wilderness. Drawing parallels between his life and the misadventures of his character Brian Robeson, Paulsen tells of the courage it took to endure harsh northern winters, learning to live off the land and eating any-thing he could find or catch, including raw turtle eggs. In his humorous and lively storytelling style, Gary Paulsen recounts near misses with moose, hunting trips using nothing more than a handmade bow and arrow, and his attempt to save a heart attack victim who eventually became the inspiration for the pilot in *Hatchet. Guts* offers readers the true stories that Paulsen later crafted into compelling fiction. (JAK)

5.21    ★ White, Ruth. **Memories of Summer.** Farrar, Straus & Giroux, 2000. ISBN 0-374-34945-2. 134 pp. (I).

This novel tells the moving story of a teenager's descent into mental illness through the eyes of her younger sister. Set in 1955, Lyric, her father, and her older sister Summer leave the coal mines of Glory Bottom, Virginia, for a better life in Flint, Michi-gan. After the move, pretty and popular Summer, "who always did have funny ways about her," begins to slip into schizo-phrenic episodes. Lyric and her father cope with shame, confu-sion, and uncertainty as they lovingly try to provide for Summer. Eventually, they must face the heartbreaking realities of psychiatric wards, medication, and state hospitals. Remaining devoted to her sister, Lyric learns a great deal about having com-passion toward those who are different. This novel offers loving commentary about family bonds and provides readers with a realistic picture of mental illness. (NJJ)

5.22    Woodruff, Elvira. **The Memory Coat.** Illustrated by Michael Dooling. Scholastic, 1999. ISBN 0-590-67717-9. Unpaged. (I).

When Cossacks threaten to kill all the Jews in Russia, Rachel and Grisha escape danger by fleeing to the United States with their family. Concerned about making a good impression at Ellis Island, Rachel's grandmother urges cousin Grisha to let her make him a new coat. But Grisha is reluctant to give up his old coat, the only reminder he has of his deceased mother. Readers will experience the fears and challenges faced by immigrants as they attempt to pass inspection on Ellis Island—a test Grisha fails. Fortunately, some quick thinking keeps the family together in their new country. Michael Dooling's oil paintings add warmth and drama to this story of loving memories and new beginnings. The book closes with factual information about Ellis Island and immigration, extending readers' knowledge about the arrival of many future U.S. citizens. Books that connect especially well with this one are the following: Kimberly Brubaker Bradley's *Weaver's Daughter* (Delacorte, 2000), *Samir and Yonatan* by Daniella Carmi (Levine/Scholastic, 2000), and Jane Yolen and Heidi Yolen Stemple's *The Wolf Girls: An Unsolved Mystery from History* (Simon & Schuster, 2001). (JAK)

## Catastrophe, Tragedy, and Hardship

5.23   Beard, Darleen Bailey. **Twister.** Illustrated by Nancy Carpenter. Farrar, Straus & Giroux, 1999. ISBN 0-374-37977-7. Unpaged. (P).

Imagine a hot summer afternoon of gentle porch swinging interrupted by the thunderous roar of an approaching tornado. This picture book recounts such a perilous experience as two children run for the cellar while their mother rushes next door to help an elderly neighbor. The thrill and the fear of a natural disaster come alive in the dark, spidery cellar, where time seems to stand still. As they wait for the all-clear sign, the children tap their toes and "count to a hundred and three," zigzag their flashlights, make wall shadows, and compare scars. They also wait while the silence is devoured by the ferocious roar of a striking twister. The story ends with everyone safe. The fierce beauty of such a disaster lingers for readers through Bailey's sensory images and Nancy Carpenter's illustrations, both of which capture the power of this natural phenomenon. Consider pairing this with Mary Pope Osborne's *Twister on Tuesday* (Random House, 2001). (NJJ)

5.24   Calabro, Marian. **The Perilous Journey of the Donner Party.** Clarion, 1999. ISBN 0-395-86610-3. 192 pp. (I).

The fateful journey of the Donner Party's mid-nineteenth-century expedition from Springfield, Illinois, to the California territory has been well documented and is recounted in books, in films, and on Web sites. But rarely has the true tale of hardship and survival been seen through the eyes of a child. Marian Calabro's *The Perilous Journey of the Donner Party* focuses primarily on the viewpoint and experiences of twelve-year-old Virginia Reed. Meticulously researched, alive in detail, and profiling other members of the party, Calabro's story is a gripping and personal narrative, making it accessible to young readers. Photographs and reproductions of art and artifacts, a reprint of a letter sent to a cousin by young Virginia Reed, and a list for further reading support the vivid retelling of this ill-fated journey. (NJJ)

5.25 ★ Kurtz, Jane. **River Friendly, River Wild.** Illustrated by Neil Brennan. Simon & Schuster, 2000. ISBN 0-689-82049-6. Unpaged. (I).

This compelling collection of eighteen free verse poems tells the story from a young girl's perspective of the 1997 flood that destroyed Grand Forks, North Dakota. The book begins with an author's note recounting her personal experience surviving the flood and paying tribute to the townspeople and the various agencies that assisted throughout the years of recovery. It continues with a poem that reflects the calm, constant presence of the Red River before a freak blizzard in April. Subsequent poems take readers through the efforts of sandbagging, evacuation, returning home, and cleaning up. Kurtz's poetry effectively captures this time of loss, and Neil Brennan's warm-toned, oil-glaze illustrations echo the underlying emotions. (NJJ)

5.26 ★ Murphy, Jim. **Blizzard!** Scholastic, 2000. ISBN 0-590-67309-2. 136 pp. (I).

One of civilization's biggest obstacles is weather, particularly when it is unexpected and unwelcome. Such was the case in March 1888 when two massive storm systems converged on northeastern United States, changing conditions from picnic weather to between twenty-one and fifty-five inches of drifting snow virtually overnight. This 2001 Orbis Pictus honor book grabs readers' attention from the first page as it relates the dramatic story of dwindling supplies, snapped power lines, trapped trains, ships lost at sea, and over eight hundred deaths in New York City, all because of the storm dubbed The Great White Hurricane. Murphy's painstaking research, coupled with his ability to personalize the storm, makes this book a page-turner. Accompanied by sepia-toned archival photographs and original art from the period, *Blizzard!* brings history to life through selected anecdotes, newspaper accounts, and a compelling narrative. (NJJ)

**5.27**  O'Brien, Patrick. **The Hindenburg.** Holt, 2000. ISBN 0-8050-6415-X. Unpaged. (ALL).

Hugo Eckener explored the invention of dirigibles and eventually designed the largest and fastest airship ever built. This dramatic picture book relates the history of dirigibles from the first airship, created by Count Ferdinand von Zepplin, to Eckener's "fabulous silvery fish that seemed to float in the ocean of air." Through compelling text and muted watercolor and gouache illustrations, O'Brien tells of early airships that not only transported passengers, but also dropped bombs on England during World War I. The *Hindenburg* was the ultimate pleasure craft, carrying thirty-six passengers and a crew of sixty-one, with private rooms, a shower, library, and well-stocked gourmet kitchen. The explosion on its ninth journey occurred over New Jersey and is speculated to have been caused by static electricity that ignited the hydrogen inside the airship. Additional facts are provided at the conclusion of this captivating account. (CG)

**5.28**  Polacco, Patricia. **The Butterfly.** Philomel, 2000. ISBN 0-399-23170-6. Unpaged. (I).

Set in France during the German occupation of World War II, this picture book for older children introduces sophisticated subjects such as Nazism, resistance, and Jewish persecution in an emotionally charged yet captivating story. Monique, a French girl, discovers a Jewish family living in a secret part of the basement of her building. At first Monique thinks the girl, Sevrine, is a ghost, but through nighttime encounters, they become friends. A butterfly becomes their symbol of freedom, but when she releases one from a window, Sevrine is noticed by a neighbor, and the basement is no longer a safe hiding place. Sevrine's family must flee once again, and Monique is forced to learn some terrible truths about the world's brutality. Insightful weaving of fact with fiction can serve as a vehicle for discussing issues and voices from the past. Polacco's detailed trademark illustrations provide a portrait of fear, courage, friendship, and hope. (CG)

★ Yin. **Coolies.** Illustrated by Chris Soentpiet. Philomel, 2001. ISBN 0-399-23227-3. Unpaged. (ALL). (See **16.33**.)

## Death and Despair

**5.29**    Atkins, Jeannine. **A Name on the Quilt: A Story of Remembrance.** Illustrated by Tad Hills. Atheneum, 1999. ISBN 0-689-81592-1. Unpaged. (I).

This quiet picture book shows how a family gathers to pay tribute to the life of a much-loved relative, even as they struggle to understand his death. Lauren is stung by Uncle Ron's death and irritated by her younger brother's behavior. As she shares her own memories of her uncle, she realizes her brother has memories too. Eventually Lauren helps her brother stitch his contribution—a pair of red socks given to him by Uncle Ron—into a quilt panel. Sensitive and somber, the story ends as Lauren wraps herself in the quilt, just as Uncle Ron enveloped her in his protective arms. Tad Hills's soft-hued illustrations are rendered in colored pencil and watercolor, acrylic, and oil pastels, and provide a quiet cushion for the painful emotions of the text. Information about the AIDS Memorial Quilt Project accompanies the story. Pair this with Theresa Nelson's novel, *Earthshine* (Orchard, 1994). (NJJ)

**5.30**    Bunting, Eve. **Rudi's Pond.** Illustrated by Ronald Himler. Clarion, 1999. ISBN 0-395-89067-5. 32 pp. (ALL).

Inspired by a true story, this picture book deals with the deep and profoundly affecting human emotions associated with the death of a friend. Even though Rudi, the narrator's best friend, is sick, the two friends share a mutual love of nature and paint the garden gate to commemorate nature's beauty. When Rudi dies, friends and classmates help pay tribute to their friend by writing a book of poems and building a pond near the knobby oak tree at school. Soon after the narrator hangs a hummingbird feeder she built with Rudi on the tree, a hummingbird appears at the school window each day, as if a messenger from her friend. This author and illustrator team continue their sensitive collaboration with spare but powerful text, accompanied by watercolors that perfectly suit the book's theme. (NJJ)

**5.31**    ★ Couloumbis, Audrey. **Getting Near to Baby.** Putnam, 1999. ISBN 0-399-23389-X. 211 pp. (I).

Sometimes family members mean well, but their good intentions are untimely and inappropriate. Such is the case in this Newbery honor book as it tells a poignant and surprisingly humorous story of twelve-year-old Willa Jo and Little Sister, who have recently moved to Aunt Patty's in the wake of their baby sister's death. Good-hearted but bossy, "It wasn't enough Aunt Patty had her own opinion, she like to have everyone else's, too" (p. 36). Aunt Patty offers to care for her nieces in the misguided belief that their mother needs time alone. As she hovers too close, the girls climb onto the roof, and the memory of their baby sister unfolds. While Willa Jo's distinctly southern voice tells the story of familial love and loss with both lightness and grief, Little Sister never speaks, mute since Baby died. This novel honors a flawed yet loving family and reveals complex and deeply felt emotions. (NJJ)

**5.32**    Gray, Dianne E. **Holding Up the Earth.** Houghton Mifflin, 2000. ISBN 0-618-00703-2. 210 pp. (I).

Hope was in first grade when a collision with a drunk driver claimed her mother's life. During the next eight years, Hope drifted from one foster home to another until she was placed with her current foster mother, Sarah, who has plans to spend the summer with her own mother on the farm in Nebraska where both women were raised. Gray has drawn from her own experiences of life in rural Nebraska to write this heartwarming novel of a young girl coming to terms with the long-ago loss of her mother. During the summer on the farm, Hope finds peace through the stories of generations of strong young women who not only survived the harshness of prairie living, but also learned to thrive on the simple comforts the land has to offer. (JAK)

## Considering the Future

**5.33**    Kessler, Christine. **Jubela.** Illustrated by JoEllen McAllister Stammen. Simon & Schuster, 2001. ISBN 0-689-81895-5. Unpaged. (P).

*Jubela* is based on a true story of a baby rhinoceros in Swaziland whose mother is killed by poachers. Hungry, afraid, exhausted, and alone, Jubela wanders the African plains until he eventually finds an old mother rhino who adopts him and teaches him how to graze. Kessler's simple yet sensitive poetic prose tells a heartbreaking story of an endangered species, while Stammen's stunning pastel illustrations capture the sweep of the savanna, the struggle to survive, and the tragedy of death. An author's note provides additional information about Jubela and makes a plea for conservation of endangered species. (CG)

**5.34**   ★ Lasky, Kathryn. **Interrupted Journey: Saving Endangered Sea Turtles.** Photographs by Christopher G. Knight. Candlewick, 2001. ISBN 0-7636-0634-9. Unpaged. (ALL).

Sea turtles face many obstacles such as humans with fishing nets, speedboats, and sharks and other predatory fish. Lasky examines the Kemp's Ridley Turtle plight and, through informational text, details the discovery of a dying sea turtle and the attempts by veterinarians, marine biologists, and volunteers to save its life and others of this endangered species. The narrative travels from New England, where the turtles are medically treated, to the Florida Keys, where they are released back into the sea. Knight's clear photographs show the process from capture to release in this engaging book about how human intervention can assist the survival of a species. (CG)

**5.35**   Philbrick, Rodman. **The Last Book in the Universe.** Scholastic, 2000. ISBN 0-439-08758-9. 223 pp. (I).

In a future where memory no longer exists and pleasures of all sorts can be found through mind probes, a boy called Spaz is joined by an old man named Ryter and a feral child known as Little Face on a journey in a futuristic society that developed after the Big Shake. It is a world of chaotic civilization, except for a place called Eden, where a small group of Proovs (genetically improved humans) lives. In this fast-paced and suspenseful novel, Spaz's adventure begins when he is sent to bust down Ryter's stackbox (residence). Shortly thereafter, news about a family member sends Spaz on a heroic quest, accompanied by the old man and his crazy, wonderful ideas. This chilling tale about courage and challenge, moral choices and consciousness, illuminates the power of story to help people remember and to keep living. (NJJ)

**5.36**   Robbins, Ken. **Thunder on the Plains: The Story of the American Buffalo.** Atheneum, 2001. ISBN 0-689-83025-4. Unpaged. (ALL).

"In 1875 there were perhaps fifty million of them. Just twenty-five years later nearly every one of them was gone." Ken Robbins's *Thunder on the Plains: The Story of the American Buffalo* reveals the sad truth of how reckless and wasteful slaughter by newly arrived settlers drove the buffalo to the brink of extinction. Once a magnificent and flourishing species, these shaggy creatures were revered by Native Americans and called "tatonka" (spirit) by the Lakota Sioux. But by 1910, only about five hundred buffalo remained. Over time, laws were passed and preserves were established to save these creatures from extinction. Photographs and archival paintings provide a historical visual for this brief introductory history of the buffalo. (NJJ)

5.37    Sedwick, Marcus. **Floodland.** Delacorte, 2001. ISBN 0-385-32801-X. 148 pp. (I).

In this futuristic novel, global warming has caused the seas to rise, resulting in cities turning into islands and civilization crumbling. When ten-year-old Zoe Black is accidentally left behind by her parents as they escape in the last visiting supply ship, she sets off alone in a small rowboat to find them. After crossing the great sea, Zoe makes it as far as tiny Eels Island, where she must survive a nightmarish world run by a band of wild children. The only adult on the island, mad William, holds out hope that the world she longs for still exists, giving Zoe the will to strike out in search of the promise of civilization and family. This novel offers readers a resourceful heroine while raising thought-provoking questions about global warming and the future. Laurence Pringle's *Global Warming: The Threat of Earth's Changing Climate* (SeaStar, 2001) is a natural nonfiction companion to this novel because it clarifies that global warming is an urgent environmental problem. The information it provides may answer readers' questions about the situation in *Floodland.* (NJJ)

5.38    Singer, Marilyn. **Tough Beginnings: How Baby Animals Survive.** Illustrated by Anna Vojtech. Holt, 2001. ISBN 0-8050-6164-9. Unpaged. (ALL).

"It's tough to begin on the beaches. . . . It's tough to begin in the seas. . . . It's hard to hang on to your mother. . . . It's hard to jump out of the trees. . . ." These phrases are introductory sentences into a look at the challenges baby animals face as they grow into adulthood. This nonfiction picture book explains how baby sea turtles must race from the sand to the safety of the sea just moments from hatching. In similar tales of infant danger, baby Komodo dragons must care for themselves to avoid running into predators, including their cannibalistic parents, and the baby giraffe will be abandoned by its mother if it does not stand within an hour of its birth. Warm watercolor illustrations appear as double-page spreads, providing a rich background for these informative survival stories. Another book about the difficulties of being young and alone is Lois Lowry's *Gathering Blue* (Houghton Mifflin, 2000). (NJJ)

# 6 School Life

Marjorie R. Hancock

*Contributing reviewers included Jeri A. Clouston, Pam K. Evans, and Janet L. Kellogg.*

---

**Criteria for Excellence**

- The book content strongly and clearly relates to the common experience of school life for elementary children.
- The book meets the standards for quality literature by exhibiting well-written text and/or quality illustrations.
- Children show a genuine interest in reading/listening to the book and respond to it in a positive fashion.
- Children readily relate the book to their own school life experiences.
- The book becomes a requested read-aloud or popular independent reading choice among students in the classroom.

---

## Anticipating the First Day of School

★ Kirk, David. **Little Miss Spider at Sunny Patch School.** Scholastic, 2000.

Millman, Isaac. **Moses Goes to School.** Farrar, Straus & Giroux, 2000.

★ Poydar, Nancy. **First Day, Hooray!** Holiday House, 1999.

## Experiencing School Culture

Best, Cari. **Shrinking Violet.** Illustrated by Giselle Potter. Farrar, Straus & Giroux, 2001.

★ Borden, Louise. **The Day Eddie Met the Author.** Illustrated by Adam Gustavson. Margaret K. McElderry Books, 2001.

★ Finchler, Judy. **Testing Miss Malarkey.** Illustrated by Kevin O'Malley. Walker, 2000.

Kalman, Bobbie. **SCHOOL from A to Z.** Crabtree, 1999.

## Challenging Multicultural Obstacles to Schooling

Bognomo, Joël Eboueme. **Madoulina: A Girl Who Wanted to Go to School.** Boyds Mills, 1999.

★ Howard, Elizabeth Fitzgerald. **Virgie Goes to School with Us Boys.** Illustrated by E. B. Lewis. Simon & Schuster, 2000.

★ Nelson, Vaunda Micheaux. **Beyond Mayfield.** Putnam, 1999.

## Laughing at Humorous School-Related Scenarios

★ Brown, Marc. **Arthur's Teacher Moves In.** Little, Brown, 2000.

★ Cleary, Beverly. **Ramona's World.** Illustrated by Alan Tiegreen. Morrow, 1999.

MacDonald, Amy. **No More Nasty.** Illustrated by Cat Bowman Smith. Farrar, Straus & Giroux, 2001.

★ Palatini, Margie. **Bedhead.** Illustrated by Jack E. Davis. Simon & Schuster, 2000.

## Sharing Common Experiences and Special Talents

★ Harper, Jessica. **I Forgot My Shoes.** Illustrated by Kathy Osborn. Putnam, 1999.

Hurwitz, Johanna. **The Just Desserts Club.** Illustrated by Karen Dugan. Morrow, 1999.

Kline, Suzy. **Molly's in a Mess.** Illustrated by Diana Cain Bluthenthal. Putnam, 1999.

Krensky, Stephen. **Arthur and the Poetry Contest.** Little, Brown, 1999.

Mills, Claudia. **You're a Brave Man, Julius Zimmerman.** Farrar, Straus & Giroux, 2000.

Priceman, Marjorie. **Emeline at the Circus.** Knopf, 1999.

## Meeting Teachers Who Make a Difference

Adler, David A. **School Trouble for Andy Russell.** Illustrated by Will Hillenbrand. Harcourt, 1999.

Bartlett, Susan. **Seal Island School.** Illustrated by Tricia Tusa. Viking, 1999.

★ Borden, Louise. **Good Luck, Mrs. K.!** Illustrated by Adam Gustavson. Margaret K. McElderry Books, 1999.

★ Hill, Kirkpatrick. **The Year of Miss Agnes.** Margaret K. McElderry Books, 2000.

Stanley, George E. **The Cobweb Confession.** Illustrated by Salvatore Murdocca. Aladdin, 2001.

## Exploring the Role of Family in School Success

Johnson, Delores. **My Mom Is My Show-and-Tell.** Marshall Cavendish, 1999.

★ Mills, Claudia. **Gus and Grandpa and Show-and-Tell.** Illustrated by Catherine Stock. Farrar, Straus & Giroux, 2000.

## Feeling Good in and out of School

Banks, Kate. **Howie Bowles, Secret Agent.** Farrar, Straus, & Giroux, 1999.

★ Clements, Andrew. **The Janitor's Boy.** Simon & Schuster, 2000.

Gorman, Carol. **Dork in Disguise**. HarperTrophy, 2000.

McDonald, Megan. **Judy Moody.** Illustrated by Peter Reynolds. Candlewick, 2000.

★ McKissack, Patricia C. **The Honest-to-Goodness Truth.** Illustrated by Giselle Potter. Atheneum, 2000.

Mills, Claudia. **Lizzie at Last.** Farrar, Straus & Giroux, 2000.

---

The primary common denominator of childhood experience in the lives of elementary readers is school life. Children effortlessly relate to stories of the first day of school, the class clown, a favorite teacher, a best friend, and serious and humorous everyday incidents in the classroom. Identifying with school characters and school-related scenarios invites personal response and active engagement in reading. The books in this chapter will trigger vivid memories and yield authentic connections to the everyday business of going to school. Characters, settings, episodes, and resolutions parallel the day-to-day lives of school-age readers through tales of embarrassing moments, inspiring teachers, exciting field trips, missing homework, and intriguing classrooms that will keep children turning pages and coming back for more.

The books chosen for this chapter take many forms: picture books, transitional chapter books, series books, and chapter books. These titles also span a variety of literary genres: realistic fiction, nonfiction, historical fiction, and fantasy. There are books about school life for all interest and reading levels. Kindergarten and first-grade teachers can share boldly illustrated picture books through read-alouds that capture the joys and trials of going to school. As children move toward early, independent reading in second and third grade, the easy-to-read transitional chapter book fills their needs. The blend of simple illustrations and short chapters in these books builds confidence in readers and spurs them on to read more and more often. Independent readers easily become hooked on titles that focus on school life, and these fourth-through sixth-grade readers constantly seek out and quickly digest new titles from familiar authors.

Because so many children's books relate to school life, the contributors to this chapter had much sorting and selecting to do. We used the following literary and response criteria to determine our top choices for inclusion in the chapter:

- The book content strongly and clearly relates to the common experience of school life for elementary children.
- The book meets the standards for quality literature by exhibiting well-written text and/or quality illustrations.
- Children show a genuine interest in reading/listening to the book and respond to it in a positive fashion.
- Children readily relate the book to their own school life experiences.
- The book becomes a requested read-aloud or popular independent reading choice among students in the classroom.

These standards raised expectations beyond teacher choices to include children's responses and preferences for school life books. The children's reading tastes and perspectives provide the most important criteria for inclusion of books in this chapter.

The selected titles fit naturally into several school-related categories for organizing the chapter. The following categories explain the types of books included within this framework:

- *Anticipating the first day of school:* Titles about the first day of kindergarten/first grade as well as first days and a fresh start in a new school.
- *Experiencing school culture:* Titles that take the reader inside the school environment during past and present times, as well as serious and humorous treatment of current issues related to schools.
- *Challenging multicultural obstacles to schooling:* Titles related to both racial and gender barriers to acquiring an education and the unjustified mistreatment of children within the historic school setting.
- *Laughing at humorous school-related scenarios:* Titles that share embarrassing incidents and funny happenings that form the day-to-day core and reality of school life.
- *Sharing common experiences and special talents:* Titles that explore the individuality of student interests and abilities framed within the common events of the school day.
- *Meeting teachers who make a difference:* Titles about memorable teachers who effectively touch their students' lives each day because of their special personalities and unique teaching styles.
- *Exploring the role of family in school success:* Titles that reflect the critical support and presence of family members, both serious and humorous, in the school experience.
- *Feeling good in and out of school:* Titles focused on defining oneself, not only as a student but also as a person, by building on

interests and personal strengths and becoming comfortable with and proud of oneself as a unique individual.

The thread that weaves throughout all the titles is the universal experience of attending school while learning about ourselves and others within the familiar environment of the school community.

## Anticipating the First Day of School

6.1    ★ Kirk, David. **Little Miss Spider at Sunny Patch School.** Scholastic, 2000. ISBN 0-439-08727-9. Unpaged. (P).

It's her first day at Sunny Patch School and Miss Spider can't wait to learn new things like climbing and clinging and hiding and curling! Too soon she learns she hasn't the knack for hiding or chirping or humming. She isn't strong enough to drill with her tongue, and she doesn't like digging in dung. Is there *anything* she can do well? Yet when Little Miss Spider hears a bug cry out that he is stuck in the spout, she climbs to the top and helps him get out. The proud principal gives her a star, with a reminder that "'Our gifts, they are many: We hop, fly and crawl. But kindness,' he said, 'is the finest of all!'" David Kirk blends appealing, rhymed text with enchanting, brilliantly hued oil illustrations. This is a wonderful story to share with those nervous and wide-eyed students on the first day of school. They come wanting to learn so much so fast, only to find that for some it's easy and for others it's a challenge. But, just like Miss Spider, they all have their own special talents. (JLK)

6.2    Millman, Isaac. **Moses Goes to School.** Farrar, Straus & Giroux, 2000. ISBN 0-374-35069-8. Unpaged. (P).

Charming, sensitive watercolors draw the reader into Moses's school, a New York City school for the deaf. On this first day of school, the children gather on the playground and busily communicate in American Sign Language as they recount their summer adventures. John has new hearing aids, Dianne has a cute new baby sister, and Moses is sporting new glasses. As Moses's day progresses, readers learn there are similarities and differences between Moses's school and those for hearing children. Because American Sign Language differs from spoken and written English, children with hearing impairments find learning to read and write in English as much of a challenge as hearing children find learning a new language. As students listened to this tender story, their fingers and hands were itching to learn American Sign Language just like Moses and his friends. An author's note and visual inserts of simple signing help readers accomplish this goal. (JLK)

6.3    ★ Poydar, Nancy. **First Day, Hooray!** Holiday House, 1999. ISBN 0-8234-1437-X. Unpaged. (P).

So the first day of school is tomorrow. Why all the fuss? Mom has Ivy trying on new shoes and buying a new lunchbox. Bus Driver Wheeler learns her route, Janitor Handy buffs the halls, Principal Master checks his notes, and Mrs. Bell hangs the alphabet letters and makes a nametag for Ivy Green. As the sun sets on the last day of summer vacation, everyone settles for the night. All over town, school personnel and students fall asleep to dream about their own first day of school: the bus driver misses a stop, the principal wears pajamas to school, Mrs. Bell loses the nametags, and Ivy forgets her lunch. Fortunately, morning comes and the waiting is over! Ivy meets the bus and goes to school, where everything is ready on time. This memorable read-aloud invites children's recollections of anticipating the first day of school. Related first-day-of-school titles include Nancy Carlson's *Look Out Kindergarten, Here I Come!* (Viking, 1999) and Rosemary Wells's *Timothy Goes to School* (Viking, 2000). (JLK)

Rosenberry, Vera. **Vera's First Day of School.** Holt, 1999. ISBN 0-8050-5936-9. Unpaged. (P). (See **8.21.**)

## Experiencing School Culture

6.4    Best, Cari. **Shrinking Violet.** Illustrated by Giselle Potter. Farrar, Straus & Giroux, 2001. ISBN 0-374-36882-1. Unpaged. (P).

Violet has always been the shyest student in school and the guaranteed target of Irwin's teasing. When Violet learns that her class will be performing a school play about the solar system, she panics about having to speak from the stage. But her insightful teacher provides her the off-stage role of Lady Space, and Violet becomes the star of the play. Giselle Potter's festive, whimsical artwork captures the expressions of school characters amid vibrant colors and patterns. During a class read-aloud of this book, the children cheered for Violet as she ultimately dealt with Irwin and gained recognition through her own performance. (MRH)

Bial, Raymond. **One-Room School.** Houghton Mifflin, 1999. ISBN 0-395-90514-1. 48 pp. (ALL). (See **2.20.**)

**6.5**  ★ Borden, Louise. **The Day Eddie Met the Author.** Illustrated by Adam Gustavson. Margaret K. McElderry Books, 2001. ISBN 068-98340-55. Unpaged. (ALL).

The most exciting day of the whole school year is the day a real author comes to visit Eddie's school. The third graders prepare for the visit by reading all the author's books and preparing questions to ask her. Yet when the author arrives and the students have a chance to ask questions, Eddie's raised hand goes unacknowledged. Later on, however, Eddie gets a special opportunity to share his insightful question with the author: "How do you write books that have parts meant for me?" Based on her own rewarding visits to schools, Louise Borden shares the delightful impact of a boy's special question on an author. The endpapers abound with the names of schools the real author has visited, and the watercolor illustrations bring an author visit to life. This title not only invited response to previous or upcoming author visits, but some children also spontaneously ran to the classroom bookshelves to share autographed books from previous author visits. (MRH)

Clements, Andrew. **Jake Drake, Know-It-All.** Illustrated by Dolores Avendano. Simon & Schuster, 2001. ISBN 0-689-83918-9. 88 pp. (I). (See **19.26.**)

**6.6**  ★ Finchler, Judy. **Testing Miss Malarkey.** Illustrated by Kevin O'Malley. Walker, 2000. ISBN 0-8027-8737-1. Unpaged. (ALL).

Most teachers and students have experienced standardized testing and its increasingly prominent role in curriculum and evaluation in recent years. Finchler simultaneously shares the folly to which teachers, administrators, and parents stoop in the hopes of ensuring good scores on THE TEST and captures the accompanying stress and frustrations in otherwise sane people. Her humorous use of staff member names, such as Mrs. Slopdown (the cafeteria lady) and Mr. Fitanuff (the gym teacher) only adds to the zaniness of this book. O'Malley's colorful, cartoonlike illustrations ensure a chuckle, including Principal Wiggins literally flipping his wig. Teachers and students should linger over its message: keep a balanced perspective between testing and reaching authentic classroom goals. (PKE)

**6.7**    Kalman, Bobbie. **SCHOOL from A to Z.** Crabtree. 1999. ISBN 0-86505-388-X. Unpaged. (P).

This informational alphabet book presents school-based photographs of children in a variety of activities in the classroom and on the playground, from academics to fine arts to sports. Children project active learning and cooperative social skills while at work and play. The bold alphabet letters on each page are reflected in the alliterative text emphasizing words that begin with each letter. Each page features eye-inviting, colorfully decorated borders with apples, school bells, books, and pencils. The eager, energetic expressions on the faces of teachers and children tell a story of their own. A third grader responded, "The kids in this book make learning look fun!" Viewing the photographs invited personal connections to our own elementary school. (PKE)

## Challenging Multicultural Obstacles to Schooling

**6.8**    Bognomo, Joël Eboueme. **Madoulina: A Girl Who Wanted to Go to School.** Boyds Mills, 1999. ISBN 1-56397-769-9. Unpaged. (P).

Based on the life of a poverty-stricken child in Cameroon, West Africa, this book confronts the struggles of an eight-year-old girl as she dreams of going to school. Madoulina's single mother enlists her daughter's help to provide a living for the family by selling fritters. While her younger brother's schooling is deemed a necessity for his future, her mother believes that Madoulina only needs to know how to care for her future household. Madoulina's educational aspirations are realized when the village teacher, Mr. Garba, finds a solution to the problem. Readers learn that not all children possess the right to an education as U.S. children do. Both the well-written text and watercolor illustrations provide a springboard for discussing cultural and gender issues related to education. (PKE)

★ Bridges, Ruby. **Through My Eyes.** Scholastic, 1999. ISBN 0-590-18923-9. 64 pp. (I). (See **2.4.**)

**6.9**    ★ Howard, Elizabeth Fitzgerald. **Virgie Goes to School with Us Boys.** Illustrated by E. B. Lewis. Simon & Schuster, 2000. ISBN 0-689-80076-2. Unpaged. (ALL).

During Reconstruction following the Civil War, the hope of learning to read and write fills the hearts and minds of newly freed black citizens. Persistent Virgie insists that her five brothers take her to the Quaker school seven miles from home where they must stay all week to receive their education. In spite of big brother retorts of school being "too far," "too long," and "too hard" and Virgie being "too little," she makes the trek and proudly enters the schoolhouse. Virgie firmly vows that "Someday I'll read all these books!" as she tenderly fingers the bookcase treasures. Based on the life of Cornelius C. Fitzgerald, the author's grandfather, the story portrays school as the first step in African Americans' journey toward freedom. E. B. Lewis's vivid watercolors capture Virgie's bright smile, independent spirit, and undying determination, while the story stands as testimony to children of all colors who view education as a doorway to personal freedom. (MRH)

6.10 ★ Nelson, Vaunda Micheaux. **Beyond Mayfield.** Putnam, 1999. ISBN 0-399-23355-5. 138 pp. (I).

Mayfield Crossing is an all-American town where citizens look after one another. The innocence of the town, however, is shaken by the turmoil of the 1960s, with violence and race riots peaking in the distant South. Sam Wood, one of the town's favorite sons, falls victim to violence and murder when he becomes a member of the Freedom Riders fighting for civil rights. Meg Turner's experience with racism helps her understand why her friend Sam loses his life fighting against bigotry in Mississippi. Meg, who is black, questions why she is blamed for stealing a pen from her substitute teacher, Mrs. Davis, who is white. Meg finds the missing pen and returns it, but Mrs. Davis refuses to believe she didn't steal it. Meg and her friends also discover they misjudged Old Hairy, a recluse who lives outside of Mayfield. A sixth-grade student said she could readily relate to Meg because substitute teachers make her angry and because she herself has been ridiculed because of her color. She highly recommended this book because it discusses the delicate subject of racism while being both honest and enjoyable to read. (JAC)

## Laughing at Humorous School-Related Scenarios

6.11 ★ Brown, Marc. **Arthur's Teacher Moves In.** Little, Brown, 2000. ISBN 0-316-11979-2. Unpaged. (P).

Horror of horrors! Is Arthur's teacher, Mr. Ratburn, really moving into Arthur's house? Arthur tries to plead his case, telling his parents that this is not only wrong—it's weird! But Mr. Ratburn needs their help since the snow collapsed his roof, and Arthur just has to get used to it. Soon Arthur learns that Mr. Ratburn watches cartoon videos, does magic tricks, wears regular clothes, and eats cake. Having Mr. Ratburn around isn't so bad until Arthur goes to school and finds his friends are treating him differently. They don't believe him when he says he studied hard to get an A on a test, Binky is calling him a teacher's pet, and Francine doesn't want to be around him. After Arthur tells his parents and Mr. Ratburn about the teasing, Arthur's teacher wants to help. But how? At lunch the next day, Arthur learns that Mr. Ratburn will no longer be staying with Arthur's family. He needs to be closer to his house, so he will be staying with Francine's family—and then Binky's, and then Muffy's, Buster's, and Fern's! First graders respond warmly to these familiar characters and understand the irony of the solution. Over twenty-five titles in Marc Brown's Arthur chapter book series provide young, independent readers a variety of interesting plots blended with familiar characters. *Arthur's Underwear* (Little, Brown, 1999) and *Binky Rules* (Little, Brown, 2000) are two more hilarious examples. (JLK)

6.12    ★ Cleary, Beverly. **Ramona's World.** Illustrated by Alan Tiegreen. Morrow, 1999. ISBN 0-688-16816-7. 192 pp. (ALL).

Ramona Quimbly looks forward to her fourth-grade year at Cedarcrest School and being with her old friends, Janet and Yard Ape. This year Ramona meets a new best friend, Daisy Kidd, who asks her to play dress-up at the Kidd's house. While playing "wicked witch and princess," Daisy accidentally shoves Ramona into the "dungeon" in the attic. Ramona triumphantly breaks through lathe and plaster through the dining room ceiling but isn't hurt. At Ramona's tenth or "zeroteenth" birthday party, she realizes Yard Ape likes her, because he runs over to her party with his friends and they eat birthday cake. Life is good for this "zeroteenager," as Beverly Cleary continues the saga of one of America's favorite, most-loved classic book characters. (JAC)

6.13    MacDonald, Amy. **No More Nasty.** Illustrated by Cat Bowman Smith. Farrar, Straus & Giroux, 2001. ISBN 0-374-35529-0. 172 pp. (I).

It was bad enough having a substitute teacher that day; imagine Simon's embarrassment when the substitute turned out to be his great aunt Matilda! Right off the farm in her orange-flowered dress, mismatched shoes, and fruit-laden hat, Aunt Mattie has a "heads up" on the sink-the-sub tactics of Simon's fifth-grade class. Not your typical sub, Aunt Mattie breaks rules and has a language all her own to deal with her students and the dismayed teachers in the school. This hilarious sequel to *No More Nice* (Farrar, Straus & Giroux, 2000) takes a humorous look at school and a fresh view of learning and leaves the reader with an appreciation for the art of a cunning substitute teacher. (MRH)

**6.14** ★ Palatini, Margie. **Bedhead.** Illustrated by Jack E. Davis. Simon & Schuster, 2000. ISBN 0-689-82397-5. Unpaged. (P).

Anyone who has experienced a "bad hair day" can readily identify with Oliver's hair, which is totally unruly. Not only is his hair in a giant snarl, like "a cat's coughed-up fur ball," but also, to make matters worse, it's picture day at school. When all the gooping, glooping, spritzing, spraying, and moussing fails, Oliver stuffs his bedhead under a battered baseball cap. Davis's exaggerated, cartoonlike illustrations in full-page layouts blend with Palatini's alliteration and playful word choice to make this book a natural draw for children. A third grader, sporting a huge grin on his face, responded, "That's the silliest looking family I ever saw!" This book gives readers license to laugh at themselves as they realize that everyone experiences embarrassing moments and that no individual is perfect or needs to be. (PKE)

## Sharing Common Experiences and Special Talents

Clements, Andrew. **The Landry News.** Illustrated by Salvatore Murdocca. Simon & Schuster, 1999. ISBN 0-689-81817-3. 123 pp. (I). (See **19.2.**)

**6.15** ★ Harper, Jessica. **I Forgot My Shoes.** Illustrated by Kathy Osborn. Putnam, 1999. ISBN 0-399-23149-8. Unpaged. (P).

Delightful, bold illustrations and captivating rhyme remind us that we all have those busy, hurried mornings when everybody forgets something. With her hair flying back, the sister rushes out the door forgetting to feed the puppy. The puppy retaliates by eating part of the sofa. The bus driver forgets to stop at the corner, so Mama has to drive a vanload of children to school. In her haste, Mama forgets her purse. Everybody forgets it is Pamela's birthday. Even Daddy forgets his coat and the brother forgets his backpack. But worst of all, the one who tells this sad tale forgets her shoes. Undiscouraged, she certainly hopes that "the sun remembers to set tonight, and everyone remembers to snooze. And the first thing I'll do when I wake up tomorrow, is put my feet into my shoes!" Children laughed out loud as they recalled mornings a mom had to drive them to school in her pajamas or the day they wore two different socks to school. The story is silly but so true to life and our own experiences. (JLK)

6.16    Hurwitz, Johanna. **The Just Desserts Club.** Illustrated by Karen Dugan. Morrow, 1999. ISBN 0-688-16266-5. 95 pp. (ALL).

Cricket Kaufman and her sixth-grade friends from Edison Armstrong School try luscious recipes to chase away boredom, earn money to help those less fortunate, and serve at a surprise celebration for their teacher's birthday. Children will not only enjoy the four chapters that make up this book, but also savor the numerous delicious recipes that follow each chapter, including Use Your Noodle Cookies and Mystery Ingredient Chocolate Cake. The friendly competition and cooperation between the girls and boys provide a healthy example for developing relationships. Eight-year-old Sarah shared, "After reading the book, I tried one of the cookie recipes. Not everyone in my family liked them, but I thought they were good, and they were fun to make!" This is an inspiring book for the budding baker and contagious for the avid reader of other Class Clown series titles such as *Llama in the Library* (Morrow, 2000). (PKE)

6.17    Kline, Suzy. **Molly's in a Mess.** Illustrated by Diana Cain Bluthenthal. Putnam, 1999. ISBN 0-399-23131-5. 71 pp. (ALL).

Third grader Molly Zander is the kind of friend we all hope to have sometime in our lives. She has an imagination that takes her places even though it sometimes gets her into trouble. Ever since kindergarten, Molly has done interesting and unusual things. When she forgot to bring something from home that starts with the letter *T*, she pulled up her t-shirt to show her tummy and had to sit in the "quiet chair." But the most unfortunate event that ever happened to Molly takes place during a fire drill. Molly loses control of the basketball she is holding and bounces it off the North School principal's head, dislodging his toupee. Once again, her overzealous nature lands her in trouble.

Molly's abilities to keep a secret and be a best friend provide sound reasons for third graders to read this book. (PKE)

6.18    Krensky, Stephen. **Arthur and the Poetry Contest.** Little, Brown, 1999. ISBN 0-316-12062-6. 60 pp. (P).

After being goaded by Fern to enter the poetry contest, the students in Mr. Ratburn's class begin their writing task. In spite of their bravado about the ease of writing poems, Arthur and Buster find they have their work cut out for them. When Jack Prelutsky visits the library as a guest speaker, Arthur and the others realize how much fun poetry really can be. Prelutsky teaches them that a poem might be about something important or dramatic, but it can also be about everyday things that sometimes take an unexpected turn. Even though the students write their poems so they won't have to join the Poetry Club, they opt to become members after all. This read-aloud provides a motivating introduction to a poetry unit. (PKE)

6.19    Mills, Claudia. **You're a Brave Man, Julius Zimmerman.** Farrar, Straus & Giroux, 2000. ISBN 0-374-38708-7. 152 pp. (I).

The summer brims with activity for twelve-year-old Julius Zimmerman as he reluctantly enrolls in Intensive Summer Language Learning. Julius eventually learns to speak French well enough to have a part in a summer play. At the same time, Julius also faces the challenge of babysitting three-year-old Edison. Julius actually potty trains Edison during an act of the play, *Cinderella.* Julius also helps his friend Octavia realize her acting potential by building her confidence. One of our sixth-grade girls identified Octavia as her favorite character because of her outgoing personality. This reader also laughed when Julius couldn't understand his French assignments or what the French teacher said. Written in a lighthearted manner, the book delicately celebrates the success of underachieving students whose talents may lie in areas outside the academic classroom. (JAC)

6.20    Priceman, Marjorie. **Emeline at the Circus.** Knopf, 1999. ISBN 0-679-87685-5. Unpaged. (P).

Emeline's teacher, Ms. Splinter, takes her second-grade class to the circus. With books in hand and her teacher voice, Ms. Splinter gives instructions on how to enjoy the circus: "Sit up straight. No shouting. No fighting. No fidgeting. No standing on the seats. No wandering off." As Ms. Splinter reads lists of facts about the elephant, the llama, the acrobats, and the trapeze artist, the reader watches Emeline enjoy the circus as only a mischievous child can. The playful illustrations reveal Emeline taking a ride on the elephant's trunk, meeting a clown and riding a horse, being rescued by the strongman, and climbing on the high trapeze. As Emeline flies and somersaults through the air, she is finally spotted by Ms. Splinter, but not before she has experienced all the excitement of the circus. As the final page turns, students' natural responses to this book include personal memories of school field trips or family adventures to the circus. (JLK)

## Meeting Teachers Who Make a Difference

6.21    Adler, David A. **School Trouble for Andy Russell.** Illustrated by Will Hillenbrand. Harcourt, 1999. ISBN 0-15-202190-6. 129 pp. (ALL).

Andy Russell has a problem. His imagination carries him away from his classroom work, and he often misses what is being taught and doesn't hear the assignments. Ms. Roman assigns him additional homework in hopes that he'll learn to pay attention. When Ms. Roman becomes ill, Ms. Salmon takes over as the substitute, to Andy's relief. But Andy finds his troubles are far from over when Ms. Salmon sends him to the principal's office for something he didn't do. He soon realizes that the grass isn't always greener on the other side of the fence. When he visits Ms. Roman at the hospital, he begins to appreciate her good qualities. This book invites students to explore relationships between children and adults and inspires reading of other books in the Andy Russell series such as *Andy and Tamika* (Harcourt, 1999). (PKE)

6.22    Bartlett, Susan. **Seal Island School.** Illustrated by Tricia Tusa. Viking, 1999. ISBN 0-670-88349-2. 69 pp. (ALL).

Life on Seal Island, located off the coast of Maine, is different from life elsewhere. Only forty-nine people live on the island. Two special things happen to Pru Stanley during third grade. She finds a note in a bottle, which initiates a new friendship off the island, and she loves Miss Sparling, the new teacher. Until now it has been difficult to retain a teacher for more than one year due to the loneliness and isolation of the island. Pru and her friend Nicholas hatch a plan to earn enough money to buy a dog for Miss Sparling so that she will have company and not want to leave. But they soon discover that keeping Miss Starling on Seal Island is not their only problem. Will there be enough children attending the school to allow it to stay open? The unusual backdrop of a school on an island will likely intrigue young readers. (PKE)

6.23 ★ Borden, Louise. **Good Luck, Mrs. K.!** Illustrated by Adam Gustavson. Margaret K. McElderry Books, 1999. ISBN 0-689-82147-6. Unpaged. (ALL).

Based on a real third-grade teacher's struggle with cancer, this poignant story deeply touched the hearts of both adult and student reviewers. Mrs. K had always been a special teacher whose students treasured her as they became "detectives, explorers, or travelers" without ever leaving her classroom. Through their imaginations, she took them to the many places she had visited. Watercolor illustrations capture the playful spirit that brought joy to Mrs. K.'s classroom as she teased and danced with her students. Even with the onset of cancer, Mrs. Kempczinski taught her students that a spirit can remain intact even when illness makes a body weak. When visiting at the end of the school year, Mrs. K. inspired the children with hope for the future as she planned to return to third grade. "And she *did* come back in the fall." (PKE)

6.24 ★ Hill, Kirkpatrick. **The Year of Miss Agnes.** Margaret K. McElderry Books, 2000. ISBN 0-689-82933-7. 115 pp. (I).

Children in the Athabascan village of Alaska are apprehensive yet excited about October 1948, the month they meet their new teacher from England. Miss Agnes Sutterfield immediately gets them involved in their education as they learn about themselves, about Alaska, and about the world. The boys in the class are excited to see where their traplines are located on a map. Frederika, known as Fred, learns that she has a love for writing stories. Miss Agnes opens up a new world to Fred's hearing-impaired sister, Bokko, by teaching her sign language so she can communicate. Bokko's enthusiasm for signing grows on her reluctant mother and the people of the village as they too learn to use sign language. Everything is perfect with Miss Agnes except her plans to stay for only one school year before returning to England. The children share a tearful goodbye before they leave for the annual journey to fish camp. Upon returning, however, Fred sees a light in the schoolhouse, recognizes Miss

Agnes in the window, and realizes her teacher plans to stay. Memories of special teachers form a natural response to this powerful classroom read-aloud. (JAC)

**6.25**    Stanley, George E. **The Cobweb Confession.** Illustrated by Salvatore Murdocca. Aladdin, 2001. ISBN 0-689-82197-2. 76 pp. (ALL).

Mr. Merlin, science teacher extraordinaire, and his third graders have gained a reputation for solving mysteries. When Todd's baseball cards are stolen from his home, Mr. Merlin connects a study of spiders and cobwebs with a solution to the mystery. This is book 4 in the Third-Grade Detectives series. Other titles in the series include *The Clue of the Left-Handed Envelope* (**21.22**), *The Puzzle of the Pretty Pink Handkerchief,* and *The Mystery of the Hairy Tomatoes* (Aladdin, 2000). Supersleuths will enjoy the science-related activities at the end of each book. (MRH)

### Exploring the Role of Family in School Success

Bercaw, Edna Coe. **Halmoni's Day.** Illustrated by Robert Hunt. Dial, 2000. ISBN 0-8037-2444-6. Unpaged. (ALL). (See **16.1.**)

dePaola, Tomie. **26 Fairmount Avenue.** Putnam, 1999. ISBN 0-399-23246-X. 56 pp. (ALL). (See **4.25.**)

**6.26**    Johnson, Delores. **My Mom Is My Show-and-Tell.** Marshall Cavendish, 1999. ISBN 0-7614-5041-6. Unpaged. (P).

This heartwarming story expertly captures the changing emotions of a boy whose mother has been invited to share information about her career with his class. Walking to school, David gives his mom a list of "don'ts": Don't tell long stories. Don't call me Pumpkin. Don't tell me to tuck in my shirt. Don't tell jokes. Don't show baby pictures. Don't talk about that crazy kind of stuff. Mom assures David she will only talk about her job, but David notices that her warm smile is gone, and suddenly he is ashamed. Looking down, he sees that his mom's shoe is untied, so he ties it for her. She feels "magic" in her feet and begins shuffling and twirling down the street. David tries to stop her, but she is on the school steps. David's friends see her and begin to laugh. As parent show-and-tell begins, David proudly overcomes his embarrassment and introduces his mother as "the best teacher and the best mother in the world." (JLK)

**6.27** ★ Mills, Claudia. **Gus and Grandpa and Show-and-Tell.** Illustrated by Catherine Stock. Farrar, Straus & Giroux. 2000. ISBN 0-374-32819-6. 47 pp. (P).

Gus, a second grader, cannot think of a single thing to share for show-and-tell. It seems that everyone has something so much better to show or tell about than he does—that is, until he begins looking through Grandpa's pictures of Colorado and listening to his stories about growing up. Gus knows he could never tell the stories as effectively as Grandpa, and an idea is born for the best show-and-tell yet. As Grandpa entertains Gus's classmates with exciting happenings of his past, young and old readers alike will be reminded of how much each generation has to share with others. Claudia Mills has blessed the audience of her popular Gus and Grandpa series for beginning readers with this intergenerational book that warms the hearts of children. (PKE)

## Feeling Good in and out of School

**6.28** Banks, Kate. **Howie Bowles, Secret Agent.** Farrar, Straus, & Giroux, 1999. ISBN 0-374-33500-1. 89 pp. (ALL).

Any child who has had to move to a new school will relate to Howie Bowles. Nervous about going to an unfamiliar school in a new town, Howie wakes up from a dream in which he becomes a secret agent responsible for solving a crime. This is just the beginning for Agent Bean Burger! Howie convinces the other students that he really is a secret agent, until he realizes that with this new identity he can't ever really be himself. Children easily identified with the dilemma Howie faces until he learns that being himself is a good thing. He experiences great relief when his teacher assigns him to the case of finding the missing Howie Bowles! This transitional series chapter book, with plentiful dialogue and intermittent pencil sketches, is a perfect match for newly independent readers. (PKE)

**6.29** ★ Clements, Andrew. **The Janitor's Boy.** Simon & Schuster, 2000. ISBN 0-689-81818-1. 140 pp. (I).

What begins as a prank against the janitor of the school ends up being a sticky mess for fifth grader Jack Rankin. He has a problem with his new school's janitor: he's Jack's dad! When some boys tease Jack about being the janitor's son, Jack retaliates by making an intricately designed spiderweb out of smelly bubble gum on a desk in music class. His plan has one drawback—he doesn't realize he can and will get caught. Jack's punishment is to help his dad and the other janitors for three weeks. Working with the janitors provides Jack access to the school's keys, which begins an adventure in school towers and tunnels. A fifth-grade student who read the book liked the fact that Jack didn't overreact to the boys who were making fun of his dad. He said it was funny when Jack went up into the bell tower and scared pigeons away, startling himself as well. The message lies in Jack's learning a new respect for his dad. Students can respond with familiar episodes of embarrassment at and pride in their parents. (JAC)

**6.30**  Gorman, Carol. **Dork in Disguise.** HarperTrophy, 2000. ISBN 0-06-024866-1. 164 pp. (I).

No more being Mr. Studious for new sixth grader Jerry Flack at Hawthorne Middle School. This year Jerry wants to be Mr. Cool to impress the popular gang, including Cinnamon O'Brien. But Jerry soon discovers that he feels better when he acts like himself by being smart and a member of the Science Club. He also has more fun with smart, witty Brenda McAdams, with whom he has a great deal in common. A sixth-grade reader said she liked the part of the book when Jerry and other students were at the fair and he left the group of cool kids to join his real friends. This reader liked Brenda the best because Brenda is truly a friend who admires Jerry because of who he is, not because he is cool. Between its humorous episodes, this book contains an important message worthy of response. (JAC)

Lewis, Maggie. **Morgy Makes His Move.** Illustrated by Michael Chesworth. Houghton Mifflin, 1999. ISBN 0-395-92284-4. 74 pp. (P). (See **19.5.**)

**6.31**  McDonald, Megan. **Judy Moody.** Illustrated by Peter Reynolds. Candlewick, 2000. ISBN 0-7636-0685-5. 160 pp. (ALL).

Judy Moody represents the typical third grader who experiences the gamut in moods. When her teacher, Mr. Todd (Mr. Toad to Judy), assigns the class "The Me Collage," Judy actually discovers a lot about herself and others. She realizes that Frank Pearl is much more interesting than she first thought and that she has a lot in common with him. She discovers the kinds of things she finds funny and what she is interested in, and learns that sometimes she can turn a bad mood event into a good one. Readers will appreciate the humor of Judy's brother Stink and the qualifications for joining the T.P. Club. This book provides an effective springboard for helping students evaluate themselves as individuals. An eight-year-old girl proclaimed, "Judy Moody is the bomb!" Judy's range of moods continues in *Judy Moody Gets Famous!* (Candlewick, 2001). (PKE)

6.32 ★ McKissack, Patricia C. **The Honest-to-Goodness Truth.** Illustrated by Giselle Potter. Atheneum, 2000. ISBN 0-689-82668-0. Unpaged. (P).

After being caught in a lie about finishing her chores, Libby vows to tell only the truth. But her good intentions go awry when she arrives at school. She tattles on friends who have not completed their homework, embarrasses those who forgot their lunch money, and loudly reports a hole in Ruthie May's sock. When Libby cannot understand why her friends shun her, Mama tells her that truth shared at the wrong time and in the wrong way can be hurtful. "But the honest-to-goodness truth is never wrong." With growing understanding, Libby apologizes to the victims of her truth telling and learns that diplomacy stands at the core of friendship. Giselle Potter's witty and whimsical illustrations capture both Libby's righteous attitude and the dismay of her teacher and friends. Children readily respond to this read-aloud with personal tales of consequences of their own lies and reasons why they are now committed to telling the "honest-to-goodness truth." (MRH)

6.33 Mills, Claudia. **Lizzie at Last.** Farrar, Straus & Giroux, 2000. ISBN 0-374-34659-3. 152 pp. (I).

It's a new beginning for Lizzie Archer this school year. Lizzie is going into seventh grade and wants to shed her old-fashioned image of white antique dresses and poetry writing. She now wears modern, colorful t-shirts and blue jeans to look like everyone else. "Straight-A" Lizzie even gets answers wrong in math so that Ethan doesn't think she's too smart. Gradually, she discovers the old Lizzie was much more interesting than the new Lizzie and decides to bring her back—vintage clothes, poetry writing, and all. A sixth-grade student said the book had a powerful message for her—students don't have to change to fit in at school. (JAC)

# 7 Early Experiences with Literature

**Joan I. Glazer**

*Contributing reviewers included Margaret Bierden, E. Sharon Capobianco, Mary Lee Griffin, Madeline F. Nixon, and Laurie Parkerson.*

---

**Criteria for Excellence**

- Literary and artistic quality
- Appealing format that entices young readers
- Patterns or repetitions that help young readers function independently
- Text that is challenging but not overwhelming for beginning readers

---

## Emergent Literacy

Conrad, Donna. **See You Soon, Moon.** Illustrated by Don Carter. Knopf, 2001.

★ Marzollo, Jean. **I Love You: A Rebus Poem.** Illustrated by Suse MacDonald. Scholastic, 2000.

Robinson, Fay. **Fantastic Frogs!** Illustrated by Jean Cassels. Scholastic, 1999.

## Rhythms, Rhymes, and Repetition

★ Hoberman, Mary Ann. **"It's Simple," Said Simon.** Illustrated by Meilo So. Knopf, 2001.

Hooper, Patricia. **Where Do You Sleep, Little One?** Illustrated by John Winch. Holiday House, 2001.

Hort, Lenny. **The Seals on the Bus.** Illustrated by G. Brian Karas. Holt, 2000.

Loomis, Christine. **Astro Bunnies.** Illustrated by Ora Eitan. Putnam, 1999.

Opie, Iona, editor. **Here Comes Mother Goose.** Illustrated by Rosemary Wells. Candlewick, 1999.

Roop, Connie, and Peter Roop. **Octopus under the Sea.** Illustrated by Carol Schwartz. Scholastic, 2001.

Sierra, Judy. **Preschool to the Rescue.** Illustrated by Will Hillenbrand. Harcourt, 2001.

★ Sloat, Teri. **Farmer Brown Shears His Sheep: A Yarn about Wool.** Illustrated by Nadine Bernard Westcott. DK Ink, 2000.

Stojic, Manya. **Rain.** Crown, 2000.

Taback, Simms. **Joseph Had a Little Overcoat.** Viking, 1999.

## Concept Books

Bang, Molly. **When Sophie Gets Angry—Really, Really Angry . . . .** Scholastic, 1999.

Bauer, Marion Dane. **If You Had a Nose Like an Elephant's Trunk.** Illustrated by Susan Winter. Holiday House, 2001.

Florian, Douglas. **A Pig Is Big.** Greenwillow, 2000.

Lobel, Anita. **One Lighthouse, One Moon.** Greenwillow, 2000.

★ Schaefer, Lola M. **This Is the Rain.** Illustrated by Jane Wattenberg. Greenwillow, 2001.

Sis, Peter. **Madlenka.** Farrar, Straus & Giroux, 2000.

Wong, Janet S. **Buzz.** Illustrated by Margaret Chodos-Irvine. Harcourt, 2000.

## Alphabet Books

Arnosky, Jim. **Mouse Letters: A Very First Alphabet Book.** Clarion, 1999.

Cline-Ransome, Lesa. **Quilt Alphabet.** Illustrated by James E. Ransome. Holiday House, 2001.

Demarest, Chris L. **Firefighters A to Z.** Margaret K. McElderry Books, 2000.

Hobbie, Holly. **Toot & Puddle: Puddle's ABC.** Little, Brown, 2000.

Lester, Mike. **A Is for Salad.** Putnam & Grosset, 2000.

Rose, Deborah Lee. **Into the A, B, Sea: An Ocean Alphabet.** Illustrated by Steve Jenkins. Scholastic, 2000.

★ Sloat, Teri. **Patty's Pumpkin Patch.** Putnam, 1999.

## Early Chapter and Series Books

Ada, Alma Flor. **Daniel's Mystery Egg.** Illustrated by G. Brian Karas. Harcourt, 2000.

Avi. **Abigail Takes the Wheel.** Illustrated by Don Bolognese. HarperCollins, 1999.

★ Banks, Kate. **Howie Bowles and Uncle Sam.** Illustrated by Isaac Millman. Farrar, Straus & Giroux, 2000.

Bos, Burny. **Fun with the Molesons.** Translated by J. Alison James. Illustrated by Hans de Beer. North-South, 2000.

Cazet, Denys. **Minnie and Moo and the Thanksgiving Tree.** DK Ink, 2000.

Gantos, Jack. **Rotten Ralph Helps Out.** Illustrated by Nicole Rubel. Farrar, Straus & Giroux, 2001.

Greene, Stephanie. **Owen Foote, Frontiersman.** Illustrated by Martha Weston. Clarion, 1999.

★ Horowitz, Ruth. **Breakout at the Bug Lab.** Illustrated by Joan Holub. Dial, 2001.

Howe, James. **Pinky and Rex and the Just-Right Pet.** Illustrated by Melissa Sweet. Atheneum, 2001.

Rylant, Cynthia. **The Cobble Street Cousins: Some Good News.** Illustrated by Wendy Anderson Halperin. Simon & Schuster, 1999.

Sachar, Louis. **A Magic Crystal.** Illustrated by Amy Wummer. Random House, 2000.

Thomas, Shelley Moore. **Good Night, Good Knight.** Illustrated by Jennifer Plecas. Dutton, 2000.

———————

The books in this chapter have qualities that encourage young children to want to read and take their first steps toward reading independently. The stories are filled with suspense, fun, and memorable characters. When children feel the excitement that stories generate, they see reading as an activity that brings pleasure and thus are eager to learn.

The language in these books often rhymes or contains patterns in refrains or phrases. For the emergent reader, these qualities provide a clue to what a word may be, and a combination of memory and logic allows the child to successfully unlock the words. Because the language often has a lilting quality, it is pleasurable to hear and read. Children may reread a story often, each time becoming more fluent and gaining deeper understandings.

Concept books and alphabet books, a form of concept book, allow young readers to explore a single concept through many examples. Some of the alphabet books are straightforward, showing a match between letter and sound through the examples given. Others play with language, creating a puzzle to be solved, or use the alphabet as an organizing structure to explore another concept fully. These books call attention to how language and letters function as they tell their story.

Early chapter books present an opportunity for readers to move toward lengthier and more complex stories. Many of these books are part of a series, so young readers come to know the Molesons, Owen Foote, and Cynthia Rylant's Cobblestone Cousins and will want to read about the further adventures of these characters. Becoming familiar with the characters, setting, and general plot structure of one book in a series helps young readers be successful with other books in the series.

In organizing this chapter, we used the following categories:

- *Emergent literacy.* Books listed in this section have elements that make then accessible to young children in the earliest stages of learning to read. They may be wordless, allowing the illustrations alone to convey the story; rebus, in which pictures are used within the text; or books with simple repetitive text that children can mimic easily.

- *Rhythm, rhymes, and repetition.* These books have patterns, either in language with rhymes or refrains or in story structure, that help readers both predict and remember the text.

- *Concept books.* Books in this section explore many aspects of a single concept. The text is clear and focused, though the concepts vary in complexity.

- *Alphabet books.* Such books obviously use the alphabet as the central organizing structure, but some support early reading because they match words and illustrations, whereas others provide support through thematic selection of content.

- *Early chapter and series books.* Books listed here challenge young readers as they transition from books with many illustrations and little text to those that have more text than illustrations. The short chapters provide an introduction to the structure of more sophisticated books.

## Emergent Literacy

7.1    Conrad, Donna. **See You Soon, Moon.** Illustrated by Don Carter. Knopf, 2001. ISBN 0-375-80656-3. Unpaged. (P).

This simple text telling of a child and his parents driving at night to visit Grandma repeats words and phrases in ways that allow beginning readers to recognize them easily. Certainly, they will recognize *moon* by the middle of the book. The child says goodbye to the objects in his bedroom, where he sees the moon through the window, and then he watches it as he sits with his blanket in the backseat of the car. Children may relate their own experiences of watching the moon from a moving automobile, noting how it remains visible and seems to follow them. The illustrations, created with foam board, plaster, and acrylic paint, are clear and attractive and could be used in a game in which the child finds the word in the text to match an object in the illustration. (JIG)

7.2    ★ Marzollo, Jean. **I Love You: A Rebus Poem.** Illustrated by Suse MacDonald. Scholastic, 2000. ISBN 0-590-37656-X. Unpaged. (P).

"Every bird loves a tree / Every flower loves a bee / Every lock loves a key / And I love you." Thus begins this simple but delightful rebus poem. Each loving relationship is given a two-page spread, with text on the left-hand page and a full-page color illustration by Caldecott honor book illustrator Suse Mac-Donald on the right. There are sixteen lines of text in all, with "And I love you" repeated at the end of each four-line stanza. The reader will find each rebus easy to guess, as the pictures are clear and each line rhymes. Beginning readers will be surprised by the ease with which they find themselves reading this book. For more advanced readers, the complete poem without rebus pictures is printed on the last page of the book. This is a fun read and great for stimulating children to write their own rebus stories. (ESC)

7.3     Robinson, Fay. **Fantastic Frogs!** Illustrated by Jean Cassels. Scholastic, 1999. ISBN 0-590-52269-8. 32 pp. (P).

*Fantastic Frogs!* is a fabulous introduction to the growth, food, habitats, colors, and shapes of different kinds of frogs. Early readers can satisfy their curiosity about the lives of frogs with this Hello Reader! science book. Brightly colored illustrations accurately depict a variety of frogs in their habitats. A chart at the back of the book gives the names of the different frogs and the pages on which they appear. This is a great resource for getting a young child hooked on reading nonfiction. (MB)

## Rhythms, Rhymes, and Repetition

Fox, Mem. **Harriet, You'll Drive Me Wild!** Illustrated by Marla Frazee. Harcourt, 2000. ISBN 0-15-201977-4. Unpaged. (P). (See **19.11.**)

Harrison, David L. **Farmer's Garden: Rhymes for Two Voices.** Illustrated by Arden Johnson-Petrov. Boyds Mills, 2000. ISBN 1-56397-776-1. Unpaged. (P). (See **10.17.**)

7.4     ★ Hoberman, Mary Ann. **"It's Simple," Said Simon.** Illustrated by Meilo So. Knopf, 2001. ISBN 0-375-81201-6. Unpaged. (P).

Friendly animals dare Simon to growl like a dog, stretch like a cat, and jump like a horse. All of this is "'simple,' said Simon." He meets his match when a tiger comes on the scene and challenges him to the same activities. After accepting the challenge to jump on the tiger's back, Simon realizes he is in trouble. Unlike the Gingerbread Boy, however, Simon escapes from the tiger by swimming away. When this story is read to second graders, they wanted to know the fate of the tiger. We don't know, but speculating is an interesting exercise. The ink-and-watercolor illustrations add to the simplicity of the story. (MB)

**7.5**   Hooper, Patricia. **Where Do You Sleep, Little One?** Illustrated by John Winch. Holiday House, 2001. ISBN 0-8234-1668-2. Unpaged. (P).

Earth tones depict the charming quiet of a forest filled with creatures large and small. That night the field mouse, the owl, the wren, the spider, the rabbit, the chipmunk, and the fawn come together at the edge of the forest as they approach a lighted stable outside the town walls. The stable is awake with domestic animals and a light from a manger. This bedtime poem is illustrated with oils on handmade paper. The animals are represented by cutouts arranged in layers and photographed against embossed backgrounds. The poem, in couplets, asks the question of where the animals make their beds. The answers will comfort children as they nestle to sleep in their own beds. While this is a year-round bedtime share, the subtle message of the Nativity holds a special meaning for some families. (MFN)

**7.6**   Hort, Lenny. **The Seals on the Bus.** Illustrated by G. Brian Karas. Holt, 2000. ISBN 0-8050-5952-0. Unpaged. (P).

In this rollicking version of the classic children's song "The Wheels on the Bus," boisterous animals share a ride with a human family on the city bus. First, the seals hop on, going "errp, errp, errp." Noisy geese, monkeys, sheep, and rabbits, among others, join the seals in going "up and down." The tiger bus driver tries unsuccessfully to quiet everyone by going "roar, roar, roar." When skunks board the bus going "ssss, ssss, ssss," the people on the bus cry "help, help, help," and everyone disembarks at the carnival. The lively, highly expressive mixed-media illustrations perfectly capture the sense of mounting chaos. Watching the expressions on the human's faces is almost as much fun as guessing what type of creature will board the bus next. Primary children will know the original song and thus be able to enjoy this adaptation as well as recognize the predictable pattern. (LP)

Lass, Bonnie, and Philemon Sturges. **Who Took the Cookies from the Cookie Jar?** Illustrated by Ashley Wolff. Little, Brown, 2000. ISBN 0-316-82016-4. Unpaged. (P). (See **13.21.**)

**7.7**     Loomis, Christine. **Astro Bunnies.** Illustrated by Ora Eitan. Putnam, 1999. ISBN 0-399-23175-7. Unpaged. (P).

Astro bunnies decide to go exploring in outer space, taking readers along on a trip far beyond the stars where all kinds of adventures await. The bunnies don space suits with pockets, float through the air, gather moondust, chart stars, and even meet three-eared bunnies from another planet. Loomis packs well-chosen action verbs into economically rhymed phrases in order to engage even the youngest listener. Eitan's soothing gouache artwork greatly enriches the story by adding imaginative details to the sparse text. Even though they are only minimally sketched, the bunnies' faces and poses are expressive. Story and illustrations combine to produce a gentle, rather ethereal, dreamlike effect. The adventure ends with the completely satisfying and reassuring "bunnies ALWAYS come back home." (LP)

**7.8**     Opie, Iona, editor. **Here Comes Mother Goose.** Illustrated by Rosemary Wells. Candlewick, 1999. ISBN 0-7636-0683-9. Unpaged. (P).

This large edition of Mother Goose rhymes is perfect for sharing with groups of children. Wells's illustrations add humor and extended action to the rhymes. For example, the full complement of the man with seven wives, each with seven sacks, each sack with seven cats, and each cat with seven kits, as seen by the man going to St. Ives, is shown in three double-page spreads. Many familiar rhymes are included but so too are lesser-known ones. Do check "What are little girls made of," as the answer is the reverse of the usual rhyme. This book bears repeated oral reading. Children can be encouraged to look closely at the illustrations and describe what they notice. (JIG)

**7.9**     Roop, Connie, and Peter Roop. **Octopus under the Sea.** Illustrated by Carol Schwartz. Scholastic, 2001. ISBN 0-439-20635-9. Unpaged. (P).

In rollicking prose, the narrative follows an octopus as it creeps, crawls, and finds a "meal [of a] crab, a shrimp, a tiny eel." Like the gentle roll of the ocean, the predictable rhyming text, complemented by Schwartz's colorful, detailed illustrations, supports young readers' meaning making. This is the kind of book emergent readers will want to revisit for the language, information about the octopus—"an octopus can be the size of a snail"—and drama of the narrative: as "quick as you can blink, an octopus shoots out dark, black ink," escaping a host of predators. (MLG)

7.10   Sierra, Judy. **Preschool to the Rescue.** Illustrated by Will Hillenbrand. Harcourt, 2001. ISBN 0-15-202035-7. Unpaged. (P).

There's a sleepy, creepy, deeper-than-you'd-think mud puddle on the preschool playground that is swallowing up all types of vehicles that pass by. In they go, with a slurp, glurp, blurp, flurp, and a plurp. When the rain stops and the preschoolers go out to play, they rescue what the reader discovers are toy vehicles from the gluey, gooey, muckity, mighty, icky, naughty mud. The wonderful use of repetitive rhyming language makes this book easy to read independently and enjoyable as a read-aloud. The bright, colorful illustrations are done in a mixed media, and the sleepy, creepy mud is a sight to behold, with yellow eyes and a bulbous nose looking over the deeper-than-you'd think puddle. This book will easily become a class favorite. (ESC)

7.11   ★ Sloat, Teri. **Farmer Brown Shears His Sheep: A Yarn about Wool.** Illustrated by Nadine Bernard Westcott. DK Ink, 2000. ISBN 0-7894-2637-4. Unpaged. (P).

It's spring, and a note on the calendar reminds Farmer Brown it's time to shear his sheep. A quick clipping gives him bags of wool but leaves his sheep cold and shivering. Covered only by goose bumps, they follow Farmer Brown as he takes the wool for processing, pleading at each stop, "We want it back." Finally, as the sheep roll the now-dyed yarn around themselves, Farmer Brown recognizes how cold they are and knits each one a cardigan. Now each year the sheep are eager "to feel the clip and hear the buzz, and wear bright sweaters over fuzz." The rhymes are catchy and onomatopoetic, while humor pervades both text and illustrations. Children can easily chime in on the refrain, and the story lends itself to dramatization. (JIG)

7.12   Stojic, Manya. **Rain.** Crown, 2000. ISBN 0-517-80086-1. Unpaged. (P).

This beautifully written description of rain on the African savanna opens when the red soil is hot, dry, and cracked. Each animal senses the coming rain; the porcupine smells it, the baboons hear it, and the rhino feels it as drops splash. After the storm has passed, the grasses grow greener and the trees sprout fresh leaves. Later still, the soil once again dries out and begins to crack under a harsh sun. Each sense is highlighted, first as the rain comes and then as it leaves its reminders—a water hole filled or shade provided by sprouting leaves. The book is a stimulating experience for the senses, with descriptive language, expressive illustrations, and changes in print size that lend emphasis to the action. (JIG)

**7.13** Taback, Simms. **Joseph Had a Little Overcoat.** Viking, 1999. ISBN 0-670-87855-3. Unpaged. (P).

Taback was awarded the 2000 Caldecott Medal for this colorful rendition of the Yiddish folk song "I Had a Little Overcoat." Not believing in waste, Joseph cannot bring himself to throw out his overcoat, even though it has become "old and worn." Cleverly placed die-cut holes show the reader what Joseph will make next as he cuts into the remaining good cloth, creating a jacket, a vest, a scarf, a handkerchief, and a tie. Finally, the material becomes so worn that there's only enough left to make a button. When Joseph loses that button, his indefatigable spirit has him "make a book about it." Which shows "you can always make something out of nothing." The strong visual appeal, along with the repetitive language, makes this a favorite for readers of many age groups. (ESC)

## Concept Books

**7.14** Bang, Molly. **When Sophie Gets Angry—Really, Really Angry . . . .** Scholastic, 1999. ISBN 0-590-18979-4. Unpaged. (P).

Sophie is having a bad day. Her sister grabs a toy away from her, angering Sophie and making her fall over a toy truck. To add insult to injury, her mother says she must share the toy with her sister. Sophie "roars a red, red roar" and then becomes a volcano "ready to explode." Rather than exploding, she "runs and runs . . . and cries," before climbing a tree and letting the calmness of nature comfort her. Feeling better, Sophie returns home, where everyone is glad to see her. This is a good conversation starter for ways to deal with anger. Bang's full-page illustrations and use of color to show emotion are bold and dramatic. This is a Caldecott honor book and recipient of the Charlotte Zolotow Award. (ESC)

Banks, Kate. **A Gift from the Sea.** Illustrated by Georg Hallensleben. Farrar, Straus & Giroux, 2001. ISBN 0-374-32566-9. Unpaged. (P). (See **8.11**.)

**7.15**   Bauer, Marion Dane. **If You Had a Nose Like an Elephant's Trunk.** Illustrated by Susan Winter. Holiday House, 2001. ISBN 0-8234-1589-9. Unpaged. (P).

Realistic paintings in multihued watercolors take the reader through a fanciful day in a young girl's imagination. Real and imagined meetings with animals make the child wonder what it would be like to have animal attributes such as feet like a fly or a tail like a lizard. Resolving the wonderings with love of self and family and her own human characteristics and abilities allows the child to "sleep snugly" in her own "sweet bed." Both adults and children will enjoy this book as they imagine the possibilities of what life would be like if they could have the wings of a swift or the cheeks of a chipmunk. Creativity and higher-level thinking will be stimulated as the imagination soars during and after the reading of this book. (MFN)

**7.16**   Florian, Douglas. **A Pig Is Big.** Greenwillow, 2000. ISBN 0-688-17125-7. Unpaged. (P).

What is big? This is the idea Douglas Florian examines in this brightly illustrated book. The pig is big—too big to fit on the book cover. But a cow is bigger, as the cleverly rhyming text explains. When readers turn the page, they can see that a car is even bigger than a cow; in fact, the car neatly holds both animals. The text progresses through things of ever increasing size, until it finally arrives at the universe, "the biggest thing of all. Compared to it, all things seem small." Through humorous rhymes and lively, colorful illustrations, Florian provides an enjoyable means of exploring the concept of relative size. Although both text and paintings are sophisticated, their warmth and humor render them inviting to young readers. (LP)

★ Freymann, Saxton, and Joost Elffers. **How Are You Peeling? Foods with Moods.** Scholastic, 1999. ISBN 0-439-10431-9. Unpaged. (P). (See **8.27.**)

**7.17**   Lobel, Anita. **One Lighthouse, One Moon.** Greenwillow, 2000. ISBN 0-688-15539-1. 40 pp. (P).

The book cover suggests that readers think of this concept book as "three acts in one play." The first act, "All Week Long," is days of the week, each day depicting different shoes in a different color. The second act, "Nini's Year," is the months of the year. The cat who was watching the shoes in the first act is the star of the second act, catching snowflakes in January, chasing kites in May, smelling the turkey in November, and waiting for "good things" (the birth of kittens) in December. The third act, "One Lighthouse, One Moon," has the cat as observer once again, this time on the seashore, seeing first one lighthouse and then other objects or animals in amounts from two to ten. The book presents the concepts clearly and is probably best shared one act at a time. (JIG)

7.18    ★ Schaefer, Lola M. **This Is the Rain.** Illustrated by Jane Wattenberg. Greenwillow, 2001. ISBN 0-688-17039-0. Unpaged. (P).

The author explains the water cycle in a vividly descriptive yet simply phrased cumulative poem. Beginning with the ocean, "blue and wet," the water cycle progresses through the processes of evaporation, condensation, and precipitation, and then flows from the land back into the blue, wet ocean where the cycle begins again. Through judicious word choice, Schaefer also manages to convey a sense of geologic time, an important concept often omitted from primary texts on the water cycle. The rhyming verse is stunningly illustrated with computer-generated collages that demand as much attention as the text, as their bright colors and humorous surprises breathe life into the poem's words. The combination of poem and illustrations makes a wonderfully effective way to introduce the water cycle to primary students. (LP)

7.19    Sis, Peter. **Madlenka.** Farrar, Straus & Giroux, 2000. ISBN 0-374-39969-7. Unpaged. (P).

On an unnamed block in the biggest little city in the world, Madlenka enjoys an adventure by announcing her good news to her shopkeeper friends: "Hey, everyone . . . my tooth is loose!" On this one block in New York City, Madlenka—or Madeleine in France, Madela in India, Maddalena in Italy, Magda in Germany, Magdalena in Spain, or Mandala in Asia —spreads the good news around her multicultural neighborhood. Viewed from many perspectives, the thin black-and-white lines of the block are contrasted with colorful images of different ethnicities. Sis portrays a variety of cultures using cutouts and miniature drawings of the neighborhood shopkeepers' goods, treasures, and traditions. After reading the story, children will enjoy exploring the borders and hidden pictures that capture the essence of each culture that makes Madlenka's block a miniature world.  (MFN)

**7.20** Wong, Janet S. **Buzz.** Illustrated by Margaret Chodos-Irvine. Harcourt, 2000. ISBN 0-15-201923-5. Unpaged. (P).

A small boy watches a bee eating breakfast outside his window as his parents go through the routine of getting ready for work. The boy discovers the recurring sound of "BUZZZbuzzzBUZZZbuzz" from his parents' snores, an alarm clock, Daddy's razor, a lawn mower, a coffee grinder, a blender, and his toy airplane. The boy buzzes the garage door so his daddy can be off to work. A doorbell buzz welcomes Grandma, who has come to stay with him while Mommy "can fly BUZZ outside like a busy bee." Margaret Chodos-Irvine, in her first picture book, combines appealing block shapes of cut-paper collage with the delicacy of woodcuts. She shows a boy comfortable in his world, especially in the stance of his small body, with a large shadow filling the door of his parents' bedroom as he shouts, "Wake up!" (MB)

## Alphabet Books

**7.21** Arnosky, Jim. **Mouse Letters: A Very First Alphabet Book.** Clarion, 1999. ISBN 0-395-55386-5. Unpaged. (P).

Using brush and ink with an acrylic wash, Jim Aronsky depicts a mouse constructing the alphabet. Who can resist a character with so much imagination? The mouse displays emotions such as surprise, inquisitiveness, satisfaction, puzzlement, discovery, trickiness, sadness, anger, fear, determination, tiredness, and finally contentment. This book may well encourage readers to construct their own alphabets out of three-dimensional finds from nature after seeing how the mouse created letters from twigs and tall grass. This very first alphabet book will certainly fit into any library, classroom, home, or pocket. (MFN)

**7.22** Cline-Ransome, Lesa. **Quilt Alphabet.** Illustrated by James E. Ransome. Holiday House, 2001. ISBN 0-8234-1453-1. Unpaged. (P).

This lovely alphabet book features each letter of the alphabet individually boxed in a quilt square, a four-line rhyming riddle, and a one- or two-page spread illustrating the corresponding answer. The letter *O*, for example, is accompanied by the following riddle:

Sweeping the sky, searching the ground
Wings outstretched, eyes shiny and round
A nightbird draped on an evening flight
Hunting for prey by the glow of moonlight.

Figured it out? If not, the gorgeous acrylic painting of an owl flying straight off the page will surely give it away. The language used in the poems can be a bit sophisticated for a beginning reader, but the lyrical flow of the riddles makes for a challenging guessing game and provides adequate context to support comprehension. The illustrations of the country-inspired topics heighten the delight of solving the puzzles. (LP)

7.23   Demarest, Chris L. **Firefighters A to Z.** Margaret K. McElderry Books, 2000. ISBN 0-689-83798-4. Unpaged. (P).

They are familiar figures in the primary social studies unit on community helpers. Now taking on a completely new dimension as American heroes are the firefighters who answer the call to put out fires and save lives: "A is for Alarm that rings loud and clear." The strong pastel illustrations complement the bold text of this informative book by Chris L. Demarest, himself a volunteer firefighter in Meriden, New Hampshire. Verses such as "C is for Chief, whose experience we trust" set the tone for a book that shows respect for these professionals and the work they do. This is an alphabet book on a serious topic to be studied by our youngest citizens not only during National Fire Prevention Month (October), but also all year long. (MFN)

7.24   Hobbie, Holly. **Toot & Puddle: Puddle's ABC.** Little, Brown, 2000. ISBN 0-316-36593-9. Unpaged. (P).

One day Puddle the pig decides to teach his friend Otto the turtle how to write his name. When Puddle realizes that his friend does not know the alphabet, he decides to teach him the letters first. Using watercolors, he paints a picture for each letter, beginning with "Ant alone with apple" and ending with "Zooming zucchini." Each letter has a full-page illustration accompanied by a cleverly worded descriptive phrase. In the end, Otto learns to write not only his own name but also the names of his friends Toot and Puddle. For children who are learning the alphabet and the sounds commonly associated with the letters, this is a great teaching tool. For children who already know the alphabet, the clever captions make it a fun read. (ESC)

7.25   Lester, Mike. **A Is for Salad.** Putnam & Grosset, 2000. ISBN 0-399-23388-1. Unpaged. (P).

An interesting take on alphabet books, Lester's *A Is for Salad* has the reader figure out what each letter actually represents. All is presented in a hilarious way, such as *T* standing for a tiger wearing polka-dotted underpants and *A* for an alligator eating a salad. The animals are drawn with a variety of comically exaggerated expressions certain to invite chuckles. When this book was shared with second graders, some serious-minded students were concerned that the mixed-up concept would confuse children learning the alphabet. But after seeing the endpapers, which show the appropriate words for the letters, they relaxed and enjoyed the book. A note of caution: when given the assignment to come up with their own illustrations, some children found it difficult to grasp the concept. One of the most delightful creations, however, was a pink and blue elephant throwing peanuts in her or his mouth to illustrate that *E* is for peanuts. (MB)

7.26    Rose, Deborah Lee. **Into the A, B, Sea: An Ocean Alphabet.** Illustrated by Steve Jenkins. Scholastic, 2000. ISBN 0-439-09696-0. Unpaged. (P).

Deborah Lee Rose invites readers to join her for a swim in an absolutely splendid sea. There's a sea creature for every letter of the alphabet (she fudges a bit on *X*). Each creature and its activities are described in only a few words, and the choice of verbs make this book shimmer. Insects "prance" and Jellies "dance." Selections are sometimes rhyming, other times alliterative, and always accurate and delightful. Steve Jenkins has illuminated the book with his trademark paper collage illustrations, capturing the texture of the animals and creating a sense of underwater translucence. The illustrations are bright and bold but not so bright as to lose the effect of an undersea world. The author includes a one- or two-sentence note about each sea creature at the end of the book. (LP)

7.27    ★ Sloat, Teri. **Patty's Pumpkin Patch.** Putnam, 1999. ISBN 0-399-23010-6. Unpaged. (P).

Readers are invited to tour Patty's busy pumpkin patch from early spring though a post–Halloween harvest and from A to Z in this lovely multilayered book. First, the rhyming text describes the process of planting, growing, and harvesting pumpkins to be sold just in time for Halloween fun. Second, a bright border along the bottom of each page contains a thematic illustration for each letter of the alphabet. (Unfortunately, there is no glossary to explain the terms.) Third, the vividly colored, sharply detailed acrylic paintings on each page repeat the illustration from the border, challenging readers to seek and find. All of this adds up to a lively, informative, and enjoyable outing. (LP)

## Early Chapter and Series Books

7.28    Ada, Alma Flor. **Daniel's Mystery Egg.** Illustrated by G. Brian Karas. Harcourt, 2000. ISBN 0-15-216237-2. Unpaged. (P).

This early reader recounts Daniel's discovery of a small white egg that he claims is the "best egg ever!" Convinced that his egg holds a small quiet creature, Daniel listens patiently to the wild speculations of his friends—"maybe it's an ostrich with a long neck . . . or an alligator with big teeth." Brian Karas's drawings over collage complement the tale, their tone and color changing as the story moves from the world of Daniel and his friends to the speculative world of their imaginations. It will come as no surprise to readers that one day out of the egg a small, nice, quiet lizard is hatched, "the best lizard ever!" (MLG)

7.29    Avi. **Abigail Takes the Wheel.** Illustrated by Don Bolognese. HarperCollins, 1999. ISBN 0-06-444281-0. 54 pp. (P).

According to the author's note, *Abigail Takes the Wheel* is based on a story that first appeared in an 1881 children's magazine, a story that he believes is true. The tale of brave Abigail skillfully navigating the busy waters of New York Harbor certainly rings true. Abigail and her brother Tom ride to school each day on their father's freight boat, the *Neptune.* One morning, two ships collide in the treacherous narrows, and Abigail's father must board one of the disabled ships, leaving Abigail and Tom to steer the *Neptune* through the harbor to dock at Pier Forty-two. Avi spins his exciting tale in six short chapters that keep readers turning pages, peering over Abigail's shoulder as she brings the boat to safety. An author's note and map of New York Harbor lend contextual authenticity to this well-written "I CAN READ" book. (MLG)

7.30    ★ Banks, Kate. **Howie Bowles and Uncle Sam.** Illustrated by Isaac Millman. Farrar, Straus & Giroux, 2000. ISBN 0-374-351116-3. 85 pp. (P).

Howie Bowles, born on Friday the thirteenth, is convinced that all his luck is bad. He has trouble with math, his siblings get all his parents' attention, and then the worst happens. A letter from the Internal Revenue Service tells him he owes Uncle Sam, "whoever that is," $112.15. Howie has only $15.17 and must raise the rest in a week. When he is warned of imprisonment, Howie dons a suit and tie and tries to get a loan from the bank. As all attempts to earn money fail, Howie says his farewells at home and at school. He is saved when his mother discovers the letter and straightens out the problem. Short chapters and likeable characters make this a great follow-up to *Howie Bowles, Secret Agent* (Farrar, Straus & Giroux, 1999; **6.28**). Math jokes and the focus on the importance of minding your numbers make this a great book to combine with math studies. (MB)

**7.31**   Bos, Burny. **Fun with the Molesons.** Translated by J. Alison James. Illustrated by Hans de Beer. North-South, 2000. ISBN 0-7358-1353-1. 44 pp. (P).

Dug Moleson narrates vignettes about his mole family's everyday activities that turn into fun-filled adventures. This addition to the series about Dug, his twin sister, his stay-at-home father, his mother who works in an office, and his grandmother who is in an electric wheelchair will be welcomed by readers of the earlier works. Three of the chapters show Father as a bit of a bungler, with Mother coming to his rescue. Grandmother shows strength and humor when a movie theater will sell her and the children tickets but cannot accommodate her wheelchair. Each of the stories presents an interesting dilemma that could be used for problem-solving activities with children. (MB)

**7.32**   Cazet, Denys. **Minnie and Moo and the Thanksgiving Tree.** DK Ink, 2000. ISBN 0-7894-2654-4. 48 pp. (P).

Minnie and Moo, the cream-puff-eating cows, are back in a Thanksgiving escapade. The turkeys are anxious about being Thanksgiving dinner even though the farmers are vegetarians. After Minnie and Moo hide the turkeys in the oak tree, the chickens demand the same protection, as do the ducks, the geese, the pigs, the sheep, and even an ostrich. This ludicrous situation, as well as the large print, four or five sentences per page, and the four-page "chapters," will appeal to the newly independent reader. *The Center for Children's Books Bulletin* called this series "the cream of the beginning-reader crop." (MB)

dePaola, Tomie. **26 Fairmount Avenue.** Putnam, 1999. ISBN 0-399-23246-X. 56 pp. (P). (See **4.25**.)

**7.33**    Gantos, Jack. **Rotten Ralph Helps Out.** Illustrated by Nicole Rubel. Farrar, Straus & Giroux, 2001. ISBN 0-374-36355-2. 47 pp. (P).

Gantos's irrepressible red cat of picture book fame has successfully invaded the beginning chapter book territory with the new Rotten Ralph Rotten Reader series. Sarah is faced with the challenge of producing a school project on ancient Egypt, and Ralph has offered to help. But, as Ralph's fans well know and as his new readers will soon learn, Ralph is a feline recipe for disaster. While Sarah learns interesting facts about ancient Egypt, well-intentioned Ralph spreads his own personal brand of mayhem. He builds a pyramid out of library books, scribbles hieroglyphics on the library walls, and similarly wrecks Sarah's various attempts to put together her project. Finally, a successful project is ready and Ralph's help is both welcomed and appreciated. The short chapters are written with manageable amounts of text, and the illustrations enhance the sense of chaos that pervades this humorous story. (LP)

**7.34**    Greene, Stephanie. **Owen Foote, Frontiersman.** Illustrated by Martha Weston. Clarion, 1999. ISBN 0-395-61578-X. 88 pp. (P).

This backyard woods adventure story will get those "reluctant to read chapter books" types interested. Greene has added a third adventure to the life of second grader Owen Foote. In this narrative, big boy bullies are held at bay as Owen and his friend Joseph try to enjoy a "Daniel Boone" lifestyle. With Daniel Boone's sayings as his guide, Owen finds confidants in his family and plots with Joseph to outwit intruders. This is a sure winner with young children who are at an independent developmental stage and long to explore the lives of frontiersmen and women while not leaving home. Greene has captured the interests, fears, and delights of the typical second grader. (MFN)

**7.35**    ★ Horowitz, Ruth. **Breakout at the Bug Lab.** Illustrated by Joan Holub. Dial, 2001. ISBN 0-8037-2510-8. 48 pp. (P).

This first-person narrative relates the adventures of a young boy and his brother Leo in their mother's bug lab, where she keeps robber flies, who "carry their food with their feet," and a hissing cockroach named Max. All dressed for the dedication of the lab's new Ruby L. Gold Nature Center, the boys accompany their mother to the lab, where she admonishes them to behave, especially around the guest of honor, Ruby L. Gold, "a lady who loves nature, even bugs." Left alone in the lab, the boys inadvertently allow Max to escape. A wild search ensues until the boys finally discover Max on a ceiling. Told in simple, straightforward prose, this engaging story will provide pleasure and success for young readers looking for their first chapter book. (MLG)

7.36    Howe, James. **Pinky and Rex and the Just-Right Pet.** Illustrated by Melissa Sweet. Atheneum, 2001. ISBN 0-689-82861-6. 40 pp. (P).

In another charming addition to the Pinky and Rex series, Pinky's family is deciding on the "just-right pet." Pinky desperately wants a dog, but his mom says dogs are "too much work," and his younger sister Amanda has her heart set on a cat. Pinky senses an ally in his dad until they pull into the supermarket parking lot and spy a sign saying, "free kittens." Everyone except Pinky falls in love with Patches the kitten, chosen and named by Amanda, and Pinky bids goodbye to his dreams of a puppy. Once home, Amanda declares herself Patches's mother and carries the kitten everywhere. At night, however, Patches hops into Pinky's bed, where she sleeps curled up and purring like a "motor running." Young readers will delight in this gentle tale of Pinky's growing love for the tiny kitten, his doggy dreams all but forgotten as he assumes his new role as Patches's dad. (MLG)

7.37    Rylant, Cynthia. **The Cobble Street Cousins: Some Good News.** Illustrated by Wendy Anderson Halperin. Simon & Schuster, 1999. ISBN 0-689-81713-4. 55 pp. (P).

Cynthia Rylant debuts a new series with this early chapter book about the Cobble Street cousins. While their parents are traveling, three cousins, Lily, Rosie, and Tess, come to stay with young, vibrant Aunt Lucy, who owns a flower shop and is in love with Michael, a botanist. To fill their days and contribute something meaningful to their close-knit community, the three girls set about writing a newsletter that they distribute to neighbors and friends. The newsletter, printed in its four-page, hand-written entirety, is one of the special delights of this well-told tale of village life. The soft, richly detailed sepia illustrations complement the story, drawing the reader into the Cobble Street world. Children will enjoy using this book as a model for their own class newspaper. (MLG)

7.38 Sachar, Louis. **A Magic Crystal.** Illustrated by Amy Wummer. Random House, 2000. ISBN 0-679-89002-5. 81 pp. (P).

This eighth in the Marvin Redpost series is a made-to-order answer for the child who wants another chapter book by Louis Sachar. Sachar, a Newbery Award–winning author, has divided this humorous fiction for the novice independent reader into nine captivating chapters. The fast movement of familiar scenes will engage both boys and girls. Readers may wonder if there really is magic in Marvin's classmate Casey's crystal, since the two friends seem to get everything that each of them wishes for. The problem gets really interesting when Marvin wishes that Casey would "shut up" and she does. Will Casey ever speak again? Marvin's confusion with language will have young readers laughing as they sort out and reread conversations. The references to events told in previous books will entice those new to Marvin's adventures to find other books from the series. (MFN)

7.39 Thomas, Shelley Moore. **Good Night, Good Knight.** Illustrated by Jennifer Plecas. Dutton, 2000. ISBN 0-525-46326-7. 47 pp. (P).

In the rhythmic language of the finest early readers, Shelley Moore Thomas tells of the good and generous knight who time and again leaves his post in the "crumbly, tumbly tower" to respond to the plaintive roars of three baby dragons. In their "deep, dark cave," the dragons wait in their jammies for the knight to bring a glass of water, tell a bedtime story, sing a song, and tuck them into bed. When the knight responds to the "largest, loudest roar of all," he discovers that what the dragons really want is a kiss goodnight. After kissing each dragon's "scaly little cheek," the knight returns to his castle to go to sleep. This charming, predictable text is one young readers will revisit often for the sheer joy of the language, the sweet illustrations of dragons in jammies, and the ever-patient knight attending to their every whim. (MLG)

# 8 Picture Books

**Linda Leonard Lamme and Roseanne Russo**

*Contributing reviewers included Be Astengo, Theda Buckley, Katrina Hall, Ruth Lowery, Diane Masla, Debbie Savage, Nancy Rankie Shelton, and Anna Sperring.*

---

## Criteria for Excellence

- Creative, compelling, artful illustrations that convey the tenor and meaning of the work and engage young readers
- Clear, powerful writing that engages young readers
- Intriguing design or combination of text and illustration
- Substantive, thought-provoking messages or entertainment value
- Authenticity with regard to culture and topic

---

## Relationships

★ Bahr, Mary. **If Nathan Were Here.** Illustrated by Karen A. Jerome. Eerdmans, 2000.

★ Fraustino, Lisa Rowe. **The Hickory Chair.** Illustrated by Benny Andrews. Scholastic, 2001.

Johnson, Dinah. **Quinnie Blue.** Illustrated by James Ransome. Holt, 2000.

Jordan, Deloris, with Roslyn Jordan. **Salt in His Shoes: Michael Jordan in Pursuit of a Dream.** Illustrated by Kadir Nelson. Simon & Schuster, 2000.

Lyon, George Ella. **One Lucky Girl.** Illustrated by Irene Travis. DK, 2000.

Pinkney, Sandra. **Shades of Black: A Celebration of Our Children.** Photographs by Myles C. Pinkney. Scholastic, 2000.

Schur, Maxine Rose. **The Peddler's Gift.** Illustrated by Kimberly Bulcken Root. Penguin, 1999.

Shank, Ned. **The Sanyasin's First Day.** Illustrated by Catherine Stock. Marshall Cavendish, 1999.

★ Smith, Maggie. **Desser the Best Ever Cat.** Knopf, 2001.

Spinelli, Eileen. **Night Shift Daddy.** Illustrated by Melissa Iwai. Hyperion, 2000.

### Fascination with the Earth

Banks, Kate. **A Gift from the Sea.** Illustrated by Georg Hallensleben. Farrar, Strauss & Giroux, 2001

★ Barner, Bob. **Fish Wish.** Holiday House, 2000.

★ Berkes, Marianne. **Marsh Music.** Illustrated by Robert Noreika. Millbrook, 2000.

Chall, Marsha Wilson. **Sugarbush Spring.** Illustrated by Jim Daly. Lothrop, Lee & Shepard, 2000.

Christian, Peggy. **If You Find a Rock.** Photographs by Barbara Hirsch Lember. Harcourt, 2000.

London, Jonathan. **Panther: Shadow of the Swamp.** Illustrated by Paul Morin. Candlewick, 2000.

Shannon, David. **The Rain Came Down.** Scholastic, 2000.

### Places

Bradby, Marie. **Momma, Where Are You From?** Illustrated by Chris K. Soentpiet. Orchard, 2000.

Collier, Bryan. **Uptown.** Holt, 2000.

Kurtz, Jane. **Faraway Home.** Illustrated by E. B. Lewis. Harcourt, 2000.

Rosenberry, Vera. **Vera's First Day of School.** Holt, 1999.

Stewart, Sarah. **The Journey.** Illustrated by David Small. Farrar, Straus & Giroux, 2001.

### Humor

★ Child, Lauren. **I Will Never Not Ever Eat a Tomato.** Orchard, 2000.

Dodd, Emma. **Dog's Colorful Day: A Messy Story about Colors and Counting.** Dutton, 2000.

★ Faulkner, Keith. **The Big Yawn.** Illustrated by Jonathan Lambert. Millbrook, 1999.

★ Feiffer, Jules. **Bark, George.** HarperCollins, 1999.

★ Freymann, Saxton, and Joost Elffers. **How Are You Peeling? Foods with Moods.** Scholastic, 1999.

Laden, Nina. **Roberto: The Insect Architect.** Chronicle, 2000.

Lum, Kate. **What! Cried Granny: An Almost Bedtime Story.** Illustrated by Adrian Johnson. Dial, 1999.

Nolan, Lucy. **The Lizard Man of Crabtree County.** Illustrated by Jill Kastner. Marshall Cavendish, 1999.

### Imagination

★ Gay, Marie-Louise. **Stella, Star of the Sea.** Douglas & McIntyre, 1999

Gollub, Matthew. **The Jazz Fly: Starring the Jazz Bugs.** Illustrated by Karen Hanke. Tortuga, 2000.

Guthrie, Woody. **Bling Blang.** Illustrated by Vladimir Radunsky. Candlewick, 2000

Hamanaka, Sheila. **I Look Like a Girl.** HarperCollins, 1999.

Mallat, Kathy. **Trouble on the Tracks.** Walker, 2001.

Smith, Linda. **When Moon Fell Down.** Illustrated by Kathryn Brown. HarperCollins, 2001.

★ Wallace, Karen. **Scarlette Beane.** Illustrated by Jon Berkeley. Dial, 1999.

---

While delving into recently published picture books, our reviewers experienced a feast for the eye, the ear, and the mind. We were amazed at the beauty and diversity in the books we reviewed. Publishers today appear to be giving attention to:

- the match between the pictures and the text
- the cultural authenticity of the stories and the illustrations
- the tenor of the words and the mood of the illustration
- the need for information as well as entertainment, story, or rhyme
- the creative nature of format and design

As with all good picture books, the illustrations are as integral to the story as the text. The illustrations include many different media—print techniques, collage, and computer art are common, in addition to the more traditional paintings and photography. More illustrators use multiple media in books published today.

The quality of the stories is as impressive as the art. Realistic picture books today range from those that record ordinary events, such as finding a rock or enjoying a rainy day, to those that share milestone occurrences, such as the first day of school or living through a tornado. We found realistic books to be exceptionally genuine, dealing with touching issues such as the death of a pet or a friend. The morals and ethics presented in these books celebrate nonconformity, advocacy, and environmental awareness. By reading these books, children are sure to make connections to their own lives.

Our fantasy choices, on the other hand, were outlandish, contemporary in humor, and imaginative; the humor was heightened by comical and quirky illustrations. Many of the books are just plain fun! We found a book about a dog with an eating disorder, a book about a finicky sibling, and a book about a granny who is a superhero. Absurd humor abounds, with personified plants dressed in outlandish accessories, a foolish peddler who has no common sense, and a Lizard Man who tricks the town's citizens.

Our collection also includes outstanding yet simple informational texts in picture book format. Picture books are a perfect way for children to learn about the world outside their families, and illustrations make that learning multisensory. Through picture books, they can travel with an Amish girl on her first visit to a city, explore a wetland, learn about jazz, or visit Harlem.

The quality of writing and language in all of our selections is fresh, unique, and modern. Writers use a few carefully selected words in the telling of tales or crafting of informative pieces. Their poetic language provides a model for a writing curriculum. In fact, many of these books opened the door for students to share their own stories about their first day in kindergarten, a rainy day, pets, and family members. The children's responses to these books were emotional as well as intellectual. They begged to take them home, and one child even hugged a book to show how much he liked it!

We found picture books that could be read for a multitude of purposes: solving student conflict, welcoming a new student, dealing with death, classroom instruction in all subjects, and pure enjoyment. We found picture books appropriate for reading to a whole class and picture books for sharing with just one child. Moreover, picture books increasingly have appeal to people of all ages. Out of all the books in our collection, we labeled fourteen as appropriate for readers of all ages and four as appropriate for intermediate readers. These are the truly exceptional books with many layers of meaning that are poignant at any level.

These past three years have produced a bumper crop of excellent literature for children. When reading our chapter, it is important to remember that most of the other chapters in this book contain picture books relevant to their chapters, books that could have been included in our list. In a time when the public seems more concerned about test scores than about what children are reading, these books provide teachers with excellent opportunities to model a true love of reading. Children who spend their school days in classrooms with libraries containing books like the ones in this chapter will be drawn into reading in multiple ways.

Our selections fit into five themes: relationships, fascination with the earth, sense of place, humor, and imagination. Powerful relationships often propel interesting children's stories. Our collection focuses on the companionship individuals have with family, friends, animals, and community. Through artistic styles ranging from realism to primitive, readers will be swept into these authentic stories of family life. Parents are featured in *Night Shift Daddy* (Spinelli, 2000) and *One Lucky Girl* (Lyon, 2000). Michael Jordon's mother wrote *Salt in His Shoes* (Jordan, 2000). Children's relationships with grandparents are featured in *Quinnie Blue* (Johnson, 2000) and *The Hickory Chair* (Fraustino, 2001). *If Nathan Were Here* (Bahr, 2000) describes a child's method of mourning the death of a best friend, while *Desser, the Best Ever Cat* (Smith, 2001) involves a family's relationship with a cat who dies. Both *The Peddler's Gift* (Schur, 1999) and *The Sanyasin's First Day* (Shank, 1999) are cultural stories that involve relationships of individuals to the wider community.

Many picture books lavishly portray the environment with lush realistic paintings, photographs, or imaginative depictions of ethereal settings. *Marsh Music* (Berkes, 2000) and *Panther: Shadow of the Swamp* (London, 2000) sensitively present the rhythms of a southern wetlands ecosystem. In *Fish Wish* (Barner, 2000), a child explores an underwater ecosystem, while in *Sugarbush Spring* (Chall, 2000) a northern woodland family celebrates the annual maple syrup sugaring-off. Two books translate ordinary experiences into special ones for appreciating nature. *If You Find a Rock* (Christian, 2000) shows a child's fascination with rocks after learning geological information about how the earth was formed, and *The Rain Came Down* (Shannon, 2000) turns a dreary rainy day into an opportunity to appreciate the sun.

Some books focus on recollectors of the past. The illustrations in this type of book are often realistic or expressionistic, reflecting the mood created by the memory of the special place. Two books explore family history, with parents telling stories of their youth in distant places. In *Momma, Where Are You From?* (Bradby, 2000), a child listens to her mother's stories of the South when she was a child; in *Faraway Home* (Kurtz, 2000), a father tells of growing up in Ethiopia as a way of letting his daughter in on a life she has never experienced. Closer to home, *Uptown* (Collier, 2000) highlights a city teaming with life and activity, while in *The Journey* (Stewart, 2001) a child travels from her Amish village to the big city of Chicago to experience a life she could never have imagined. In keeping with new experiences in special places, Vera attends kindergarten for the first time in *Vera's First Day of School* (Rosenberry, 1999).

We found many humorous stories in picture book formats. The comedy grows out of both illustrations and texts. Bright colors, inventive characters, and outlandish design distinguish the books in this section. *Bark, George* (Feiffer, 1999) and *What! Cried Granny: An Almost Bedtime Story* (Lum, 1999) are progressive narratives that catapult readers into a spiral of absurdity. Adding to the group of ridiculous sequential stories are *Dog's Colorful Day: A Messy Story about Colors and Counting* (Dodd, 2000) and *The Big Yawn* (Faulkner, 1999). Foods inspire preposterous tales in *I Will Never Not Ever Eat a Tomato* (Child, 2000) and *How Are Your Peeling? Foods with Moods* (Freymann and Elffers, 1999). *Roberto: The Insect Architect* (Laden, 2000) presents new ideas in urban planning.

Children possess a natural sense of wonder and curiosity that can be enhanced by engagement with an outstanding array of imaginative picture books that play with language as well as illustrations. A young boy repeatedly asks questions about sea life in *Stella, Star of the Sea* (Gay, 1999). The playful musical talents of insect musicians sound forth in *The Jazz Fly* (Gollub, 2000), which comes with a CD, and *Bling Blang* (Guthrie, 2000) presents a folk song about cooperation. Two books are about self-fulfillment and accomplishing our personal goals and dreams. *I Look Like a Girl* (Hamanaka, 1999) highlights the remarkable potential of many different types of girls. When moon falls to Earth, he sees everything in a new perspective and falls in love with our "wondrous world" in *When Moon Fell Down* (Smith, 2001). Perspective also comes into play in *Trouble on the Tracks* (Mallet, 2001); not until the last page do readers learn that the train is only a toy, not the real thing. These books stretch the mind and leave tunes and ideas lingering in the minds of readers.

Using these books, art teachers at all levels can guide students in a study of illustrators as artists. Classroom teachers will find the books a wonderful way to extend their curriculum into the world of fine arts by having students learn about illustrations and illustrators. Interestingly, children's responses to the books in our chapter were often comments about the art. One child said, "The pictures are beautiful," and another commented, "Quinnie Blue looks like a girl in our class" (meaning that the illustrations in the book are very lifelike); still another said, "I like the colors in the pictures." Others inquired about the media, asking how the illustrator created the pictures. A thorough presentation and discussion of these picture books with children *must* involve exploring the artwork.

## Relationships

★ Allen, Debbie. **Dancing in the Wings.** Illustrated by Kadir Nelson. Dial, 2000. ISBN 0-8037-2501-9. Unpaged. (P). (See **11.21.**)

8.1      ★ Bahr, Mary. **If Nathan Were Here.** Illustrated by Karen A. Jerome. Eerdmans, 2000. ISBN 0-8028-5187-8. Unpaged. (ALL).

A young boy recalls the companionship of his best friend, Nathan, who has just died. His memories, illustrated in luminescent yellow tones, depict the fun they had together. He remembers how he and Nathan teased Nathan's sister from their tree house and how they would jump exuberantly through puddles on their way to school. In somber, dark colors, the story then moves to the present, following the boy's now solitary journey home from school and into the empty tree house. His teacher has invited the class to donate to a memory box. In the end, he sees that others are also missing Nathan and that they might be of comfort to one another. Children suffering from the loss of a loved one will find sympathy and comfort in this poignant book. (DM)

8.2    ★ Fraustino, Lisa Rowe. **The Hickory Chair.** Illustrated by Benny Andrews. Scholastic, 2001. ISBN 0-590-52248-5. Unpaged. (ALL).

Louis and his beloved Gran enjoy many activities together. Born without sight, Louis's favorite activity is sitting beside Gran while she reads aloud to him from her carved hickory chair. When Gran dies, her will instructs family members to search for notes tucked throughout her home, bequeathing a favorite item to each of them. Although Louis finds many notes for others, there doesn't seem to be one for him. Feeling sad and forgotten, Louis accepts the hickory chair from his family since it evokes the comfort of Gran's lap. Andrews's illustrations in oil-and-fabric collage are spare in details and riveted on the characters, featuring bright explosions of color against pastel backgrounds. The elongated pictures are unique and perhaps metaphorical for the long lineage of Louis's family. Here is a story to satisfy the youngest through the oldest, with a perfect happy ending to please all. (DM)

8.3    Johnson, Dinah. **Quinnie Blue.** Illustrated by James Ransome. Holt, 2000. ISBN 0-8050-4378-0. Unpaged. (ALL).

Hattie Lottie Annie Quinnie Blue is the rhythmical name shared by a young girl and her grandmother. Third graders made lots of positive comments about James Ransome's boldly colored oil paintings, which vividly enhance the reader's journey through the traditions of this African American family as grandmother and granddaughter ponder the similarities in their childhood experiences, despite their difference in age. This book is ideal for the beginning of the school year when children are learning one another's names and sharing the origins of their names. *Quinnie Blue* inspired children in a kindergarten class to tell their own stories about family names. Many children will see themselves in this warmhearted story that recollects handclap rhymes, grass between the toes, backyard swings, and relatives who live just "over yonder." (DS/TB)

8.4    Jordan, Deloris, with Roslyn Jordan. **Salt in His Shoes: Michael Jordan in Pursuit of a Dream**. Illustrated by Kadir Nelson. Simon & Schuster, 2000. ISBN 0-689-83371-7. Unpaged. (ALL).

Michael Jordan's family shares a personal story that emphasizes the importance of following your dreams. A young boy who is rejected by his playmates does not give up and today, as an adult, speaks to children about staying positive and believing in themselves. Mikey, the shortest player on the court, is picked on by Mark and goes home defeated. Mike's family provides encouragement: his mother tells him to "put salt in his shoes and say a prayer every night" and with patience he will grow. The real growth is in Mike's attitude as he diligently practices. He returns to the courts when he finally realizes that height is not the measure of a good player. Oil paintings complement the story by depicting emotions and actions with equal importance. Fourth-grade students remarked on the unnecessary behavior of the antagonist, Mark, and connected this book to *Wings* by Christopher Myers (Scholastic, 2000; **24.32**), one student saying: "Don't pay attention to negative people. You have to believe in yourself." (NRS)

★ Littlesugar, Amy. **Freedom School, Yes!** Illustrated by Floyd Cooper. Philomel, 2001. ISBN 0-399-23006-8. Unpaged. (I). (See **15.3**.)

8.5    Lyon, George Ella. **One Lucky Girl**. Illustrated by Irene Travis. DK, 2000. ISBN 0-7894-2613-7. Unpaged. (ALL).

One afternoon the sky darkens and a tornado unexpectedly whisks away a family's trailer, with Becky, an infant, asleep inside. The aptly named Hawkeye spots Becky's crib in a nearby field, as Becky is awakening from "the wildest ride in her life." Travis's watercolor illustrations capture the family's original contentment, the terror of the tornado, and the relief of a family who survives, all in a way that allows readers to identify with the family. In this story, Lyon honors a working-class family living in a trailer park, and the ethnic diversity in the neighborhood and the sense of community are well developed for such a short book. This story is based on real experiences and should be shared as part of emergency preparation instruction in every classroom and home. (NRS/KH/DM)

★ Miller, William. **The Piano.** Illustrated by Susan Keeter. Lee & Low, 2000. ISBN 1-880000-98-9. Unpaged. (P). (See **11.37.**)

Millman, Isaac. **Moses Goes to School.** Farrar, Straus & Giroux, 2000. ISBN 0-374-35069-8. Unpaged. (P). (See **6.2.**)

★ Myers, Christopher. **Wings.** Scholastic, 2000. ISBN 0-590-03377-8. Unpaged. (I). (See **24.32.**)

8.6     Pinkney, Sandra. **Shades of Black: A Celebration of Our Children.** Photographs by Myles C. Pinkney. Scholastic, 2000. ISBN 0-439-14892. Unpaged. (ALL).

With up close and personal photographs accompanied by lyrical language, the Pinkneys offer a poignant reminder that no single word can adequately describe an entire community of people. There are instead, as the title declares, many "shades of black." Sandra Pinkney's metaphorical phrases, such as "I am the midnight blue of a licorice stick" and "My hair is the straight edge of a blade of grass and the twisted corkscrew in a rope," describe skin tones, hair texture, and eye color and provide models of expressive language for young writers. My students sat enraptured by the pictures and commented on other kids they knew who looked like the children in the book. Combine this story with Karen Katz's *The Colors of Us* (Holt, 1999; **17.16**) to enhance a unit on self, family, diversity, and community. (DS)

Ryan, Pam Muñoz. **Amelia and Eleanor Go for a Ride.** Illustrated by Bryan Selznick. Scholastic, 1999. ISBN 0-590-96075-X. Unpaged. (ALL). (See **3.20.**)

8.7     Schur, Maxine Rose. **The Peddler's Gift.** Illustrated by Kimberly Bulcken Root. Penguin, 1999. ISBN 0-8037-1978-7. 32 pp. (I).

Young Leibush is delighted when the foolish peddler, playfully called "Shnook," comes to visit his rural village, for Shnook is a terrible businessman, cursed to lose more than he sells. When Leibush's mother selects her wares, the price is always miraculously one ruble, the exact amount she has to spend. As Shnook is leaving Leibush's home, Leibush quietly pockets one of Shnook's beautiful dreidels, thinking that the foolish Shnook will never know the difference. Laden with guilt, Leibush cannot sleep that night. Ashamed, he rushes into the night to seek Shnook and confess his crime. Shnook receives him with such kindness and love that Leibush realizes that Shnook has *never* been foolish, only generous. Pastels dominate the watercolor and colored-pencil drawings. Older children love this enchanting story about a simpleton who turns out to be the wisest of all. (DM)

8.8     Shank, Ned. **The Sanyasin's First Day.** Illustrated by Catherine Stock. Marshall Cavendish, 1999. ISBN 0-7614-5055-6. Unpaged. (I).

Today is a day of new beginnings for many people in and around a city in India. A *sanyasin*, or holy man, begins the spiritual discipline of relying on the charity of others for food. A woman starts her new career as a plumber. A policeman starts his first day directing traffic. A farmer goes to town for the first time to sell rice. Each offers up a prayer for help and guidance on this day, and each touches the life of another to inadvertently put rice in the *sanyasin*'s bowl. Beautiful, busy watercolors realistically portray the crowded streets and character of an Indian city. This story eloquently conveys a valuable message about the interdependence and interconnectedness of people and is a great addition to any curriculum focus on a culture seldom depicted in U.S. children's books. (BA)

8.9     ★ Smith, Maggie. **Desser the Best Ever Cat.** Knopf, 2001. ISBN 0-375-81056-0. Unpaged. (P).

A young girl relates the story of a stray cat, adopted by her father when he was single, who became such an integral part of the family that he is later included in wedding pictures. The girl calls the cat "Desser" because she can't pronounce his name, Dexter. She tells of Desser's daily life: sleeping on her bed, playing with her, and waiting for her to come home from school. Just as the little girl grows older, so too does Desser, who ages with grace and dies with dignity. He is buried in the backyard, surrounded by all that he loved. In spite of their sadness, a month later the family adopts a kitten named Ginger. The girl shows Ginger pictures of Desser and tells of his exploits. The soft watercolor illustrations of typical cat antics demonstrate the affection between Desser and his family. This book stimulates lots of talk and writing about pets. (LLL)

**8.10** Spinelli, Eileen. **Night Shift Daddy.** Illustrated by Melissa Iwai. Hyperion, 2000. ISBN 0-7868-0495-5. Unpaged. (P).

As evening shadows stretch across the pages, a little girl and her father go through their nightly bedtime ritual of sharing a snack and snuggling together to read a book. Then Daddy calls her "little sleepyhead" and tenderly kisses her good night. After the little girl is tucked in bed, Daddy goes to his job as a night shift custodian. In the morning, the two of them repeat their routine, only this time Daddy is the "sleepyhead" going to bed. The faces of the little girl and her father radiate a sweet delight in their morning and evening patterns. The illustrations are tinted with a comfortable duskiness as nighttime approaches, making this a perfect bedtime book for parents, especially fathers, to read to their own little sleepyheads. Children in school enjoy writing about the rituals they enjoy with their dads. (DM)

Willis, Jeanne. **Susan Laughs.** Illustrated by Tony Ross. Holt, 2000. ISBN 0-8050-6501-6. Unpaged. (P). (See **19.25.**)

## Fascination with the Earth

**8.11** Banks, Kate. **A Gift from the Sea.** Illustrated by Georg Hallensleben. Farrar, Straus & Giroux. 2001. ISBN 0-374-32566-9. Unpaged. (P).

A young boy, unaware of the tremendous history in the life of a rock, picks up a rock on the beach and takes it home as a souvenir. From the dinosaur age, through the ice age, from a volcano, to the bottom of the ocean, and then to the sandy beach, the historical journey of this rock is described. The young boy comes to realize that his precious rock is a cherished gift from the sea. The exquisite watercolors illuminate the rock's journey through time. Young children responding to an oral reading of this tale exclaimed at the "fireworks" of the volcanic eruptions, the "great big" dinosaurs roaming the earth, and how such a small rock could have such an exciting past. (RL)

**8.12** ★ Barner, Bob. **Fish Wish.** Holiday House, 2000. ISBN 0-8234-1482-5. Unpaged. (P).

A boy gazes at a cheerful, blue-eyed fish, wondering what it would be like to be in that fish's fins, thus beginning an imaginative journey under the sea. The fish (boy) awakens on a coral reef and journeys through octopus arms and "clouds of jellyfish," eventually resting in a sea of starfish. Various kinds of colorful paper and common items such as buttons combine to create a simple but delightful collage of a friendly undersea world. A key to ocean creatures and notes on coral reefs add to the informational value of the book. Young children listened attentively to the story and browsed through the information at the end, making it an ideal book for an introduction to undersea life. (DM)

**8.13**  ★ Berkes, Marianne. **Marsh Music.** Illustrated by Robert Noreika. Millbrook, 2000. ISBN 0-7613-1850-X. Unpaged. (P).

When the noises of traffic have stilled, sit outside and listen to the harmonies and cacophonies of nocturnal animals. The tone for this particular romp in the swamp is set through a quote by the late Dr. Archie Carr, a well-known zoologist and environmentalist: "Frogs do for the night what birds do for the day." Berkes's rhyming text intones the rhythm of the evening, composing a dazzling musical number for the amphibian philharmonic. But Noreika's delightfully exquisite and whimsical illustrations transform these words into a frog fantasia! Although the anthropomorphic depictions of the animals might bother some, the precise identification of each frog and the appendix identifying the cast of characters will intrigue every young scientist. For those who enjoy listening to the cadence of frogs, this book is a terrific early field guide. (RR)

Brown, Ruth. **Ten Seeds.** Knopf, 2001. ISBN 0-375-80697-0. Unpaged. (P). (See **9.3.**)

**8.14**  Chall, Marsha Wilson. **Sugarbush Spring.** Illustrated by Jim Daly. Lothrop, Lee & Shepard, 2000. ISBN 0-688-14907-3. Unpaged. (ALL).

A child accompanies her grandpa and his horses as they tap the maple trees, preparing to draw the sap. The next morning the whole family collects the sap and takes it to the sugarhouse, where it is boiled down into syrup. Chall's stirring text and Daly's realistic oil paintings create an authentic picture of country life in the North, providing clear information about how maple sugar is made. Our Florida children connected the story to their own experiences of making cane syrup and were fascinated with the idea of making snow angels and eating hot syrup poured over snow. The illustrations pull the children into the story and made fourth-grade students feel a part of the sugaring process. "Look at the little boy" and "Wow, I feel like I am there" were just a few of the comments that filled the room as we read. (LLL/NRS)

8.15    Christian, Peggy. **If You Find a Rock.** Photographs by Barbara Hirsch Lember. Harcourt, 2000. ISBN 0-15-239339-0. Unpaged. (ALL).

The shapes, textures, sizes, and colors of rocks usually go unnoticed. In this book, however, stunning color photographs highlight the beauty and the sense of peace and serenity of rocks. The children in the book find numerous uses for various kinds of rocks: skipping rocks, chalk rocks, resting rocks, worry rocks, climbing rocks, and, best of all, memory rocks, which remind one of a place, a feeling, or an important person. This book helps readers appreciate nature, remember the importance of reflection, and relive the fascination with the simple things we often take for granted. After reading *If You Find a Rock,* first and second graders spent many days looking for and exploring rocks. (AS)

8.16    London, Jonathan. **Panther: Shadow of the Swamp.** Illustrated by Paul Morin. Candlewick, 2000. ISBN 1-56402-623-X. Unpaged. (ALL).

Against the swampy backdrop of the Everglades, a tale of the mysterious, elusive Florida panther unfolds. Walking silently through tropical underbrush of strangler fig and saw palmetto, the panther is in search of prey. The reader follows the panther on her journey, getting acquainted with a snowy egret, an alligator, an armadillo, and an ibis, until the cat pounces on and kills a wild hog. After eating her fill and burying her catch, she returns to her den and feeds her young. The exquisite oil-on-canvas paintings pull the reader into the landscape and capture the expressions of the panther. As an afterword, the author provides a brief explanation of the ecosystem of the Everglades and the plight of the endangered Florida panther. This book can be used to spark discussion about human responsibility and endangered species. (BA)

8.17    Shannon, David. **The Rain Came Down.** Scholastic, 2000. ISBN 0-439-05021-9. Unpaged. (P).

As the rain pours from the sky, unrest seems to come over everyone and everything. The chickens squawk, the dog barks, and people in the city begin to yell at one another. The rain is slowing down traffic and everyone is in a hurry! Each drop that falls seems to make the day more miserable. When the rain finally stops and the sun shines, everyone and everything finds peace in its warmth and enjoys the day again. Each page in this book is filled with color. The people and animals are realistically drawn, thanks to Shannon's careful attention to detail. Reading this book on a dreary, rainy day prompted my third-grade students to write about ways to make a rainy day fun. (TB)

★ Waldman, Neil. **The Starry Night.** Boyds Mills, 1999. ISBN 1-56397-736-2. Unpaged. (ALL). (See **11.20.**)

## Places

8.18    Bradby, Marie. **Momma, Where Are You From?** Illustrated by Chris K. Soentpiet. Orchard, 2000. ISBN 0-531-30105-2. Unpaged. (P).

"Where are you from, Momma?" a little girl asks as she helps her mother in the kitchen. In response, the mother revisits her childhood, recalling things such as washing the laundry in a wringer machine, a fisherman who sold his wares from the back of a wagon, and treats of ice chips from the iceman. She also recalls her older siblings traveling across town to attend school. The lifelike illustrations are brilliant with color, portraying a childhood full of warmth despite poverty and segregation. Like the daughter in the story, readers understand that the love in the mother's family created the wonderful memories. For the little girl, the sweetness of being part of a big, extended family is realizing that she shares in Momma's family origins. Young audiences quickly capture the mood of Momma's reminiscing, recalling stories their own parents and grandparents tell about growing up in the United States. (RL/DM)

8.19    Collier, Bryan. **Uptown.** Holt, 2000. ISBN 0-8050-5721-8. Unpaged. (ALL).

A young boy takes readers on a journey through his neighborhood, allowing them to experience the richness of Harlem's culture and the depth of its character. Collier uses a collage technique, bold colors, and reflected light to make Harlem come alive with the energy and richness of its people. Restaurants that are open all night, city lights, brownstones, the Apollo Theater, jazz, and the Metro-North train present a positive image of Harlem. Like *Harlem: A Poem* by his father, Walter Dean Myers, a book Bryan Collier also illustrated (Scholastic, 1997), *Uptown* gives readers a cultural experience and exposure to neighborhood pride. As one second grader commented, "It reminds me about this morning. My mom was talking culture, where you know a lot about where you live." Bottom line? Harlem is home. (AS)

Coy, John. **Strong to the Hoop.** Illustrated by Leslie Jean-Bart. Lee & Low, 1999. ISBN 1-880000-80-6. Unpaged. (ALL). (See **12.24.**)

8.20    Kurtz, Jane. **Faraway Home.** Illustrated by E. B. Lewis. Harcourt, 2000. ISBN 0-15-200036-4. Unpaged. (I).

When Desta's father announces that he must leave the United States to care for his ailing mother in Ethiopia, Desta begins to worry that he won't return. To lessen her fears, her father vividly describes his homeland and his childhood, helping his daughter picture his life in another part of the world. Lewis's double-page watercolor illustrations of the Ethiopian landscape make the father's descriptions come to life and contrast with the close up, photolike paintings of Desta and her father. When Desta begs for more stories of her father's youth, he promises that more will come—when he returns. Kurtz provides a beautiful narration, highlighting the themes of love, family, and immigration. Many children will notice the contrasting cultures and comment on how different Desta's life in the United States is from her father's childhood in Ethiopia. *Faraway Home* evokes genuine curiosity about specific cultural histories and spurs authentic discussion of life choices. (RL/NRS)

8.21    Rosenberry, Vera. **Vera's First Day of School.** Holt, 1999. ISBN 0-8050-5936-9. Unpaged. (P).

Tomorrow is Vera's first day of school. She is "big at last!" and about to embark on new adventures. What greater adventure than the first day of kindergarten? Vera Rosenberry relies on her own childhood memories to portray that special day with both humor and sensitivity. Through endearing watercolor illustrations, we see Vera, filled with a mixture of emotions ranging from giddy excitement to tearful anxiety, encounter her big day.

The children in her class are culturally diverse, and what a treat it is when readers meet the kindergarten teacher, Mr. Kline. If you teach kindergarten, this book deserves a place in your collection. The story resonated with several kindergarten children in my class who admitted to "scary feelings" about starting school. *Vera's First Day of School* will help teachers, students, and their families celebrate that marvelous milestone that comes with being "big at last." (DS)

8.22 Stewart, Sarah. **The Journey.** Illustrated by David Small. Farrar, Straus & Giroux, 2001. ISBN 0-374-33905-8. Unpaged. (ALL).

Today, Hannah's dream of visiting a big city is coming true. As a birthday gift from her aunt Clara, Hannah, an Amish girl, is in Chicago having exciting and eye-opening experiences. Each day brings new and wondrous adventures as she walks through department stores, cranes her neck at skyscrapers, and sees people of more shades than she ever imagined. She reveals her impressions in her daily letters to "Dear Diary," drawing comparisons to life at home. David Small, in his characteristically lively pen-and-watercolor illustrations, begins telling the tale in the cover art, depicting Hannah saying goodbye to Aunt Clara by the horse-drawn carriage, sweeping across the countryside to the city-bound bus, and then into Chicago—all before the first letter is written! A distinguished duo, Stewart and Small combine their talents again as they did in *The Gardener* (Farrar, Straus & Giroux, 1997) and *The Library* (Farrar, Straus & Giroux, 1995) to create this charming story. (BA)

## Humor

8.23 ★ Child, Lauren. **I Will Never Not Ever Eat a Tomato.** Orchard, 2000. ISBN 0-7636-1188-3. Unpaged. (P).

Feeding a fussy eater like Lola is certainly a challenge, until her ever-resourceful and creative older brother Charlie masterminds a formula for a feasting adventure. With a cleverness held only by older siblings, Charlie takes Lola on a culinary escapade through a galaxy of distinctively and deliciously dubbed edibles, sampling everything along the way. This tasty morsel is a perfect launch for the kindergarten or early elementary class that is embarking on an exploration of the senses and nutrition. Third graders, themselves members of the "I Will Never Eat . . ." club, loved the idea of *moon squirters* (tomatoes) and *ocean nibbles* (fish sticks) and were fascinated by the illustrations. A child's mix of cartoonlike drawings with realistic photos creates an appetizing environment for these tasty tricks. (TB/RR)

**8.24** Dodd, Emma. **Dog's Colorful Day: A Messy Story about Colors and Counting.** Dutton, 2000. ISBN 0-525-46528-6. Unpaged. (P).

Meet Dog, all white except for one black spot on his ear. Dog is a busy little guy. As he goes through his day, he gets jam, paint, grass, chocolate, pollen, ice cream, mud, orange juice, and marker splashed, squirted, or drawn on him until, at day's end, he is a white dog with ten spots—all of different colors! This humorous tale follows Dog on his various adventures, instructing children on colors and numbers along the way. Sound words such as *splat, splish, squash,* and *squish* signal the onslaught of substances and make this a fun read-aloud. Children laugh at adorable Dog's antics, anticipating and naming each new color. The illustrations are bright, bold, and colorful in a cartoon style, filling entire double-page spreads. This jolly little book is sure to add color to many a dull day. (BA)

**8.25** ★ Faulkner, Keith. **The Big Yawn.** Illustrated by Jonathan Lambert. Millbrook, 1999. ISBN 0-7613-1029-0. Unpaged. (P).

Anything but a snoozer, this whimsical story takes an amusing look at the nocturnal habits of some of our favorite beasts. Set in the rain forest, the alliterative text brings us to the "tallest treetops," over "lush leaves," and through a "smelly swamp." There we encounter a bug, a parrot, a snake, a gorilla, a crocodile, and a tiger at sunset, with mouths wide open in big yawns. The most ingenious feature of the book is the peepholes cut out of the animals' yawning mouths. At each turn of the page, a new yawn appears, building to a cumulative crescendo of yawning critters. The illustrations are brightly colored, comical, highly stylized, and set against a black background for extra brilliance. Children love to create sound effects for each animal. This is an excellent participation book for a multisensory approach to rain forest appreciation and for large group participation. (BA)

**8.26** ★ Feiffer, Jules. **Bark, George.** HarperCollins, 1999. ISBN 0-06-205185-7. Unpaged. (P).

George is an unconventional canine pup with a remarkable appetite for language acquisition, much to the chagrin of his mama. With her frustration level high and her patience low, Mama takes George to visit a long-limbed veterinarian, who, in a most professional manner (and with the longest latex gloves ever seen!), extracts an explanation for these talents from George's innards. Feiffer's comical illustrations complete his tongue-in-cheek text to present a worthwhile addition to any public, school, or classroom library where participation in story time is encouraged. Children readily supply the animal sounds for George's overwrought mother as one animal after another is pulled from George's throat. Preschoolers through third graders squeal over the silliness as they join in the probe for George's real voice. Use this book to kick off multicultural units focusing on communication. (RR/BA)

**8.27**    ★ Freymann, Saxton, and Joost Elffers. **How Are You Peeling? Foods with Moods.** Scholastic, 1999. ISBN 0-439-10431-9. Unpaged. (P).

Feast your eyes on these deliciously flamboyant fruits and vivacious vegetables that are as passionate as they are palatable. With an eye for "produce potential," masters of makeover Freymann and Elffers transform lowly legumes into culinary comedians. Blending foods and moods, they serve up a sumptuous emotional smorgasbord. With the help of black-eyed peas and an Exacto knife, the authors create an insecure onion, a confused kiwi, and a green pepper that growls at a frightened red pepper. Teachers eagerly snatch up this book for a humorous and light approach to conflict resolution in the classroom. Children giggled and pointed at the comical comestibles and were often overcome with a strange desire to eat their vegetables. (BA/RR)

**8.28**    Laden, Nina. **Roberto: The Insect Architect.** Chronicle, 2000. ISBN 0-8118-2465-9. Unpaged. (I).

For Roberto, a termite who forged his own path in life, wood was to be seen, wood was to be played with, but wood was *not* to be eaten! Mocked by the other termites in his colony, Roberto set off for the big city, arriving in Bug Central Station with high hopes and lofty dreams. Though unemployed, unwanted, and downtrodden, Roberto was determined to succeed despite the odds. Accordingly, he carved out a niche for himself as developer and architect, building functional, interesting, and affordable housing for all of his insect friends. Working in mixed-media collage, Laden has fashioned a fascinating tongue-in-cheek look at the benefits society reaps from nonconformity. Fifth and sixth graders studying urban development and problem solving will enjoy and benefit from meeting Roberto. (RR)

8.29 Lum, Kate. **What! Cried Granny: An Almost Bedtime Story.** Illustrated by Adrian Johnson. Dial, 1999. ISBN 0-8037-2382-2. Unpaged. (P).

Patrick is a proficient procrastinator. He is having his first sleep-over at his granny's, but when she tells him it's bedtime, he replies, "But Granny! I don't have a bed here." Most grandparents would just plop down a sleeping bag and couch cushions—end of story. But this is Wonder-Granny! Horrified at her lack of preparation, Granny quickly sets to work. She chops down a tree, takes out her tools, builds a bed, paints it blue, adds a mattress, and plunks it in Patrick's bedroom. The predictable rhythm of Lum's text, along with Granny's unpredictable behavior, is embellished by Johnson's quirky and comical illustrations. Children love to repeat the recurring phrases and laugh out loud at Wonder-Granny's antics. A superb choice for women's history units, this book shows that women really can do anything. (BA)

8.30 Nolan, Lucy. **The Lizard Man of Crabtree County.** Illustrated by Jill Kastner. Marshall Cavendish, 1999. ISBN 0-7614-5049-1. Unpaged. (ALL).

Nothing ever happens in sleepy Crabtree County until the day James Arthur dresses up like a bush in hopes of creating some excitement for himself. Quite unintentionally, he sets rumors flying. How? When the bugs make a home in James Arthur's underpants, he has to run to Miss Bunch's pond to wash them out. Miss Bunch sees a wild green man running by! By the time James Arthur gets home that day, the word is out: there is a Lizard Man in Crabtree County residing in Miss Bunch's pond. In spite of James Arthur's valiant efforts to spy on the Lizard Man, he misses him every time. Young audiences are quick to catch on that James Arthur is causing the town's ruckus and laugh at his unintentional pranks. The expressive oil-on-paper illustrations adeptly capture the story's humor and action and are sure to spark lively classroom conversations. (BA)

★ Palatini, Margie. **Bedhead.** Illustrated by Jack E. Davis. Simon & Schuster, 2000. ISBN: 0-689-82397-5. Unpaged. (P). (See **6.14.**)

## Imagination

★ Fleischman, Paul. **Weslandia.** Illustrated by Kevin Hawkes. Candlewick, 1999. ISBN 0-763-60006-7. Unpaged. (ALL). (See **14.27.**)

**8.31**　★ Gay, Marie-Louise. **Stella, Star of the Sea.** Douglas & McIntyre, 1999. ISBN 0-88899-337-4. Unpaged. (P).

Stella and her little brother Sam are spending a glorious day at the seashore. Having been there once before, Stella is a "sea expert." Eagerly she dashes into the ocean, encouraging Sam to come too. But Sam is too full of questions, such as "Where do starfish come from?" Luckily, Stella conjures imaginative answers: "Starfish are shooting stars that fell in love with the sea." Preschool and early elementary children were especially charmed by the humor. Third graders thoroughly enjoyed the story, easily relating to a situation in which a younger sibling "really gets on your nerves," and they loved Stella's creative answers to Sam's constant questions. The splendid watercolor and cut-paper illustrations invoke jubilation. Stella, with her wild red curls and inflatable pink seahorse, and Sam, with his green plaid trunks and golden straw hair, dash into a turquoise sea. All young children will delight in the sweetness of this tale of sibling love. (BA/TB)

**8.32**　Gollub, Matthew. **The Jazz Fly: Starring the Jazz Bugs.** Illustrated by Karen Hanke. Tortuga, 2000. ISBN 1-889910-17-1. 30 pp. (ALL).

Here is the answer to the question, "What is jazz?" A fly cannot find his way into town, where he is supposed to play drums at a jazz club. First he asks the frog, "ZA-baza, BOO-zaba, ZEE-zah RO-ni?" and the frog, not understanding the fly's question, replies, "RRibit." This continues with other animals until the fly makes it to the club, where the other musicians are already playing. When the manager demands a "new beat," the jazz fly incorporates all the animal noises he encountered earlier into his music. When read aloud, the words swing with a cool, syncopated beat. Illustrations are sleek, with a predominance of blacks and grays and just a touch of pastel coloring, complementing the jazz theme. A CD accompanies the book, enhancing the story with rich instrumentals and Gollub's ultra-jazzy reading of the text. (DM)

**8.33**　Guthrie, Woody. **Bling Blang.** Illustrated by Vladimir Radunsky. Candlewick, 2000. ISBN 0-7636-0769-X. Unpaged. (ALL).

How do you build a truly happy home? With a little gouache, collage, splashes of drawings by children, and a toolbox full of music and merriment! Radunsky's playful illustrations provide the perfect decor for this harmonious abode built by folk music's premier architect, Woody Guthrie. Though locating the sheet music on the reverse side of the dust jacket makes reading the music a challenge, who cares? From cover to cover, every part of this book serves a function and is thoroughly entertaining. At first glance, teachers might reserve this book for younger readers, but my fourth graders enjoyed its imaginativeness and the friendship theme as well as the music. This is a perfect addition to units about cooperation and families, as well as a terrific participation song that will be hummed by all the whole day through. (NRS/RR)

**8.34** Hamanaka, Sheila. **I Look Like a Girl.** HarperCollins, 1999. ISBN 0-688-14625-2. Unpaged. (P).

She is fierce like a tiger and playful like a dolphin. She soars like the condors and is as wild as horses running free. She is a girl. Written in lyrical, poetic prose, this young girl's narrative of herself draws readers through the lovely landscape of pages and into a journey of potentials and possibilities. Hamanaka emphasizes that *all* children are *all* these things. The beautiful oil painting illustrations realistically portray girls of many different ethnic backgrounds inhabiting the spirit of the animals they represent. Each girl is represented as strong and proud, determined to realize her full potential. The message is potent and eloquently stated. Read this book to young children early and often to inspire and remind them to be everything they can be. (BA)

Johnson, D. B. **Henry Hikes to Fitchburg.** Houghton Mifflin, 2000. ISBN 0-395-96867-4. Unpaged. (ALL). (See **24.2**.)

Madrigal, Antonio Hernández. **Blanca's Feather.** Illustrated by Gerardo Suzán. Rising Moon, 2000. ISBN 0-87358-743-X. Unpaged. (P). (See **17.17**.)

**8.35** Mallat, Kathy. **Trouble on the Tracks.** Walker, 2001. ISBN 0-8027-8771-1. Unpaged. (P).

With markers and colored pencils, Mallat's bold and life-size illustrations set the stage for an adventurous train ride as the conductor calls "ALL ABOARD" and passengers hurry onto the train. As the engineer makes his final check, we learn that he is worried about meeting trouble ahead. For a while, the train glides along its familiar route, but soon it does meet trouble, and readers are treated to a surprising twist. This tantalizing tale of feline mischief makes a read-aloud session especially fun as children realize that Trouble is a black house cat and the tracks are part of a little boy's toy train set. What looked in the beginning like a life-size train rolling through vividly colored landscapes of forests, farms, and villages is really an elaborate set that is too tempting for the young engineer's cat to resist. (DS)

★ Nikola-Lisa, W. **Can You Top That?** Illustrated by Hector Viveros Lee. Lee & Low, 2000. ISBN 1-880000-99-7. Unpaged. (P). (See **15.25.**)

8.36   Smith, Linda. **When Moon Fell Down.** Illustrated by Kathryn Brown. HarperCollins, 2001. ISBN 0-06-028301-7. Unpaged. (P).

One starry evening the moon falls to Earth and lands in a farmer's field. Moon is soon joined by a curious but adventuresome cow and sets off on a trek through the nearby town. Moon delights in seeing familiar sights from his new perspective: he discovers, for example, that trees have trunks and horses have knees. Charmed by simply peering through the windows of shops he knows only by their shingled rooftops, Moon falls in love with our "wondrous world." Brown's illustrations glow as softly as a moonlit night in spring and lend a warm, peaceful feeling to Smith's enchanting, poetic story. Young readers raised on nursery rhymes are likely to find this pairing of the moon and a cow a familiar sight. *When Moon Fell Down* will be a fun addition to a unit on nursery rhymes or friendship. (DS)

8.37   ★ Wallace, Karen. **Scarlette Beane.** Illustrated by Jon Berkeley. Dial, 1999. ISBN 0-8037-2475-6. Unpaged. (P).

In a house the size of a garden shed, Scarlette Beane is born with a beet-red face and green fingers. She is a joy to her parents, who know she will grow up to do something wonderful. Her ten green fingers turn out to be better than ten green thumbs, and with some seeds and a little dirt, Scarlette is able to grow the most amazing things. Young readers are awestruck by the gargantuan size of the vegetables, and soup stirred up in a cement mixer evokes some hearty chuckles. Berkeley's bright, joyful acrylic paintings will inspire all readers to believe they are born with the power to grow from where they are "planted" and accomplish greatness. Teachers can create a delightful story time about spring, planting, or gardens by coupling *Scarlette Beane* with a lively telling of the Russian tale *The Great Big Enormous Turnip.* (BA)

Williams-Garcia, Rita. **Catching the Wild Waiyuuzee.** Illustrated by Mike Reed. Simon & Schuster, 2000. ISBN 0-689-82601-X. Unpaged. (P). (See **15.28.**)

Wood, Audrey. **Jubal's Wish.** Illustrated by Don Wood. Scholastic, 2000. ISBN 0-439-16964-X. Unpaged. (P). (See **14.8.**)

# 9 Mathematics in Our World

**Phyllis Whitin and David Whitin**

*Contributing reviewers included Teresa Hurtares, Hye Sook Kang, and Mirella Rizzo.*

---

**Criteria for Excellence**
- Mathematical accuracy, functional use, and accessibility of ideas
- Varied opportunities for response
- Aesthetic dimension of language, form, and/or illustrations
- Gender, racial, and cultural inclusiveness

---

## Counting and Number Operations

Anderson, Lena. **Tea for Ten.** Farrar, Straus & Giroux, 2000.

Appelt, Kathi. **Bats on Parade.** Illustrated by Melissa Sweet. Morrow, 1999.

Brown, Ruth. **Ten Seeds.** Knopf, 2001.

Capucilli, Alyssa Satin. **Mrs. McTats and Her Houseful of Cats.** Illustrated by Joan Rankin. Margaret K. McElderry Books, 2001.

Cuyler, Margery. **100th Day Worries.** Illustrated by Arthur Howard. Simon & Schuster, 2000.

Dodds, Dayle Ann. **The Great Divide.** Illustrated by Tracy Mitchell. Candlewick, 1999.

Freymann, Saxton, and Joost Elffers. **One Lonely Seahorse.** Scholastic, 2000.

Guettier, Benedicte. **The Father Who Had 10 Children.** Dial, 1999.

Hendra, Sue. **Numbers.** Candlewick, 1999.

★ Hoban, Tana. **Let's Count.** Greenwillow, 1999.

Isadora, Rachel. **1 2 3 Pop!** Viking, 2000.

★ Lesser, Carolyn. **Spots: Counting Creatures from Sky to Sea.** Illustrated by Laura Regan. Harcourt Brace, 1999.

MacDonald, Suse. **Look Whooo's Counting.** Scholastic, 2000.

★ Schmandt-Besserat, Denise. **The History of Counting.** Illustrated by Michael Hays. Morrow, 1999.

Schwartz, David M. **On Beyond a Million: An Amazing Math Journey.** Illustrated by Paul Meisel. Random House, 1999.

★ Tang, Greg. **The Grapes of Math: Mind-Stretching Math Riddles.** Illustrated by Harry Briggs. Scholastic, 2001.

Thorne-Thomsen, Kathleen, and Paul Rocheleau. **A Shaker's Dozen.** Chronicle, 1999.

Wells, Rosemary. **Emily's First 100 Days of School.** Hyperion, 2000.

## Measurement, Statistics, and Classification

Jenkins, Emily. **Five Creatures.** Illustrated by Tomek Bogacki. Farrar, Straus & Giroux, 2001.

Jocelyn, Marthe. **Hannah's Collections.** Dutton, 2000.

Maestro, Betsy. **The Story of Clocks and Calendars: Marking a Millennium.** Illustrated by Giulio Maestro. Lothrop, Lee & Shepard, 1999.

Mollel, Tololwa M. **My Rows and Piles of Coins.** Illustrated by E. B. Lewis. Clarion, 1999.

Nagda, Ann Whitehead, and Cindy Bickel. **Tiger Math: Learning to Graph from a Baby Tiger.** Holt, 2000.

★ Schwartz, David M. **If You Hopped Like a Frog.** Illustrated by James Warhola. Scholastic, 1999.

Sullivan, George. **Any Number Can Play.** Cartoons by Anne Canevari Green. Millbrook, 2000.

## Shapes, Patterns, and Puzzles

Agee, Jon. **Sit on a Potato Pan, Otis! More Palindromes** Farrar, Straus & Giroux, 1999.

Fleischman, Paul. **Lost! A Story in String.** Illustrated by C. B. Mordan. Holt, 2000.

Franco, Betsy. **Grandpa's Quilt.** Illustrated by Linda Bild. Children's Press, 1999.

Harris, Trudy. **Pattern Fish.** Illustrated by Anne Canevari Green. Millbrook, 2000.

Hoban, Tana. **Cubes, Cones, Cylinders, & Spheres.** Greenwillow, 2000.

Luciani, Brigitte. **How Will We Get to the Beach?** Illustrated by Eve Tharlet. North-South, 2000.

Swinburne, Stephen R. **Guess Whose Shadow?** Boyds Mills, 1999.

Wyatt, Valerie. **The Math Book for Girls and Other Beings Who Count.** Illustrated by Pat Cupples. Kids Can Press, 2000.

Zaslavsky, Claudia. **Number Sense and Nonsense.** Chicago Press, 2001.

Traditionally, mathematics classrooms have been quiet places. Teachers dispensed assignments and students spent time in solitary practice. The National Council of Teachers of Mathematics (NCTM) has addressed this troublesome issue in *Principles and Standards for School Mathematics* (2000) by identifying oral and written communication as one of its key process standards. Children's literature can be one important avenue to promoting talking and writing in the mathematics classroom. Good books help readers recognize the relevance of mathematics in their everyday lives and present mathematics as a way of thinking.

It was important to view potential books for this chapter through both mathematical and literary lenses. Four criteria guided the process: (1) books should reflect mathematical accuracy, functional use, and accessibility of ideas; (2) books should offer varied opportunities for response; (3) books should encompass an aesthetic dimension; and (4) books should promote NCTM's Equity Principle, which highlights gender, racial, and cultural inclusiveness.

Accuracy is of paramount importance in choosing children's literature for the mathematics classroom. Tana Hoban, for example, uses the accurate terms *cube* and *sphere* instead of *box, ball,* or even the less desirable *circle* in *Cubes, Cones, Cylinders, & Spheres* (2000). Accessibility of mathematical ideas is especially important in illustrations found in counting books. Objects need to be clearly portrayed so that readers can easily match a numeral to the corresponding set.

Books that meet the second criterion of varied response lead readers to conduct further research, pose questions, view the natural world in a fresh way, or devise multiple solutions to problems. These books have a multiage appeal. We rejected titles in which symbols, algorithms, or terminology dominate the story, as well as books that target a narrow audience identified at a specific "skill level." Such books place the reader in a passive role or restrict the range of potential responses. *Bats on Parade* (Appelt, 1999) can clarify the difference. Although the illustrations include specific equations, the book also highlights intriguing geometric and numerical patterns found in square numbers for readers to pursue.

Third, good books for the mathematics classroom have an aesthetic appeal. The poetic language in *Spots: Counting Creatures from Sky to Sea* (Lesser, 1999) delights the ear, while the depiction of the earth's ten biomes evokes awe and wonder. Simple string figures arouse the imagination in *Lost! A Story in String* (Fleischman, 2000). David M. Schwartz astonishes readers with facts about animals and their abilities in *If You Hopped Like a Frog* (1999). Highlighting the aesthetic dimension of mathematics helps dispel the belief that mathematics is unfeeling, irrelevant, and unrewarding, a belief that can lead to math dysfunction.

Finally, books should contribute to gender, racial, and cultural equity. In *The Math Book for Girls and Other Beings Who Count* (2000), Valerie Wyatt gives firsthand accounts of women who excel in mathematical and scientific professions. Denise Schmandt-Besserat highlights the resourcefulness of a wide range of people in *The History of Counting* (1999). Despite some excellent examples, however, it is clear that more progress is needed in this area.

We have organized the books listed in this chapter into three categories:

- Counting and Number Operations
- Measurement, Statistics, and Classification
- Shapes, Patterns, and Puzzles

Many of the books in the first category appeal to a wide age range because of their interdisciplinary connections. *A Shaker's Dozen* (Thorne-Thomsen & Rocheleau, 1999), for instance, depicts the life and craftsmanship of Shaker society. *One Lonely Seahorse* (Freymann & Elffers, 2000) portrays imaginative sea creatures created from fruits, vegetables, and spices. Books in this category also offer a variety of counting-on strategies that highlight patterns and illustrate meaningful contexts for basic number operations. *The Father Who Had 10 Children* (Guettier, 1999) shows counting by 2s, 5s, and 10s, and *Look Whooo's Counting* (MacDonald, 2000) and *Bats on Parade* (Appelt, 1999) illustrate the sequence of square numbers using numerals as well as arrays. Other books in this category illustrate the concept of equivalence, an important concept for children to understand since it underlies the meaning of the four basic operations and is an essential component of algebraic thinking. Several of the books in this chapter highlight this concept by grouping objects in arrangements that invite readers to count them in different ways. Particularly effective examples include *The Grapes of Math* (Tang, 2001), *Let's Count* (Hoban, 1999), and *1 2 3 Pop!* (Isadora, 1999).

In the category Measurement, Statistics, and Classification, more interdisciplinary connections appear. In *Hannah's Collections* (Jocelyn, 2000), a young girl uses the attributes of shells, leaves, and feathers (as well as a host of other objects) to classify her personal treasures in various ways. *Tiger Math: Learning to Graph from a Baby Tiger* (Nagda & Bickel, 2000) uses a series of pie, line, and bar graphs to tell the true story of a Siberian tiger cub. Several books also highlight a multicultural perspective. *My Rows and Piles of Coins* (Mollel, 1999) describes a young

Tanzanian boy who earns money to buy a bicycle in order to help his mother carry goods to the marketplace. *The Story of Clocks and Calendars* (Maestro, 1999) recognizes the historical contributions of many cultures by describing the inventive ways they kept track of time.

A variety of books about shape and design are included in the category Shapes, Patterns, and Puzzles. An interesting text set would be to pair *Cubes, Cones, Cylinders, & Spheres* (Hoban, 2000) with *Guess Whose Shadow?* (Swinburne, 1999). The former looks at three-dimensional figures, whereas the latter explores the two-dimensional shadows cast by such shapes. Recognizing a diversity of patterns is an essential part of mathematical thinking, and this category illustrates various patterns, such as the changing area pattern of a quilt (Franco, 1999), reversible patterns in the form of palindromes (Agee, 1999), and linear patterns with a repeating core of elements (Harris, 2000).

Mathematics is a sense-making endeavor. It makes sense when it is functional, purposeful, and connected to the lives of children. Incorporating the books in this chapter into the classroom is an excellent way to highlight the relevance of mathematics to daily living.

### Reference

National Council of Teachers of Mathematics. (2000). *Principles and standards for school mathematics.* Reston, VA: Author.

## Counting and Number Operations

**9.1**    Anderson, Lena. **Tea for Ten.** Farrar, Straus & Giroux, 2000. ISBN 91-29-64557-3. Unpaged. (P).

One can be a lonely number as Hedgehog sits home alone, hoping that friends will come by for a visit. One by one friends knock on the door, and a counting book from one to ten unfolds. The layout of the book works well: a rhyming text and entering visitor are shown on the left; the cumulative group of guests is depicted on the right as they gather around the kitchen table sipping tea and eating cookies. The plus-one pattern of the counting numbers is effectively illustrated by each new visitor entering from the left. The growing group of visitors is also shown in smaller subgroups for easier counting. For instance, Hedgehog holds the new visitor Teddy, the duck rests on the dog's shoulder, and the elephant sits on the bench to show that $2 + 2 + 1 = 5$. Soft watercolor illustrations enhance the homey appeal of this inviting counting book. (DW)

**9.2**  Appelt, Kathi. **Bats on Parade.** Illustrated by Melissa Sweet. Morrow, 1999. ISBN 0-688-15665-7. Unpaged. (ALL).

Lively rhyme and comical illustrations invite readers to join the spectators who watch the bats' grand marching band. Each instrumental group marches in neat arrays of consecutive square numbers, culminating with one hundred sousaphones in ten rows of ten. The full assembly of arrays then marches in order across a two-page spread. As the parade ends, the 385 bats take flight, while a mouse below carries a banner that clarifies the sum: $1 + 4 + 9 + 16 + 25 + 36 + 49 + 64 + 81 + 100 = 385$. Throughout the book, younger children can use the illustrations to count the total number of bats in each array. Older students can also compare the area model of multiplication with the set model (i.e., three sets of four wheels each), as well as investigate the many numerical and geometric patterns found in square numbers. (PW)

**9.3**  Brown, Ruth. **Ten Seeds.** Knopf, 2001. ISBN 0-375-80697-0. Unpaged. (P).

Simply told, this delightful subtraction story begs to be read and reread. The collection of ten sunflower seeds on the first page is reduced one by one, either by being consumed by wildlife or being damaged by natural pests, pets, or humans. The one surviving plant, however, successfully produces ten seeds (or more) on the last page. The illustrations, resplendent with lush greens and warm browns, complement the text by adding detail to the story line and providing the context for vocabulary such as *seedlings*, as well as for the scientific information, such as a picture of the shriveled leaves and dying bud on the page that reads, "Two buds . . . too many greenflies." The book is a wonderful addition to a study of the plant cycle, the food chain, and gardening. (PW)

**9.4**  Capucilli, Alyssa Satin. **Mrs. McTats and Her Houseful of Cats.** Illustrated by Joan Rankin. Margaret K. McElderry Books, 2001. ISBN 0-689-83185-4. Unpaged. (P).

Mrs. McTat and her cat Abner live a contented life. But their daily routine is disrupted by the arrival of two cats at her door, followed by three, four, five, and six more, which Mrs. McTat names in alphabetical order. Although the predictable sequence of new groups is interrupted when only four cats appear next, the book concludes in a satisfactory and logical way. The twenty-sixth pet is not a cat, but a puppy named Zoom. Inviting water-color illustrations highlight a range of feline personalities, appearances, and activities, nicely complementing the playful rhymes. The book invites counting, predicting, and adding consecutive numbers and can lead to investigating triangular numbers (1, 3, 6, 10, 15 . . .), an opportunity rarely found in math-related books for young readers. Children might enjoy comparing this book to *The Very Kind Rich Lady and Her One Hundred Dogs* (Candlewick, 2001). (PW)

**9.5**    Cuyler, Margery. **100th Day Worries.** Illustrated by Arthur Howard. Simon & Schuster, 2000. ISBN 0-689-82979-5. Unpaged. (P).

Jessica's classmates have no trouble creating collections for the 100th-day celebration: five bags of twenty peanuts, ten piles of ten paper clips, and four jars of twenty-five peppermints. After much worrying, Jessica solves the problem with her family's help. Her resulting project is an assembly of minicollections. Some represent different combinations for ten, such as six brown, three green and one sparkly rock; others highlight monetary values, such as ten pennies or ten nickels. Jessica ingeniously completes her project by pasting the ten Xs from a note her mother tucked in her lunchbox. Cartoonlike illustrations accentuated by sketchy "worry lines" complement the text. This book begs to be reread for both its story and its wide range of mathematical ideas. A similar book that effectively demonstrates ways to group one hundred objects is Trudy Harris's *100 Days of School* (Millbrook, 1999). (HSK)

**9.6**    Dodds, Dayle Ann. **The Great Divide.** Illustrated by Tracy Mitchell. Candlewick, 1999. ISBN 0-7636-0442-9. Unpaged. (ALL).

A group of eighty racers bolt from the starting line, eager to win the great cross-country race. They encounter several difficulties along the way, however, and the number of racers begins to dwindle. A wide canyon causes the tires of forty racers to pop, while forty others continue on the course. Forty racers soon become twenty as some racers are swirled about in the whirlpools of a river. The pack continues to divide itself, from twenty, to ten, to five. The author cleverly devises a solution for this odd number and concludes the story with an unexpected winner. The simple yet colorful illustrations portray the racers in the bright costumes of queens, clowns, dancers, convicts, and pirates. The story has the potential to generate discussion on such topics as odd and even numbers, symmetry, and division. (TH)

**9.7**    Freymann, Saxton, and Joost Elffers. **One Lonely Seahorse.** Scholastic, 2000. ISBN 0-439-11014-9. 10 pp. (P).

Told in light verse, this story follows a single seahorse as she discovers increasingly larger groups of fellow sea creatures. Close examination shows that every plant and animal is actually composed of something edible. A key at the close of the story reveals their true identities: chloggia beets, a variety of mushroom, ginger, horseradish, and more. In addition, the creatures can be counted by grouping animals in different ways. Ten angelfish (peppers), for example, are composed of four red, four yellow, and two green peppers (4 + 4 + 2). The seven eels (cranberry beans) are physically arranged in groups of four and three. Two of the three puffer fish (horned melons) swim in the foreground, while a third swims in the distance. More than a well-designed counting book, this story easily can lead to investigations of the names, shapes, and textures of produce. (PW)

**9.8**    Guettier, Benedicte. **The Father Who Had 10 Children.** Dial, 1999. ISBN 0-8037-2446-2. Unpaged. (P).

Each day a busy father takes care of ten children. His daily tasks entail counting by ones, twos, fives, and tens as he prepares ten bowls of spaghetti, twenty meatballs, fifty broccoli spears, and one hundred raspberries. Other interesting groupings include two groups of five cereal bowls and two sets of five children as they scurry off to school. A weary father seeks rest from these daily labors. He builds a boat, leaves the children with their grandmother, and sets sail around the world. But this devoted parent soon realizes something is missing and quickly returns home to bring his children on the trip. The childlike drawings and written text, set against stark backgrounds of white or blue, accentuate the preeminent role that children play in the story. This book will invite children to do their own skip-counting of classmates and family members. (DW)

**9.9**    Hendra, Sue. **Numbers.** Candlewick, 1999. ISBN 0-7636-0893-9. Unpaged. (P).

This delightful flip-and-find book follows a predictable pattern. First, an animal poses a question, such as a chimpanzee who asks children to count its fingers. The opposite page contains three flaps with possible answers represented by the numeral, the written word, and an array of the corresponding number of dots. Beneath each flap lies the real treat of the book. Not only is the correct answer confirmed under one flap, but the other choices give additional animal facts or invite readers to count another part of the illustration. Although the answer for a chimpanzee's fingers is ten, the statement under a flap notes that a chimp has two ears to "hear sounds from a long way away." The information under another flap mentions the five berries in the illustration and continues, "I love eating fruit!" Emergent readers will enjoy counting and learning facts about favorite animals. (PW)

9.10   ★ Hoban, Tana. **Let's Count.** Greenwillow, 1999. ISBN 0-688-16008-5. Unpaged. (P).

Similar to her earlier counting book, *Count and See* (Greenwillow, 1972), the author uses color photographs to show numbers one through fifteen, twenty through fifty (by tens), and one hundred. One strength of the book is that each number is represented in several ways: a numeral, a number word, a string of white dots, and a photograph. Each page offers children different ways to count: seven drums can be classified by their size or their placement in space; the number two is shown with other accompanying sets of two, such as two ice cream cones, two napkins, and two hands; and twenty mannequin heads wearing sunglasses can be counted as twenty heads or forty eyes. These multiple opportunities for exploration and discovery make Tana Hoban's books some of the best available for children. (DW)

9.11   Isadora, Rachel. **1 2 3 Pop!** Viking, 2000. ISBN 0-670-88859-1. Unpaged. (ALL).

This bright, vibrant counting book reflects a pop-art style of color and pattern, counting from one through twenty, one hundred, five hundred, one thousand, and finally one million. Although it offers an interesting counting experience for younger children, the book also displays groups of objects for older students to analyze. All square numbers (four, nine, sixteen, one hundred), for instance, are illustrated in square formations of two by two, three by three, and so forth. Triangular numbers are suggested by the fifteen acrobats arranged in descending rows of 1 + 2 + 3 + 4 + 5. Prime numbers are portrayed more subtly because they are not arranged in rows and columns. The symmetry of many even numbers is highlighted by two equal sets, such as two groups of four superheroes. These different groupings of objects can generate discussions about number relationships, opening up many possible number topics to explore. (DW)

**9.12**   ★ Lesser, Carolyn. **Spots: Counting Creatures from Sky to Sea.** Illustrated by Laura Regan. Harcourt Brace, 1999. ISBN 0-15-200666-4. Unpaged. (ALL).

This intriguing counting book integrates mathematics and science in a wondrous way: it counts from one to ten using a variety of creatures whose bodies show unique patterns of spots and who live in ten different biomes. The illustrations add visual information about each biome, such as the verdant tropical forest or the filtered blue light of the open ocean. The brief, poetic language conveys characteristics of each creature, such as the "loping, gazing, nibbling spots" of the reticulated giraffe. The book concludes with horizontal bands of each creature's spots covering a two-page spread, highlighting the beauty and diversity of their patterning. Endnotes provide more information about the animals and biomes. This book invites students of any grade to investigate these creatures and their biomes further and to find other examples of patterning in the natural world. (DW)

**9.13**   MacDonald, Suse. **Look Whooo's Counting.** Scholastic, 2000. ISBN 0-590-68320-9. Unpaged. (ALL).

This seemingly simple book invites a range of explorations. Owl counts different animals she finds in groups from one to ten. Hidden in the illustrations is a surprise: the numerals themselves are contained within the animals' bodies. The curled horns of six sheep, for instance, each show the numeral 6, and the eight-legged spiders have bodies shaped as an 8. On each page, the counting sequence (1, 2, 3, 4, 1, 2, 3, 4 . . .) is found under Owl's outstretched wings. The cut-paper illustrations are silhouetted against a blue background, keeping the text uncluttered and accentuating the shapes of the numerals. Younger children will enjoy counting and finding the numerals, while older children can calculate the sum for each page and investigate the many patterns of square numbers. All ages will be inspired to design alternative animals that hide numerals. (PW)

**9.14** ★ Schmandt-Besserat, Denise. **The History of Counting.** Illustrated by Michael Hays. Morrow, 1999. ISBN 0-688-14118-8. 45 pp. (I).

Eminent archaeologist Denise Schmandt-Besserat introduces readers to the fascinating history of our number system. The strength of the book lies in its recognition of many cultural contributions. The author discusses the counting systems of several peoples, including the Veddas of Sri Lanka, who had only a few general words, such as "a single" and "another one," to communicate quantity. The author also poses the question of why it took thousands of years to invent a system of abstract numbers. Her answer demonstrates that it was not a matter of a particular group's intelligence but rather a matter of need: the rise of cities and the increase of commerce made it necessary to develop more precise systems for counting. This book can provide a basis for investigating various numeration systems in more detail. (DW)

**9.15** Schwartz, David M. **On Beyond a Million: An Amazing Math Journey.** Illustrated by Paul Meisel. Random House, 1999. ISBN 0-385-32217-8. Unpaged. (I).

Once again David Schwartz responds to children's fascination with large numbers in a book inspired by his own classroom demonstrations in which he uses popcorn to illustrate the powers of ten. The lively format invites readers' active participation. Each two-page spread consists of information provided by Professor X and his dog Y; children's questions and observations, all noted in speech bubbles; and sidebars with statistics that provide applications of these large quantities. The benchmark facts include a wide range of topics, from the number of mosquitoes a brown bat consumes per hour (six hundred) to the number of Tootsie Rolls manufactured daily (37 million). Common misconceptions, such as calling "infinity" or "bajillion" numbers, are addressed, although the colloquial term "a trillion" (as opposed to one trillion) is tolerated. This book can be a useful tool to explain exponential notation and to inspire additional statistical research. (PW)

**9.16** ★ Tang, Greg. **The Grapes of Math: Mind-Stretching Math Riddles.** Illustrated by Harry Briggs. Scholastic, 2001. ISBN 0-439-21033-X. Unpaged. (ALL).

Calculating sums strategically becomes a brain-tickling game in this highly engaging collection of math riddles. Strategies follow four basic ideas: (1) group items, such as mentally combining bunches of cherries to make sets of ten; (2) stay open-minded by scanning groups vertically or diagonally rather than horizontally; (3) find patterns and symmetry, such as taking half of a set of mushrooms on a pizza and multiplying by two; and (4) use operations flexibly, such as imagining a complete five-by-seven array of windows and subtracting the ones with no light. To invite multiple solutions to the problems, children might first examine an illustration, compare ideas with peers, and then read Tang's rhymed clues. Endnotes, complete with diagrams, give details about each example. This book could spark a yearlong investigation in which children create their own picture riddles drawn from everyday events. (PW)

9.17    Thorne-Thomsen, Kathleen, and Paul Rocheleau. **A Shaker's Dozen.** Chronicle, 1999. ISBN 0-8118-2299-0. Unpaged. (ALL).

This counting book contains photographs of Shaker life and artifacts as well as a short text and endnotes that provide additional information. Some photographs depict Shaker men, women, and children; others show a wide range of their artifacts, such as tools, brooms, hats, and dolls. One photograph highlights a Shaker home, with a graceful semicircular arch that frames the doorways. Interesting geometric patterns are woven into their handmade rugs. The photographs are set against a white backdrop that accentuates the simple Shaker life while highlighting the detailed precision of their handiwork. This book could spark further research on this fascinating element of U.S. history. (DW)

9.18    Wells, Rosemary. **Emily's First 100 Days of School.** Hyperion, 2000. ISBN 0-868-0507-2. Unpaged. (P).

Over the course of one hundred days, Emily discovers a wide range of uses for numbers in her daily life. Some numbers represent monetary value (twenty-five cents in a quarter), time (six-o'clock is dinner time), or measurement (thirty-six inches in a yard). Other examples show how humans use numbers to organize (street numbers) or to establish conventional groups (a deck of cards). Several examples are arbitrary, such as twenty-eight peas. Although some examples are difficult for young readers to understand (such as forty-five-degree angles), the book can be used to inspire children to hunt for numbers in their lives. Since the story would probably be used as a catalyst for discussion, we recommend not attempting to read it in one sitting. Wells's endearing watercolor illustrations add to the appeal of the story, and bold numbers set in boxes highlight the numerical sequence. (PW)

## Measurement, Statistics, and Classification

**9.19**   Jenkins, Emily. **Five Creatures.** Illustrated by Tomek Bogacki. Farrar, Straus & Giroux, 2001. ISBN 0-374-32341-0. Unpaged. (P).

In this imaginative counting book, a young girl describes the three humans and two cats who live in her house. She cleverly describes these inhabitants in different ways by classifying them according to a variety of attributes. Sometimes humans are grouped together, such as three who can button buttons; sometimes cats form an exclusive set, such as those who eat mice. At other times, humans and animals share a common characteristic, such as four who can open cupboards (two adults, one child, and one ingenious cat!). The book's strength is its flexible use of classification schemes through a variety of comparisons. Although intended for younger students, this book could be used creatively by K–5 teachers to demonstrate the skill of classifying in intriguing ways. (DW)

**9.20**   Jocelyn, Marthe. **Hannah's Collections.** Dutton, 2000. ISBN 0-525-46442-5. Unpaged. (P).

Hannah likes to collect treasures so much that her room "looks like a museum." When faced with the dilemma of which of her many collections to bring to school, Hannah examines each one. The colorful mixed-media collages invite readers to join Hannah in the process. Not only does she have a wide range of objects, such as buttons, used Popsicle sticks, rings, creatures, barrettes, shells, and feathers, but she also arranges each in unique ways. Hannah sorts the buttons by size, shape, and color; arranges the Popsicle sticks in geometric patterns; distributes the five rings on her ten fingers in three ways; and orders the creatures by height. The story ends when Hannah decides to combine several collections to make the first of her "sculpture" collections. The book inspires children to talk about their own collections and to create new ones. (PW)

**9.21**   Maestro, Betsy. **The Story of Clocks and Calendars: Marking a Millennium.** Illustrated by Giulio Maestro. Lothrop, Lee & Shepard, 1999. ISBN 0-688-14548-5. 48 pp. (I).

This informative story demonstrates how the measurement of time developed from human need, how it varied from culture to culture, and how it has changed throughout history. The author explains that although the earliest humans saw time in the changing seasons and the cycles of the moon, sun, and stars, geographical factors influenced variations. The Sumerians, for example, had two seasons, summer and winter, while the Egyptians added a third, the flooding of the Nile. Maestro emphasizes the Christian Gregorian calendar since it's the one most widely used today, but she discusses others as well, such as the Hebrew, Chinese, and Islamic calendars, and mentions briefly the growing debate about modifying the Gregorian calendar to a more inclusive, international form. Generous, colorful illustrations and informative endnotes complement and enrich the historical narrative. (DW)

**9.22**   Mollel, Tololwa M. **My Rows and Piles of Coins.** Illustrated by E. B. Lewis. Clarion, 1999. ISBN 0-395-75186-1. 32 pp. (ALL).

In the country of Tanzania, a young boy named Saruni is saving money to buy a bicycle. He wants to use a bicycle rather than his rickety wheelbarrow to help his mother carry heavy loads of produce to the marketplace. Saruni earns money helping his family at the market, secretly counting and arranging his rows and piles of coins. The repetitive language and the placement of Saruni's growing piles of coins against a white backdrop accentuate his love of and determination to help his family. The warmth of the watercolor illustrations conveys the love of family and the energy of the bustling marketplace. Even after Saruni purchases a bicycle in an unexpected way, he is already saving money to buy a cart to assist his mother further. This story is an invitation to discuss ways to save money to help others in a school community. (DW)

**9.23**   Nagda, Ann Whitehead, and Cindy Bickel. **Tiger Math: Learning to Graph from a Baby Tiger.** Holt, 2000. ISBN 0-8050-6248-3. 29 pp. (ALL).

The story of T. J., a motherless Siberian tiger cub who struggles to survive in a Denver zoo, is told by two parallel means: as a narrative and as a series of graphs. Through the narrative and photographs, readers learn details of veterinary practice and the endearing antics of the growing cub. The graphs complement the text with statistical information such as the population of tigers in the wild, T. J.'s weight compared to his father's, and the number of ounces of meat he consumes. The various graph formats reflect their purposes: line graphs convey change over time, for instance, and circle graphs show part-to-whole relationships. Fourth graders found the graphs readable and informative. They also fell in love with T. J. and wanted to read the book for themselves after hearing it once. (TH)

9.24    ★ Schwartz, David M. **If You Hopped Like a Frog.** Illustrated by James Warhola. Scholastic, 1999. ISBN 0-590-09857-8. Unpaged. (ALL).

Hypothetical comparisons draw readers into this story immediately: "If you hopped like a frog, you could jump from home plate to first base in one mighty leap. / If you were as strong as an ant, you could lift a car." Large, bold illustrations enhance the humorous side of these comparisons. The informative endnotes describe the author's mathematical calculations and invite readers to do some of their own comparing. Readers are challenged, for instance, to discover what they could eat if they ate three times their own body weight (shrew comparison) or what they could see at a distance of fifteen hundred meters (eagle comparison). The text creates in readers not only an awe for and fascination in the natural world, but also an appreciation for how mathematics can help us better understand that world. (TH)

9.25    Sullivan, George. **Any Number Can Play.** Cartoons by Anne Canevari Green. Millbrook, 2000. ISBN 0-7613-1557-8. 64 pp. (I).

Do you know why basketball players rarely wear a jersey number larger than fifty-five? What is the relationship between football players' positions and their jersey numbers? Readers will find the answers to these and related sports trivia questions in this highly entertaining book. Basketball referees, for example, identify a player who fouls with hand signals; number twenty-four is two fingers on the left hand and four on the right. A particularly rib-tickling cartoon pokes fun at a dilemma from the 1950s when George Mikan wore number ninety-nine: a ref is lying on his back, eighteen fingers and toes waving in the air, muttering, "I hate it when Mikan fouls. . . ." Fans will appreciate the many uses of numbers in sports and will be inspired to collect additional facts as well. An index is included. (PW)

## Shapes, Patterns, and Puzzles

9.26    Agee, Jon. **Sit on a Potato Pan, Otis! More Palindromes.** Farrar, Straus & Giroux, 1999. ISBN 0-374-31808-5. Unpaged. (I).

"Eegad, Agee!" He's done it again! The master of palindromes has created his third volume of fascinating phrases that can be read exactly the same forward and backward. The whimsical drawings enhance the humorous appeal of over sixty clever, reversible oddities. Two prison guards commiserate over the loss of an escapee: "We lost a fatso, Lew." A farmer and his wife wonder, "Do geese see god?" And Santa Claus rolls paint on his apartment walls as his wife mutters, "Red? No wonder." This book invites children to create their own palindromes using numbers as well as words. Some numbers are natural palindromes, such as 121 and 55. Others can be changed into palindromes by reversing the digits and adding the two numbers, such as 52 + 25 = 77. Some numbers take more than one reversal. Let children investigate and see for themselves. (DW)

9.27    Fleischman, Paul. **Lost! A Story in String.** Illustrated by C. B. Mordan. Holt, 2000. ISBN 0-8050-5583-5. Unpaged. (I).

When a storm causes the electricity to go out, Grandmother entertains her granddaughter by telling the story of a resourceful young child who survives a blizzard. As she speaks, Grandmother creates a series of string figures to accompany her tale: a gate, a dog's head, the North Star, and five others. As the story ends, the granddaughter realizes that Grandmother is that brave child. Inspired, she takes a string and begins a story of her own. The patterns and lines in the ink-on-clayboard illustrations echo the shapes of Grandmother's fingers and the string. Endnotes give a history of string figures and clear instructions for making each of the figures in the story. After some practice, children can enact the story themselves and then, like the granddaughter, create some of their own. (PW)

9.28    Franco, Betsy. **Grandpa's Quilt.** Illustrated by Linda Bild. Children's Press, 1999. ISBN 0-516-26551-2. 31 pp. (P).

Rarely is a book from a set of easy readers (Rookie Reader) both an appealing story and a mathematical goldmine, but this book is exactly that. Grandpa has a problem: his triangle-and-square patterned quilt doesn't cover his toes. His loving grandchildren snip apart the thirty-six quilt blocks and reassemble them in various ways. They change the geometric design but retain the six-by-six-square shape. Only when they place the blocks in a four-by-nine array is Grandpa completely covered. By reenacting the story with paper squares and triangles, children can prove for themselves that while the area of a rectangle remains constant, the perimeter can change. They can explore factors for thirty-six as well as factors for other composite numbers. The illustrations may also inspire children to create quilt designs using the same (or different) quantities of squares and triangles depicted in the book. (PW)

**9.29**  Harris, Trudy. **Pattern Fish.** Illustrated by Anne Canevari Green. Millbrook, 2000. ISBN 0-7613-1712-0. Unpaged. (P).

Each sea creature or plant and every set of sounds or movements illustrates a basic pattern for children to discover. Here, borders of color give clues to the pattern featured on the double-page spreads. One page, for example, shows a border of green and pink, following the AABB pattern. The illustration depicts a sea horse decorated with an AABB pattern of yellow and blue, and the text reads, "chomp-chomp-munch-munch" as the seahorse nibbles seaweed growing in groups of short, short, tall, tall blades. When a shark appears, the six differently patterned creatures disperse, leaving the shark to splash-turn-swish-dive (ABCD) on its own. The book is a natural invitation for children to find patterns in the sights, movements, and sounds around them and to invent their own. Endnotes explain the conventional notation of patterns without being overly didactic. (MR)

**9.30**  Hoban, Tana. **Cubes, Cones, Cylinders, & Spheres.** Greenwillow, 2000. ISBN 0-688-15325-9. 24 pp. (ALL).

Colorful photographs invite readers to find different shapes in their environment. The diversity of objects is one of the book's strengths: cones are shown as hats, bushes, and roofs; spheres appear as bubbles, lights, and hot air balloons; cylinders become smokestacks and drums; and cubes are depicted as blocks and dice. In addition to the identification of shapes, this book may invite other mathematical discussions. Rugs and hay are shown as rolled-up cylinders, so children might investigate other ways to transform shapes. The photograph of sugar cubes in a jar might prompt a discussion of volume. The open-ended nature of this book makes it appealing for all ages. (DW)

**9.31** Luciani, Brigitte. **How Will We Get to the Beach?** Illustrated by Eve Tharlet. North-South, 2000. ISBN 0-7358-1268-3. 28 pp. (P).

Readers are invited to play a guessing game as a mother decides to go to the beach with her baby and four objects: a turtle, an umbrella, a thick book, and a ball. When her car will not start, she tries various modes of transportation to get to the beach. Each time she is unsuccessful in bringing all her objects along. She tries a bus, for example, but the turtle is not allowed on the bus. She tries a bike, but the ball will not fit on the bike. A farmer and his cart finally come to the rescue. The predictable format encourages young readers to guess which object will not be able to go on the trip. The illustrations are uncluttered and depict each scene across the two-page spread. They also effectively highlight the part-to-whole relationship of five objects separated into the subsets of four and one. (HSK)

**9.32** Swinburne, Stephen R. **Guess Whose Shadow?** Boyds Mills, 1999. ISBN 1-56397-724-9. Unpaged. (P).

"Your shadow can be behind you, below you, or next to you," states this photo-essay for young readers. Captions explain how shadows form, and photographs illustrate their varied size, position, and shape. One photograph shows large shadowy branches of a tree framing two small children at a water fountain; another depicts the spindly form of a spider casting delicate curved shadows on a leaf. Several pages invite children to play a shadow guessing game and to discover the answers by turning the page. A foreword gives more detailed scientific information. Children will enjoy experimenting with their own shadows, finding interesting shapes, and measuring shadows as they change in length and direction. Teachers might use the book as a model to follow as children create their own class photo-essay of shadow riddles. (PW)

**9.33** Wyatt, Valerie. **The Math Book for Girls and Other Beings Who Count.** Illustrated by Pat Cupples. Kids Can Press, 2000. ISBN 1-55074-830-0. 64 pp. (I).

A modern-day fairy godmother who uses math and science instead of a magic wand leads readers into a variety of mathematical puzzles and activities. Investigations include using one's own body parts as measures, creating three-dimensional shapes, playing with patterns, and devising secret-code invitations. The key strength of the book lies in its connection of a particular mathematical topic with the occupations of women in the real world. After readers are invited to explore the concept of probability using coins and dice, for instance, the author introduces a wildlife biologist who discusses how she uses probability to estimate the size of a caribou herd. A financial advisor examines the importance of graphs in her work, and an environmental engineer shows how she uses the concept of area to determine the amount of contaminated soil in a polluted region. This is a readable, accessible, and engaging book. (DW)

9.34    Zaslavsky, Claudia. **Number Sense and Nonsense.** Chicago Press, 2001. ISBN 1-55652-378-5. 140 pp. (I).

Readers are introduced to a variety of mathematical topics in this inviting and appealing book that exemplifies NCTM's *Principles and Standards for School Mathematics* (2000). Sections include odd and even numbers, prime and composite numbers, money and other measures, riddles, puzzles, and calculator tricks. A strong and vibrant multicultural strand runs throughout the book as well. Readers learn about other numeration systems, a Liberian stone game, a brief history of zero, the Egyptian method of division, and historical figures such as Carl Friedrich Gauss, the great German mathematician, and Tom Fuller, an African American slave brought to America in 1724. Each section concludes with a "Try this" paragraph that invites readers to explore and extend the topics presented. The emphasis is on sense-making strategies that require reasoning and explaining. (DW)

# **10** Poetry

**Amy A. McClure**

*Contributing reviewers included Joan C. Bownas, Lisa A. Dapoz, Karen Hildebrand, Peggy S. Oxley, Lillian B. Webb, and Linda A. Woolard.*

---

**Criteria for Excellence**

- Provides examples of excellent poetic crafting: fresh use of language, inventive comparisons, unusual perspectives, effective rhyming (if rhymed verse)
- Appeals to children yet extends their taste of what is "good" poetry
- Contains content related to children's lives

---

### Nature

Baird, Audrey. **Storm Coming!** Illustrated by Patrick O'Brien. Boyds Mills, 2001.

Florian, Douglas. **Winter Eyes.** Greenwillow, 1999.

★ Graham, Joan Bransfield. **Flicker Flash.** Illustrated by Nancy Davis. Houghton Mifflin, 1999.

★ Johnston, Tony. **An Old Shell: Poems of the Galápagos.** Illustrated by Tom Pohrt. Farrar, Straus & Giroux, 1999.

Nye, Naomi Shihab. **Salting the Ocean: 100 Poems by Young Poets.** Illustrated by Ashley Bryan. Greenwillow, 2000.

Paolilli, Paul, and Dan Brewer. **Silver Seeds: A Book of Nature Poems.** Illustrated by Steve Johnson and Lou Fancher. Viking, 2001.

★ Schertle, Alice. **A Lucky Thing.** Illustrated by Wendell Minor. Harcourt Brace, 1999.

Schnur, Steven. **Summer: An Alphabet Acrostic.** Illustrated by Leslie Evans. Clarion, 2001.

★ Siebert, Diane. **Cave.** Illustrated by Wayne McLoughlin. HarperCollins, 2000.

★ Van Laan, Nancy. **When Winter Comes.** Illustrated by Susan Gaber. Atheneum, 2000.

Yolen, Jane. **Color Me a Rhyme: Nature Poems for Young People.** Photographs by Jason Stemple. Boyds Mills, 2000.

### People

Chaconas, Dori. **On a Wintry Morning.** Illustrated by Stephen T. Johnson. Viking, 2000.

George, Kristine O'Connell. **Toasting Marshmallows.** Illustrated by Kate Kiesler. Clarion, 2001.

Yolen, Jane, and Heidi E. Y. Stemple. **Dear Mother, Dear Daughter.** Illustrated by Gil Ashby. Boyds Mills, 2001.

### Animals

Chapman, Nancy Kapp. **Doggie Dreams.** Illustrated by Lee Chapman. Putnam, 2000.

★ George, Kristine O'Connell. **Little Dog Poems.** Illustrated by June Otani. Clarion, 1999.

Harrison, David L. **Farmer's Garden: Rhymes for Two Voices.** Illustrated by Arden Johnson-Petrov. Boyds Mills, 2000.

Johnston, Tony. **It's about Dogs.** Illustrated by Ted Rand. Harcourt, 2000.

Lewis, J. Patrick. **Good Mousekeeping: And Other Animal Home Poems.** Illustrated by Lisa Desimini. Atheneum, 2001.

Schertle, Alice. **I Am the Cat.** Illustrated by Mark Buehner. Lothrop, Lee & Shepard, 1999.

Seeber, Dorthea P. **A Pup Just for Me; a Boy Just for Me.** Illustrated by Ed Young. Philomel, 2000.

Yolen, Jane. **How Do Dinosaurs Say Goodnight?** Illustrated by Mark Teague. Scholastic, 2000.

### Curricular Connections

Grimes, Nikki. **Is It Far to Zanzibar? Poems about Tanzania.** Illustrated by Betsy Lewin. Lothrop, Lee & Shepard, 2000.

★ Hopkins, Lee Bennett, selector. **My America: A Poetry Atlas of the United States.** Illustrated by Stephen Alcorn. Simon & Schuster, 2000.

Hopkins, Lee Bennett, selector. **Spectacular Science: A Book of Poems.** Illustrated by Virginia Halstead. Simon & Schuster, 1999.

★ Katz, Bobbi. **We the People.** Illustrated by Nina Crews. HarperCollins, 2000.

Michelson, Richard. **Ten Times Better.** Illustrated by Leonard Baskin. Marshall Cavendish, 2000.

### Fresh Perspectives on Ordinary Things

Adoff, Arnold. **Touch the Poem.** Illustrated by Lisa Desimini. Scholastic, 2000.

★ Grimes, Nikki. **A Pocketful of Poems.** Illustrated by Javaka Steptoe. Clarion, 2001.

Grimes, Nikki. **Shoe Magic.** Illustrated by Terry Widener. Orchard, 2000.

★ Hopkins, Lee Bennett, selector. **Yummy! Eating through a Day.** Illustrated by Renée Flower. Simon & Schuster, 2000.

Nye, Naomi Shihab. **Come with Me: Poems for a Journey.** Illustrated by Dan Yaccarino. Greenwillow, 2000.

Stevenson, James. **Candy Corn: Poems.** Greenwillow, 1999.

Stevenson, James. **Cornflakes: Poems.** Greenwillow, 2000.

Stevenson, James. **Just around the Corner: Poems.** Greenwillow, 2001.

Willard, Nancy. **The Moon & Riddles Diner and the Sunnyside Café.** Illustrated by Chris Butler. Harcourt, 2001.

Wong, Janet S. **Night Garden.** Illustrated by Julie Paschkis. Margaret K. McElderry Books, 2000.

## Sports

★ Smith, Charles R. Jr. **Short Takes: Fast-Break Basketball Poetry.** Dutton, 2001.

Thayer, Ernest Lawrence. **Casey at the Bat: A Ballad of the Republic Sung in the Year 1888.** Illustrated by Christopher Bing. Handprint, 2000.

---

Children are naturally drawn to poetry. They love the rhythms of jump rope rhymes, advertising jingles, and rap music. As teachers and librarians, we can capitalize on this enthusiasm and help children develop a taste for poetry that goes beyond superficial verse to pieces that stretch their imaginations and increase their appreciation for inventive language use. We can do this by exploring poetry naturally through talk and reflection, examining what has touched children emotionally, what has caused curiosity or joy, and what has led a group of children to catch their breath in wonder.

Our committee examined virtually every poetry book published between 1999 and 2001, searching for the collections that best exemplified poetic writing but also appealed to children. During our monthly meetings, we discussed which books were instant hits and which ones took some teacher encouragement to capture a group's interest. We also found some collections that were initially popular but eventually lost their appeal because there wasn't enough "meat" to sustain interest. Thus, children's preferences and interests were central to our decisions about what should be annotated in this chapter. We strongly believed, however, that only collections of well-crafted poetry should be included, so if a book appealed to children but wasn't good poetry, it was eliminated.

Our final list of books seemed to fall naturally into several categories, supporting research on children's poetry preferences that suggests children prefer poetry about nature, animals, familiar everyday situations, and people. They tend to dislike esoteric, free verse poetry with subtle, abstract imagery. But we also found that we could expand their taste for more complex poetry by sharing it enthusiastically and taking time to explore why these poems were more interesting and pleasing to the ear. To our delight, children returned again and again to the complex poems as they learned to appreciate their subtleties. Sharing high-quality poetry that focused on appealing topics seemed to be the key.

Following are the categories for our favorite collections:

- *Nature:* From geographic regions to plant life to seasons, we found nature to be a perennially popular topic in poetry. Children responded eagerly to poetic descriptions of the natural world, frequently writing their own poetic descriptions of the world they themselves observed.

- *People:* Our children enjoyed a wide range of poetry about families, friends, and familiar experiences such as camping out or taking a winter walk. They could easily identify with the mother-daughter conflicts in Jane Yolen and Heidi Stemple's *Dear Mother, Dear Daughter* (2001), the snuggly, warm feeling of sitting around the campfire as described in *Toasting Marshmallows* (George, 2001), and the joy of special time with a parent in *On a Wintry Morning* (Chaconas, 2000).

- *Animals:* Animal poems are very popular with children. Our students particularly enjoyed the dog poetry; something about it sparked their interest and enthusiasm. (We have to admit we particularly enjoyed them too!) Yet they also were intrigued by the unusual imagery in *Good Mousekeeping* (Lewis, 2001), the humorous descriptions in Nancy Kapp Chapman's *Doggie Dreams* (2000), and the mysterious, sensual language of Alice Schertle's *I Am the Cat* (1999).

- *Curricular Connections:* We are always looking for ways to integrate poetry into the academic curriculum. The books we selected do this successfully. Lee Bennett Hopkins's *My America* (2000), for example, takes readers on a poetic journey across the United States. Richard Michelson's *Ten Times Better* (2000) mixes mathematical concepts and poetry. Nikki Grimes in *Is It Far to Zanzibar? Poems about Tanzania* (2000) provides a lively glimpse of an African country, about which we might previously have shared only dry facts.

- *Fresh Perspectives on Ordinary Things:* One of the special delights of reading poetry is that it can help us see our world in new ways. Poetry breaks up our conventional perceptions, opening up new views on our everyday lives. We found that, with some gentle encouragement, children found delight in this quality of poetry. Comments such as "I never thought of it like this before" and "Wow, what a neat description" were common when we shared the books in this section. From unusual descriptions of shoes in *Shoe Magic* (Grimes, 2000) to comparisons of hot and cold sand in *Touch the Poem* (Adoff, 2000), we found that the collections in this category sparked children's imaginations.

- *Sports:* Today's children are vitally interested in sports. Sharing sports poetry is a guaranteed way to encourage children's enthusiasm for the genre.

## Nature

**10.1**   Baird, Audrey. **Storm Coming!** Illustrated by Patrick O'Brien. Boyds Mills, 2001. ISBN 1-56397-887-3. 32 pp. (ALL).

How do you know a storm is coming? The barometer falls, thunder rumbles, "churning clouds with heavy eyebrows brush the skies," and Grandpa's toe aches. Soon lightning "sparks fly / from a giant's hobnailed boots" (p. 18) and thunder rolls in an "avalanche of sound" (p. 17). This collection uses simple, child-like imagery to describe an impending storm, its eruption into full force, and the quiet aftermath of puddles, rainbows, and that special smell of "wet bark, . . . soft, smooshy grass / and black / garden dirt" (p. 32). O'Brien's soft watercolor washes aptly reflect how the day becomes dark and then light as the storm subsides. We found that children were drawn to the images described in this book, inevitably making comparisons with their own rainy day experiences. The topic's universal appeal, along with the relatively unsophisticated imagery, makes this collection particularly useful for children who have had limited exposure to poetry. Teachers can pair these poems with those found in other collections about rain, such as Carolyn Lesser's *Storm on the Desert* (Harcourt Brace, 1997) and Thomas Locker's *Water Dance* (Harcourt Brace, 1997). (AAM)

**10.2**   Florian, Douglas. **Winter Eyes.** Greenwillow, 1999. ISBN 0-688-16458-7. 48 pp. (ALL).

Florian treats readers to a sophisticated variety of winter imagery, allowing them to appreciate all the pluses and minuses of this cold and sometimes dreary season and treating us to examples of ways in which winter assails our senses. In "Sled," a concrete poem, Florian depicts the work and then the reward of this often long-awaited winter activity. "Sugaring Time" could be read as an apt accompaniment to Kathryn Lasky's informational book of the same title (Macmillan, 1988) and to Jessie Haas's *Sugaring* (Greenwillow, 1996). Children will particularly like the pair of poems contrasting our love-hate relationship with winter. Florian's simple watercolor-and-colored-pencil illustrations add to but do not overpower the beauty of his vivid sensory descriptions. (LBW)

10.3    ★ Graham, Joan Bransfield. **Flicker Flash.** Illustrated by Nancy Davis. Houghton Mifflin, 1999. ISBN 0-395-90501-X. Unpaged. (ALL).

In *Flicker Flash,* Joan Bransfield Graham's concrete poems on light explode across the page into luminescent rhyme. Nancy Davis's bright, whimsical pictures are perfect for these twenty-three verses lapped in descriptive energy, ready to ignite your mind and "solar power you out of your bed." Mimicking the hard edge of cut paper and exhibiting flushes of color that seem lightly applied, Davis's harmonious illustrations aptly reflect Graham's word images, which bounce off the tip of the tongue— "Spotlight hot light / Give-it-all-you-got light / Wow light now light / Time to take a bow light." Students enjoyed acting out the poems as well as creating their own concrete and descriptive poetry. (LAW)

10.4    ★ Johnston, Tony. **An Old Shell: Poems of the Galápagos.** Illustrated by Tom Pohrt. Farrar, Straus & Giroux, 1999. ISBN 0-374-35648-3. 54 pp. (I).

Johnston traveled to the Galápagos Islands in 1995 and felt moved to write these paeans to the animals, plants, geological formations, and history of these unique islands. Each poem focuses on an individual creature and its relationship to its universe. The poems are beautiful in and of themselves, and together they constitute a hymn of praise to this strange and fragile environment. The sensitively delivered environmental message is never didactic. Rather, Johnston urges us to revere the islands, learn from them, and leave them unharmed. Using a variety of poetic forms, Johnston captures the essence of the islands' flora and fauna. Historical allusions in several poems and the author's note about the history of the island could lead students to further investigation. The gray-toned illustrations enhance without overpowering the text. (LBW)

★ Kurtz, Jane. **River Friendly, River Wild.** Illustrated by Neil Brennan. Simon & Schuster, 2000. ISBN 0-689-82049-6. Unpaged. (I). (See **5.25.**)

10.5 Nye, Naomi Shihab. **Salting the Ocean: 100 Poems by Young Poets.** Illustrated by Ashley Bryan. Greenwillow, 2000. ISBN 0-688-16193-6. 111 pp. (I).

Naomi Nye collected these poems from her students twenty-five years ago when she was a writer-in-residence at schools throughout the country. The poets were in grades 1 through 12, although grade levels are not listed. The poems are free verse and deal with worries, feelings, memories, and people in the lives of the writers. The title poem, for example, tells of childhood visits to the ocean. The poet's mother would take a salt-shaker and salt the ocean each time. He writes, "Now that I know my mother isn't responsible for the salty ocean / It takes some of the fun out of going to the beach" (inside cover). Nye includes anecdotes from her teaching days in the index. Students who enjoy reading thoughtful poetry written by others their age will find this a welcome anthology. (JCB)

10.6 Paolilli, Paul, and Dan Brewer. **Silver Seeds: A Book of Nature Poems.** Illustrated by Steve Johnson and Lou Fancher. Viking, 2001. ISBN 0-670-88941-5. Unpaged. (P).

These teams of writers and artists have created a beautiful book of simple acrostic poems, taking the reader from sunrise through the day to dark of night. Each is composed of a single metaphoric sentence that describes a concept. The poems are arranged on double-page spreads containing full-color illustrations with the word floating across the pages. Clouds are compared to "Creamy scoops of ice cream," while fog is "Folds and folds of spun sugar." The title of the book refers to a poem about stars: "Silver seeds / Tossed in the air." The images created by the harmony of the words and the pictures are easily grasped by younger children and could serve as models for their own writing. (LBW)

10.7 ★ Schertle, Alice. **A Lucky Thing.** Illustrated by Wendell Minor. Harcourt Brace, 1999. ISBN 0-15-200541-2. 32 pp. (I).

The first and last poems in this book create a set of bookends about the process of writing poetry. They enclose the remainder of the poems, images of nature that the writer views from the window of her barn/studio. In "The Barn," Schertle compares an old creaking barn first to a ship riding out a storm at night and later, as the sun rises, to a beached wreck. She completes the metaphor by describing "the stamping, snorting voyagers" exiting "two by two." The title poem tells of a robin who envies chickens in a coop being fed by a farmer, while the chickens envy the robin its freedom. A mole invites the reader to "come on down" and "wear the earth like a glove." Each of Wendell Minor's realistic yet dreamy watercolor illustrations includes the image of a piece of paper or a writing tool, suggesting that ideas for poems are present everywhere for those who are observant. (LBW)

10.8    Schnur, Steven. **Summer: An Alphabet Acrostic.** Illustrated by Leslie Evans. Clarion, 2001. ISBN 0-618-02372-0. Unpaged. (ALL).

As in the companion books about autumn and spring, Schnur here takes us on an alphabetic journey through the season with pithy acrostic poems that travel right to the heart of each subject. Evans's colorful linoleum-cut illustrations double the treat for the reader. A unique feature of these poems is that for the most part they are composed of one sentence, which contains words that begin with each of the letters of the subject. For the subject "daisy," "Dragonflies dart / And hover, / Inspecting white flowers with / Sunlike / Yellow centers." Students from second grade through the intermediate grades will be able to use Schnur's technique and higher-level thinking skills to describe both theme-related objects and book characters. A fifth grader, for example, responded to the historical fiction title *Brady* by Jean Fritz (Coward, McCann & Geoghegan, 1960) by writing the following acrostic in Schnur's style: "Being friends with / Range is hard when you don't want / Animals to / Die / Young." (LBW)

10.9    ★ Siebert, Diane. **Cave.** Illustrated by Wayne McLoughlin. HarperCollins, 2000. ISBN 0-688-16447-1. Unpaged. (I).

Diane Siebert is a master at revealing the secrets of the natural world in evocative poetry for children. This book is no exception. Here she describes the geologic formations, inhabitants, and characteristics of limestone caves in rhythmic lines that bring children into the heart and soul of these fascinating places: "I am the cave, / cool and dark / Where time unending leaves its mark / As natural forces build and hone / A crystal world from weeping stone." Because everything is described from the "first-person" perspective of the cave, readers come to know intimately its innermost secrets as they explore its depths. We found that although the vocabulary is at times quite advanced (due to its scientific accuracy), children were spellbound by the rhythmic, almost sensuous poetry and the beautiful acrylic paintings, which work together to convey meaning. This is an excellent companion to nonfiction cave books such as Gail Gibbons's *Caves and Caverns* (Harcourt Brace, 1993), Jenny Wood's *Cave* (Puffin, 1990), and Larry Brimner's *Caves* (Children's Press, 2000), as well as *Heartland* (Crowell, 1989) and *Mojave* (Crowell, 1988), Siebert's other poetic essays on the natural world. (AAM)

10.10  ★ Van Laan, Nancy. **When Winter Comes.** Illustrated by Susan Gaber. Atheneum, 2000. ISBN 0-689-81778-9. 36 pp. (P).

As this poem is read aloud, children just naturally join in on the repeated refrain, "Where oh where do all the leaves [various animals, songbirds, fish, etc.] go / When winter comes and the cold winds blow?" Depicted in luminous acrylic paintings on bristol board, two loving parents walk with their child and small dog through a hushed and lovely landscape on a snowy day, seeking the winter resting places of nature's creations. Authentic information is presented as the family moves along under a gentle fall of snowflakes until at last they return home, where the parents tuck *their* little one "In a warm, warm bed / . . . ," soon to be "Snuggling deep. / Fast asleep." This marriage of beautiful artwork and inviting poetry draws attentive response from young listeners, who inevitably say, "Please read it again!" (PSO)

10.11  Yolen, Jane. **Color Me a Rhyme: Nature Poems for Young People.** Photographs by Jason Stemple. Boyds Mills, 2000. ISBN 1-56397-892-X. 32 pp. (ALL).

Jane Yolen has teamed again with son Jason Stemple to create *Color Me a Rhyme.* For each of the thirteen included colors there is a harmonious double-paged spread. Stemple's photographs of nature's patterns were the catalysts for Yolen's free verse, which features a color quote on one side of the page and five words of different intensity for each hue on the other side. All of this inspires students to delve deeper into their word palettes to create clarity of emotion and understanding as they write. A favorite of my third-grade students was Stemple's pink thistle photograph matched to Yolen's "A surge of sunlight / Shocks through stem and thistle hairs. A punk pink hairdo" (p. 19). Just as Yolen selected from Stemple's photos to fashion her poems, students can generate their own writings from photos or direct observations of nature. (LAW)

## People

★ Alarcón, Francisco X. **Angels Ride Bikes and Other Fall Poems/Los ángeles andan en bicicleta.** Illustrated by Maya Christina Gonzalez. Children's Book Press, 1999. ISBN 0-89239-160-X. 32 pp. (ALL). (See **17.11.**)

10.12  Chaconas, Dori. **On a Wintry Morning.** Illustrated by Stephen T. Johnson. Viking, 2000. ISBN 0-670-89245-9. Unpaged. (P).

"Daddy, take the baby out / Take the bonny baby out. / Show the baby all about, / On a wintry morning." This rhythmic, repetitive book describes a father and baby outing on a cold and snowy day. From bundling up, through snowy adventures, to the warmth of returning to a cozy nap, the patterns of this poem were noticed immediately by second graders, who joined in on repeated refrains from the beginning to "Sleep for now, and very soon / We'll share a wintry afternoon." Watercolor and pastel paintings contribute richly to this charming story poem. Comparing it with Douglas Florian's poems in *Winter Eyes* (Greenwillow, 1999; **10.2**) and Nancy Van Laan's in *When Winter Comes* (Atheneum, 2000; **10.10**), the children embraced this poem as a favorite paean to winter. (PSO)

10.13  George, Kristine O'Connell. **Toasting Marshmallows.** Illustrated by Kate Kiesler. Clarion, 2001. ISBN 0-618-04597-X. 48 pp. (ALL).

Embark on a family camping adventure with these twenty-nine free verse and rhyming poems. Share George's wonderfully descriptive metaphors, as in "Sleeping Bag": "I'm a caterpillar in a cozy cloth cocoon that zips" (p. 10). From pitching the tent, toasting marshmallows, feeling warm around the campfire, skipping stones, sleeping under the stars, to being back home with great memories of the trip, Kate Kiesler's rich acrylic paintings set the reader right inside the woods, hillsides, and meadows detailed in the poems. Hike, watch, and listen to George's lyrical thoughts: "The best paths / are whispers / in the grass / . . . hide themselves / until the right / someone / comes along / . . . lead you / to where / you didn't know / you wanted to go" (p. 13). Not only will students be able to share their own camping and nature adventures but, after reading this book, they also will be enriched by the author's poetic insights. (LAW)

Grimes, Nikki. **My Man Blue: Poems.** Illustrated by Jerome Lagarrigue. Dial, 1999. ISBN 0-8037-2326-1. Unpaged. (P). (See **15.13.**)

★ Medina, Jane. **My Name Is Jorge on Both Sides of the River: Poems.** Illustrated by Fabricio Vanden Broeck. Boyds Mills, 1999. ISBN 1-563-97811-3. 48 pp. (ALL). (See **5.9.**)

★ Mora, Pat. **Love to Mamá: A Tribute to Mothers.** Illustrated by Paula S. Barragán M. Lee & Low, 2001. ISBN 1-58430-019-1. Unpaged. (ALL). (See **17.18.**)

Wong, Janet S. **The Rainbow Hand: Poems about Mothers and Children.** Illustrated by Jennifer Hewitson. Simon & Schuster, 1999. ISBN 0-689-82148-4. Unpaged. (ALL). (See **4.9.**)

10.14 Yolen, Jane, and Heidi E. Y. Stemple. **Dear Mother, Dear Daughter.** Illustrated by Gil Ashby. Boyds Mills, 2001. ISBN 1-56397-886-5. 40 pp. (I).

This is the perfect book for middle school girls and their mothers because it encourages them to communicate with each other. Jane Yolen and Heidi Stemple, who are mother and daughter, express their thoughts in companion poems on universal adolescent issues and concerns such as the death of a grandparent, a crush, phone privileges, gym excuses, and boredom. The daughter initiates each concern, and the mother responds. The authors acknowledge that communicating by writing a poem about a problem can often be more helpful than talking, since it helps keep emotions from interfering with resolving the situation. (JCB)

## Animals

**10.15**   Chapman, Nancy Kapp. **Doggie Dreams.** Illustrated by Lee Chapman. Putnam, 2000. ISBN 0-399-23443-8. Unpaged. (P).

"Some dogs dream as people do— / Hard to believe, and yet it's true!" So begins this rollicking collection of poems describing dogs and people in reversed positions—e.g., dogs in restaurants, people not allowed; dogs on buses for hounds only; and dogs daring and heroic, objects of human admiration and devotion. These shaped and rhythmic poems are the delight of primary grade children who relish the humorous juxtapositions and are intrigued by the accompanying oil-on-canvas paintings ("with the occasional dog hair mixed in"). Second graders had fun comparing and contrasting this book with Tony Johnston's *It's about Dogs* (Harcourt, 2000; **10.18**), Jack Prelutsky's *Dog Days: Rhymes around the Year* (Random House, 2001), and Kristine O'Connell George's *Little Dog Poems* (Clarion, 1999; **10.16**) and imagining that "when dogs dream / . . . they just may be / Very much like you and me." (PSO)

★ Florian, Douglas. **Lizards, Frogs, and Polliwogs: Poems and Paintings.** Harcourt, 2001. ISBN 0-15-202591-X. 48 pp. (ALL). (See **13.15.**)

**10.16**   ★ George, Kristine O'Connell. **Little Dog Poems.** Illustrated by June Otani. Clarion, 1999. ISBN 0395-82266-1. 40 pp. (P).

In this book of gentle poems, we go through the day with Little Dog, from early morning when he wakes his little girl with his "Cold Nose" to "Bedtime." Between dawn and dusk, Little Dog's adventures include an encounter with his "Enemy," a poem in which he barks and chases until finally "the vacuum cleaner learns its lesson" (p. 7). Second graders compared this particular poem with Sylvia Cassedy's "Vacuum Cleaner" from *Zoomrimes: Poems about Things That Go* (HarperCollins, 1993). In "Morning Nap," when Little Dog curls up to become "exactly the same size as the sunny spot" (p. 11), they also noted how similar he was to Valerie Worth's cat, who in "Sun" from *All the Small Poems and Fourteen More* (Farrar, Straus & Giroux, 1994) curls up in "warm yellow squares on the floor" (p. 9). In easy-to-read format with lovely watercolors, this book is a delight for primary children. After reading it, they particularly enjoy creating their own poems about "little dog" adventures. (PSO)

**10.17** Harrison, David L. **Farmer's Garden: Rhymes for Two Voices.** Illustrated by Arden Johnson-Petrov. Boyds Mills, 2000. ISBN 1-56397-776-1. Unpaged. (P).

David Harrison has written a rhythmic "read-it-again" book of conversations between a farm dog and inhabitants of the farmer's garden. The dog asks two or three questions of each animal and vegetable he encounters. Most of the poems are similar in rhythm and form and follow this example: "Beetle, Beetle why so fast? / Out of my way! I must get past! / Beetle, Beetle where do you run? / Away from Lizard / and out of the sun." The illustrator's own dog is delightfully drawn in pastels. Primary children enjoy memorizing and reciting these poems, as well as creating similar poems about other farm animals. (JCB)

**10.18** Johnston, Tony. **It's about Dogs.** Illustrated by Ted Rand. Harcourt, 2000. ISBN 0-15-202022-5. 48 pp. (ALL).

*It's about Dogs* is a wonderful marriage between Tony Johnston's poetically described memories of, recollections about, and evocations of dogs and Ted Rand's brilliant watercolor illustrations that leap from the pages directly into readers' hearts. The poems evoke "oohs" and "aahs" when read aloud to both children and adults. "Shadow," a parody of the lead-in to a radio program of the 1940s, causes adults to laugh aloud, while children understand the humor and frustration caused by the Labrador who hides all manner of treasures. Children were particularly enthralled by "Spell," with its double-page illustration of a pleading dog peeking from underneath a checkered tablecloth. This lovable pet communicates "Feed me" with his "unblinking eyes" (p. 13). After experiencing Johnston's poems about all manner of dogs, students will be eager to write their own pet tributes. (LBW)

**10.19** Lewis, J. Patrick. **Good Mousekeeping: And Other Animal Home Poems.** Illustrated by Lisa Desimini. Atheneum, 2001. ISBN 0-689-83161-7. Unpaged. (P).

J. Patrick Lewis poses this thought-provoking question to animals: "Where would you stay . . . just for a day?" Their answers, describing their perfect homes, are delightfully illustrated and explained. Lisa Desimini's whimsical artwork enhances Lewis's rich and clever language: "Oh, where would a flamingo go? / She'd go to a Flamingalow, / A flaming hot pink bungalow /

Beside the steamy jungle-o." Desimini paints the Flamingolow
bright orange with a feathered roof and long, leglike stilts over
the water. Fittingly, the dragon's home is equipped with a smoke
alarm, and the skunk's home is constructed with fragrant flowers. This book is sure to be a favorite and to spark children's
imaginations about their favorite animals' dream homes. (LAD)

10.20    Schertle, Alice. **I Am the Cat.** Illustrated by Mark Buehner.
         Lothrop, Lee & Shepard, 1999. ISBN 0-688-13153-0. Unpaged.
         (ALL).

Exquisite word pictures abound in this book as the poems shift
from reality to myth and back. One poem tells of the flying cat's
fall from grace after drinking the moon, thus explaining the cat's
white chin and its aristocratic, proud personality. "Sophie, Who
Taunted the Dogs," a four-page detailed narrative, has a surprise
ending. The full-page humorous illustrations show the historical
importance of the cat in Egypt and the many situations a cat
encounters throughout the day. Close inspection of each page
will uncover hidden animals. Children with cats will identify
with the cats' behavior and have similar stories to share about
their own pets. This is a good book to compare with Lois Duncan's *I Walk at Night* (Viking, 2000), which features a cat reflecting on its past. (JCB)

10.21    Seeber, Dorthea P. **A Pup Just for Me; a Boy Just for Me.** Illus-
         trated by Ed Young. Philomel, 2000. ISBN 0-399-23403-9. (P).

Dorthea Seeber has created two heartfelt stories about a dog and
a boy who find each other. Starting from one end of the book, she
tells the story from the dog's point of view. From the other end,
the boy's search for the perfect pet evolves. Both stories end
simultaneously in the middle of the book. This poetry/story
book fascinated my students because of its unique upside-down,
two-books-in-one format. The children commented that it really
doesn't matter which side is read first. After the initial reading,
they immediately asked me to read it again, starting with the
other side. Ed Young's bold and simple paper collage illustrations emphasize the range of both human and dog emotions,
from loneliness to joy. The unique format inspired some students
to try writing their own "upside-down" books. (LAD)

10.22    Yolen, Jane. **How Do Dinosaurs Say Goodnight?** Illustrated by
         Mark Teague. Scholastic, 2000. ISBN 0-590-31681-8. Unpaged. (P).

Most children dread bedtime, but not if it includes huge, humorous dinosaur paintings and wonderful, witty rhymes. Jane Yolen and Mark Teague make bedtime delightful by featuring dramatic dinosaurs who mimic typical childlike behaviors. This book was the most popular poetry selection in my first-grade classroom. The children giggled as the pouting dinosaurs refused to go to bed, and they enjoyed acting out the bedtime procrastination scenes while reciting the rhythmic text: "How does / a dinosaur say / good night / when Papa / comes in / to turn off / the light? . . . Does a / dinosaur / stomp / his feet / on the floor / and shout: / 'I want / to hear / one book / more!'?" The children were amused at the surprise ending in which the dinosaurs ultimately don't put up a fight at bedtime. (LAD)

## Curricular Connections

10.23    Grimes, Nikki. **Is It Far to Zanzibar? Poems about Tanzania.** Illustrated by Betsy Lewin. Lothrop, Lee & Shepard, 2000. ISBN 0-688-13157-3. Unpaged. (ALL).

Take a visit to East Africa in this lively book of poems about daily life in Zanzibar and Tanzania: "Go to Zanzibar to see / a nutmeg bush, a cashew tree, / cloves and ginger growing wild, / chili peppers hot and mild." From crowded buses where friendly chaos reigns ("people jam the open door, / Bright cloth bundles crowd the floor") to descriptions of native foods, from the seasons to visits home, Grimes has provided a vivid glimpse of this culture. Swahili words sprinkled throughout give readers a feel for the rhythm of the language. Although the poems are uneven in quality, we found that children were fascinated by them and enjoyed comparing their own lives with those described in the poems. The book is also a good resource for studying a part of the world that is typically neglected in U.S. schools. Lewin's cartoon-style watercolor illustrations reflect the irreverent, exuberant feeling of the poetry. (AAM)

10.24    ★ Hopkins, Lee Bennett, selector. **My America: A Poetry Atlas of the United States.** Illustrated by Stephen Alcorn. Simon & Schuster, 2000. ISBN 0-689-81247-7. 83 pp. (I).

Arranged into seven geographic regions and Washington, D.C., each section of this anthology contains a map of the region and brief facts about the states, followed by the poetry. Poems by many diverse poets, including Nikki Giovanni, Myra Cohn

Livingston, Langston Hughes, Shonto Begay, X. J. Kennedy, and Lee Bennett Hopkins, provide a kaleidoscope of perspectives on each region. Stephen Alcorn's beautifully rendered paintings add to the regional quality of this geographic look at the United States in poetry. Earlier collections of poetry that deal with the United States in history will work well with this volume. (KH)

10.25    Hopkins, Lee Bennett, selector. **Spectacular Science: A Book of Poems.** Illustrated by Virginia Halstead. Simon & Schuster, 1999. ISBN 0-689-81283-3. 37 pp. (ALL).

"What Is Science?" by Rebecca Kay Dotlich opens this beautifully illustrated book of poetry. After Dotlich explains that science is "so many things," the rest of the poetry Hopkins has selected looks at aspects of the natural world such as seeds, microscopes, prisms, rocks, insects, dinosaur bones, and more. Favorite poets represented in this collection include Alice Schertle, Valerie Worth, Jane Yolen (to whom the book is dedicated), Aileen Fisher, Lilian Moore, David McCord, Carl Sandburg, and others. The colorfully bold illustrations add to the intrigue of the mysteries of science but also represent the interaction of science and child. This book could be useful not only in language arts classes but also in science classes to help children ponder the aesthetics of science. *Spectacular Science* is an excellent companion to Hopkins's *Marvelous Math: A Book of Poems* (Simon & Schuster, 1997). (KH)

10.26    ★ Katz, Bobbi. **We the People.** Illustrated by Nina Crews. HarperCollins, 2000. ISBN 0-688-16531-1. 102 pp. (I).

The poems in *We the People* will be appreciated by students who possess some knowledge of U.S. history. In her author note, Katz says that a historical event comes alive for her when "I can experience it through a specific person—someone whose face I can see and whose feelings I can imagine, someone with a name." Using biographies, journals, diaries, letters, photos, and paintings as her sources, Katz comments on events in U.S. history in the voices of the famous, the not so well known, and fictitious people who might have viewed a specific event. "At the Station, Part I" and "At the Station, Part II," for example, chronicle the fictitious Charlotte Doolittle's impressions and memories as President Lincoln's train passes through Columbus, Ohio, on its way to his inauguration and again as his body is carried back to

Springfield, Illinois, after his assassination. Brief quotes related to the situation highlighted by the poem appear at the bottom of each page, such as Lincoln's statement, "The ballot is stronger than the bullet." *We the People* can serve as a model for children to write poems from the viewpoint of ordinary citizens during specific historic periods. (LBW)

10.27 Michelson, Richard. **Ten Times Better.** Illustrated by Leonard Baskin. Marshall Cavendish, 2000. ISBN 0-7614-5070-X. 40 pp. (ALL).

Mixing mathematical concepts and poetry, Michelson and Baskin have created a unique and captivating book in which pairs of animals compete to be best, based on numerical facts. "What number's best? There can be no debate — / tarantulas know that the greatest is EIGHT /" (p. 22). But the peacock replies, "You're hairy and scary, but you must be blind. See, / I have EIGHTY eyes, and that's just behind me" (p.25). Using multiples of ten, Michelson presents animal information, first in the poems and then in a final illustrated compendium. Each compendium entry concludes with a ten-based problem for readers to solve. This book of witty poems and striking watercolors is fun to compare with other mathematical poetry books, such as Florence Perry Heide, Judith Heide Gilliland, and Roxanne Heide Pierce's *It's about Time!* (Clarion, 1999). In great demand among our young readers, this is a book made for sharing. (PSO)

## Fresh Perspectives on Ordinary Things

10.28 Adoff, Arnold. **Touch the Poem.** Illustrated by Lisa Desimini. Scholastic, 2000. ISBN 0-590-4797-09. Unpaged. (ALL).

Adoff's poems are replete with sensory images that delight children. The experiences he describes are concrete and familiar yet unusual. Students enjoy the unexpected ways in which the poems explore the sense of touch, from the stroking of one's own cheek, to the sense of being suspended in a bath full of warm sudsy water, to the feeling of cold ice cream on one's tongue. In "Happy on the Beach," the reader is reminded of the burning heat of surface sand as well as the cool damp feeling of feet buried in sand. Lisa Desimini's mixed-media collages, comprising photos, paintings, paper, and computer graphics, add immeasurably to the sensory impact of the book. Students will take pleasure in writing their own free verse poems that focus on everyday experiences involving their own sense of touch. (LBW)

**10.29** ★ Grimes, Nikki. **A Pocketful of Poems.** Illustrated by Javaka Steptoe. Clarion, 2001. ISBN 0395-93868-6. 30 pp. (ALL).

This happy book is an excellent pairing of art and poetry. We meet Tiana, a young black girl with "a pocketful of words," in the first poem. Her favorite words are *spring, shower, pigeon, moon, hot, Harlem, caterpillar, homer, pumpkin, snow, angels, gift,* and *haiku.* Each of these words then has its own poem. In the moon poem, Tiana says, "I slip under its silver light / and pull it to my chin, like a quilt. / Full moon, magic in silver, speaks to me, drowning the sound of sirens" (p. 12). Steptoe's inventive collages use many unusual objects including faucets, sponges, wire, feathers, dirt, and straws, making the double-page illustrations remarkably bright and cheerful. (JCB)

**10.30** Grimes, Nikki. **Shoe Magic.** Illustrated by Terry Widener. Orchard, 2000. ISBN 0-531-3028-65. 32 pp. (ALL).

Shoes are important to children: every teacher recognizes the happy announcement, "I've got new shoes!" Therefore, from "The shoe rack / Is stacked / with promise, / with dreams waiting / to wake" (p. 5) to "Slippers," the closing poem, this collection was an immediate hit with second graders. The children related these lively, joyous poems about shoes of many kinds with shoes in their own lives. Glowing illustrations, created with acrylics on bristol board, added greatly to the book's appeal. This book is also an introduction to a study of shoes and those who wear them. Complementary books of fiction include Elizabeth Winthrop's *Shoes* (Harper & Row, 1986) and Johanna Hurwitz's *New Shoes for Silvia* (Morrow, 1993), while Ann Morris's *Shoes, Shoes, Shoes* (Lothrop, Lee & Shepard, 1995) presents information about shoes world wide. *Shoe Magic* did indeed cast its spell! (PSO)

**10.31** ★ Hopkins, Lee Bennett, selector. **Yummy! Eating through a Day.** Illustrated by Renée Flower. Simon & Schuster, 2000. ISBN 0-689-81755-X. 32 pp. (ALL).

This delicious collection of carefully selected dietary poems was received with delight by young readers of all ages. The poems are fun to read aloud. For example, "Pasta Perfect"—"Ravioli / Macaroni / Vermicelli / in the pot. / Tortellini / Cappellini steamy hot" (p. 22) has the rhythm of a jump rope rhyme and is fun to compare with Jack Prelutsky's "Spaghetti! Spaghetti!" in *Rainy, Rainy Saturday* (Greenwillow, 1980), while crispy "Potato Chip" pairs nicely with Myra Cohn Livingston's "Street Song" (*The Way Things Are, and Other Poems,* Atheneum, 1974). Children have fun comparing food poems in this book with those in Arnold Adoff's *Eats* (Lothrop, Lee & Shepard, 1979) and *Chocolate Dreams* (Lothrop, Lee & Shepard, 1984). From "Morning Smells" to final "Thanks," these poems, enhanced by novel and vibrant paintings, provide a culinary feast for the senses. (PSO)

10.32  Nye, Naomi Shihab. **Come with Me: Poems for a Journey.** Illustrated by Dan Yaccarino. Greenwillow, 2000. ISBN 0-688-15947-8. 32 pp. (ALL).

Journeys, whether actual or imagined, are the focus of the sixteen poems in this collection, which reflects a more childlike side of Nye's poetry than is found in many of her other collections. Poems that cross time and often ask questions join Dan Yaccarino's mixed-media illustrations to create a thoughtful perspective. The opening poem on the inside book jacket begins the journey: "A journey can lead / east and west, from / north to south, up down, / over, under, in between / and next to. A journey can last / a minute, an hour, a year / a month, a lifetime." Nye gives children who are ready for more serious poetry much to think about. (KH)

10.33  Stevenson, James. **Candy Corn: Poems.** Greenwillow, 1999. ISBN 0-688-15837-4. 56 pp. (ALL).

Stevenson, James. **Cornflakes: Poems.** Greenwillow, 2000. ISBN 0-688-16718-7. 48 pp. (ALL).

Continuing the series begun with *Sweet Corn: Poems* (Greenwillow, 1995) and *Popcorn: Poems* (Greenwillow, 1998) are these two new tasty morsels. Using a variety of fonts and typefaces, tempos and subjects, Stevenson presents poems both humorous and touching. In these two books, as in the first two, he dwells on recurring themes: people, junkyards, old dilapidated buildings, rusting things, weather, and street and water scenes. Children as well as adults are drawn to his poignant poems and telling comments, such as "Along the rusty railroad track / A building stands / That must have been important once. / Now rain goes through the open doors, / Vines climb up the walls (*Candy Corn,* p. 30), and "Along the shore / The perfect shell / Awaits the perfect child" (*Cornflakes,* p. 34). Each free verse poem has an appealing tale to tell that draws children into an appreciation of the subtle images of good poetry. (PSO)

10.34　Stevenson, James. **Just around the Corner: Poems.** Greenwillow, 2001. ISBN 0-688-17303-9. 56 pp. (ALL).

Once more Stevenson combines free verse commentary with watercolor paints and black pen drawings to express his views on life. His humor is tinged with sadness as he spotlights the everyday people, things, and events around us. Children are drawn to his latest "corn(er)" poems as he helps them become observers of the small things in life. "Old Shoes,"—"Tough as nails / They've been around . . . / Worn down, fixed-up, split apart, / . . . Now it's time for them to rest indoors, / Next to the softies" (p. 34)—agrees philosophically with Deborah Chandra's "Grandpa's Shoes" (*Rich Lizard: And Other Poems,* Farrar, Straus & Giroux, 1993). And in "Trees," master wordsmith Stevenson shows compassion for "The Christmas captives / Tied with twine / Lean against each other on the city sidewalk, / Whispering of the frozen woods back home" (p. 26). (PSO)

10.35　Willard, Nancy. **The Moon & Riddles Diner and the Sunnyside Café.** Illustrated by Chris Butler. Harcourt, 2001. ISBN 0-15-201941-3. 40 pp. (ALL).

Based on a postcard from her childhood, Willard has created this odyssey of Shoofly Sally and her Everything Dog as they wander in search of an incredible café. Along the way, they treat us to poems in many forms, including a ballad, a limerick, rhythm 'n blues, and Mother Goose–related rhymes, such as "a thousand heifers rock and roll. / They hoof it high, / they hoof it low, / across the Milky Way." Young readers are intrigued by both Willard's lovely nonsense verse and Butler's paper sculpture illustrations made with enamel paint and Elmer's glue on bristol board, which has been backlit and photographed. Children are eager to try the fourteen easy recipes from the M & R Diner and the Sunnyside Café listed at the end of the book. (PSO)

10.36　Wong, Janet S. **Night Garden.** Illustrated by Julie Paschkis. Margaret K. McElderry Books, 2000. ISBN 0-689-82617-6. 28 pp. (I).

In Janet Wong's *Night Garden*, fifteen poems from the world of dreams set readers' minds spinning, searching, seeking, and soaring. "Deep in the earth / a tangle of roots / sends up / green shoots / and dreams grow / wild" (p. 1). Julie Paschkis's gouache-on-paper illustrations intertwine through Wong's nighttime visions and reflect a positive spirit. From speaking foreign words you do not know, to flying, to talking in your sleep, to the "news-at-seven-true nightmare," Wong's poems mirror the mystery and magic of dreams: "There is a place / where the museum houses thousands of paintings / seen nowhere else . . . , where the library is filled with brand new books / waiting for you to open them first, / to tell stories only you could know, . . . / There is such a place, / hidden deep / in me" (p. 28). Not only will readers see themselves in these poems and make connections, but they will also be ready to weave their own night garden web of words. (LAW)

## Sports

Adoff, Arnold. **The Basket Counts.** Illustrated by Michael Weaver. Simon & Schuster, 2000. ISBN 0-689-80108-4. 46 pp. (I). (See **12.29.**)

★ Smith, Charles R. Jr. **Rimshots: Basketball Pix, Rolls, and Rhythms.** Dutton, 1999. ISBN 0-525-46099-3. 31 pp. (I). (See **12.32.**)

10.37 ★ Smith, Charles R. Jr. **Short Takes: Fast-Break Basketball Poetry.** Dutton, 2001. ISBN 0-525-46454-9. 32 pp. (I).

This is the third book in Charles Smith's basketball series, which also includes *Rimshots* (Dutton, 1999; **12.32**), and *Tall Tales: Six Amazing Basketball Dreams* (Dutton, 2000). The poetry in this collection reflects the quick reality of the game, from fast breaks to trash talk on the court, and will appeal to basketball players and/or readers who are looking for upbeat contemporary poetry. In addition to rhymed pieces, readers will find haiku, free verse, and a glossary in the back defining the elements of poetry used by the author. (KH)

10.38 Thayer, Ernest Lawrence. **Casey at the Bat: A Ballad of the Republic Sung in the Year 1888**. Illustrated by Christopher Bing. Handprint Books, 2000. ISBN 1-929766-00-9. 30 pp. (ALL).

Christopher Bing has a grand-slam winner in this scrapbook-design version of Thayer's original poem "Casey at the Bat." To make the book look like an authentic scrapbook from 1888, Bing has overlaid mementos, artifacts, and baseball memorabilia throughout the poem, even yellowing the edges of the 1988 *Mudville Monitor* newspaper clippings before presenting the poem itself. Not just a poem but also a history of the period, including the obituary of Ernest Thayer on the final endpapers, this edition is a classic in itself, richly deserving its Caldecott Honor Book Award. Children will enjoy comparing this version of the poem with earlier ones. (KH)

# 11 Fine Arts

**Glenna Sloan**

*Contributing reviewers included Jane LoBosco, Michelina M. Gannon, Melissa Gonzalez, Lola Lauri, Karen Maroney, Joan Masotti, Mary Kate McDonald, Patricia Munsch, and Elizabeth Schneider.*

---

**Criteria for Excellence**
- Language of high literary quality
- Outstanding illustrations in all books
- Illustrations complement text in informational books
- Appealing overall design
- Evidence of thorough research and authenticity in informational books
- Memorable characters, plots, themes, and language in fiction
- Appealing for children K–6 in content and presentation

---

## Architecture

Crosbie, Michael J. **Arches to Zigzags: An Architecture ABC.** Photographs by Steve Rosenthal and Kit Rosenthal. Abrams, 2000.

★ Greenberg, Jan, and Sandra Jordan. **Frank O. Gehry: Outside In.** DK Ink, 2000.

Macaulay, David. **Building Big.** Houghton Mifflin, 2000.

★ Rubin, Susan G. **There Goes the Neighborhood: Ten Buildings People Loved to Hate.** Holiday House, 2001.

## Art and Artists

Brenner, Barbara. **The Boy Who Loved to Draw: Benjamin West.** Illustrated by Olivier Dunrea. Houghton Mifflin, 1999.

★ Browne, Anthony. **Willy's Pictures.** Candlewick, 2000.

★ Catalanotto, Peter. **Emily's Art.** Atheneum, 2001.

Christelow, Eileen. **What Do Illustrators Do?** Clarion, 1999.

★ Cummings, Pat, compiler and editor. **Talking with Artists. Volume 3.** Clarion, 1999.

★ Elleman, Barbara. **Tomie dePaola: His Art and His Stories.** Putnam, 1999.

Emberley, Ed. **Ed Emberley's Fingerprint Drawing Book.** Little, Brown, 2000.

Finley, Carol. **Aboriginal Art of Australia: Exploring Cultural Traditions.** Lerner, 1999.

★ Gherman, Beverly. **Norman Rockwell: Storyteller with a Brush.** Atheneum, 2000.

★ Greenberg, Jan, and Sandra Jordan. **Vincent van Gogh: Portrait of an Artist.** Delacorte, 2001.

Lacey, Sue. **Sports and Leisure.** Copper Beach, 2000.

Lasky, Kathryn. **First Painter.** Paintings by Rocco Baviera. DK Ink, 2000.

★ Marciano, John Bemelmans. **Bemelmans: The Life and Art of Madeline's Creator.** Viking, 1999.

Ross, Michael Elsohn. **Nature Art with Chiura Obata.** Illustrated by Wendy Smith. Carolrhoda, 2000.

Sohi, Morteza E. **Look What I Did with a Shell.** Walker, 2000.

★ Waldman, Neil. **The Starry Night.** Boyds Mills, 1999.

## Dance and Dancers

★ Allen, Debbie. **Dancing in the Wings.** Illustrated by Kadir Nelson. Dial, 2000.

★ Calhoun, Dia. **Aria of the Sea.** Winslow, 2000.

★ Glover, Savion, and Bruce Weber. **My Life in Tap.** Morrow, 2000.

★ Marshall, James. **Swine Lake.** Illustrated by Maurice Sendak. HarperCollins, 1999.

★ McMahon, Patricia. **Dancing Wheels.** Photographs by John Godt. Houghton Mifflin, 2000.

★ Tallchief, Maria, with Rosemary Wells. **Tallchief: America's Prima Ballerina.** Illustrated by Gary Kelley. Viking, 1999.

★ Varriale, Jim. **Kids Dance: The Students of Ballet Tech.** Dutton, 1999.

## Drama and Dramatists

Conford, Ellen. **Annabel the Actress, Starring in "Just a Little Extra."** Illustrated by Renee Andriani. Simon & Schuster, 2000.

★ Coville, Bruce. **William Shakespeare's Romeo and Juliet.** Illustrated by Dennis Nolan. Dial, 1999.

★ Ganeri, Anita. **The Young Person's Guide to Shakespeare.** Designed by Anita Ganeri. Harcourt Brace, 1999.

## Music and Musicians

Austin, Patricia. **The Cat Who Loved Mozart.** Illustrated by Henri Sorenson. Holiday House, 2001.

★ Cutler, Jane. **The Cello of Mr. O.** Illustrated by Greg Couch. Dutton, 1999.

★ Dahlberg, Maurine. **Play to the Angel.** Farrar, Straus & Giroux, 2000.

★ George-Warren, Holly. **Shake, Rattle, and Roll: The Founders of Rock and Roll.** Illustrated by Laura Levine. Houghton Mifflin, 2001.

Haskins, James. **One Nation under a Groove: Rap Music and Its Roots.** Hyperion, 2000.

★ Koscielniak, Bruce. **The Story of the Incredible Orchestra.** Houghton Mifflin, 2000.

★ Miller, William. **The Piano.** Illustrated by Susan Keeter. Lee & Low, 2000.

★ Weatherford, Carol Boston. **The Sound That Jazz Makes.** Illustrated by Eric Velasquez. Walker, 2000.

## Puppetry

Gauch, Patricia Lee. **Poppy's Puppet.** Illustrated by David Christiana. Holt, 1999.

---

Through experience with the arts, children discover new ways of knowing the world, often finding in themselves proclivities—even talents—they never dreamed they had. In elementary, middle, and high school education, studies in the arts receive lip service but often little more. When school budgets are cut, music, art, and drama, widely regarded as dispensable frills, are the first to be eliminated from the curriculum.

Author and educator Maxine Greene in May 2000 delivered the speech "The Slow Fuse of the Possible" at the annual Educating the Imagination Lecture sponsored by the Teachers and Writers Collaborative. Greene deplored the fact that in some schools where children don't do well in reading and math, the arts are taken away in order to spend more time on those subjects. The arts, she insisted, educate the imagination, and imagination, in Emily Dickinson's words, lights the slow fuse of the possible.

Nothing can replace active participation in the arts. But good books—factual or fictional—about dancers; music and musicians; actors, plays, and playwrights; and artists and their works have the potential to open minds and imaginations to new possibilities. "The arts may never change the world," said Greene, "but they may change the people who can change the world."

Through the books in this chapter, readers can learn what it is like to study dance and what it takes to excel in this demanding art. Two examples are *Tallchief: America's Prima Ballerina* (Tallchief, 1999) and *Aria of the Sea* (Calhoun, 2000). The former is a picture book in which luminous paintings enhance a story told in Maria Tallchief's own words. Some children have stereotypic or negative notions about ballet: "It's just for girls in tutus." *Kids Dance: The Students of Ballet Tech* (Varriale, 1999) is a book to set them straight.

Books included here demonstrate that it takes as much perseverance and perspiration as talent and inspiration to make one's mark in the arts. *Bemelmans: The Life and Art of Madeline's Creator* (Marciano, 1999) and *My Life in Tap* (Glover, 2000) are two excellent examples. The biography *The Boy Who Loved to Draw* (Brenner, 1999) tells how a career in art began as a dream in the imagination of a young child; this and other annotated books show that the road toward the fulfillment of a childhood ambition is often long with many detours. The way in which music can lift the spirits to help individuals transcend hardships is the theme of more than one book on our list, such as *Play to the Angel* (Dahlberg, 2000) and *The Cello of Mr. O* (Cutler, 1999).

Some books, such as *What Do Illustrators Do?* (Christelow, 1999), provide information about careers in the arts or offer technical information about artwork, as does *Building Big* (Macaulay, 2000). Others are stories in which the arts are woven into fictional plots, as in the picture book *The Piano* (Miller, 2000) and *Play to the Angel* (Dahlberg, 2000), a book for older readers.

In selecting the books reviewed here, three words have guided the committee: *excellence, interest,* and *variety.* From the books available, we included those we found to be of highest quality in design, writing, and illustration. We looked for substance. If a book contained illustrations, we required that they be complementary, enhancing and illuminating the text. All our choices are visually appealing. Among our selections are important books we believe will endure to become classics. We chose books with appeal for children, especially those that pique interest in finding out more about a topic or those that engender a sense of wonder. To help us select books of particular interest to young readers, we asked students in elementary and middle level classrooms for their critical opinions; these guided us in making our choices for the chapter.

Our ultimate purpose in book selection is to interest children in the arts through a variety of approaches and genres. Children often find their way to art through crafts; for instance, Lois Ehlert, creator of many fine picture books for children, as a child experimented with collage at a card table set up in a corner of her artist parents' studio. For this reason, the chapter includes selected craft and instructional art books recommended by children, as well as picture books, chapter books, information books, fiction, and biography. Readers will find an ABC book,

*Arches to Zigzags* (Crosbie, 2000); a story in an easy-to-read format, *Annabel the Actress, Starring in "Just a Little Extra"* (Conford, 2000); a how-to book, *Start with Art: Sports and Leisure* (Lacey, 2000); and an informational book that includes a CD, *The Young Person's Guide to Shakespeare* (Ganeri, 1999).

Although the books span a range of difficulty from easy to challenging, we believe that all are capable of inviting substantive response. Among the wide range of books are those to read independently, share in classroom groups, or use by individuals or classes for research. Some are meant to be read as whole entities, from cover to cover; others are designed for browsing. However the books are presented to children, we hope that pleasure will be the first consideration. May readers find among our choice of books on the arts at least one to kindle the spark of interest in this or that art that lies within us all.

## Architecture

**11.1**   Crosbie, Michael J. **Arches to Zigzags: An Architecture ABC.** Photographs by Steve Rosenthal and Kit Rosenthal. Abrams, 2000. ISBN 0-8109-42186. 48 pp. (P).

This large-format book teaches young children the ABCs of architecture through questions that stimulate readers to consider anew the structural world around them. Engaging interactive text introduces arches, gargoyles, hinges, I-beams, zigzags, and more while further engaging the eye with high-quality photographs of these architectural elements. An appendix gives the location of each photographic example and definitions of terms. Books on architecture, especially for younger readers, are rare. This excellent one belongs in every collection. (GS)

**11.2**   ★ Greenberg, Jan, and Sandra Jordan. **Frank O. Gehry: Outside In.** DK Ink, 2000. ISBN 0-7894-2677-3. 47 pp. (I).

In a rare study of architecture for young people, the authors choose an architect known for daring originality in his designs, among them the dramatic Guggenheim Museum in Bilbao, Spain. Accounts of Frank Gehry's early life, accompanied by his own comments, provide a sense of how childhood experience can influence adulthood. The ubiquitous fish in his designs echo memories of the beautiful disappearing carp that each week swam briefly in his grandmother's bathtub before becoming food in the ritual of the Jewish Sabbath. Dramatically illustrated with glossy photographs and eye-catching graphics, this large-format book has eye appeal and an accessible, informative text. Gehry's story, often in his own words, inspires. "There are no rules, no right or wrong. I work intuitively," says this hardworking creative artist, a lifetime learner who is as energetic as ever in his seventies. Included is a glossary of architectural terms and a bibliography of related readings. (GS)

11.3     Macaulay, David. **Building Big.** Houghton Mifflin, 2000. ISBN 0-395-96331-1. 192 pp. (ALL).

Perhaps the most famous of Macaulay's excellent books is *Cathedral: The Story of Its Construction* (Houghton Mifflin, 1974). A companion volume, in a format large enough to do justice to its subject, *Building the Book Cathedral* (Houghton Mifflin, 1999) explains, with detailed sketches, the entire bookmaking process. In *Building Big,* Macaulay invites readers to look closely at the structures that surround them: domes, dams, bridges, tunnels, skyscrapers. He explains the whys and hows of construction of such landmarks as the Empire State Building, the U.S. Capitol dome, and Chicago's Sears Tower. He also poses questions about architectural marvels: Why this shape and not another? Why steel instead of another building material? His answers reflect his consistently meticulous research and attention to detail. This book is an excellent guide for budding architects as well as those fascinated with large structures. (ES)

11.4     ★ Rubin, Susan G. **There Goes the Neighborhood: Ten Buildings People Loved to Hate.** Holiday House, 2001. ISBN 0-8234-1435-3. 96 pp. (I).

With examples from buildings such as McDonald's restaurants to cultural icons such as the Eiffel Tower, Rubin regales the reader with entertaining facts about famous structures hated in their early days by the public. Photographs, together with a witty, readable text, engage the reader from the first words of the introduction. White type on blue pages interspersed throughout add interest and variety to the detailed text, and the actual comments of detractors add sparkle to the accounts. Mark Twain, writing about the Washington Monument, called it the "memorial chimney" with "cow sheds about its base." One critic wrote that the ramp of the Guggenheim Museum in New York City was "more appropriate in a parking garage than in a museum." This fine example of well-researched material entertainingly reported is an interesting, amusing introduction to architecture that also fosters critical awareness of physical surroundings. (GS)

## Art and Artists

**11.5**   Brenner, Barbara. **The Boy Who Loved to Draw: Benjamin West.** Illustrated by Olivier Dunrea. Houghton Mifflin, 1999. ISBN 0-395-85080-0. Unpaged. (P).

The tenth child in a large colonial family, Benjamin West, destined to become the first world-famous American painter, was obsessed with drawing from a young age. His obsession led his elders to think him lazy and irresponsible. Suppressing his talent proved impossible, especially when a "real live artist," William Williams, predicted West's success. Study and effort eventually made Benjamin West a successful painter whose works were admired by King George III of England. The text is based on West's own account of his childhood, and Brenner has focused on anecdotes with appeal for child readers. Dunrea's stylized pictures convey a strong sense of the colonial period. Prints of some of West's paintings are included. (GS)

**11.6**   ★ Browne, Anthony. **Willy's Pictures.** Candlewick, 2000. ISBN 0-7636-0962-5. Unpaged. (ALL).

Browne chooses Willy, the popular chimp hero of five other books, to bring to children "a celebration of painting and the visual world." "I love the idea," says Browne, "of introducing children to paintings they might not ordinarily know." Playing with the images in famous paintings, the 2000 Hans Christian Andersen Award–winner for illustration provides children with a hilarious but sound introduction to great artworks in this spectacular large-format book. Willy is painter and narrator throughout this tour of masterpieces, each altered to tell a new story with apes as subjects. Botticelli's 1485 painting *The Birth of Venus* appears but titled *The Birthday Suit,* featuring a startled-looking ape in a shower cap, paws covering her privates. Browne's outrageous, masterfully executed versions of the paintings should be compared with the originals, which are included in full color with succinct explanatory descriptions in a foldout appendix. (GS)

**11.7**    ★ Catalanotto, Peter. **Emily's Art.** Atheneum, 2001. ISBN 0-689-83831-X. 32 pp. (P).

An exceptionally talented artist in the first grade, Emily paints her beloved dog Thor with larger-than-life ears because he "hears everything." She enters the painting of Thor in a contest but loses when the judge admires but utterly misunderstands the symbolism of the work, mistaking Thor for a rabbit. Emily buries her painting, vowing never to paint again. Through an insightful discussion by the first-grade children in Emily's class, Catalanotto exposes the impossibility of ranking art works, especially by those who imperfectly understand what makes good art. Through his masterful use of acrylic, gouache, and watercolor, the artist creates a visual masterpiece, his luminous backgrounds juxtaposed with his sympathetic, remarkably realistic rendering of young children's painting. This exquisite book combines important insights about art with the portrayal of a sensitive, compassionate child character. (KM)

**11.8**    Christelow, Eileen. **What Do Illustrators Do?** Clarion 1999. ISBN 0-395-90230-4. 40 pp. (P).

Presented in a colorful, cartoonlike format and style, this book offers children insight into a book illustrator's life. The author describes in detail the many decisions an illustrator must make while illustrating a book and as an example shows two artists creating illustrations for "Jack and the Beanstalk." Each has an individual way of working; their separate visions of the story characters and events are unique and equally beautiful. Used in conjunction with an earlier book by the same author, *What Do Authors Do?* (Clarion, 1995), this book provides a behind-the-scenes look at the creativity required for bookmaking. Children learn valuable lessons about the crafts of writing and illustrating while enjoying the humor and wit of pictures and text. (MG)

**11.9**    ★ Cummings, Pat, compiler and editor. **Talking with Artists. Volume 3.** Clarion, 1999. ISBN 0-395-89132-9. 93 pp. (ALL).

Pat Cummings adds a third to her two previous volumes of *Talking with Artists.* In format, Volume 3 is consistent with the others, each of its thirteen conversations introduced with a monologue by the artist subject. Answers follow to questions children might ask the artists: Where do you get your ideas? Do you have any children? Any pets? Do you ever put people you know in your pictures? What do you use to make your pictures? How did you get to do your first book? In this inviting book planned to delight young readers, the artist's pets are pictured along with photos of the artist both as a young child and as a grown-up. Examples of work are provided, in some cases early drawings and sketches saved from childhood. Whether leafing through the pages to become acquainted with artists or researching their favorite illustrator, children will enjoy meeting, among others, Jane Dyer, Kevin Hawkes, Ted Lewin, and Paul Zelinsky. (PM)

**11.10**   ★ Elleman, Barbara. **Tomie dePaola: His Art and His Stories.** Putnam, 1999. ISBN 0-399-23129-3. 218 pp. (ALL).

Barbara Elleman, known for her insightful critical commentaries on children's literature, creates in this comprehensive, meticulously researched work a detailed portrait of a well-known and much appreciated artist-author of children's books. The creator of Strega Nona, Big Anthony, Jamie O'Rourke, and Fin M'Coul appears as large as life in this sympathetic treatment of dePaola and his art. Color photographs, prints of his paintings, and reproductions of excerpts from dePaola's many books lavishly support a readable text. Organization by topic facilitates research: A Life; Autobiographical Tales; Religious Books; Christmas Stories; Folktales; Strega Nona; Story Making; Informational Books; Mother Goose and Other Collections; Patterns, Visual Themes, and Motifs; Publishing History; Creating the Book; dePaola Off Page; and dePaola's Non-Book Art. (GS)

**11.11**   Emberley, Ed. **Ed Emberley's Fingerprint Drawing Book.** Little, Brown, 2000. ISBN 0-316-23638-1. Unpaged. (P).

Artist Ed Emberley has produced a number of drawing books to foster the creativity of the youngest artists. Among them are *Ed Emberley's Drawing Book of Animals* (Little, Brown, 1970), *Ed Emberley's Drawing Book of Faces* (Little, Brown, 1975), and *Ed Emberley's Drawing Book: Make a World* (Little, Brown, 1972). This latest book shows young artists how to make unique pictures using fingerprints and "a few scribbles, dots, and lines." Through drawings in the introductory pages, technical advice is provided, along with illustrations of required materials. What follows is a colorful parade of astonishing creatures created with only fingers, some paint, and a few simple line drawings. These examples become progressively more complex, ending with those in a section Emberley calls Advanced Finger-Painting. He makes the point that, since all fingerprints are unique, each artwork will be one of a kind. As the artist says in a postscript to the reader, "Much has been left for you to explore and discover." This is a delightful how-to book that young readers and prereaders will enjoy. (GS)

**11.12**   Finley, Carol. **Aboriginal Art of Australia: Exploring Cultural Traditions.** Lerner, 1999. ISBN 0-8225-2076-1. 64 pp. (ALL).

Here children have the opportunity to study Australian Aboriginal cultures through their artwork. The book briefly describes Aboriginal history, notes their current political struggles, and introduces the concept of Dreamtime, the Aboriginal creation myth. Aboriginal culture and belief are explained through references to the symbols, patterns, and stories in their artwork. Having discussed the symbolism in several paintings, the author challenges readers to provide an interpretation for a typical painting. The photographs of the beautiful Australian landscape, juxtaposed with the ancient paintings, give readers a sense of the Aboriginal reverence for their land and its creatures. Third graders who read this book found the simply drawn symbols and patterns easily understandable and the earth tones of the illustrations appealing. (LL)

**11.13**   ★ Gherman, Beverly. **Norman Rockwell: Storyteller with a Brush.** Atheneum, 2000. ISBN 0-689-82001-1. 57 pp. (I).

A time line provides the important dates in the life of Norman Rockwell, the artist who told stories of American life in paintings from 1912 to 1964. Rockwell's famous works, many of them painted for covers of *The Saturday Evening Post,* seem to prove the adage that a picture is worth a thousand words. Asking students to put into words a painted Rockwell "story" is one way to hone story-writing skills. The comprehensive, readable text, containing biographical facts and anecdotes about Rockwell, is liberally adorned with prints of his paintings, many full page and in color. Admitting that some critics judge Rockwell's works to be dated and sentimental, the author maintains that, besides presenting valuable insights into a period of U.S. history, Rockwell's universal themes touch the human spirit. Implicit throughout is the message that polished artworks result from meticulous effort. (GS)

**11.14** ★ Greenberg, Jan, and Sandra Jordan. **Vincent van Gogh: Portrait of an Artist.** Delacorte, 2001. ISBN 0-385-32806-0. 144 pp. (I).

Greenberg and Jordan follow the life of Vincent van Gogh in a sensitive biography that reads with the drama and suspense of a novel. Was he an inspired lunatic or a committed artist? The authors invite readers to judge for themselves from the facts they present. We learn about van Gogh's different careers, his erratic behavior, his constant restless movement through Europe. We hear that he taught himself his craft through persistent practice and repetition. Through his letters, we hear his own voice reflecting his hopes, dreams, and changing moods. Full-color reproductions of van Gogh's more famous works are included, along with pictures of his family and home. The book is an example of fine research well reported. (KM)

**11.15** Lacey, Sue. **Sports and Leisure.** Copper Beech, 2000. ISBN 0-7613-1210-2. 32 pp. (P).

Other titles in Start with Art, a practical how-to series of books about art, are *People, Animals, Still Life,* and *Landscapes. Sports and Leisure* is subtitled *Understanding Art with Lots of Practical Step-by-Step Projects for the Young Artist.* The practical and unintimidating instructional approach appealed to the children who used this book. In the first few pages, readers learn something about how to work like an artist, and the rest of the book guides them through experimentation with various media and styles: ink drawings, etchings, collage, cardboard sculptures, circus mobiles, and papier-mâché "pottery" bowls. Accompanying each how-to project is a full-color reproduction of examples of work that artists created in each medium or style. Georges Seurat's 1891 painting *Le Cirque* is shown with an explanation of pointillism, the painting technique he perfected. Each project is suited to the young child's abilities and features easily procured materials. Colorful pages are packed with information and inspiration for young artists. (GS)

**11.16** Lasky, Kathryn. **First Painter.** Paintings by Rocco Baviera. DK Ink, 2000. ISBN 0-7894-2578-5. Unpaged. (ALL).

Lasky combines her usual meticulous research with imagination to take readers into the prehistoric world where a young woman, the first painter, attempts to appease the gods and through her art bring rain to a famine-ridden land. In the rock walls of the cave where she paints, Mishoo, the artist, finds her subjects and coaxes out their shapes with her colors. "Am I catching spirits or being caught myself?" she wonders. Using organic materials that would have been available in prehistoric times, Rocco Baviera creates memorable pictures, dark with mystical beauty. (MG)

11.17   ★ Marciano, John Bemelmans. **Bemelmans: The Life and Art of Madeline's Creator.** Viking, 1999. ISBN 0-670-88460-X. 151 pp. (ALL).

Using photographs, illustrations from his grandfather's books, and excerpts from letters, published writings, and private journals, the grandson of Ludwig Bemelmans provides a fitting celebration of Madeline's creator. Marciano says, "No conventional biography could capture what my grandfather was as a writer and artist. Only his work can do that" (p. vii). Access to his grandfather's files yields pages rich with sketches, drawings, drafts of text, and paintings. The many aspects of this detailed, lavishly illustrated account of Bemelmans' life, not written specifically for children but certainly of interest to them, are linked through John Marciano's readable commentary. Of particular interest to young readers is the chapter "The Making of a Madeline Book." Early sketches that led to the final versions of those perennial favorites are here, as well as notes on ideas that didn't work. This fine work expresses both the joy and the labor involved in the creative process. (GS)

11.18   Ross, Michael Elsohn. **Nature Art with Chiura Obata.** Illustrated by Wendy Smith. Carolrhoda, 2000. ISBN 1-57505-378-0. 48 pp. (ALL).

This book doubles as biography and art. On the one hand, it is the story of Chiura Obata, a Japanese American artist who painted pictures both of his family's time of internment at Topaz, a World War II internment camp for Japanese Americans, and famous sites in the United States such as Yosemite National Park. On the other hand, it is a book on how to sketch and paint using the techniques of Obata. In sidebars throughout the book, the author gives detailed instructions on creating nature art. The book may be used for exploration in art technique, especially for younger children; for older students, learning what the Obata family endured during World War II is equally interesting. (ES)

**11.19** Sohi, Morteza E. **Look What I Did with a Shell.** Walker, 2000. ISBN 0-80-27-8722-3. Unpaged. (ALL).

A companion book to *Look What I Did with a Leaf* (Walker, 1993), this is a young child's introduction to creating through crafts. Readers learn how to use an array of shells to make a shell creature or nature scenes or to decorate a picture frame. The text is readable, with easy-to-follow directions for making the shell sculptures. As an informational bonus, the author provides a field guide containing information about fifteen types of shells. Through this informative, lively book, readers are invited to explore nature and be creative. Second graders used both books with remarkable results. (MKM)

**11.20** ★ Waldman, Neil. **The Starry Night.** Boyds Mills, 1999. ISBN 1-56397-736-2. Unpaged. (ALL).

Vincent van Gogh's works caught artist Neil Waldman's imagination in his childhood. Learning from his reading that van Gogh lived a life of hardship, Waldman dreamed of bringing the artist to New York to escape them. This unique book is the imaginative realization of this dream. Waldman shows the painter New York landmarks, which are painted by Waldman as van Gogh might have rendered them. Through memorable paintings and the words of young Bernard, who speaks for him, Waldman communicates to young readers his enduring passion for the great artist and his works. Readers, realizing that van Gogh never visited New York to paint these pictures, understand something of the power of imagination coupled, in this case, with an artist's skill. (ES)

## Dance and Dancers

**11.21** ★ Allen, Debbie. **Dancing in the Wings.** Illustrated by Kadir Nelson. Dial, 2000. ISBN 0-8037-2501-9. Unpaged. (P).

Choreographer Debbie Allen is the winner of two Emmy Awards for the TV series *Fame*, an actress on Broadway and in films, and author of *Brothers of the Knight* (Dial, 1999), a modern retelling of the fairy tale "The Twelve Dancing Princesses." In both books about the joys of dance, the stories are told through equally hip text and pictures, the latter created in lively living color by Kadir Nelson, first in pencil, then photocopied, and finished in oil paint. Inspiration for *Dancing in the Wings*, the story of a self-conscious, gangly girl who yearns to be a ballerina, was Allen's sixteen-year-old daughter, a ballet student. At first Sassy dances in the wings, too tall to dance in the line with other, shorter dancers and too large to be lifted aloft by any of the boys in her dance class. Talent, perseverance, and an astute teacher eventually take her from the wings to the stage. (MG)

**11.22** ★ Calhoun, Dia. **Aria of the Sea.** Winslow, 2000. ISBN 1-890817-25-2. 264 pp. (I).

*Aria of the Sea* is a coming-of-age story about the dilemmas young people face in planning their futures. An event-filled narrative, strong in characterization, reveals how rigorous and demanding is the discipline of ballet. Living in a strange, stratified society, a thirteen-year-old commoner, Cerinthe, is allowed, only because of outstanding talent, to attend the elite School of the Royal Dancers. There she contends with imperious instructors, a challenging regimen, and the torment of a well-born student rival. Extraordinary courage and independence of spirit bring Cerinthe success as a dancer. But is this the life she wants? A young man urges her to abandon dancing and marry him. With proven ability as a healer, Cerinthe is invited to enroll in the healers' school. Ultimately, Cerinthe makes a decision about her future: "I will be myself!" she cries in the last lines of a book in which, in places, language and plot soar to an aria's lyrical heights. (GS)

**11.23** ★ Glover, Savion, and Bruce Weber. **My Life in Tap.** Morrow, 2000. ISBN 0-688-15629-0. 79 pp. (ALL).

This collaboration with journalist Bruce Weber includes over fifty photographs that feature Savion tap dancing and give a history of the art form. In his twenties, Glover is a phenomenon in the entertainment world, winner of countless awards as a star on Broadway, on television, and in film. He has performed at, among other places and events, the White House, the Super Bowl, and the Academy Awards. He also formed his own tap company, Not Your Ordinary Tappers. Savion receives high praise from Gregory Hines in the foreword: "Savion Glover has redefined tap dancing." Readers will be both impressed and inspired by the way Savion moves toward mastery of his art. Another powerful book about a male dancer is *Dance* (Hyperion, 1998), written by modern dance virtuoso Bill T. Jones and Susan Kuklin, with dramatic photographs by Kuklin of Jones in motion. (JM)

11.24   ★ Marshall, James. **Swine Lake.** Illustrated by Maurice Sendak. HarperCollins, 1999. ISBN 0-06-205171-7. Unpaged. (ALL).

Who could resist a book by two masters of the art of the picture book, especially a work that exists for "pure fun"? A wolf, hungry for a tasty meal of succulent pig, sees his opportunity when he notices an advertisement for *Swine Lake* by the Boarshoi Ballet, a dance company of pigs. Disguised and seated alone in a box in the theater for the performance, the wolf awaits the right moment to leap onto the stage. When he does leap, he is carried away by the music, joins the dance, and can't bring himself to capture a pig. Here is another masterpiece from a creator of memorable characters, among them Viola Swamp, George, Martha, the Stupids, and Emily Pig, all the legacy of James Marshall, who died in 1992. Sendak's distinctive style sparkles in pictures that perfectly complement and extend with wit and humor Marshall's delightfully deadpan, tongue-in-cheek text. (GS)

11.25   ★ McMahon, Patricia. **Dancing Wheels.** Photographs by John Godt. Houghton Mifflin, 2000. ISBN 0-395-88889-1. 48 pp. (ALL).

Lively, conversational text and fascinating photographs tell the remarkable story of Mary Verdi-Fletcher's realization of her dream to dance despite the fact that she uses a wheelchair. This photo-essay describes Dancing Wheels, the company Mary founded, which features both stand-up and sit-down dancers, the latter using their legs, arms, backs, necks, and faces for expression—along with their wheelchairs. In workshop sessions and performances, the dancers rehearse and perform dances created by their choreographer-director. The impressive results of their efforts are recorded in an easily read, interesting text and bright, action-filled photographs. Perseverance against all odds is the central theme underlying this real-life account. The group's motto is inspiration for every reader: Think about what you can do, not about what you can't. (MMG)

11.26   ★ Tallchief, Maria, with Rosemary Wells. **Tallchief: America's Prima Ballerina.** Illustrated by Gary Kelley. Viking, 1999. ISBN 0-670-88756-0. 28 pp. (ALL).

"There was only one great American dancer," Rosemary Wells's mother often told her. "Tallchief." Discovering that her mother, a former member of the corps de ballet of the Ballets Russes de

Monte Carlo, was somewhere on the stage when sixteen-year-old Maria Tallchief first saw the Russian ballet, Wells decided to write this book with the now seventy-five-year-old dancer. The result is an often lyrical first-person account of the celebrated ballerina's early life. Born in 1925 on an Osage Indian reservation in Fairfax, Oklahoma, Maria studied as a young girl in Los Angeles. At age seventeen, she traveled to New York City to join "the world of my angels," the ballet company that had been her inspiration. In illustrations warmed by earth tones, Kelley both evokes Tallchief's Native American heritage and celebrates dance and dancers. Pictures and words combine in a testimony to the focused effort required to make dreams come true. (GS)

11.27    ★ Varriale, Jim. **Kids Dance: The Students of Ballet Tech.** Dutton, 1999. ISBN 0-525-45536-1. Unpaged. (ALL).

Asked what they knew of ballet, one class of third graders spoke of boring dances to classical music by girls in tutus. *Kids Dance,* about the children of Ballet Tech, a public school in New York City, quickly erased those notions. Illustrated by photographs of actual students and enlivened by descriptions in the students' own words of the hard work, fun, and satisfaction of learning to dance, the book gives a sense of the rigor of the academic and dance schedule required to graduate. The real-life photographs make nonsense of stereotypical perceptions about ballet: there are as many boys as girls in the school and not a tutu to be seen. (LL)

## Drama and Dramatists

11.28    Conford, Ellen. **Annabel the Actress, Starring in "Just a Little Extra."** Illustrated by Renee Andriani. Simon & Schuster, 2000. ISBN 0-689-81405-4. 64 pp. (P).

This easy-to-read text tells of ten-year-old Annabel who lives to act. She sees her big chance to be discovered when a movie is made in her town. Determined pushiness, combined with luck and a little acting ability, wins her a part as an extra. Conford creates engaging characters in Annabel, her friends, her family, and the moviemakers and then lets them loose in a humorous story. Illustrations, such as the color cover of Annabel cavorting for the camera, and back-and-white line drawings throughout, add to the humor. Having discovered Ellen Conford, younger readers, eager for enjoyable, simply written books they can read independently, will want to search the library for more of her works. (MG)

**11.29**  ★ Coville, Bruce. **William Shakespeare's Romeo and Juliet.** Illustrated by Dennis Nolan. Dial, 1999. ISBN 0-8037-2462-4. Unpaged. (I).

Just as he does in *William Shakespeare's Macbeth* (Dial, 1997), Coville combines his own prose with excerpts from Shakespeare's play in a version well suited for use with students not quite ready to handle the complications of the play's entire text. Nolan's watercolor-and-pencil pictures illuminate the text and add a visual dimension to the emotions expressed by the characters in words. This book is useful as an introduction to Shakespeare and to the play. Experienced readers of Shakespearean text might compare this retelling to the actual work or copy Coville's technique to present another Shakespearean play. (ES)

**11.30**  ★ Ganeri, Anita. **The Young Person's Guide to Shakespeare.** Designed by Anita Ganeri. Harcourt Brace, 1999. ISBN 0-15-202101-9. 55 pp. (I).

Anita Ganeri uses an appealing layout of photographs, text, and sidebars to integrate information about Shakespeare's life and times with his plays in a book particularly appropriate for young students' first introduction to the master. Little-known facts about William Shakespeare and his works are included in this visually appealing and accessible illustrated account. A valuable addition to the book is an accompanying compact disk containing excerpts from the playwright's works expertly performed by the Royal Shakespeare Company. One class of sixth graders found this introduction to Shakespeare intriguing, interesting, and, best of all, not intimidating. Ganeri has also authored *The Young Person's Guide to the Orchestra* (Harcourt Brace, 1996) and *The Young Person's Guide to the Ballet* (Harcourt Brace, 1998). (ES)

## Music and Musicians

**11.31**  Austin, Patricia. **The Cat Who Loved Mozart.** Illustrated by Henri Sorenson. Holiday House, 2001. ISBN 0-8234-1535-X. Unpaged. (P).

This tale, based on fact, according to its teller, is told in simple, rhythmic prose and sympathetically brought to life through Sorenson's complementary, realistic oil-on-canvas paintings. The cat that Jennifer, an accomplished young pianist, adopts and names Amadeus after the great composer, Wolfgang Amadeus

Mozart, refuses to participate in typical cat pastimes such as playing with a ball or jumping for the end of a dangling string. What he does like to do is sit with Jennifer as she practices the Mozart sonata she will play in a contest, adding to her confidence and pleasure. A note on Mozart's life is included, along with a list of related readings. (GS)

**11.32**   ★ Cutler, Jane. **The Cello of Mr. O.** Illustrated by Greg Couch. Dutton, 1999. ISBN 0-525-46119-1. Unpaged. (P).

Mr. O, a cellist, is disliked because he keeps to himself in a war-torn community peopled only by women, children, the elderly, and the sick. Yet, when morale is lowest, Mr. O daily carries a chair and his magnificent cello to the town square and plays "grand" songs that lift the people's spirits. When his cello is destroyed, Mr. O continues to play—on a harmonica. Shared with a culturally diverse class, this picture book evoked a variety of significant responses to the many important ideas implicit in it, among them the demoralizing effects of war, the mistake of being too quick to judge others, and the power of music to lift the spirits. Greg Couch's often poignant watercolor paintings, glowing in reds, browns, and yellows, create a tapestry effect as they extend visually the simple, understated text movingly narrated in the voice of a young child. (JM)

**11.33**   ★ Dahlberg, Maurine. **Play to the Angel.** Farrar, Strauss & Giroux, 2000. ISBN 0-374-35994-6. 186 pp. (I).

The author creates a courageous, strong-willed character in twelve-year-old Greta Radky. Living in 1938 in Vienna, Greta experiences the Nazi occupation of Austria, with its attendant horrors. Jews and those who endeavor to help them are persecuted through torture, imprisonment, and death. Greta is instrumental in helping Herr Hummel, her mysterious German piano teacher with a "past," escape the Nazis a second time. Talented and dedicated to becoming a concert pianist, Greta must contend with a mother who, inconsolable over the death of her gifted pianist son, withholds recognition, affection, and support from her daughter. This is an inspirational story of determination and the triumph of will over physical and psychological handicaps. *Torn Thread* by Anne Isaacs (Scholastic, 2000) is another such story, a true one, of young women coping amid the atrocities of World War II. The two books reinforce each other in celebration of the human spirit. (GS)

**11.34**  ★ George-Warren, Holly. **Shake, Rattle, and Roll: The Founders of Rock and Roll.** Illustrated by Laura Levine. Houghton Mifflin, 2001. ISBN 0-618-05540-1. 32 pp. (ALL).

This is a simple text that will delight and enlighten elementary school readers interested in how the music of their times began. With just enough information and colorful pictures in American primitive style, this is a good-humored, amusing look at the artists who founded rock and roll in the 1950s. Fifteen stars, including Elvis Presley, Chuck Berry, and James Brown, receive a spread each with a description of their childhood, their musical backgrounds, some of their hit songs, and notes of the little eccentricities that made them memorable. The author explains how the artists added a distinctive sound as they shaped and changed music forever. Art complements text to create a joyous romp. The book is also a model for research students might want to undertake on other subjects. (KM)

**11.35**  Haskins, James. **One Nation under a Groove: Rap Music and Its Roots.** Hyperion, 2000. ISBN 078680478-5. 165 pp. (I).

Sixth graders enjoyed this book about the roots of rap, the popular musical form they find exciting. A thoroughly researched report, complete with quotations from rappers and critics, the book provides solid information from a balanced viewpoint on this controversial subject. Most notable is the historical perspective provided. Modern rappers didn't appear on the scene out of nowhere. The roots of their art evolved from the centuries-old griot tradition of West Africa as well as from work songs, spirituals, and blues of Africans enslaved in the Americas. Particularly notable is the attractive design of the book. Most of the photographs and sketches, appearing without borders, become an integral part of the text; rap lyrics printed in a funky font introduce each chapter. A comprehensive bibliography is included in this serious study of a controversial genre. (JLB)

**11.36**  ★ Koscielniak, Bruce. **The Story of the Incredible Orchestra.** Houghton Mifflin, 2000. ISBN 0-395-96052-5. Unpaged. (ALL).

Although the text is simple and straightforward in this introduction to musical instruments of the symphony orchestra, it is a useful and interesting resource for readers of all ages. Explanatory text and accurate but informal pictures trace the development of the orchestra and its instruments over four hundred years, explaining how instrumental innovations change the sound of the ensemble. The book touches on jazz and trends in modern music and invites readers to contemplate what may be next in a tradition that consistently incorporates the old and the new. Other books on the orchestra include Anita Ganeri's *The Young Person's Guide to the Orchestra,* with CD (Harcourt, 1996) and Karla Kuskin's classic *The Philharmonic Gets Dressed* (Harper, 1982). (KM)

11.37   ★ Miller, William. **The Piano.** Illustrated by Susan Keeter. Lee & Low, 2000. ISBN 1-880000-98-9. Unpaged. (P).

Set in the Deep South in the early 1900s, this picture book tells of a friendship between a little African American girl and an older white woman. A mutual love of music brings the two together. Tia, walking in a wealthy part of town, hears music through the windows of a fine house. By good fortune, she manages to secure a job as maid to Miss Hartwell, its owner. One day she is discovered as she tentatively tries to make music on her mistress's piano. Her understanding employer, sensing the girl's overwhelming need to learn, agrees to give Tia piano lessons; in return, the child offers a home remedy for Miss Hartwell's painful arthritic hands. William Miller, author of several Lee & Low books, including *Richard Wright and the Library Card* and *The Bus Ride,* again proves his storytelling skill. Susan Keeter's pictures vividly reflect the text. (GS)

11.38   ★ Weatherford, Carole Boston. **The Sound That Jazz Makes.** Illustrated by Eric Velasquez. Walker, 2000. ISBN 0-8027-8720-7. Unpaged. (I).

This large-format book traces, in dramatic pictures and lively rhymed text, the history of American jazz from its African origins to current rap and hip-hop versions. Oil paintings by Eric Velasquez effectively capture the action and drama of this dynamic art form. Starting with the African *kalimba* dances and music, the book takes readers on board slave ships and through American cotton fields and sharecropping, showing how music helped a people survive hard times. Honky-tonk, the blues, and gospel music are all described here, and the jazz greats of Harlem along with present-day rap and hip-hop artists are celebrated in vivid sound and color. One group of New York City fifth graders, all rap fans, were fascinated to discover the basis of their favorite music in their own African ancestry; they chose to use the book's rhythmic text for a choral speaking presentation. (PM)

## Puppetry

**11.39** Gauch, Patricia Lee. **Poppy's Puppet.** Illustrated by David Christiana. Holt, 1999. ISBN 0-8050-5291-7. 32 pp. (P).

David Christiana provides dreamy, stylized watercolors for this fantasy about a puppet maker and puppeteer who "listens to the wood" when he carves a puppet. In the case of a puppet named Clarinda, however, he doesn't hear well and tries to make her a ballerina against her will. Despite Poppy's efforts to control her, Clarinda expresses herself in her own creative way. To young children, puppetry seems like magic; here its magical nature is captured in words and pictures. (MKM)

# 12 Sports, Games, and Hobbies

**Sylvia M. Vardell**

*Contributing reviewers included Kate Hunnicutt and Kellie Hale.*

---

### Criteria for Excellence
- Appeals to child readers, particularly those with specialized interests in sports
- Relevant to the sports enthusiast but also enriching as a reading experience
- Literary quality, especially the criteria for good nonfiction: accuracy, organization, design, style
- Inclusion of access features such as glossaries and indexes
- Distinctive style, language, and voice

---

## Sports Biographies

Christopher, Matt. **At the Plate with . . . Mark McGwire.** Little, Brown, 1999.

Christopher, Matt. **At the Plate with . . . Sammy Sosa.** Little, Brown, 1999.

Christopher, Matt. **In the Goal with . . . Briana Scurry.** Little, Brown, 2000.

Christopher, Matt. **On the Field with . . . Derek Jeter.** Little, Brown, 2000.

Christopher, Matt. **On the Field with . . . Terrell Davis.** Little, Brown, 2000.

Christopher, Matt. **On the Track with . . . Jeff Gordon.** Little, Brown, 2000.

★ Cline-Ransome, Lesa. **Satchel Paige.** Illustrated by James E. Ransome. Simon & Schuster, 2000.

★ Freedman, Russell. **Babe Didrikson Zaharias: The Making of a Champion.** Clarion, 1999.

Golenbock, Peter. **Hank Aaron: Brave in Every Way.** Illustrated by Paul Lee. Harcourt Brace, 2001.

Kaminsky, Marty. **Uncommon Champions: Fifteen Athletes Who Battled Back.** Boyds Mills, 2000.

Mandel, Peter. **Say Hey! A Song of Willie Mays.** Illustrated by Don Tate. Hyperion, 2000.

Stewart, Mark. **Venus & Serena Williams: Sisters in Arms.** Millbrook, 2000.

Sutcliffe, Jane. **Jesse Owens.** Illustrated by Janice Lee Porter. Carolrhoda, 2001.

★ Winter, Jonah. **Fair Ball! 14 Great Stars from Baseball's Negro Leagues.** Scholastic, 1999.

## Sports Nonfiction

Ajmera, Maya, and John Ivanko. **Come Out and Play.** Charlesbridge, 2001.

Anderson, Joan. **Rookie: Tamika Whitmore's First Year in the WNBA.** Photographs by Michelle V. Agins. Dutton, 2000.

Buckley, James Jr. **Strikeout Kings.** Dorling Kindersley, 2001.

Geng, Don. **Play-by-Play Baseball.** Photographs by Andy King. LernerSports, 2001.

Gibbons, Gail. **My Baseball Book.** HarperCollins, 2000.

Gibbons, Gail. **My Basketball Book.** HarperCollins, 2000.

Gibbons, Gail. **My Football Book.** HarperCollins, 2000.

Gibbons, Gail. **My Soccer Book.** HarperCollins, 2000.

Kuklin, Susan, and Sheryl Swoopes. **Hoops with Swoopes.** Hyperion, 2001.

Miller, Marla. **All-American Girls: The U.S. Women's National Soccer Team.** Pocket, 1999.

★ Oxlade, Chris, and David Ballheimer. **Olympic Games.** Knopf, 1999.

Page, Jason. **Soccer.** Two-Can, 2000.

Roberts, Robin. **Basketball the Right Way.** Millbrook, 2000.

Roberts, Robin. **Basketball Year: What It's Like to be a Woman Pro.** Millbrook, 2000.

Roberts, Robin. **Careers for Women Who Love Sports.** Millbrook, 2000.

Roberts, Robin. **Sports for Life: How Athletes Have More Fun.** Millbrook, 2000.

Sotzek, Hannelore. **Golf in Action.** Crabtree, 2001.

★ Sullivan, George. **Don't Step on the Foul Line: Sports Superstition.** Illustrated by Anne Canevari Green. Millbrook, 2000.

## Sports Fiction

Christopher, Matt. **Cool as Ice.** Little, Brown, 2001.

Christopher, Matt. **Inline Skater.** Little, Brown, 2001.

Christopher, Matt. **Skateboard Renegade.** Little, Brown, 2000.

Christopher, Matt. **Soccer Duel.** Little, Brown, 2000.

Christopher, Matt. **Tennis Ace.** Little, Brown, 2000.

Christopher, Matt. **Wheel Wizards.** Little, Brown, 2000.

*Soccer Cats Series*

Christopher, Matt. **The Captain Contest.** Illustrated by Daniel Vasconcellos. Little, Brown, 1999.

Christopher, Matt. **Hat Trick.** Illustrated by Daniel Vasconcellos. Little, Brown, 2000.

Christopher, Matt. **Heads Up.** Illustrated by Daniel Vasconcellos. Little, Brown, 2000.

Christopher, Matt. **Master of Disaster.** Illustrated by Daniel Vasconcellos. Little, Brown, 2001.

Christopher, Matt. **Operation Babysitter.** Illustrated by Daniel Vasconcellos. Little, Brown, 1999.

Christopher, Matt. **Secret Weapon.** Illustrated by Daniel Vasconcellos. Little, Brown, 2000.

Coy, John. **Strong to the Hoop.** Illustrated by Leslie Jean-Bart. Lee & Low, 1999.

Lynch, Chris. **Gold Dust.** HarperCollins, 2000.

Miller, William. **Night Golf.** Illustrated by Cedric Lucas. Lee & Low, 1999.

★ Rappaport, Doreen, and Lyndall Callan. **Dirt on Their Skirts: The Story of the Young Women Who Won the World Championship.** Illustrated by E. B.Lewis. Dial, 2000.

**Sports Stories You'll Have a Ball With.** SeaStar, 2001.

## Sports Poetry

Adoff, Arnold. **The Basket Counts.** Illustrated by Michael Weaver. Simon & Schuster, 2000.

★ Hopkins, Lee Bennett, selector. **Sports! Sports! Sports! A Poetry Collection.** Illustrated by Brian Floca. HarperCollins, 1999.

Kennedy, X. J. **Elympics.** Illustrated by Graham Percy. Philomel, 1999.

★ Smith, Charles R. Jr. **Rimshots: Basketball Pix, Rolls, and Rhythms.** Dutton, 1999.

## Games and Hobbies

Berg, Barry. **Opening Moves.** Photographs by David Hautzig. Little, Brown, 2000.

Harper, Piers. **Checkmate at Chess City.** Candlewick, 2000.

Ross, Kathy. **The Best Birthday Parties Ever! A Kid's Do-It-Yourself Guide.** Illustrated by Sharon Lane Holm. Millbrook, 1999.

Ross, Kathy. **Crafts to Make in the Winter.** Illustrated by Vicky Enright. Millbrook, 1999.

★ **The Ultimate LEGO Book.** Dorling Kindersley, 1999.

It would be easy to assume that sports books are most appropriate for children who are athletic and already interested in sports. But as we read and shared the books on this topic, we were surprised by how many of these books had a wider appeal and varied instructional possibilities. Those of us who focus on teaching reading and the language arts may think sports books are suitable for physical education but just don't have a place in our reading or language program. Conversely, teachers of physical education often believe they have no role in teaching or promoting reading in their gym classes. Both are making a mistake. In the books listed here are many possibilities for deep reading, critical analysis, and literary appreciation in the reading or language arts class. Also included are resources for providing information (nonfiction, how-to books) and even inspiration (poems, rhymes, biographies) in the physical education or coaching setting. Either way, we are doing children a disservice when we ignore the rich experiences many of them have outside of school playing team sports, competing as individual athletes, or simply pursuing recreational games and hobbies. The books selected here offer underutilized opportunities to connect children with books that are interesting to them, as well as to model for them how books can be relevant to their lives outside the classroom.

Five categories of books are listed for the general topic of sports, games, and hobbies:

- sports biographies
- sports nonfiction
- sports fiction
- sports poetry
- games and hobbies

These are the categories that emerged as we read and shared the most recently published books on the topic. Many excellent stand-alone titles as well as series nonfiction books on how to play various sports continue to be published. These books target readers who are already interested and involved in the sport. But sports literature includes much more than informational literature for the athlete; it also includes a growing body of biographies about athletes. These biographies are taking more varied forms about diverse subjects. Several excellent picture book biographies maximize the relationship between art and narrative to capture a life story, and collective biographies tell the stories of less well-known individuals such as disabled athletes or players in the Negro Leagues. Contemporary athletes in the news and major women players of the U.S. Women's National Soccer Team and the Women's

National Basketball Association are featured in the latest biographies for young people. Also, some major award-winning authors such as Russell Freedman are writing sports biographies. Any of these books would be well worth including in a study of the genre of biography or in leading students to explore biographies for recreational reading.

When it comes to recreational, or "free choice," reading, many excellent nonfiction or informational books are available. These are great books for matching with individual children based on their unique talents and interests. Many titles have a wider appeal, however, and will interest children who are simply curious about a sport or sporting event. The Eyewitness series, for example, drew an enthusiastic response from our students as they browsed through *Olympic Games* (Oxlade & Ballheimer, 1999), which was particularly popular during the Sydney Summer Games in 2000 and the Salt Lake City Winter Games in 2002, or through *Football* (Buckley, 1999) and *Baseball* (Kelley & Buckley, 2000). A relatively new trend in sports nonfiction is the creation of younger versions of topical books for the primary grades, such as the DK Readers series and Gail Gibbons's series of small sports books. Girls are now more commonly featured in the content and images of sports books as well as in the range of sports depicted, from golf to horseback riding to martial arts.

Sports fiction also includes a greater variety than might be expected. Although sports author Matt Christopher still dominates the field, with fifty-nine chapter books featuring sports themes, readers have many other choices, including picture books appropriate across the grades, such as John Coy's *Strong to the Hoop* (1999) about boys and basketball, or Doreen Rappaport and Lyndall Callan's *Dirt on Their Skirts* (2000) about girls and baseball. Christopher's newest series of "I CAN READ"–style Soccer Cats books were fast reading and quickly shared among our students. The range of subjects in sports fiction is also becoming more diverse. Christopher's latest titles include skateboarding (a big hit with our audiences) and wheelchair basketball. African American and women athletes are also getting long overdue attention. In addition, sports books for younger readers are finding their way into print, often illustrated by major artists working in children's literature, such as E. B. Lewis.

The increased number of sports poetry titles was a refreshing treat for those of us who love poetry and see the potential for active participation in the oral sharing of verse. The possibilities for movement and performance are even greater when the poems are about sports and athletes. The sports poetry books include both humorous and more serious verse, as well as a range of styles and voices suitable across all grade levels. In addition, the work of Arnold Adoff and of Charles R. Smith offer interesting styles of poetry for students to consider when they attempt their own poetry writing. When it comes to sports biographies and fiction, baseball seems to be the most popular subject, but in sports poetry, basketball is king. Students can be encouraged to explore their own extracurricular interests as they write about their experiences and share their worlds.

The final subtopic, games and hobbies, is a grab bag of nonfiction books about chess, crafts, and toys. Here we can direct students to specific titles that target their individual interests. One teacher shared *Opening Moves* (2000) by Barry Berg (about a five-year-old chess champion) with her after-school chess club, and one competitive fifth grader commented that he found it interesting to read, "To lose is to learn." Most surprising of all is the fact that the number one book from this entire collection was the Dorling Kindersley title about LEGO blocks. *The Ultimate LEGO Book* (1999) drew comment after comment from students, who pored over the pictures of LEGO creations such as robots, models, and famous faces, including those of Albert Einstein and the Statue of Liberty. If we had any doubts that sports and hobby books were relevant to the class as a whole, this book helped change our minds.

The LEGO book also helped us shape our criteria for inclusion in this chapter. We had to rank "kid appeal" number one. It was soon apparent that to be considered viable in the classroom, sports books had to be tested by actual readers. But since some titles whose literary worthiness was questionable still found an appreciative audience in the student with a specialized interest, we also looked for quality texts, especially in the criteria for good nonfiction: accuracy, organization, design, and style. In our annotations, we have noted the access features and other "extras" that authors have included to maximize the reader's learning experience. Things such as glossaries and indexes are not extras, for example, when a reader is hunting for a clear understanding of what it means to "bunt." In selecting fiction and poetry, we have also considered issues of style, language, and voice, striving to choose books that are relevant to the sports enthusiast but also simply enriching as a reading experience. As in all things, balance is the goal. Sports books need to be timely, but they can also endure over time if they are written and illustrated with care.

A growing emphasis in the books we reviewed is on a kind of sports appreciation:

- an awareness of what is needed to be an informed spectator
- a deeper understanding of the beauty of a game well played

- a validation of the life lessons to be learned from discipline and teamwork
- a sensibility of the human being behind the celebrity athlete
- an appreciation of the contribution of sports to the history of our society

These are all worthy topics for children to encounter as they grow up with books. Sports for life and fitness for health are important themes. No classroom or library should be without a selection of contemporary, quality trade books about sports, games, and hobbies for children.

## Sports Biographies

12.1    Christopher, Matt. **At the Plate with . . . Mark McGwire.** Little, Brown, 1999. ISBN 0-316-13457-0. 116 pp. (I).

Christopher, Matt. **At the Plate with . . . Sammy Sosa.** Little, Brown, 1999. ISBN 0-316-13477-5. 108 pp. (I).

Christopher, Matt. **In the Goal with . . . Briana Scurry.** Little, Brown, 2000. ISBN 0-316-13507-0. 112 pp. (I).

Christopher, Matt. **On the Field with . . . Derek Jeter.** Little, Brown, 2000. ISBN 0-316-13508-9. 119 pp. (I).

Christopher, Matt. **On the Field with . . . Terrell Davis.** Little, Brown, 2000. ISBN 0-316-13552-6. 109 pp. (I).

Christopher, Matt. **On the Track with . . . Jeff Gordon.** Little, Brown, 2000. ISBN 0-316-13469-4. 111 pp. (I).

This list represents a few in the series of over twenty biographies about contemporary athletes. Each is clearly written, beginning with the athlete's childhood and progressing through his or her young life to the present. In lively and engaging writing, each chapter pivots around a central event or incident in the athlete's life. The books reveal how the featured athlete became interested in the sport, which incidents or events have been critical to his or her success, and how determination and practice have helped the individual succeed. A small collection of black-and-white photographs and a chart of personal statistics are also offered in the center of each book. (SMV)

12.2    ★ Cline-Ransome, Lesa. **Satchel Paige.** Illustrated by James E. Ransome. Simon & Schuster, 2000. ISBN 0-689-81151-9. Unpaged. (ALL).

This picture book biography of baseball legend Satchel Paige is absorbing from beginning to end. The folksy narrative has an oral quality ideal for reading aloud. The large paintings throughout the book capture the life and times of Satchel Paige in bold and glowing colors. His achievement as a pitcher in the Negro Leagues and then in the majors, as well as his genuine love for the game of baseball, comes vividly to life. This is an outstanding addition to the growing collection of richly illustrated picture books about famous ballplayers, such as *Lou Gehrig: The Luckiest Man* by David Adler (Gulliver Books, 1997) and *Home Run: The Story of Babe Ruth* by Robert Burleigh (Silver Whistle, 1998). (SMV)

**12.3** ★ Freedman, Russell. **Babe Didrikson Zaharias: The Making of a Champion.** Clarion, 1999. ISBN 0-395-63367-2. 192 pp. (I).

The life of "the greatest woman athlete of all time" (p. 10) unfolds in Freedman's usual comprehensive and engaging style, with a dozen readable chapters in chronological order from her birth to immigrant parents to her death as a world famous athlete. Every flip of the page includes black-and-white photographs that capture Didrikson in motion in a variety of sports and scenes. Freedman provides details and quotes that convey her personality ("She ran the soles off a pair of tennis shoes every two weeks" [p. 10]) as well as the times she lived in (the founder of the modern Olympics felt women's sports were "against the laws of nature" [p. 12]). Freedman details Didrikson's prizes and statistics in basketball, track and field (Olympic gold medalist), tennis, baseball, bowling, diving, and golfing (her favorite sport), as well as her impact on the image of American womanhood. Notes, sources, credits, and index are all included. (SMV)

**12.4** Golenbock, Peter. **Hank Aaron: Brave in Every Way.** Illustrated by Paul Lee. Harcourt Brace, 2001. ISBN 0-152-02093-4. 32 pp. (P).

Hank Aaron, the boy, the man, and the athlete, is sensitively portrayed in this dramatic picture book biography. The lean story line follows him from his humble beginnings, emphasizing his father's baseball teaching and his mother's moral modeling. Aaron's joy in playing, as well as his dreams and goals, unfold in believable fashion. His desire to break Babe Ruth's long-standing record and the racial tension that accompanied this feat are handled with dignity and care. For older students, combine this title with *Satchel Paige* by Lesa Cline-Ransome (Simon & Schuster, 2000; **12.2**) and *Say Hey! A Song of Willie Mays* by Peter Mandel (Hyperion, 2000; **12.6**) to consider the emerging role of the African American athlete in the world of U.S. sports. (SMV)

**12.5**  Kaminsky, Marty. **Uncommon Champions: Fifteen Athletes Who Battled Back.** Boyds Mills, 2000. ISBN 1-56397-787-7. 147 pp. (I).

Here are fifteen stories of individuals who have coped with extreme challenges to achieve success as athletes. Read about, among others, Erik Weihenmayer, the first blind mountain climber; Michelle Akers plays soccer despite severe chronic fatigue syndrome; Ruben Gonzalez rose from homelessness to become grand master of racquetball; Gail Devers won Olympic medals in track despite Graves' disease; baseball player Jim Eisenreich battled Tourette's syndrome; and John Lucas, a professional basketball player, fought drug and alcohol addiction. Details make each story real and personal, such as the fact that Weihenmayer prepared for mountain climbing by racing up stairs of forty-story skyscrapers strapped into a fifty-pound backpack. And Diana Golden Brosnihan, cancer survivor and skier (on one leg), reminds us, "I didn't ski on one leg to be courageous—The commitment required to be an athlete is the same whether all your body parts are working or not" (p. 86). (SMV)

**12.6**  Mandel, Peter. **Say Hey! A Song of Willie Mays.** Illustrated by Don Tate. Hyperion, 2000. ISBN 0-78682417-4. 32 pp. (ALL).

This is another picture book biography of a major baseball player that is well worth adding to a classroom library. Like *Satchel Paige* by Lesa Cline-Ransome (Simon & Schuster, 2000; **12.2**), this story celebrates the accomplishments of a very special African American athlete. Hall of Fame centerfielder Willie Mays comes to life through angular and stylized portraits that integrate computer-generated art. The narrative moves along with an appealing repetitive refrain that centers on Mays's nickname, the Say Hey Kid. Facts about his life and his ball career are interwoven: his birth in Alabama, his rise in the Negro Leagues, and his famous catch and throw in the 1954 World Series. The overall effect is informative and lively, capturing Mays's life and personality with zest and enthusiasm. (SMV)

**12.7**   Stewart, Mark. **Venus & Serena Williams: Sisters in Arms.** Millbrook, 2000. ISBN 0-7613-1803-8. 48 pp. (ALL).

Tennis-playing sisters Venus and Serena Williams are the subject of this biography, one in the New Wave series about contemporary athletes. In ten short chapters, the author focuses on the Williams sisters' experiences growing up in the world of tennis (rather than details of school and family life). There are color photographs on every page, quotes from fellow athletes, and Did You Know? facts such as "The street gangs of Compton were so proud of Venus and Serena that they agreed to a 'ceasefire' whenever the girls were practicing" (p. 14). Even the controversy over their father's coaching and leadership is discussed. One African American fifth-grade girl said this book was "Girl power + tennis spirit = A good book." (Other New Wave subjects include Kobe Bryant, Alex Rodriguez, Terrell Davis, Derek Jeter, Tim Duncan, and Mia Hamm.) (SMV)

**12.8**   Sutcliffe, Jane. **Jesse Owens.** Illustrated by Janice Lee Porter. Carolrhoda, 2001. ISBN 1-57505-451-5. 48 pp. (P).

One of the eight On My Own biographies produced by Carolrhoda, this book packs an incredible amount of information in a very digestible forty-eight pages. Divided into three sections, Oakville, Alabama 1920, Athlete in Training, and Olympic Star, *Jesse Owens* features many interesting details about this Olympic gold medalist. Readers learn, for example, that his name became "Jesse" when a teacher misunderstood him saying his name was "J.C." The abundant use of stylized color illustrations adds to the mood as well as to the content of the book. A photograph of Owens, an author's afterword, and a list of important dates conclude this admirable book about "the world's fastest human" (p. 28). (SMV)

**12.9**   ★ Winter, Jonah. **Fair Ball! 14 Great Stars from Baseball's Negro Leagues.** Scholastic, 1999. ISBN 0-590-39464-9. 32 pp. (ALL).

This homage to fourteen great African American baseball players is laid out like a series of collectible baseball cards. Each double-page spread includes full-page paintings of every player framed in a box with their names hand-lettered at the bottom, as well as a "back of the card" narrative description and list of vital statistics, including name (and nickname), career dates, teams served, positions played, height, weight, and birth and death information. The narratives are detailed and lively, with facts such as: Satchel Paige played until he was fifty-nine years old (the oldest ever), Josh Gibson hit a home run out of Yankee Stadium (no one else has ever done that), and Bingo DeMoss always played second base with a toothpick in his mouth. Written with an obvious sense of racial pride, *Fair Ball!* introduces the reader to a new world of baseball legends. (SMV)

## Sports Nonfiction

12.10    Ajmera, Maya, and John Ivanko. **Come Out and Play.** Charlesbridge, 2001. ISBN 1-57091-385-4. Unpaged. (P).

This informational picture book uses two simple refrains to engage the young reader or listener: "To play means . . . [swinging, jumping, climbing]" and "You can play . . . [all kinds of games, in the water, on your own]." Each two-page spread then shows examples of play using color photographs of children engaged in a variety of play activities in countries all over the world. Teachers (including physical education teachers and coaches) can read the simple narrative line to prompt actual play or a discussion of favorite play activities and then return to the photo captions to list examples of play in a variety of cultural contexts. Much like Ann Morris and Ken Heyman's photoconcept books *Houses and Homes* (Mulberry, 1995) and *On the Go* (Mulberry, 1994), *Come Out and Play* makes a simple point about the universality of a childhood experience while weaving in a message about global awareness. (SMV)

12.11    Anderson, Joan. **Rookie: Tamika Whitmore's First Year in the WNBA.** Photographs by Michelle V. Agins. Dutton, 2000. ISBN 0-525-46412-3. 40 pp. (I).

At age thirteen in Tupelo, Mississippi, Tamika Whitmore decided to play basketball as a possible ticket to a college education. It worked. Tamika's growing up, her earliest training with her mother, her college years, and her eventual signing with the New York Liberty team of the WNBA after finishing college are all described here. Large full-color photographs are generously placed throughout the book to help communicate Tamika's personality. Smooth, flowing narrative engages the reader with revealing details that even nonsports enthusiasts should find interesting. Tamika likes to write poetry in her spare time, is afraid of flying, has a serious demeanor, and calls her mom nearly every day. A list of Tamika's 1999 player statistics and a glossary of basketball terms are also included. (SMV)

**12.12**  Buckley, James Jr. **Strikeout Kings.** Dorling Kindersley, 2001. ISBN 0-7894-7347-X. 48 pp. (P).

This is one of the new Dorling Kindersley (DK) Readers, with the usual physical format of an "I CAN READ" book in its size, shape, length, chapter divisions, and large typeface. This nonfiction reader, however, also includes a glossary, an index, and informational sidebars on every page. In addition, *Strikeout Kings* uses the effective Eyewitness series formula of cutout color photographs on a stark white background. The visual appeal of the book is outstanding. Its use of baseball photos and sidebar tidbits, along with its focus on favorite pitchers, should make it popular with emerging readers who are also sports fans. Other current sports-related books in the DK Readers series include *Super Short Stops* by James Buckley (2001) and *Going for Gold!* by Andew Donkin (1999). (SMV)

**12.13**  Geng, Don. **Play-by-Play Baseball.** Photographs by Andy King. LernerSports, 2001. ISBN 0-8225-9880-9. 80 pp. (I).

This new nonfiction series title provides an introduction to and overview of the sport of baseball for the intermediate reader. The half-dozen chapters include information and illustrations that will be helpful to a novice player or spectator. For more advanced athletes or enthusiasts, there is effective use of boxes, inserts, and boldface to highlight additional game history and strategies. A glossary, index, and list of related books and organizations are also helpful. The many color photographs portray boys and girls (and even women) of many backgrounds actively participating. Also in this new series is *Play by Play Mountain Biking* by Andy King (2001). (SMV)

**12.14**  Gibbons, Gail. **My Baseball Book.** HarperCollins, 2000. ISBN 0-688-17137-0. Unpaged. (P).

Gibbons, Gail. **My Basketball Book.** HarperCollins, 2000. ISBN 0-688-17140-0. Unpaged. (P).

Gibbons, Gail. **My Football Book.** HarperCollins, 2000. ISBN 0-688-17139-7. Unpaged. (P).

Gibbons, Gail. **My Soccer Book.** HarperCollins, 2000. ISBN 0-688-17138-9. Unpaged. (P).

The small size and shape of this series of sports books lends itself to sharing with young children. The trademark watercolor illustrations by Gail Gibbons fill every page. Her usual use of captions and labels in her drawings provides another layer of text that can be perused on repeated readings. Brief explanations for the basics and rules of each sport are provided in the simple narrative at the bottom of each page. Hypothetical teams (e.g., the Rockets and the Dragons) are used to describe an example game in play. With the guidance of a knowledgeable adult, these books can serve as helpful introductions to the sports. A glossary of terms concludes each book. (SMV)

**12.15** Kuklin, Susan, and Sheryl Swoopes. **Hoops with Swoopes.** Hyperion, 2001. ISBN 0-7868-0551-X. Unpaged. (P).

This picture book is almost a poem, with action verbs and short phrases spread out among the photographs of WNBA star Sheryl Swoopes playing basketball: "Sheryl Swoopes shoots hoops. Jump. Catch. Step. Shoot." In her colorful red shorts and blue sports top, Swoopes's image draws the eye as she moves across the pages. Although Swoopes is an especially strong role model for girls, all children should enjoy the way sports vocabulary such as "defend," "dribble," and "down the court" is incorporated in captionlike fashion. The book might inspire them to move and play or even photograph and narrate their own athletic activities. Pair this book with *Rimshots: Basketball Pix, Rolls, and Rhythms* by Charles Smith (Dutton, 1999; **12.32**) to compare the use of basketball-related words and images on the page. (SMV)

**12.16** Miller, Marla. **All-American Girls: The U.S. Women's National Soccer Team.** Pocket, 1999. ISBN 0-671-03599-1. 176 pp. (I).

For fans of women's soccer, this book is chock-full of interesting information. It profiles the fourteen members of the U.S. Women's National Team (WNT) that won the Olympic gold medal in 1996. Each team member is interviewed, with the following information shared in clear, readable prose and quotes: Personal statistics, (previous) soccer teams and growing up years, her play with the WNT including best game moment, superstitions each woman holds, "in the zone" (high moments) as well as injuries and bloopers, "soccer is my life" anecdotes including background on her jersey number (and its significance), and sources of inspiration and advice to young athletes.

An epilogue and appendixes provide post-Olympic information. A center section of color photographs depicts the major players as children and as adults today. This is an ideal book for browsing, reading up on favorite players, or comparing statistics and experiences across players. (SMV)

**12.17** ★ Oxlade, Chris, and David Ballheimer. **Olympic Games.** Knopf, 1999. ISBN 0-7894-6292-3. 64 pp. (ALL).

In the usual Eyewitness series format, this book focuses on the subject of the Olympic Games with nearly two dozen subtopics getting the standard photocaption treatment. The history of the ancient games and their reestablishment in 1896 are presented, but the book also includes extensive information about the Paralympics, as well as the tools and techniques for considering Olympic-level competition. Fitness, styles of clothing and shoes, equipment, and even the various shapes and sizes of body needed for competing in various sports are discussed. A global inclusion of athletes and anecdotes from around the world (not just the United States) is refreshing. An index is also provided. The series also includes *Football* by James Buckley Jr. (1999), *Baseball* by James Kelley and James Buckley (2000), *Super Bowl* by James Buckley Jr. (2000), and *Soccer* by Hugh Hornby and Andy Crawford (2000). (SMV)

**12.18** Page, Jason. **Soccer.** Two-Can, 2000. ISBN 1-58728-0019. 32 pp. (I).

This informational book in the Sports Club series is designed for both the novice and the more experienced soccer player. Organized as a series of double-page spreads, each one focuses on a different skill or aspect of the game of soccer, including rules, dribbling, passing, heading, shooting, and defending. Each section includes "in training" maneuvers to try and Hot Tips or Top Tactics for more advanced players. Computer-generated cartoon characters of players (both girls and boys) are named, given a team position, and used to demonstrate each rule or technique. The effect is a clear and inviting introduction to the game that includes a glossary of soccer phrases, an index, and a brief list of other resources. One fifth-grade girl reviewing the book said, "A marvelous book. I think I'll try some of the tips." The series also includes *Basketball: Learn How to Be a Star Player* by Matt Parselle (Two-Can, 2000). (SMV)

**12.19**    Roberts, Robin. **Basketball the Right Way.** Millbrook, 2000. ISBN 0-7613-1409-1. 48 pp. (I).

Roberts, Robin. **Basketball Year: What It's Like to Be a Woman Pro.** Millbrook, 2000. ISBN 0-7613-1406-7. 48 pp. (I).

Roberts, Robin. **Careers for Women Who Love Sports.** Millbrook, 2000. ISBN 0-7613-1408-3. 48 pp. (I).

Roberts, Robin. **Sports for Life: How Athletes Have More Fun.** Millbrook, 2000. ISBN 0-7613-1407-5. 48 pp. (I).

Sports announcer Robin Roberts has produced a series of nonfiction books written especially for girl readers with an interest in sports. Together they feature a wide array of topics, from training, game tactics, fan relationships, traveling, family life, and role of the coach to career options and teamwork. Each book includes a helpful table of contents, an index, and a list of resource books and Web sites. Although the books are somewhat text heavy, a generous use of color photographs and informative captions makes them effective for skimming and scanning. The series helps meet a need for more information about women athletes, particularly about the increasing variety of roles women can play in the world of sports. (SMV)

**12.20**    Sotzek, Hannelore. **Golf in Action.** Crabtree, 2001. ISBN 0-7787-0168-9. 32 pp. (I).

This Sports in Action series of nonfiction books provides a clear and helpful introduction to many popular sports for the novice sports enthusiast. Beginning with a table of contents listing the dozen or so topics included in each book and ending with a short glossary and index, each book is well organized and easy to understand. The authors make good use of subheadings, captions, key words, boxed items, and color drawings and photographs, so the layout of information is clear and logical. The focus is on the child learning about the sport, not on the professional athlete. In addition, images include children (and adults) of various ages and races learning to play. Try pairing this informational book with the fictional story *Night Golf* by William Miller (Lee & Low, 1999; **12.26**). The series also currently includes books on soccer, baseball, hockey, basketball, volleyball, football, horseback riding, martial arts, and figure skating. (SMV)

**12.21** ★ Sullivan, George. **Don't Step on the Foul Line: Sports Superstition.** Illustrated by Anne Canevari Green. Millbrook, 2000. ISBN 0-7613-1558-6. 64 pp. (I).

This nonfiction book is filled with anecdotes and statistics about the "routines and rituals, and charms and omens, [that] are as much a part of sports as sweating and chewing gum" (p. 4). From the most visible superstition of stepping on (or avoiding) the foul line during a game to keeping a rabbit's foot (or a whole rabbit) close at hand, hundreds of examples of sports superstitions are described and detailed. Learn about the most common mascots (eagles), historical recollections (Babe Ruth thought butterflies were unlucky), and who the most superstitious players are (usually the oldest and longest-playing athletes). Fifth-grade readers said, "It was good to know that athletes have superstitions" and "It's funny to know athletes are weird too." The anecdotal narrative is interspersed with black-and-white cartoons that students found "hilarious." (SMV)

## Sports Fiction

**12.22** Christopher, Matt. **Cool as Ice.** Little, Brown, 2001. ISBN 0-316-13489-9. 148 pp. (I).

Christopher, Matt. **Inline Skater.** Little, Brown, 2001. ISBN 0-316-12071-5. 150 pp. (I).

Christopher, Matt. **Skateboard Renegade.** Little, Brown, 2000. ISBN 0-316-13487-2. 136 pp. (I).

Christopher, Matt. **Soccer Duel.** Little, Brown, 2000. ISBN 0-316-13474-0. 148 pp. (I).

Christopher, Matt. **Tennis Ace.** Little, Brown, 2000. ISBN 0-316-13519-4. 116 pp. (I).

Christopher, Matt. **Wheel Wizards.** Little, Brown, 2000. ISBN 0-316-13611-5. 120 pp. (I).

These titles are just the latest chapter books in Christopher's fifty-nine-book series of sports fiction. Each novel contains the same ingredients: a straightforward and linear plot, simple vocabulary, plenty of dialogue and action, and stock, identifiable characters. The series contains a growing variety of topics, including sports such as dirt biking and skate boarding, as well as a protagonist who is also a wheelchair athlete. Although the focus is on competitive sports and on using teamwork to achieve athletic success, side issues about life lessons to learn are often included. As one fifth-grade boy put it after reading *Skateboard Renegade,* "It taught you that you don't always have to follow the leader and that a friend is always there for you no matter what." (SMV)

**12.23    Soccer Cats Series:**

Christopher, Matt. **The Captain Contest.** Illustrated by Daniel Vasconcellos. Little, Brown, 1999. ISBN 0-316-14169-0. 64 pp. (ALL).

Christopher, Matt. **Hat Trick.** Illustrated by Daniel Vasconcellos. Little, Brown, 2000. ISBN 0-316-10669-0. 54 pp. (ALL).

Christopher, Matt. **Heads Up.** Illustrated by Daniel Vasconcellos. Little, Brown, 2000. ISBN 0-316-13504-6. 54 pages. (ALL).

Christopher, Matt. **Master of Disaster.** Illustrated by Daniel Vasconcellos. Little, Brown, 2001. ISBN 0-316-13555-0. 55 pages. (ALL).

Christopher, Matt. **Operation Babysitter.** Illustrated by Daniel Vasconcellos. Little, Brown, 1999. ISBN: 0-316-13723-5. 55 pp. (ALL).

Christopher, Matt. **Secret Weapon.** Illustrated by Daniel Vasconcellos. Little, Brown, 2000. ISBN 0-316-13458-9. 56 pages. (ALL).

Soccer Cats is a new sports fiction series by Matt Christopher that targets the "I CAN READ" niche of reading material. They are hardbound chapter books with ten chapters of approximately two to four pages each. Full-page black-and-white action sketches are generously sprinkled throughout the narrative and help move the story forward. The focus is on the sport of soccer, with the Soccer Cats team of eleven members (and four substitutes) serving as the rotating protagonists. Although these books are simple in format and seem designed for the primary level, the language is full of sports lingo (e.g., "throw-in," "touchline," "striker") that may be challenging for emerging readers. Surprisingly, our "test team" of gifted fifth-grade readers devoured these books and shared them widely with friends and younger siblings. Their responses focused on the thematic qualities: "These books are about believing in yourself, determination, and teamwork." (SMV)

**12.24** Coy, John. **Strong to the Hoop.** Illustrated by Leslie Jean-Bart. Lee & Low, 1999. ISBN 1-880000-80-6. Unpaged. (ALL).

This picture book, the story of a ten-year-old boy eager to join in on a pickup game of basketball with the "big boys," offers multiple options for student engagement. The boy's experience, common to many budding athletes, may prompt discussion and sharing of personal stories. The story's language is casual, fast-paced, and full of basketball slang, lending itself to a reader's theater presentation or spontaneous dramatic interpretation. The illustrations use photographs of real children collaged into paintings that have a spontaneous, vivid quality. Students may enjoy creating original art that tells a story with photos of themselves superimposed onto drawings or scenes cut out of magazines. (SMV)

**12.25** Lynch, Chris. **Gold Dust.** HarperCollins, 2000. ISBN 0-06-028174-X. 196 pp. (I).

Richard Riley Moncrief is a seventh grader growing up in Boston in 1975. He lives and breathes baseball, especially when it comes to his beloved team, the Red Sox. When a new boy, Napoleon Charlie Ellis from the Dominican Republic, comes to town, Richard's ideas about many things are challenged, and an interesting, if prickly, friendship develops. With the arrival of touted rookies Fred Lynn and Jim Rice—the Gold Dust Twins—to the Sox roster, Richard decides he and Napoleon will be the next Gold Dust Twins. Told in a fresh first-person voice, the narrative is lively with believable dialogue and crisp with insights about growing up. This chapter book will appeal not only to those who enjoy sports stories or the novels of Chris Lynch, but also to the fans of the writing style of E. L. Konigsburg or Jerry Spinelli. (SMV)

**12.26** Miller, William. **Night Golf.** Illustrated by Cedric Lucas. Lee & Low, 1999. ISBN 1-880000-79-2. Unpaged. (ALL).

James is a little boy who finds a discarded golf bag in the garbage, swings an old rusted club, and instantly feels a kinship with the game of golf. Unfortunately, James is African American growing up in a time when golf was a game played only by rich white men in country clubs. Still, he is eager to get near a golf course and eventually gets the chance to caddy. He works alongside a black man named Charlie who teaches him the game of "night golf," played in the moonlight on the same course. Finally, James gets his chance to "shine" in the daylight, showing off his newfound talents. An author's note and time line of the history of African Americans in golf provide a historical context essential for understanding this picture book as a whole. (SMV)

12.27   ★ Rappaport, Doreen, and Lyndall Callan. **Dirt on Their Skirts: The Story of the Young Women Who Won the World Championship.** Illustrated by E. B. Lewis. Dial, 2000. ISBN 0-8037-2042-4. Unpaged. (ALL).

Told through the eyes of a fictitious little girl named Margaret, this is a vignette of one game played in the All-American Girls Professional Baseball League. The story gives a general play-by-play account of a 1946 championship game between the Racine Belles and the Rockford Peaches. Details of playing and score-keeping are told in sports lingo set against the historical back-drop of the post–World War II era. Margaret's identification with the real ball player Sophie Kurys reinforces her willingness to cope with skinned knees and "dirt on her skirts" in order to play ball. With endpapers that reprint black-and-white photographs of actual team members of the Belles and the Peaches, a roster of their actual individual and team statistics, and an explanatory author's note, this book is a loving homage to female athletes. (SMV)

12.28   **Sports Stories You'll Have a Ball With.** SeaStar, 2001. ISBN 1-58717-085-X. 64 pp. (P).

This appealing mini-anthology in the Reading Rainbow Readers series includes short stories and poems about sports by authors such as Nikki Grimes, Megan McDonald, Jean Marzollo, and Lee Bennett Hopkins. In the "I CAN READ" format, colorful cartoon characters along with large print and short chapters are particularly engaging for the emerging reader. The sports themes include the elation as well as the anxiety of participating in athletic activities. One story even focuses on the cultural differences in sports experienced by a child for whom English is a second language. This title is a natural companion to the poetry collection *Sports! Sports! Sports!* selected by Lee Bennett Hopkins (HarperCollins, 1999; **12.30**). (SMV)

## Sports Poetry

**12.29** Adoff, Arnold. **The Basket Counts.** Illustrated by Michael Weaver. Simon & Schuster, 2000. ISBN 0-689-80108-4. 46 pp. (I).

Adoff's trademark poetic style is here wrapped around the topic of basketball. His use of free verse, concrete poetry, and wordplay is combined with the energetic and stylized illustrations of Michael Weaver. From a game of pickup basketball to the playing of wheelchair athletes, Adoff's topics cover a range of basketball connections. His use of space, repetition, and capitalization (or lack of it) are all poetic techniques students often enjoy imitating and experimenting with themselves. Combine this book with Charles Smith's *Rimshots: Basketball Pix, Rolls, and Rhythms* (Dutton, 1999; **12.32**) to discuss their similarities and differences and to invite students to share their own experiences of the ball, the court, and the moves they know best. (SMV)

**12.30** ★ Hopkins, Lee Bennett, selector. **Sports! Sports! Sports! A Poetry Collection.** Illustrated by Brian Floca. HarperCollins, 1999. ISBN 0-06-027801-3. 48 pp. (ALL).

Hopkins has created an "I CAN READ" book of poetry that is both poetic and athletic. The dozen poets who have written sports-related poems here have managed to capture the energy and emotion of playing sports in words and lines that are manageable for the emerging reader. Their images and experiences are those that children can relate to, while their use of language is effective and often clever. Characters in the colorful cartoon illustrations are energetic and playful and include both boys and girls. The pictures help the beginning reader anticipate the sport being depicted in each poem, easing their comprehension of sports vocabulary and vivid words. Although the format is designed for the young child, many of the poems would be just as fun and effective with older children when read out loud or performed chorally. (SMV)

**12.31** Kennedy, X. J. **Elympics.** Illustrated by Graham Percy. Philomel, 1999. ISBN 0-399-23249-4. Unpaged. (P).

NCTE Award for Excellence in Poetry for Children–winner X. J. Kennedy brings his usual blend of humor and wordplay to the subject of the Olympics, except here the competitors are all elephants! Each elephant character gets her or his own poem spread against the backdrop of a large and colorful double-page illustration, perfect for young readers. But Kennedy's clever use of language will also appeal to older readers, who will catch the puns and plays on words, as when an elephant character wins "by a nose"! This is a fun and appealing introduction to the Olympic traditions (Summer Games, Winter Games, gold medals, etc.), as well as to the sly and humorous style of X. J. Kennedy. (SMV)

12.32   ★ Smith, Charles R. Jr. **Rimshots: Basketball Pix, Rolls, and Rhythms.** Dutton, 1999. ISBN 0-525-46099-3. 31 pp. (I).

This collection of poems and story vignettes is an in-your-face urban experience of basketball playing. The sepia-toned photographs throughout the book capture faceless players in active poses playing pickup games on outdoor courts. The combination of vivid language and creative use of typeface on oversized white pages creates an effect of constant energy and motion. Most of the text is in first person, drawing the reader into the book with a sense of immediacy and engagement. Many of the poems are concrete, using the expansive white space to spread the poem out in a visual representation of the action, such as "Fastbreak," "The sweetest roll," and "The Scorer." Other "list" poems such as "I remember," "Excuses, excuses," and "Everything I Need to Know in Life, I Learned from Basketball" beg for student involvement in choral readings or in writing extensions. (SMV)

## Games and Hobbies

12.33   Berg, Barry. **Opening Moves.** Photographs by David Hautzig. Little, Brown, 2000. ISBN 0-316-91339-1. 44 pp. (ALL).

Meet five-year-old chess champion Michael Thaler and his family as they foster Michael's gift for playing chess. Through the child's point of view, we learn about Michael's seven "Lessons I Have Learned," which are (1) Prepare, (2) Respect your opponent, (3) Focus, (4) Patience, (5) Develop a plan, (6) Winning and losing, and (7) Chess isn't everything. One fifth-grade student who read the book enjoyed these "kid" insights, responding, "I think 'to lose is to learn' is good info." In addition, extensive diagrams and directions for playing chess are provided and described in the chapter "Defending My Title." The final section focuses on Michael's family and the rest of his life, including his goals of becoming a chess master by age ten, playing piano in Carnegie Hall, and playing Little League baseball. (SMV)

12.34   Harper, Piers. **Checkmate at Chess City.** Candlewick, 2000. ISBN 0-7636-0921-8. 26 pp. (I).

Designed to teach the basics of how each chess piece moves, this book uses a kind of "Where's Waldo" style of illustration to engage the reader. Each set of double-page spreads is filled with color and detail from edge to edge. Black-and-white chessboards at various angles dominate the scene, inviting the reader to play the game of chess right in the book. A fantasy battle provides the challenge for each move, which is also clearly indicated with descriptions and diagrams. Some support and explanation from an experienced player, however, will surely be necessary to help novice players move beyond understanding each chess piece to grasp game strategy as a whole. One fifth-grade reader declared it "very challenging." (SMV)

12.35   Ross, Kathy. **The Best Birthday Parties Ever! A Kid's Do-It-Yourself Guide.** Illustrated by Sharon Lane Holm. Millbrook, 1999. ISBN 0-7613-1410-5. 79 pp. (I).

Visually, this book is very busy with a great deal of information packed into every page. Although this might seem overwhelming to young readers, most of our student readers were so intrigued with all the party ideas that they didn't mind. A dozen different party themes are provided, from "the three bears" to a "firefighter" party. For each theme, specific directions are given for a theme cake, party invitations and decorations, hats, games, and party favors. Directions can be somewhat complicated, so adult assistance may be necessary, and the baking clearly assumes adult involvement. (SMV)

12.36   Ross, Kathy. **Crafts to Make in the Winter.** Illustrated by Vicky Enright. Millbrook, 1999. ISBN 0-7613-0319-7. 63 pp. (ALL).

This book presents simple craft activities related to winter holidays and seasonal events for children of all ages to make. A table of contents lists the roughly two-dozen activities described in the book. Each craft is presented in a double-page spread with clear directions and colorful drawings delineating each step. The sequence is clear, with each craft page listing materials and tools needed for the activity in a rebus style, the combination of words and pictures enabling even young children to follow along. The activities themselves are fun and useful, and few of them require extensive adult supervision (beyond the use of scissors). (SMV)

**12.37   ★ The Ultimate LEGO Book.** Dorling Kindersley, 1999. ISBN 0-7894-4691-X. 124 pp. (ALL).

This was, hands down, the most popular of all the sports books with the fifth graders who perused the sports collection. The history and variety of LEGO toys created by the company by the same name founded in Denmark in 1934 is presented in the now familiar DK approach with captions and color photographs on a stark white background. The multitude of photos of all sizes creates an effect that is both inviting and stimulating. The book includes the following general categories of topics: The LEGO Story, LEGO Master Builders, LEGOLands—The Parks, and Imagination Unlimited. An intriguing index also allows browsers to seek out images and information on a range of topics, such as LEGO robots, LEGO models, and famous faces in LEGO bricks, such as Albert Einstein and the Statue of Liberty. The students literally could not put this book down, and much sharing and discussion occurred spontaneously as they pored over it. (SMV)

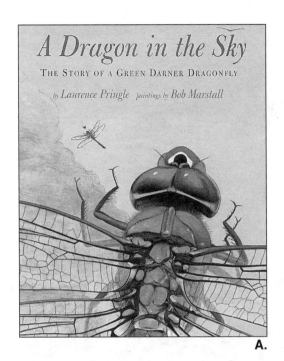

**A.**

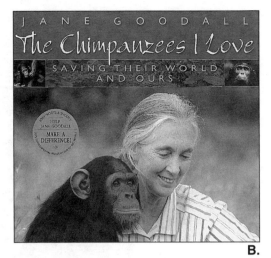

**B.**

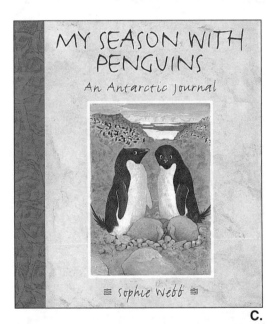

**C.**

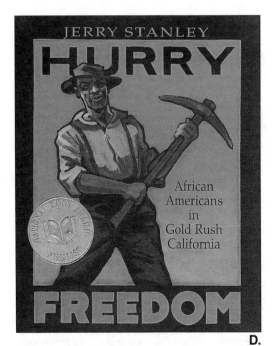

**D.**

**A.** *A Dragon in the Sky: The Story of a Green Darner Dragonfly,* Laurence Pringle/Bob Marstall (**1.31**).
**B.** *The Chimpanzees I Love: Saving Their World and Ours,* Jane Goodall (**1.27**).   **C.** *My Season with Penguins: An Antarctic Journal,* Sophie Webb (**1.34**).   **D.** *Hurry Freedom: African Americans in Gold Rush California,* Jerry Stanley (**2.28**).

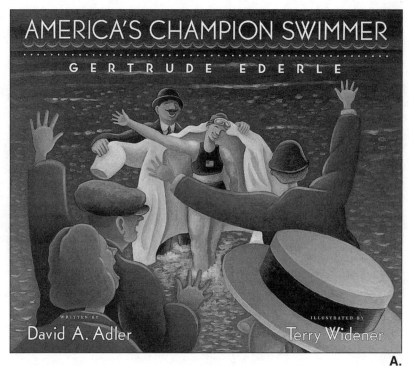

**A.**

**B.**

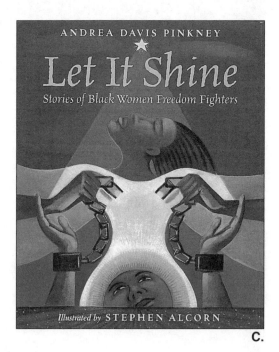

**C.**

**A.** *America's Champion Swimmer: Gertrude Ederle,* David A. Adler/Terry Widener (**2.1**). **B.** *Nazi Germany: The Face of Tyranny,* Ted Gottfried/Stephen Alcorn (**2.34**). **C.** *Let It Shine: Stories of Black Women Freedom Fighters,* Andrea Davis Pinkney/Stephen Alcorn (**2.15**).

**A.**

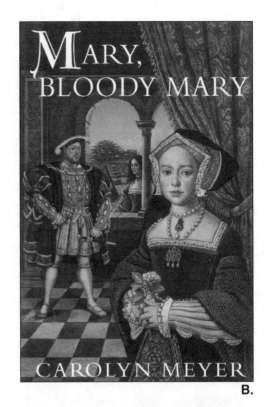

**B.**

**C.**

**D.**

**A.** *The Gate in the Wall,* Ellen Howard (**3.15**). **B.** *Mary, Bloody Mary,* Carolyn Meyer (**3.3**). **C.** *Anna of Byzantium,* Tracy Barrett (**3.1**). **D.** *Ties That Bind, Ties That Break,* Lensey Namioka (**3.19**).

A.

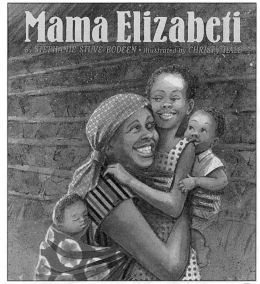

B.

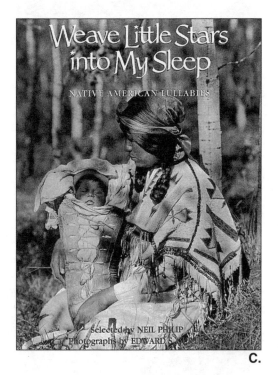

C.

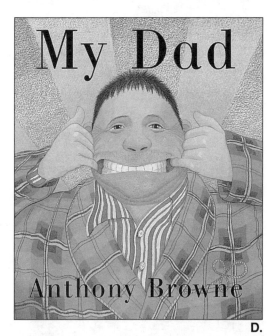

D.

**A.** *The Trip Back Home,* Janet S. Wong/Bo Jia (**4.31**). **B.** *Mama Elizabeti,* Stephanie Stuve-Bodeen/Christy Hale (**4.17**). **C.** *Weave Little Stars into My Sleep: Native American Lullabies,* Neil Philip/Edward S. Curtis (**4.27**). **D.** *My Dad,* Anthony Browne (**4.2**).

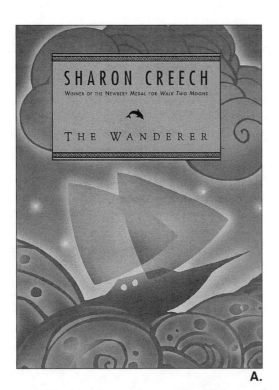

**A.** *The Wanderer,* Sharon Creech/David Diaz (**5.8**).   **B.** *Spirit of Endurance: The True Story of the Shackleton Expedition to the Antarctic,* Jennifer Armstrong/William Maughan (**5.2**).   **C.** *The Memory Coat,* Elvira Woodruff/Michael Dooling (**5.22**).

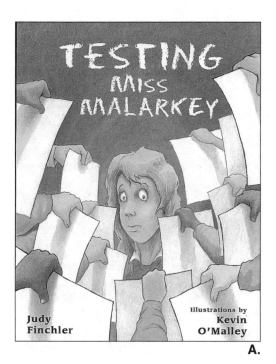

**A.**

**B.**

**C.**

**D.**

**A.** *Testing Miss Malarkey,* Judy Finchler/Kevin O'Malley (**6.6**). **B.** *Arthur's Teacher Moves In,* Marc Brown (**6.11**). **C.** *Little Miss Spider at Sunny Patch School,* David Kirk (**6.1**). **D.** *The Year of Miss Agnes,* Kirkpatrick Hill (**6.24**).

**A.**

**B.**

**C.**

**D.**

**A.** *"It's Simple," Said Simon,* Mary Ann Hoberman/Meilo So (**7.4**). **B.** *Into the A, B, Sea: An Ocean Alphabet,* Deborah Lee Rose/Steve Jenkins (**7.26**). **C.** *A Gift from the Sea,* Kate Banks/Georg Hallensleben (**8.11**). **D.** *This Is the Rain,* Lola M. Schaefer/Jane Wattenberg (**7.18**).

A.

B.

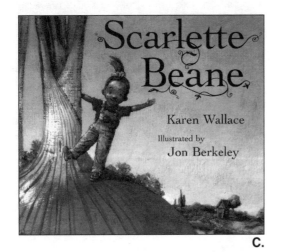

C.

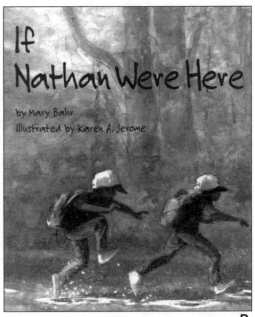

D.

**A.** *I Will Never Not Ever Eat a Tomato,* Lauren Child (**8.23**). **B.** *Desser the Best Ever Cat,* Maggie Smith (**8.9**). **C.** *Scarlette Beane,* Karen Wallace/Jon Berkeley (**8.37**). **D.** *If Nathan Were Here,* Mary Bahr/Karen A. Jerome (**8.1**).

A.

B.

C.

D.

**A.** *Tiger Math: Learning to Graph from a Baby Tiger,* Ann Whitehead Nagda and Cindy Bickel (**9.23**).
**B.** *If You Hopped Like a Frog,* David M. Schwartz/James Warhola (**9.24**).   **C.** *The Story of Clocks and Calendars: Marking a Millennium,* Betsy Maestro/Giulio Maestro (**9.21**).   **D.** *Hannah's Collections,* Marthe Jocelyn (**9.20**).

**A.**

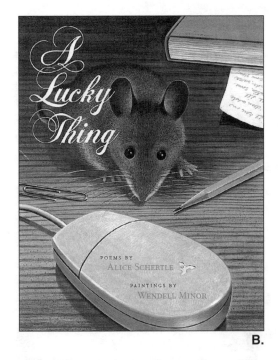

**B.**

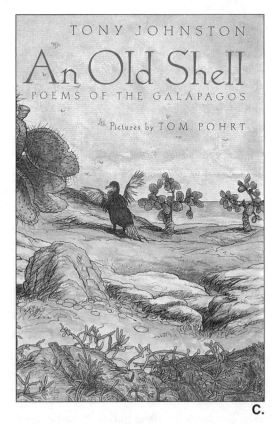

**C.**

**A.** *Yummy! Eating through a Day,* Lee Bennett Hopkins/Renée Flower (**10.31**). **B.** *A Lucky Thing,* Alice Schertle/Wendell Minor (**10.7**). **C.** *An Old Shell: Poems of the Galápagos,* Tony Johnston/Tom Pohrt (**10.4**).

**A.**

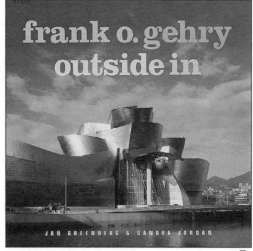

**B.**

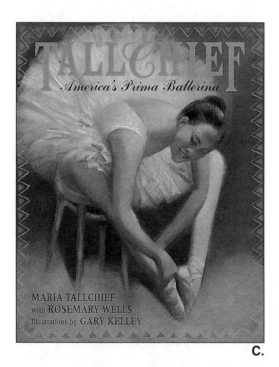

**C.**

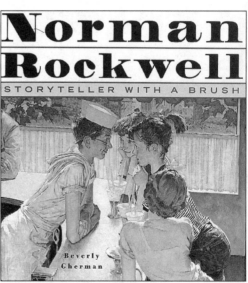

**D.**

**A.** *Kids Dance: The Students of Ballet Tech,* Jim Varriale (**11.27**).  **B.** *Frank O. Gehry: Outside In,* Jan Greenberg and Sandra Jordan (**11.2**).  **C.** *Tallchief: America's Prima Ballerina,* Maria Tallchief with Rosemary Wells/Gary Kelley (**11.26**).  **D.** *Norman Rockwell: Storyteller with a Brush,* Beverly Gherman (**11.13**).

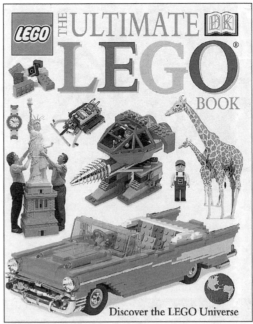

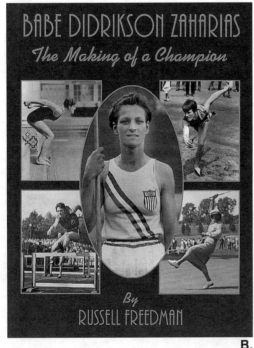

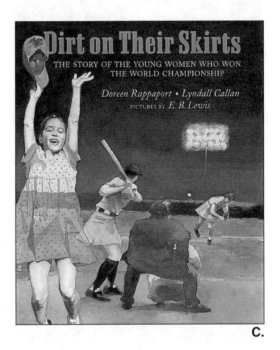

**A.** *The Ultimate LEGO Book* (**12.37**).   **B.** *Babe Didrikson Zaharias: The Making of a Champion,* Russell Freedman (**12.3**).   **C.** *Dirt on Their Skirts: The Story of the Young Women Who Won the World Championship,* Doreen Rappaport and Lyndall Callan/E. B. Lewis (**12.27**).

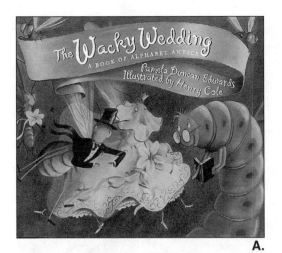

**A.**

**B.**

**C.**

**D.**

**A.** *The Wacky Wedding: A Book of Alphabet Antics,* Pamela Duncan Edwards/Henry Cole (**13.7**).
**B.** *Does a Kangaroo Have a Mother, Too?* Eric Carle (**13.11**). **C.** *Fed Up! A Feast of Frazzled Foods,*
Rex Barron (**13.6**). **D.** *Lizards, Frogs, and Polliwogs: Poems and Paintings,* Douglas Florian (**13.15**).

**A.**

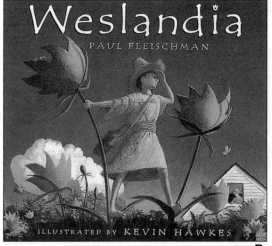

**B.**

**C.**

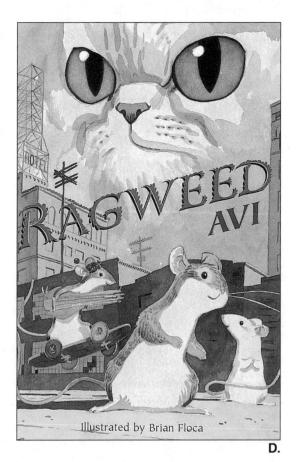

**D.**

**A.** *Island of the Aunts,* Eva Ibbotson/Kevin Hawkes (**14.28**).   **B.** *Weslandia,* Paul Fleischman/Kevin Hawkes (**14.27**).   **C.** *Zigazak! A Magical Hanukkah Night,* Eric A. Kimmel/Jon Goodell (**14.11**). **D.** *Ragweed,* Avi/Brian Floca (**14.1**).

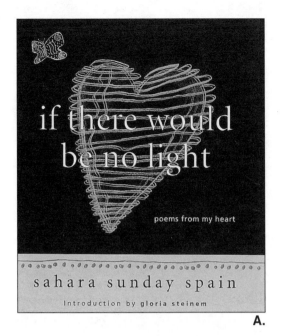

**A.**

**B.**

**C.**

**D.**

**A.** *If There Would Be No Light: Poems from My Heart,* Sahara Sunday Spain (**15.20**). **B.** *Can You Top That?* W. Nikola-Lisa/Hector Viveros Lee (**15.25**). **C.** *Summertime from* Porgy and Bess, George Gershwin, DuBose Heyward, Dorothy Heyward, and Ira Gershwin/Mike Wimmer (**15.12**). **D.** *The Grandad Tree,* Trish Cooke/Sharon Wilson (**15.23**).

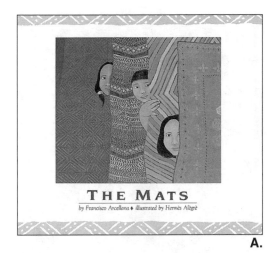

**A.**

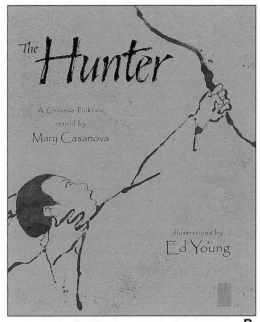

**B.**

**C.**

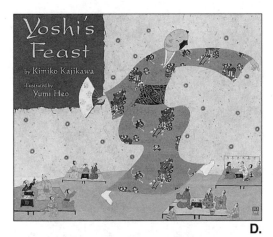

**D.**

**A.** *The Mats,* Francisco Arcellana/Hermès Alègrè (**16.21**).   **B.** *The Hunter: A Chinese Folktale,* Mary Casanova/Ed Young (**16.12**).   **C.** *A Single Shard,* Linda Sue Park (**16.31**).   **D.** *Yoshi's Feast,* Kimiko Kajikawa/Yumi Heo (**16.16**).

**A.**

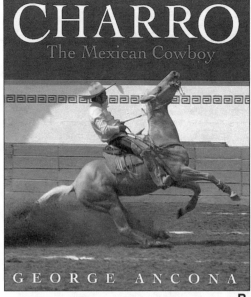

**B.**

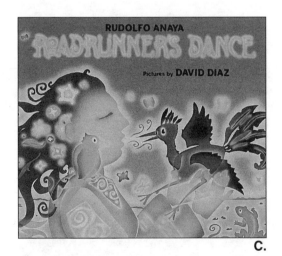

**C.**

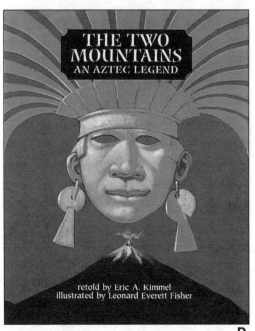

**D.**

**A.** *Coolies,* Yin/Chris Soentpiet (**16.33**). **B.** *Charro: The Mexican Cowboy,* George Ancona (**17.12**). **C.** *Roadrunner's Dance,* Rudolfo Anaya/David Diaz (**17.2**). **D.** *The Two Mountains: An Aztec Legend,* Eric A. Kimmel/Leonard Everett Fisher (**17.23**).

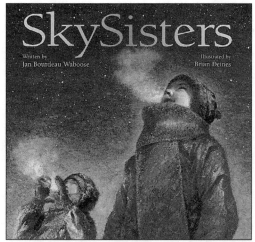

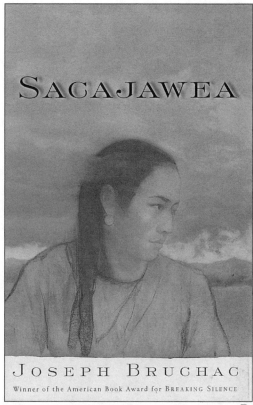

**A.** *SkySisters*, Jan Bordeau Waboose/Brian Deines (**18.21**). **B.** *Sacajawea: The Story of Bird Woman and the Lewis and Clark Expedition*, Joseph Bruchac (**18.4**). **C.** *Esperanza Rising*, Pam Muñoz Ryan (**17.38**). **D.** *Lakota Hoop Dancer*, Jacqueline Left Hand Bull and Suzanne Haldane (**18.10**).

**A.**

**B.**

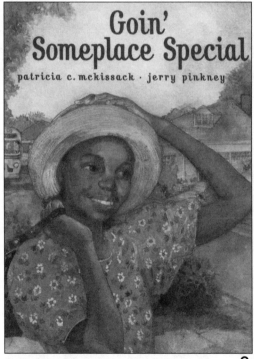

**C.**

**D.**

**A.** *O'Sullivan Stew: A Tale Cooked Up in Ireland,* Hudson Talbott (**19.41**).   **B.** *Harriet, You'll Drive Me Wild!* Mem Fox/Marla Frazee (**19.11**).   **C.** *Goin' Someplace Special,* Patricia C. McKissack/Jerry Pinkney (**19.38**).   **D.** *The Raft,* Jim LaMarche (**19.31**).

**B.**

**C.**

**A.** *Orwell's Luck,* Richard Jennings (**20.21**).   **B.** *Clever Cat,* Peter Collington (**20.16**).   **C.** *Farewell, My Lunchbag: From the Tattered Casebook of Chet Gecko, Private Eye,* Bruce Hale (**21.18**).

**A.**

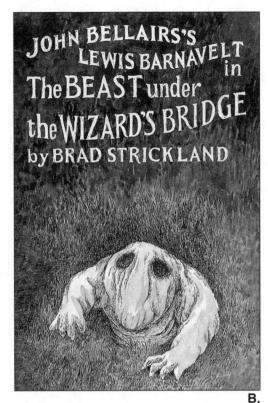

**B.**

**C.**

**A.** *Who Stole the Gold?* Udo Weigelt/Julia Gukova (**21.13**). **B.** *John Bellairs's Lewis Barnavelt in The Beast under the Wizard's Bridge,* Brad Strickland (**21.30**). **C.** *Sammy Keyes and the Hollywood Mummy,* Wendelin Van Draanen (**21.23**).

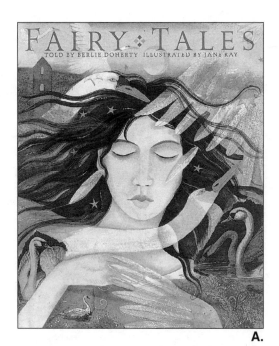

A.

B.

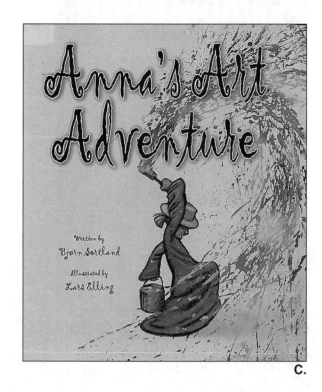

C.

**A.** *Fairy Tales,* Berlie Doherty/Jane Ray (**22.35**). **B.** *The Collector of Moments,* Quint Buchholz (**23.12**). **C.** *Anna's Art Adventure,* Bjørn Sortland/Lars Elling (**23.18**).

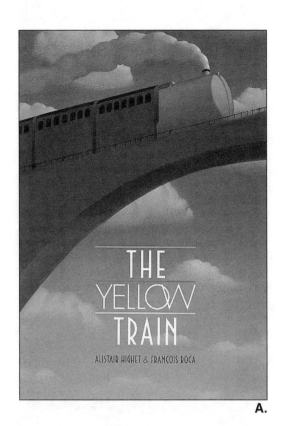

A. *The Yellow Train,* Alistair Highet/François Roca (**23.4**).    B. *Fox,* Margaret Wild/Ron Brooks (**23.20**).
C. *A Day, a Dog,* Gabrielle Vincent (**23.19**).

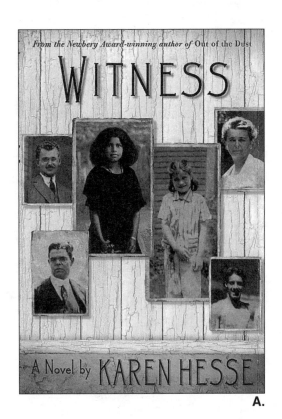

**A.**

**B.**

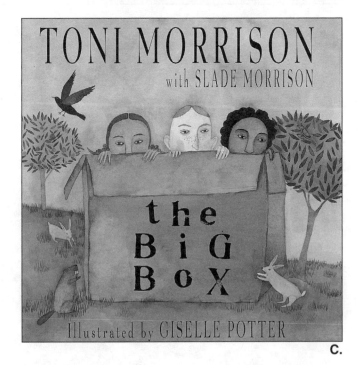

**C.**

**A.** *Witness,* Karen Hesse (**24.1**).  **B.** *Stargirl,* Jerry Spinelli (**24.5**).  **C.** *The Big Box,* Toni Morrison with Slade Morrison/Giselle Potter (**24.24**).

# 13 Literature and Language Play

**Michael F. Opitz**

*Contributing reviewers included Teresa Ginn, Helen O'Donnell, and William O'Donnell.*

---

**Criteria for Excellence**

- Features some sort of language play
- Lends itself to further language exploration activities
- Provides appropriate content for primary-age children
- Suitable as a read-aloud
- Child-tested

---

## Rhyme

Barrett, Judi. **I Knew Two Who Said Moo: A Counting and Rhyming Book.** Illustrated by Daniel Moreton. Atheneum, 2000.

Brown, Ruth. **Mad Summer Night's Dream.** Dutton, 1999.

★ Lorenz, Lee. **Pig and Duck Buy a Truck: A Book of Colors.** Simon & Schuster, 2000.

★ Spence, Rob, and Amy Spence. **Clickety Clack.** Illustrated by Margaret Spengler. Viking, 1999.

Walton, Rick. **Little Dogs Say "Rough!"** Illustrated by Henry Cole. Putnam, 2000.

## Alliteration

★ Barron, Rex. **Fed Up! A Feast of Frazzled Foods.** Putnam, 2000.

★ Edwards, Pamela Duncan. **The Wacky Wedding: A Book of Alphabet Antics.** Illustrated by Henry Cole. Hyperion, 1999.

Hausman, Bonnie. **A to Z: Do You Ever Feel Like Me? A Guessing Alphabet of Feelings, Words, and Other Cool Stuff.** Photographed by Sandi Fellman. Dutton, 1999.

★ Moxley, Sheila. **ABCD: An Alphabet Book of Cats and Dogs.** Little, Brown, 2001.

Wojtowycz, David. **Animal Antics from 1 to 10.** Holiday House, 2000.

## Repetition

★ Carle, Eric. **Does a Kangaroo Have a Mother, Too?** HarperCollins, 2000.

Narahashi, Keiko. **Two Girls Can!** Margaret K. McElderry Books, 2000.

★ Parr, Todd. **The Feelings Book.** Little, Brown, 2000.

Winter, Rick. **Dirty Birdy Feet.** Illustrated by Mike Lester. Rising Moon, 2000.

## Poetry

★ Florian, Douglas. **Lizards, Frogs, and Polliwogs: Poems and Paintings.** Harcourt, 2001.

Mathers, Pete. **A Cake for Herbie.** Atheneum, 2000.

Wise, William. **Dinosaurs Forever.** Illustrated by Lynn Munsinger. Dial, 2000.

## Songs

Arnosky, Jim. **Rattlesnake Dance.** Putnam, 2000.

Guthrie, Woody. **Howdi Do.** Illustrated by Vladimir Radunsky. Candlewick, 2000.

Kellogg, Steven. **Give the Dog a Bone.** SeaStar, 2000.

Lass, Bonnie, and Philemon Sturges. **Who Took the Cookies from the Cookie Jar?** Illustrated by Ashley Wolff. Little, Brown, 2000.

★ Maguire, Gregory. **Crabby Cratchitt.** Illustrated by Andrew Glass. Clarion, 2000.

★ Westcott, Nadine Bernard. **Skip to My Lou.** Little, Brown, 2000.

## Other

Cuyler, Margery. **Road Signs: A Harey Race with a Tortoise.** Illustrated by Steve Haskamp. Winslow, 2000.

Gardiner, Lindsey. **Here Come Poppy and Max.** Little, Brown, 2000.

Heap, Sue. **Baby Bill and Little Lil.** Kingfisher, 1999.

Jay, Alison. **Picture This . . .** Dutton, 2000.

★ Leslie, Amanda. **Flappy, Waggy, Wiggly.** Dutton, 1999.

★ Rosenberry, Vera. **Run, Jump, Whiz, Splash.** Holiday House, 1999.

Simmons, Jay. **Daisy Says Coo!** Little, Brown, 2000.

Tobias, Tobi. **Serendipity.** Illustrated by Peter H. Reynolds. Simon & Schuster, 2000.

Literature and language play are meant for each other. This is a lesson that well-known authors have taught us over the years with their playful texts. What better way for children to learn about the sounds of their language and the fun that can be had with language than by listening to or reading a book filled with opportunities to savor and play with sounds. Youngsters can't help but catch the repetitive and rhyming aspects of language as they sense the invitation to chime in saying the words and experiencing their sounds as they roll off their tongues, out of their mouths, and into their ears.

Reading aloud children's literature that focuses on specific language elements is one of the best ways to foster phonological awareness (i.e., the awareness that spoken language comprises sound units such as words within sentences, syllables within words, and phonemes within syllables and words). Texts such as these draw learners' attention to features such as rhyme, alliteration, phoneme substitution, and phoneme segmentation. Many children discover and attend to sounds in language by experiencing books such as these. Just the same, some children may need more explicit instruction to develop all levels of phonological awareness (i.e., word, syllable, and phonemic awareness). In these cases, phonological awareness activities can be used as an extension of a literacy experience such as a read-aloud so that children can see how the activity connects to reading and writing. In fact, the results of some studies have shown that children who engage in meaningful, connected activities actually perform as well as or better on phonological awareness tasks than children who complete isolated tasks.

Fortunately for the children we teach, several authors and illustrators continually help advance the idea that learning about language by playing with it can be a fun and rewarding activity. The words and images of several of these authors and illustrators are featured in this chapter. But make no mistake. This chapter is a sampling rather than a complete list of the many fine books published between 1999 and 2001. We could only include so many.

Given the number of books available to us for this project, we needed to employ criteria to help us select books. As you read through the annotations, you'll notice that all of the books:

- feature some sort of language play so that children's attention can focus on the author's intended meaning and the highlighted language feature (e.g., rhyme, alliteration) simultaneously.

- lend themselves to further language exploration activities. Ideas for further language play are sprinkled throughout the annotations and resulted from actually using the books with children.

- provide appropriate content for primary-age children (preschool through second grade).

- are good read-alouds (although we recognize that some children may be able to read some of them independently).

- are trade books. That is, the books are written to communicate ideas to the intended audience rather than to use specific words a given number of times based on some set formula. Consequently, all of the books featured in this chapter can be found in local libraries and bookstores.

- are child tested. While the books were being used with children, we watched their reactions. We also asked for their opinions. Again, their words are sprinkled throughout the annotations.

We also thought it would be a good idea to categorize the books for easy access. We decided to organize according to the predominant language features used by the authors to form five categories: rhyme, alliteration, repetition, poetry, and songs. We soon discovered, however, that we needed to have an "other" category for books that dealt with language play in other ways. Riddle books fall into this category, as do books in which the authors and illustrators played with the spacing of the text. Several of the words in Vera Rosenberry's *Run, Jump, Whiz, Splash* (Holiday House, 1999), for example, are stretched over a page in larger print, suggesting that the word be said in the same manner.

When thinking about using these books with children, we offer these suggestions to invite success:

- Enjoy the book with the children. Encourage children to participate by gathering them together and inviting them to make some predictions based on what they see on the cover.

- Read and reread the book to familiarize the students with the language of the text.

- Call children's attention to the language used in the story. For a book in which much rhyming is used, for example, you might comment, "*Sat, bat.* Hey! Those words rhyme! This author uses a lot of rhyming words in this book. Did you hear any others as I was reading?"

- Several of the annotations in this chapter include a response activity that helps children explore the language play aspect of the book. We encourage you to use the activity as is or modify it to fit your unique needs.

- Display the book for further exploration. Some children will want to see the book again. Some will pretend to read the book, making up the story as best as they can recall. Others will read the story as printed. Providing children with these experiences is an excellent way to help them connect spoken and written language.

Most important, we encourage you to use some or all of the books in this chapter to convey an important message to children: learning about the sounds of language is an enjoyable, rewarding activity that helps us better understand ourselves and our world. It's a kick!

## Rhyme

**13.1**   Barrett, Judi. **I Knew Two Who Said Moo: A Counting and Rhyming Book.** Illustrated by Daniel Moreton. Atheneum, 2000. ISBN 0-689-82104-2. Unpaged. (ALL).

Using the numbers one to ten, this book allows children to explore a variety of rhymes created by using different spellings for the same sound. Each rhyme invites children to observe likeness and difference among words. The rhymes can be read as a whole or individually, as each can stand alone. Try this on for size: "I knew <u>two</u>/ who said <u>moo</u>/ all dressed in <u>blue</u>/ sitting in a <u>shoe</u>/ on the <u>avenue</u>/ with noses they <u>blew</u>/ because of the <u>flu</u>/ getting a <u>shampoo</u>/ before the <u>barbecue</u>/ given by the <u>kangaroo</u>/ and the <u>ewe</u>/ at the <u>zoo</u>/ <u>WHEW</u>!" (emphasis added). Once children have been exposed to the different spellings and rhymes, individuals or pairs of students can be invited to construct one of their own to share with the class. (TG)

**13.2**   Brown, Ruth. **Mad Summer Night's Dream.** Dutton, 1999. ISBN 0-525-46010-1. Unpaged. (P).

Want to get children talking about their dreams? If so, you need this book. The real becomes the unreal when normal, everyday objects go berserk. Birds blossom! Flowers sing! Opposites such as these will have children talking about how Brown created each of the word pairs. After discussing the book with my students, we made a list of the events in the story, placing each object and action on separate cards. After displaying the cards in the card holder, children were invited to straighten them out—to make the unreal real once again. We also created some hinkpinks (i.e., two rhyming words used consecutively to answer a riddle such as "What do you say to a bad cat? Scat, cat!") to draw students' attention to how rhyme was used in the book. (WOD)

Harris, Trudy. **Pattern Fish.** Illustrated by Anne Canevari Green. Millbrook, 2000. ISBN 0-7613-1712-0. Unpaged. (P). (See **9.29.**)

13.3    ★ Lorenz, Lee. **Pig and Duck Buy a Truck: A Book of Colors.** Simon & Schuster, 2000. ISBN 0-689-83780-1. Unpaged. (P).

If you want to show children how colors can be blended to make additional colors, this book is for you. Pig and duck contemplate what they will do with their extra money. After much thought, they decide to buy a truck. But this soon presents a major problem: they can't decide on a color because each has a different favorite. Enter the used truck salesman, who solves the problem while indirectly showing how to blend colors to make new colors. Dialogue such as "I like yellow. / I like red. / How about an orange one instead?" ensues. Told in rhyme, this text encourages children to supply missing rhyming words if the reader pauses long enough for them to chime in. It is also an excellent book for teaching students more about how sounds can be blended together to make words (i.e., phoneme blending). Teachers might say riddles such as, "I'm thinking of a color that was in the story; it is /r/ /e/ /d/. What's the color?" (HOD)

13.4    ★ Spence, Rob, and Amy Spence. **Clickety Clack.** Illustrated by Margaret Spengler. Viking, 1999. ISBN 0-670-87946-0. Unpaged. (P).

With colorful, engaging illustrations that accompany the Spences' rhythmic text, Spengler helps create a fun train ride with a noisy group of animals. Not only do the animals make noise, but the train does as well. How can it stop from groaning with all of that animal weight? The text encourages involvement as it progresses. "This is funny!"; "It sure has lots of noise!" commented a couple of children. Much initial consonant substitution makes this a perfect book to use for phonemic awareness. Using rhyming words from the text, statements such as the following can be shared with students: "Take the /s/ off of *sack* and add some new sounds to *-ack* to make the words that tell where the train went." The book also lends itself well to dramatization. Children can take on the role of different animals and board the train as the story is reread. (HOD)

13.5    Walton, Rick. **Little Dogs Say "Rough!"** Illustrated by Henry Cole. Putnam, 2000. ISBN 0-399-23228-1. Unpaged. (P).

Did you ever wonder what animals are really saying when they make their animal noises? Wonder no more as Walton provides text that reveals answers to questions about just what animals are saying when they make their sounds. Cole's amusing illustrations are sure to put smiles on children's faces as they have fun making the animal sounds using the elongated words (e.g., *cooooool mooooon*) spelled out in Walton's clever text. The elongated words are also excellent examples for showing children how sounds can be stretched and blended together to form words. We had fun stretching and blending names of objects in the classroom. (TG)

## Alliteration

**13.6** ★ Barron, Rex. **Fed Up! A Feast of Frazzled Foods.** Putnam, 2000. ISBN 0-399-23450-0. Unpaged. (ALL).

All of us get fed up now and then, but who would ever imagine that food does too? Here, readers learn about, for example, "anxious apples" and "cabbage crying over coleslaw." Barron captures a range of emotions through the "moody foods" presented in the text. The illustrations do an excellent job of depicting the emotion of each food discussed. This book can be used as a catalyst for discussion about emotions, different types of foods, and, in terms of phonological awareness, words that begin alike. Students can pretend to go shopping by sitting in a circle and stating something they will buy that begins with a given sound. Older students might want to try their hand at creating a similar book using different foods or objects. (MFO)

**13.7** ★ Edwards, Pamela Duncan. **The Wacky Wedding: A Book of Alphabet Antics.** Illustrated by Henry Cole. Hyperion, 1999. ISBN 0-7868-2248-1. Unpaged. (P).

You haven't attended a wedding until you've attended this alliterative one! Queen Ant and Faithful Flying Ant decide to get married and get off to a good start ("An army of ants attended a wedding once on an April afternoon."), but disaster soon ensues. The foolish fly lets some fruit fall on the groom's head. The couple is not to be deterred, however, and they persist through every letter of the alphabet and appear to be living happily ever after. Cole's lush, large illustrations are sure to attract children, especially when they realize there is a hidden letter and object associated with the letter featured on the page. A natural follow-up is to complete a sound-matching activity in which the teacher states a sound used on one of the pages and then asks students to recall words on the page that have that sound. Children also have a great time trying to get through each verse without getting their tongues twisted! (MFO)

**13.8**    Hausman, Bonnie. **A to Z: Do You Ever Feel Like Me? A Guessing Alphabet of Feelings, Words, and Other Cool Stuff.** Photographs by Sandi Fellman. Dutton, 1999. ISBN 0-525-46216-3. Unpaged. (P).

Developed from a real first-grade class project, this book includes bright, attractive photographs of children. For each letter of the alphabet, Hausman invites children to guess the feelings represented by the children's body language in the photographs, using both picture and text. As an added help, the word is printed somewhere in the border, along with pictures of other objects that begin with the same letter. Children had fun ("I like it!"; "These pages are fun!") as they continued to build vocabulary for reading and writing. As children stated words with a given sound, I wrote them on corresponding charts and displayed them in the room. (WOD)

Hobbie, Holly. **Toot & Puddle: Puddle's ABC.** Little, Brown, 2000. ISBN 0-316-36593-9. Unpaged. (P). (See **7.24.**)

**13.9**    ★ Moxley, Sheila. **ABCD: An Alphabet Book of Cats and Dogs.** Little, Brown, 2001. ISBN 0-316-59240-4. Unpaged. (P).

Painting and photographs are combined to show different dogs and cats completing tasks for every letter of the alphabet. Whether it's "Arnold is an amazing aviator" or "Yolanda yearns for a yellow yo-yo," these dogs and cats are sure to help children learn the alphabet and the sounds associated with each letter in meaningful and unique ways. The book closes with a two-page spread showing miniature-sized versions of the illustrations used throughout the text. One way this page can be used is to isolate one of the pictures and have students see if they can recall the corresponding verse. Students can then be encouraged to bring in pictures of their own pets and create verses for them. Having children repeat the verses as quickly as possible would be a fun way to repeat sounds and to see how long tongues can move untwisted! (MFO)

**13.10**  Wojtowycz, David. **Animal Antics from 1 to 10.** Holiday House, 2000. ISBN 0-8234-1552-X. Unpaged. (P).

We've all stayed in hotels, but have any of us stayed in a hotel that specializes in numbers? That's exactly what this hotel does, and different animals from one to ten come to stay. Beginning with "one warthog wearing a wig" and ending with "ten tigers in tutus," this book is sure to help children learn basic counting while also focusing on the letters and sounds of the alliterative text. The illustrations breathe life and humor into the story; there's just something about seeing tigers in tutus that says more than words can! Encourage children to think of other animals that could stay at the hotel and have them make up corresponding alliterative verses. These could then be shared with others and later combined to form a book for the classroom library. (MFO)

## Repetition

**13.11**  ★ Carle, Eric. **Does a Kangaroo Have a Mother, Too?** Harper-Collins, 2000. ISBN 0-06-028768-3. Unpaged. (P).

Using repetitive text, Carle informs youngsters that baby animals have mothers too! While conveying this message, he also provides the names of animal babies, parents, and groups depicted in the illustrations used throughout the book. In his classic style, Carle provides children with yet another enjoyable reading experience as they use the simple text and supportive illustrations to learn more about animals. To help children further understand that words are made up of syllables, use animal names from the book. State them in syllables and invite students to blend the syllables to state the word. You might say, for example, "One of the animals in the book is a /kang/ /a/ /roo/. What's the animal?" (MFO)

★ Cronin, Doreen. **Click, Clack, Moo: Cows That Type.** Illustrated by Betsy Lewin. Simon & Schuster, 2000. ISBN 0-689-83213-3. Unpaged. (P). (See **24.22.**)

**13.12**  Narahashi, Keiko. **Two Girls Can!** Margaret K. McElderry Books, 2000. ISBN 0-689-82618-4. Unpaged. (P).

Using watercolor illustrations and simple, repetitive text, Narahashi provides a look at some of the many activities girls can engage in. Among the many activities shown in the text, the two girls in this story hold hands, stay dry, get mad, play leapfrog, and dance. They do all of these activities together. And, as noted at the end of the story, these activities are suited for larger groups as well. To help children understand that language is made up of words, frame each word and ask children to clap each time they hear a word. Children will have fun doing all of the activities the two girls do, as well as making a list of additional activities that two or more can do. (MFO)

13.13   ★ Parr, Todd. **The Feelings Book.** Little, Brown, 2000. ISBN 0-316-69131-3. Unpaged. (P).

Here's a book that helps children explore their feelings and come to realize that others sometimes feel just as they do. With the repetitive phrase "Sometimes I feel," children are invited to experience what causes others to feel the way they do at times. In fact, different children commented, "I know how that feels!" when the book was shared with them. The colorful and simple illustrations evoked student responses such as "I like the bright colors and the simple illustrations!" After dramatizing the book, an activity in which different groups of children acted out a feeling and the others in the class tried to guess what it was, we decided to make a class book entitled "Sometimes I Feel." Each student completed the sentence "Sometimes I feel" and drew a picture. These were then compiled into the class book. I also used the book to help children further understand that many words contain more than one syllable. I would say a word from the story and ask children to show a happy face if they heard more than one word part (i.e., syllable) and a sad face if they heard only one. (WOD)

13.14   Winter, Rick. **Dirty Birdy Feet.** Illustrated by Mike Lester. Rising Moon, 2000. ISBN 0-87358-768-5. Unpaged. (P).

Are you thinking of getting white carpeting for your house? If so, you might want to read this book first. Little sister and her brother watch as the cat, dog, big brother, dad, and mom each take a turn trying to get rid of a bird that accidentally falls down the chimney during dinner. Now, trying to get a bird out of a house is hard enough, but when you include the cat and dog in your efforts, a huge mess is sure to be the result. In cumulative and repetitive text, Winter engages children in the different attempts to rid the house of the bird. The lively illustrations add to their frantic efforts and the mess that ensues. Professional cleaning, anyone? (WOD)

## Poetry

**13.15** ★ Florian, Douglas. **Lizards, Frogs, and Polliwogs: Poems and Paintings.** Harcourt, 2001. ISBN 0-15-202591-X. 47 pp. (ALL).

Perhaps one of the best ways to teach children about different animal groupings is to use the poetry collections written and illustrated by Douglas Florian. This one is no exception. Twenty-one short reptile and amphibian poems describe various reptiles and amphibians. Each poem is accompanied by a full-page watercolor illustration that captures the essence of the poem. The challenge and fun for children is in distinguishing the factual information from the fantasy that go together to create each rhyme. To further focus on how rhyme is used, reread the poems and pause long enough for students to fill in the rhyming words. (MFO)

**13.16** Mathers, Pete. **A Cake for Herbie.** Atheneum, 2000. ISBN 0-689-83017-3. Unpaged. (P).

Herbie the duck and his best friend Lottie the hen go to the grocery store, where Herbie spots a sign about a poetry contest in which the winner will be rewarded with a cake. Herbie decides he will join the competition and works hard to compose a poem for every letter of the alphabet. When the big day arrives and Herbie begins to read his poems aloud, the audience gets bored and they let him know it. Embarrassed, Herbie leaves without finishing and tries to regain his composure in the alley. This is the beginning of discovering new friends who appreciate his poetry and those who like cake as much as he does. The book has much to say about the value of friendship and valuing oneself. It is a perfect book for engaging children in a discussion about being considerate of others' feelings as well as for showing children how rhymes are created. Using words from the book, say each pair and ask children to tell you what was changed in the second word in the pair to make it rhyme with the first word (i.e., phoneme substitution). (TG)

Paolilli, Paul, and Dan Brewer. **Silver Seeds: A Book of Nature Poems.** Illustrated by Steve Johnson and Lou Fancher. Viking, 2001. ISBN 0-670-88941-5. Unpaged. (P). (See **10.6.**)

**13.17** Wise, William. **Dinosaurs Forever.** Illustrated by Lynn Munsinger. Dial, 2000. ISBN 0-8037-2114-5. Unpaged. (ALL).

Here is a collection of poems that can be used to capitalize on an interest shared by most children. Each dino-rhyme provides humorous information about a specific dinosaur. Dinosaurs who like to bake chocolate cakes and who dress up to go to a dino ball are just two of the many activities that the dinosaurs in these dino-rhymes like to do. All of these activities are captured in brilliant watercolors. Look for factual information about dinosaurs as well. This is an excellent book for helping children distinguish between what is real and what is fantasy in an entertaining way. To help children further understand that words are used to create text, choose one of the poems and write each line on a different sentence strip. Ask students to watch as you cut each line into words and count every time a word is cut off the line. Ask them to state how many words were used to create a given line. (MFO)

## Songs

**13.18** Arnosky, Jim. **Rattlesnake Dance.** Putnam, 2000. ISBN 0-399-22755-5. Unpaged. (P).

Can a rattlesnake dance? He sure can in this story, though little does he know this when he first slithers into a cave to find some rest. In the cave, the rattlesnake begins to shake and dance and is joined by others who do the same. A complete musical score with accompanying lyrics is provided at the opening of the book for those musically inclined. Tips for doing the rattlesnake dance are provided on the last page. With its accompanying lively illustrations, this story is sure to have everyone moving and singing. Point out the rhyming words used to create the dance. Say one word from the book and ask students to take off the beginning sound and add another sound to create a word from the book that rhymes with the first word (i.e., phoneme manipulation). (MFO)

**13.19** Guthrie, Woody. **Howdi Do.** Illustrated by Vladimir Radunsky. Candlewick, 2000. ISBN 0-7636-0768-1. Unpaged. (P).

Folk musician Woody Guthrie and illustrator Vladimir Radunsky team up—albeit posthumously on Guthrie's part—to provide a lively book and CD-ROM for a song that was originally written in the 1960s. "Howdie Do" is a song about a dog who feels compelled to say, "Howdi Do!" to every animal he meets. He also likes to "shakey paw." The recurring chorus, "Howjee, heejee, hijee, hojee / Howdi do, sir, doodle do!," got my children singing and moving as I read the book and had them listen to the CD. The nonsense words are a wonderful way to show them that goofing around with language can be an enjoyable activity. In fact, we had fun going through the book to find all of the non-sensical rhyming word pairs. "This is a cool song book!" was heard from more than one child. (HOD)

**13.20** Kellogg, Steven. **Give the Dog a Bone.** SeaStar, 2000. ISBN 1058717-001-9. 33 pp. (P).

"This Old Man" is a popular song that first appeared in the early twentieth century, and it's gone through many variations since its inception. This is yet another rendition sure to delight and entertain children. After the first verse, the text is original and includes several kinds of dogs (250 in all). By the time this version of the traditional song ends, the old man is surrounded by his best friends, the dogs. The action-packed text invites children to perform such actions as clap and stomp. In fact, as Kellogg notes in the endnotes, this song can be used to teach language, counting, rhythm, and coordination. The musical score is provided in the back of the book. I followed the author's suggestion and had students clap each time they heard a word to help them understand that words are used to create their language. (MFO)

**13.21** Lass, Bonnie, and Philemon Sturges. **Who Took the Cookies from the Cookie Jar?** Illustrated by Ashley Wolff. Little, Brown, 2000. ISBN 0-316-82016-4. Unpaged. (P).

In this adaptation of a playground song, children can help Skunk solve the mystery of who took the cookie as he asks each of his animal friends the question, "Who took the cookie from the cookie jar?" The surprise ending reveals that the ants took the cookies and purposefully left a trail of crumbs so that all animals in the story could find them and enjoy eating the cookies together. I used several of the authors' suggestions for how the book can be read and found that the children enjoyed the song and game before and after the story. To focus on phonemes, students whose name began with a given sound were invited to take the cookie from the cookie jar. Students commented, "It's fun to sing and play this book!" (HOD)

**13.22**    ★ Maguire, Gregory. **Crabby Cratchitt.** Illustrated by Andrew Glass. Clarion, 2000. ISBN 0-395-60485-0. 32 pp. (P).

Poor Crabby Cratchitt! She's crabby because she can't get any rest, thanks to the hen on her farm who continually makes noise. Rather than buy earplugs to block out the sound, Crabby goes to great lengths to get rid of the hen in this action-packed text. Only when the fox captures and almost eats the hen does Crabby realizes how much she likes the hen and that she doesn't want too much quiet. In fact, she learns to use the cluckings as a lullaby. The text is set to the tune of "Old MacDonald Had a Farm," a song most children know and love, making it more likely that they will be able to sing along after they've heard the story a few times. My students commented, "This is a food storybook!" and "I like singing it!" Indeed, I used the book to point out rhyming words while children sang along. (HOD)

**13.23**    ★ Westcott, Nadine Bernard. **Skip to My Lou.** Little, Brown, 2000. ISBN 0-316-93091-1. Unpaged. (P).

This is an adaptation of a familiar song ("Flies in the sugarbowl, / Shoo fly shoo. / Cats in the buttermilk, / Two by two. / Pigs in the parlor, / What'll I do? / Skip to my Lou, / My darling!") that promises to have children singing and dancing as to the previous versions. This rendition tells of a young boy who is left in charge of the family farm by his parents. Unfortunately for him, the farm animals wreak havoc in the farmhouse. All's well that ends well, however; everything is put back in order before the parents return home. My students enjoyed singing along, and some made comments such as "I liked the sheep unzipping their wool!" They were also able to identify the rhyming words with ease. (HOD)

## Other

**13.24**    Cuyler, Margery. **Road Signs: A Harey Race with a Tortoise.** Illustrated by Steve Haskamp. Winslow, 2000. ISBN 1-890817-23-6. Unpaged. (P).

In this adaptation of the well-known Aesop fable, signs are everywhere. Once again, Tortoise and Hare are racing to the finish line. This time, however, they encounter several signs that provide direction and support. One sign, for example, reads, "Harey Up." As in the traditional tale, Tortoise wins the race because he uses the signs to guide him right to the finish line. Hare, on the other hand, lets the signs lead him astray. After reading the book, children can make different signs that can be used to retell the story. Creating these signs also provides students with practice in hearing sounds in words, thus increasing phonological awareness. (WOD)

**13.25** Gardiner, Lindsey. **Here Come Poppy and Max.** Little, Brown, 2000. ISBN 0-316-60346-5. Unpaged. (P).

Poppy loves to imitate all sorts of animals, and her dog Max loves to imitate Poppy imitating different animals. Many different actions ensue as these two lovable characters use their imaginations to do their imitations. The colorful illustrations capture each imitation, bringing it to life. This is a perfect book to dramatize since children can take on the role of Poppy or Max and act out the imitations. After reading this book, students typically made the following comments, "This is a fun book!"; "I want to keep this book. Can I?"(HOD)

**13.26** Heap, Sue. **Baby Bill and Little Lil.** Kingfisher, 1999. ISBN 0-7534-5196-4. Unpaged. (P).

Baby Bill and Little Lil set out to find a pet fishy, and their friends accompany them to the sea to assist as needed. Thanks to a big wave, however, Baby Bill looses his pail in the sea and is unable to fulfill his wish. But as luck would have it, the sea washes the pail to shore right side up, and inside is a pet fish. A bit of a stretch? Perhaps. But my students appeared to enjoy the story, especially the parts we read chorally. To focus on phonological awareness, we then used a pail to catch words that had more than one syllable. I wrote some of the words from the story on fish shapes and gave each student a word. Next, I read the word. If the word had one part, it went in the pail, and if it had more than one part, it remained in the ocean. (TG)

**13.27** Jay, Alison. **Picture This . . .** Dutton, 2000. ISBN 0-525-46380-1. Unpaged. (P).

The one or two words in large type make this look like a simple text, but a closer look reveals more. Each page hints at a nursery rhyme, and there is an item from the previous page on each succeeding page. Looking for the item in the new picture can be fun and challenging. Obviously, the pictures are a big part of this book. My students were excited about finding something from the previous page on the page they were reading. This is an excellent book for expanding children's vocabularies while teaching them about looking for clues and about rhyming. After the students had a lot of practice with rhyming, I selected words from the various rhymes and had children stand if the two words rhymed and stay seated if they didn't. We then talked about the sound that was changed in one of the words to create a rhyming word for each pair. (TG)

13.28  ★ Leslie, Amanda. **Flappy, Waggy, Wiggly.** Dutton, 1999. ISBN 0-525-46182-5. Unpaged. (P).

In this interactive text, children are encouraged to lift flaps to find answers to riddles provided in the text and illustrations. One question, for example, asks, "Who has a waggy yellow tail and a stick-licky tongue?" The animal that answers this riddle is revealed once the flap is lifted. I've had difficulty finding appropriate riddle books for grade K–1, but this book is perfect. The text is large enough for the whole group to see and read together. I also use it to give students some practice with phoneme blending. I reread a riddle and state the animal's name, sound by sound. The children then blend the sounds together and state the word. Children commented, "I wish I could have this book."; "This is so much fun!"; "I can guess *all* of these!" The next project is to launch a class-made riddle book using the pattern provided in the text. (HOD)

13.29  ★ Rosenberry, Vera. **Run, Jump, Whiz, Splash.** Holiday House, 1999. ISBN 0-8234-1378-0. Unpaged. (P).

What do people do in different seasons? Through simple text and captivating illustrations, this book presents specific activities that children like to engage in for each season. Both text and illustrations also describe the seasons and take children on a whirlwind tour of spring, summer, fall, and winter. The text is often written in a way that stretches out a word, which makes this book suitable for showing children how authors use typographic clues to convey their message and that sounds are often stretched and blended to form meaningful words. (TG)

13.30  Simmons, Jay. **Daisy Says Coo!** Little, Brown, 2000. ISBN 0-316-79764-2. Unpaged. (P).

Have children gather around and listen to the sounds that Daisy Duck's animal friends make as each talks to Daisy in its own language. Daisy gets so wrapped up in talking to her friends that her mother comes looking for her. Mother's quack is one sound that Daisy instantly recognizes, and she is reunited with her by the end of the story. The story is told using simple text with repetitive lines that entice children to read chorally when they recognize a familiar line. It's also an excellent choice when helping children understand that words are used to create sentences. I used sentence strips and had children watch and count as I cut the words off the sentence strip. The watercolor illustrations are a perfect match for the text. These, combined with the repetitive nature of the text, made it possible for many of my students to read the book independently after a simple introduction. (HOD)

13.31   Tobias, Tobi. **Serendipity.** Illustrated by Peter Reynolds. Simon & Schuster, 2000. ISBN 0-689-83373-3. Unpaged. (ALL).

What could be better than having something turn out to be happy when you don't expect it to be so? In this book, children experience the meaning of serendipity when they read or listen to this collection of unrelated situations in which good fortune unexpectedly occurs. I had students write and illustrate their own serendipitous experiences for a class book. I also used the book to focus on syllables in spoken language and asked students to clap each time they heard a word part. (TG)

# 14 Fantasy Literature

Daniel P. Woolsey

*Contributing reviewers included Evelyn Alessi, Darlene Bressler, Colleen Clester, Carol Harris, Thomas Herman, Traci Kozak-Krist, Mary Lingenfelter, Darice Mullen, Marcia H. Tyrrell, Scott Vonderheide, Nancy Walters, and Sherry Wilson.*

---

**Criteria for Excellence**

- Literary quality (e.g., memorable language, compelling illustrations, believable and engaging characters, convincing plot, significant themes)
- A strong element of the magical or fantastic
- Writing that helps us to "suspend our disbelief"
- Presence of originality and unique elements
- Images and ideas that stay with us after the reading is done
- Ideas that change the way we look at the world

---

## Animal Fantasy

★ Avi. **Ragweed.** Illustrated by Brian Floca. Avon, 1999.

Dunrea, Olivier. **Bear Noel.** Farrar, Straus & Giroux, 2000.

Hurwitz, Joanna. **PeeWee's Tale.** Illustrated by Patience Brewster. SeaStar, 2000.

Lester, Helen. **Hooway for Wodney Wat.** Illustrated by Lynn Munsinger. Houghton Mifflin, 1999.

Marcellino, Fred. **I, Crocodile.** HarperCollins, 1999.

McPhail, David. **Mole Music.** Holt, 1999.

Whybrow, Ian. **Sammy and the Dinosaurs.** Illustrated by Adrian Reynolds. Orchard, 1999.

Wood, Audrey. **Jubal's Wish.** Illustrated by Don Wood. Scholastic, 2000.

## Literary Fairy Tales

Cole, Brock. **Larky Mavis.** Illustrated by Brock Cole. Farrar, Straus & Giroux, 2001.

Helldorfer, M. C. **Night of the White Stag.** Illustrated by Yvonne Gilbert. Random House, 1999.

★ Kimmel, Eric A. **Zigazak! A Magical Hanukkah Night.** Illustrated by Jon Goodell. Doubleday, 2001.

Mitchell, Adrian. **Nobody Rides the Unicorn.** Illustrated by Stephen Lambert. Scholastic, 1999.

★ Schmidt, Gary. **Straw into Gold.** Clarion, 2001.

Silverman, Erica. **Raisel's Riddle.** Illustrated by Susan Gaber. Farrar, Straus & Giroux, 1999.

## Heroic Fantasy

★ Beaverson, Aiden. **The Hidden Arrow of Maether.** Delacorte, 2000.

Billingsley, Franny. **The Folk Keeper.** Atheneum, 1999.

★ Pattison, Darcy. **The Wayfinder.** HarperCollins, 2000.

Pierce, Tamora. **Squire.** Random House, 2001.

Russell, Barbara Timberlake. **The Taker's Stone.** DK Ink, 1999.

Thompson, Kate. **Wild Blood.** Hyperion, 2000.

## Science Fiction Fantasy

Bell, Hilari. **Songs of Power.** Hyperion, 2000.

Bunting, Eve. **Wanna Buy an Alien?** Illustrated by Tim Bush. Clarion, 2000.

Scieszka, Jon. **Baloney (Henry P.).** Illustrated by Lane Smith. Viking, 2001.

Waugh, Sylvia. **Space Race.** Delacorte, 2000.

## Enchanted Realism

Almond, David. **Skellig.** Delacorte, 1999.

Fine, Anne. **Bad Dreams.** Delacorte, 2000.

★ Fleischman, Paul. **Weslandia.** Illustrated by Kevin Hawkes. Candlewick, 1999.

★ Ibbotson, Eva. **Island of the Aunts.** Illustrated by Kevin Hawkes. Dutton, 2000.

King-Smith, Dick. **The Merman.** Illustrated by Roger Roth. Crown, 1999.

Mayer, Mercer. **The Rocking Horse Angel.** Illustrated by Mercer Mayer. Marshall Cavendish, 2000.

McLerran, Alice. **Dragonfly.** Absey, 2000.

★ Wiesner, David. **Sector 7.** Clarion, 1999.

Wilson, Gena. **Ignis.** Illustrated by P. J. Lynch. Candlewick, 2001.

## Shifts in Time

★ Bowler, Tim. **River Boy.** Margaret K.McElderry Books, 2000.

Griffin, Peni R. **The Ghost Sitter.** Dutton, 2001.

Heneghan, James. **The Grave.** Farrar, Straus & Giroux, 2000.

Osborne, Mary Pope. **Christmas in Camelot.** Illustrated by Sal Murdocca. Random House, 2001.

Sleator, William. **Rewind.** Dutton, 1999.

Woodruff, Elvira. **The Ghost of Lizard Light.** Illustrated by Elaine Clayton. Knopf, 1999.

---

*antasy literature* is the broad term for stories that fulfill the primal human need to imagine alternate realities and to explore the unexplainable and the impossible. The stories reviewed in this chapter examine all sorts of fantastic impossibilities, ranging from dusty old dinosaur toys that plod to life as they are lovingly cleaned by an attentive youngster, to encounters by modern-day children with a mythical merman, to ghostly travelers from a time long past, to alien visitors. Rooted in wishes and dreams and in tales that are as old as the human race, these enchanting stories satisfy our yearning for "a sudden glimpse of something strange and wonderful" (Hunter, 1990, p. 58).

## Evaluating Fantasy Literature

Over five hundred fantasies for children were published in the United States during the three-year period from 1999 to 2001, and we read the vast majority of them. As we made the difficult decisions about which of these fantasy books to include on our final list, our circle of readers agreed on several criteria for selection. At the most fundamental, we looked for literary excellence, raising questions such as: Is the language memorable? Is the setting convincingly realized? Are the characters believable and engaging? Is the story line intriguing and well paced? Of course, these are the kinds of questions that thoughtful readers ask of all stories. These matters take on special significance for fantasy literature, however, for fantasy writers must create worlds, characters, and actions that are so engaging and compelling that we are willing to put aside our natural skepticism to give ourselves to them fully.

Along with literary merit, we looked for stories with a strong element of the fantastic and ones in which that thread of enchantment is presented in a unique way. Visitors from outer space seek to live on Earth in many science fiction stories. In contrast, the alien father and son spy team in Sylvia Waugh's *Space Race* (2000) must overcome incredible odds in their desperate efforts to *leave* Earth. Equally strange is the otherworldly creature called Skellig in the eponymously titled book (1999). Author David Almond leads readers down the thin pathway between fantasy and reality and across the borders between this world and the next.

We also looked for stories that engaged our hearts and minds long after the last page was turned and for images and ideas that changed the way we look at the world. None of us could resist the winsome charm of Wesley, the underappreciated nonconformist who spends his summer vacation creating the backyard world of *Weslandia* (1999). On a deeper level, however, Paul Fleischman's clever story serves as a metaphor for the transforming power of imaginative play, and this is a message we ponder and savor as we continue reading and discussing fantasy stories with children.

Of course, we had to exclude many books from our final list, and for several reasons aside from literary concerns. We were aiming to create a well-balanced list and one that included many types of fantasy and the works of many different authors whose fantasy stories would be understood and enjoyed by children in kindergarten through sixth grade. Many recently published fantasies are aimed at a young adult audience rather than our target audience. We set our sights high, but we felt that some books, such as Philip Pullman's popular *The Amber Spyglass* (2000), aim too far over the heads of this target audience for inclusion here. During the three-year span covered by this text, three Harry Potter books were published. Although they are notable fantasies, these much-heralded publications were not included here so that we could highlight other lesser-known fantasies that are too good to miss.

## Categorizing Fantasy Literature

Fantasy is arguably the richest and most varied of all literary genres. We wanted to gather books that would highlight that diversity, ones that would appeal to readers with a broad range of experiences, reading abilities, and interests. Therefore, we organized the books into six categories and included books that are accessible and appealing to a wide variety of readers.

Animal fantasies are stories in which animals act and interact in extraordinary and often very human ways, such as the vain reptilian protagonist in *I, Crocodile* (Marcellino, 1999) and the engaging rodent hero of *Hooway for Wodney Wat* (Lester, 1999), who overcomes his speech impediment and sends a schoolyard bully packing. Whether published in picture book form or as an easy chapter book with illustrations, such as *PeeWee's Tale* (Hurwitz, 2000) and *Ragweed* (Avi, 1999), these stories are written in a simple and direct style and imbued with a good measure of humor. These are all elements that delight younger children. Such stories are considered "low fantasy": they are set in a world that is generally portrayed realistically, though one that involves anthropomorphized animals.

Another way to interest children in fantasy literature is to introduce them to literary fairy tales. Though original stories by modern authors, these narratives adhere to the conventions of folk and fairy tales. As Jane Yolen (1996, p. 15) wisely notes, "Stories lean on stories, art on art." Thus, past experiences with Cinderella variants will provide children with a sturdy foothold in the world of *Raisel's Riddle* (Silverman, 1999), and an enjoyment of *Zigazak! A Magical Hanukkah Night* (Kimmel, 2001) will emerge from a general familiarity with the wonders and dangers of magic.

At the other end of the spectrum are the more complex fantasy stories that are often called "high fantasy," and we have divided these into two categories, heroic fantasy and science fiction fantasy. Many heroic fantasy stories are set in a "long ago and far away" world invented by the author, and they build on the ancient archetypes of myth and epics. The books in Tamora Pierce's Protector of the Small series are classic examples of this type of fantasy. These books and others of this type, such as *The Folk Keeper* (Billingsley, 1999), involve courageous preadolescent heroines who discover their inner resources and come of age while battling both self-doubt and the exterior evil that threatens. Other books in this category, such as *The Taker's Stone* (Russell, 1999) and *Wild Blood* (Thompson, 2000), are set in a recognizable modern world in which the brave actions of their protagonists avert both personal and widespread disaster.

Science fiction fantasies share many of these qualities, but here the struggles for survival are played out in a futuristic world, one in which often there is interaction between earthlings and visitors from other planets. In most science fiction fantasy, such as *Songs of Power* (Bell, 2000) and *Space Race* (Waugh, 2000), the tone is serious and the mood intense; other stories in this category are playful and lighthearted, like that of the fast-talking space traveler in *Baloney (Henry P.)* (Scieszka, 2001).

Situated between the boundaries of low and high fantasy are stories of enchanted realism. Here we included narratives in which magical objects, characters, or events intrude into a realistically depicted contemporary world, thus heightening the suspense and intrigue of the story. A mundane trip to the beach, for example, is made extraordinary by the visitation of the merman in *The Merman* (King-Smith, 1999), and in *Sector 7* (Wiesner, 1999), the cloudy skies above the Empire State Building take on a marvelous, unearthly splendor.

Other authors use a real-world setting and realistically drawn characters but manipulate time in order to put ordinary individuals into extraordinary situations. In books employing shifts in time, characters discover that the borders between today, yesterday, and tomorrow are more permeable than they expect. In *Rewind* (Sleator, 1999), for example, a seventh grader is allowed to repeatedly relive the days just before a fatal car accident in a desperate attempt to alter the events that led to his death. And Jess, the sensitive girl in *River Boy* (Bowler, 2000), becomes acquainted with a mysterious boyhood version of her beloved grandfather who helps her come to terms with her grandfather's impending death. The books in these last two categories differ from the high fantasies in that they are set in a recognizable modern world. Just as significant, in these fantasies the changes and growth occur at a level that is personal rather than universal.

This brief excursion through our categories is intended to entice you to read the more detailed reviews of each of the selected books in the annotations that follow, but also to suggest the array of delights to be found within the wide-ranging boundaries of fantasy literature. All of these works of literature are created by inventive authors who possess what Virginia Woolf called "a sense of the unseen" (1958, p. 64). All of these authors offer readers of all ages a glimpse of new worlds.

### References

Hunter, Mollie. (1990). "One World." In *Talent is not enough: Mollie Hunter on writing for children*. New York: Harper & Row.

Woolf, Virginia.(1958). *Granite and rainbow: Essays*. New York: Harcourt, Brace.

Yolen, Jane. (1996). *Touch magic: Fantasy, faerie & folklore in the literature of childhood*. Little Rock, AR: August House.

## Animal Fantasy

**14.1**     ★ Avi. **Ragweed.** Illustrated by Brian Floca. Avon, 1999. ISBN 0-380-97690-0. 178 pp. (I).

This prequel to *Poppy* (Orchard, 1995) and *Poppy and Rye* (Avon, 1998) recounts Ragweed's early life. The story is easy to read, while spinning a tale that readers can imagine actually taking place in their own neighborhood. Ragweed is a lively, often naive field mouse who is determined to independently explore the world. He sets off for the city without any particular plan and with no idea of the cruel realities of life for his city kindred. Upon arrival he comes face to face with F.E.A.R. and its nasty feline leader, Silversides, whose only goal is to exterminate all mice. Ragweed is saved by Clutch, a funny, streetwise mouse who introduces him to city culture, an odd new language, and love. Unexpectedly, Ragweed becomes a hero when he develops a plan to exterminate F.E.A.R. Ragweed's travels and exploits quickly capture the attention of readers who are certain to root for the underdog. (TK-K)

**14.2**    Dunrea, Oliver. **Bear Noel.** Farrar, Straus & Giroux, 2000. ISBN 0-374-39990-5. Unpaged. (P).

Christmas Eve holds the promise of the coming of Bear Noel to the North Woods. As he comes, the trampling of snow, jingling of bells, singing, and laughing build breathless anticipation for the gifts he will bestow for the animals' feast. His greatest gift, however, is freedom from fear as all of the wood's creatures listen for his arrival and spread the good news that he is coming. This cumulative and repetitive tale evokes the peace and joy associated with Christmas. Dunrea's realistic illustrations depict the stark beauty of a cold, snowy night while conveying the warmth, eagerness, and goodwill of the celebration. Young readers will delight in the actions of the animals, the rhythmic language of the text, and the compelling illustrations. (DB)

**14.3**    Hurwitz, Johanna. **PeeWee's Tale.** Illustrated by Patience Brewster. SeaStar, 2000. ISBN 1-587-17027-2. 96 pp. (P).

After beginning life in a New York City pet shop, PeeWee finds himself at home in a Manhattan apartment. His new owner, nine-year-old Robbie, quickly learns to love the guinea pig even though he would have preferred a dog. Robbie's mother, however, despises the rodent and arranges for his abandonment in Central Park. Unprepared for life in the wild, the sensitive and bright PeeWee appears destined for an early demise until he is befriended by a savvy squirrel named Lexi. Notwithstanding his inexperience, PeeWee has one skill none of the other animals possess—he can read. His mother taught him to read the letters on the scraps of paper in his cage, and in the end PeeWee's unique ability makes him a hero. This engaging tale offers readers the joy of wordplay, poetry, and humor while inviting them to value the lessons of friendship and freedom. (DB)

**14.4** Lester, Helen. **Hooway for Wodney Wat.** Illustrated by Lynn Munsinger. Houghton Mifflin, 1999. ISBN 0-395-92392-1. 32 pp. (P).

Given Helen Lester's amusing story and the whimsical and irresistible illustrations by Lynn Munsinger, readers will quickly become captivated by the shy, innocent Rodney who endures merciless teasing from his rodent classmates because he cannot pronounce his *r*'s. The tide turns when a new student named Camilla Capybara barges into the classroom. Now Rodney's classmates are too busy protecting themselves from the bigger, smarter, meaner Camilla to bother with Rodney. But Rodney's speech problem turns him into a hero. When he is chosen to be leader in "Simon Says," Rodney directs, "Go west!" and all of the rodents except Camilla collapse in a happy heap for a rest. Camilla stomps West, never to be seen again. This enchanting story will delight and amuse young listeners while also allowing them to reflect on the importance of tolerance and the need to deal gently with the feelings of others. (CH)

**14.5** Marcellino, Fred. **I, Crocodile.** HarperCollins, 1999. ISBN 0-062-05168-7. Unpaged. (ALL).

A contented crocodile spends most of his days by the Nile snoozing and eating a delectable variety of nearby animals. But one day the famous Napoleon visits Egypt and can't resist the idea of having his very own crocodile in his Parisian palace gardens, so the lazy creature is scooped up and whisked away to Napoleon's garden. Overnight the crocodile becomes a celebrity. He is feeling very important when the fickle Napoleon becomes interested in something else and orders crocodile pie for dinner. The crocodile's clever escape will delight young readers as much as his antics on the Nile and in the French garden. A picture book for young and old alike, this hilarious story is filled with rich vocabulary and delightful illustrations. The humorous story and nineteenth-century setting provide an entertaining vehicle to interest students in a study of Napoleon, crocodiles, Egypt, the Nile, or France. (DM)

**14.6** McPhail, David. **Mole Music.** Holt, 1999. ISBN 0-8050-2819-6. Unpaged. (P).

Mole lives in an underground home where he keeps busy creating tunnels and living an ordinary life until one day he wonders if there is more to life. While contemplating his problem, Mole notices a man playing a violin on television and is overcome by a desire to become a musician. Mole buys a violin, practices daily, and eventually becomes a skillful violinist who plays only for himself. Or so he thinks. The music telegraphs up the roots of the tree that spreads over his tunnel, and the soothing music affects everyone who comes near. The musical magic even averts a battle, causing soldiers to put down their weapons as their anger is transformed into tranquility. This gentle and evocative story for beginning readers could be used to inspire children to work on their own writing as they listen to music. (SW)

**14.7** Whybrow, Ian. **Sammy and the Dinosaurs.** Illustrated by Adrian Reynolds. Orchard, 1999. ISBN 0-531-30207-5. Unpaged. (P).

Sammy knows, just as every child does, that dinosaurs are as real today as when they roamed the earth. While cleaning the attic with his grandmother, he finds an old dusty box containing a collection of broken and bent dinosaurs. Sammy carefully fixes and washes them, and then he stores each dinosaur in a bucket. After some determined library research, Sammy is able to tell each dinosaur its name, and they shuffle to life in his bucket, just loud enough for Sammy to hear. One day Sammy and his dinosaurs become separated when he accidentally leaves them on the train, but he is able to accurately identify and reclaim them, proving once and for all that they are definitely "Sammy's dinosaurs." Ian Whybrow has created a delightful story that will easily capture a young child's imagination. (MHT)

**14.8** Wood, Audrey. **Jubal's Wish.** Illustrated by Don Wood. Scholastic, 2000. ISBN 0-439-16964-X. Unpaged. (P).

*Jubal's Wish* invites us to join the fantastic world of Jubal, with his unselfish attitude and endearing demeanor. It is a beautiful summer day and Jubal, an optimistic toad, wants to enjoy the day picnicking with his friends. Gerdy Toad is in a simply horrible mood and refuses to even entertain the idea of wasting her day on a picnic when she has so much work to get done. The dispirited Captain Lizard is plainly in no mood for friends and cannot be bothered to picnic. Jubal momentarily questions himself until a wizard appears. The wizard offers Jubal a wish, but cautions, "Dreams and wishes, wishes and dreams, sometimes they work and sometimes they don't." Nonetheless Jubal makes wishes that are guaranteed to improve his friends' circumstances. Or are they? The bold, larger-than-life illustrations attract attention and are so powerful that the story is told practically without words. (TK-K)

## Literary Fairy Tales

**14.9** Cole, Brock. **Larky Mavis.** Illustrated by Brock Cole. Farrar, Straus & Giroux, 2001. ISBN 0-374-34365-9. Unpaged. (P).

A lark is defined as "a merry, carefree adventure; frolic" and "innocent or good-natured mischief; a prank." The first definition aptly describes Brock Cole's main character, Larky Mavis. The second explains what happens in the story. Mavis is a free-spirited, itinerant young woman who angers and bewilders the more established adults in the community when she finds a creature inside a peanut shell that she loves and cares for, naming it Heart's Delight. The schoolmaster, parson, doctor, and storekeeper each in turn finds the creature a nuisance, and they plot to get rid of her in accordance with their ideas about what she is. But Larky refuses to give up Heart's Delight and is unexpectedly carried off by the angel that Heart's Delight has become. "Where did they go? . . . just maybe, it was far, far away, to another land altogether, where babies grow in peanut shells." (ML)

**14.10** Helldorfer, M. C. **Night of the White Stag.** Illustrated by Yvonne Gilbert. Random House, 1999. ISBN 0-385-32261-5. Unpaged. (P).

In this allegorical story, a young boy, Finder, seeks the king to beg food for his starving family. On the way, he encounters a blind old man who is searching for a white stag. Together they find the stag, and the magical animal's red blood restores the poor man's sight. When Finder finally reaches the ornately adorned king, he discovers that the old blind man *is* the king. Finder and his family are cared for by the king and the white stag forever after. Helldorfer and Gilbert combine vivid language with subtle illustrations. Readers of this enchanting story are first drawn to the book's design: the choreography of illustrations and words on each page creates fabulous works of art, dreamlike and yet realistic in detail. The richly descriptive text is bordered with a unique set of symbolic drawings that hint at the message as the story unfolds. (ML)

**14.11**  ★ Kimmel, Eric A. **Zigazak! A Magical Hanukkah Night.** Illustrated by Jon Goodell. Doubleday, 2001. ISBN 0-385-32652-1. Unpaged. (P).

In this hilarious tale of enchantment run amok, two mischievous devils create chaos in a small village on the first night of Hanukkah. With a magical word—"Zigazak!"—dreidels dance, candles explode into fireworks, and latkes and household pets soar through the air as panicked villagers race for sanctuary at the house of the wise rabbi. The less-than-brilliant devils are no match for the resolute and crafty rabbi, but as they engage in a battle of wills, the rabbi demonstrates to the villagers that "sparks of holiness exist in all things, even in devils' tricks." Kimmel's rollicking narrative and Goodell's expressive, action-packed double-page spreads capture the excitement and hilarity of this magical night while also highlighting the power of goodness and wit over the darkness. This is a great read-aloud during the holiday season and throughout the year. (DPW)

**14.12**  Mitchell, Adrian. **Nobody Rides the Unicorn.** Illustrated by Stephen Lambert. Scholastic, 1999. ISBN 0-439-11204-4. Unpaged. (P).

Fearful of being poisoned, a greedy king turns for help to a quiet, gentle beggar girl with no family. He sends Zoe into the forest to lure a unicorn to her side by softly singing a song that came to her in a dream. When the unicorn approaches, it is apprehended by the cruel king's helper, Dr. Slythe. Zoe is heavyhearted to think that the unicorn is now in danger, so she sets the unicorn free. This courageous act leads to her banishment and a new name: Nobody! Goodness rules in the end as Zoe finds her way to the secret valley of the unicorns. Children will appreciate the dreamy nature of this fantasy book and enjoy the play on words in the title. (CH)

**14.13**  ★ Schmidt, Gary D. **Straw into Gold.** Clarion, 2001. ISBN 0-618-05601-7. 172 pp. (I).

Tousle has spent his life living with a mysterious little magical man in a small cottage and has begun to wonder about the world beyond the clearing and his own place in that world. Adventure lures him to the wide world beyond the cottage and leads Tousle and his companion, the blind but insightful Innes, on a quest to solve the king's riddle, find the banished queen, and unlock the secrets of his past. Tousle's role in setting the kingdom right culminates in the discovery of his special gift and his purpose in life. This fast-paced adventure with surprising twists and turns will delight readers by offering a new perspective on the story of Rumpelstiltskin while leading them to consider what they hold most dear. (DB)

**14.14**  Silverman, Erica. **Raisel's Riddle.** Illustrated by Susan Gaber. Farrar, Straus & Giroux, 1999. ISBN 0-374-36168-1. Unpaged. (P).

"What's more precious than rubies, more lasting than gold? / What can never be traded, stolen, or sold? / What comes with great effort and takes time, but then / Once yours, will serve you again and again?" (p. 32). Instead of a prince searching for the beautiful owner of a glass slipper, a rabbi's son searches for the extraordinarily beautiful young woman who told him this riddle at a holiday celebration and then suddenly ran away at the sound of midnight. He is enchanted not only by her beauty but also by her display of rare intelligence. He knows he must find her, but little does he know that she is the poor servant girl working in his own home. With many references to Jewish traditions, the author gives us a lovely "Cinderella" variant rich with beautiful language and evocative illustrations that capture the feelings of this story. (NW)

## Heroic Fantasy

**14.15**  ★ Beaverson, Aiden. **The Hidden Arrow of Maether.** Delacorte, 2000. ISBN 0-385-32750-1. 177 pp. (I).

As Linn begins her quest to find the City of the Trees, a path magically opens before her. She is escaping a brutal stepfather who is trying to force her to become a Ranite, a member of an evil cult that is taking over her homeland of Maether. Before his death, Linn's father left her the Lysetome, the holy book of their people, and it is her secret study of this book that guides her. Not until the last chapter does the full importance of Linn's role in the salvation of her civilization become clear to the reader. Beaverson has woven a gripping quest tale rooted in Scandinavian lore and rich in symbolism and descriptive language. The characters are well developed and the landscape is believable even with the blend of realism and fantasy. This appealing story will capture the interest of independent readers. (ML)

**14.16**  Billingsley, Franny. **The Folk Keeper.** Atheneum, 1999. ISBN 0-689-82876-4. 162 pp. (I).

Corinna has hidden her true identity and disguised herself as a boy so that she can be a Folk Keeper, one who uses her knowledge of charms and the ways of the Folk to protect the household from the angry spirits. All was going well for Corinna, now Corin, when Lord Merton requests that Corin become the Folk Keeper at his estate. "Corin" jumps at the chance but finds it a difficult duty. A secret connecting all of the characters is soon revealed, and the reader is propelled breathlessly through the unpredictable story to a surprising and satisfying conclusion. Corinna is a memorable heroine who moves fluidly between the two secondary worlds that Billingsley has so skillfully created. Corinna's love for Lord Merton's stepson Finian gives an interesting twist to this story of intrigue and folklore. (SW)

**14.17**  ★ Pattison, Darcy. **The Wayfinder.** HarperCollins, 2000. ISBN 0-688-17080-3. 208 pp. (I).

Eleven-year-old Win Endras is a Wayfinder, one who has the gift of locating anything in the fantasy world of G'il Rim. He experiences great grief and self-doubt when he is unable to save his sister, who wanders too close to the Great Rift. Then the prince of the Heartland arrives with the devastating news of a rapidly spreading plague, and Win is recruited to find the healing waters of the Well of Life, located deep in the Rift. Joined on the quest by the haughty Lady Kala, a telepathic hound, the reluctant Win encounters a talking eagle, a deadly crocodile, and many other dangers while locating the well and solving the mystery of his sister's disappearance. Pattison has created a fast-paced, suspenseful story with credible characters in this intriguing, believable fantasy world. Students will enjoy the novel as an independent read or as a read-aloud. (CC)

**14.18**  Pierce, Tamora. **Squire.** Random House, 2001. ISBN 0-679-88916-7. 399 pp. (I)

It is the year 456 H.E. (Human Era), and Keladry is fourteen years old and a squire. She's proven her desire to become a knight and serve the king of Tortall by completing the first four years of rigorous physical and mental training in what has traditionally been a boy's world. Kel now faces four years of battles, competitions, adventures, and even love under the direction of an experienced knight. She must then pass the ultimate test, known as the Ordeal, alone in a magical room called The Chamber. Kel sees firsthand that not all survive this trial. Keladry is an extraordinarily strong character who easily captures the reader's heart. This suspenseful and well-written text is the third book in the Protector of the Small series, along with *First Test* (1999) and *Page* (2000). All will attract and inspire any young girl embarking on the adventures of life. (NW)

**14.19**  Russell, Barbara Timberlake. **The Taker's Stone.** DK Ink, 1999. ISBN 0-789-42568-8. 231 pp. (I).

Fourteen-year-old Fischer doesn't really feel he belongs anywhere. Even within his own family he is often scrutinized, and now he has been sent to spend summer vacation with his cousin David. After sneaking out of the house one evening, Fischer is cajoled into taking something that is not his. Unknowingly, he has taken some ancient stones that possess magical powers. Suddenly, Fischer and David are compelled to help Thistle, a Keeper of the stones, reunite with her father and fight the leader of darkness, the evil Belial, who desires to rule the world. Fischer must make daring decisions that force him to chose between good and evil, and the intense story forces readers to examine their own moral convictions. Once they pick up the book, readers can't distance themselves from the characters; they become one of the characters in this desperate battle for survival. (TK-K)

**14.20**  Thompson, Kate. **Wild Blood.** Hyperion, 2000. ISBN 0-786-80572-2. 261 pp. (I).

The final tale in the Switchers trilogy, *Wild Blood* compels the reader to explore an ancient Irish world. Populated by fairies, this wild world is home to those with the ability to switch from one species to another. A modern-day switcher, Tess is unaware of her ancestry and the source of the wild blood running through her veins. She faces a complex challenge of faith and courage in the days leading up to her fifteenth birthday, when she must decide what form she will take for the rest of her life. Her choices determine not only who she becomes but also the future of her family and ancestors. This convincing tale invites the reader to peek into an alternate reality and consider whether we believe what we see or see what we believe. Multidimensional characters and gripping foreshadowing help propel the plot and fascinate the reader. (DB)

## Science Fiction Fantasy

**14.21**    Bell, Hilari. **Songs of Power.** Hyperion, 2000. ISBN 0-786-80561-7. 219 pp. (I).

Hilari Bell taps our fascination with ocean worlds in her story of an underwater colony on an earth of the near future. This is a survival story on multiple levels. A terrorist attack has infected the earth's food supply with a deadly virus, and scientists are desperately seeking new methods for harvesting food from the sea. The stalwart protagonist, fifteen-year-old Imina, grieves at the death of the shaman grandmother who raised her, but it is her growing grasp of her own magical powers that saves the colony from the menace of a mysterious force that is sabotaging their work and threatening lives. This fast-paced story explores the conflicts between science, ancient wisdom, and magic and spins a compelling coming-of-age tale as Imina learns to trust herself and others. It is a superb read-aloud, notable for its blend of science fiction fantasy, legendary magic, and seat-gripping suspense. (DPW)

**14.22**    Bunting, Eve. **Wanna Buy an Alien?** Illustrated by Tim Bush. Clarion, 2000. ISBN 0-395-69719-0. 92 pp. (I).

Ben receives a mysterious birthday present in the mail from his friend Jason. The box of souvenirs from outer space is supposed to be a great gag gift from a mail order company. Ben doesn't see the humor in it. Instead, he becomes increasingly frightened by its contents, which include an invitation from an alien named Iku to visit the planet Cham. When the appointed meeting time arrives and a real spaceship lands near his house, Ben and his friends Jason and Paloma face a terrible dilemma. Is the alien's offer an exciting opportunity for adventure or a one-way trip to a horrible end? The author's use of the grammatical present tense increases the story's suspense and pace but may prove awkward for reading aloud. The conversational style and first-person narrative broaden the accessibility of this science fiction tale to young and reluctant readers. (SV)

**14.23**    Scieszka, Jon. **Baloney (Henry P.).** Illustrated by Lane Smith. Viking, 2001. ISBN 0-670-89248-3. 31 pp. (P).

Henry P. Baloney is an alien, but he has problems just like any Earth child. Unless he comes up with a good excuse for being late again, his teacher will give him lifelong detention. Henry's tale is that of an imaginative child in a tight spot, and his inventive monologue includes many strange and seemingly alien words: he is late for *szkola* because he misplaced his *zimulus* and he was looking for it when the *razzo* blasted off. Initial confusion turns to delight as readers build meanings from the illustrations and context clues. In a fascinating afterword, Scieszka explains that he has invented the words by combining Earth languages. Coupled with Lane Smith's typically off-kilter illustrations, this hilarious tale keeps readers moving through the book to discover what creative excuses Henry will conjure up next, while also delighting in its playful language and illustrations. (DM)

**14.24** Waugh, Sylvia. **Space Race.** Delacorte, 2000. ISBN 0-385-32766-8. 241 pp. (I).

Six-year-old Thomas and his father Patrick quietly come to Earth from the planet Ormingat to observe Earthling behavior. After five happy years, Thomas's father tells him they must return home. Thomas is devastated, not wanting to leave his best friend and his beloved motherly neighbor Stella. Then an accident with a runaway truck injures Thomas and separates the father and son. In shock and mute, Thomas is hospitalized, but Patrick must find his son and then get to the spaceship in time for the programmed departure. Many questions linger: Will Patrick find Thomas in time? Will Thomas rediscover his identity, and will he agree to return to Ormingat? This heartwarming story depicts the strong love between a parent and child and leaves readers pondering the question of whether aliens could be any different from us. (SW)

## Enchanted Realism

**14.25** Almond, David. **Skellig.** Delacorte, 1999. ISBN 0-385-32653-X. 182 pp. (I).

Michael is an anxious, displaced child who misses his home and worries about his gravely ill sister. While his distracted parents care for the baby and settle into the new house, Michael explores a ramshackle garage and discovers an extraordinary creature named Skellig. The origins and nature of this fragile winged being are shrouded in mystery, but in the story's moving climax he dances with the baby on the eve of the heart surgery that saves her life. Through experiences with Skellig and his growing friendship with his intelligent and perceptive friend Mina,

Michael learns to deal with his fears and see beauty even in the commonplace and the terrible. Almond's ability to create a palpably eerie mood and to build suspense, his perceptive portrayal of engaging characters, and his lyrical prose make for a moving and unforgettable story that will long linger in readers' hearts and minds. (DPW)

**14.26**  Fine, Anne. **Bad Dreams.** Delacorte, 2000. ISBN 0-385-32757-9. 133 pp. (I).

This story about a young girl with supernatural powers will hook readers from the beginning to the very end. Melanie's teacher assigns her to help a new girl, Imogen, become acquainted with her new surroundings. An avid reader, Melanie grows frustrated with her new friend's reluctance to read, but as she observes her more carefully, Melanie realizes that whenever Imogen touches the cover of a book, she is able to feel the emotions of the characters and to predict the story's outcome. Gradually she realizes that Imogen's torment and unpopularity have to do with a necklace she always wears that was given to her by her mother. When Melanie secretly disposes of the necklace, Imogen is finally freed from its spell. Anne Fine creatively weaves reality and fantasy as she highlights the difficulties we all face when making decisions that affect another person's life. (CC)

**14.27**  ★ Fleischman, Paul. **Weslandia.** Illustrated by Kevin Hawkes. Candlewick, 1999. ISBN 0-763-60006-7. Unpaged. (ALL).

Attention! Nerds of the universe unite! Although intelligent and unconventional, Wesley is tormented by peers and convinced by his frustrated conformist parents that he is "an outcast from the civilization around him." But left to his own devices during a particularly long and hot summer vacation, Wesley creates an entire world within the confines of his own backyard. Unusual plants, self-made clothes, and an inventive counting system all contribute to this brave new place appropriately called Weslandia. Through this story of self-derived entertainment and exploration, readers discover a simpler way of life that ultimately leads to a more satisfying level of appreciation and social acceptance. (TH)

**14.28**  ★ Ibbotson, Eva. **Island of the Aunts.** Illustrated by Kevin Hawkes. Dutton, 2000. ISBN 0-525-46484-0. 276 pp. (I).

A tropical wildlife refuge on an island paradise run by three aging, animal-loving sisters provides an exhilarating backdrop for an uproarious tale of epic proportions. As the story opens, Aunts Etta, Coral, and Myrtle, who reside with their elderly father, have come to grips with their own mortality. Without children, no one will be left to carry on their legacy of caring for the magical and mystical animals they've rescued. That is, until Aunt Etta contrives a plan to visit London with the primary goal of kidnapping neglected children of people who are either too busy or otherwise indisposed to care for them. Thus is set in motion an elaborate scheme of "mad aunt" mayhem for the sole purpose of perpetuating a new generation of island caretakers. Ibbotson's tale combines the childlike ingenuity of desperate adults and the soul-searching adventures of innocent young imaginations. (TH)

**14.29**  King-Smith, Dick. **The Merman.** Illustrated by Roger Roth. Crown, 1999. ISBN 0-517-80030-6. 102 pp. (I).

This prolific author has once again written an appealing book that will capture the hearts and attention of newly independent readers. Zeta, a winsome ten-year-old, first meets the sagacious merman Marinus while on vacation with her family off the coast of Scotland. Over 140 years old, Marinus shares his wisdom and love for the sea with Zeta. Even more important, he helps her overcome her fears and face life with a newfound awareness and confidence. Through the character of Marinus, King-Smith deftly reveals a wealth of information about the ocean and its inhabitants. Zeta returns home a much wiser young lady, as will the readers of this engaging book. (ML)

**14.30**  Mayer, Mercer. **The Rocking Horse Angel.** Illustrated by Mercer Mayer. Marshall Cavendish, 2000. ISBN 0-761-45072-6. Unpaged. (P).

Little does the young boy realize the extraordinary events that will occur when he discovers a rocking horse in his attic. The horse was to have been his Christmas present, and his parents had hidden the horse in a place the boy didn't usually go without permission. But one day something lures him to the attic, and there he discovers a beautiful dappled-gray rocking horse. He climbs on the horse and his magical adventures begin. Through a series of dreamlike visits, conversations, and enchanted journeys, the boy learns to trust the horse. When he becomes terribly ill, the rocking horse proves to be the "angel" that takes him on an unforgettable journey to healing. The brilliant and vivid computer-generated illustrations help guide readers in and out of worlds of fantasy and reality. (NW)

14.31    McLerran, Alice. **Dragonfly.** Absey, 2000. ISBN 1-888-84222-9. 142 pp. (I).

Where would you hide a dragon that has outgrown every building you own? How would you secretly exercise this flying dragon without creating an uproar in your neighborhood and community? If you added a nosy librarian neighbor and a former member of a motorcycle gang, the possibilities are endless. McLerran has woven these details into a credible story, yet readers know it's a fantasy. *Dragonfly* is a lighthearted, fast-moving story with a surprise ending. Readers have numerous opportunities to predict what will happen next, although their predictions will undoubtedly differ from what actually happens to Dragonfly. (ML)

14.32    ★ Wiesner, David. **Sector 7.** Clarion, 1999. ISBN 0-395-74656-6. Unpaged. (ALL).

While on a field trip to the top of the Empire State Building, a boy is befriended by an impish cloud and is taken on a journey through the sky to Sector 7 Headquarters, a bizarre Grand Central Station for clouds. When the boy discovers the clouds' boredom with their typical assigned designs, he creates new ones that delight them. Although the authorities try to censor such fancifulness, the clouds will not be stopped, and the skies over Manhattan will never be the same. This wordless picture book is another story of wonder, friendship, and fun from the same author who took readers on other flying adventures in *Tuesday* (Clarion, 1991) and *June 29, 1999* (Clarion, 1992). Young and old alike will enjoy pouring over the incredibly rich and fantastic illustrations that creatively invite them to tell the story, borrowing from their own imaginations. (SV)

14.33    Wilson, Gina. **Ignis.** Illustrated by P. J. Lynch. Candlewick, 2001. ISBN 0-763-61623-0. Unpaged. (P).

Ignis was a well-loved and admired young dragon who lived with the other dragons in Dragonland. He could run the fastest and fly the highest. But Ignis knew in his heart that he wasn't a real dragon, for he possessed no fire. What good is a dragon who can't breathe fire? And so the sad yet determined Ignis sets off on a quest to find his fire. On the journey, he makes several new friends who encourage him and make him feel a special warmth inside. As he continues to the top of a mountain, he discovers an old volcano but no fire. The dejected dragon begins to cry, accidentally swallowing a spark left from the volcano, and immediately it produces changes in Ignis. He's breathing fire! The author has created a lovely, heartwarming fantasy that is brought to life by the enchanting illustrations. (NW)

## Shifts in Time

14.34 ★ Bowler, Tim. **River Boy.** Margaret K. McElderry Books, 2000. ISBN 0-689-82908-6. 155 pp. (I).

Jess has a special relationship with her grandfather because she is the only one who can reach through his dark moods and spur on his artistic creativity. At the beginning of the story, Grandfather has suffered a serious heart attack, but even so the family travels to his childhood home. While she explores the river that runs through the backyard, Jess meets a stranger who seems to appear and disappear without warning. She struggles to understand the nature of this boy. Is he real or a spirit from the past? When the image of this same boy appears in Grandfather's painting, Jess is determined to find out more. Against this backdrop, Jess and Grandfather begin their last journey together. The story carries the reader through the intricacies of family relationships and explores the connection between generations. Finally, Jess and the reader understand the importance of Grandfather's last painting, *River Boy*. (EA)

14.35 Griffin, Peni R. **The Ghost Sitter.** Dutton, 2001. ISBN 0-525-46676-2. 131 pp. (I).

Peni R. Griffin has written a riveting and realistic ghost story that makes a wonderful class read-aloud. Ten-year-old Susie died in an accident with a firecracker fifty years earlier on the Fourth of July. Unfortunately, Susie does not realize that she is dead and now a ghost of her former self. Families move into her house one after another, with only the small children able to see and hear Susie. Finally Charlotte and her family move in, and

Charlotte's little brother Brandon becomes the next child for Susie to "babysit." Charlotte perseveres and eventually unravels the mystery of Susie's life and death. The action quickly moves to a climax on July fourth when an unexpected reunion finally sets Susie free from her earthly life. This unusual ghost story will entice students to further explore this genre. (MHT)

**14.36**  Heneghan, James. **The Grave.** Farrar, Straus & Giroux, 2000. ISBN 0-374-32765-3. 242 pp. (I).

In 1974, Tom Mullen is a thirteen-year-old boy who has been repeatedly shuffled from one foster home to another. He has formed few ties with the people in his life. When construction exposes a mass grave near his home, Tom is drawn to it. As he explores the building site, he falls into the grave and wakes up in Ireland in the midst of the potato famine. By saving the life of Tully Monaghan, Tom becomes involved in Tully's family's life. During his travels back and forth between 1974 and 1847, Tom discovers the secrets of the mass grave. Heneghan explores the possibilities of time travel in a believable manner, and we are seamlessly carried between the two time periods. The troubles and triumphs of the two sets of characters are masterfully interwoven to create a story that will stay with the reader long after the last page is read. (EA)

**14.37**  Osborne, Mary Pope. **Christmas in Camelot.** Illustrated by Sal Murdocca. Random House, 2001. ISBN 0-375-81373-X. 115 pp. (I).

Christmas. . . . Camelot. . . . Just the names evoke worlds of fantasy, mystery, and happiness. Mary Pope Osborne's latest adventure in the Magic Tree House series finds Jack and Annie spinning their way into the midst of King Arthur's Court in an effort to save Camelot from the Dark Wizard's spell of gloom that has been cast over the entire kingdom. Finding Sir Lancelot and two other knights missing, and the remainder of King Arthur's Court frozen in time by the Christmas Knight, Jack and Annie venture off on a quest into the Otherworld, and return with the joy-restoring Water of Memory and Imagination. Their brave journey will not only keep Camelot's memory joyously alive, but also ensure further adventures from the magic tree house itself. Osborne's tale of adventure beautifully melds Celtic legend with Christmas tradition, celebrating the imaginations of early chapter book readers. (TH)

**14.38** Sleator, William. **Rewind.** Dutton, 1999. ISBN 0-525-46130-2. 120 pp. (I).

What if you could rewind your life from a certain event and change the outcome? This intriguing premise makes *Rewind* a perfect novel for a class read-aloud. Peter dies in a car accident, but he is given a chance to change the fatal accident. He must pick a point in time to return to his life where he feels that he can change the chain of events that led up to his death. This novel clearly illustrates that adults as well as children are often unaware of the consequences of their words and actions. Peter is forced to examine his life before he can alter these events in order to avert his death. If Peter fails, he will be permanently dead. The final events quickly move to a surprising but completely believable conclusion, giving the reader much to ponder. (MHT)

**14.39** Woodruff, Elvira. **The Ghost of Lizard Light.** Illustrated by Elaine Clayton. Knopf, 1999. ISBN 0-679-89281-8. 176 pp. (I).

This haunting middle grade ghost story will have reluctant readers racing to uncover a 150-year-old mystery. Fourth grader Jack and his family relocate from Iowa when his father accepts an elementary school principal position. Their new house turns out to be an old lighthouse keeper's home on the coast of Maine. One foggy night, Jack awakens when the ghost of Nathaniel Witherspoon appears in his bedroom. After Jack's terror subsides, he listens to Nathaniel's tale of the shipwreck that ended his young life and the mystery surrounding his father's death. Woodruff does a wonderful job of developing highly believable characters. The two boys, one real and the other a ghost, form a close friendship as both boys deal with a father-son conflict. The ghost and a family boating accident provide the means by which Jack eventually reverses his father's poor opinion of him and solves the old mystery. (CC)

# 15 African American Literature

**Elizabeth Bridges Smith**

*Contributing reviewers included Coralea Collins and Mary Lynn Heimback.*

---

**Criteria for Excellence**

- The text must be well written.
- The illustrations must be attractive and engaging for young people.
- The text and illustrations must be nonstereotypical.
- The text and illustrations must represent African American culture authentically and accurately.
- The text and illustrations must be original, bringing new or unique perspectives to the reader.
- The text and illustrations must be developmentally appropriate for the K–grade 6 reader/listener.

---

## Connections to the Past

Clinton, Catherine. **The Black Soldier: 1492 to the Present.** Houghton Mifflin, 2000.

Hopkinson, Deborah. **Under the Quilt of Night.** Illustrated by James E. Ransome. Atheneum, 2001.

★ Littlesugar, Amy. **Freedom School, Yes!** Illustrated by Floyd Cooper. Philomel, 2001.

Monceaux, Morgan, and Ruth Katcher. **My Heroes, My People: African Americans and Native Americans in the West.** Illustrated by Morgan Monceaux. Frances Foster Books, 1999.

Pinkney, Andrea Davis. **Mim's Christmas Jam.** Illustrated by Brian Pinkney. Harcourt, 2001.

Rappaport, Doreen. **Martin's Big Words: The Life of Dr. Martin Luther King Jr.** Illustrated by Bryan Collier. Hyperion, 2001.

Robinet, Harriette Gillem. **Walking to the Bus-Rider Blues.** Atheneum, 2000.

★ Woodson, Jacqueline. **The Other Side.** Illustrated by E. B. Lewis. Putnam, 2001.

## Connections to Rhythm

Axtell, David. **We're Going on a Lion Hunt.** Holt, 1999.

Bishop, Rudine Sims. **Wonders: The Best Children's Poems of Effie Lee Newsome.** Illustrated by Lois Mailou Jones. Boyds Mills, 1999.

★ Dunbar, Paul Laurence. **Jump Back, Honey: Poems.** Illustrated by Ashley Bryan, Carole Byard, Jan Spivey Gilchrist, Brian Pinkney, Jerry Pinkney, and Faith Ringgold. Hyperion, 1999.

★ Gershwin, George, DuBose Heyward, Dorothy Heyward, and Ira Gershwin. **Summertime from *Porgy and Bess*.** Illustrated by Mike Wimmer. Simon & Schuster, 1999.

Grimes, Nikki. **My Man Blue: Poems.** Illustrated by Jerome Lagarrigue. Dial, 1999.

Grimes, Nikki. **Stepping Out with Grandma Mac.** Illustrated by Angelo. Orchard , 2001.

★ hooks, bell. **Happy to Be Nappy.** Illustrated by Chris Raschka. Hyperion, 1999.

Lester, Julius. **The Blues Singers: Ten Who Rocked the World.** Illustrated by Lisa Cohen. Hyperion, 2001.

Lewis, J. Patrick. **Freedom Like Sunlight: Praisesongs for Black Americans.** Illustrated by John Thompson. Creative Editions, 2000.

★ Okutoro, Lydia Omolola (ed.). **Quiet Storm: Voices of Young Black Poets.** Hyperion, 1999.

Smith, Will. **Just the Two of Us.** Illustrated by Kadir Nelson. Scholastic, 2001.

Spain, Sahara Sunday. **If There Would Be No Light: Poems from My Heart.** HarperCollins, 2001.

## Connections to One Another

Burrows, Adjoa J. **Grandma's Purple Flowers.** Lee & Low, 2000.

Cameron, Ann. **Gloria's Way.** Illustrated by Lis Toft. Farrar, Straus & Giroux, 2000.

★ Cooke, Trish. **The Grandad Tree.** Illustrated by Sharon Wilson. Candlewick, 2000.

Grimm, Edward. **The Doorman.** Illustrated by Ted Lewin. Orchard, 2000.

★ Nikola-Lisa, W. **Can You Top That?** Illustrated by Hector Viveros Lee. Lee & Low, 2000.

Pegram, Laura. **Daughter's Day Blues.** Illustrated by Cornelius Van Wright & Ying-Hwa Hu. Dial, 2000.

Williams, Sherley Anne. **Girls Together.** Illustrated by Synthia Saint James. Harcourt Brace, 1999.

Williams-Garcia, Rita. **Catching the Wild Waiyuuzee.** Illustrated by Mike Reed. Simon & Schuster, 2000.

★ Woodson, Jacqueline. **Miracle's Boys.** Putnam, 2000.

## Connections to the Spirit

Brown, Margaret Wise. **A Child Is Born.** Illustrated by Floyd Cooper. Hyperion, 2000.

★ Johnson, James Weldon. **Lift Every Voice and Sing: A Pictorial Tribute to the Negro National Anthem.** Hyperion, 2000.

Ladwig, Tim. **The Lord's Prayer.** Eerdmans, 2000.

---

There has been no shortage of African American books published for children grades K–6 during the 1999–2001 period. While many titles for the secondary audience have been published, there has been concern about the developmental appropriateness and quality of literature written for the K–6 student. Books for this age group that reflect the diversity of the African American past, present, and future are lacking.

After examining hundreds of African American titles, we can safely report that the recurrent theme is still the story of slavery and escape. Again and again, we found stories in both picture and chapter book formats that did not represent African American culture authentically and accurately. In a few instances, these titles presented information in a unique way or from a different perspective. Most often, however, they followed the same pattern: slave is unhappy, slave endures hardships, white person befriends the slave, slave escapes. This treatment not only stereotypes the slavery period, but it also fails to offer readers new or unique perspectives. Such books must be presented in a nonstereotypical manner. Also, while slavery did occur, the harsh realities are difficult to present to a primary audience in a developmentally appropriate way. We had to examine not only the quality and accuracy but also the appropriateness of these stories for the intended age group.

As we developed this list, it became clear that we had to search for stories that portray African American culture and heritage in multiple ways, not just from the perspective of the unhappy slave. Books with illustrations had to meet an additional standard. Not only should the text reflect unique and varied perspectives, but the illustrations also needed to be authentic, attractive, and engaging for the young reader. The books included here fall into four categories: connections to the past, connections to one another, connections to rhythm, and connections to spirit. The concept of connections comes from the ideal of unity in diversity; in other words, in the multiplicity of individuals is a common cultural experience.

The titles included in the section Connections to the Past reflect the diversity of the African American experience. They show the African American as slave, but they also take readers from that time period through the civil rights movement. Thus, they address a broader time frame, which more accurately reflects African American heritage.

Song and poetry have been an essential part of the African American oral tradition, and the books in Connections with Rhythm reflect that tradition. This section includes poetry from Paul Laurence Dunbar to Nikki Grimes. This melodious collection includes titles that represent actual songs, as well as explanations of musical genre and autobiographies of musicians.

Building and maintaining relationships with family and friends is the basis for the Connection with One Another section. Each of the titles here focuses on how children connect to adults, how adults connect to children, and how children connect with one another. The giving and sharing of wisdom and advice are central to many of the narratives included here.

Finally, Connections to Spirit is a section that includes titles reflecting the faith and religious convictions of African American culture. Rather than focusing on a specific denomination, these titles look at issues and topics common across all faiths. The significant element in this section is the representation of holy figures with African or African American characteristics.

## Connections to the Past

★ Cline-Ransome, Lesa. **Satchel Paige.** Illustrated by James E. Ransome. Simon & Schuster, 2000. ISBN 0-689-81151-9. Unpaged. (ALL). (See **12.2.**)

15.1    Clinton, Catherine. **The Black Soldier: 1492 to the Present.** Houghton Mifflin, 2000. ISBN 0-395-67722-X. 117 pp. (I).

Catherine Clinton succeeds in creating a well-crafted history book full of factual information about African American soldiers, who are often overlooked as war heroes. Each chapter represents a time period or war action during which the United

States used African American patriots to defend the country. Many students are unaware that African slaves fought to defend America's freedom during wars beginning as early as the 1500s. The final chapter discusses the present state of African Americans in the military. Included in this section is information on Colin Powell, the first African American to be appointed to the position of chairman of the Joint Chiefs of Staff. (CM)

**15.2**    Hopkinson, Deborah. **Under the Quilt of Night.** Illustrated by James E. Ransome. Atheneum, 2001. ISBN 0-689-82227-8. Unpaged. (ALL).

Written in short bursts of prose poems, this story shows slaves as they follow the route of the Underground Railroad, are chased by slave catchers, and are aided by abolitionists on their way to freedom. *Under the Quilt of Night* is a good companion book to *Sweet Clara and the Freedom Quilt* (Knopf, 1993), also by the Hopkinson-Ransome team. Ransome's broad brush strokes, done in oil paint, and Hopkinson's lyrical prose add to the emotion of the story. This is a great book to use not only with units on slavery but also with units on the family and with tales related to quilting and patterns. Children will experience vicariously the hardships of the journey as well as the exhilaration of freedom. (MLH)

**15.3**    ★ Littlesugar, Amy. **Freedom School, Yes!** Illustrated by Floyd Cooper. Philomel, 2001. ISBN 0-399-23006-8. Unpaged. (I).

Based on the1964 Mississippi Freedom School Summer Project, Littlesugar has crafted a story from a history many know little about. The protagonist of the story, Jolie, expresses her fear and uncertainty when her family volunteers to house the new teacher hired for the Freedom School. Jolie and her family suffer bricks thrown through their windows and hate notes before they experience the worst tragedy, the burning of the church where the Freedom School was to be held. Littlesugar shows Jolie's slow transformation and that understanding the necessity for the school makes her committed to learn more about her heritage. Cooper's characteristic artwork, developed using a kneaded eraser with a watercolor wash, reflects the power of this story. The book makes a great companion source with Debbie Wiles's *Freedom Summer* (Atheneum, 2001; **24.13**). Both books help students understand the civil rights movement from the perspective of the "everyday" person. (EBS)

Miller, William. **Night Golf.** Illustrated by Cedric Lucas. Lee & Low, 1999. ISBN 1-880000-79-2. Unpaged. (ALL). (See **12.26.**)

**15.4** Monceaux, Morgan, and Ruth Katcher. **My Heroes, My People: African Americans and Native Americans in the West.** Illustrated by Morgan Monceaux. Frances Foster Books, 1999. ISBN 0-374-30770-9. 64 pp. (I).

Monceaux uses oil pastels, paint, markers, and collage to portray African Americans, Native Americans, and persons of mixed race who were influential in settling the Old West. This book is an important contribution to history, chronicling the lives and contributions of persons typically unmentioned in social studies textbooks. Included in this work are brief biographies of Toussaint L'Ouverture, the leader of a successful slave revolt; black cowboy Nat Love; Bass Reaves, a black marshal and minister; a buffalo soldier named Moses Williams; and rodeo bulldogger Bill Pickett. Monceaux also includes additional information about these leaders in graffitilike illustrations. (MLH)

Nobisso, Josephine. **John Blair and the Great Hinkley Fire.** Illustrated by Ted Rose. Houghton Mifflin, 2000. ISBN 0-618-01560-4. Unpaged. (ALL). (See **5.4.**)

**15.5** Pinkney, Andrea Davis. **Mim's Christmas Jam.** Illustrated by Brian Pinkney. Harcourt, 2001. ISBN 0-15-201918-9. Unpaged. (P).

Christmas is a family time, according to Saraleen and Royce, the brother and sister team in this marvelous book. Along with their mom, Mim, they miss their father, Pap, who is in New York helping with the building of the subway system. Recognizing that Christmas won't be the same without him, Mim makes a traditional treat, her belly-hum jam, and encourages the children to ship it off to him as a gift. Once the jam arrives, it has an almost magical effect on the subway foremen, who give the "sandhogs" the day off as a result. Andrea Davis Pinkney has created story with a dual purpose: showing a family's Christmas celebration and relating the history of the building of the New York subway system, including vocabulary specific to that period and profession. Brian Pinkney's characteristic illustrations are done with huma dyes and acrylic on scratchboard. Teachers are encouraged to use this book when students are reading stories of the building of the railroad system in western

United States. Students can compare the hardships faced by those involved in the work of building our country's early transportation systems. (MLH)

15.6    Rappaport, Doreen. **Martin's Big Words: The Life of Dr. Martin Luther King, Jr.** Illustrated by Bryan Collier. Hyperion, 2001. ISBN 0-786-80714-8. Unpaged. (ALL).

Both a Caldecott Award honor book and a Coretta Scott King Award honor book, *Martin's Big Words* is a visually and textually powerful presentation. The story is told from a young child's perspective, providing readers with snippets not only of the life of the civil rights leader, but also of his speeches and sermons. The message of the book is clear: "You are as good as anyone." Because the focus is on equity and belief in self, *Martin's Big Words* is a powerful addition to a curriculum focus on King's life as well as a message of self-esteem. Collier uses watercolor and cut-paper collage to create strong, rich images of King as both a child and an adult. Rappaport includes valuable resources and references at the end of the book for an extended study about Dr. Martin Luther King, Jr. (MLH)

15.7    Robinet, Harriette Gillem. **Walking to the Bus-Rider Blues.** Atheneum, 2000. ISBN 0-689-83191-9. 146 pp. (I).

This wonderful example of historical fiction by Harriette Robinet tells of the Jim Crow era, when black and white separation was the norm and inequality was legal in the southern states. The setting of the story is Montgomery, Alabama, during the bus boycotts. Alfa Merryfield, the narrator, is twelve years old and working at a local grocery store. He prides himself on using the money he makes to assist with the rent for the tarpaper home he shares with his sister and grandmother. When money begins disappearing from home and from the local grocery, the family is accused of theft. Alfa and his sister work to solve the mystery of the missing money in an effort to bring honor back to their family name. Historical facts are effectively integrated within this engaging story. (CM)

15.8    ★ Woodson, Jacqueline. **The Other Side.** Illustrated by E. B. Lewis. Putnam, 2001. ISBN 0-399-23116-1. Unpaged. (ALL).

Clover, a young African American girl, is curious about the fence that separates her house from a neighbor child's. She doesn't understand why her momma insists that it just isn't safe for her to play with the little white girl who likes to sit on that fence. Together, Woodson and Lewis have created a story that reflects the confused emotions of a young girl when confronted with issues of race and segregation. Lewis's rich watercolors give readers the visual impression that there are more similarities than there are differences between the two girls. In a few powerful words, Woodson breathes life into Clover, who ignores her mother's warning and befriends Annie, her neighbor. They share a touching reflection on the last page of the book: "'Someday somebody's going to come along and knock this old fence down,' Annie said. And I nodded, 'Yeah,' I said. 'Someday.'" (MLH)

## Connections to Rhythm

**15.9** Axtell, David. **We're Going on a Lion Hunt.** Holt, 1999. ISBN 0-8050-6159-2. Unpaged. (P).

Many adults fondly remember the camp chant "Going on a bear hunt." Axtell has given the old chant a new twist by making the main character a lion. Two African American sisters set out to find a lion by using their imaginations to travel through the tall grasses, swamps, and lakes of Africa. When at last they find him, the frightened pair makes a quick return to the safety of their own home despite their earlier declarations of not being afraid. The oil-on-canvas-board illustrations have a textured quality that gives them a life of their own. The repetition of the standard refrain is contagious, encouraging young children to join in the reading. (MLH)

**15.10** Bishop, Rudine Sims. **Wonders: The Best Children's Poems of Effie Lee Newsome.** Illustrated by Lois Mailou Jones. Boyds Mills, 1999. ISBN 1-563-9778-85. 40 pp. (P).

Bishop says in her introduction, "Although she published well over 150 poems for children, Newsome's work as a children's poet has been largely forgotten. She was, however, a pioneer, and this collection is an attempt to reintroduce her and the spirit of her work to a new generation of children" (p. 8). This collection by Newsome, an African American poet from the 1920s and 1930s, reflects an interest in nature—trees, flowers, spiders, and fireflies. Artist Lois Jones has displayed work all over the world and is best known for her textile designs, paintings, and drawings. This book represents an important contribution to the history of children's book publishing, particularly African American children's literature. (EBS)

15.11 ★ Dunbar, Paul Laurence. **Jump Back, Honey: Poems.** Illustrated by Ashley Bryan, Carole Byard, Jan Spivey Gilchrist, Brian Pinkney, Jerry Pinkney, and Faith Ringgold. Hyperion, 1999. ISBN 0-7868-0464-5. Unpaged. (ALL).

"Little brown baby wif spa'klin eyes. Come to yo' pappy an' set on his knee. What you been doin' suh—makin' san' pies?" Six award-winning illustrators pay tribute to the famous African American poet Paul Laurence Dunbar in this collection of his lyric and dialect work. A wonderful classroom addition, the book includes a brief biography of the poet written by Brian Pinkney and Andrea Davis Pinkney. Included in an afterword are the memories and thoughts of each of the artists about the influence Dunbar's work had on their own lives and work. Because each of the poems is illustrated by a different artist, children have the opportunity to see a range of mediums and styles, including gouache, acrylic and oil, scratchboard, and pencil and watercolor. (EBS)

15.12 ★ Gershwin, George, DuBose Heyward, Dorothy Heyward, and Ira Gershwin. **Summertime from *Porgy and Bess*.** Illustrated by Mike Wimmer. Simon & Schuster, 1999. ISBN 0-689-80719-8. Unpaged. (I).

This richly illustrated book is set to the lyrics of "Summertime" from the Gershwin musical *Porgy and Bess*. Mike Wimmer uses oil paintings to illustrate a warm summer day in the life of an African American family. While the scenes of swimming, fishing, and attending church are not at all a part of the original context of the song, Wimmer's renderings bring the music of a classic folk opera to contemporary readers. The tenderness of family relationships is evident in the paintings, especially in the illustrations of the father cradling the baby to the lyric "there's a nothin' can harm you." The musical score is included on the final page of the book for interested readers. (EBS)

15.13 Grimes, Nikki. **My Man Blue: Poems.** Illustrated by Jerome Lagarrigue. Dial, 1999. ISBN 0-8037-2326-1. Unpaged. (P).

Nikki Grimes tells the story of a young boy, new to a neighborhood, wrestling to find his place in the world. A man his mother is familiar with, simply called Blue, befriends him. Together they form a strong mentoring relationship. Blue, referred to as a gentle giant, helps the young boy negotiate the streets of this tough neighborhood and reinforces his self-esteem. Blue is quick to make short statements filled with sound advice: "You know I'll be right here in case you fall" (p. 10) and "Anger is a waster, . . . use your lips for something more than pouting" (p. 12). The richly textured illustrations by Jerome Lagarrigue use acrylic on Canson paper. This is a wonderful book for teachers to use in units on self-esteem, neighborhoods, or heroes and she-roes. (MLH)

15.14    Grimes, Nikki. **Stepping Out with Grandma Mac.** Illustrated by Angelo. Orchard, 2001. ISBN 0-531-30320-9. 38 pp. (I).

Grandma Mac is not your typical grandmother. She doesn't bake cookies or pinch cheeks. She doesn't hide candy or crochet. Instead, Grandma Mac is a self-assured woman of few words who seldom verbalizes her emotions. Poems, told from the point of view of Grandma Mac's ten-year-old granddaughter, give an amusing view of their relationship, and the focus on etiquette and the differences between the generations will evoke smiles. Angelo's pencil illustrations are realistic and seem to lift off the page, complementing the poetic text. This book makes a great addition to teachers' sources dealing with family and relationships, particularly those that depict nonstereotypical situations. (EBS)

15.15    ★ hooks, bell. **Happy to Be Nappy.** Illustrated by Chris Raschka. Hyperion, 1999. ISBN 0-7868-0427-0. Unpaged. (P).

Hooks, widely known for her work on feminist theory and political activism, has created a wonderful children's verse that describes the variety of African American hair. Rashka's color washes give a visual vibrancy to the rhythmic text. Instead of using the word *nappy* in a pejorative way, hooks uses it to describe the beauty of black hair: "Hair for hands to touch and play! / Hair to take the gloom away!" Together this author and illustrator have created a book that will work well in classroom units on diversity and self-esteem. *Happy to be Nappy* is a good companion to Rita Williams-Garcia's book *Catching the Wild Waiyuuzee* (Simon & Schuster, 2000; **15.28**). (EBS)

**15.16**   Lester, Julius. **The Blues Singers: Ten Who Rocked the World.**
Illustrated by Lisa Cohen. Hyperion, 2001. ISBN 0-7868-0463-7.
47 pp. (I).

This wonderful collection of brief biographies features significant figures in the world of blues music. Lester not only gives
information about their musical careers, but also emphasizes the
difficulties each of them faced on the way to fame. Cohen, a self-
taught artist, illustrates the book with large stylized paintings,
giving each singer a larger-than-life aura. The anecdotes of the
singers are framed by story, that of a grandfather explaining the
blues to a grandchild. In his definition of the blues, the grandfather states, "The words of a blues song might be sad, but the
music and the beat wrap around your heart like one of your
grandmother's hugs" (p. 5). Although the book gives no clear
definition of the blues, it does share with the reader the impact of
many great singers. This book would be an excellent companion
to other music-related books for young children, including
William Miller's *The Piano* (Lee & Low, 2000; **11.37**) and George
Weiss's *What a Wonderful World* (Atheneum, 1995). (EBS)

**15.17**   Lewis, J. Patrick. **Freedom Like Sunlight: Praisesongs for Black
Americans.** Illustrated by John Thompson. Creative Editions,
2000. ISBN 1-56846-163-1. 40 pp. (I).

Written by a European American, this collection of prose poems
are tributes to many historical African American figures. John
Thompson has created full-page illustrations that face each of
Lewis's poems. The pictures vary: for Langston Hughes, a desk
is shown; for Martin Luther King, a crying female; and for
Wilma Rudolph, images of her crossing the finish line at the
Olympics. Lewis varies his poetic style throughout the text:
some are simple four line verses; others are complex forms of
free or unrhymed verse. While there has been some controversy
about the cover of the book (a prison image of Malcolm X), this
should not be a deterrent to using it. With the autobiographical
notes at the back, the beautiful images, and the well-written
poetry, this book is a must for all libraries. (MLH)

**15.18**   ★ Okutoro, Lydia Omolola, editor. **Quiet Storm: Voices of Young
Black Poets.** Hyperion, 1999. ISBN 0-78668-0461-0. 102 pp. (I).

Teenagers of African descent penned all sixty-one poems in this
collection. Okutoro has categorized the poems according to eight

themes: "Wearing our Pride"; "We, the Observers"; "Mother-lands and the Hood"; "Trip to my Soul"; "Love Rhythms"; "the Struggle Continues"; "After Tomorrow"; and "To Our Elders." The poems range in style and quality, but they share an emotional intensity that must be acknowledged. Because each section is framed by a poem from a noted African American poet (e.g., Maya Angelou and Nikki Giovanni), the book is a useful tool for educators, encouraging young people to write poetry of their own. In addition, the poems show an intense connection across all African cultures and heritages that could serve as discussion points in classrooms. (EBS)

**15.19** Smith, Will. **Just the Two of Us.** Illustrated by Kadir Nelson. Scholastic, 2001. ISBN 0-439-08792-9. Unpaged. (ALL).

Rapper, musician, and actor Will Smith has taken the lyrics of his popular remake of Bill Withers's classic "Just the Two of Us" and created a special picture book that illustrates the bond between father and son. Readers will find it hard not to tap their feet and sing along as they move through the text of this delightful book. Kadir Nelson uses pencil and oil paint to show tender moments between the father and son, capturing the intensity of emotion when the father holds his newborn, places his young son on his shoulder for a ride, and has a heart-to-heart talk with him at the beach. (EBS)

**15.20** Spain, Sahara Sunday. **If There Would Be No Light: Poems from My Heart.** HarperCollins, 2001. ISBN 0-06-251740-6. 113 pp. (ALL).

Sahara Sunday Spain, a bright, talented, nine-year-old African American girl, has created a collection of spirit-filled, almost mystical poetry. Her work focuses on nature, love, and self-image. While simple, the messages are powerful and could prove to be the impetus for much classroom poetry writing. Of her own work, Spain says, "feels like I swallow the words down from the sky and they come up again as poems, already complete and entire" (book jacket). Although her illustrations are connected to her developmental level, they are candid representations of each of her poems and reflect an understanding of symbolism and imagery not seen in the work of many children her age. Sahara Sunday Spain's writing serves as an inspiration for other talented young writers as they hone their own skills. (EBS)

## Connections to One Another

**15.21** Burrows, Adjoa J. **Grandma's Purple Flowers.** Lee & Low, 2000. ISBN 1-880000-73-3. 30 pp. (P).

This is a lyrical story of a young girl and her grandmother. The girl loves to go through the park and down the hill to visit her grandmother, picking purple flowers as she goes. Purple is her grandmother's favorite color. Grandmother always has a smile, a hug, and some special treat for her granddaughter. But age catches up to grandmother; she begins to move slower, cook less, and have less energy. Eventually the grandmother dies, and this young girl is left feeling that nothing will be the same. In her first book, Burrows has crafted a story that connects the girl's sadness with winter and her eventual movement toward memory and hope with the purple blossoms of an oncoming spring. The cut-paper collage and acrylic illustrations masterfully support the text. Teachers will find this book especially useful for children dealing with the loss of a loved one, as well as a useful resource for a unit on the life cycle. (MLH)

**15.22** Cameron, Ann. **Gloria's Way.** Illustrated by Lis Toft. Farrar, Straus & Giroux, 2000. ISBN 0-374-32670-3. 96 pp. (P).

Ann Cameron's story about Gloria is a sequel to the Huey and Julian tales. In this book, Gloria gets a chance to be the center of attention, getting in trouble wherever she goes. Each chapter is an independent story, showing an adult who helps Gloria learn life lessons in the midst of her troubles. In the chapter "The Question," for example, Gloria's mother gives her advice on how to judge a true friend: "Friends come and go, but your best friend is always you. As long as you like you, lots of other people will, and deep down you'll be happy" (p. 72). This book is a wonderful way to introduce important life lessons. The pencil sketches by Lis Toft help the reader visualize the humorous moments from each chapter. (CM)

**15.23** ★ Cooke, Trish. **The Grandad Tree.** Illustrated by Sharon Wilson. Candlewick, 2000. ISBN 0-7636-0815-7. Unpaged. (P).

"And sometimes things die, like trees, like people . . . like Grandad. But they don't go away forever. They stay . . . because we remember" (pp. 19–20). Cooke has written a simple yet eloquent tribute to the cycle of life, acknowledging that all things change and all things die, but their memory can last forever in our hearts and minds. The children in this story remember special family stories of their grandfather climbing a coconut tree as a boy, playing a fiddle as a man, and watching them pick apples and build snowmen when he is too old to join in their activities. After his death, they plant a tree, recognizing that caring for this tree will help them remember special times with their grandad. Wilson used pastels to illustrate this loving and tender story about relationships and life. (EBS)

15.24  Grimm, Edward. **The Doorman.** Illustrated by Ted Lewin. Orchard, 2000. ISBN 0-531-3028-6. Unpaged. (P).

There is always someone special in a neighborhood, someone who holds a place in everyone's heart. Such is the case with John, the doorman, in a large New York City apartment building. He knows each tenant by name, remembers special occasions, checks on elderly tenants, and sees to the delivery of packages and mail. So the tenants are saddened when they are told that John has had a heart attack and passed away. Instead of being didactic, this book encourages children to remember the positives about a lost loved one and to use those memories to help move through the grieving process. Lewin's characteristic paintings are done in dark watercolor hues that give visual detail to the events of John's typical day. (MLH)

Johnson, Angela. **When Mules Flew on Magnolia Street.** Illustrated by John Ward. Knopf, 2000. ISBN 0-679-89077-7. 105 pp. (I). (See **21.5.**)

★ Miller, William. **The Piano.** Illustrated by Susan Keeter. Lee & Low, 2000. ISBN 1-880000-98-9. Unpaged. (P). (See **11.37.**)

15.25  ★ Nikola-Lisa, W. **Can You Top That?** Illustrated by Hector Viveros Lee. Lee & Low, 2000. ISBN 1-880000-99-7. Unpaged. (P).

This is a wonderful story of children participating in one-upmanship. Embedded in this game of "who's better than who" is a counting book and repetitive pattern that will attract the youngest listener. "I got a fish with one fin," boasts one boy. "A fish with one fin," another answers, "I got a mouse with two tails!" The story is filled with characters trying to outdo one another with their wild, make-believe possessions. The game comes to a halt when one young man jokingly asks his friends to produce all the animals they boasted about. The text gives readers and listeners the opportunity to count from one to ten and back. Lee's illustrations, done in gouache, india ink, and watercolor, give life to the fantastic animals and wild imaginings of each of the children. (EBS)

15.26 Pegram, Laura. **Daughter's Day Blues.** Illustrated by Cornelius Van Wright and Ying-Hwa Hu. Dial, 2000. ISBN 0-8037-1557-9. Unpaged. (P).

There is a Father's Day and a Mother's Day, so why isn't there a special day set aside for daughters? This is the question Phyllis Mae asks her grandmother one Mother's Day morning. J. T., her toddler brother, has no concern about any special day and ruins the cake that had been prepared for the Mother's Day celebration. Using watercolors and pencils on illustration board, Van Wright and Hu bring the characters to life. The humor and turmoil of the family take on an almost fantastic touch when plan after plan is foiled by the antics of J. T. This is a fun read that encourages creative thought and discussion from young readers. (EBS)

15.27 Williams, Sherley Anne. **Girls Together.** Illustrated by Synthia Saint James. Harcourt Brace, 1999. ISBN 0-15-230982-9. Unpaged. (ALL).

Williams has penned a wonderful celebration of friendship and sisterhood in this vibrant book that focuses on the simple themes of play and togetherness. Several girls from the projects gather together to play dress-up, dance, and go on bike rides as they work to escape daily chores and younger siblings. Their play carries them into a nearby neighborhood where they climb spring trees and dress up in magnolia blossoms. The sheer joy of their friendship and the time they can spend together is important to them. Saint James's bold colors and distinct lines, done in acrylic on canvas, complement the narrator's inner-city language patterns. The author's descriptions of each of the girls show the diversity and beauty within this community. (MLH)

15.28 Williams-Garcia, Rita. **Catching the Wild Waiyuuzee.** Illustrated by Mike Reed. Simon & Schuster, 2000. ISBN 0-689-82601-X. Unpaged. (P).

The Wild Waiyuuzee does everything she can to avoid being caught by the Shemama. Williams-Garcia uses rhythm and sound to create a tale that mixes make-believe and realism. Young listeners and readers will quickly realize that the Wild Waiyuuzee is actually a young girl trying her best to avoid getting her hair combed. But despite her efforts to run and hide, "Shemama caught that Wild Waiyuuzee and Patti Patti Rub Rub put nut-nut oil on that nut-nut head." Using Adobe Photoshop, Mike Reed painted images that reflect the imagination of a young girl. The mixture of iguanas, high grass, turtles, and rocks with a dining room table and bed from the girl's home draws children into this fun tale. (EBS)

**15.29** ★ Woodson, Jacqueline. **Miracle's Boys.** Putnam, 2000. ISBN 0-399-23113-7. 133 pp. (I).

Jacqueline Woodson has written a powerful novel about three African American brothers living on their own in contemporary Harlem. Ty'ree is the levelheaded older brother who has given up dreams of college and taken on the responsibility of caring for his younger brothers. Charlie is the middle child who often finds himself on the wrong side of the law; he has served time at the Rahway House for troubled boys. The narrator, Lafayette, is thirteen and struggling to find himself in the midst of loss and turmoil. The brothers' memories of the roles they played in the deaths of their parents—their father was a drowning victim and their mother went into a diabetic coma—haunt the three boys. The text is a gritty and compulsive read, reflecting not only the struggles of African American young men, but also the power of family and love. It is a worthy winner of the 2001 Coretta Scott King Award. (EBS)

## Connections to the Spirit

**15.30** Brown, Margaret Wise. **A Child Is Born.** Illustrated by Floyd Cooper. Hyperion, 2000. ISBN 0-7868-0673-7. Unpaged. (ALL).

This warm, simple retelling of the Nativity story was found among Margaret Wise Brown's manuscripts after her death. In short verse, the reader is taken through the classic story of Jesus' birth from the calling of the shepherds to the gathering of Wise Men and animals at the manger. "O come, country shepherds, O follow the light And welcome the baby this blessed night" Floyd

Cooper has used layered oil washes and kneaded eraser to create soft, warm images. The portrayal of the holy family, shepherds, and visitors to the manger as persons representing multiple races makes this book valuable in both presentation and interpretation. (EBS)

15.31    ★ Johnson, James Weldon. **Lift Every Voice and Sing: A Pictorial Tribute to the Negro National Anthem.** Hyperion. 2000. ISBN 0-7868-0626-5. Unpaged. (ALL).

The Negro national anthem, "Lift Every Voice and Sing," was originally written and composed by James Weldon Johnson and his brother, J. Rosamond Johnson. The brothers had been asked to create a piece appropriate for a high school assembly program. The result was a song that in the first verse reflects faith, in the second, belief, and the in third, the prayers of the African American people. Several previously published books about this anthem designed for children are illustrated by notable African American illustrators such as Elizabeth Catlett and Jan Spivey Gilchrist. This variation is particularly remarkable because of the dramatic black-and-white photographs that represent the history of the African American people from slavery through the civil rights movement. The book represents a powerful addition to a classroom library and can be used by teachers at multiple grade levels to support units on poetry, empowerment, nationalism, or self-esteem. (EBS)

15.32    Ladwig, Tim. **The Lord's Prayer.** Eerdmans, 2000. ISBN 0-8028-5180-0. Unpaged. (P).

Ladwig is best known for his contemporary illustrations of biblical texts, and this book is in the same vein. By showing a young girl helping her handyman father repair the yard and home of an elderly neighbor, Ladwig gives new meaning to the Lord's Prayer. The text has been simplified for the youngest of readers, providing abstract concepts from the Bible presented in concrete terms. Ladwig used watercolor with a glazing technique to create the rich illustrations in this book. Characters' faces are expressive, particularly when the elderly woman places a necklace with the text of the prayer around the young girl's neck in thanks for her help and her honesty. (EBS)

# 16 Asian and Pacific Island Literature

Yvonne Siu-Runyan and Shelby Anne Wolf

---

**Criteria for Excellence**

- Books reflect realities and genuine ways of life.
- Books transcend images and offensive stereotyping.
- Books provide accurate information and details such as histories, heritages, cultures, languages, and religions.
- Books reflect the diverse family structures and roles of our changing world rather than promote old notions of family structure and roles.
- Books contain illustrations or photographs that accurately reflect the racial and cultural diversity.
- Books portray the cultural group through skillful plotting, thoughtful characterization, and aesthetically crafted language.

---

## Families/Between Generations

Bercaw, Edna Coe. **Halmoni's Day.** Illustrated by Robert Hunt. Dial, 2000

Bunting, Eve. **Jin Woo.** Illustrated by Chris Soentpiet. Clarion, 2001.

English, Karen. **Nadia's Hands.** Illustrated by Jonathan Weiner. Boyds Mills, 1999.

Gilles, Almira Astudillo. **Willie Wins.** Illustrated by Carl Angel. Lee & Low, 2001.

★ Lee, Marie G. **F Is for Fabuloso.** Avon, 1999.

Lewis, Rose. **I Love You Like Crazy Cakes.** Illustrated by Jane Dyer. Little, Brown, 2000.

★ Lin, Grace. **Dim Sum for Everyone.** Knopf, 2001.

Look, Lenore. **Henry's First-Moon Birthday.** Illustrated by Yumi Heo. Atheneum, 2001.

Look, Lenore. **Love as Strong as Ginger.** Illustrated by Stephen T. Johnson. Atheneum, 1999.

Namioka, Lensey. **Yang the Eldest and His Odd Jobs.** Illustrated by Kees de Kiefte. Little, Brown, 2000.

Pak, Soyung. **Dear Juno.** Illustrated by Susan Kathleen Hartung. Viking, 1999.

## Seeing Culture through Folk Literature

★ Casanova, Mary, reteller. **The Hunter: A Chinese Folktale.** Illustrated by Ed Young. Atheneum, 2000.

★ Compestine, Ying Chang. **The Runaway Rice Cake.** Illustrated by Tungwai Chau. Simon & Schuster, 2001.

Compestine, Ying Chang. **The Story of Chopsticks.** Illustrated by YongSheng Xuan. Holiday House, 2001.

Holt, Daniel D., selector and translator. **Tigers, Frogs, and Rice Cakes: A Book of Korean Proverbs.** Illustrated by Soma Han Stickler. Shen's Books, 1999

★ Kajikawa, Kimiko. **Yoshi's Feast.** Illustrated by Yumi Heo. DK Ink, 2001.

Myers, Tim. **Basho and the Fox.** Illustrated by Oki S. Han. Marshall Cavendish, 2000.

San Souci, Daniel, reteller. **In the Moonlight Mist: A Korean Tale.** Illustrated by Eujin Kim Neilan. Boyds Mills, 1999.

★ Xuan, YongSheng. **The Dragon Lover and Other Chinese Proverbs.** Shen's Books, 1999.

★ Young, Russell. **Dragonsong: A Fable for the New Millennium.** Illustrated by Civi Chen. Shen's Books, 2000.

## Appreciating One's Cultural Heritage

Arcellana, Francisco. **The Mats.** Illustrated by Hermès Alègrè. Kane/Miller, 1999.

★ Hamanaka, Sheila, and Ayano Ohmi. **In Search of the Spirit: The Living National Treasures of Japan.** Morrow, 1999.

★ Kapono, Henry. **A Beautiful Hawaiian Day.** Illustrated by Susan Szabo. Mutual, 2000.

McCoy, Karen Kawamoto. **Bon Odori Dancer.** Illustrated by Carolina Yao. Polychrome, 1999.

Wong, Janet S. **This Next New Year.** Illustrated by Yangsook Choi. Farrar, Straus & Giroux, 2000.

★ Yamate, Sandra S. **Char Siu Bao Boy.** Illustrated by Carolina Yao. Polychrome, 2000.

## Living and Learning History

Cooper, Michael L. **Fighting for Honor: Japanese Americans and World War II.** Clarion, 2000.

★ Fa, Lu Chi, with Becky White. **Double Luck: Memoirs of a Chinese Orphan.** Holiday House, 2001.

Heisel, Sharon E. **Precious Gold, Precious Jade.** Holiday House, 2000.

★ Hoobler, Dorothy, and Thomas Hoobler. **The Ghost in the Tokaido Inn.** Philomel, 1999.

★ Park, Linda Sue. **A Single Shard.** Clarion, 2001.

★ White, Ellen Emerson. **The Royal Diaries: Kaiulani, the People's Princess.** Scholastic, 2001.

★ Yin. **Coolies.** Illustrated by Chris Soentpiet. Philomel, 2001.

## Navigating Cultures in Modern Times

★ Na, An. **A Step from Heaven.** Front Street, 2001.

★ Yep, Laurence. **The Amah.** Putnam, 1999.

★ Yep, Laurence. **Dream Soul.** HarperCollins, 2000.

## Growing Up and Coming of Age

★ Germain, Kerry. **Surf's Up for Kimo.** Illustrated by Keoni Montes. Island Paradise, 2000.

Salisbury, Graham. **Lord of the Deep.** Delacorte, 2001.

---

Our nation's schools are becoming increasingly multiracial. Though we all like to think of ourselves as open to diversity in our nation and the world, unfortunately, stereotypical thinking still plays a powerful role in how we deal with people whose heritage is different from our own. Stereotyping peoples and cultures has disastrous effects—politically, educationally, socially, and personally—and cannot be erased easily from our hearts and minds.

In the 2000 U.S. census, 281.4 million people were counted in the United States, a 13.2 percent increase from the 1990 census population (Humes & McKinnon, 2000). In March 1999, the Asian and Pacific Islander population was 10.9 million, constituting 4 percent of the total population. But the term "Asian and Pacific Islander" is an umbrella term that encompasses a huge variety. So before we proceed to the books written for and about these peoples, we need to stop and define who they are. The U.S. Census Bureau defines the "Asian" population in the United States as those sharing roots with any of the original peoples of the Far East, Southeast Asia, or the Indian subcontinent including Cambodia, China, India, Japan, Korea, Malaysia, Pakistan, the Philippine Islands, Thailand, and Vietnam. "Pacific Islander" refers to those whose heritage begins with any of the original peoples of Hawaii, Guam, Samoa, or other Pacific islands.

Clearly, the Asian and Pacific Islander population is not a homogeneous group. Instead, it comprises twenty-nine distinct Asian and Pacific Islander subgroups who speak over a hundred different languages and are diverse in terms of national affiliation, history, culture, heritage, and religious belief. Some of the Asian American groups, such as the Chinese and Japanese, have been in the United States for five generations, while others such as the Hmong, Vietnamese, Laotians, and Cambodians are comparatively recent immigrants. Most Pacific Islanders, on the other hand, have been U.S. citizens ever since their homelands were annexed as territories over forty years ago or, as in the case of the Hawaiian Islands, became the fiftieth state in the union.

Because many Asian and Pacific Islander stories have never been written in English or even shared orally with the larger U.S. population, there are large gaps in our understanding of the history of these highly diverse groups—internationally, nationally, and locally. When she returned home in the fall of 2001, for instance, Yvonne asked her relatives about their stories of the period when the Japanese bombed Pearl Harbor. She discovered new information not told in books published on World War II. Specifically, she hadn't known that her Hawaiian aunties were playing in the yard when they saw not U.S. planes but Japanese planes flying toward Pearl Harbor, or that her relatives spent many nights at the mortuary with other local people because their homes were damaged.

When children read and discuss literature that accurately represents Asian and Pacific Island peoples, they learn new ways of thinking and being and will hopefully become better citizens of our multicultural, multiracial world. Without a better understanding of all peoples—that is, appreciating and understanding commonalities as well as contrasts—barriers to world peace will continue to strengthen, and peace will be more difficult to achieve.

Unfortunately, as we reviewed books for this chapter, we found that only a limited number of Asian and Pacific Island books for children were available. This is particularly discouraging because approximately three to five thousand children's books are published annually in the United States. Yvonne vividly remembers growing up in Hawaii and reading only stories about white boys and girls who were middle or upper class; they certainly weren't people with whom she was familiar. The only place she was able to read books that reflected her cultural background was at the public library, where she found Hawaiian folktales. Never did she read stories with Asian children in them other than the classic folktales *The Five Chinese Brothers* and *Peach Boy*. Yvonne's strong interest in folktales is thus no accident. In Shelby's teaching of multicultural children's literature in her university classes, she has found it difficult to find Asian/Pacific Island literature that extends beyond the old tales into modern times. While folktales are a critical part of any group's heritage, children need to read texts and see images that reflect their current lives. Thus, even in the 1999, 2000, and 2001 books reviewed in this chapter, folktales and historical fiction predominate, and realistic fiction, such as Lensey Namioka's latest story of the Chinese American Yang family or An Na's story of a modern Korean family, are all too rare.

With so few books accurately portraying Asian and Pacific Islanders, children who make up this diverse group will continue to be distanced from the texts they read. In addition, children of other cultural and ethnic groups will continue to stereotype and hold misconceptions about Asian and Pacific Island peoples—Americans as well as indigenous individuals. Teachers can avoid presenting stereotypical and inadequate images by discussing the books being read, as well as the culture(s) represented, before, during, and after reading. But teaching about cultures can be tricky; presenters of Asian and Pacific Island literature are too often unaware of their own stereotypical thinking. Sadly, certain assumptions continue to prevail: Chinese people usually work in banks, restaurants, and laundries; Asian females are submissive; Asian children do well in school; Pacific Islanders are plantation workers. Asian and Pacific Island peoples are not alike; instead, these peoples are diverse and as different from one another as the individuals of any other group.

While we would like to see more books that accurately and thoughtfully portray Asian and Pacific Islanders, we did notice a positive trend—that more stories were written and illustrated by authors and illustrators of the culture portrayed in the text than in the past.

In the annotations for this chapter on Asian and Pacific Island literature for children, we concentrated on authenticity as well as aesthetic qualities (Wolf, Ballentine, & Hill, 1999) using the following criteria:

1. Does the book reflect the realities and ways of life of Asian and Pacific Island peoples? That is, does the book really tell about how the characters live? Or do the realities of life in the book promote stereotypical conceptions? Is the author writing from the point of view of an imagined rather than the actual culture?

2. Does the book transcend images and offensive stereotyping about Asian and Pacific Island peoples? Are the characters well rounded and complex rather than simplistic? In short, does the book offer other ways of understanding the characters instead of promoting common misinformation?

3. Does the book provide accurate information and details such as histories, heritages, cultures, languages, and religions of Asian and Pacific Island peoples? Are the cultural aspects in the book accurate? Does the author explain his or her research process and sources in the book?

4. Does the book reflect the diverse family structures and roles of our changing world? Or does it promote old notions of family structure and roles?

5. Does the book contain illustrations or photographs that accurately reflect the racial and cultural diversity of Asian and Pacific Island peoples? Are the illustrations accurate?

6. Does the book portray the cultural group through skillful plotting, thoughtful characterization, and aesthetically crafted language? Does the language communicate accurate and rich images and engage the reader in the text? If the text incorporates a native language within the English text, is the language used thoughtfully rather than sporadically tossed in to make the story appear authentic?

During the selection process, we quite purposefully omitted books that didn't live up to our criteria. We decided not to include books that took stories from other lands and simply transferred them to an Asian/Pacific Island setting. Demi's *The Emperor's New Clothes* (2000), for example, is a relatively slight retelling of Hans Christian Andersen's original, surprisingly set in China. In her author's note, Demi makes a valiant attempt to relate the Dane's tale to the Chinese concept of "chí," the essence of life, but the argument seems weak and the writing itself too spare.

We also decided not to include books in which an author's genuine interest in a particular culture was still not enough to create an accurate portrayal. Mercer Mayer's *Shibumi and the Kitemaker* (1999), for example, tells of an emperor of a "far-away kingdom" in Japan who builds a garden with high walls to separate his daughter from the squalor of the city. But Shibumi climbs a chestnut tree, and when she sees the horror below, she determines to make a change. She flies away on the biggest kite ever made and warns her father that she will not come down until the city is as lovely as the palace. The rest of the story follows the emperor's attempts to meet his daughter's demands and Shibumi's final return. Although intriguing in its strong political statements, Mayer's story misses in several ways. First of all, although Mayer is intrigued by Japanese culture, he acknowledges in his author's note that "Westerners are rarely allowed to see into the Japanese heart." Thus, the tale of Shibumi is not based on Japanese folk literature but is instead grounded in Mayer's imagined culture. Second, his artwork, all done on the computer, is visually stunning but lacks association with Japanese art beyond the superficial features of kimonos, cranes, and strong samurai. It is as though Mayer himself is flying high on his computer-generated kite, and his view distances us from Japanese culture rather than bringing us closer.

Finally, we eliminated tales that characterized cultures in pedantic and stereotypical ways. One example is V. J. Pacilio's *Ling Cho and His Three Friends* (2000). This tedious tale of rhymed couplets is set in China, though the author and illustrator have no recognizable experience with the culture. There is no endnote to explain the origin of the story, and the rhymes are forced, with only rare nods to Chinese life. The story recounts how Ling Cho, a prosperous farmer, tries to care for his neighbors. But when he finds a way and his friends ultimately deceive him, the "wise, kind" Ling Cho pedantically denies them further assistance and then endlessly lectures the one man who was the most honest. While the illustrations lighten the weight of the tale, one can't help but wonder whether images that emerge more from the imagination than research might perpetuate harmful stereotypes.

### References

Humes, K., & McKinnon, J. (2000). *The Asian and Pacific Islander population in the United States: March, 1999.* U.S. Census Bureau Current Population Reports, Series P20–529. Washington, DC: U.S. Government Printing Office.

Wolf, S. A., Ballentine, D., & Hill, L. (1999). The right to write: Preservice teachers' evolving understandings of authenticity and aesthetic heat in multicultural literature. *Research in the Teaching of English, 34*(1), 130–84.

## Families/Between Generations

**16.1** Bercaw, Edna Coe. **Halmoni's Day.** Illustrated by Robert Hunt. Dial, 2000. ISBN 0-8037-2444-6. Unpaged. (ALL).

This moving, intergenerational story, illustrated in exquisite oil paintings, crosses cultural, language, place, and time barriers. Many young people feel the way Jennifer does when family members are different from the dominant culture. Jennifer's *halmoni,* or grandmother, is visiting from Korea just in time for Grandparents' Day at school. Though Jennifer is excited about the event, she is also worried, because Halmoni does not speak English very well, wears strange clothes, and does not understand U.S. culture. When it is Halmoni's turn to receive her award and share a memory, she talks about her childhood in war-torn Korea. Halmoni ends her story explaining that the greatest joy of being a grandparent is seeing how the parts of herself, her husband, and her parents live on through her children and their children. (YSR)

16.2    Bunting, Eve. **Jin Woo.** Illustrated by Chris Soentpiet. Clarion, 2001. ISBN 0-395-93872-4. 30 pp. (P).

This is a tender tale of a European American family's adoption of Jin Woo, a Korean child, told from the older sibling's point of view. While David's parents can hardly wait for the arrival of their new son, David can. One illustration shows David's parents at the airport, smiling as they first gaze at the baby. But David is somberly watching his parents, wondering about their ability to love him and the new baby as well. Events turn around as David coaxes Jin Woo into his first laugh on the car ride home. More important, after tucking the baby in his crib, both parents concentrate on David, sharing a "letter from Jin Woo" that reassures David about the capacity of his parents' love. Eve Bunting's moving prose is magnified in Soentpiet's stunning illustrations, which are all the more convincing because Soentpiet himself was adopted from Korea. (SAW)

16.3    English, Karen. **Nadia's Hands.** Illustrated by Jonathan Weiner. Boyds Mills, 1999. ISBN 1-56397-667-6. Unpaged. (ALL).

As a member of a large Pakistani American family, Nadia has been chosen to be the flower girl for Auntie Laila's wedding. In this role, she will wear a *shalwar* and *kameez* (popular Pakistani clothing) and have her hands painted with *mehndi* (henna paste) in intricate designs. Although she has the usual worries about her role, her real concern is what will happen when she goes to school with "hands that looked as if they belonged to someone else." The story ends on a happy note as Nadia comes to appreciate her heritage through the love of her extended family. The story highlights some of the issues children of dual cultures must face in mainstream school. The illustrations enhance the text with the reddish-gold glow of henna throughout. (SAW)

16.4    Gilles, Almira Astudillo. **Willie Wins.** Illustrated by Carl Angel. Lee & Low, 2001. ISBN 1-58430-033-7. Unpaged. (ALL).

Willie is having a bad day. He strikes out in a Little League baseball game, and now he must find a bank to bring to school. Dad has just what Willie needs—an *alkansiya,* or coconut shell, that has been made into a bank. The best part of the *alkinsiya* is that inside is a treasure from his uncle. At the end of the month, Willie's teacher announces that now is the time to unlock their banks. Willie uses a small hammer to crack open his *alkinsiya.* To his surprise, the treasure is a San Francisco Giants card dated 1964 with a picture of Willie Mays on it. The children with whom we shared this book commented on Angel's bold, detailed acrylic illustrations and how they capture the expressive faces of Willie and his father. Although many children had eaten coconut, they knew little about the tree or the fruit. They asked many questions about coconut trees, where they grow, what coconuts look like, and how one opens a coconut to get the milk and the meat. (YSR)

16.5 ★ Lee, Marie G. **F Is for Fabuloso.** Avon, 1999. ISBN 0-380-97648-X. 176 pp. (I).

Caught between two cultures, Korean and American, Jin-Ha often feels bewildered. Though she loves American food, she still has a craving for hot, spicy, garlicky Korean foods. Jin-Ha's father, a scholar in Korea, now works for a car mechanic. Her mother does not speak much English and embarrasses Jin-Ha in public. When Jin-Ha's mother is embarrassed by another customer in the bank because she doesn't speak English well, she wonders, "What kind of place is America? In Korea no one would ever say 'Learn Korean!' to an American. In fact, if an American spoke any Korean at all, they would probably all be amazed" (p. 2). This sensitive story shows a modern-day immigrant family's struggle to survive in a new country and a young girl's determination to forge a new American identity while at the same time preserve her culture and honor her immigrant parents' values. (YSR)

16.6 Lewis, Rose. **I Love You Like Crazy Cakes.** Illustrated by Jane Dyer. Little, Brown, 2000. ISBN 0-316-52538-3. Unpaged. (ALL).

Based on the author's own experience, this tender and loving story chronicles a woman's journey to adopt a baby girl from China. Jane Dyer's watercolors express the mood of the story and complement the text. When this book was shared with parents who have adopted baby girls from China, all agreed that this book does indeed capture their feelings and thoughts. Several had already read this book to their adopted Chinese daughters, reporting that it had a profound influence on the family, opening up conversations. As one child said to her mother, "I didn't know you went through all that trouble just to adopt me." Following this statement, the mother and father were able to talk about why they chose to adopt their little girl from China. (YSR)

**16.7** ★ Lin, Grace. **Dim Sum for Everyone.** Knopf, 2001. ISBN 0-375-81082-X. Unpaged. (P).

The author explains that when dining in a dim sum restaurant, you can "tap three fingers on the table" when you want to thank your waiter. So here's a three-finger tap to Lin for serving up this tale of the deliciously varied dishes of dim sum. The text is simple, but the illustrations bring the text to life. A family arrives, selects, and shares their favorite dishes. Some pictures provide captivating views of the bustling restaurant with waitresses rolling their carts of food, waiters pouring tea, and families eating with delight. But the close-up views of the central family—mother, father, and three little girls—are even more charming. The picture of young Mei-Mei peeking over the cart of sweet tofu proves one translation of *dim sum* as "point" (dim) and "heart" (sum)—for Mei-Mei's directed gaze clearly demonstrates her heart's (and stomach's) desire! (SAW)

**16.8** Look, Lenore. **Henry's First-Moon Birthday.** Illustrated by Yumi Heo. Atheneum, 2001. ISBN 0-689-82294-4. Unpaged. (P).

Jenny's baby brother is having his first moon, or one-month birthday, a traditional Chinese celebration to welcome the newborn. Together, Jenny and her *gnin gnin*, parental grandmother, handle all the preparations—dying eggs with the lucky color red, making pigs' feet and ginger soup, and cleaning the house. It might be wise for teachers to point out that the Chinese dialect used throughout the text is Cantonese, not Mandarin. Discussing dialect is important because there are many dialects of Chinese spoken throughout Asia, and all of them are different. Heo's pencil, oil, and collage illustrations are lively and colorful, working cohesively with the story line to capture the spirit of the text. The illustrations have a childlike quality, which gives the reader the impression that Jenny actually drew the pictures herself. After hearing this story, children talked and wrote about the celebrations their families have to welcome newborns. Discussions like these open doors of understanding and appreciation for the many ways all cultures celebrate important events. (YSR)

**16.9**   Look, Lenore. **Love as Strong as Ginger.** Illustrated by Stephen T. Johnson. Atheneum, 1999. ISBN 0-689-81248-5. Unpaged. (ALL).

This intergenerational story, based on the author's own experiences, tells how Katie spends Saturdays with her beloved grandmother, or *gnin gnin,* a cannery worker in Seattle who has large rubber gloves that are *chiubungbung,* or "stinky-stinky." Katie watches her grandmother swing a heavy mallet cracking crabs from morning until evening. Gnin Gnin's hard work buys bus fare to work and a fish for dinner, which she cooks exquisitely with "love as strong as ginger and dreams as thick as black-bean paste." The soft pastel illustrations set a perfect mood and enhance the story of a young girl who gains a deep respect for the grandmother who works so hard yet maintains a noble spirit and an infectious sense of humor. This book can serve as an excellent springboard for students to write about their parents' and grandparents' work and the uniqueness of their own family's cultural heritage. (YSR)

**16.10**   Namioka, Lensey. **Yang the Eldest and His Odd Jobs.** Illustrated by Kees de Kiefte. Little, Brown, 2000. ISBN 0-316-59011-8. 121 pp. (I).

This fourth book in the delightful series about the Yang family describes how First Brother works at a series of jobs to replace his damaged violin, though he loses some enthusiasm for music in the process. The narrator is the third eldest sister who explains the subtle and not-so-subtle differences between Chinese and American culture. She even lets us in on some of the differences among the Chinese and Japanese when she has her first Japanese meal, noting that even the chopsticks differ. The picture of Ying-mei taking her first bite of *wasabi* with her hair standing on end is hilarious. Beyond the surface differences in food and utensils, the beauty of this tale lies in the devotion of the Yang family to one another. Indeed, it is family love and Yang the Eldest's rediscovery of the joy of music that bring this story to its uplifting conclusion. (SAW)

**16.11**   Pak, Soyung. **Dear Juno.** Illustrated by Susan Kathleen Hartung. Viking, 1999. ISBN 0-670-88252-6. Unpaged. (ALL).

Juno receives a letter from his grandmother but is disappointed when his parents are too busy to read it to him since he cannot read Korean. When he opens the letter on his own, Juno discovers a picture of his grandmother and her cat and a dried flower from her garden. When Juno's parents finally read the letter to him, they are surprised at how much he already knows just from the picture. Juno then decides to draw pictures to send to his grandmother because she will understand what he wants to say, even without words. This book shows children that pictures can say as much, maybe more, than words. To understand this concept, children can investigate and experiment with drawing pictures instead of writing words to communicate messages to friends or family members, demonstrating another way of knowing and sharing. (YSR)

## Seeing Culture through Folk Literature

16.12   ★ Casanova, Mary, reteller. **The Hunter: A Chinese Folktale.** Illustrated by Ed Young. Atheneum, 2000. ISBN 0-689-82906-X. Unpaged. (ALL).

This Chinese tale tells of a brave young hunter, Hai Li Bu, who rescues a pearly snake from the maw of a crane. Offered any reward he desires, he chooses to understand the language of animals so that he can provide sustenance for his village. The gift comes with a stone and a warning, however, for if he ever reveals his secret, he too will turn to stone. The selfless hunter ultimately reveals the secret, but only to save his community. While the tale is a lovely one, the true treasure is Ed Young's illustrations, with black brush-stroke figures stark against warm earth tones. The most moving illustration is that of the hunter offering his truth, with the white of his luminous stone reflected in the tears in his eyes. An added gem is the single red box of Chinese calligraphy that captures the essence of each page. (SAW)

16.13   ★ Compestine, Ying Chang. **The Runaway Rice Cake.** Illustrated by Tungwai Chau. Simon & Schuster, 2001. ISBN 0-689-82972-8. Unpaged. (ALL).

Chinese New Year provides a backdrop for this story of a young boy and his family who have enough rice flour to make one *niangao*, or holiday rice cake. The cake suddenly comes to life and runs away. When an old woman catches the cake, the Changs let the starving woman eat it even though they are just as hungry. When they return home, neighbors recognize the family's generosity and pitch in to make a sumptuous feast and celebration, complete with a dragon, firecrackers, and dancers. The tale is enhanced with an informative note on Chinese New Year and two recipes for *nian-gao.* As a first-time illustrator, Tungwai Chau has effectively matched colorful acrylics with the bounty of the text. Because the children who read this book were unfamiliar with Chinese New Year, they found the story intriguing and enjoyed learning about the traditions of another culture. They were also impressed with the compassion of the family. The children loved the colorful, action-oriented illustrations portraying the traditions surrounding the Chinese New Year. (YSR)

16.14 Compestine, Ying Chang. **The Story of Chopsticks.** Illustrated by YongSheng Xuan. Holiday House, 2001. ISBN 0-8234-1526-0. Unpaged. (ALL).

Kúai is always hungry. One day when his family is waiting for the food to cool, Kúai uses twigs to pierce food too hot to pick up with his hands. Seeing this new way of eating, his family joins him. To honor Kúai, his mother suggests they call them "Kúai zi" to honor Kúai. At a wedding, Kúai sneaks in sticks. Enamored with this new way of eating, other people get their own sticks. Eventually all the people in town eat with sticks. Before long people are using them in every part of China. At the end of the book, the author provides information about chopsticks along with a recipe for Sweet Eight Treasures Rice Pudding. Xuan's cut-paper illustrations emboldened with strong black lines animate this entertaining story. Though at first glance the illustrations look Japanese, they are in fact Chinese. (YSR)

16.15 Holt, Daniel D., selector and translator. **Tigers, Frogs, and Rice Cakes: A Book of Korean Proverbs.** Illustrated by Soma Han Stickler. Shen's Books, 1999. ISBN 1-885-008-10-4. Unpaged. (I).

Holt has compiled an intriguing collection of bilingual Korean-English texts with twenty Korean *sok-dams,* or folk sayings, each written in Korean and English. Each proverb focuses on a significant folk symbol or Korean belief held throughout all of Korean society and reminds readers of basic truths. At the end of the book, Holt categorizes the proverbs into three areas—character, cooperation and accomplishment, and eating—and then brilliantly explains the meaning of each. Stickler's accompanying full-page watercolor illustrations effectively blend color and design to clarify and provide insights into each Korean proverb. This exceptional book is not only a work of art but also a work of wisdom that helps us see human frailties and offers suggestions for living. It is an excellent resource for those interested in Korean culture. (YSR)

16.16 ★ Kajikawa, Kimiko. **Yoshi's Feast.** Illustrated by Yumi Heo. DK Ink, 2001. ISBN 0-7894-2607-2. Unpaged. (P).

This is a feast of a book with delectable prose and delicious illustrations. Yoshi the fan maker spends each night eating a simple bowl of rice but adds zest to his meals by sniffing the air of his neighbor Sabu's broiling eels. Eager to keep his money in his money box, "Yoshi enjoyed with his nose what he would not pay to put in his mouth." Disgruntled, Sabu presents Yoshi with a bill for *smelling* his eels, but Yoshi returns the favor by paying Sabu with only the *sound* of his money, dancing about with his money box. The two neighbors finally reach a happy resolution when the combination of Yoshi's dancing and Sabu's cooking draws more customers, and both men find themselves rich and full. The swirling, twirling illustrations combine handmade Japanese papers with pencil and oil. Even the print dances, following the lines of Yoshi's undulating limbs. (SAW)

16.17 Myers, Tim. **Basho and the Fox.** Illustrated by Oki S. Han. Marshall Cavendish, 2000. ISBN 0-7614-5068-8. Unpaged. (ALL).

This is a delightful story about the Japanese poet Basho, renowned for his extraordinary haiku. Myers, a haiku writer himself, has long been an admirer of both the economy and the evocative nature of Basho's poetry. In the tale, Basho loves the taste of wild cherries in summer. One day, however, he finds his favorite tree raided by a local fox dressed in a vibrantly colored kimono. When Basho protests, the fox challenges him to create a haiku worthy of a fox's listening. Basho works hard to polish his poems, but the first two he offers are ridiculed by the fox, even Basho's most famous poem: "An old pond, / A frog jumps in. / The sound of water." In a last desperate attempt, Basho finally succeeds because his haiku features a fox. Korean-born Oki Han's watercolors add to the lively humor of the text, especially the image of the fox in full kimono. (SAW)

16.18 San Souci, Daniel, reteller. **In the Moonlight Mist: A Korean Tale.** Illustrated by Eujin Kim Neilan. Boyds Mills, 1999. ISBN 1-56397-754-0. Unpaged. (ALL).

This enchanting retelling of a Korean folktale follows a compassionate woodcutter who saves the life of a deer and is rewarded with a heavenly wife. When she pines for her celestial home, the woodcutter ignores the deer's instructions and gives her the garments she needs to make the passage home. The deer offers him a chance to regain his wife, but he once again forgoes his own desires and allows his elderly mother access to heaven in his place. At this point, the "heavenly king" intervenes, and the woodcutter is rejoined with his family, adding luster to the firmament. The well-researched illustrations are particularly beautiful. Neilan uses strong brush strokes to enhance her acrylics, which are bathed in light and capture the feeling of the world during the Chosun Dynasty of long ago. (SAW)

16.19 ★ Xuan, YongSheng. **The Dragon Lover and Other Chinese Proverbs.** Shen's Books, 1999. ISBN 1-885008-11-2. Unpaged. (I).

Based on the original texts found in historical documents, Xuan selected five Chinese proverbs that portray important truths. The timeless wisdom of these proverbs shows us that there is much to learn from the animal kingdom. These five profound yet simple sayings that have helped Chinese people for centuries are written in both Chinese and English. The intricate, vibrant, and delicate illustrations, using cut-paper artwork, objectify and embellish each proverb. Each page contains both English and Chinese text with illustrative borders that enhance the mood of the book. The publisher's note at the end of the book explains the source for each proverb. According to the author, "The value of these morals is so universal that they are worth retelling to our own children, for their application to contemporary life." (YSR)

16.20 ★ Young, Russell. **Dragonsong: A Fable for the New Millennium.** Illustrated by Civi Chen. Shen's Books, 2000. ISBN 1-885008-12-0. Unpaged. (ALL).

This wondrous story carries Chiang-An, the youngest dragon, around the world in search of a treasure able to last the next thousand years. As Chiang-An travels the world, he meets a dragon in each place who shares new wisdom and gives him a meaningful gift. When Chiang-An finally flies home, he transforms all he has learned into the gift of hope wrapped in a song. When the other dragons question his gift, Chiang-An sings the most beautiful song, weaving the themes and melodies of the four dragons he met into one song that fills a person's spirit and heart, providing hope for a brighter tomorrow. The dragons are extremely pleased and agree that Chiang-An deserves to be Keeper of the Mountain. Chen's stunning illustrations of misty mornings, shimmering waters, and opalescent skies splendidly enhance Young's words to create an incredible book for the new millennium. (YSR)

## Appreciating One's Cultural Heritage

**16.21**   Arcellana, Francisco. **The Mats.** Illustrated by Hermès Alègrè. Kane/Miller, 1999. ISBN 0-916291-86-3. Unpaged. (ALL).

A young girl growing up in the Philippines learns the importance of traditions and how they are expressed in the gift of mats presented to each family member by her proud and loyal father. Alègrè's vivid drawings, splashed with tropical colors, depict the excitement of the family, the beauty of mats, the uniqueness of each individual, and the reverence for family members who are gone but still cherished. The children who read this book learned that sickness and death occur in cultures other than their own and that it is important to remember the people who have died. *The Mats* is an excellent book to read aloud to children as an introduction to discussing with them the importance of families and traditions in all cultures. Children may draw or write about their own special family celebrations and share the unique qualities of each person within their own cultures. (YSR)

**16.22**   ★ Hamanaka, Sheila, and Ayano Ohmi. **In Search of the Spirit: The Living National Treasures of Japan.** Morrow, 1999. ISBN 0-688-14607-4. 48 pp. (I).

This extraordinary book describes the careful craft of artisans who extend and elaborate on traditions passed down from sixteenth-century Japan. These traditions might have been lost in the mechanization following World War II had the government not had the foresight to offer grants to the "Bearers of Important Intangible Cultural Assets." The one hundred recipients—popularly known as Living National Treasures—use the support to continue their work and train apprentices. Of the one hundred, Hamanaka and Ohmi describe the art of six masters: a *yuzen* dyer (a kimono artisan), a bamboo weaver, a *bunraku* puppet master, a sword maker, a Noh actor, and a *neriage* potter. While clear photographs and delicate step-by-step paintings detail the art forms, the living treasure of this book lies in its lyrical description of each master's philosophical dedication to his art. (SAW)

**16.23** ★ Kapono, Henry. **A Beautiful Hawaiian Day.** Illustrated by Susan Szabo. Mutual, 2000. ISBN 1-56647-346-2. Unpaged. (P).

This lavishly illustrated story tells of Kaleo, who finds a magical seashell as she walks along the shoreline. When she puts the seashell to her ear, she closes her eyes and hears a most beautiful sound. Suddenly Kaleo is swept back into time and meets the young King Kamehameha. The young king shows Kaleo his favorite spot at the top of a steep cliff. As Kaleo looks at the magnificent beauty that surrounds her, she tells the king of her home—the tall buildings, pollution, homeless population, and crime. King Kamehameha takes Kaleo to a sacred place where two waterfalls cascade into a pond. He tells her a legend of the waterfall and how it represents eternal love. When the young king returns Kaleo to her time, she realizes the importance of respecting and honoring the ocean, the land, the sky, and the peoples of Hawaii. (YSR)

**16.24** McCoy, Karen Kawamoto. **Bon Odori Dancer.** Illustrated by Carolina Yao. Polychrome, 1999. ISBN 1-879965-16-X. Unpaged. (ALL).

Keiko has high hopes for performing the traditional dance at the Obon festival, but she can't get her feet to move correctly. With the help of an understanding teacher and good friends, the performance goes well, despite one small mishap with the *kachi-kachi* sticks. The importance of honoring our ancestors, the beauty of the Obon celebration, and the value of friendship are all depicted in this whimsical book with an important message. While the illustrations are lighthearted and colorful, they effectively convey the beauty of the festival and the dancers' colorful kimonos. This book is an excellent read-aloud for young children interested in the celebrations and traditional clothing of Asian cultures as well as how friends can help one another. After hearing this story, some students commented on the beautiful costumes and many expressed a desire to see a real Obon celebration. (YSR)

**16.25**     Wong, Janet S. **This Next New Year.** Illustrated by Yangsook Choi.
              Farrar, Straus & Giroux, 2000. ISBN 0-374-35503-7. Unpaged. (P).

In lyrical, lilting verse, Wong describes Chinese New Year preparations in her Chinese Korean house. The house is swept clean of
last year's dust, food is prepared for the celebration, and clothes
are washed and pressed for wearing. Choi's animated and energetic double-page illustrations capture the spirit of this important celebration using vibrant, bold colors. The author note at the
end of the book also describes Chinese New Year preparations
and symbols in the Wong family. Chinese New Year is celebrated
by almost all Chinese Americans, so this story is perfect to read
to all children. Since children might be confused by the fact that
this story is about a Chinese Korean American family, teachers
would be wise to point out that the Asian text/words shown in
the illustrations are Korean, not Chinese, and that though both
Korean and Chinese written languages may look alike, they are
in fact different. (YSR)

**16.26**     ★ Yamate, Sandra S. **Char Siu Bao Boy.** Illustrated by Carolina
              Yao. Polychrome, 2000. ISBN 1-879965-19-4. Unpaged. (ALL).

Charlie loves *char siu bao* (Chinese barbequed pork buns). He
brings it to school for lunch every day, but the other children
tease him. They wonder how he can eat it and think it looks terrible. Charlie tries eating what the other kids eat, but misses eating
*char siu bao.* Then Charlie has an idea. He asks his grandmother to
make *char siu bao* to share with his friends. The boys and girls
sniff and poke at their *bao.* Then Mike, Charlie's best friend, tentatively takes a bite and announces, "Hey, this is good!" Before long
everyone is eating *char siu bao.* This tender story portrays tension
between conformity and individuality as well as pride in a culture. At the end, there is a recipe for making *char siu bao.* (YSR)

## Living and Learning History

**16.27**     Cooper, Michael L. **Fighting for Honor: Japanese Americans
              and World War II.** Clarion, 2000. ISBN 0-395-91375-6. 118 pp. (I).

Over the past decade, we've been enlightened about the racially
motivated internment of Japanese Americans during World War
II through books such as *Baseball Saved Us* by Ken Mochizuki
(Lee & Low, 1993), *I Am an American: A True Story of Japanese
Internment* by Jerry Stanley (Crown, 1994), and *Bat 6* by Virginia

Euwer Wolff (Scholastic, 1998). *Fighting for Honor* is a welcome addition because it explores the stories of many Japanese Americans who volunteered for army service. The irony of fighting for a country that arrested and interned their families as well as condoned the theft and destruction of their property is clear. What makes the book all the more compelling, however, is the bravery of the 100th/442nd battalion. The battle scenes, especially the dangerous rescue of the "Lost Battalion" and Senator Daniel Inouye's leadership role, are particularly gripping. Black-and-white photographs, a chronology, endnotes, and references all add to the authenticity of the text. (SAW)

16.28 ★ Fa, Lu Chi, with Becky White. **Double Luck: Memoirs of a Chinese Orphan.** Holiday House, 2001. ISBN 0-8234-1560-0. 212 pp. (I).

Lu Chi Fa's parents die in 1944 when he is only three years old. Chairman Mao Zedong's Cultural Revolution is in progress, and China is in political turmoil and suffering severe poverty. Because times are hard, Lu Chi is shuffled from one relative to another and is eventually sold to a communist chief. Enduring hunger and beatings, he nevertheless survives. In 1969, Lu Chi immigrates to the United States where he makes a new life for himself. At the end of this heartfelt, stirring memoir, a time line of three events is chronicled: the year and the Chinese astrological sign, Lu Chi's experiences, and events of the Chinese Cultural Revolution. This time line provides an important backdrop to help readers make sense of the events that occurred during Lu Chi Fa's life and how these events were intertwined. (YSR)

16.29 Heisel, Sharon E. **Precious Gold, Precious Jade.** Holiday House, 2000. ISBN 0-8234-1432-9. 186 pp. (I).

Set in a western mining town at the end of the gold rush era, Angelena befriends An Li despite the racism and fear that surround the community. The tauntings, threats, beatings, and even murders that the Celestials (Chinese immigrants) endured at the hands of U.S. miners speak volumes about the prevalence of prejudice during these times. Because of her friendship with An Li, Angelena learns about the Chinese culture. Despite the tension that erupts, An Li and Angelena remain fast friends until the day An Li leaves with her family to work on the railroads on the Columbia River. This moving book provides a glimpse into the lives of the Chinese immigrants who worked in the mines and on the railroads and who had a significant impact on our American way of life. (YSR)

16.30    ★ Hoobler, Dorothy, and Thomas Hoobler. **The Ghost in the Tokaido Inn.** Philomel, 1999. ISBN 0-399-23330-X. 224 pp. (I).

In eighteenth-century Japan, Judge Ooka was known for his ability to solve crimes through careful reasoning. In this novel, the Hooblers have taken the tender leaves of this history and brewed a complex tale of samurai suspense. Their story's protagonist is Seiki, a fourteen-year-old merchant's son, who longs to rise above his class to samurai status. He has his chance when he witnesses the theft of a valuable gift to the shogun, and with Judge Ooka's assistance he follows the path of the crime to its thrilling conclusion. Like the tea that Seiki drinks, the novel is smooth and full of subtle flavors, with fascinating insights into the place of duty, honor, and respect in shogun-era Japan. (SAW)

16.31    ★ Park, Linda Sue. **A Single Shard.** Clarion, 2001. ISBN 0-395-97827-0. 152 pp. (I).

As the first Asian American to win the Newbery Medal, Linda Sue Park delivers a fascinating story of early Korea. The young protagonist, Tree Ear, is an orphan apprenticed to Min, the village's master potter. Tree Ear volunteers to travel to faraway Songdo to deliver two of Min's superb vases to an important emissary. Along the way, he is robbed by thieves, who hurl the vases from a cliff. Tree Ear considers making the same leap in shame but instead retrieves a single shard from one of the vases and continues to Songdo. Rather than reject the shard, the emissary sees the quality of the work: "'Radiance of jade and clarity of water'—that is what is said about the finest celadon glaze. . . . I say it of this one" (p. 138). Like celadon, Park's prose shows clarity and craft, and her helpful author's note, which explores the history of celadon pottery as well as shares insights into twelfth-century life in Korea, enhances the tale. (SAW)

16.32    ★ White, Ellen Emerson. **The Royal Diaries: Kaiulani, the People's Princess.** Scholastic, 2001. ISBN 0-439-12909-5. 238 pp. (I).

In this well-researched book written in diary form, White has captured the life events as well as the moods and feelings of Princess Kaiulani. White's expert use of Hawaiian words throughout this story lends authenticity to the text and teaches readers something about the Hawaiian language, and students will learn a lot about the history of the Hawaiian Islands. At the end of the book, the author provides a family tree of the Kalákaua family, with pictures as well as information about the Hawaiian language. This book is a must-read for anyone studying the history of the Hawaiian Islands. (YSR)

**16.33** ★ Yin. **Coolies.** Illustrated by Chris Soentpiet. Philomel, 2001. ISBN 0-399-23227-3. Unpaged. (ALL).

In this stunning book, Yin takes a deprecatory term—coolies—and transforms it into a celebration of the heroic contributions of Chinese Americans in building the transcontinental railroad. The central tale is of two brothers, Shek and Little Wong, who leave China and are hired by Central Pacific to help build the western half of the U.S. railroad. Their tribulations are intense, though Shek and Wong remain determined to stay together. Soentpiet's double-page spreads are dazzling. Illustrations of the United States like Soentpiet's are all too rare because, in actuality, when the railroad was completed, everyone was invited to the celebration except the coolies. In Soentpiet's illustration, the brothers are pictured standing in the back of the crowd. Shek comments: "Call us what you will, it is our hands that helped build the railroad." Through Yin's and Soentpiet's capable hands, readers develop a more accurate and personal portrayal of the early history of multicultural America. (SAW)

## Navigating Cultures in Modern Times

**16.34** ★ Na, An. **A Step from Heaven.** Front Street, 2001. ISBN 1-886910-58-8. 176 pp. (I).

The winner of the 2002 Michael L. Printz Award for Excellence in Young Adult Literature, this poignant narrative details the life of Young Ju from her immigration to the United States from Korea at the age of four until she begins college. In her youth, Young Ju believes that the United States is heaven. Her uncle explains that while the United States is not paradise, perhaps it is just a step away. But the journey Young Ju and her family have to travel makes it clear that the distance is far wider. Faced with language difficulties and crushing poverty, Young Ju's family struggles to survive. Her father loses the battle and becomes an alcoholic whose violence erupts against his wife and children until a climactic scene in which Young Ju calls the police. This stunning first novel from Korean-born An Na is sure to grip the minds and hearts of intermediate readers if they have a teacher courageous enough to discuss a world that is far more than a step away from heaven. (SAW)

16.35   ★ Yep, Laurence. **The Amah.** Putnam, 1999. ISBN 0-399-23040-8. 181 pp. (I).

Yep has once again captured the experiences of Chinese American children born to immigrant parents. Jealousy and anger are emotions Amy Chin frequently feels when her mother becomes an amah (a Chinese nanny) to Miss Stephanie, the daughter of a wealthy widower. Though Amy's life has not been easy since the death of her father, she now has to take on many added responsibilities that she dislikes. Then, because Mr. Sinclair, Stephanie's father, works long hours, Stephanie moves in with the Chin family and sleeps in Amy's bed. This realistic novel shows the tension among the family members in both households and how they cope with this most difficult situation. In the end, Mrs. Chin and Mr. Sinclair learn about their daughters, while Amy and Stephanie better understand their parents and each other and thus are able to forge a new relationship. (YSR)

16.36   ★ Yep, Laurence. **Dream Soul.** HarperCollins, 2000. ISBN 0-06-028390-4. 245 pp. (I).

Yep's continuing story of the Lee family tells of their first Christmas in West Virginia. The only thing the three Lee children want for Christmas is to be allowed to celebrate it. When Miss Lucy, the family's landlady, invites them to celebrate Christmas with her, Mr. and Mrs. Lee initially resist. After much cajoling, the parents agree, but only if the children are good all the time. Each day brings new temptations for the Lee children, who get caught in one of their naughty adventures. Joan, the eldest, befriends glamorous Victoria Barrington. How Joan wishes she were Victoria and had a father like Mr. Barrington! A crisis forces Joan to gain new understanding of her parents, her heritage, and what parental love is all about. Chinese American children will be able to see themselves in this realistic book and appreciate the hardships immigrant Chinese parents endure to make a better life for their children. (YSR)

## Growing Up and Coming of Age

**16.37** ★ Germain, Kerry. **Surf's Up for Kimo.** Illustrated by Keoni Montes. Island Paradise, 2000. ISBN 0-9705889-0-9. Unpaged. (P).

Kimo wants to surf, but first he has to become a strong swimmer and learn how the waves break on the shore. One day Kimo's mother tells him about the first wave she caught. That night Kimo dreams about gliding across the waves. The next morning Kimo awakes and runs to the beach. He paddles the old surfboard hard, but the waves are rough, his arms ache, and he keeps missing the waves. Then Kimo hears another surfer say, "Hey, kid, that one's got your name on it." Kimo remembers his mother's words and soon he is riding the waves just like his brothers. Beautifully illustrated by Hawaiian artist Keoni Montes, this book is a feast for the eyes. The bold, vibrant illustrations provide information about Hawaii's native plants and animals, and at the end of the book a glossary of terms describes the various plants that adorn the bottom of each page. (YSR)

**16.38** Salisbury, Graham. **Lord of the Deep.** Delacorte, 2001. ISBN 0-385-72918-9. 182 pp. (I).

Mikey is a thirteen-year-old deckhand who works with his stepdad Bill on his charter boat, the *Crystal-C,* off the Kona coast on the big island of Hawaii. When Bill takes Mikey with him on a charter, Mikey finds himself in a difficult situation. Mikey wonders how Bill could demean himself for the charter and must deal with his conflicting feelings toward himself and Bill. Should he approach Bill, and if he does, what should he say? Finally, when Mikey has the courage to approach Bill, his response is not what Mikey expects. In a fit of emotion, Mikey jumps off the *Crystal-C.* Swimming back to shore, he feels restless and empty. As he thinks about other charters, Mikey realizes that not all of them have been like this one, not even once. With this realization, Mikey is flooded with understanding and calls out to Bill, "I'll be there to clean up when you get in, okay?" (YSR)

# 17 Hispanic American Voices and Experiences

Caryl G. Crowell

*Contributing reviewers included Carol Cribbet-Bell, Kathy Lohse, Elizabeth M. Redondo, and Katrina Smits.*

---

**Criteria for Excellence**

- Literary and artistic quality
- Hispanic authors and illustrators
- Evidence of careful research or long-standing ties to Hispanic communities
- Cultural authenticity that respects regional variation with regard to historical or contemporary topics
- Rich, natural-sounding language in both English and Spanish and in code-switching (the use of both languages within an utterance)

---

## Traditional and Contemporary Tales

★ Álvarez, Julia. **The Secret Footprints.** Illustrated by Fabian Negrin. Knopf, 2000.

★ Anaya, Rudolfo. **Roadrunner's Dance.** Illustrated by David Diaz. Hyperion, 2000.

Gerson, Mary-Joan. **Fiesta Feminina: Celebrating Women in Mexican Folklore.** Illustrated by Maya Christina Gonzalez. Barefoot, 2001.

Hayes, Joe. **Little Gold Star/Estrellita de oro: A Cinderella Cuento.** Retold in Spanish and English. Illustrated by Gloria Osuna Pérez and Lucia Angela Pérez. Cinco Puntos, 2000.

★ Kimmel, Eric A. **The Runaway Tortilla.** Illustrated by Randy Cecil. Winslow, 2000.

Montes, Marisa, reteller. **Juan Bobo Goes to Work: A Puerto Rican Folktale.** Illustrated by Joe Cepeda. HarperCollins, 2000.

Pitcher, Caroline. **Mariana and the Merchild: A Folktale from Chile.**
Illustrated by Jackie Morris. Eerdmans, 2000.

★ Sierra, Judy. **The Beautiful Butterfly: A Folktale from Spain.** Illustrated by
Victoria Chess. Clarion, 2000.

Soto, Gary. **Chato and the Party Animals.** Illustrated by Susan Guevara. Putnam, 2000.

★ Stevens, Jan Romero. **Carlos Digs to China/Carlos excava hasta la China.**
Illustrated by Jeanne Arnold. Northland, 2001.

## Celebrations

★ Alarcón, Francisco X. **Angels Ride Bikes and Other Fall Poems/Los ángeles
andan en bicicleta.** Illustrated by Maya Christina Gonzalez. Children's
Book Press, 1999.

★ Ancona, George. **Charro: The Mexican Cowboy.** Harcourt Brace, 1999.

★ Garza, Carmen Lomas. **Magic Windows/Ventanas mágicas.** Translated by
Francisco X. Alarcón. Children's Book Press, 1999.

Garza, Carmen Lomas. **Making Magic Windows: Creating Papel
Picado/Cut-Paper Art With Carmen Lomas Garza.** Children's Book
Press, 1999.

Hoyt-Goldsmith, Diane. **Las Posadas: An Hispanic Christmas Celebration.**
Photographed by Lawrence Migdale. Holiday House, 1999.

Jiménez, Francisco. **The Christmas Gift/El regalo de Navidad.** Illustrated by
Claire B. Cotts. Houghton Mifflin, 2000.

★ Katz, Karen. **The Colors of Us.** Holt, 1999.

Madrigal, Antonio Hernández. **Blanca's Feather.** Illustrated by Gerardo
Suzán. Rising Moon, 2000.

★ Mora, Pat. **Love to Mamá: A Tribute to Mothers.** Illustrated by Paula S. Barragán M. Lee & Low, 2001.

## Ancient Traditions

Amado, Elisa. **Barrilete: A Kite for the Day of the Dead.** Photographs by
Joya Hairs. Groundwood, 1999.

Amado, Elisa. **Un barrilete para el Día de los muertos.** Groundwood, 1999.

★ Castillo, Ana. **My Daughter, My Son, the Eagle, the Dove: An Aztec Chant.**
Illustrated by Susan Guevara. Dutton, 2000.

Fisher, Leonard Everett. **Gods and Goddesses of the Ancient Maya.**
Holiday House, 1999.

Kimmel, Eric A. **Montezuma and the Fall of the Aztecs.** Illustrated by
Daniel San Souci. Holiday House, 2000.

★ Kimmel, Eric A. **The Two Mountains: An Aztec Legend.** Illustrated by
Leonard Everett Fisher. Holiday House, 2000.

Montejo, Victor. **Popol Vuh: A Sacred Book of the Maya.** Translated by David Unger. Illustrated by Luis Garay. Douglas & McIntyre, 1999.

Montejo, Victor. **Popol Vuj: Libro sagrado de los Maya.** Illustrated by Luis Garay. Groundwood, 1999.

Mora, Pat. **The Night the Moon Fell.** Illustrated by Domi. Groundwood, 2000.

Mora, Pat. **La noche que se cayó la luna.** Illustrated by Domi. Groundwood, 2000.

Rockwell, Anne. **The Boy Who Wouldn't Obey: A Mayan Legend.** Harper-Collins, 2000.

Vande Griek, Susan. **A Gift for Ampato.** Illustrated by Mary Jane Gerber. Groundwood, 1999.

## Overcoming Obstacles

★ Anaya, Rudolfo. **Elegy on the Death of César Chávez.** Illustrated by Gaspar Enríquez. Cinco Puntos, 2000.

★ Bertrand, Diane Gonzales. **Trino's Choice.** Arte Público, 1999.

Bertrand, Diane Gonzales. **Trino's Time.** Arte Público, 2001.

Campos, Tito. **Muffler Man/El hombre mofle.** Illustrated by Lamberto Alvarez and Beto Alvarez. Arte Público, 2001.

Encinas, Carlos. **The New Engine/La máquina nueva.** Kiva, 2001.

Figueredo, D. H. **When This World Was New.** Illustrated by Enrique O. Sanchez. Lee & Low, 1999.

★ Garland, Sherry. **Voices of the Alamo.** Illustrated by Ronald Himler. Scholastic, 2000.

Herrera, Juan Felipe. **The Upside Down Boy/El niño de cabeza.** Illustrated by Elizabeth Gómez. Children's Book Press, 2000.

Laufer, Peter. **Made in Mexico.** Illustrated by Susan L. Roth. National Geographic Society, 2000.

Laufer, Peter. **Hecho en México.** Illustrated by Susan L. Roth. National Geographic Society, 2000.

★ Lourie, Peter. **Rio Grande: From the Rocky Mountains to the Gulf of Mexico.** Boyds Mills, 1999.

★ Rodríguez, Luis. **It Doesn't Have to Be This Way: A Barrio Story/No tiene que ser así: Una historia del barrio.** Illustrated by Daniel Galvez. Children's Book Press, 1999.

Ryan, Pam Muñoz. **Esperanza Rising.** Scholastic, 2000.

★ Winter, Jonah. **¡Béisbol! Latino Baseball Pioneers and Legends.** Lee & Low 2001.

As our group considered the piles of books we received from publishers, selecting those we determined to be the best, we couldn't get past the feeling that we were not reading as many books for the years 1999 to 2001 as we had for the previous three years when we prepared the 1999 edition of *Adventuring with Books.* Were we already seeing the impact of changes in the publishing world caused by the rising anti-immigrant–antibilingual education feelings in our country? With no hard evidence to support our nagging suspicions (we had not kept records of how many books we received from publishers for the 1999 edition), we made our choices based on criteria discussed below and later carried out some cursory data collection and analysis. We have both good news and not such good news to report.

The good news is that over half of the books we've included were written and/or illustrated by Hispanic writers and artists, including familiar names such as Carmen Lomas Garza, Francisco Alarcón, Gary Soto, and Jan Romero Stevens. In addition, we present several books written by authors who are better known as writers for older readers and adults, such as Rudolfo Anaya and Julia Álvarez. When an author or illustrator draws from his or her own life, we generally assume the story to be a culturally accurate telling or a less biased presentation of a nonfiction topic. These books speak to us with strong voices about authentic experiences and real issues. The illustrations often display characteristics of a rich Hispanic artistic tradition. Together, the stories and illustrations result in books that are vibrantly alive, even when they discuss historical themes. Such cultural authenticity was important in our decision to include or not include a book. If the author or illustrator of a book was not from the culture being depicted, we looked for evidence of careful research or long-standing contact with that community. Such is the work of Joe Hayes, Leonard Everett Fisher, Diane Hoyt-Goldsmith, and others.

A note of caution is needed, however. Although we eliminated books we felt were clearly stereotypical in presentation, a few were balanced by such strong stories and artistic illustrations that we've included them on our list. Some Hispanic communities do still have adobe buildings and farmers dressed in white with wide-brimmed hats, but many others do not. We have commented on the stereotyping where necessary and hope that adults will engage children in critical reading and discussion. Balancing these books with others that are more representative of current issues may be difficult because of the small number of books we received on contemporary story themes, a topic shift we've noticed since our work on the 1999 edition of *Adventuring with Books.*

Language use was another critical factor in our decisions. Most of the books included are written in English, although many use Spanish words throughout. Usually, readers will be able to ascertain the meaning of the Spanish words from the text, although glossaries are frequently included. We also felt that in most cases Spanish was used to lend authenticity rather than serving the more didactic purpose of teaching the language. Gary Soto remains the master of code-switching, including Spanish words with the natural rhythm and cadence of bilingual speakers, who often include both languages in the same utterance. A few books have separate English and Spanish editions, and others use both languages together in the same book. In these instances, we checked for rich vocabulary, interpretations rather than direct translations, and naturally flowing language in both English and Spanish. We also noticed that most of the bilingual books privilege English in positioning the dual texts on the page.

We have grouped the books into four categories that we think may help teachers and librarians include these books of particular interest to Hispanic American students with other books for a wider audience. The collection of traditional and contemporary tales includes modern fiction and folklore from the United States and several Spanish-speaking countries. *Little Gold Star/Estrellita de oro* (2000) by Joe Hayes and Eric Kimmel's *The Runaway Tortilla* (2000) would make wonderful companions to traditional stories of Cinderella and the Gingerbread Man. The category of celebrations has been defined to include not only major holidays, but also everyday celebrations of life and diversity and less common traditions such as the Blessing of the Animals. The collection of books about the ancient civilizations of Central and South America—the Aztec, the Maya, and the Inca—are breathtakingly beautiful and superbly written. They stand together as an excellent text set or can be read with other books on related topics or of the same genre. Finally, the books about overcoming obstacles are stories of people, both famous and ordinary, who faced difficulties and triumphed, changing their own lives and sometimes those of others.

Now for the not-so-good news. Researchers such as Rosalinda Barrera who are more familiar than we are with the publishing process suggest that it's still too soon to tell if laws outlawing bilingual education in California and Arizona and possibly in other states will affect the numbers of books published on Hispanic themes, despite the ever increasing growth of the Hispanic reading audience. Nevertheless, titles targeted for Hispanic children remain a "disproportionately small part of the large body of U.S. children's literature" (Barrera, Quiroa, & West-Williams, 1999, p. 326). According to Joel Taxel and Holly M. Ward

(2000), the recent mergers of publishing companies into fewer but larger multinational houses holding many imprints is leading to a decline in the variety of books published and threatens the future publication of books that might appeal to specialized segments of the reading public.

For the 1999 *Adventuring with Books* chapter on Hispanic American literature, we reviewed books from thirty-one different publishers, including some major companies that have not a single book included on this year's list and a few small publishers that have since been gobbled up by bigger outfits or disappeared altogether. This year's list represents only twenty-one publishers, and 25 percent of the titles on the list come from just five smaller but still independent presses. A quick perusal of the spring 2001 catalogs from major publishers such as Orchard, Simon & Schuster, and Harcourt Brace revealed that they had depressingly few titles (or none) related to Hispanics and not many more on their backlists. Instead, the preponderance of titles related to cartoon shows and movies. It seems that fewer and bigger publishers and booksellers, and a desire for bigger bottom lines, means that books of dubious quality with mass appeal that move off the shelves quickly are being published. We worry about the fate of quality books for special audiences if the presses interested in publishing these works and cultivating new Hispanic authors go the way of our favorite independent bookstores. Will all children continue to see themselves in literature and also learn about the world that sets them apart? We hope so.

### References

Barrera, R. B., Quiroa, R. E., & West-Williams, C. (1999). Poco a poco: The continuing development of Mexican-American children's literature in the 1990s. *The New Advocate, 12*(4), 315–30.

Taxel, J., & Ward, H. M. (2000). Publishing children's literature at the dawn of the 21st century. *The New Advocate, 13*(1), 51–59.

## Traditional and Contemporary Tales

**17.1**   ★ Álvarez, Julia. **The Secret Footprints.** Illustrated by Fabian Negrin. Knopf, 2000. ISBN 0-679-89309-1. Unpaged. (ALL).

Julia Álvarez, in her first children's book, introduces us to the charming legend of the *ciguapas*, a tribe of beautiful creatures with golden skin and long black hair who live in caves under the sea, leaving the safety of their homes only at night to hunt for food on land. The *ciguapas* remain undetected by humans due to a unique characteristic—their feet are on backward and leave footprints going in the opposite direction whenever they come onto land. One afternoon, Guapa, an exceptionally beautiful member of the tribe, is overcome with curiosity about humans, and the secret of the *ciguapas* is nearly revealed. The *ciguapas* learn of the kindness of humans, and Guapa always remembers the consideration shown to her by a particular boy. Fabian Negrin's radiant tropical paintings, reminiscent of Gauguin's work, enhance the magical quality of this Dominican folktale. (KS)

17.2    ★ Anaya, Rudolfo. **Roadrunner's Dance.** Illustrated by David Diaz. Hyperion, 2000. ISBN 0-7868-0254-5. Unpaged. (P).

In the tradition of Pueblo storytellers, Anaya brings us this contemporary creation story about Roadrunner, the clown of the Southwest deserts and an enemy of snakes everywhere. When Rattlesnake takes control of the road, allowing no one to pass, Desert Woman calls upon all the animals to work with her in creating a new animal to help them. Each animal contributes a different part, unrelated to any others. At first the newly fashioned Roadrunner is clumsy and inept, but practice at the urging of his creator turns him into a dancing, graceful challenge for Rattlesnake. The bold, unconventional illustrations of Caldecott Award–winning artist David Diaz appear to be airbrushed stencils and are both brilliant and translucent. The first- and second-grade desert dwellers who listened to this tale agreed that roadrunners did appear to be made up of many disjointed parts. (CGC)

17.3    Gerson, Mary-Joan. **Fiesta Feminina: Celebrating Women in Mexican Folklore.** Illustrated by Maya Christina Gonzalez. Barefoot, 2001. ISBN 1-84148-365-6. 64 pp. (ALL).

This carefully researched and beautifully illustrated volume contains eight stories about powerful women drawn from the rich Mexican cultural traditions of Aztec, Mayan, Mixtec, Yaqui, and other peoples of Mexico. All of the women in these stories possess special talents and qualities that enable them to meet and surpass challenges. Readers will find familiar protagonists such as the Virgin of Guadalupe and Malintzin alongside others less known on this side of the border. Each story is accompanied by at least one full-page illustration along with several smaller images and border motifs, all done in the vibrant acrylics of Maya Christina Gonzalez, an award-winning artist. (CCB)

**17.4** Hayes, Joe. **Little Gold Star/Estrellita de oro: A Cinderella Cuento.** Retold in Spanish and English. Illustrated by Gloria Osuna Pérez and Lucia Angela Pérez. Cinco Puntos, 2000. ISBN 0-938317-49-0. 30 pp. (ALL).

In this bilingual retelling of a traditional New Mexican tale, the heroine, Arcía, convinces her father to marry a widowed neighbor and later suffers at the hands of her jealous stepsisters and stepmother. One day while Arcía is washing at the river, a hawk visits her and imprints her forehead with a golden star for doing his bidding. Her envious stepsisters search for and encounter the hawk, treat it unkindly, and receive their just desserts—one, a donkey's ear, and the other, a cow's horn growing out of her forehead. The bright, bold, acrylic paintings by the mother-and-daughter illustrators are primitive in style, in keeping with early folk art. An author's note explains the origins of the story. A nice comparison text would be *Little Gold Star: A Spanish-American Cinderella Tale* by Robert D. San Souci (HarperCollins, 2000), a traditional version from New Mexico with more formal watercolor illustrations. (KS)

**17.5** ★ Kimmel, Eric A. **The Runaway Tortilla.** Illustrated by Randy Cecil. Winslow, 2000. ISBN 1-890817-18-X. Unpaged. (P).

Eric Kimmel creates a fun, Rio Grande version of the Gingerbread Man, about a tortilla longing for freedom from the *taqueria* El Papagayo, The Happy Parrot. The tortilla rolls past braying donkeys, leaping jackrabbits, rowdy rattlers, bold buckaroos, and finally into the mouth of Señor Coyote. The rhythm of the story, the number sequencing of the animals, and the repetition are predictable story elements used to perfection. Randy Cecil paints in bright oils, capturing the colors and intense heat of the Southwest. His Diego Rivera–style figures of Tía Lupe and Tío Jose, the owners of El Papagayo, lead a chase full of silly, lighthearted action that will have young readers chanting aloud, "Run as fast as fast can be. You won't get a bite of me. Doesn't matter what you do. I'll be far ahead of you!" The children who listened to this story told us to give it two stars! (CCB)

**17.6** Montes, Marisa, reteller. **Juan Bobo Goes to Work: A Puerto Rican Folktale.** Illustrated by Joe Cepeda. HarperCollins, 2000. ISBN 0-688-16233-9. Unpaged. (P).

Juan Bobo is a familiar character in many Puerto Rican folktales. This "Simple John" misunderstands directions given to him by his mother when she sends him to find work, cautioning him not to lose the money he earns. Juan Bobo sets off each day with good intentions and a strong sense of duty but bungles every task. Despite his blunders, the neighbors recognize his efforts with caring and affection. Although Spanish words are sprinkled throughout this book, it's easy to determine the meanings from the context of the story. Just in case readers need it, a glossary of the Spanish words is included. Joe Cepeda's cartoon-style illustrations, done in bright and thickly applied paints, support the text and lend texture to this comical tale. (KL)

17.7    Pitcher, Caroline. **Mariana and the Merchild: A Folktale from Chile.** Illustrated by Jackie Morris. Eerdmans, 2000. ISBN 0-8028-5204-1. Unpaged. (ALL).

Mariana, old and alone in her hut by the sea, longs for companionship but is shunned by the village children. After a terrible squall, Mariana finds a crab shell bearing an unexpected treasure: a merchild, the daughter of a sea spirit. Mariana's heart is immediately filled with love for the child, and she promises to care for her until the sea is safe and calm enough for her return. The sea spirit visits every day, feeds the child, and teaches her how to swim. Mariana is happy raising the merchild and dreads the day she will have to return her to the sea. When the day arrives, Mariana is accompanied and comforted by the village children, who have become her friends. Morris's vivid watercolor illustrations evoke a tender mood that complements the rich, descriptive language of this enchanting traditional tale. (KS)

17.8    ★ Sierra, Judy. **The Beautiful Butterfly: A Folktale from Spain.** Illustrated by Victoria Chess. Clarion, 2000. ISBN 0-395-90015-8. 32 pp. (ALL).

A beautiful butterfly is courted by a series of animals in this retelling of a classic Spanish folktale. The butterfly considers each animal's request to marry, asking, "How will you sing to our babies?" She rejects all of the animals because of their unpleasant songs until the mouse serenades her "in a small sweet voice." They marry and all is well until the mouse is swallowed by a large fish while fetching water from the pond. The butterfly receives much sympathy from those around her, but the king's act of mourning causes all to laugh, including the fish, who then coughs up the mouse groom. This folktale delighted a kindergarten class that found much to say about tiny details in the brightly colored, sepia pen-and-ink and gouache illustrations. (KL)

17.9    Soto, Gary. **Chato and the Party Animals.** Illustrated by Susan Guevara. Putnam, 2000. ISBN 0-399-23159-5. Unpaged. (ALL).

Readers who savored the antics of Soto's barrio characters in *Chato's Kitchen* (Putnam, 1995) will find similar delights in Chato's newest adventure. As the coolest cat in *el barrio* plans a birthday *pachanga* for his friend Novio Boy, he spares no details but forgets to invite the guest of honor. With his usual aplomb, Chato saves the day, and the birthday surprise is a real surprise. Soto is a master at code-switching, inserting Spanish words into the text using the natural cadences and the substitution patterns of true bilingual speakers. Although most readers will ascertain the meanings of Spanish words from the text, a glossary is also available. Susan Guevara's acrylics on scratchboard enliven the party atmosphere across bold, double-page spreads. This book is a witty celebration of Hispanic barrio life that is sure to make everyone laugh. (EMR)

17.10    ★ Stevens, Jan Romero. **Carlos Digs to China/Carlos excava hasta la China.** Illustrated by Jeanne Arnold. Northland, 2001. ISBN 0-87358-764-2. Unpaged. (ALL).

Readers who have grown to love Carlos throughout his many adventures will not be disappointed in this new adventure. A class field trip to a local Chinese buffet convinces Carlos to dig to China, a story idea that was something of a stretch for us as adult reviewers. Predictably, he does not reach his destination but is content to be seated around a table of familiar foods, surrounded by family, friends, and community. As always, Stevens treats us to a traditional recipe, this time *arroz dulce*. Jeanne Arnold's bold acrylic illustrations reflect the local color of Carlos's New Mexico community. Although Carlos fans will also enjoy *Carlos and the Carnival/Carlos y la feria* (Northland, 1999) and perhaps see his adventures with crooked carnival games as a more reasonable plot, *Carlos Digs to China* deserves our attention. It is the last in the series of these bilingual picture books due to Stevens's untimely death. (KS)

## Celebrations

**17.11** ★ Alarcón, Francisco X. **Angels Ride Bikes and Other Fall Poems/Los ángeles andan en bicicleta.** Illustrated by Maya Christina Gonzalez. Children's Book Press, 1999. ISBN 0-89239-160-X. 32 pp. (ALL).

Following the successes of two earlier volumes of poetry, Alarcón produces another splendid collection celebrating the wonders of fall and family in Los Angeles, the "Promised Land where people from all over the world can make their dreams come true" (p. 31). The poems cover topics such as the first day of school, neighborhood personalities, cultural celebrations of autumn, and family traditions. Written bilingually in language that is equally rich in both English and Spanish, the layouts privilege neither language, choosing to alternate their placement on the pages. By applying acrylic paints over enlarged photographs of friends, relatives, and strangers, Maya Christina Gonzalez's spirited images convey the joys and trials of everyday lives filled with possibilities. (EMR)

Ancona, George. **Carnaval.** Harcourt Brace, 1999. ISBN 0-15-201793-3. Unpaged. (ALL). (See **2.30.**)

**17.12** ★ Ancona, George. **Charro: The Mexican Cowboy.** Harcourt Brace, 1999. ISBN 0-15-201047-5. Unpaged. (ALL).

After reading this book, I wanted to study to become a *charro.* Through Ancona's intimately personal photographs and text, the reader is introduced to Don Pablo and his family, who have lived the *charro* traditions all their lives. Readers learn about La Charreada, the rodeo competition that includes bull riding, roping, horse handling, and the women's equestrian ballet. The *charro*'s traditional clothing is beautifully photographed and explained so readers understand its special significance. Spanish words for the clothing, events, and customs of this Mexican sport are adroitly woven into the text so that readers can comprehend their meaning without using the included glossary. (CCB)

**17.13** ★ Garza, Carmen Lomas. **Magic Windows/Ventanas mágicas.** Translated by Francisco X. Alarcón. Children's Book Press, 1999. ISBN 0-89239-157-X. 30 pp. (ALL).

Garza, Carmen Lomas. **Making Magic Windows: Creating Papel Picado/Cut-Paper Art with Carmen Lomas Garza.** Children's Book Press, 1999. ISBN 0-89239-159-6. 61 pp. (I).

This new series of stories from Carmen Lomas Garza about her family, their celebrations, her life as an artist, and the legends of the Aztecs is the winner of the Pura Belpré Award for 2000. Each bilingually told story is illustrated with a full-page *papel picado* (cut paper) of amazing detail. The companion book is a how-to guide for making *papel picado*. The carefully written directions are easy to follow, although they are provided only in English. A group of intermediate-age girls spent hours of their vacation creating the designs in this book. Also included are safety tips for handling the necessary tools. Both books would be a fine addition to a text set on celebrations or arts around the world in either a regular or a fine arts classroom. (KL)

**17.14**  Hoyt-Goldsmith, Diane. **Las Posadas: An Hispanic Christmas Celebration.** Photographed by Lawrence Migdale. Holiday House, 1999. ISBN 0-8234-1449-3. 32 pp. (I).

In *Las Posadas* by Hoyt-Goldsmith, readers learn about a Hispanic Christmas tradition as they follow eleven-year-old Kristen through her preparations for the processions. The history of Las Posadas and music to several traditional songs are accompanied by photo captions, labels, and maps that allow primary children access to a text better suited for intermediate students. Readers will find considerable detail in the colorful photographs, recipes, a glossary, an index, and a pronunciation guide. A good related book is Tomie dePaola's *The Night of Las Posadas* (Putnam, 1999). This tender story concerns the goodness of ordinary people caught up in the magic of Las Posadas. Lupe and Roberto are to play the roles of Mary and Joseph but get stuck in a snowstorm. Miraculously, the holy couple does appear in the procession but disappear before the actors arrive. DePaola's fresco-style acrylic paintings on handmade watercolor paper and a strong narrative provide a multifaceted perspective on this holiday. (CCB)

**17.15**  Jiménez, Francisco. **The Christmas Gift/El regalo de Navidad.** Illustrated by Claire B. Cotts. Houghton Mifflin, 2000. ISBN 0-395-92869-9. Unpaged. (I).

Panchito's migrant family is moving again to find work. It's the Christmas season and food and money are getting scarce. Their departure is briefly interrupted by a young couple trying to sell their personal belongings to buy food and shelter. Panchito's family cannot help, however, since they also are struggling. Panchito worries that he may not receive the new ball he so desperately wants as a gift, but he trusts his parents will find a way. On Christmas morning, Panchito and his siblings are disappointed with their gifts of candy until they see that Father has given Mother a beautifully embroidered handkerchief purchased from the young couple. This true story, drawn from Jiménez's childhood and told in Spanish and English, is a fine Christmas tale about giving and receiving. The acrylic paintings on watercolor paper are richly detailed with dramatic facial expressions and lighting that create just the right mood. (CCB)

**17.16**   ★ Katz, Karen. **The Colors of Us.** Holt, 1999. ISBN 0-8050-5864-8. Unpaged. (ALL).

Karen Katz shows us the richness of ethnic diversity through the eyes of her seven-year-old daughter Lena. As the two walk through the neighborhood, Lena compares the skin colors of her friends and neighbors to cinnamon, butterscotch, peaches, ginger, and every other shade of brown imaginable. To represent the diverse palette of skin colors, one needs more than a box of multicultural crayons. Katz uses collage, gouache, and colored pencils to create childlike images of ethnic differences and varying skin colors. Kindergarten through fifth-grade children found themselves comparing their own skin colors to foods and other objects in their everyday lives. Artist and writer Katz has captured children's natural metaphorical language in this delightful celebration of difference. (EMR)

**17.17**   Madrigal, Antonio Hernández. **Blanca's Feather.** Illustrated by Gerardo Suzán. Rising Moon, 2000. ISBN 0-87358-743-X. Unpaged. (P).

Everyone is preparing for the blessing of their animals by the padre in honor of Saint Francis of Assisi. When it's time to leave for church, Rosalia cannot find Blanca, her hen. Unable to locate her pet, Rosalia decides to take one of Blanca's white feathers to be blessed. Other people tease Blanca for this, but the padre reassures her, "That was a good idea. At least I can bless one of her feathers." When Rosalia returns home, there is Blanca, surrounded by little fluffy chicks. Rosalia rubs the feather against her hen and the chicks, blessing each one. This story will bring a sigh of relief and comfort to young readers. The text is paired with richly textured paintings by well-known Mexican illustrator Gerardo Suzán. In this gentle story, children will find reassurance that family love and concern for pets is a shared value among many people. (CCB)

**17.18** ★ Mora, Pat. **Love to Mamá: A Tribute to Mothers.** Illustrated by Paula S. Barragán M. Lee & Low, 2001. ISBN 1-58430-019-1. Unpaged. (ALL).

Pat Mora has collected the voices of thirteen Latino poets celebrating the bond between mothers, grandmothers, and children. An endnote gives short biographies of the poets who contributed, including such well-known writers as Francisco Alarcón, Pat Mora, and Judith Ortiz Confer, as well as lesser-known Chicano poets and a fifteen-year-old newcomer. Most poems are written in English with Spanish embedded like candy in a piñata. Pat Mora's poem "Song to Mother," at the close of the volume, clearly sings the love of life, laughter, and quiet times with these important people in our lives. Each page illustrated by Paula Barragán, a first-time illustrator, is rendered in pencil, cut paper, and gouache and then scanned into a computer for further design with Adobe Illustrator. This book will no doubt inspire many young writers to compose a very special Mother's Day gift. (EMR)

## Ancient Traditions

**17.19** Amado, Elisa. **Barrilete: A Kite for the Day of the Dead.** Photographs by Joya Hairs. Groundwood, 1999. ISBN 0-88899-366-8. Unpaged. (ALL).

Amado, Elisa. **Un barrilete para el Día de los muertos.** Photographs by Joya Hairs. Translated by Claudia M. Lee. Groundwood, 1999. ISBN 0-88899-367-6. Unpaged. (ALL).

In separate English and Spanish editions, Amado and Hairs take readers to Santiago Sacatepéquez, Guatemala, where the people fly some of the largest kites in the world to celebrate the Day of the Dead. This informative yet approachable text chronicles the building of the kites and the daily village life among these descendants of the Quiché Maya. Small and large black-and-white and color photographs illustrate each step in the creation of these giant tissue paper kites. The camera's perspective helps readers appreciate their size so well that a class of first and second graders was moved to mark one off on the floor of their classroom. A list of the words for *kite* used in different Hispanic countries will remind readers that the cultures of Spanish-speaking peoples are not monolithic. (CGC)

**17.20**  ★ Castillo, Ana. **My Daughter, My Son, the Eagle, the Dove: An Aztec Chant.** Illustrated by Susan Guevara. Dutton, 2000. ISBN 0-525-45856-5. Unpaged. (ALL).

In this well-researched treasure, Ana Castillo shares excerpts from the *huehuehtlatolli*, the ancient teachings of Aztec parents used to mark a rite of passage. Two chants, one for a daughter, the dove, and another for a son, the eagle, mark the milestones of growing up and becoming an adult. The messages of self-respect and respect for all living things are as vibrantly alive now as they were in pre-Hispanic Mexico. Susan Guevara's paintings on *amate*, or bark paper, represent both the modern and the ancient worlds. Using historical documents as resources, Guevara places Aztec glyphs on each page to illuminate Castillo's chants and also creates contemporary visual stories of the girl and the boy, who eventually marry and have a child of their own. In author's and illustrator's notes, readers can find additional information about Aztec culture and the use of metaphor in their "picture writing." (CGC)

**17.21**  Fisher, Leonard Everett. **Gods and Goddesses of the Ancient Maya.** Holiday House, 1999. ISBN 0-8234-1427-2. Unpaged. (ALL).

Using the art, glyphs, and sculpture of the ancient Maya, Fisher describes twelve important Mayan gods and goddesses, explaining their roles in Mayan culture and beliefs. The bright acrylic illustrations are faithful to the author's resources. The introduction provides important background information about the Maya, their origins, accomplishments, and decline. A pronunciation guide and bibliography are included. On the opening endpapers, a map of major Mayan sites in Central America places the Mayan world in its contemporary setting. The closing endpapers explain and demonstrate how the Maya used three symbols to write the numbers used to mark the pages. *The Mystery of the Maya: Uncovering the Lost City of Palenque* (Boyds Mills, 2001), a similar book by Peter Lourie, uses wonderful photographs and a strong first-person narrative that allow us to accompany the author through the heart of the Mexican jungle to Palenque and secrets hidden from view for centuries. Readers desiring more detailed information on Mayan culture and the archaeological excavations that have revealed their world should look to Lourie's book. (CGC)

**17.22** Kimmel, Eric A. **Montezuma and the Fall of the Aztecs.** Illustrated by Daniel San Souci. Holiday House, 2000. ISBN 0-8234-1452-3. Unpaged. (ALL).

With his usual storyteller's skill, Kimmel brings us a gripping account of the last days of the Aztec empire and its fall to the invading Spanish army of Hernán Cortés. Kimmel's version explores the mythology surrounding these events and concludes that, most likely, Cortés took advantage of a civilization already in decline, and with the help of its enemies, starvation, and disease, toppled the extensive Aztec realm. San Souci's watercolor paintings bring us face to face with participants on both sides in detailed double-page spreads. An author's note, glossary, and a list of suggested books for further reading complete this rich telling of an event that changed the world. (CGC)

**17.23** ★ Kimmel, Eric A. **The Two Mountains: An Aztec Legend.** Illustrated by Leonard Everett Fisher. Holiday House, 2000. ISBN 0-8234-1504-X. Unpaged. (ALL).

Borrowing from a legend of the Nahua people, modern descendants of the Aztecs, Kimmel weaves the story of Ixcoçauqui, son of the sun god, and Coyolxauhqui, daughter of the moon goddess. The two lovers meet when Ixcoçauqui ignores his father's orders to stay within his garden wall and are allowed to marry when they both agree to stay in heaven and never descend to earth. These children of the gods, however, break their vows and are turned into mortals as punishment. When the lovers die, the gods change them into the mountain Iztaccihuatl, which means "the Lady of the Snows," and the volcano Popocatepetl, the "Smoking Hill." The vibrancy of Kimmel's storytelling is matched by Fisher's heavily textured and brightly colored acrylic paintings. A glossary will help those who become tongue-tied when pronouncing the Aztec names. (CGC)

**17.24** Montejo, Victor. **Popol Vuh: A Sacred Book of the Maya.** Translated by David Unger. Illustrated by Luis Garay. Douglas & McIntyre, 1999. ISBN 0-88899-334-X. 85 pp. (I).

Montejo, Victor. **Popol Vuj: Libro sagrado de los Maya.** Illustrated by Luis Garay. Groundwood, 1999. ISBN 0-88899-344-7. 85 pp. (I).

The Maya's highly developed civilization and written language allowed them to keep accurately dated and detailed histories that were transcribed using the Latin alphabet in 1558 and described as the Popol Vuh, "the book we can no longer see." Translated into Spanish in 1701 by Fray Francisco Ximénez, the book has been passed through the centuries to us today. Montejo has produced this adapted version of the Popol Vuh with younger readers in mind. Within its covers, readers will discover Mayan stories of creation, accounts of the gods and demigods who ruled the universe, and the lineage of Mayan lords who maintained traditions until their imprisonment and torture at the hands of their Spanish captors. Garay's pen-and-ink and watercolor illustrations lend texture and a characteristically somber mood to this history of a doomed civilization. Both editions include a categorized glossary to help readers keep track of the K'iche' Maya words. (CGC)

17.25 Mora, Pat. **The Night the Moon Fell.** Illustrated by Domi. Groundwood, 2000. ISBN 0-88899-398-6. Unpaged. (P).

Mora, Pat. **La noche que se cayó la luna.** Illustrated by Domi. Groundwood, 2000. ISBN 0-88899-399-4. Unpaged. (P).

In separate English and Spanish editions, Pat Mora adapts this Mopan Mayan legend from Belize concerning the creation of the Milky Way and the moon's journey across the sky. Tumbled from the sky by a blowgun's arrow, Luna lands in pieces at the bottom of the sea, where she is helped to rise again by a school of glowing fish. The lyrical text, interspersed with poetic chants, captures the imagination of young readers and listeners and reads equally well in both languages. Domi's translucent wet-into-wet washes cover the double-page spreads from edge to edge. These colorfully luminescent paintings were likened to those of Paul Klee by a class of first and second graders. A brief author's note documents the origins of this delightful tale. (CGC)

17.26 Rockwell, Anne. **The Boy Who Wouldn't Obey: A Mayan Legend.** HarperCollins, 2000. ISBN 0-688-14881-6. Unpaged. (ALL).

In this well-researched book, Anne Rockwell adapts an ancient Mayan legend about Chac, the god of rain, and the time he stole a boy from Earth to be his servant. After enduring punishments for failing to satisfy his demanding master, the boy gets even by stealing the tools Chac uses to make rain, wind, lightning, and thunder, accidentally causing a violent storm. Rockwell's pen-and-ink and watercolor paintings reveal the events of the tale and feature a monkey, the writer of stories in Mayan mythology, and a sky band motif on every set of pages. The foreword and notes by the author provide references and information that set the story in time and place. Leonard Everett Fisher's volume on *Gods and Goddesses of the Ancient Maya* (Holiday House, 1999; **17.21**) is a marvelous reference companion to Rockwell's tale. (CGC)

**17.27** Vande Griek, Susan. **A Gift for Ampato.** Illustrated by Mary Jane Gerber. Groundwood, 1999. ISBN 0-88899-358-7. 109 pp. (I).

Vande Griek ties this fictional account of an Inca priestess-in-training to the discovery of a mummified ice maiden on the slopes of Nevado Ampato, in the Peruvian Andes, in 1995. Each chapter begins with a brief account describing the mummy's appearance, clothing, or anthropologists' theories about the circumstances surrounding her death. From here, the author imagines the story of Timta, who will be offered in ritual sacrifice to the gods of the volcano that threatens her village. Readers follow Timta's preparations for this "greatest honor of all" and her eventual escape up the side of the mountain. Vande Griek's research has allowed her to include known details of Inca life and language, lending authenticity to her fiction. A glossary and recommendations for further reading make this small treasure suitable for research as well as pleasure reading. (CGC)

## Overcoming Obstacles

**17.28** ★ Anaya, Rudolfo. **Elegy on the Death of César Chávez.** Illustrated by Gaspar Enríquez. Cinco Puntos, 2000. ISBN 0-938317-51-2. 26 pp. (I).

In a moving and eloquent elegy, Rudolfo Anaya honors the life and "the spirit of the man," Mexican American labor activist César Chávez. The poem begins with an announcement of Chávez's death and encourages readers to keep the work of Chávez alive in their hearts and daily living. The airbrush paintings by Gaspar Enríquez capture the mood of the poem in photographic style, often overlapping images that chronicle the lives of the farmworkers and the labor movement. Included in the book is a chronology of Chávez's life and a dust jacket that opens to reveal a display poster. Along with notes from the author, this text rewards Chávez with his much deserved place in history and motivates readers to sustain his vision of a more just world. (KL)

**17.29** ★ Bertrand, Diane Gonzales. **Trino's Choice.** Arte Público, 1999. ISBN 1-55885-279-4. 124 pp. (I).

Bertrand, Diane Gonzales. **Trino's Time.** Arte Público, 2001. ISBN 1-55885-317-0. 170 pp. (I).

Trino has witnessed the brutal beating of a local merchant and is being warned by the gang to keep quiet about what he has seen. He finds refuge in a bookstore, where he meets a group of youngsters with different values and interests from those of his current friends. A whole new world opens up to Trino as he is introduced to poetry as a form of self-expression. When Rosca tempts him with a plan to make some quick money, Trino, with little adult guidance available, struggles to make the right decision. *Trino's Choice* is a dramatic and gritty young adult novel that speaks to the choices faced by some youths. After this book was read to them, fifth-grade listeners clamored to hear *Trino's Time* (Arte Público, 2001), the sequel. Even though the stories border on stereotyping urban Latino families, they will appeal to many preteen and teenage readers. (KS)

**17.30** Campos, Tito. **Muffler Man/El hombre mofle.** Illustrated by Lamberto Alvarez and Beto Alvarez. Arte Público, 2001. ISBN 1-55885-318-9. Unpaged. (ALL).

Chuy Garcia dreams of the day that he and his mother will be able to join his father in the United States. When Chuy seeks employment at the muffler shop where his father used to work, he discovers that his father was the artist who crafted the muffler man, a metal sculpture that has greeted customers for years. When Chuy and his mother finally arrive in the United States, they discover that life is much more difficult than they had imagined. Chuy encourages his dad to create a sculpture similar to the one in Mexico. The sculptures prove to be popular, providing the Garcia family with a means of support and a source of pride. Enriching this dual language text, the distinctive illustrations by the father and son team of Lamberto Alvarez and Beto Alvarez were created using conventional scratchboard and then scanned into digital images to be further enhanced using computer technology. (KS)

**17.31** Encinas, Carlos. **The New Engine/La máquina nueva.** Kiva, 2001. ISBN 1-885772-24-6. Unpaged. (ALL).

The lesson of change and acceptance is well told in this story of an eight-year-old boy's memory of the arrival of the diesel locomotive to his town. His father works shoveling coal into the firebox on old steam locomotives, a job threatened by the new technology. Memories of family conversations about changing work, the worried expressions on his father's face, and the opportunity for learning come full circle when the boy becomes a man confronting a new computer. The characters in this book share a family love and concern that are heartwarming and rich in Hispanic traditions. Encinas's striking photo collages are fresh and unique in their high-tech format. (CCB)

**17.32** Figueredo, D. H. **When This World Was New.** Illustrated by Enrique O. Sanchez. Lee & Low, 1999. ISBN 1-880000-86-5. Unpaged. (P).

Danilito travels on airplanes with his family to the United States, leaving the sultry Caribbean ocean and palm trees, only to arrive in a wintry city, scared and worried about his new life. On Danilito's first day of school, his papá wakes him early to see something magical. They both take their first walk in snow, throwing snowballs and leaving a trail of footprints behind. As they look back at their path, Danilito realizes that his father will always be right beside him and that he will be all right in his new country. The illustrations, in acrylic on watercolor paper, effectively capture both the warmth of the Caribbean and the cold U.S. winter. This book would be a good addition to a text set on families, immigration, or change. (KL)

**17.33** ★ Garland, Sherry. **Voices of the Alamo.** Illustrated by Ronald Himler. Scholastic, 2000. ISBN 0-590-98833-6. Unpaged. (ALL ).

Creating first-person narratives to bring voices of the past to life, Sherry Garland constructs a time line of the history of the Alamo and the region surrounding it. Beginning her time line in 1500, just prior to the arrival of Spanish explorers, the author writes with dignity and balance for the Native Americans, Spaniards, Mexicans, Texans, and Americans who occupied the land. Each double-page spread represents a different inhabitant or event leading up to the Mexican-American War and subsequent efforts to preserve the Alamo site. Himler's watercolor-and-gouache illustrations bleed off the edges of the pages and into the text, adding visual testimony to the grim faces and stories of determination depicted in this book. One primary class used the book as a model for creating a time line of their own city's history. The historical notes, bibliography, and suggestions for further readings make it even more suitable for intermediate readers and researchers. (EMR)

17.34    Herrera, Juan Felipe. **The Upside Down Boy/El niño de cabeza.** Illustrated by Elizabeth Gómez. Children's Book Press, 2000. ISBN 0-89239-162-6. 32 pp. (ALL).

When his migrant family settles in one place, Juanito is able to go to school for the first time. In this memoir, Herrera refers to himself as The Upside Down Boy to describe his sense of bewilderment as he struggles to understand English, school and schedules, and his new world. His teacher recognizes his musical and artistic gifts and encourages him to express himself. Juanito's parents relate their own stories of schooling, telling him that "each word, each language has its own magic" (p. 23). This tender, bilingual story touched the hearts of kindergartners, who responded by sharing their own feelings and stories about coming to school, being scared, and not understanding what was happening. In her first children's book, Elizabeth Gómez has captured the disequilibrium and adjustments of new beginnings in vibrant acrylic paintings on rag paper. (KL)

17.35    Laufer, Peter. **Made in Mexico.** Illustrated by Susan L. Roth. National Geographic Society, 2000. ISBN 0-7922-7118-1. Unpaged. (ALL).

Laufer, Peter. **Hecho en México.** Illustrated by Susan L. Roth. National Geographic Society, 2000. ISBN 0-7922-7925-5. Unpaged. (ALL).

On a trip to discover the origin of his son's guitar, Laufer travels to Paracho, in Michoacán, México. Although the village's guitar-making expertise is known mostly in the world of mariachi musicians, the author quickly learns "there's more than mariachi music in Mexico." The guitars of Paracho are used by mariachi, jazz, and classical musicians throughout Mexico and the world. In addition to describing the building of a guitar, Laufer contrasts the poverty and desperation of the border communities with the relatively rich life that the guitar industry has afforded the people of Paracho. Stunning collage illustrations by Susan Roth are made with papers and scrap materials from both sides of the border and feature chips of wood from the guitar shop floors. Separate English and Spanish editions highlight the pride of these talented people and their efforts to perpetuate their musical skills and traditions through their children. (KL)

17.36 ★ Lourie, Peter. **Rio Grande: From the Rocky Mountains to the Gulf of Mexico.** Boyds Mills, 1999. ISBN 1-56397-706-0. 46 pp. (I).

Lourie's journey along the Rio Grande River begins in Colorado, at the river's headwaters, and follows its course through New Mexico, along the Mexico–Texas border, and out to the Gulf of Mexico. The book begins with a map to clearly define the run of the river. A lively and informative text, illustrated with contemporary and archival photographs, reveals the geography, history, and culture of the land and the people this river touches as it flows. Mountain men, miners, outlaws, migrants, and historical figures come to life on the pages. Along the way, Lourie visits pueblos in New Mexico, accompanies the U.S. Border Patrol, rafts through the white water of Big Bend National Park, and dives into the Gulf of Mexico. He writes with sensitivity about the critical issues surrounding immigration and Native American customs, giving the reader a better understanding of the unique role of this special river. (CCB)

17.37 ★ Rodríguez, Luis. **It Doesn't Have to Be This Way: A Barrio Story/No tiene que ser así: Una historia del barrio.** Illustrated by Daniel Galvez. Children's Book Press, 1999. ISBN 0-89239-161-8. 31 pp. (I).

Monchi, a poetry-writing, storytelling, carefree child, is approached by a youth of the Encanto Locos gang to become a junior member. With no other options in sight, Monchi prepares to be "jumped in" but is warned not to go by his cousin Dreamer. The night of his initiation, a rival gang appears on the scene and Dreamer is unintentionally shot. As the family waits at the hospital, Monchi realizes that his life can take another path. His tío Rogelio tells him, " I know that you want to be a man, but you have to decide what kind of man you want to be" (p. 27). Rodríguez draws this story from his own seven-year experience as a gang member. The Spanish and English texts alternate position on the pages. Galvez, an experienced public muralist, uses a photorealist style and real people as models to make Monchi's close call that much more authentic. (KL)

**17.38**   Ryan, Pam Muñoz. **Esperanza Rising.** Scholastic, 2000. ISBN 0-439-12041-1. 262 pp. (I).

Twelve-year-old Esperanza Ortega lives the life of a pampered only child on her parent's hacienda in northern Mexico in the 1930s. Suddenly her life takes a drastic turn when her father is ambushed and killed by bandits. The only option for Esperanza, her mother, and the family's loyal servants is to flee to the United States as migrant laborers. Esperanza's challenge of adjusting to a new way of life is compounded by her mother's illness, harsh working conditions, the lack of acceptance by her own people, and economic hardships brought on by the Great Depression. Throughout the course of one year, traced in chapters named for the crop being harvested, Esperanza matures from a spoiled child into a young woman who is able to let go of the past and embrace the challenges of the future. (KS)

**17.39**   ★ Winter, Jonah. **¡Béisbol! Latino Baseball Pioneers and Legends.** Lee & Low, 2001. ISBN 1-58430-012-4. Unpaged. (I).

The stunning acrylic paintings resembling baseball trading cards are the initial attention grabbers in this lively look at baseball's greats from Latin America, but the stories of these amazing players will sustain the attention of readers even if they're not baseball aficionados. The fourteen players portrayed in this volume played sometime between 1900 and 1960 and are not necessarily household names. The accounts of each player's accomplishments and style, however, will inspire even non-baseball fans. Many of these pioneers suffered the effects of racism, playing in the Negro Leagues before Jackie Robinson broke the color barrier and paved the way for his Latino counterparts. Winter's vivid biographies deftly balance the achievements of each player with the obstacles he faced, presenting readers with an inspiring volume of determination and pride. (KS)

# **18** Indigenous Peoples

Wendy C. Kasten, Jodi Dodds-Kinner,
and Danielle G. Gruhler

---

**Criteria for Excellence**

- Author's credentials demonstrate that the individual has the knowledge to write about an indigenous group.
- Text and illustrations are respectful of native peoples in language, tone, terminology, and illustrations, including sensitivity to stereotyping.
- Text and illustrations are authentic and accurate to the native group.
- In cases of sacred stories or written down oral narratives, narrative style is consistent with native storytelling styles (rather than westernized), and the author has permission to use or ownership of the story.
- The book appeals to children.

---

Ahenakew, Freda. **Wisahkecahk Flies to the Moon.** Illustrated by Sherry Farrell Racette. Pemmican, 1999.

★ Bruchac, Joseph. **Crazy Horse's Vision.** Illustrated by S. D. Nelson. Lee & Low, 2000.

★ Bruchac, Joseph. **Pushing Up the Sky: Seven Native American Plays for Children.** Illustrated by Teresa Flavin. Dial, 2000.

Bruchac, Joseph. **Sacajawea: The Story of Bird Woman and the Lewis and Clark Expedition.** Harcourt, 2000.

★ Erdrich, Louise. **The Birchbark House.** Hyperion, 1999.

Goble, Paul. **Storm Makers Tipi.** Atheneum, 2001.

★ Harrell, Beatrice Orcutt. **Longwalker's Journey.** Dial, 1999.

Hazen-Hammond, Susan. **Thunder Bear and Ko: The Buffalo Nation and Nambe Pueblo.** Photographs by Susan Hazen-Hammond. Dutton, 1999.

Kusugak, Michael Arvaarluk. **Who Wants Rocks?** Illustrated by Vladyana Langer Krykorka. Annick, 1999.

★ Left Hand Bull, Jacqueline, and Suzanne Haldane. **Lakota Hoop Dancer.** Photographs by Suzanne Haldane. Dutton, 1999.

★ National Museum of the American Indian. **When the Rain Sings: Poems by Young Native Americans.** Simon & Schuster, 1999.

Nelson, S. D. **Gift Horse: A Lakota Story.** Abrams, 1999.

Penman, Sarah, editor. **Honor the Grandmothers: Dakota and Lakota Women Tell Their Stories.** Minnesota Historical Society Press, 2000.

Raczek, L. T. **Rainy's Powwow.** Illustrated by Gary Bennett. Rising Moon, 1999.

Rose, LaVera. **Grandchildren of the Lakota.** Photographs by Cheryl Walsh Bellville. Carolrhoda, 1999.

★ Schick, Eleanor. **Navajo Wedding Day: A Diné Marriage Ceremony.** Marshall Cavendish, 1999.

★ Smith, Cynthia Leitich. **Jingle Dancer.** Illustrated by Cornelius Van Wright & Ying-Hwa Hu. Morrow, 2000.

Staub, Frank. **Children of the Tlingit.** Photographs by Frank Staub. Carolrhoda, 1999.

★ Tapahonso, Luci. **Songs of Shiprock Fair.** Illustrated by Anthony Chee Emerson. Kiva, 1999.

Tohe, Laura. **No Parole Today.** West End, 1999.

★ Waboose, Jan Bordeau. **SkySisters.** Illustrated by Brian Deines. Kids Can Press, 2000.

---

Of all the ethnic or cultural minority groups within North America and particularly the United States, indigenous peoples, those still living and those long gone, have been the most poorly served in formal education. They also have been the least understood and respected in the school curriculum. Even most well-intentioned teachers and other professionals are inadequately informed about unique native issues and thus inadvertently reinforce stereotypes and perpetuate misinformation.

Learning about Native Americans rarely goes beyond the legend of Thanksgiving and a study of surface culture, including dress, home building, foods, crafts, symbols, and daily living habits. Issues of deep culture, which include ways of knowing, believing, and valuing, are rarely addressed. For most readers, the only conduit to such knowledge is through literature.

We have taken on the challenge of reading and selecting books that provide an accurate portrayal of North American indigenous cultures. Even with our collective experience, we have relied on the credentials of native writers and the advice of native peoples to ensure this list has integrity.

Much has been written of late about the insider/outside controversy. Some believe that no one who is not a member of a specific culture, with that privileged knowledge of an insider perspective, can write about that culture. Others believe that developing an insider perspective is exactly what a skilled writer does and that writers cannot be restricted to writing only within and about their own experience. What is clear to us is that if one takes on the perspective of an insider, then one also has embarked on a treacherous journey with a huge responsibility to write with the greatest of care and accuracy.

This is especially difficult to do when writing about indigenous cultures, because ways of knowing and worldviews are so different. We have learned that the uniqueness of indigenous cultures encompasses a breadth that could take a lifetime to fully comprehend (Gilliland, 1988; Kasten, 1992; Locust, 1988; Nelson, 1983; Paul, 1981; Rhodes, 1989). Another challenge is that native groups are not unified in their beliefs, and the differences between groups sometimes outweigh the threads they share.

Our way of dealing with these issues is to rely on writers who are themselves native or part native in ethnicity. Their voices are the best vehicle we have to educate teachers about native issues, peoples, and history. Some publishers and authors, however, don't appreciate or understand the need to verify authenticity. In reviewing several collections of native stories, for example, we found that the authors were non-native, and no acknowledgement was included that native peoples had been consulted or that the authors had credentials or had done research about the cultures.

Stories generally hold an esteemed position, one of respect and sacredness, for indigenous peoples. Stories are connected to the history and often the religion of a culture. They are living entities in the hands of esteemed storytellers, and they are the property of the people who own them. In many native cultures, it is taboo to tell someone else's story without requesting permission to do so. So for someone to hear a story and then simply write and publish their own version of it is theft, however well intentioned the motivation. We need to afford the stories of others the same respect many of us have for intellectual property and copyright laws. Given these standards, when we found books of "native stories" by non-native retellers, with no mention of permission, cooperation with tribal councils, or other attempts to respect the story property, we decided not to include these books in this chapter.

We present, then, this list of fiction, nonfiction, and poetry titles that we believe are reliable sources and that we also thoroughly enjoyed. We have highlighted the author's affiliation and the community to which the story belongs in the annotations. We have also noted the illustrator's affiliation where appropriate. We hope this helps teachers make selections for classroom and personal use.

Sources are available to help educators make informed choices and be wise consumers of books on indigenous peoples. We recommend that educators make use of the information at http://www.Oyate.org. On this Web site, books are reviewed and discussed by native people; they also mention books to avoid. We also recommend *Multicultural Review,* a periodical found in university libraries. Another good source of accurate information is the American Museum of the American Indian and *Expressive Arts,* published by Cornell University.

### References

Gilliland, H., with Reyhner, J. (1988). *Teaching the Native American.* Dubuque, IA: Kendall/Hunt.

Kasten, W. C. (1992). Bridging the horizon: American Indian beliefs and whole language learning. *Anthropology and Education Quarterly 23*(2), 108–119.

Locust, C. (1988). Wounding the spirit: Discrimination and traditional American Indian belief systems. *Harvard Educational Review 58*(3), 315–30.

Nelson, R. K. (1983). *Make prayers to the raven: A Koyukon view of the northern forest.* Chicago: University of Chicago Press.

Paul, A. (1981). Cultural aspects that affect the Indian student in public schools. *Bilingual Resources 4*(2-3), 32–34.

Rhodes, Robert. (1989). Native American learning styles. *Journal of Navajo Education VII*(1), 33–41.

**18.1**   Ahenakew, Freda. **Wisahkecahk Flies to the Moon.** Illustrated by Sherry Farrell Racette. Pemmican, 1999. ISBN 0921827571. Unpaged. (ALL).

This story was told to the author by her Cree great uncle, Edward Ahenakew, who wrote and translated the story into English from the Cree language. The book presents the text in both English and Cree and tells the story of Wisahkecahk, a recurring character in Cree stories, who desires to ride the moon across the evening sky. He journeys to the moon on a crane, and his clumsy return explains the existence of mud holes, or "muskegs." This selection is an authentic native folktale that honors two languages. Illustrator Sherry Farrell Racette is a Timiskaming native of Manitoba. (WCK)

**18.2**   ★ Bruchac, Joseph. **Crazy Horse's Vision.** Illustrated by S. D. Nelson. Lee & Low, 2000. ISBN 1-880000-94-6. Unpaged. (ALL).

This authentic and moving picture book, a collaboration between native storyteller Bruchac and native illustrator Nelson (Lakota Sioux), tells a story handed down over generations. The great chief Crazy Horse had a vision as a young man that foretold the destiny of his people. This is the personal story of the man who was Crazy Horse—how he got his name and of events in his youth that shaped his views and decisions. The art is "influenced by the traditional ledger book style of my ancestors," according to the illustrator. Crazy Horse is an important historic figure in U.S. history, and this book provides insight into his background and motivation. (WCK/JDK)

18.3    ★ Bruchac, Joseph. **Pushing Up the Sky: Seven Native American Plays for Children.** Illustrated by Teresa Flavin. Dial, 2000. ISBN 0-8037-2168-4. 94 pp. (ALL).

Bruchac, of Abenaki heritage, has transformed the stories of seven different native nations into plays for children. Provided are suggestions for props, scenery, costumes, and staging with an emphasis on simplicity and authenticity that honor the peoples from whom these stories originate. Included are plays from the stories of the Abenaki, Ojibway, Cherokee, Cheyenne, Snohomish, Tlingit, and Zuni tribes. Flavin's dreamlike rich-color paintings and simple black-line illustrations add visual interest to the plays, which can be adapted for groups of various sizes. Historical notes about each cultural group are provided for each play. (DGG)

18.4    Bruchac, Joseph. **Sacajawea: The Story of Bird Woman and the Lewis and Clark Expedition.** Harcourt, 2000. ISBN 0-15-202234-1. 199 pp. (I).

This story is based on historical information about Sacajawea, the young Shoshone woman who was an essential member of the Lewis and Clark Expedition. Bruchac writes the story as though Sacajawea and William Clark, who had a strong friendship, are alternately telling the story of the expedition to Pomp, the nickname for Sacajawea's baby son, who was carried along. The contrasting storytelling styles of those chapters based on Clark and those on Sacajawea show cultural differences. This novel-length selection would be a wonderful addition to a study on this historical topic. (WCK)

18.5    ★ Erdrich, Louise. **The Birchbark House.** Hyperion, 1999. ISBN 0-7868-0300-2. 244 pp. (I).

This historical novel by a native Ojibway author describes the life of a young girl, Omakaya, whose people were wiped out by disease (smallpox or measles) and who was subsequently adopted by a neighboring native village. Told from the girl's perspective, aspects of native life are portrayed as the girl discovers her unique gifts. This novel would enhance the study of westward expansion by presenting a native perspective, especially the manner in which native peoples were exposed to devastating diseases brought by white settlers for which they had no immunities. The novel is extremely engaging as the main character faces typical concerns about growing up. (WCK)

**18.6**    Goble, Paul. **Storm Makers Tipi.** Atheneum, 2001. ISBN 0689-84137-X. Unpaged. (ALL).

Well-known author Paul Goble, a non-native author, delivers another Blackfoot legend that provides details about practices associated with the tipi, including its building and meaningful decorative embellishments. In addition to the characteristically vivid illustrations, patterns and diagrams demonstrate tipi construction sufficient to reproduce as a classroom project. First, however, this is a story of Sacred Otter and Morning Plume, the former of whom had a dream that changed the lives of the community. The book ends with a photo of present-day tipis at a Blackfoot summer camp in Montana and Alberta, Canada. (WCK)

**18.7**    ★ Harrell, Beatrice Orcutt. **Longwalker's Journey.** Dial, 1999. ISBN 0803723806. 133 pp. (I).

Based on the author's own great-great-grandfather, this historical novel describes the journey of a father, son, and roguish pony who walked ahead of their people on The Trail of Tears from their southeastern Choctaw home to midwestern Indian territory. They survived one of the worst Arkansas storms ever recorded and arrived at the reservation land in advance of their people, to prepare for their eventual arrival. Many of their people perished along the way. The boy's pony provides joy and relief on the treacherous long walk, during which resourcefulness is the key to survival. The relationship between father and son is developed beautifully. This story depicts an often overlooked and shameful event in U.S. history, making it an important contribution to classroom studies of this era. (WCK)

**18.8**    Hazen-Hammond, Susan. **Thunder Bear and Ko: The Buffalo Nation and Nambe Pueblo.** Photographs by Susan Hazen-Hammond. Dutton, 1999. ISBN 0-525-46013-6. Unpaged. (I).

This engaging photo-essay picture book is about an eight-year-old Nambe Pueblo boy. The narrative takes the reader on a journey as Thunder Bear and his people help care for the buffalo. Thunder Bear's people rescue buffalo from sport hunters by convincing the state of New Mexico to allow some of the animals to live at Nambe Pueblo. The important balance between the present and respect for the past as a source of knowledge is evident throughout this book. The photographs provide a fascinating look at the rich traditions of the Nambe Pueblo people, and the attractive format and design successfully portray Thunder Bear learning about his culture. (JDK)

**18.9**    Kusugak, Michael Arvaarluk. **Who Wants Rocks?** Illustrated by Vladyana Langer Krykorka. Annick, 1999. ISBN 1-55037-588. Unpaged. (ALL).

Canadian Inuit storyteller and writer Kusugak explains that this fable-style tale "came to him" in Dawson City, Yukon. His character of Old Joe, a gold prospector, dreams of riches. When he strikes gold, he yells so loud about his discovery that others come and stake claims on the quickly depleting resource, and Old Joe finds that he does not have enough to get rich. When he settles in an area resplendent with beauty, he realizes he has other kinds of riches, and he hasn't destroyed anything to get them. Krykorka's pen-and-watercolor illustrations communicate the coldness of the landscape as well as the dreaminess of the story. (WCK)

**18.10**   ★ Left Hand Bull, Jacqueline, and Suzanne Haldane. **Lakota Hoop Dancer.** Photographs by Suzanne Haldane. Dutton, 1999. ISBN 0-525-45413-6. Unpaged. (I).

The explicit and detailed photographs illustrate Kevin Locke performing the traditional Lakota hoop dance. Locke is a member of the Lakota Nation on the Standing Rock Reservation in South Dakota. *Lakota Hoop Dancer* looks not only at the hoop regalia, songs, and dance, but also at the importance of keeping the Lakota culture alive. The glossary and recommended readings are helpful to young readers who want to find out more about northern Plains Indians. Kevin Locke is a modern-day role model for native children to emulate, while non-native children reading the book will realize that this culture is alive and well today. (JDK)

**18.11**    ★ National Museum of the American Indian. **When the Rain Sings: Poems by Young Native Americans.** Simon & Schuster, 1999. ISBN 0-689-82283-9. 76 pp. (ALL).

This is a collection of poems by student writers from Ojibwe, Lakota, Omaha, Navajo, Cochiti-Kiowa, Tohnono O'odham, Hopi, and Ute communities, with an introduction providing important supportive information about each native community represented. The topics of the poems vary but include highly personal works about growing up native. Each section begins with an artistic representation of the community, with pages decorated on the upper edge with authentic native designs. These youthful living voices will enhance multicultural understanding. (WCK)

**18.12**    Nelson, S. D. **Gift Horse: A Lakota Story.** Abrams, 1999. ISBN 0-8109-4127-9. Unpaged. (ALL).

This touching story by S. D. Nelson is about the relationship between a young boy, Flying Cloud, and his horse. Nelson is a member of the Standing Rock Sioux tribe in the Dakotas, and his great-great-grandfather's name was Flying Cloud. The author's notes tell the reader that Nelson often wondered what growing up must have been like for Flying Cloud. From his curiosity, Nelson came to write this Lakota tale in which the lives of the Lakota people are portrayed as the story of Flying Cloud becoming a man unfolds. Early one morning, for example, horse thieves attack, and several of the tribe's horses, including Storm, Flying Cloud's horse, are stolen. The intentions of the raiding party were to make contact with and rescue the horses without injury to the enemy. This is a positive image of Native American warriors. The superb wood panel and acrylic paint illustrations, influenced by the ledger book drawings of the Plains Indian artists, help create an engaging tale. (JDK)

**18.13**    Penman, Sarah, editor. **Honor the Grandmothers: Dakota and Lakota Women Tell Their Stories.** Minnesota Historical Society, 2000. ISBN 0-87351-384-3. 147 pp. (I).

First-person historical narratives of four remarkable native women are offered in this volume. Celane Not Help Him, the granddaughter of Iron Hail, who survived the Battle of Little Big

Horn and the Wounded Knee Massacre of 1890, died in 1998. Stella Pretty Sounding Flute, born in 1924, from the Crow Creek Reservation in South Dakota, runs a cottage quilting industry. Cecilia Hernandez Montgomery, born an Oglala Dakota in 1910, still passes on traditional stories at schools. Iola Columbus, a Sisseton Wahpeton Dakota, passed away in 1997 at age sixty-nine; she was the first woman in Minnesota to be elected tribal chair. These stories make social studies classes come alive as well as honor the voices of native women. (WCK)

18.14    Raczek, L. T. **Rainy's Powwow.** Illustrated by Gary Bennett. Rising Moon, 1999. ISBN 0-87358-686-7. Unpaged. (ALL).

Filled with information about American Indian powwows and dances, this book tells the story of a young girl in search of the type of dance best suited to what she is about. A descriptive glossary at the conclusion helps explain powwow and dance terminology used in the text. Raczek is a non-native author but one who has had personal involvement with powwows. We hesitated to include this book as it got mixed reviews from native adults, but we decided to include it because the native children who read it liked it. (JDK)

18.15    Rose, LaVera. **Grandchildren of the Lakota.** Photographs by Cheryl Walsh Bellville. Carolrhoda, 1999. ISBN 1-57505-279-2. 41 pp. (I).

LaVera Rose, a member of the Rosebud Sioux tribe, has written *Grandchildren of the Lakota* as a celebration of the Lakota people. The beautiful photographs by Cheryl Walsh Bellville and the narrative depict contemporary life in South Dakota. In some ways, Lakota children are very much like most U.S. children, but their Lakota culture does make them unique. Not all Lakota families live on the reservation, but they are still tied to their people. The book is made more interesting by following specific children throughout the story, such as Brittany, a seven-year-old who lives outside the reservation in Onida. She often visits her relatives on the Rosebud Reservation, where her mother is from. This book portrays positively and realistically the lives of native people today. (JDK)

18.16    ★ Schick, Eleanor. **Navajo Wedding Day: A Diné Marriage Ceremony.** Marshall Cavendish, 1999. ISBN 0-7614-5031-9. Unpaged. (ALL).

Gentle colored-pencil illustrations invite readers to experience the daylong celebration that is a Navajo marriage ceremony. As seen through the eyes of a young girl who is not Navajo, readers embark on a journey that takes them from the early morning food preparation of the bride's family, to the midday meal, to dressing the bride in traditional wedding clothing, to the sunset marriage ceremony in the hogan, to the evening feast. This text brings together the past, present, and future of Navajo people as a young couple marries. (DGG)

18.17   ★ Smith, Cynthia Leitich. **Jingle Dancer.** Illustrated by Cornelius Van Wright and Ying-Hwa Hu. Morrow, 2000. ISBN 0-688-16241-X. Unpaged. (ALL).

This delightful story by Cynthia Leitich Smith depicts the tradition of jingle dancing. Readers learn about this traditional dance of native women in which their dresses are adorned with metal decorations made from tobacco tins that give their dresses a jingling sound. The main character is Jenna, who wants to participate in the jingle dance at the next powwow. She studies by repeatedly watching a videotape of her grandmother dancing. When she realizes she needs enough jingles before the powwow to "make her dress sing," she goes to the women in her family for help. Included in the story are excellent role models for young girls: cousin Elizabeth, for example, is an attorney. *Jingle Dancer* includes a wonderful blend of contemporary life and tradition. The watercolor illustrations reflect the warmth and affection family members have for one another. The author's notes explain the history of jingle dancing and of the Ojibway (Chippewa/Anishinabe) people. (JDK)

18.18   Staub, Frank. **Children of the Tlingit.** Photographs by Frank Staub. Carolrhoda, 1999. ISBN 1-575-053333-0. 48 pp. (I).

This book, one in The World's Children series, depicts the modern-day life of the Tlingit people of southeastern Alaska. Each two-page spread features sharp and expressive photos and descriptive text about a particular aspect of Tlingit culture. The lives of children are presented, showing the ways in which history and tradition affect their lives today. Children are depicted dressing salmon after traditional salmon camps and learning the art of wood carving, but readers also see them drinking root beer and learning about computers. Our native reviewers liked the fact that this book talks about both past and present. (JDK)

18.19 ★ Tapahonso, Luci. **Songs of Shiprock Fair.** Illustrated by Anthony Chee Emerson. Kiva, 1999. ISBN 1-885772-11-4. Unpaged. (P).

The brightly colored illustrations and the poetic imagery in the *Songs of Shiprock Fair* make the reader feel a part of the celebration of the oldest fair in the Navajo Nation, held every year in Shiprock, New Mexico, where author Luci Tapahonso was born and raised. She was honored in 1992 when she was selected as the grand marshal of the fair parade. Family is an important element in the book as evidenced by all ages attending and enjoying the fair together. The festivities reflect the deep sense of spirituality of the Navajo people: "The Yeibicheii dancers symbolize the Holy Ones, who come each year to offer thanks for the abundant harvest, for good health, and for strong families." Luci Tapahonso successfully draws the reader into this magical time with family and friends at the Shiprock Fair. (JDK)

18.20 Tohe, Laura. **No Parole Today.** West End, 1999. ISBN 0-931122-93-7. 47 pp. (I).

Tohe, a professor at Arizona State University and Diné (Navajo) writer, has compiled these memories of her survival of one of the notorious Indian boarding schools. In the past, many native children were forcibly removed from their families and sent away to these schools to be "assimilated" into white society. This book is a no-nonsense account of the author's experiences told in both narrative and poetry. This selection would lend an authenticity to social studies lessons as a primary source of information, yet it is written in a style accessible to young people. (WCK)

18.21 ★ Waboose, Jan Bordeau. **SkySisters.** Illustrated by Brian Deines. Kids Can Press, 2000. ISBN 1-55074-697-9. Unpaged. (ALL).

Deines's impressionistic oil paintings and Waboose's precise and lyrical prose tell the story of two Ojibway sisters traveling at night up Coyote Hill to witness the "sky spirits"—the Northern Lights that appear in the sky over their village in northern Ontario. Allie, the older sister, is charged with the care of her younger sister, Alex, as they make their way alone through the night. They make tracks through the snow, pluck icicles off tree branches, silently watch a rabbit and deer, and then make the final trek up the hill. Lying in the snow at the top of the hill, they watch the "sky sisters." The beauty of the sisters' journey, as well as of their relationship, is captured in both words and pictures as they playfully make their way through the wilderness together. (DGG)

# 19 Gender Issues

**Shirley B. Ernst**

*Contributing reviewers included Jane Cook, Linda Duckstein, Kelly Emerson, Heidi Mehringer-Macina, and Pat Shimchick.*

---

**Criteria for Excellence**

- Literary quality (authentic and universal themes, rich and descriptive language, believable and interesting plot, strong characterization, quality illustrations)
- Characters who can serve as solid gender role models
- Characters and situations to which children can relate
- Characters who move away from stereotypical behavior
- Characters who have strong, positive relationships with others
- Characters who demonstrate growth toward maturity throughout the book

---

### Finding or Redefining Oneself

Buchanan, Jane. **Hank's Story.** Farrar, Straus & Giroux, 2001.

Clements, Andrew. **The Landry News.** Illustrated by Salvatore Murdocca. Simon & Schuster, 1999.

★ Crisp, Marty. **My Dog, Cat.** Illustrated by True Kelley. Holiday House, 2000.

Gantos, Jack. **Jack on the Tracks: Four Seasons of Fifth Grade.** Farrar, Straus & Giroux, 1999.

Lewis, Maggie. **Morgy Makes His Move.** Illustrated by Michael Chesworth. Houghton Mifflin, 1999.

Mead, Alice. **Soldier Mom.** Farrar, Straus & Giroux, 1999.

Myers, Walter Dean. **Bad Boy: A Memoir.** HarperCollins, 2001.

Ray, Mary Lyn. **Basket Moon.** Illustrated by Barbara Cooney. Little, Brown, 1999.

Shavik, Andrea. **You'll Grow Soon, Alex.** Illustrated by Russell Ayto. Walker, 2000.

## Relationships with Family and Friends

Brisson, Pat. **Bertie's Picture Day.** Illustrated by Diana Cain Bluthenthal. Holt, 2000.

Fox, Mem. **Harriet, You'll Drive Me Wild!** Illustrated by Marla Frazee. Harcourt, 2000.

Greene, Stephanie. **Owen Foote, Money Man.** Clarion, 2000.

Hamilton, Virginia. **Bluish.** Scholastic, 1999.

★ Holt, Kimberly Willis. **When Zachary Beaver Came to Town.** Holt, 1999.

Kornblatt, Marc. **Understanding Buddy.** Margaret K. McElderry Books, 2001.

Ripken, Cal Jr., and Mike Bryan. **Cal Ripken, Jr.: My Story.** Adapted by Dan Gutman. Dial, 1999.

Voigt, Cynthia. **It's Not Easy Being Bad.** Atheneum, 2000.

## Breaking Out of a Mold/Mold-Breakers: Eschewing Stereotypes

Bunting, Eve. **Peepers.** Harcourt Brace, 2001.

Hurst, Carol Otis. **Rocks in His Head.** Illustrated by James Stevenson. Greenwillow, 2001.

★ Joinson, Carla. **A Diamond in the Dust.** Dial, 2001.

Macy, Sue, and Jane Gottesman. **Play Like a Girl: A Celebration of Women in Sports.** Holt, 1999.

McGill, Alice. **Molly Bannaky.** Illustrated by Chris K. Soentpiet. Houghton Mifflin, 1999.

Moss, Marissa. **Emma's Journal: The Story of a Colonial Girl.** Harcourt Brace, 1999.

Ogburn, Jacqueline K. **The Magic Nesting Doll.** Illustrated by Laurel Long. Dial, 2000.

Willis, Jeanne. **Susan Laughs.** Illustrated by Tony Ross. Holt, 2000.

## Self-Image: Powerful and Dynamic Characters

Clements, Andrew. **Jake Drake, Know-It-All.** Illustrated by Dolores Avendano. Simon & Schuster, 2001.

Williams, Karen Lynn. **One Thing I'm Good At.** Lothrop, Lee & Shepard, 1999.

## Intergenerational

Best, Cari. **Three Cheers for Catherine the Great!** Illustrated by Giselle Potter. DK, 1999.

Eccles, Mary. **By Lizzie.** Dial, 2001.

Fogelin, Adrian. **Anna Casey's Place in the World.** Peachtree, 2001.

LaMarche, Jim. **The Raft.** HarperCollins, 2000.

★ Martin, Terri. **A Family Trait.** Holiday House, 1999.

Mills, Claudia. **Gus and Grandpa and the Two-Wheeled Bike.** Illustrated by Catherine Stock. Farrar, Straus & Giroux, 1999.

## Journeys: Mental, Physical, or Spiritual Excursions

Avi. **The Secret School.** Harcourt, 2001.

Brown, Don. **A Voice from the Wilderness: The Story of Anna Howard Shaw.** Houghton Mifflin, 2001.

Clements, Andrew. **The School Story.** Simon & Schuster, 2001.

Curtis, Christopher Paul. **Bud, Not Buddy.** Delacorte, 1999.

★ McKissack, Patricia C. **Goin' Someplace Special.** Illustrated by Jerry Pinkney. Atheneum, 2001.

## Making a Difference in the World

★ Bunting, Eve. **The Summer of Riley.** HarperCollins, 2001.

Matas, Carol. **The War Within: A Novel of the Civil War.** Simon & Schuster, 2001.

Talbott, Hudson. **O'Sullivan Stew: A Tale Cooked Up in Ireland.** Putnam, 1999.

### *Women Changing the World Series*

Buscher, Sarah, and Bettina Ling. **Mairead Corrigan & Betty Williams: Making Peace in Northern Ireland.** Feminist Press, 1999.

Harlan, Judith. **Mamphela Ramphele: Challenging Apartheid in South Africa.** Feminist Press, 2000.

Ling, Bettina. **Aung San Suu Kyi: Standing Up for Democracy in Burma.** Feminist Press, 1999.

Silverstone, Michael. **Rigoberta Menchú: Defending Human Rights in Guatemala.** Feminist Press, 1999.

Sreenivasan, Jyotsna. **Ela Bhatt: Uniting Women in India.** Feminist Press, 2000.

———

Children need exemplary gender role models to help them face the challenges in today's world. In this chapter, you will find summaries of high-quality children's books published between 1999 and 2001 whose characters possess the sterling qualities that exemplify positive gender role models. You will find many exceptional characters—brave girls, sensitive boys, stereotype-smashing grandmas and grandpas, soldiers, fathers, princesses, teachers, and bold rebels—who will make you and your students laugh, cry, feel, and think.

To create this chapter, we formed a team of six educators: a university professor, two reading specialists, a classroom teacher, a special education teacher, and a staff developer. All have expertise in literacy and a passion for children's literature. The team met periodically in person and sent e-mails back and forth between meetings as assignments were doled out and tasks were accomplished. We were a congenial group who laughed and ate lots of pizza and chips to fortify our bodies and minds.

At our initial meeting, we brainstormed selection criteria. In keeping with previous editions of this book, we recognized that we first must select high-quality literature. Books that met this definition would be those in which we saw themes that were authentic and universal, in which language was rich and descriptive, in which the plot was believable and interesting, and in which the characters were ones with whom readers might identify. In addition, for picture books we needed to select those with illustrations of the highest quality.

Once we had determined the general qualities of the books we would select, we decided we wanted to find books that had one or more characters who could serve as solid gender role models, who supported one another, and whose relationships with others of all ages were strong. We discussed whether the characters needed to be human or whether it would be appropriate to include books with male or female animals that represented positive gender roles. We finally decided to include books with human characters to whom children could relate and characters who were authentic and perhaps flawed: humans, not saints.

As we completed our annotations, we realized that a number of themes were emerging. We found, for example, that characters who exemplify positive gender role models usually make a difference in the world, they often break out of the stereotypical mold and find or redefine themselves in the process, and most have strong relationships with family and friends. We ended up with seven categories into which we divided the books:

> *Finding or Redefining Oneself:* In all of the books in this section, the characters grow and mature as they work their way through a variety of problems and situations. They learn lessons about themselves as they move from being egocentric to empathetic, and they represent boys and girls

who solve problems, coming to terms with themselves without resorting to stereotypical gender behavior.

*Relationships with Family and Friends:* The characters in these books share unique relationships with others as they search to find their place within a group. Their relationships reflect interactions with friends and family; they quarrel, they are noisy and make mistakes, but they respect and trust others and stand up for those who need their support.

*Breaking Out of a Mold/Mold-Breakers: Eschewing Stereotypes:* In many books for children, the characters reflect traditionally acceptable behavior that often fits a historical gender stereotype. In such books, one might find girls to be passive, weak, silly, and dependent and boys to be brave, rough, messy, aggressive, and adventurous. The characters in the books in this section all "break" such traditional gender stereotypes while at the same time meeting their goals, overcoming obstacles, and simply having fun.

*Self-Image: Powerful and Dynamic Characters:* Characters in the following books deal with a variety of issues and in doing so strengthen their sense of self. While relationships with others form an important aspect of each of these stories, it is the growth of self-esteem that made these characters role models in our eyes.

*Intergenerational:* The characters in these books all share a common thread of family relationships across the generations. Many of these relationships are with grandparents, but others are with foster families or younger and older siblings.

*Journeys: Mental, Physical, or Spiritual Excursions:* Life is a journey, and the characters in these books venture on a variety of journeys. Along the way, the characters demonstrate that they can solve problems rather than waiting to have others take care of things for them. They learn to fend for themselves, they ask for advice from others, and they reach a satisfying ending place, although it is not always the one toward which they set out.

*Making a Difference in the World:* In these books, the characters struggle through war, poverty, and injustice to create a better world.

## Finding or Redefining Oneself

**19.1**  Buchanan, Jane. **Hank's Story.** Farrar, Straus & Giroux, 2001. ISBN 0-374-32836-6. 136 pp. (I).

Life is difficult for Hank, a twelve-year-old who is sent on the Orphan Train with his brother Peter in search of a new family and home. Shortly after their arrival, Peter runs away to avoid the beatings from Mr. Olson, their bitter adoptive father. Hank is left alone and abandoned to face Mr. Olson's rage. He is forced to work from dawn till dark on the farm and then withstand the beatings he no longer shares with Peter. The local bully also harasses him. When Molly McIntire, an eccentric local woman who rescues wounded and discarded animals, befriends Hank, his life turns a corner. Through all of the challenges Hank faces, he perseveres, serving as a positive role model for all young boys. Hank's story is a believable and inspiring narrative of the life an orphan faced in the United States in the early 1900s. (JC)

**19.2**  Clements, Andrew. **The Landry News.** Illustrated by Salvatore Murdocca. Simon & Schuster, 1999. ISBN 0-689-81817-3. 123 pp. (I).

Cara Landry, a fifth-grade student and budding journalist, decides to publish a newspaper, *The Landry News,* and in the first edition exposes the weaknesses of her teacher, Mr. Larson, who each day has his students start on mindless activities while he reads his newspaper and drinks coffee. Cara's writing is blunt, candid, controversial, and honest, which gets her into trouble and creates a chain of events that eventually pulls the entire community together. Cara learns a lot about herself when she faces issues concerning the proper etiquette of being an editor and knowing when to advocate for the rights of people and the First Amendment. This fast-paced, thought-provoking story of a girl who takes a stand against apathy keeps readers wanting to find out what will happen next. It's a great starting point for teaching about a newspaper's format and its place in society and the politics surrounding a published piece of information. (HMM)

**19.3**  ★ Crisp, Marty. **My Dog, Cat.** Illustrated by True Kelley. Holiday House, 2000. ISBN 0-8234-1537-6. 106 pp. (I).

Wishing is Abbie's main hobby, and he makes three heartfelt wishes: he wants to have a boy's name, he wants to be taller, and he wants to have a big black dog named Killer who will protect him from the school bully. Abbie thinks one of his wishes has come true when his aunt leaves her new dog with him while she goes traveling. Unfortunately, instead of a big black dog, she leaves him a tiny Yorkshire terrier named Cat. As he gets to know Cat and they experience the world together, Abbie learns that heart is much more important than size. Delightful pencil sketches of Abbie and Cat punctuate each chapter. With its universal theme of courage triumphing over brute force, this charming book appeals to boys and girls alike but provides an especially good role model for boys, who might identify with Abbie. (JC)

19.4 Gantos, Jack. **Jack on the Tracks: Four Seasons of Fifth Grade.** Farrar, Straus & Giroux, 1999. ISBN 0-374-33665-2. 182 pp. (I).

Growing up is not easy, especially when you are a fifth-grade boy who is moving from North Carolina to Florida, has an unbearable sister, and is drawn to all things gross and disgusting. Readers will chuckle as they follow Jack Henry's adventures with cats and trains and a teacher who describes boys as snakes and snails and puppy dog tails. What's endearing about Jack is his constant pursuit of becoming a better person, even though that goal eludes him throughout the book. This book demonstrates the value of writing, especially for boys, since Gantos's childhood journals were the inspiration for this story; illustrated journal pages appear at the beginning of each of the nine chapters. Teachers can use this book to inspire journal writing in intermediate classes. (SBE)

19.5 Lewis, Maggie. **Morgy Makes His Move.** Illustrated by Michael Chesworth. Houghton Mifflin, 1999. ISBN 0-395-92284-4. 74 pp. (P).

When third grader Morgy MacDougal-MacDuff moves from California to Massachusetts, he has much more than homesickness with which to contend. He has to figure out what a *spa* and a *mar* are and what *wam* means. In addition, he becomes the favorite target of Ferguson, the fifth-grade bully who stuffs leaves down Morgy's back. Morgy doesn't want to tell the teacher or "look Ferguson in the eye and tell him to stop," as his father suggests. He does, however, solve the problem in his own nonviolent way, and as each new problem surfaces, Morgy manages, with a little help from family and friends, to get things under control. This simply written book combines story text with letters between Morgy and the friend he left in California. Some black-and-white illustrations bring the characters to life. This is an excellent book for primary grade independent readers. (SBE)

**19.6** Mead, Alice. **Soldier Mom.** Farrar, Straus & Giroux, 1999. ISBN 0-374-37124-5. 152 pp. (I).

The touching story of a mother of two who is called to serve in the Gulf War in 1990 is told through the perspective of her daughter Jasmyn, a seventh grader. Jasmyn is a multilayered character who faces adversity, but her inner strength pulls her through the most difficult times. Adolescent readers will appreciate Jasmyn's distress as she struggles with missing her mom, living with her mother's boyfriend, changing her schedule to help her family, trying to make the basketball team, and generally growing up. Readers also get a sense of Jasmyn's mother as she faces the conflict between defending her family and defending her country. Both female characters are wonderful role models as they exhibit respect, dependability, and strength. This is an especially good book for readers who might find themselves in a similar situation. (KE)

★ Mollel, Tololwa M. **Subira Subira.** Illustrated by Linda Saport. Clarion, 2000. ISBN 0-395-91809-X. 32 pp. (ALL). (See **22.17**.)

**19.7** Myers, Walter Dean. **Bad Boy: A Memoir.** HarperCollins, 2001. ISBN 0-06-029523-6. 206 pp. (I).

Children need strong role models, and they need to know that it is possible to become contributing members of society even if they have had a shaky start. Such a role model is what Walter Dean Myers provides in *Bad Boy: A Memoir.* Children will benefit from learning that someone who spent as much time as he did in the principal's office and who was in trouble both in and out of school could become the prolific writer of so many wonderful books for children and young adults. In this memoir, Myers takes the reader on a journey through his growing up years in Harlem, where he struggled to find his own niche in a world in which being a black male meant being different, often in a negative way. That niche included finding himself as a reader and a writer, which makes him a particularly strong role model for boys. (SBE)

**19.8**   Ray, Mary Lyn. **Basket Moon.** Illustrated by Barbara Cooney. Little, Brown, 1999. ISBN 0-316-73521-3. Unpaged. (ALL).

When the moon was round—a basket moon—the boy's father took their baskets to sell in Hudson. The boy so badly wanted to go too, but his father always said no, not until he was old enough. So he waited and watched and helped peel splint and tried some weaving. On the boy's ninth birthday, his father said he was old enough to go. Impressed with the sights and sounds of Hudson, he was looking forward to telling his mother about them when someone taunted him with "A tisket, a tasket, a hillbilly basket! That's all a bushwhacker knows." Embarrassed, he rejects all that has to do with basket making. Not until he learns the language of the wind is he able to overcome this taunting and make baskets again. This gentle story of a boy coming to terms with what is important in his life is beautifully illustrated by Barbara Cooney. (SBE)

**19.9**   Shavik, Andrea. **You'll Grow Soon, Alex.** Illustrated by Russell Ayto. Walker, 2000. ISBN 0-8027-8736-3. Unpaged. (P).

Alex is very unhappy because he's so short. He asks everyone for advice, and each person offers different suggestions. He follows their advice exactly but doesn't grow a smidgen taller. Then his very tall uncle gives him a peek into life as a tall person and its shortcomings. This new perspective and some secret advice from his uncle help Alex focus on the important things in life, and finally Alex is happy. Russell Ayto's illustrations plant the reader squarely in Alex's shoes, beginning with endpapers depicting the world as experienced through Alex's eyes. While being short is often especially problematic for boys, the message here goes beyond the issue of being tall or short; rather, it speaks to the universal wish for whatever a person lacks in order to be happy. Readers of all ages will be able to infer the message spelled out with few words and simple pictures. (PS)

## Relationships with Family and Friends

**19.10**   Brisson, Pat. **Bertie's Picture Day.** Illustrated by Diana Cain Bluthenthal. Holt, 2000. ISBN 0-8050-6281-5. 69 pp. (P).

Second grader Bertie has big plans for Monday. It's school picture day, and his teacher wants everyone to look "spiffy!" He'll wear his blue jacket, his red polka-dot tie, and a big smile. But over the weekend, Bertie loses his front tooth and gets his first shiner, and his little sister Eloise gives him a "terribly interesting" haircut. Pat Brisson and Diana Cain Bluthenthal bring back the delightful siblings from *Hot Fudge Hero* (1997) for another charming escapade. From kickball games to accidental head butts, this endearing story recalls the simple pleasures of being able to drink your milk with a straw through a "square hole," saving up silver dollars, and sharing with brothers and sisters. Kids will easily relate to Bertie and Eloise, who already make the world a happier place. (LD)

Ehrlich, Amy. **Joyride.** Candlewick, 2001. ISBN 0-7636-1346-0. 241 pp. (I). (See **4.3.**)

19.11  Fox, Mem. **Harriet, You'll Drive Me Wild!** Illustrated by Marla Frazee. Harcourt, 2000. ISBN 0-15-201977-4. Unpaged. (P).

Harriet is a pesky child. During the course of one day, she knocks over a glass of juice, dribbles jam all over her jeans, drips paint on the carpet, and pulls the tablecloth off the table. Since Harriet's mother doesn't like to yell, she simply responds with "Harriet, my darling child. Harriet, you'll drive me wild." Finally, when Harriet rips open a pillow instead of napping, Harriet's mother loses her patience and begins to yell. After tears and apologies all around, they laugh as they pick up the feathers together. This endearing picture book paints a picture of an exasperating but lovable little girl who has a patient but human mother who loves her very much. Mem Fox's rhythmic and predictable text and Marla Frazee's charming pencil and transparent drawing ink illustrations are a perfect combination to support emergent readers while entertaining parents and teachers. (JC)

19.12  Greene, Stephanie. **Owen Foote, Money Man.** Clarion, 2000. ISBN 0-618-02369-0. 88 pp. (P).

Eight-year-old Owen is interested in earning money with his friend Joseph in order to buy some pets, and there are plenty of salamanders, newts, snapping turtles, goldfish, cats, and dogs in this sequel to *Owen Foote, Frontiersman*. Owen tries to find work so he can earn money. Each chapter presents a moneymaking scheme that helps Owen learn that life's work can be hard but that it should make the individual happy, and each chapter ends with a description of Owen's feelings, using succinct imagery typical of an eight-year-old. Greene uses humor to portray realistic family life, including sibling rivalry. The adults in this book—mother, father, and a grandfatherly neighbor—are marvelous role models: they treat Owen as if his opinions matter. Owen is delightful, learning from each mistake. (PS)

Grimes, Nikki. **My Man Blue: Poems.** Illustrated by Jerome Lagarrigue. Dial, 1999. ISBN 0-8037-2326-1. Unpaged. (P). (See **15.13.**)

19.13   Hamilton, Virginia. **Bluish.** Scholastic, 1999. ISBN 0-590-28879-2. 127 pp. (I).

This poignant story about three friends, Dreenie, Tuli, and Natalie (called Bluish by her friends), is set in New York City. It's a story of friendship, of compassion, of understanding. Natalie has acute lymphoblastic leukemia and thus is in a wheelchair and often out of school for medical reasons. She wears a knitted cap and earlier in her illness has knitted similar caps for her classmates. When they all wear them, she says, "We're all the same; we're different too. Now you all look just like me" (p. 80). The characters in the story represent a diverse range in race, religion, and socioeconomic status. This would be an excellent book to use in middle grades to encourage discussions about caring for others. (SBE)

19.14   ★ Holt, Kimberly Willis. **When Zachary Beaver Came to Town.** Holt, 1999. ISBN 0-8050-6116-9. 227 pp. (I).

When a trailer advertising an invitation to see Zachary Beaver, the fattest boy in the world, pulls into town, Toby is not impressed. He has other things to think about. His mother has left for Nashville to enter the National Amateurs' Country Music Competition at the Grand Ole Opry, and Toby worries that she won't come back. He can't get a girl, Scarlett Stalling, out of his mind, and his best friend's brother is serving in Vietnam. But Toby and his friend Cal find themselves involved with Zachary when Paulie Rankin, Zachary's guardian, disappears. Through a series of adventures and misadventures, the three boys become friends. Humorous and sensitive at the same time, this book demonstrates friendship at its best and at its most vulnerable. Readers will laugh and cry with Toby as he works his way through his fears and problems. (SBE)

★ Joseph, Lynn. **The Color of My Words.** HarperCollins, 2000. ISBN 0-06-028232-0. 138 pp. (I). (See **4.34.**)

19.15   Kornblatt, Marc. **Understanding Buddy.** Margaret K. McElderry Books, 2001. ISBN 0-689-83215-X. 113 pp. (I).

Buddy is a withdrawn, depressed boy who is new to Sam's class. While Sam knows that Buddy's mother was killed in a car accident during the summer, he doesn't tell any of his classmates. He just comes to Buddy's aid when other classmates pick on him. Sam's best friend doesn't understand why he is defending the weird, withdrawn boy, causing a rift between the two friends. Sam is Jewish and Buddy is a Jehovah's Witness. The author uses these religions to support the underlying issues in the story such as death, peer pressure, and broken friendships. The problems Sam experiences in this fast-paced and thought-provoking book mirror the problems many of our children face today with relationships and family. (HMM)

19.16   Ripken Cal Jr., and Mike Bryan. **Cal Ripken, Jr.: My Story.** Adapted by Dan Gutman. Dial, 1999. ISBN 0-8037-2348-2. 115 pp. (I).

Sports fans will delight in this autobiographical look at Cal Ripken's personal life and career. The book starts with Cal as the motivated child of a close family and follows him through his teenage years, his time in the minor leagues, and then his record-breaking years in the major leagues. Readers will be struck by the respectful manner in which Cal plays baseball, treats others, and lives his life; his lifelong philosophy is that by being the best you can be each and every day, your work will be rewarded. The book reveals how close-knit the Ripken family is and the importance of family in any person's life, whether or not its lived in the limelight. Photos of Cal and his family are included. (KE)

19.17   Voigt, Cynthia. **It's Not Easy Being Bad.** Atheneum, 2000. ISBN 0-689-82473-4. 244 pp. (I).

Best friends Margalo and Mikey enter junior high. The girls have decided that their goal is to be part of the popular group. How should they go about it when everything is different in junior high? Margalo, a student of human nature, suggests that friends aren't the people you like; they're the ones you hang with. Mikey, a straightforward, action-oriented physical individual who lives with her divorced dad, argues that "hang with" means hang by the neck until you're dead. Voigt has created two characters with whom readers will easily identify. The two nonconformists use internal and external dialogue to communicate the pain and frustration of wanting to belong. They approach the challenge in opposite ways, giving the reader valuable insight into the struggle of maintaining identity when the rules have changed. (PS)

Williams, Sherley Anne. **Girls Together.** Illustrated by Synthia Saint James. Harcourt Brace, 1999. ISBN 0-15-230982-9. Unpaged. (ALL). (See **15.27.**)

★ Yep, Laurence. **The Amah.** Putnam, 1999. ISBN 0-399-23040-8. 181 pp. (I). (See **16.35.**)

## Breaking Out of a Mold/Mold-Breakers: Eschewing Stereotypes

**19.18** Bunting, Eve. **Peepers.** Harcourt Brace, 2001. ISBN 0-15-260297-6. Unpaged. (ALL).

Two young boys help their father with an autumn tour bus business. Each fall when the "leaf peepers" come out to see the fall foliage, the boys mock and giggle at them. The boys do not understand or appreciate the beauty around them, so they mimic the tourists by saying, "Oh! Look! Look how beautiful!" When the season is over, things begin to quiet down in town. Then, one night, while looking into the sky to view the stars, the boys discover the beauty in nature. They admit they are embarrassed about admiring nature the way the tourists did the foliage, but the boys have grown up just a bit. This book is filled with wonderful similes along with illustrations that are bursting with beautiful autumn colors. (HMM)

Corey, Shana. **You Forgot Your Skirt, Amelia Bloomer! A Very Improper Story.** Illustrated by Chesley McLaren. Scholastic, 2000. ISBN 0-439-07819-9. Unpaged. (P). (See **2.5.**)

**19.19** Hurst, Carol Otis. **Rocks in His Head.** Illustrated by James Stevenson. Greenwillow, 2001. ISBN 0-06-029403-5. Unpaged. (ALL).

Carol Hurst writes the story of her father's passion for rock collecting, following him through his childhood and adulthood, when he was eager to share rocks he carried in his pocket. In the days when the Ford Model T was becoming popular, the rock collection was first kept at the gas station Hurst's father built with his own father but eventually moved to his house because, during the Depression, people couldn't afford cars or their repairs. The collection of rocks was labeled, categorized, and cared for by Hurst's father, and his dream came true when the local museum director asked him to work as curator of mineralogy. This is a great book for those children who need an example both of breaking the mold and following their passion. James Stevenson's sketchlike illustrations are a nice touch and complement the text. (HMM)

19.20    ★ Joinson, Carla. **A Diamond in the Dust.** Dial, 2001. ISBN 0-8037-2511-6. 197 pp. (I).

Sixteen-year-old Katy has lived in the hardscrabble mining town of Buckeye City, Iowa, all her life, experiencing many hardships: the terror of mining accidents; filthy piles of coal dust her mother sweeps out of the house daily; coughing spasms that rack her miner father, who will almost certainly die of black lung; and inescapable poverty. She fears the total control the mine has over the families in town. Katy glimpses a life beyond Buckeye City through the books she has read at school and through the shared memories of her friend Miss Katy, an older woman and former vaudeville star. The author has created rich characters in the women in this story: mothers, wives, daughters, sisters, and girlfriends of the miners. Readers will identify with brave Katy's unavoidably painful struggle to live a life different from her mother's. (PS)

19.21    Macy, Sue, and Jane Gottesman. **Play Like a Girl: A Celebration of Women in Sports.** Holt, 1999. ISBN 0-8050-6071-5. 32 pp. (ALL).

In this exuberant celebration of women in sports, the saying "You play like a girl," once an insult, becomes a compliment. The power of women engaging in various sports comes through in both the illustrations and the text. Photographs of women running, swimming, coaching volleyball, skiing, and engaging in a variety of other sports are accompanied by textual comments by the athletes themselves. For example, "With head thrown back and right arm raised in victory, I shout YES to the morning sky. It is one of the smallest words in the English language but also one of the largest.

It is a word of infinite power and possibility" (p. 29, Zoe Koplowitz, marathoner). Both team and individual sports are represented in this book, which is a marvelous source for encouraging girls to be active in whatever sport they choose. (SBE)

19.22   McGill, Alice. **Molly Bannaky.** Illustrated by Chris K. Soentpiet. Houghton Mifflin, 1999. ISBN 0-395-72287-X. Unpaged. (I).

In 1683, at the age of seventeen, Molly Bannaky was exiled to an American colony because the cow she was milking tipped over a pail of milk. The factual story of this remarkable woman begins in England but soon moves to America, where Bannaky earns her freedom after working as an indentured servant for seven years. She stakes her own claim and then turns a plot of land with a one-room cabin into a thriving one-hundred-acre farm. This achievement comes with the help of an African slave, whom she eventually frees and marries. Molly teaches her grandchildren to read, and one of them, Benjamin Banneker, becomes the first black man to write an almanac, among many other notable achievements. Oversized pages and double-page watercolor illustrations glow with life and historical accuracy, enhancing the challenges this woman faced and met. (NJJ)

19.23   Moss, Marissa. **Emma's Journal: The Story of a Colonial Girl.** Harcourt Brace, 1999. ISBN 0-15-202025-X. Unpaged. (I).

Although, as the author tells readers in an endnote, there is no record of a young girl spying for American rebels during the Revolutionary War, there is evidence that many women did indeed serve as spies during that period. Using the vehicle of a journal to tell Emma's story, Moss takes readers into what the life of a colonial girl might have been like during the revolutionary period. Both fictional characters and real ones people this journal excursion that takes place between July 18, 1774, and July 18, 1776. Emma's spying experience of hearing the British generals plan their strategy in the room below her is based on the true experience of Lydia Darragh, one woman who did act as a spy. The yellow, lined journal pages, enhanced with sketches, have an authentic journal feel to them, and the map on the front endpapers helps readers better visualize Emma's experience. (SBE)

Moss, Marissa. **True Heart.** Illustrated by C. F. Payne. Harcourt, 1999. ISBN 0-15-201344-X. Unpaged. (ALL). (See **3.18.**)

**19.24**   Ogburn, Jacqueline K. **The Magic Nesting Doll.** Illustrated by Laurel Long. Dial, 2000. ISBN 0-8037-2414-4. Unpaged. (I).

Young Katya sets out into the world with only a small wooden toy in her pocket. A gift from her dying grandmother, the little *matryoshka*, or nesting doll, is said to contain powerful magic. "If your need is great, help will come," her grandmother promised. When Katya finds herself in a frozen city of darkness, she knows what she must do. A wicked spell has been cast on the handsome young tsar, changing him into a sleeping prince of living ice. Determined to break the evil spell, Katya uses physical strength and agility to gain entry to the palace. With gorgeous illustrations that evoke Russian folk art, this original story is a fairy tale with a modern twist. Katya is courageous, strong, and smart and saves her prince with magical beasts and a classic solution. This is a nice alternative to the "boy saves girl" story format. (LD)

★ Rappaport, Doreen, and Lyndall Callan. **Dirt on Their Skirts: The Story of the Young Women Who Won the World Championship.** Illustrated by E. B. Lewis. Dial, 2000. ISBN 0-8037-2042-4. Unpaged. (ALL). (See **12.27.**)

**19.25**   Willis, Jeanne. **Susan Laughs.** Illustrated by Tony Ross. Holt, 2000. ISBN 0-8050-6501-6. Unpaged. (P).

Susan laughs and sings. She rides and swings. She gets angry and sad. She is good and bad. She hugs and hears. She feels and fears. Through simple text and engaging pencil-and-crayon illustrations, this picture book introduces beginning readers to a girl who experiences all the same feelings they do. She is "just like me and just like you" despite the physical challenges she faces. The author and illustrator present a happy little girl who never perceives her physical challenges as disabilities, so neither does the reader. It's not until the final page that readers see Susan in a wheelchair. This book can be easily read and understood by primary-level children, yet the message is significant for children of all ages. (JC)

## Self-Image: Powerful and Dynamic Characters

Best, Cari. **Shrinking Violet.** Illustrated by Giselle Potter. Farrar, Straus & Giroux, 2001. ISBN 0-374-36882-1. Unpaged. (P). (See **6.4.**)

**19.26** Clements, Andrew. **Jake Drake, Know-It-All.** Illustrated by Dolores Avendano. Simon & Schuster, 2001. ISBN 0-689-83918-9. 88 pp. (I).

In Andrew Clements's newest series, Jake recounts his life in school from the wise perspective of a fourth grader. Hoping to win the grand prize in the science fair, he is determined to be the best without losing his friends and becoming a know-it-all. Jake explores the scientific method in more than magnets as he solves problems and arrives at conclusions. In *Jake Drake, Bully Buster* (2001), another book in the series, Jake looks back at his school career as a "bully magnet" and explains how he learned to deal with the harassment and intimidation of "Super Bully" Link Baxter in second grade. An expert on the subject, Jake instructs readers in the right and wrong way to deal with a bully. Wise-cracking Jake speaks the language of a typical kid as he confronts the real problems facing kids in school today. (LD)

**19.27** Williams, Karen Lynn. **One Thing I'm Good At.** Lothrop, Lee & Shepard, 1999. ISBN 0-688-16846-9. 144 pp. (I).

Julie Dorinsky is a girl experiencing difficulty at home and at school. Her father is trying to change professions due to health problems, and her mother has returned to work while Julie cares for her younger brother. Julie finds reading difficult and feels that her friends are smarter than she is, resulting in low self-esteem. Julie is good at one thing; she spends time teaching her four-year-old brother safety tips while she babysits. Her brother's knowledge eventually saves their father's life. This story focuses on friendship and family dynamics in today's fast-paced world. The characters are believable and there's an important lesson to be learned. This story would be helpful for children experiencing problems with parents who are out of work, on disability, or changing careers. It is also a good book for students with low self-esteem who are looking for a contemporary role model. (HMM)

## Intergenerational

**19.28** Best, Cari. **Three Cheers for Catherine the Great!** Illustrated by Giselle Potter. DK, 1999. ISBN 0-789-42622-6. Unpaged. (ALL).

This is a tender and poignant tale of the relationship between Sara and her Russian grandmother, who is nicknamed Catherine the Great by her large and loving family. Catherine the Great announces that for her birthday this year she would like to have a celebration with her loved ones, but "NO PRESENTS," as she already has everything she could ever need or want. The uplifting message—that the best presents come from the heart—is apparent as Catherine's entire family struggles to find the perfect "nonpresent" for her. Sara discovers that the best nonpresent she can give her grandmother is to teach Catherine how to read and write English. Students of all ages will enjoy this story of Sara's creative problem solving, family relationships, the joy of learning to read, and gifts from the heart. Colorful watercolor illustrations will enchant all readers. (KE)

19.29   Eccles, Mary. **By Lizzie.** Dial, 2001. ISBN 0-8037-2608-2. 116 pp. (I).

After she finds her mother's old typewriter in the closet, Lizzie decides that since she can't travel the way her mother did, she will write her own stories on the typewriter. Month by month, readers travel through Lizzie's year as a nine-year-old. They agonize with her over her relationships with her little sister and her older brother and cheer for her as she overcomes her difficulties with each of them. They laugh as she organizes and carries out a yard sale to earn money for skates. They also empathize as she worries about the new school year and the teacher to whose class she is assigned. Throughout it all, however, Lizzie is a problem solver, even if the solutions are sometimes problems in themselves. (SBE)

19.30   Fogelin, Adrian. **Anna Casey's Place in the World.** Peachtree, 2001. ISBN 1-56145-249-1. 207 pp. (I).

It's tough being a foster child, especially for Anna, who has been shuffled from relative to relative after her grandmother, with whom she lived, died. As a way of taking charge of her own world, Anna makes neighborhood maps and keeps one stone from each place. Insisting that Eb, another child in her foster home, be part of her world, she makes friends with neighbor children and befriends a homeless Vietnam veteran. In the process, she sets in motion the situation that results in her finding "her place." Anna is a spunky and appealing character, and her heartwarming story reaffirms the role that good intergenerational relationships play in the life of a child. (SBE)

Gray, Dianne E. **Holding Up the Earth.** Houghton Mifflin, 2000. ISBN 0-618-00703-2. 210 pp. (I). (See **5.32.**)

**19.31** LaMarche, Jim. **The Raft.** HarperCollins, 2000. ISBN 0-688-13977-9. Unpaged. (P).

Nicky reluctantly goes to spend what he expects will be a boring summer in the Wisconsin woods with his grandma who doesn't even own a television. His fears materialize as she keeps him busy stacking firewood, helping clean the rain gutters, and fishing for bluegills. But then he finds a raft covered with animal drawings that resemble ancient cave paintings, and Nicky's relationship with his grandma and the world changes. This beautifully illustrated story contains bits and pieces of the author's boyhood summers, captivating the reader in a child's magical engagement with the raft, the river, the woods, the animals, and Nicky's grandma. These experiences teach Nicky how to see the world through an artist's eyes. The engaging plot and double-page, muted watercolor illustrations capture the reader's attention from beginning to end. (JC)

**19.32** ★ Martin, Terri. **A Family Trait.** Holiday House, 1999. ISBN 0-8234-1467-1. 157 pp. (I).

Eleven-year-old Iris Mae Watson wants to have fun during vacation with her friends in the clubhouse they've discovered on Ol' Man Hazard's property, an old hunting cabin that was the scene of his grisly and untimely death last fall. Her grandmother, with whom she and her mother live, insists that she finish her reading assignment, *Silas Marner,* before vacation. Of course, Iris and the Voodoo Club are more interested in solving the mystery of the neighbor's death and the coincidental robbery in town. Iris's grandfather suggests that she may be having so much difficulty with her mother and grandmother because all three of them share the same family traits: they are tough, stubborn as his dang tractor, and focused on doing things their own way. Martin has fashioned in Iris a complex and real character who struggles to understand and accept her family and herself as she arrives at the solution to the town's mystery as well as her own family mysteries. (PS)

**19.33** Mills, Claudia. **Gus and Grandpa and the Two-Wheeled Bike.** Illustrated by Catherine Stock. Farrar, Straus & Giroux, 1999. ISBN 0-374-32821-8. 47 pp. (P).

Gus is perfectly content riding his bike with training wheels until his neighbor, Ryan, starts riding a brand-new five-speed bike complete with handbrakes and water bottle. Gus's father surprises Gus with a new bike just like Ryan's and tries to teach Gus how to ride without training wheels. Gus is frustrated until he visits his grandpa. Grandpa and Gus fix up an older bike and then, when they take it out for a test ride, Grandpa teaches Gus the timeless lesson of how to ride a bike. Short chapters, simple word choices, and colorful watercolor illustrations will attract primary readers. The universal experiences of learning to ride a two-wheeled bike and spending quality time with grandparents will engage readers of all ages. (KE)

## Journeys: Mental, Physical, or Spiritual Excursions

**19.34**  Avi. **The Secret School.** Harcourt, 2001. ISBN 0-15-216375-1. 153 pp. (I).

Living in the Colorado mountains around 1925, Ida dreams of becoming a teacher. She must first finish eighth grade, however, and then move on to high school. When her town's one-room school is forced to close, headstrong Ida realizes that the only way to attain her dream is to open a "secret school" with herself as the head teacher and her peers as the students. Ida faces many obstacles, including a confused school board, the classroom management of her students, as well as the added demands of lesson planning while studying for her exit exams. Avi has created a dynamic and remarkable female character who will stop at nothing to follow her dream. This novel gives young readers a glimpse into the realities of becoming a teacher and the hardships one might face on such a journey. Readers will applaud as Ida successfully overcomes each battle. (KE)

**19.35**  Brown, Don. **A Voice from the Wilderness: The Story of Anna Howard Shaw.** Houghton Mifflin, 2001. ISBN 0-618-08362-6. Unpaged. (ALL).

"By most measures, Anna Howard Shaw's life was hard and filled with struggle" begins this beautifully written and cleverly illustrated biography. Anna began her journey when she came to the United States at age four in 1851. The daughter of abolitionists, at twelve she accompanied her family into the wilderness of Michigan to build a new home. Despite the fact that women were discouraged from pursuing careers and independent thinking in those years, Anna grew up to become a leader in the women's rights movement. She was a pioneer, a physician, a minister, a teacher, and a suffragette—a most extraordinary role model of strength, courage, and determination. This story shows how important it is for both boys and girls to be knowledgeable about the lives of young women in the past as they struggled to find their niche in a world that was not yet ready for them. (LD)

**19.36**   Clements, Andrew. **The School Story.** Simon & Schuster, 2001. ISBN 0-689-82594-3. 196 pp. (I).

Andrew Clements, the author of *Frindle* (1996), returns with a fabulous new novel that once again captures the emotions of elementary school. A young author writes her own novel after hearing from her editor mother that "school stories" are big sellers. Natalie shares her novel with her best friend, who decides that it *must* be published. Zoe, Natalie, and their English teacher start using pseudonyms and discover the complicated world of children's book publishing. Natalie's book does make it into her mother's hands, although her mother has no idea it is her daughter's work, and the book is published, with the identity of the author still a mystery. This story-within-a-story novel contains excellent examples of spunky and endearing characters who will capture the reader's interest, and underlying themes of a young girl missing her father, cheating, honesty, revising, and hard work add depth. (KE)

**19.37**   Curtis, Christopher Paul. **Bud, Not Buddy.** Delacorte, 1999. ISBN 0-385-32306-9. 245 pp. (I).

Times were tough in 1936, especially for ten-year-old Bud, an orphan. His most precious belonging is his suitcase in which he keeps all his belongings, including some rocks and several fliers left by his mother. These fliers lead Bud to believe that his father is Herman E. Calloway, a famous musician, and when the new foster home he is sent to doesn't work out very well, Bud decides to use the fliers to find his father. Readers will laugh and cry as they follow Bud on his journey and will rejoice at the ending that doesn't quite turn out the way Bud thinks it will. Bud is a strong character, with a set of "rules and things" that he uses to explain his life. He uses his wits rather than force to get himself out of the troubles that surround him, and he is a good role model for boys in today's world. (SBE)

Gantos, Jack. **Joey Pigza Loses Control.** Farrar, Straus & Giroux, 2000. ISBN 0-374-39989-1. 196 pp. (I). (See **4.5.**)

**19.38**   ★ McKissack, Patricia C. **Goin' Someplace Special.** Illustrated by Jerry Pinkney. Atheneum, 2001. ISBN 0-689-81885-8. Unpaged. (ALL).

Although 'Tricia Ann wants to go by herself to "someplace special," her grandmother is reluctant to let her go, not because she's too young, but because the Jim Crow laws are still in effect in 1950s Nashville. 'Tricia Ann has to sit in the back of the bus, can't sit on a "whites only" bench, and is yelled at when swept by a crowd into the grand lobby of an old hotel. Her grandmother's words, "You are somebody, a human being—no better, no worse than anybody else in this world. Gettin' someplace special is not an easy route. But don't study on quittin', just keep walking straight ahead—and you'll make it," give 'Tricia Ann the courage to keep on—and she reaches her final destination, the public library, which bears a sign that says all are welcome. Jerry Pinkney's full-page illustrations will delight readers as they journey with the author through a story based on her own life experiences. (SBE)

## Making a Difference in the World

★ Bridges, Ruby. **Through My Eyes.** Scholastic, 1999. ISBN 0-590-18923-9. 64 pp. (I). (See **2.4.**)

**19.39**   ★ Bunting, Eve. **The Summer of Riley.** HarperCollins, 2001. ISBN 0-06-029141-9. 170 pp. (I).

Eleven-year-old William feels lost and alone. His parents have divorced and his grandfather has died suddenly. William's mother takes him to the pound to adopt a dog, hoping that will help heal his heartache. Riley, a nearly purebred yellow Labrador, captures William's attention and heart. Unfortunately, Riley has one very bad habit—chasing horses. When Riley chases the neighbor's retired racehorse, the Sultan of Kaboor, he is sentenced to death. William is heartbroken but doesn't give up hope of saving Riley's life. He and his "totally unsurpassed" friend Grace spend the summer trying to free Riley. William is a resourceful and creative problem solver and Grace is a dedicated friend. Together they begin a petition campaign that uses modern technology in their quest to save Riley's life. Eve Bunting's riveting story compels readers to keep turning the pages, hoping for Riley's reprieve. (JC)

★ Freedman, Russell. **Babe Didrikson Zaharias: The Making of a Champion.** Clarion, 1999. ISBN 0-395-63367-2. 192 pp. (I). (See **12.3.**)

**19.40**   Matas, Carol. **The War Within: A Novel of the Civil War.** Simon & Schuster, 2001. ISBN 0-689-82935-3. 151 pp. (I).

"The war has changed everything. And it has changed me." So starts *The War Within*, historical fiction in the form of a journal kept by Hannah Green, a young girl who lives in Holly Springs, Mississippi, in 1862. Hannah's family has owned a general store in town for many years, but they have been commanded to evacuate the territory under General Order #11, issued by General Grant, simply because they are Jewish. Through Hannah's journal entries, the reader is drawn into the turmoil of the Confederate South and the horrors of the Civil War. As the Greens follow the Union army to Memphis, Hannah bravely struggles with the war outside and the war within as she learns that the Civil War is not just about slavery. The end of the story finds her a more caring and stronger person. Carol Matas offers the reader historical accuracy and thought-provoking imagery of a troubling time in U.S. history. (JC)

**19.41**   Talbott, Hudson. **O'Sullivan Stew: A Tale Cooked Up in Ireland.** Putnam, 1999. ISBN 0-399-23162-5. Unpaged. (ALL).

The king snatches the horse of Crookhaven's witch to pay for taxes, and when no one comes to her aid, she becomes angry and curses the town. When cows stop giving milk, gardens die, and fishermen's nets come up empty, Kate O'Sullivan convinces her father and brothers to help steal the horse back. They are caught and sentenced to hang, so, in the tradition of Scheherazade, Kate tells stories to the king to save her family. Her tales are hilarious, colorful, and most inventive, and they secure the freedom of Kate's father and brothers. When the king asks her to marry him, she tells him she is going on an adventure and he might try again in five years. Kate is a true protagonist, clever, funny, witty, and a strong role model. The colorful illustrations are supportive of the text and relay the humorous mood. This adventuresome tale is a great read-aloud when teaching Irish tales and story-telling and will make readers laugh. (HMM)

**19.42    Women Changing the World Series**

Buscher, Sarah, and Bettina Ling. **Mairead Corrigan & Betty Williams: Making Peace in Northern Ireland.** Feminist Press, 1999. ISBN 1-55861-200-9. 102 pp. (I).

Harlan, Judith. **Mamphela Ramphele: Challenging Apartheid in South Africa.** Feminist Press, 2000. ISBN 1-55861-227-0. 99 pp. (I).

Ling, Bettina. **Aung San Suu Kyi: Standing Up for Democracy in Burma.** Feminist Press, 1999. ISBN 1-55861-196-7. 102 pp. (I).

Silverstone, Michael. **Rigoberta Menchú: Defending Human Rights in Guatemala.** Feminist Press, 1999. ISBN 1-55861-198-3. 99 pp. (I).

Sreenivasan, Jyotsna. **Ela Bhatt: Uniting Women in India.** Feminist Press, 2000. ISBN 1-55861-229-7. 100 pp. (I).

History books have generally left out women's contributions other than those involved in traditionally women's roles, such as nursing. But it is important that both boys and girls recognize and know about the women who are making a difference in non-traditional ways as well. This series demonstrates to readers that there are contemporary women who have made and are making differences in the world. These are women who provide positive role models for readers of both genders. Each of the books includes a chronology of the subject's life events, a glossary, and suggestions for further reading. An index makes it easy for readers to find specific topics. These are excellent additions to classroom libraries, particularly in middle schools. (SBE)

# 20 Animal Stories

**Marcia F. Nash**

*Contributing reviewers included Erin Allen, Patricia Flint, Rebecca Kerr, Denise Richard, and Lia Paliota.*

---

**Criteria for Excellence**

- Quality literature (imaginative use of language, fully developed characters, well-constructed plot, compelling theme)
- Animals as topic or significant element of the content of the story

---

## Animals in Realistic Fiction

Crisp, Marty. **Black and White.** Illustrated by Sherry Neidigh. Rising Moon, 2000.

★ DiCamillo, Kate. **Because of Winn-Dixie.** Candlewick, 2000.

Freeman, Martha. **The Trouble with Cats.** Illustrated by Cat Bowman Smith. Holiday House, 2000.

Hänel, Wolfram. **Rescue at Sea!** Illustrated by Ulrike Heyne. Translated by Rosemary Lanning. North-South, 1999.

Hite, Sid. **A Hole in the World.** Scholastic, 2001.

Hurwitz, Johanna. **One Small Dog.** Illustrated by Diane deGroat. HarperCollins, 2000.

Lawson, Julie. **Bear on the Train.** Illustrated by Brian Deines. Kids Can Press, 1999.

Livingstone, Star. **Harley.** Illustrated by Molly Bang. SeaStar, 2001.

McCully, Emily Arnold. **Four Hungry Kittens.** Dial, 2001.

McNamee, Graham. **Nothing Wrong with a Three-Legged Dog.** Delacorte, 2000.

Rossiter, Nan Parson. **The Way Home.** Dutton , 1999.

Tafuri, Nancy. **Silly Little Goose!** Scholastic, 2001.

Waddell, Martin. **A Kitten Called Moonlight.** Candlewick, 2001.

## Animals in Modern Fantasy

Avi. **Ereth's Birthday.** Illustrated by Brian Floca. HarperCollins, 2000.

★ Child, Lauren. **Beware of the Storybook Wolves.** Scholastic, 2000.

Collington, Peter. **Clever Cat.** Knopf, 2000.

Elliott, David. **The Transmogrification of Roscoe Wizzle.** Candlewick, 2001.

Garland, Michael. **Last Night at the Zoo.** Boyds Mills, 2001.

Gray, Kes, and Mary McQuillan. **The "Get Well Soon" Book: Good Wishes for Bad Times.** Millbrook, 2000.

Halls, Kelly Milner. **I Bought a Baby Chicken.** Illustrated by Karen Stromer Brooks. Boyds Mills, 2000.

★ Jennings, Richard. **Orwell's Luck.** Houghton Mifflin, 2000.

King-Smith, Dick. **Lady Lollipop.** Illustrated by Jill Barton. Candlewick, 2001.

Lauber, Patricia. **Purrfectly Purrfect: Life at the Acatemy.** Illustrated by Betsy Lewin. HarperCollin, 2000.

★ McPhail, David. **Drawing Lessons from a Bear.** Little, Brown, 2000.

Ryan, Pam Muñoz. **Mice and Beans.** Illustrated by Joe Capita. Scholastic, 2001.

Wahl, Jan. **The Field Mouse and the Dinosaur Named Sue.** Illustrated by Bob Doucet. Scholastic, 2000.

---

Animals are an important and pervasive element in children's lives. It's hard to imagine a childhood without a beloved family pet or a surrogate in the form of a stuffed bedtime companion. Toys, games, movies, television, and other aspects of popular culture depend on the appeal of animals to attract children.

Animals are also among the most memorable characters in literature for children. Primary classrooms are enriched by visits from Charlotte, Clifford, Paddington, Corduroy, Frog, Toad, and many others. In later grades, new friends such as the intrepid animals of Redwall Abbey and the elusive dog from Chris Van Allsburg's work find their way into the classroom. Reading preference studies have consistently shown animal stories to be among children's favorites (Huck, Hepler, Hickman, & Kiefer 2001), although there are age and gender differences. Younger children tend to favor low fantasy animal stories with personified animals as main characters. Older children, particularly girls, prefer realistic animal stories (Goforth, 1998).

The books included in this chapter meet two criteria: (1) they are quality literature, and (2) animals are the topic or a significant element of the content of the story. First and foremost, the books chosen for this chapter are quality literature. Characteristics of quality literature include imaginative use of language, fully developed characters, a well-constructed plot, and a compelling theme.

Second, the animal or animals have to be a significant element of the content of the story. The significance of the animals in the books occurs in a number of different ways. In some of the stories, the animal's role is to offer a glimpse into the animal world. That glimpse can be realistic, romanticized, or both. In *Ereth's Birthday* (Avi, 2000), which manages to do both, readers find a grumpy old porcupine with personified emotions and reactions. Like real porcupines in nature, however, he has a solitary life, an appetite for salt, and a dangerous and cunning enemy—a fisher.

Some animal stories use the animal as a catalyst for the human characters to work out their human problems. The cats in *The Trouble with Cats* (Freeman, 2000) at first only exacerbate the problems a young girl has adjusting to her new stepdad. Eventually these same cats precipitate an event that brings the girl and her stepdad to a point of common understanding. Other animal stories capture the interface between the worlds of humans and animals. *The Way Home* (Rossiter, 1999) offers an example of an appropriate relationship between humans and wild creatures. *Silly Little Goose!* (Tafuri, 2001) and *Bear on the Train* (Lawson, 1999) depict animals coping in human environments. At their very best, animal stories help us examine our humanity. In *Because of Winn-Dixie* (DiCamillo, 2000), for example, a truly remarkable dog helps the human characters come to grips with the sweetness and sorrow they have known in their lives.

All of the stories in this chapter are either realistic fiction or modern fantasy, so the chapter is divided into those two genres. Readers seeking informational texts about animals should check out the chapter on science nonfiction.

**References**

Goforth, F. (1998). *Literature and the learner.* Belmont, CA: Wadsworth.

Huck, C., Hepler, S., Hickman, J., & Kiefer, B. (2001). *Children's literature in the elementary school* (7th ed.). Boston: McGraw-Hill.

## Animals in Realistic Fiction

20.1    Crisp, Marty. **Black and White.** Illustrated by Sherry Neidigh. Rising Moon, 2000. ISBN 0-87358-756-1. Unpaged. (P).

When Bud gets his new black-and-white dog, his mother tells him not to name it. If the dog chases the cows and scares the chickens, he won't be a good farm dog and they won't be able to keep him. Bud's mother cautions him to watch the dog closely, but the dog disappears. When Bud climbs up on the fence to try to see the dog, he sees sheep grazing. Or is that a tail wagging? Can't be. Sheep don't wag their tails. As Bud searches among the various farm animals, he senses something but can't spot the dog. That's because the farm animals are all black and white too. The new dog truly does fit in. From the first illustration, readers are in on the puzzle and will enjoy picking out the dog among the other black-and-white animals. An author's note at the end names all the black-and-white animals introduced in the book.

20.2     ★ DiCamillo, Kate. **Because of Winn-Dixie.** Candlewick, 2000. ISBN 0-7636-0776-2. 182 pp. (I).

When ten-year-old Opal Buloni's daddy sends her to the store for macaroni-and-cheese, white rice, and tomatoes, she comes back with a dog. Opal and her father have just moved to Naomi, Florida. Her mother left the family when Opal was three years old, and her father has become withdrawn, like a turtle in his shell. The stray dog, whom Opal names Winn-Dixie after the grocery store where they met, becomes her friend and confidante. All the things that happen to Opal that summer happen because of Winn-Dixie, including a memorable cast of characters she befriends and the resolution she and her father must come to about her absent mother. The characters are beautifully developed and united by the sorrows they have known and the sweetness they come to share. The plot is episodic, each chapter nearly able to stand alone, while moving the story along to a satisfying conclusion.

20.3     Freeman, Martha. **The Trouble with Cats.** Illustrated by Cat Bowman Smith. Holiday House, 2000. ISBN 0-8234-1479-5. 77 pp. (P).

Holly is starting third grade in a new school. Other things in her life are new too—a new stepdad, a new home, and her stepdad's four very frisky cats. The cats make life at home difficult by keeping Holly awake at night, chewing holes in her socks, and trying to escape when she opens the door. At school the other kids think Holly is weird because she falls asleep, has holes in her socks, and doesn't have her homework done. Clearly, Holly, the cats, and her stepdad all have some adjusting to do if they are going to live together in harmony. The story is told from Holly's point of view, with a third grader's sense of humor and irony. The black-and-white sketches add to the humor of the story, as they often capture Holly's unfortunate encounters with the cats.

**20.4** Hänel, Wolfram. **Rescue at Sea!** Illustrated by Ulrike Heyne. Translated by Rosemary Lanning. North-South, 1999. ISBN 0-7358-1045-1. 61 pp. (P).

Paul is nearly nine years old and feels that he is old enough to have a dog. His father tells him that a dog is not like a toy you can just walk into a shop and buy; you have to prove yourself worthy of a dog. Paul gets a chance to prove his worthiness when a fishing boat gets caught in a storm off the coast. Paul's father and the other men of the village set out in a lifeboat to rescue the sailors. Just as the men are rescued and the boat is about to break up, Paul sees a dog stranded on the wreck. Paul knows that if he doesn't act, the dog will die. Though this is a common theme for an easy-to-read book, *Rescue at Sea!* has an unusually serious plot. The dark illustrations are interwoven with the text, adding to the tension and the adventure of this stepping-stone chapter book.

**20.5** Hite, Sid. **A Hole in the World.** Scholastic, 2001. ISBN 0-439-09830-0. 204 pp. (I).

Paul Shackleford told a lie. It seemed like an innocent enough lie, told to cover for a friend. But it backfired. The friend got in big trouble and Paul's parents shipped him off to work on the farm of a distant relative for the summer. Paul expects to find "hokey old farmers" and endless boredom. Instead, he finds a strong-willed dog, a girl, a ghost, and himself. Paul is fifteen years old, so the book is aimed at a young adult audience, but the clever plot and the possibility of a ghost should hold younger readers who may not be interested in the low-key relationship between Paul and the girl on the farm.

**20.6** Hurwitz, Johanna. **One Small Dog.** Illustrated by Diane deGroat. HarperCollins, 2000. ISBN 0-688-17382-9. 110 pp. (I).

Curtis is having trouble adjusting to his parents' recent divorce. When he asks for a dog, his mother gives in, hoping that a dog will help Curtis through the transition. The dog Curtis chooses is cute but out of control. Curtis believes the dog can be controlled, until it begins to bite people. With the help of Curtis's dad, the dog finds a new home with people who will train him properly. Although Curtis learns that all stories don't have a happy ending, this ending is softened somewhat because he can visit the dog when he is with his dad on weekends. At the end of the book, a note by a professional dog trainer analyzes what went wrong with Curtis and his dog and gives advice about successful pet ownership.

**20.7** Lawson, Julie. **Bear on the Train.** Illustrated by Brian Deines. Kids Can Press, 1999. ISBN 1-55074-560-3. Unpaged. (P).

As Jeffrey watches, a bear comes out of the woods to eat grain that is being loaded into a hopper on a westbound train. When the bear finishes eating, he lies down on the train. Jeffrey tries to warn the bear to get off the train before it leaves because he will freeze when it snows, get wet when it rains, be scared in tunnels, and worry his friends. But the bear doesn't listen, and soon he is westbound from the prairies through the mountains to the coast. The bear continues to crisscross the country on a traveling hibernation, until he smells spring. Then, as Jeffrey watches, the bear returns to the woods to eat. This simple story is written in a lyrical style that reads like poetry. The rich oil illustrations help establish both setting and character while providing a lush travelogue for the bear's cross-country trek.

**20.8** Livingstone, Star. **Harley.** Illustrated by Molly Bang. SeaStar, 2001. ISBN 1-58717-048-5. Unpaged. (P).

When the reader meets the llama named Harley, he is living on a ranch and being trained to be a pack animal. The training is not going well, but fortunately for Harley there is a shepherd in a big field whose sheep need to be protected from wolves. Harley gets the job. Simple sentences and a playful tone invite readers into the daily life of Harley the llama. The illustrations add humor and detail. Information about the author on the jacket flap reveals that Harley is a real llama.

**20.9** McCully, Emily Arnold. **Four Hungry Kittens.** Dial, 2001. ISBN 0-8037-2505-1. Unpaged. (P).

In this wordless picture book, four hungry kittens play in the barn as their mother goes out to hunt for food. While the mother cat is away, the hungry kittens get into mischief and a bit of danger. Fortunately, they have a watchful friend who protects them when needed and helps their mother eventually return to them. For wordless storybooks to work, they have to do two things well: develop the characters and establish a clear plotline. This book succeeds on both counts. In addition, with subsequent readings, children will be able to elaborate on the characters and plot as they discover subtleties in the illustrations.

**20.10**  McNamee, Graham. **Nothing Wrong with a Three-Legged Dog.** Delacorte, 2000. ISBN 0-385-32755-2. 134 pp. (I).

Keath is used to being called "ghost" or "vanilla" or "whitey." He's the only white kid in his fourth-grade class. His best friend Lynda is called "zebra" because her father is white and her mother is African American. Keath and Lynda share a love of animals, particularly dogs. After school they work for Lynda's mother, who is a veterinarian. Their favorite dog is Lynda's three-legged dog Leftovers. Through his work with Leftovers, Keath discovers that it is permissible to stand out and that, even though he looks different, there are still ways to fit in. This story provides a realistic and humorous look at friendships, both human and animal.

**20.11**  Rossiter, Nan Parson. **The Way Home.** Dutton, 1999. ISBN 0-525-45767-4. Unpaged. (P).

In late October, Samuel and his father discover an injured Canadian goose. As they are carrying her back to the house, they notice that her mate is nearby. Both geese become their guests as the female recuperates. After a few weeks, she is strong enough to fly, and both geese leave right before the first snow. Through the winter, Samuel and his father talk about the geese and wonder if they made it to a southern haven. In spring the geese return with their family. This story realistically depicts the habits of Canadian geese. It also shows an appropriate interaction between humans and wild animals. The full-page golden-hued illustrations help establish setting and mood. Each page of text has a small inset illustration of some aspect of the environment—the geese's nest, crocuses popping up through the snow, flowering chicory—that informs as it enhances the story.

**20.12**  Tafuri, Nancy. **Silly Little Goose!** Scholastic, 2001. ISBN 0-439-06304-3. Unpaged. (P).

On a windy morning, a goose sets out to explore the farm in search of a good place to make a nest. Every time she finds a place that seems to suit her needs, another animal is occupying it. In the end, she finds a spot that is just right. The ideal nest has been there for the goose (and the reader) to discover all along. The large print, the limited text, and the repeated refrain make this book perfect for a read-aloud and subsequent independent reading for emergent and beginning readers. The map of the farm at the beginning of the book and the various nooks and crannies explored by the goose make this a good book for discussions about farm life.

**20.13** Waddell, Martin. **A Kitten Called Moonlight.** Candlewick, 2001. ISBN 0-7638-1176-X. Unpaged. (P).

Charlotte's favorite story is about a little girl and her mother rescuing a kitten on a cold winter night. Charlotte likes this story so much because it is *her* story, the story of how her kitten, Moonlight, came into her life. This gentle story is as much about the bond and trust between Charlotte and her mother as it is about the kitten they rescue together. The realistic pastel chalk illustrations extend the story and help establish the gentle mood. Further, the large print and double-page spreads make this a good choice for a read-aloud in the primary grades.

## Animals in Modern Fantasy

**20.14** Avi. **Ereth's Birthday.** Illustrated by Brian Floca. HarperCollins, 2000. ISBN 0-380-97734-6. 180 pp. (ALL).

This story, fourth in the Tales from the Dimwood Forest series, takes the reader to Dimwood Forest on a special day. It is the birthday of Erethizon Dorsatum, or Ereth, as he calls himself. Ereth is a smelly, grumpy, self-centered old porcupine. When his friends seem to have forgotten his birthday completely, Ereth takes off to treat himself to some salt, his very favorite thing. On his birthday adventure, Ereth is stalked by a fisher, encounters fur hunters, makes a promise to a dying fox, and temporarily adopts the fox's family. The story is fast paced and builds to a satisfying climax and denouement. Although personified, the animal characters are developed so thoughtfully that readers will feel they are learning a bit of natural history. It is not necessary to have read the other books in the series to understand this story, but readers may want to visit the others to enjoy more adventures of Ereth and his friends.

★ Browne, Anthony. **Willy's Pictures.** Candlewick, 2000. ISBN 0-7636-0962-5. Unpaged. (ALL). (See **11.6.**)

20.15    ★ Child, Lauren. **Beware of the Storybook Wolves.** Scholastic, 2000. ISBN 0-439-20500-X. Unpaged. (ALL).

When Herb's mother reads bedtime stories about big bad wolves, he always asks her to take the book (and its wolf inhabitants) when she leaves the room for the night. One night she forgets, and two very unpleasant wolves make their way out of the book and into Herb's room. A wicked fairy and a disgruntled fairy godmother complicate matters as Herb tries to outwit his unwanted visitors. This story artfully mixes several folktale motifs with modern sensibilities to create a delightfully clever spoof. Readers with folk and fairy tale experience will have fun discovering connections to "Little Red Riding Hood," "Cinderella," "Sleeping Beauty," "Hansel and Gretel."

20.16    Collington, Peter. **Clever Cat.** Knopf, 2000. ISBN 0-375-90477. Unpaged. (P).

Tibs the cat runs out of patience with his busy human family. He is tired of waiting to be let in and out and waiting to be fed, so he decides to take control of his life. When Tibs jumps up on the counter, opens his own cat food, and feeds himself, his family is impressed. They are so impressed that they give him a door key and a cash card to do his own shopping. When he starts eating out and going to movies, his family takes his cash card away and makes him get a job. Tibs discovers what the other cats in the neighborhood who snooze in the sun all day already know—it is possible to be too clever. The humorous, detailed illustrations are a perfect match for this funny story. The circular plot and almost explicit theme make it a good vehicle for basic discussions of these literary elements.

20.17    Elliott, David. **The Transmogrification of Roscoe Wizzle.** Candlewick, 2001. ISBN 0-7636-1173-5. 155 pp. (I).

To transmogrify means "to change or transform, especially into something funny or comical." Unfortunately for Roscoe Wizzle, he discovers that he has begun to transmogrify into a bug. Several coincidences in relation to Roscoe's change—the opening of a Gussy's fast food restaurant, the disappearance of several children, and the covering up of a toxic dump—provide clues for Roscoe and his best friend Kinchy as they try to find the cause of Roscoe's transmogrification. That sounds like a heavy load for one story, but the tone is so light and the situations so absurd that the results are good fun. With Roscoe narrating his recollections of the events, the reader is reassured from the beginning that all ends well.

20.18   Garland, Michael. **Last Night at the Zoo.** Boyds Mills, 2001. ISBN 1-56397-759-1. Unpaged. (P).

It's night at the zoo and the animals are restless, so they decide to go out for an adventure. Using coins from the seal and walrus pool and clothes from the zoo's lost-and-found, they catch a bus and head into town. Their table manners get them thrown out of the Cafe Paree, but they fit right in at the Club Boogie, where they create a new dance. After a late snack at Joe's Diner, they catch a bus, head back to the zoo, and arrive just as the sun is rising. The animals enjoy their adventure so much that they begin planning their next night's outing. The rhymed text and the bold, humorous illustrations invite repeated readings. The open ending will encourage readers to tell or write the next installment of the animals' adventures.

20.19   Gray, Kes, and Mary McQuillan. **The "Get Well Soon" Book: Good Wishes for Bad Times.** Millbrook, 2000. ISBN 0-7613-1435-0. Unpaged. (P).

It's never fun to be sick or injured. Just ask Cynthia the centipede, who sprained ninety-eight ankles playing field hockey, or Danny the dalmatian, who broke out in spots. Paul the python isn't very happy either since a gorilla tied him in a knot. And how about Connie the crocodile, who broke her tooth biting a rhino? Each of these unfortunate creatures and a few others get a double-spread illustration that shows the infirmity and the event that precipitated it. The text is limited, featuring two sentences per animal. The cartoonlike illustrations are bright, playful, and add details not in the text. Happily, all of the animals listen to their doctor, take their medicine, and get better in the end.

20.20   Halls, Kelly Milner. **I Bought a Baby Chicken.** Illustrated by Karen Stromer Brooks. Boyds Mills, 2000. ISBN 1-56397-800-8. Unpaged. (P).

After a little girl buys a chick at the general store, her sister buys two more, her father buys three more, and her mother buys four.

When the grandma, grandpa, cousin, and other extended family members join the buying spree, they finally end up with more than fifty chickens. In the end, the little girl thinks her family is lucky that she didn't want a cow. The rhymed counting format, the large print, and the humorous illustrations make this a good book for emerging readers and mathematicians.

20.21 ★ Jennings, Richard. **Orwell's Luck.** Houghton Mifflin, 2000. ISBN 0-618-03628-8. 146 pp. (I).

When a girl finds an injured rabbit sprawled across the morning paper on her lawn, she assumes it is a victim of an overzealous delivery man who "associated high speed with professional achievement" (p. 4). She names the rabbit Orwell, takes it into her life, and then discovers that he is a rabbit of many hidden talents. Orwell begins to send her coded messages, mostly through the horoscope in the newspaper: the final score of the Super Bowl game before it is played, warning of a pop quiz at school, and the winning lottery number. Circumstances keep her from cashing in on most of this good fortune, but they don't keep her from believing in Orwell's magic. This is a genuine and satisfying story about love, kindness, and hope in a world in which fortune and fate occasionally collide.

20.22 King-Smith, Dick. **Lady Lollipop.** Illustrated by Jill Barton. Candlewick, 2001. ISBN 0-7636-1269-3. 120 pp. (I).

Princess Penelope is a spoiled and unpleasant child. As her eighth birthday approaches, her parents ask what she wants for her birthday. She can, of course, have anything. Penelope wants a pig. The king proclaims that every pig keeper in the kingdom must bring one pig to the palace on Penelope's birthday. She chooses the scruffiest, ugliest pig of all, who happens to be the smartest too. Fortunately for Penelope, the pig and her trainer help the king and queen see the pig's value while helping Penelope become less spoiled. The story is light and fun, and the interspersed sketchlike illustrations add to the humor and help develop the characters.

20.23 Lauber, Patricia. **Purrfectly Purrfect: Life at the Acatemy.** Illustrated by Betsy Lewin. HarperCollins, 2000. ISBN 0-688-17299-7. 78 pp. (ALL).

It's the first day for the new class at The Acatemy, a school for cats. The Acatemy was founded by Purrfessor F. Catus of the

University of Catifornia, who believes that "the proper study of cats is cats" (p. 6). The purriculum includes everything from Cats in Nature (catnip, cattail, dandelion) to Cats in Geography (Catskill Mountains, Catalonia, Connecticat). But there is something wrong with this class, something that might ruin The Acatemy's purrfect record of having all purrfect graducats. A kitten named Dudley has followed his brother and sister to school. The school doesn't have a kittengarten, and Dudley can't keep up in the regular classes. Fortunately, the head teacher devises a way to keep Dudley and save The Acatemy's reputation. Readers will find this book outrageously "punny" and might even be inspired to use imaginative language play in their own stories.

20.24  ★ McPhail, David. **Drawing Lessons from a Bear.** Little, Brown, 2000. ISBN 0-316-56345-5. Unpaged. (P).

When the bear was young, his mother taught him to be a bear. Yet even at an early age, the bear loved to draw. He's a big bear now, but he is also an artist. In this story, the bear describes his development as an artist as he encourages young listeners and readers to think of themselves as artists too. The story is gentle and encouraging without being sentimental or preachy. Bear even uses the endpapers to teach by decorating them with a lush pencil drawing of a tree, with notes from bear about his drawing process.

20.25  Ryan, Pam Muñoz. **Mice and Beans.** Illustrated by Joe Capita. Scholastic, 2001. ISBN 0-439-18303-0. Unpaged. (P).

Rosa Maria loves to fix big meals for her big family in her tiny house. Her own mother used to say: "When there's room in the heart, there's room in the house, except for a mouse." As she prepares a meal in honor of her youngest grandchild's birthday, Rosa Maria makes a list of chores to be done so she won't forget anything. Yet she seems to be forgetting to put out a mousetrap—or has she? After the party, Rosa Maria discovers that the mice were helpful and that she has been remembering her mother's saying all wrong. What her mother actually said was: "When there's room in the heart, there's room in the house, even for a mouse." Rosa Maria decides never to set a trap again. The double-page spread illustration at the end of the story provides a satisfying conclusion and rewards readers who have been "reading" the illustrations closely.

**20.26** Wahl, Jan. **The Field Mouse and the Dinosaur Named Sue.** Illustrated by Bob Doucet. Scholastic, 2000. ISBN 0-439-09984-6. Unpaged. (ALL).

This book provides a "mouse eye view" of the discovery, lab analysis, and reconstruction of Sue, the largest and most complete *Tyrannosaurus rex* ever found. The story begins in the hills of South Dakota, where a tiny field mouse has been using one of Sue's bones as a roof for its home. When Sue is discovered and transported to the Field Museum in Chicago, the mouse goes along to find its bone. The mouse and the reader explore the laboratories and exhibits of the museum in search of food, water, shelter, and the bone. The story provides a basic insider's view of the museum and the reconstruction process. A note at the end of the book briefly describes the true story of Sue. By focusing on the mouse's perspective and introducing the information about Sue through the story, the author makes this very large topic more accessible to young readers. At the same time, enough information is provided so that the book is a satisfactory introduction to the topic for more sophisticated readers.

# 21 Solving Mysteries and Puzzles

**Diane E. Bushner and Jo Ann Brewer**

*Contributing reviewers included Andrew Allen, Donna Brady, Lisa Ellis, Elisa LaSota, and Jennifer D. Tress.*

---

**Criteria for Excellence**

- Engages the reader in trying to solve the mystery
- Plot that holds the reader's interest
- Straightforward characters
- Authentic settings
- Action and humor
- Enjoyable reading

---

## Mysteries

Cutler, Jane. **'Gator Aid.** Illustrated by Tracey Campbell Pearson. Farrar, Straus & Giroux, 1999.

★ DeFelice, Cynthia. **Death at Devil's Bridge.** Farrar, Straus & Giroux, 2000.

Duffey, Betsy. **Cody Unplugged.** Illustrated by Ellen Thompson. Viking, 1999.

★ Hearne, Betsy. **Who's in the Hall? A Mystery in Four Chapters.** Illustrated by Christy Hale. Greenwillow, 2000.

Johnson, Angela. **When Mules Flew on Magnolia Street.** Illustrated by John Ward. Knopf, 2000.

Jones, Elizabeth M. **Mystery on Skull Island.** Pleasant Company, 2001.

Kellogg, Steven. **The Missing Mitten Mystery.** Dial, 2000.

Naylor, Phyllis Reynolds. **Carlotta's Kittens and the Club of Mysteries.** Illustrated by Alan Daniel. Atheneum, 2000.

Nixon, Joan Lowery. **Gus & Gertie and the Missing Pearl.** Illustrated by Diane deGroat. SeaStar, 2000.

Palatini, Margie. **The Web Files.** Illustrated by Richard Egielski. Hyperion, 2001.

Stanley, Diane. **The Mysterious Matter of I. M. Fine.** HarperCollins, 2001.

Walsh, Ellen Stoll. **Dot & Jabber and the Great Acorn Mystery.** Harcourt, 2001.

★ Weigelt, Udo. **Who Stole the Gold?** Illustrated by Julia Gukova. Translated by J. Alison James. North-South Books, 2000.

## How to Solve a Mystery

Dickson, Louise. **Lu & Clancy's Crime Science.** Illustrated by Pat Cupples. Kids Can Press, 1999.

Mahr, Juli. **The Mailbox Mice Mystery.** Illustrated by Graham Percy. Random House, 1999.

Sobol, Donald J. **Encyclopedia Brown and the Case of the Slippery Salamander.** Illustrated by Warren Chang. Delacorte, 1999.

## Detectives

Adler, David A. **Cam Jansen and the Barking Treasure Mystery.** Illustrated by Susanna Natti. Viking, 1999.

Hale, Bruce. **Farewell, My Lunchbag: From the Tattered Casebook of Chet Gecko, Private Eye.** Harcourt, 2001.

Roy, Ron. **The Invisible Island.** Illustrated by John Steven Gurney. Random House, 1999.

Rylant, Cynthia. **The Case of the Climbing Cat.** Illustrated by G. Brian Karas. Greenwillow, 2000.

Sharmat, Marjorie Weinman. **Nate the Great and the Monster Mess.** Illustrated by Martha Weston. Delacorte, 1999.

Stanley, George E. **The Clue of the Left-Handed Envelope.** Illustrated by Salvatore Murdocca. Aladdin, 2000.

★ Van Draanen, Wendelin. **Sammy Keyes and the Hollywood Mummy.** Knopf, 2001.

Yep, Laurence. **Case of the Firecrackers.** HarperCollins, 1999.

## Ghosts, Magic, and Monsters

Amato, Mary. **The Word Eater.** Illustrated by Christopher Ryniak. Holiday House, 2000.

Cuyler, Margery. **The Battlefield Ghost.** Illustrated by Arthur Howard. Scholastic, 1999.

Guiberson, Brenda Z. **Tales of the Haunted Deep.** Holt, 2000.

★ Seabrooke, Brenda. **Haunting at Stratton Falls.** Dutton, 2000.

Shreve, Susan. **Ghost Cats.** Scholastic, 1999.

★ Strickland, Brad. **John Bellairs's Lewis Barnavelt in The Beast under the Wizard's Bridge.** Dial, 2000.

### Puzzles

Clements, Gillian. **Into the Under World.** Candlewick, 1999.

Garland, Michael. **Mystery Mansion: A Look Again Book.** Dutton, 2001.

Gorbachev, Valeri. **Where Is the Apple Pie?** Philomel, 2000.

Marzollo, Jean. **I Spy Treasure Hunt: A Book of Picture Riddles.** Photographs by Walter Wick. Scholastic, 1999.

Nilsen, Anna. **Mousemazia: An Amazing Dream House Maze.** Illustrated by Dom Mansell. Candlewick, 2000.

Spires, Elizabeth. **Riddle Road: Puzzles in Poems and Pictures.** Illustrated by Erik Blegvad. Margaret K. McElderry Books, 1999.

Steiner, Joan. **Look-Alikes, Jr.** Photographs by Thomas Lindley. Little, Brown, 1999.

---

Mysteries and puzzles involve readers in solving something. The focus of a mystery is finding out "who did it" or "what happened." Quality mysteries have a problem to be solved, well-developed characters, fast-paced action, and a logical solution to the problem. The solution is often foreshadowed through careful presentation of clues. By examining the clues carefully, readers are often able to predict the solution or solve the mystery before the author discloses the solution. This active quest for a solution is what makes mysteries popular with children.

In some mystery stories, specific detectives play a role in solving the mystery or in figuring out the clues. Mysteries for children offer a tradition of well-known detectives who inhabit children's books, from Nate the Great and Cam Jansen to the more contemporary Sammy Keyes and the trio of Josh, Dink, and Ruth Rose, the detectives in all of the A to Z mysteries. Most of these fictional detectives appear in a series of books, and children enjoy the predictability of the series and the knowledge that the detective character will solve the mystery.

Mysteries are classified as part of the genre of realistic fiction despite the fact that ghosts, magic, and monsters sometimes appear. Otherworldly creatures enter the contemporary realistic world of fiction and cause incongruities, but these creatures usually assist or enable a realistic character to solve the mystery, allowing the stories to maintain a sense of realism.

This chapter reviews books in five major categories: mysteries; how to solve a mystery; detectives; ghosts, magic, and monsters; and puzzles.

*Mysteries.* Books in this category include stories that have a strong plot driven by the need to find out who did something or what happened. Mysteries contain a character or multiple characters who are involved in determining what happened or who did what in the story. Part of solving the mystery is determining who has the needed information to solve the problem. A good mystery has enough clues that a careful reader can follow them, and the endings are not so contrived that all the threads of the story are wrapped up without any advance clues.

*How to Solve a Mystery.* A subcategory of mysteries for children is the "how to solve a mystery," or books containing specific activities that allow children to practice identifying the clues. This category is indigenous to children's literature and is not found in comparable adult literature. The focus of these books is to help the reader learn how to go about solving a mystery. Often the author examines the clues presented to help the reader determine if they contain needed or related information or if the author has thrown in a red herring.

*Detectives.* Detective stories are defined as books with strong detective characters who specialize in solving mysteries. Many of the crime solvers in children's books are well known to the readers. Children can predict before the book is read that the detective will solve the mystery, because the crime solver is part of a series of books featuring the same character who always solves the mystery. Some of the best known of these detectives are Cam Jansen, Nate the Great, and Encyclopedia Brown. Each of these characters has his or her own style of solving a mystery. Nate the Great, for example, works with his dog Sludge and makes a mess before the mystery is solved, whereas Cam Jansen successfully solves mysteries using her photographic memory.

*Ghosts, Magic, and Monsters.* Books in this category combine contemporary realistic settings and characters with unexplainable happenings that are caused by the existence of a ghost, magic, or a monster. The ghost, magic, or monster comes into the contemporary realistic setting, often from hundreds of years ago, and aids the realistic character in solving the mystery.

*Puzzles.* Puzzle books present a variety of puzzles to be solved. Most contemporary puzzle books rely heavily on a visual element. For the video generation, many puzzle books have visual elements that need to be analyzed or "read" in order for the reader to solve the puzzle.

## Mysteries

**21.1**  Cutler, Jane. **'Gator Aid.** Illustrated by Tracey Campbell Pearson. Farrar, Straus & Giroux, 1999. ISBN 0-374-32502-2. 134 pp. (I).

*'Gator Aid* is another adventure with second grader Edward Fraser and his older brother Jason. During school vacation, while looking at the lake through binoculars, Edward believes he sees an alligator. No one believes him, but the story is spread by other children and becomes more exaggerated without Edward's help. Everyone in town seems to have a different version of what is in the lake, so a professional alligator catcher is brought to town to help solve the mystery. With conflicting information, the task is more challenging than the alligator catcher imagined. Is there really something in the lake, or does Edward just have an active imagination? The author describes the events in the story from Edward's second-grade point of view, making them appealing to young readers. (DEB)

**21.2**  ★ DeFelice, Cynthia. **Death at Devil's Bridge.** Farrar, Straus & Giroux, 2000. ISBN 0-374-31723-2. 134 pp. (I).

Set in Martha's Vineyard, this novel focuses on thirteen-year-old Ben Daggert and the choices he makes. Ben has a summer job working as first mate on a charter fishing boat. While sailing, he discovers a submerged car. Ben begins to wonder about his sixteen-year-old friend Donny's role in the car submersion. Donny hires Ben and Jeff to deliver packages to summer residents on their bicycles for fifteen dollars a trip. These packages, however, turn out to contain illegal drugs. Then Ben and Jeff discover a body at Devil's Bridge and wonder if Donny is involved in the murder. Who is the gun-wielding adult looking for Donny? Although Ben makes inappropriate choices, he has his mother and police officers standing by to offer adult guidance without preaching to him. This book is well written, keeping the reader guessing all through the story. (DEB)

**21.3**   Duffey, Betsy. **Cody Unplugged.** Illustrated by Ellen Thompson. Viking, 1999. ISBN 0-670-88592-4. 96 pp. (P).

Cody's parents send him to summer camp for a week because he is becoming too dependent on television and video games. Knowing that he has to survive without electricity at camp, he reads a book called *Wilderness Survival* on the bus ride. At camp, Cody faces one challenge after another, from passing a swimming test, to getting a Native American name, to listening to ghost stories around the campfire, to hiking overnight to Bear Mountain, where Cody's camp group encounters a dangerous intruder. Will the campers know what to do? This book is a favorite with children who have read earlier titles about Cody Michaels. Consistent with earlier titles, Cody gets along well with the children he meets. (DEB)

**21.4**   ★ Hearne, Betsy. **Who's in the Hall? A Mystery in Four Chapters.** Illustrated by Christy Hale. Greenwillow, 2000. ISBN 0-688-16262-2. 32 pp. (P).

This mystery is set in an apartment house. Two families hire a babysitter to take care of the children. One babysitter leaves Lizzy and her two dogs alone for a few minutes. Lizzy hears a knock on the door and remembers not to open the door when someone claiming to be the janitor appears in the hall. This scenario is played out again when Rowan and Ryan and their pet rat are alone briefly. Finally, the two babysitters, three children, and three pets meet and plan to go to the roof. The janitor knocks again, and the babysitters find out who is in the hall. The illustrations portray the view through the peephole in the door in an insightful and consistent way. The cartoon-style illustrations convey the humor of the story, as do the choices of character names. (DEB)

**21.5**   Johnson, Angela. **When Mules Flew on Magnolia Street.** Illustrated by John Ward. Knopf, 2000. ISBN 0-679-89077-7. 105 pp. (I).

In this collection of interrelated short stories by Angela Johnson, two-time Coretta Scott King Award winner, Charlie, a young girl who lives on Magnolia Street, is the unifying force. Although it is only Charlie's second summer at her Magnolia Street address, she displays a strong sense of ownership of her neighborhood as she seeks to solve the mystery of what happened to the family next door. She discovers that the new family knows how to perform magic; experiences adventures with a new friend, Ashley; and learns of camp adventures through Billy's and Lump's experiences. Charlie solves problems, investigates, and manages everyone's life on Magnolia Street. The charcoal black-and-white line drawings highlight the imagery of the text. Individual short stories are a good read for children who might be daunted by the size of chapter books. (DEB)

**21.6**  Jones, Elizabeth M. **Mystery on Skull Island.** Pleasant Company, 2001. ISBN 1-68485-341-7. 173 pp. (I).

One of the series of "history mysteries," mystery stories set in historical times and places, this book is set in Charles Town, South Carolina, in 1724. Rachel had been living in New York with her grandparents, but her father has finally sent for her to come to South Carolina to live with him. Rachel and her new friends begin exploring an island and find evidence of pirate activity. They manage to get help and solve the mystery of what the pirates are doing on the island. While Rachel is involved with the pirate mystery, she is also trying to unravel the involvement of her future stepmother with the pirates. The action will interest readers, and the details of the setting will give them a flavor of life on the American coast in 1724. Two pages of factual information are included at the end of the book. (DEB/JAB)

**21.7**  Kellogg, Steven. **The Missing Mitten Mystery.** Dial, 2000. ISBN 0-8037-2566-3. Unpaged. (P).

While Annie and her dog Oscar are playing in the snow, she discovers that she has lost one of her red mittens. This makes a total of five mittens lost this year. Annie returns to all the places she played to look for her mitten. Each time she finds something else that is red, but it is not her mitten. Where could the mitten be? Steven Kellogg's ink-and-pencil line drawings with watercolor washes enhance the story. The pictures have less line-and-ink detail than most of Kellogg's illustrations, making this book a good choice for a read-aloud for kindergarten children. The cover of the book is worth an extended look, as it provides some clues to the mysterious disappearance of the red mitten. (DEB)

**21.8**  Naylor, Phyllis Reynolds. **Carlotta's Kittens and the Club of Mysteries.** Illustrated by Alan Daniel. Atheneum, 2000. ISBN 0-689-83269-9. 131 pp. (I).

This is the third adventure of a set of feline characters introduced in *The Grand Escape* (1993) and *The Healing of Texas Jake* (1997). The male cats in the Club of Mysteries are looking for Carlotta. Once she has her kittens, they know they have to protect the kittens from being taken to the pound by teaching them the skills they need for survival. The kittens are taught to hunt for food, walk in line, and pounce. After an outing, Catnip, one of the kittens, is missing. Will Catnip be found? What will happen to the litter of kittens since Carlotta's master doesn't want any more cats? Young readers will find the answer satisfying. (DEB)

21.9    Nixon, Joan Lowery. **Gus & Gertie and the Missing Pearl.** Illustrated by Diane deGroat. SeaStar, 2000. ISBN 1-58717-022-1. 48 pp. (P).

This chapter book presents the story of Gus and Gertie's vacation on Holiday Island, which promises to be elegant. The two penguins dress in their best vacation clothes, and Gertie even wears her valuable deep-sea pearl. The dock is deserted when they arrive, and there is no taxi driver in sight. Once it starts to rain, they take shelter in an old hotel, along with some wayward characters, even though they have been warned about the Bad Guys. Soon Gertie's pearl is missing, but because of all the photographs Gus took, they have some clues as to who took the pearl. A motorcycle officer arrives and takes charge of the investigation. He takes Gus and Gertie to the hotel where they had a reservation. Will Gertie's pearl be found, and will the hotel be as elegant as it claims? This book is a good choice for children just moving into chapter books. (DEB)

21.10    Palatini, Margie. **The Web Files.** Illustrated by Richard Egielski. Hyperion, 2001. ISBN 0-7868-2366-6. 32 pp. (P).

This clever takeoff on the old TV show *Dragnet* finds Ducktective Web investigating the case of the missing peck of purple, almost-pickled peppers, the missing tub of tartest tasty tomatoes, and the missing load of luscious leafy lettuce. Little Boy Blue has an alibi but no witnesses. Jack Horner swears he was in his corner. Little Miss Muffet has been tossed off her tuffet, and some gal named Peep is missing some sheep. Just as in the TV show, the time is listed as the ducktectives go about their work, and each segment ends with "dum de dum dum." Even though the children will not remember *Dragnet,* they will enjoy the humor and the repetitive dum de dum dum. This book was carefully designed; even the font chosen for the text resembles the typing that would have been used to file police reports years ago. (JAB)

**21.11**  Stanley, Diane. **The Mysterious Matter of I. M. Fine.** Harper-Collins, 2001. ISBN 0-688-17546-5. 201 pp. (I).

This mystery is the second novel of noted nonfiction author Diane Stanley. Strange things have been happening during the school year to some members of the student body at Franny's elementary school. Finally, Franny and a classmate, Beamer, realize there is a common element among the children who are experiencing strange sensations: they are all avid readers of I. M. Fine's chiller series. Franny and Beamer know the adults will not believe their theory, so they set about trying to discover the reason for the students' reactions to the books by devoting their summer to solving the mystery of who I. M. Fine is. They do a lot of detective work, but most surprising is the adult they call on to help them solve the mystery and prevent further harm to the readers of I. M. Fine's books. (DEB/JAB)

**21.12**  Walsh, Ellen Stoll. **Dot & Jabber and the Great Acorn Mystery.** Harcourt, 2001. ISBN 0-15-202602-9. Unpaged. (P).

This is a mystery for the youngest children, who are more likely to be listeners than readers. Walsh's well-known mouse characters are detectives trying to find out how a little oak tree has grown on one side of the meadow. They know that oak trees grow from acorns and that acorns grow on big oak trees, so they set off to find out how an acorn got from the big oak tree all the way across the meadow to start a new oak tree. They ultimately solve the mystery and then decide to eat the leftover clues. Walsh includes one page of factual information about acorns and oak trees at the end of the book. (DEB/JAB)

**21.13**  ★ Weigelt, Udo. **Who Stole the Gold?** Illustrated by Julia Gukova. Translated by J. Alison James. North-South, 2000. ISBN 0-7358-1372-8. Unpaged. (P).

Hamster discovers that his gold is missing from his home when he tries to show his shiny gold to Hedgehog. Together they set out to investigate the problem of the missing gold, asking each animal they meet along the way if they stole anything from Hamster's house. Eventually, Hedgehog determines who stole the gold and catches the animal returning it. The text is written so that observant listeners will be able to solve the mystery before the author reveals the answer. This book is a great read-aloud for first graders, who can solve the mystery if they listen carefully to the text. The illustrations enhance the tale and help the reader visualize the many animals and the outcome of the story. (DEB)

## How to Solve a Mystery

**21.14** Dickson, Louise. **Lu & Clancy's Crime Science.** Illustrated by Pat Cupples. Kids Can Press, 1999. ISBN 1-55074-552-2. 40 pp. (P).

In another of the series about Lu and Clancy, two dog detectives, Lu and Clancy present short vignettes on how to solve mysteries. In each, they present an activity to show readers how to practice some of the skills needed to be a detective. As Lu and Clancy try to find Dottie's missing puppies, they model skills such as collecting fingerprints and lip prints, analyzing different types of pens, making molds of footprints, taking an impression of a bite, and collecting evidence from hair samples. All the activities clearly describe the materials that are needed to analyze the evidence and offer clear directions as to how an aspiring detective might perform the analysis. At the end of the book, the author presents a series of clues on each suspect. The reader compares them to the evidence and then selects the guilty dognapper. (DEB)

**21.15** Mahr, Juli. **The Mailbox Mice Mystery.** Illustrated by Graham Percy. Random House, 1999. ISBN 0-679-88603-6. Unpaged. (P).

This introductory book explicitly models how to solve a mystery and provides hands-on fun for its young readers. Watson Mouse receives a package in the mail containing a booklet on how to be a famous detective. Likewise, when readers turn the page, they find an envelope with a copy of the detective manual that they can remove and read. Watson Mouse discovers that cheese is missing from his refrigerator and seeks to follow the five rules for being a detective as he attempts to solve the mystery. Throughout the book, readers discover envelopes holding removable clue cards and even a mirror. Finally, Watson Mouse solves the mystery, and readers can remove Watson Mouse's junior detective badge from its envelope. The envelopes with manipulative pieces engage readers more fully in the story line, and the colorful pen-and-ink illustrations of the mice bring the characters to life. (DEB/JAB)

21.16   Sobol, Donald J. **Encyclopedia Brown and the Case of the Slippery Salamander.** Illustrated by Warren Chang. Delacorte, 1999. ISBN 0-385-32579-7. 87 pp. (P).

Well-known crime solver Encyclopedia Brown returns to solve ten more cases. Often during the school year, Encyclopedia helps his father—who is with the police department—solve cases. During the summer, Encyclopedia heads up his own detective agency. For each of the ten short cases, the case is discussed, Encyclopedia observes some clues, and he then offers specific help in solving the case. After readers attempt to explain what Encyclopedia means by his clues, they are then referred to a specific page in the book for the solution to the case, allowing them to compare their version with the reasoning of supersleuth Encyclopedia Brown. (DEB/JAB)

## Detectives

21.17   Adler, David A. **Cam Jansen and the Barking Treasure Mystery.** Illustrated by Susanna Natti. Viking, 1999. ISBN 0-670-88516-9. 56 pp. (P).

Cam Jansen, with her photographic memory, returns in a new adventure. Cam, along with her pal Eric, his mother, and Mabel Trent, an old friend, is taking a boat ride around the city. Although a sign says that no animals are allowed on the boat, a lady in a red dress brings aboard her poodle, Little Treasure. Eventually, the woman discovers that Little Treasure is missing, and Cam and Eric offer to help her find the dog. As passengers watch the sights coming into view, Cam and Eric watch them closely while Cam activates her photographic memory. Once the dog is found, the next problem is that his jeweled dog collar is missing. Will Cam be able to find the thief and the collar before the boat docks? Most second graders can read this story easily, making it an excellent first mystery for transitional readers. (DEB)

21.18   Hale, Bruce. **Farewell, My Lunchbag: From the Tattered Casebook of Chet Gecko, Private Eye.** Harcourt, 2001. ISBN 0-15-202275-9. 107 pp. (ALL).

The Chet Gecko mystery series contains a variety of unusual characters, including geckos, lizards, cobras, and worms. Someone is stealing food from the school lunchroom during the night. Mrs. Bagoong, who is in charge of the lunchroom, asks fourth grader and private-eye Chet Gecko to solve the mystery. Since he has to attend classes, Chet and his assistant Natalie do not have much time for detective work. Chet plans an all-night stakeout where he will hide in the cafeteria to catch the thief. It is Chet, however, who is surprised and made to look like the thief. Chet is sent to the principal's office and given dishwashing duty and detention for life. As Chet's class takes part in the school open house, Chet notices some unusual things from the stage and takes off in search of the food thief. Who can it be? Many third-grade readers find this series appealing because of its unusual characters and predictability. (DEB)

**21.19**  Roy, Ron. **The Invisible Island.** Illustrated by John Steven Gurney. Random House, 1999. ISBN 0-679-89457-8. 87 pp. (P).

Three friends, Josh, Dink, and Ruth Rose, pack a picnic basket and wade out to Squaw Island. After enjoying their picnic, they explore the island, discovering a one hundred dollar bill. They want to return the money to the person who lost it, so they leave the money at the police station, where Officer Fallon tells them that if no one claims it in thirty days, the money is theirs. The next day they return to the island to look for more money and discover a cement vault containing cash. The three friends follow up on a car license plate and wonder if the people who own the car have anything to do with the money on the island. The three friends ask Officer Fallon to go to the island, where he uncovers criminal dealings. The A to Z Mystery series is popular with second and third graders because of its likeable characters and accessible writing style. (DEB)

**21.20**  Rylant, Cynthia. **The Case of the Climbing Cat.** Illustrated by G. Brian Karas. Greenwillow, 2000. ISBN 0-688-16310-6. 48 pp. (P).

Cynthia Rylant has developed a new series, the High-Rise Private Eyes, about a pair of animal detectives, Bunny Brown and Jack Jones. After an introductory chapter about the two detectives, she describes in detail the case in which Miss Nancy reports that a cat stole her binoculars from her high-rise balcony and then disappeared. In the next chapter, the two detectives assemble the clues, take notes on what they see, and decide to search for the cat at the aviary. In the final chapter, the detectives find the cat at the aviary with the stolen binoculars. This series is in an easy-to-read format and permits young readers to experience a chapter book they can read on their own. Brian Karas's illustrations extend the story, especially his portrayal of the many animal characters. (DEB)

**21.21**  Sharmat, Marjorie Weinman. **Nate the Great and the Monster Mess.** Illustrated by Martha Weston. Delacorte, 1999. ISBN 0-385-32114-7. 48 pp. (P).

Superdetective Nate the Great and his dog Sludge are brought into another case when Nate the Great receives a written note from his mother that she's lost her recipe for Monster Cookies. After searching inside the house, she starts looking outside. Nate the Great decides to search inside the house again and makes a huge mess. He is undaunted, however, and takes Sludge outside in search of more clues. After interviewing Annie and Oliver and going to the fish store, Nate the Great returns home to follow up on his clues. Which clues will help him find the recipe? His only hope of eating those Monster Cookies again is to find the recipe. Will he be successful? Will his mother find the huge mess he made in the house? Second graders find this series appealing for the easy reading style and the messes that Nate always makes. (DEB/JAB)

**21.22**  Stanley, George E. **The Clue of the Left-Handed Envelope.** Illustrated by Salvatore Murdocca. Aladdin, 2000. ISBN 0-689-82194-8. 62 pp. (P).

Mr. Merlin, a former spy, is the new third-grade teacher. He likens going to school to solving mysteries and asks if anyone in the class has a mystery to solve. Amber Lee wants to know who sent her an anonymous envelope. The first step in solving the mystery is to unlock some secret codes that hold clues to the answer. Noelle and Todd are anxious to solve the mystery before Amber Lee does. Between typical school lessons, Mr. Merlin asks additional questions to help the students think about solving the mystery, encouraging them to raise other questions. Noelle comes up with a theory about who sent the envelope that Mr. Merlin accepts, but will that person be found? For a field trip, Mr. Merlin takes the class to the police station to see how the police experts investigate evidence. The series title, Third-Grade Detectives, indicates that this book is meant to appeal to second and third graders. (DEB)

21.23 ★ Van Draanen, Wendelin. **Sammy Keyes and the Hollywood Mummy.** Knopf, 2001. ISBN 0-375-80266-5. 256 pp. (I).

Thirteen-year-old supersleuth Samantha (Sammy) Keyes lives with her grandmother in Kansas while her mother is in Hollywood trying to become a star. Sammy and her friend Marissa decide to visit Mrs. Keyes in Hollywood. Once there, Sammy finds that her mother has changed her name and dyed her hair. While Sammy and Marissa are visiting, the woman who is competing with Sammy's mother for a part in a soap opera is killed. Sammy tries to find out who the murderer is, afraid that it might be her mother. Soon Sammy's focus changes as she decides that her mother was the intended victim. The murder is complex and Sammy keeps trying to solve the case, believing that her mother is in danger. Will she be able to act quickly enough to save her mother's life? This series is popular with intermediate readers because of the sophisticated plots and believable dialogue. (DEB)

21.24 Yep, Laurence. **Case of the Firecrackers.** HarperCollins, 1999. ISBN 0-06-024449-6. 179 pp. (I).

Auntie Tiger Lil, a former movie star, returns once again to solve a case in Chinatown in Yep's Chinatown Mystery series. Television's biggest star, Clark Tom, is in town to film some scenes. Auntie Tiger Lil takes her great niece Lily, great nephew Chris, and Chris's girlfriend Evie to the set of Clark's show. A loaded gun finds its way into a scene, and an extra is charged with trying to kill Clark. In an effort to clear the extra and remove suspicion from Chris, Auntie has her friends search for clues in the attempted murder. They follow a trail of firecrackers, gangs, and bad food but do not come up with a suspect, so they return to the set where the TV show is being filmed. Will they find the culprit? The Chinese American dialogue rings true in this story, and readers will appreciate the believable character development. (DEB)

## Ghosts, Magic, and Monsters

21.25 Amato, Mary. **The Word Eater.** Illustrated by Christopher Ryniak. Holiday House, 2000. ISBN 0-8234-1468-X. 151 pp. (I).

The focus of this story is Lerner Ghanse, a new student at Cleveland Middle School. Lerner doesn't like her new school and seems destined to be part of the "out" group of students, until she finds a magical worm. By feeding the worm specific words, things disappear, such as the class test, the vending machine, and the dog next door. Lerner begins to see that her actions are not very responsible since innocent people are getting into trouble because of her actions. When a new club is started at school, Lerner is the perceived leader, thanks to the magical powers of the worm. This magical power brings great responsibility; will Lerner be able to harness this power, or will it continue out of control? The school scenes and the short, punchy sentences will appeal to intermediate readers. (DEB)

21.26   Cuyler, Margery. **The Battlefield Ghost.** Illustrated by Arthur Howard. Scholastic, 1999. ISBN 0-590-10848-4. 103 pp. (I).

The Perkins family, including nine-year-old John and his ten-year-old sister Lisa, move into an old house in Princeton, New Jersey, that adjoins one of the Revolutionary War battlefields. John and Lisa have experiences during which they feel the presence of someone else, and they begin to fear that the house is haunted, just as in all those stories they have heard. Even John's teacher recalls an old legend about a Hessian soldier who appears just after midnight every January third. The children continue to have strange experiences in the barn and while riding their horse. They decide to investigate the legend and stay up on January third to meet the ghost face to face. Will they be successful? And what good will it do to meet the ghost? (DEB/JAB)

21.27   Guiberson, Brenda Z. **Tales of the Haunted Deep.** Holt, 2000. ISBN 0-8050-6057-X. 70 pp. (I).

This nonfiction book offers accounts of mysterious maritime happenings during the past two hundred years. These unexplainable events have given rise to numerous ghost stories, and as these stories are told and retold, they have become legends of the sea. Specific chapters focus on various monsters of the sea, including pirate ghosts, sea serpents, lighthouse ghosts, and ships with minds of their own. After recounting all these legends, the author describes five situations, complete with photographs, and encourages readers to tell their own stories based on the situation. Children will enjoy the opportunity to become part of the legends and to compare different tales. The book is well researched, listing a bibliography and an index to help locate specific information. (DEB)

21.28 ★ Seabrooke, Brenda. **Haunting at Stratton Falls.** Dutton, 2000. ISBN 0-525-46389-5. 151 pp. (I).

During World War II, eleven-year-old Abby and her mother move from Florida to Stratton Falls to live with relatives while Abby's father goes to Europe to fight the Nazis. She sees wet footprints in the house, but no one has walked by. After hearing a neighbor tell the story of Felicia's ghostly Christmas visits to the Strafford home, Abby looks for the ghost and sees her around midnight near Christmas. But there is never any communication with the ghost and she soon fades from view. Abby tries to understand the significance of the ghostly visits and fears that someone in Stratton Falls is in danger and the ghost is an omen. What is the significance of this ghost and who is in danger? The strengths of this book are its well-constructed plot and sophisticated subject matter. (DEB)

21.29 Shreve, Susan. **Ghost Cats.** Scholastic, 1999. ISBN 0-590-37131-2. 162 pp. (I).

A young boy with a transient past tells the story of his family life and his love for his cats. He describes the day he found his cat dead under the table. The strangeness of this incident entices the reader to read further. The narrator proceeds to tell of his life after moving to Boston with his three siblings, his mother, and his father, who is a neurologist. Life is supposed to be "normal" there, but it's anything but. The story ends with the siblings' encounter with their dead cats. Are they ghost cats? The family members seem to think so. This story is intriguing because it introduces mystery and a lifestyle that will interest young readers. (DEB)

21.30 ★ Strickland, Brad. **John Bellairs's Lewis Barnavelt in The Beast under the Wizard's Bridge.** Dial, 2000. ISBN 0-8037-2220-6. 151 pp. (I).

Strickland has completed the unfinished manuscript of Bellairs's story. This is another adventure that focuses on the character Lewis Barnavelt, who lives with his uncle. Lewis is concerned that Uncle Jonathan is upset about the old bridge over Wilder Creek being replaced, but his uncle is not one to discuss things with Lewis. So Lewis and his best friend from school, Rose Rita Pottinger, spend most of their summer vacation trying to uncover the real story. They begin with Mrs. Zimmerman, who provides some historical background about the dead magician who once owned the land. Lewis and Rose find themselves in all sorts of adventures as they discover long hidden secrets and a monster that inhabited the area. After learning new information, Lewis and Rose go to tell Uncle Jonathan, but he and Mrs. Zimmerman are at the creek. Will Lewis and Rose get the information to them in time? Readers who have enjoyed the fast-paced plots of Bellair's mysteries will enjoy this one as well. (DEB)

## Puzzles

21.31   Clements, Gillian. **Into the Under World.** Candlewick, 1999. ISBN 0-7636-0686-3. Unpaged. (I).

Readers of this book step into the Under World and must make their way through the nine underground mazes. Each maze portrays a different topic related to the Under World, and readers need to carefully observe the visual effects in order to make it through the mazes. Clearly, readers need a strategy to solve the maze. The back of the book contains guides to solving the mazes as well as an explanation of the many places encountered in each maze. The explanation of the many places in each maze makes for interesting reading, although unfortunately the publisher has placed the maze answer key and the information about the place names on the same page so that readers can't read about the places without seeing the answer to the maze. (DEB)

21.32   Garland, Michael. **Mystery Mansion: A Look Again Book.** Dutton, 2001. ISBN 0-525-46675-4. Unpaged. (P).

Young Tommy receives an invitation from his eccentric aunt to visit her Victorian mansion. When he gets there, however, he cannot find her. Instead, he discovers rhyming clues that guide him through the house while he looks for various animals, birds, the picture gallery, and a maze. The book contains clear textual messages, specific messages written to Tommy by his aunt, and a host of creatures to find in the illustrations. The eccentric aunt is often hidden in the illustrations keeping an eye on Tommy, although Tommy doesn't see her. Will Tommy make the right decisions and find his aunt? The book combines two types of text with a search for various objects. Several children could use the book together to collaborate on finding the clues. (DEB/JAB)

**21.33** Gorbachev, Valeri. **Where Is the Apple Pie?** Philomel, 2000. ISBN 0-399-23385-7. Unpaged. (P).

This picture book is a nonsense tale written in question-and-answer format. Each double page begins with a question at the top of the page and a response at the bottom. The question, not explicitly answered in the text, is "Where is the apple pie?" The detailed pen-and-ink illustrations with watercolor washes provide fertile ground for the reader's search for clues. The reader needs to be visually observant, carrying clues from one page to another. The book is best used with individuals or a small group of children who are able to clearly see the illustrations. Children need to recognize the visual clues from many perspectives or else the meaning of the story is lost. (DEB)

**21.34** Marzollo, Jean. **I Spy Treasure Hunt: A Book of Picture Riddles.** Photographs by Walter Wick. Scholastic, 1999. ISBN 0-439-04244-5. 36 pp. (I).

*I Spy Treasure Hunt* is the tenth book in the popular I Spy series. Walter Wick built a miniature village called Smuggler's Cove and photographed the village from different perspectives, bringing color, depth, and dimension to the illustrations. The task is to locate hidden objects in the photographs. A two-line rhyming verse for each page provides the reader with clues about what to locate in the twelve scenes. Marzollo also provides an extra group of riddles, in which the reader matches the riddle to a specific picture, and offers guidance for readers as they write their own I Spy riddles. The book uses an array of photographs to encourage children to develop language skills as they solve the riddles. The book requires perseverance, and there is no answer key. (JDT)

**21.35** Nilsen, Anna. **Mousemazia: An Amazing Dream House Maze.** Illustrated by Dom Mansell. Candlewick, 2000. ISBN 0-7636-1251-0. Unpaged. (P).

Dottie is a pet mouse who escapes from her cage. The reader needs to follow Dottie through the mouse hole and lead her back to safety. Once through the mouse hole, an array of magic tunnels and twelve challenging mazes await the skill of the reader. On each double-page spread, the author provides information about the location of the maze in the dream house and then provides some explicit clues to follow in navigating the specific maze. The book relies heavily on clues and visual information, which the reader must use to solve the problem. Unlike most other puzzle books, no answer key is provided, so the reader must pay careful attention to the author's clues in order to complete the mazes. (DEB)

21.36  Spires, Elizabeth. **Riddle Road: Puzzles in Poems and Pictures.** Illustrated by Erik Blegvad. Margaret K. McElderry Books, 1999. ISBN 0-689-81783-5. 26 pp. (P).

This book is a collection of twenty-six riddles, many written in rhyme. The detailed watercolor illustrations provide visual clues to assist the reader in solving the riddle in case the text doesn't point to the answer. At the bottom of each page, the answer to the riddle is printed upside down. The riddles are enhanced by the clever text and illustrations, and the guessing game format is enjoyable for both children and adults. This book follows the pattern of an earlier riddle book, *With One White Wing: Puzzles in Poems and Pictures* (1995), by the same author and illustrator team. (DEB)

21.37  Steiner, Joan. **Look-Alikes, Jr.** Photographs by Thomas Lindley. Little Brown, 1999. ISBN 0-316-81307-9. Unpaged. (I).

Steiner creates a sequel to *Look-Alikes* (1998) that challenges a reader's search and identification ability or detective powers in locating all the objects in the brightly colored visual array. Each two-page spread contains the graphic stimulus for readers to identify all fifty-two look-alike objects. A two-line riddle offers a clue about where readers should start focusing attention. The end contains directions for solving the visual puzzles as well as a listing of terms on each double page. The book requires a sophisticated vocabulary in order to name the cleverly disguised objects, as well as patience to locate all the hidden objects. Children particularly enjoy recognizing familiar objects under the disguise of a look-alike. (DEB)

# 22 Traditional Literature

**John Warren Stewig**

*Contributing reviewers included Maggie Amberg, Jan Borden, Judith Cole, Ellen Crozier, Jane DeAngelis, Barbara Franczyk, Nancy Hill, Mayra Sanchez Negron, Michele Oxman, and Marilyn N. Ward.*

---

### Criteria for Excellence

- Visual quality: art that is distinctive in style and/or medium; art that serves the story with distinction
- Language quality: words that "sing in the ear" because of particular word choice, directness, unusual phrases, or comparisons
- Utility: stories that provide insight into cultures either underrepresented or not represented until now
- Book as object: showing obvious, careful, and aesthetic decision making about such production details as paper, binding, and font, among others

---

## Fables

Poole, Amy Lowery. **The Ant and the Grasshopper.** Holiday House, 2000.

Sogabe, Aki. **Aesop's Fox.** Harcourt Brace, 1999.

Watts, Bernadette. **The Lion and the Mouse: An Aesop Fable.** North-South, 2000.

## Single Tales in Picture Book Format

Beneduce, Ann Keay, reteller. **Jack and the Beanstalk.** Illustrated by Gennady Spirin. Philomel, 1999.

★ Bierhorst, John. **The People with Five Fingers: A Native Californian Creation Tale.** Illustrated by Robert Andrew Parker. Marshall Cavendish, 2000.

Chen, Kerstin. **Lord of the Cranes: A Chinese Tale.** Illustrated by Jian Jiang Chen. North-South, 2000.

Diakité, Baba Wagué. **The Hatseller and the Monkeys: A West African Folktale.** Scholastic, 1999.

Goode, Diane. **Cinderella, the Dog and Her Little Glass Slipper.** Scholastic, 2000.

Goode, Diane. **The Dinosaur's New Clothes.** Scholastic, 1999.

★ Hamilton, Virginia. **The Girl Who Spun Gold.** Illustrated by Leo Dillon and Diane Dillon. Scholastic, 2000.

Howland, Naomi. **Latkes, Latkes, Good to Eat: A Chanukah Story.** Clarion, 1999.

Huth, Holly. **The Son of the Sun and Daughter of the Moon: A Saami Folktale.** Illustrated by Anna Vojtech. Atheneum, 2000.

★ Kimmel, Eric A., reteller. **The Rooster's Antlers: A Story of the Chinese Zodiac.** Illustrated by YongSheng Xuan. Holiday House, 1999.

Martin, Rafe. **The Shark God.** Illustrated by David Shannon. Scholastic, 2001.

McDermott, Dennis. **The Golden Goose.** Morrow, 2000.

Mollel, Tololwa M. **Song Bird.** Illustrated by Rosanne Litzinger. Clarion, 1999.

★ Mollel, Tololwa M. **Subira Subira.** Illustrated by Linda Saport. Clarion, 2000.

★ Olaleye, Isaac O. **In the Rainfield: Who Is the Greatest?** Illustrated by Ann Grifalconi. Scholastic, 2000.

Perrault, Charles. **Cinderella: A Fairy Tale.** Illustrated by Loek Koopmans. Translated by Anthea Bell. North-South, 1999.

Perrault, Charles. **Puss in Boots.** Illustrated by Giuliano Lunelli. Retold by Kurt Baumann. Translated by Anthea Bell. North-South, 1999.

Polacco, Patricia. **Luba and the Wren.** Philomel, 1999.

Sanderson, Ruth. **The Golden Mare, the Firebird, and the Magic Ring.** Little, Brown, 2001.

San Souci, Robert D. **Peter and the Blue Witch Baby.** Illustrated by Alexi Natchev. Doubleday, 2000.

Sierra, Judy. **The Dancing Pig.** Illustrated by Jesse Sweetwater. Harcourt Brace, 1999.

Souhami, Jessica. **No Dinner! The Story of the Old Woman and the Pumpkin.** Marshall Cavendish, 2000.

Wahl, Jan. **Little Johnny Buttermilk: After an Old English Folktale.** Illustrated by Jennifer Mazzucco. August House, 1999.

Wattenberg, Jane, reteller. **Henny-Penny.** Illustrated by Jane Wattenberg. Scholastic, 2000.

## Myths and Legends

Bini, Renata, reteller. **A World Treasury of Myths, Legends, and Folktales: Stories from Six Continents.** Illustrated by Mikhail Fiodorov. Abrams, 2000.

Hausman, Gerald, and Loretta Hausman. **Cats of Myths: Tales from around the World.** Illustrated by Leslie Baker. Simon & Schuster, 2000.

Heaney, Marie. **The Names upon the Harp: Irish Myth and Legend.** Illustrated by P. J. Lynch. Scholastic, 2000.

Lattimore, Deborah Nourse. **Medusa.** HarperCollins, 2000.

Mama, Raouf, reteller. **The Barefoot Book of Tropical Tales.** Illustrated by Deidre Hyde. Barefoot, 2000.

Richards, Jean, reteller. **The First Olympic Games: A Gruesome Greek Myth with a Happy Ending.** Illustrated by Kat Thacker. Millbrook, 2000.

Vogel, Carole Garbuny. **Legends of Landforms: Native American Lore and the Geology of the Land.** Millbrook, 1999.

## Collections of Tales

★ Doherty, Berlie. **Fairy Tales.** Illustrated by Jane Ray. Candlewick, 2000.

★ Philip, Neil. **Celtic Fairy Tales.** Illustrated by Isabelle Brent. Viking, 1999.

Schwartz, Howard, and Barbara Bush, retellers. **A Coat for the Moon and Other Jewish Tales.** Illustrated by Michael Lofin. Jewish Publication Society, 1999.

Yolen, Jane. **The Fairies' Ring: A Book of Fairy Stories and Poems.** Illustrated by Stephen Mackey. Dutton, 1999.

Yolen, Jane, collector and reteller. **Not One Damsel in Distress: World Folktales for Strong Girls.** Illustrated by Susan Guevara. Harcourt Brace, 2000.

---

Our committee faced a pleasant dilemma: a plethora of possible books to include in our chapter and a limited space in which to describe the books we chose. Therefore, it became important to develop selection criteria. After much discussion, we arrived at four criteria to use in selecting our examples of traditional literature: visual quality, language quality, utility, and format.

In the visual quality category, we were looking for art that was (1) distinctive and (2) served the tale particularly well. The art might be distinctive in style or medium. Looking at the illustrations, we considered: "Is this a style uncommon in children's books, particularly in traditional literature illustration?" In looking at medium, we considered: "Is this a medium seldom used?" or "Is a familiar medium used in an unexpected, interesting way?" Together, we considered: "Is this use of style or medium memorable in itself?" and "If it is, does it still serve the story without overpowering it?" We tried to avoid books in which the style called undue attention to itself. Related to medium, we tried to avoid books in which the artist's use of medium was exemplary but didn't seem to connect with the author's intent.

In considering language quality, we were interested in books in which the language isn't simply pedestrian but has the potential to "sing" in listeners' ears. Because all the books in this chapter are rooted in oral sources, we read for interesting, sometimes quirky word choices, for a crisp directness, for an unusual, particularly melodic turn of phrase, and for striking comparisons, even in the longer works such as those included in the myths and legends category. In the case of tales that incorporate words from a language other than English, we looked to see that use of such words is integral, not intrusive.

A third criterion we adhered to was utility. That is, does the particular book chosen in some way fill in a gap in the genre of traditional literature? The last two decades has seen published a much wider array of stories from many different sources than previously. While we still revere the works of the Brothers Grimm, Peter Asbjornson and Jörgen Moe, Andrew Lang, and Charles Perrault, we now have a richer choice of countries and ethnicities from which to choose in presenting folk literature to children. And because of the conscientious work of publishers in bringing these diverse sources to print, we found that among the books we finally included are many stories unfamiliar to us. It is our hope that by including some of these lesser known or unknown stories we encourage the teachers and librarians reading this chapter to be more adventuresome in presenting such stories to children, both for the literary insights and the cultural understandings that might result.

In our selection process, we also included all the other aspects of book production in considering format. Our question was, "In what way is this book a beautiful object?" We truly believe that a book is more than simply a container for a story. Rather, the final look of a book is critically affected by the selection of paper quality, type font, binding materials, size, shape, and axis orientation. In addition, a designer's decisions about page layout and sequence can lift a book out of the ordinary into the exceptional. Though many children, and indeed the adults who work with them, remain unaware of such elements, they are not peripheral but rather vital influences on the final look of the book. We trust that readers will find the books included here distinctly individual objects, even though we have been constrained by space limitations from commenting fully on such aspects of book production.

Along with selection criteria, we considered as a group how to organize the books we chose. An inherent problem is that category systems frequently have "leaks"; no matter which system is used, it is common for a book to fit easily into more than one category. We decided that a simple system reflecting complexity and format would serve best. Therefore, readers will find the books arranged in four loose categories:

concise fables; relatively simple, short folktales in picture book format; longer, more complex myths and legends; and collections of tales, which were less numerous than single-tale books.

## Fables

**22.1** Poole, Amy Lowery. **The Ant and the Grasshopper.** Holiday House, 2000. ISBN 0-8234-1477-9. Unpaged. (P).

The author hooks readers into this Aesop tale by transporting them to Beijing, China. As the ants work to prepare for winter, grasshopper is content to live in the moment, singing and dancing for the emperor. As the seasons change and the emperor prepares to move to his winter home, grasshopper becomes quite taken with the relocation arrangements, disregarding the shifting wind and the ants' sound advice. When winter comes, the ants are comfortable and warm in their home, and grasshopper is left out in the cold to contemplate the advice he did not heed. Poole's exquisite illustrations exemplify Chinese brush painting with the addition of vivid detail and color. Traditional rice paper gives each page texture and depth. Students will be captivated by the illustrations and highly motivated to create similar images by using this ancient art technique. (JB)

**22.2** Sogabe, Aki. **Aesop's Fox.** Harcourt Brace, 1999. ISBN 0-15-201671-6. Unpaged. (P).

This picture book cleverly combines eight of Aesop's fables to create one interesting day for Fox. The day begins when Fox outwits Rooster, and then Rooster outwits Fox, followed by other animals who try to outsmart Fox. The day ends with Fox getting himself in trouble, though not for long, as Fox always seems to have a saying that will help him out. This book would be an excellent way to culminate a classroom study of several singly published fables by Aesop. The children will enjoy the bold cut-paper illustrations and the varied placement of the characters on the page. (MSN)

**22.3** Watts, Bernadette. **The Lion and the Mouse: An Aesop Fable.** North-South, 2000. ISBN 0-7358-1221-7. Unpaged. (P).

An appealing jungle setting introduces the characters of Aesop's retold story. The lion spares the life of the harmless little mouse. The mouse pledges to one day repay the lion's kindness, but the lion laughs because he is so much bigger and stronger and can't imagine needing a mouse's help. When the mighty lion gets caught in a net, he is rescued by the nibbling mouse. From then on, the lion has respect for anything weaker or smaller than himself. The author's detailed pen-and-colored-pencil illustrations help tell the story, and children will enjoy searching for all the animals in each picture. Use this with Margery Cuyler's *Road Signs: A Harey Race with a Tortoise* (Winslow, 2000; **13.24**) in a unit on Aesop. (JC)

## Single Tales in Picture Book Format

**22.4**    Beneduce, Ann Keay, reteller. **Jack and the Beanstalk.** Illustrated by Gennady Spirin. Philomel, 1999. ISBN 0-399-23118-8. 32 pp. (ALL).

Illustrator Spirin creates an elaborate world of fantasy and magic in this retelling of the favorite British tale. The earth-toned watercolor-and-tempera paintings and decorated borders are magnificent. Beneduce has added richness to this dramatic story by introducing a fairy guardian who encourages Jack to avenge the death of his father, killed by the wicked giant of enchantingly scary "fee, fi, fo, fum" infamy. (MNW)

**22.5**    ★ Bierhorst, John. **The People with Five Fingers: A Native Californian Creation Tale.** Illustrated by Robert Andrew Parker. Marshall Cavendish, 2000. ISBN 0-7614-5058-0. Unpaged. (ALL).

Coyote and his animal friends make several appearances in this native Californian creation tale. Bierhorst's animals are creative problem solvers in their approach to constructing the grand design of the world, which includes people, laughter, the moon, mountains, and valleys. Predator and prey work together in harmony as gopher builds, and eagle, bear, and deer supply food. The ancient story line foretells of a land filled with diversity where people from all over the world come together to share and mingle among their neighbors. The simple text and burnished pen-and-watercolor illustrations encourage readers to use their imaginations as they move through the story and soak up the rich images of a land coming together. (JB)

★ Casanova, Mary, reteller. **The Hunter: A Chinese Folktale.** Illustrated by Ed Young. Atheneum, 2000. ISBN 0-689-82906-X. Unpaged. (ALL). (See **16.12**.)

**22.6** Chen, Kerstin. **Lord of the Cranes: A Chinese Tale.** Illustrated by Jian Jiang Chen. North-South, 2000. ISBN 0-7358-1192-8. Unpaged. (ALL).

Tian, a wise old man, lives among the clouds with his friends the cranes. One day, dressed in rags, he goes begging through the city below, looking for people who are kind and generous. He finds only one, an innkeeper named Wang. Tian returns to Wang's inn day after day, and Wang feeds Tian and treats him with respect. In gratitude, Tian rewards Wang with fame and fortune, asking only that he teach others to share with the less fortunate. Wang learns of Tian's true identity when Tian flies to his home in the clouds on the back of a crane. Jian Jiang Chen's beautiful paintings richly complement Kerstin Chen's retelling. Both paintings and story have a quiet beauty. (MA)

**22.7** Diakité, Baba Wagué. **The Hatseller and the Monkeys: A West African Folktale.** Scholastic, 1999. ISBN 0-590-96069-5. Unpaged. (P).

BaMusa the hatseller sits down under a tree to rest. When he awakens, his hats are gone, stolen by monkeys in the branches above him. How to get his hats back? Diakité retells this tale as it was told to him when he was a child in Mali, West Africa. His paintings on ceramic tile bring BaMusa, the monkeys, and the beautiful West African countryside to life. This book is a lovely addition to the folklore shelf. Children will enjoy comparing it with *Caps for Sale* by Esphyr Slobodkina (Scholastic, 1985). (MA)

**22.8** Goode, Diane. **Cinderella, the Dog and Her Little Glass Slipper.** Scholastic, 2000. ISBN 0-439-07166-6. Unpaged. (P).

Goode's version of this familiar tale features a diverse canine cast and closely follows Marcia Brown's adaptation of Charles Perrault's version. The furniture and architecture of Cinderella's father's eighteenth-century French chateau and the prince's palatial ballroom are adorned with dog carvings. The cruel stepsisters are dressed in elaborate pastel gowns and powdered wigs ornamented with bones. Cinderella's fairy godmother is a winged dog outfitted in a romantic pink tutu, and the adoring prince is a small spaniel half Cinderella's size. Witty wordplay abounds. Cinderella's stepmother is a "well-bred" lady and the stepsisters command Cinderella to "fetch" their supper. Understanding the wisdom of kindness, Cinderella invites her stepsisters to the wedding, and they all live happily ever after. This silly retelling is useful for comparison studies of the classic tale. (MNW)

22.9    Goode, Diane. **The Dinosaur's New Clothes.** Scholastic, 1999. ISBN 0-590-38360-4. Unpaged. (P).

This version of the Hans Christian Andersen classic "The Emperor's New Clothes" takes on a humorous, delightful, and prehistoric twist with Goode's dinosaur characters. Set in Versailles, the emperor, a *Tyrannosaurus rex,* is so enamored with clothes that he hires swindlers to create new accoutrements for him. The clothes are invisible to all, though no one will admit this truth to the emperor. The final garment masterpiece is a fashion statement all its own and is brought to true light by an innocent dinosaur child. The emperor, not easily embarrassed, stands up proudly and parades around in his new suit, having learned a valuable lesson regarding his clothing weakness. Goode's illustrations are lavishly detailed. Compare this version with other variations on this tale, such as Stephanie Calmenson's *The Principal's New Clothes* (Scholastic, 1989). (JB)

22.10   ★ Hamilton, Virginia. **The Girl Who Spun Gold.** Illustrated by Leo Dillon and Diane Dillon. Scholastic, 2000. ISBN 0-590-47378-6. Unpaged. (ALL).

This is a familiar story with versions in many cultures. A peasant girl named Quashiba catches the attention of the king. Quashiba's mother tells the king her daughter spins entire fields of the finest golden thread. The king marries Quashiba and tells her she must spin three whole rooms of golden things. A tiny creature saves her by spinning gold but asks her to guess his name. Gold is used effectively in the illustrations for borders and shading, extending the theme of the story. This book could be used effectively with variants of the Rumplestiltskin tale. (JC)

22.11   Howland, Naomi. **Latkes, Latkes, Good to Eat: A Chanukah Story.** Clarion, 1999. ISBN 0-395-89903-6. 31 pp. (P).

This story will remind readers of Big Anthony's struggles with the magic kettle in *Strega Nona* by Tomi dePaola (Prentice-Hall, 1975). This time four siblings can't find a way to stop their sister's magical frying pan from cooking latkes, latkes, and more latkes. Just like Anthony, they have failed to hear the words that end the magic. The story includes key elements of Chanukah, ending with a recipe for latkes, a concise explanation of Chanukah, and directions for playing dreidel. The gouache-and-colored-pencil illustrations highlight Russian folk art motifs. Children will enjoy the characters' facial expressions and probably ask why children are wearing shorts in a very cold and drafty cabin in the middle of winter. This is a good story to use in a paired read-aloud with *Strega Nona*. (MSN)

22.12    Huth, Holly. **The Son of the Sun and Daughter of the Moon: A Saami Folktale.** Illustrated by Anna Vojtech. Atheneum, 2000. ISBN 0-689-82482-3. Unpaged. (ALL).

The son of the sun is searching for a wife. The son would like to marry Vanishia, the daughter of the moon, because earthly women, who cannot fly, are unsuitable mates. The moon hides her daughter with an old couple. Vanishia grows up and marries Luminias, a brother of the Northern Lights. The story has an unusual, tragic conclusion. Vibrant illustrations enhance this Saami folktale. (JC)

22.13    ★ Kimmel, Eric A., reteller. **The Rooster's Antlers: A Story of the Chinese Zodiac.** Illustrated by YongSheng Xuan. Holiday House, 1999. ISBN 0-8234-1385-3. Unpaged. (P).

When the Jade Emperor announces he will name each of the twelve years in his calendar after a different animal, Dragon hopes to be chosen but is too embarrassed to be seen by the emperor because his head is bald. Dragon's friend, the scheming Centipede, tricks Rooster into giving his antlers to Dragon to cover his head for "as long as he needs." After the emperor's choices are made, Rooster asks for his antlers back, but Dragon refuses to return them until his head grows hair—which no dragon has done in ten thousand years. Rooster is angry with Centipede for his trickery, and to this day Rooster and his descendants can be seen chasing and pecking at centipedes. Vivid colors enhance cut-paper illustrations as they move across a brilliant blue background. (JDA)

22.14    Martin, Rafe. **The Shark God.** Illustrated by David Shannon. Scholastic, 2001. ISBN 0-590-39500-9. Unpaged. (I).

In an extended author's note, Martin traces the antecedents of his retelling of this Hawaiian tale of life in and around the sea.

The unnamed young brother and sister, in a kind gesture, save an entangled shark, but later their impetuous touching of the king's drum endangers them, and only the Shark God can save them. Shannon's robust, richly colored paintings are so full of vigorous action that they threaten to burst the bounds of the pages, an appropriate reflection of the energy of the tale. (JWS)

22.15    McDermott, Dennis. **The Golden Goose.** Morrow, 2000. ISBN 0-688-11402-4. Unpaged. (P).

This is a charmingly told and beautifully illustrated version of the traditional Brothers Grimm tale about the virtue of kindness. Hans, the youngest of a poor woodsman's sons, kindly shares his meager lunch with a magical troll. The troll repays Hans by giving him the secret to recover the golden goose, taken from the lovely Princess Rosamund. Hans sets out to return the goose to the princess and encounters villagers along the way, who all become ensnared in the magic spell. When Hans returns the goose to the princess, the spell is broken, and the king offers his daughter's hand to Hans. Lavish acrylic-and-pencil illustrations accompany this tale of "happily ever after," which can be compared to other tales with the theme of being kind to others. (MA)

22.16    Mollel, Tololwa M. **Song Bird.** Illustrated by Rosanne Litzinger. Clarion, 1999. ISBN 0-395-82908-9. 32 pp. (P).

This is an adaptation of a folktale from southern Africa. A magical bird helps Mariamu's family get back from a monster their stolen cattle. The story's focus is on the power of a promise. Lively watercolor-and-colored-pencil illustrations capture the moods of the land, characters, and whimsical animals. Swahili songs and traditional tunes are incorporated within the story, which is characterized by playfulness and trickery. Read this aloud so that children can appreciate the sounds of the Swahili words. (JC)

22.17    ★ Mollel, Tololwa M. **Subira Subira.** Illustrated by Linda Saport. Clarion, 2000. ISBN 0-395-91809-X. 32 pp. (ALL).

This Tanzanian folktale, somewhat lengthy for young readers, is exquisitely retold. Saport's pastel artwork appears dreamlike and even eerie at times. Although this may be troublesome for very young children, the message is truly worthwhile for group sharing. Following the death of her mother, a young Tanzanian girl named Tatu is left to care for Maulidi, her troublesome younger brother. Following the urging of a spirit woman, Tatu tackles the challenge of plucking three whiskers from a lion. By accomplishing this, she hopes to calm Maulidi. Virtues such as love, patience, and endurance are expressed through both the text and the illustrations, making this story a wonderful catalyst for discussion. Although the values are directed to a younger audience (kindergarten through third grade), they are worth sharing with intermediate readers. This work is ideal for exploring interpersonal, cultural, and folk literature studies with a class. (NH)

Montes, Marisa, reteller. **Juan Bobo Goes to Work: A Puerto Rican Folktale.** Illustrated by Joe Cepeda. HarperCollins, 2000. ISBN 0-688-16233-9. Unpaged. (P). (See **17.6.**)

**22.18**   ★ Olaleye, Isaac O. **In the Rainfield: Who Is the Greatest?** Illustrated by Ann Grifalconi. Scholastic, 2000. ISBN 0-590-48363. Unpaged. (ALL).

What makes this book so attractive is the use of a relatively small amount of text on vibrantly collaged pages that represent the Nigerian rainfield, where the story takes place. The folktale recounts the contest that Wind, Fire, and Rain engage in to prove who is "the greatest." The author animates his narrative through the use of onomatopoeia to represent sounds of Wind whistling ("fuuu, fuuu"), of birds whimpering ("penye, penye"), of children huffing and puffing ("kiakia, kata-kiti"), of Fire crackling ("pere, pere"), of Rain singing ("wini-wini"), and so on. In the end, Rain is the victor, proving that "the gentlest is the greatest!" The collages combine marbled paper with painting and pictures of real-life plants, animals, and human figures. (MO)

**22.19**   Perrault, Charles. **Cinderella: A Fairy Tale.** Illustrated by Loek Koopmans. Translated by Anthea Bell. North-South, 1999. ISBN 0-7358-1052-4. Unpaged. (ALL).

This classic tale is brought back to life in a captivatingly beautiful rendition. Koopmans's illustrations catch Cinderella in magical ambiance on each page, no matter how laborious her task is or how vicious her stepmother and stepsisters are toward her. Warm colors enhance the artistically crafted pages and draw readers into Cinderella's life, giving her and the surroundings an ethereal yet lifelike quality. The story takes on an interesting twist when Cinderella returns safely home in time to change from startling beauty to housemaid and keeps both slippers. The awestruck prince announces another ball the following day in hopes of seeing Cinderella again. They do meet, she drops her glass slipper, and the story concludes with Cinderella and the prince marrying and living happily ever after. Children can compare this with other traditional Perrault versions of the tale, discussing how the various illustrations change the reader's perception of the story. (JB)

**22.20**   Perrault, Charles. **Puss in Boots.** Retold by Kurt Baumann. Illustrated by Giuliano Lunelli. Translated by Anthea Bell. North-South, 1999. ISBN 0-7358-1158-X. Unpaged. (ALL).

The text in this version of the traditional story is too lengthy for young ones to sit through, although most will delight in Lunelli's shimmering illustrations. Independent readers will enjoy the story's message but may feel pressured and frustrated by the text's length. The miller once again leaves one of his sons virtually nothing. Only a cat is bequeathed to the main character. Through the cat's magic, the miller's son wins the king's daughter's hand in marriage and becomes a prince. Parallels to today's "real world" and the "luck of the draw" are fully exposed here. Many readers will connect with this notion and begin to see the main character as someone like themselves. "What if's?" in the classroom are a must for discussion and ideal for creative writing follow-ups. Compare this story with other tellings of this tale. (NH)

Pitcher, Caroline. **Mariana and the Merchild: A Folktale from Chile.** Illustrated by Jackie Morris. Eerdmans, 2000. ISBN 0-8028-5204-1. Unpaged. (ALL). (See **17.7.**)

**22.21**   Polacco, Patricia. **Luba and the Wren.** Philomel, 1999. ISBN 0-399-23168-4. Unpaged. (P).

This Ukrainian version of "The Fisherman and His Wife" is immediately identifiable as Polacco's, based on the folk art style so characteristic of her work. Colorful double-page spreads display expressive and real characters. Luba, an addition to this old tale, is the daughter of a farming couple; she displays the characteristics of compassion, love, and unselfishness. After caring for a wren in the forest, the magical bird offers to grant Luba any wish. She declines the bird's generosity but is forced by her parents to return repeatedly to ask for greater social status. The family eventually returns to their roots, finding happiness in their simple life. This story is ideal for exploring wants, needs, and greed and can be compared with other versions of this tale. (NH)

**22.22**  Sanderson, Ruth. **The Golden Mare, the Firebird, and the Magic Ring.** Little, Brown, 2001. ISBN 0-316-76906-1. Unpaged. (I).

This complex story is an amalgamation of motifs from several Russian folktales. Here, Alexi journeys to find adventure and fortune. The characterizations of kindhearted Alexi, the impossibly demanding tsar, and shrewd Yelina the Fair, who wins her heart's desire through her own cleverness, are developed through both Sanderson's words and art. Sanderson's customary finely detailed, realistic, full-color paintings show, through costume and architecture, a distinctly different time and place. (JWS)

**22.23**  San Souci, Robert D. **Peter and the Blue Witch Baby.** Illustrated by Alexi Natchev. Doubleday, 2000. ISBN 0-385-32269-0. Unpaged. (P).

A young tsar named Peter wishes to marry. Lovely Molnya presents herself, but Peter rejects her. She becomes jealous and, changing herself into a wicked witch, places a curse on Peter. Peter falls in love with Little Sister of the Sun and journeys to her Cloud Castle. On the way, he stops to help three sad giants. Arriving at the castle, he looks through a magic window and sees his own castle in ruins. The witch has become a giant blue baby who tries to destroy the tsar. With the help of the three giants and the brother of Little Sister of the Sun, the tsar is saved. The illustrations, traditional Russian designs done in pen, ink, and watercolors, lend fairy tale enchantment to the story. (JC)

**22.24**  Sierra, Judy. **The Dancing Pig.** Illustrated by Jesse Sweetwater. Harcourt Brace, 1999. ISBN 0-15-201594-9. Unpaged. (P).

Young children love this Balinese version of Hansel and Gretel, wonderfully told by Judy Sierra. This is a familiar plot, told in many cultures, of children left home alone and set upon by a wicked monster or animal. In this story, it is the *rangsasa*, or ogress, who captures twin girls when their mother is away. But in a charming twist, a dancing pig, musical frogs, and a clever mouse save the girls. Jesse Sweetwater's acrylic, watercolor, and gouache illustrations reproduce the rich colors and patterns of Bali. Reading this in conjunction with Audrey Wood's *Heckedy Peg* (Harcourt, 1987) would make for an interesting perspective on this traditional tale. (MA)

22.25    Souhami, Jessica. **No Dinner! The Story of the Old Woman and the Pumpkin.** Marshall Cavendish, 2000. ISBN 0-7614-5059-9. Unpaged. (ALL).

A frail old woman, all skin and bone, outsmarts fierce, hungry animals on her way to visit her granddaughter by convincing them that she'll be a tastier meal on her return trip, when she's nice and fat. Happily, the granddaughter has a clever plan to get granny home in one piece. Imaginative layout of text and bold watercolor-and-charcoal illustrations that present characters peering out from unexpected perspectives draw the eye to the action. The repetition in the humorous text and the onomatopoetic, Indian-sounding "tagook . . . tagook" of the walking stick and the "galook . . . galook" of the rolling pumpkin make this a standout for read-aloud, story dramatization, or storytelling. (Although one wonders why the animals shout the American "boo!" to granny.) This rendition is based on a popular folktale told across the Indian subcontinent. (MNW)

22.26    Wahl, Jan. **Little Johnny Buttermilk: After an Old English Folktale.** Illustrated by Jennifer Mazzucco. August House, 1999. ISBN 0-87483-559-3. Unpaged. (P).

Johnny takes pails of buttermilk to market every day for his mother. Twice a witch tries to take his buttermilk and throw him into a sack, and twice he escapes and fools her into taking home the sack filled with thistles or stones. On the third day, he devises a way to outwit her for good. The vibrant acrylic illustrations and whimsical addition of a cat and a mouse delight young children, who giggle each time Johnny tricks the witch. The witch is dressed in familiar pointed black hat and cloak, but her face will not scare very young children. This is a delightful tale of good outsmarting evil that works well for read-aloud or storytelling activities. (MA)

22.27    Wattenberg, Jane, reteller. **Henny-Penny.** Illustrated by Jane Wattenberg. Scholastic, 2000. ISBN 0-439-0781702. Unpaged. (ALL).

"Shake, rattle, and roll! The sky is falling!" The classic story of Henny-Penny returns with a wild twist. Henny-Penny and her feathered friends go on a geographical journey past Stonehenge, the Great Pyramids, the Leaning Tower of Pisa, the Taj Mahal, and the Parthenon to tell the king that the sky is falling. Is the king Elvis, King Tut, or King Kong? Readers never find out. When the globe-trotting flock meets the charming but drooling Foxy-Loxy, Henny-Penny suddenly clucks that she forgot to lay her egg today and runs home. Photo collages of real animals and world landmarks, combined with clever language, create the comic quality of this modern interpretation. The text is creatively laid out in italics, boldface, lowercase, and all capitals using energetic wordplay, puns, rhyme, and alliteration that zigzag and jump across the pages. The imaginative illustrations are a delightful blend of surrealism and pop art. Comparisons can be made to traditional versions of this tale as well as more contemporary tellings such as those by Steven Kellogg and Jon Scziescka. (MNW)

## Myths and Legends

**22.28**　Bini, Renata, reteller. **A World Treasury of Myths, Legends, and Folktales: Stories from Six Continents.** Illustrated by Mikhail Fiodorov. Abrams, 2000. ISBN 0-8109-4554-1. 128 pp. (I).

Translated from Italian, this collection contains thirty-three tales from twenty-six cultures, including traditional Greek and Roman myths as well as Incan, Bantu, Mayan, and Ugandan stories. According to the introduction, these tales were "selected with children in mind." Children will be fascinated by stories filled with creatures such as a poison-spraying dragon; a many-headed, many-armed demon; and giant monkeys. Vivid illustrations will engage readers, enticing them to linger over the stories. The collection is suitable for classroom curriculum use as well as independent reading. Unfortunately, no source notes are given, but further reading is suggested. (JDA)

**22.29**　Hausman, Gerald, and Loretta Hausman. **Cats of Myths: Tales from around the World.** Illustrated by Leslie Baker. Simon & Schuster, 2000. ISBN 0-689-82320-7. 87 pp. (I).

This is more than great storytelling about cats and more cats; it is a careful study of myths from around the world, including eastern India, ancient Egypt, Middle Europe, Southeast Asia, the Bahamas, Polynesia, and Switzerland. The stories portray cats as magicians, goddesses, guardians, and tricksters. The beauty of this book lies in its large, transparent watercolors, created using wet techniques and layered washes, which bring the legends alive. The different expressions on the cats' faces help tell the stories and give greater depth and understanding. A helpful afterword gives a history of the cat in each myth. (JC)

22.30 Heaney, Marie. **The Names upon the Harp: Irish Myth and Legend.** Illustrated by P. J. Lynch. Scholastic, 2000. ISBN 0-590-68052-8. 96 pp. (I).

Both the author and the illustrator live in Dublin, and this book melds their significant talents. The watercolor-and-gouache paintings show the eerily vast expanse of Irish land and sea. In shades of blue, green, brown, and gold, the illustrations are both detailed and controlled, as well as wispy, shadowy, and mystical. Gore is often depicted (e.g., a severed head), but so are melancholy and serenity. Each of the book's three parts represents a cycle of early Irish literature. The Mythological Cycle contains stories and events leading up to the tales of the Faery or Little Folk. The Ulster Cycle tells stories of warriors of the king of Ulster and of the women in that land. The Fenian or Finn Cycle includes stories about a band of men called the Flanna, "the noblest, bravest, swiftest, strongest, and most honorable men in the land" (p. 60). Each is tested for his skill as a poet and must swear loyalty to his leader, respect women, and help the poor. Courage, strength, dignity, and trickery all play a part in these tales. The author includes a pronunciation guide, source notes, and further reading sections at the end. Creating a family tree of the characters would be an interesting classroom activity. (MO)

★ Kimmel, Eric A. **The Two Mountains: An Aztec Legend.** Illustrated by Leonard Everett Fisher. Holiday House, 2000. ISBN 0-8234-1504-X. Unpaged. (ALL). (See **17.23.**)

22.31 Lattimore, Deborah Nourse. **Medusa.** HarperCollins, 2000. ISBN 0-06-027904-4. Unpaged. (I).

The book clearly and descriptively spins the tale of this Greek mythological character, explaining why Athena cursed the beautiful Medusa and transformed her into a horrible-looking monster, her "once lustrous hair" changed into a "mass of living snakes." Anyone who looked at her would turn into stone. The second half of the book tells the adventures of Perseus as he tries to kill Medusa so that he can bring her head back to Polydectes. If he doesn't do this, he and his mother will be killed. In true mythological fashion, Perseus meets many obstacles but overcomes them with the help of the gods. The illustrations are colorful and intricate, completely surrounding the text and superbly complementing the story. (BF)

**22.32** Mama, Raouf, reteller. **The Barefoot Book of Tropical Tales.** Illustrated by Deidre Hyde. Barefoot, 2000. ISBN 1-902283-21-X. 64 pp. (ALL).

Intriguing ink-and-crayon artwork, detailed borders, and culturally representative illustrations by Hyde make this work a visual delight. Collections are difficult to do well, but Beninese storyteller Mama has retold each of the selected myths and legends of the tropics using melodious language and unique form. The detailed text and colorful language make this work desirable for group sharing. Rewrites for the intermediate grades are a natural follow-up activity. Comparisons to similar tales are an ideal activity for primary children. The illustrations are acutely representative of the natural elements from which the tropical tales originate, so sharing them is necessary every time a new story is read. (NH)

**22.33** Richards, Jean, reteller. **The First Olympic Games: A Gruesome Greek Myth with a Happy Ending.** Illustrated by Kat Thacker. Millbrook, 2000. ISBN 0-7613-13117. Unpaged. (I).

This beautifully illustrated book presents four themes/story lines: Zeus's reunion with his son, Tantalus, and the subsequent cruel trick that Tantalus plays on the gods; the punishment of Tantalus in the Underworld and the "rebirth" of his son, Pelops; Pelops's quest for a kingdom and the beautiful princess, Hippodamia; and the great chariot race against Hippodamia's father, the king. The story ends with Pelops's victory but also the death of the king. Before they wed, Pelops and his bride hold a funeral feast for the king. The invited guests are "heroes from all over Greece" who participate in "athletic games and races in remembrance of the king's great chariot race." Pelops announces that the games will be held every four years "till the end of time." The large, bold, colorful, and friezelike pictures perfectly complement the text. This book could be useful for drama studies; teachers could enact Zeus or Hera, with students responding in the roles of gods and goddesses. This would also be a good opportunity to compare this book with those by Leonard Everett Fisher. (MO)

22.34  Vogel, Carole Garbuny. **Legends of Landforms: Native American Lore and the Geology of the Land.** Millbrook, 1999. ISBN 0-7613-0272-7. 96 pp. (ALL).

These adaptations of legends from various native peoples explain natural wonders, including the Hot Springs of Arkansas, the Grand Canyon, Horseshoe Falls at Niagara Falls, and the Hawaiian Islands, by blending mythical and scientific information. Fourteen artful photographs add to young readers' understanding of and appreciation for the natural power and beauty of the geological landforms depicted. Readers will discover the ancients' native tales of fearsome dragons, gentle serpents, friendly giants, and spirit beings as they relate to the spectacular landscapes of North America. The combination of physical and spiritual descriptions expands readers' understanding of how scientists explain the natural forces that formed these landforms. Readers will see the lands around them in new ways. (EC)

## Collections of Tales

★ Bruchac, Joseph. **Pushing Up the Sky: Seven Native American Plays for Children.** Illustrated by Teresa Flavin. Dial, 2000. ISBN 0-8037-2168-4. 94 pp. (ALL). (See **18.3.**)

22.35  ★ Doherty, Berlie. **Fairy Tales.** Illustrated by Jane Ray. Candlewick, 2000. ISBN 0-7636-088708. 223 pp. (ALL).

This book contains twelve fairy tales, some familiar, such as "Cinderella" and "Little Red Riding Hood," and some unfamiliar, such as "The Firebird" and "The Wild Swans." The stories are rich in literary style and exciting vocabulary, and the illustrations are as rich as the text. Each text page is bordered in a gold design and surrounded by an illustrated background, vibrant with color and intricate in pattern. The pictures, which depict multicultural characters, invite the reader to touch the page and study the drawings and designs. The stories are interesting enough to read to first and second graders, easy enough for fourth and fifth graders to read independently, and adventurous and "gory" enough for seventh and eighth graders to enjoy. This is a great source for illustrating characteristics of fairy tales and comparing and contrasting different versions of the tales. (JB)

22.36 ★ Philip, Neil. **Celtic Fairy Tales.** Illustrated by Isabelle Brent. Viking, 1999. ISBN 0-670-88387-5. 140 pp. (ALL).

The introduction provides the history of these twenty richly illustrated Irish and Scottish "wonder tales." Some of the stories are shorter but complete, and some are longer and more complicated. Regardless of length, the stories are intriguing, engaging, and adventurous. They easily can be read out loud or silently. The tales often include the numbers three and seven, fantastic adventures, and studies of characters, good and bad. Often animals play integral parts. The illustrations are works of art, standing on their own merit. Each is framed in a design, often with a figure from the story. Part of the frame is then used on every page of that particular story. With the engaging stories and the rich illustrations, children of all ages will enjoy this book. (BF)

22.37 Schwartz, Howard, and Barbara Bush, retellers. **A Coat for the Moon and Other Jewish Tales.** Illustrated by Michael Lofin. Jewish Publication Society, 1999. ISBN 0-8276-0596-X. 96 pp. (ALL).

This collection retells fifteen Jewish folktales from around the world that emphasize primary Jewish principles and ideals. Among these are the importance of keeping a vow or a secret, of giving to charity, of saving someone who is in serious danger, and of sharing and hospitality. The stories are short and well written with clear sequencing and an obvious moral. Because of their length, they could be used as lessons in implied meaning. Each tale is accompanied by a beautiful pen-and-ink drawing. A special feature of the book is the Source and Commentary section at the end. Besides identifying the origins of the tale, this important section explains and interprets the stories. (BF)

22.38 Yolen, Jane. **The Fairies' Ring: A Book of Fairy Stories and Poems.** Illustrated by Stephen Mackey. Dutton, 1999. ISBN 0-525-46045-4. 96 pp. (ALL).

In this splendidly illustrated collection, Yolen transports readers into the magical world of fairies. The book is introduced by a short, humorous, and instructive quiz about fairies: Are they real?

What do fairies look like? Are they good or bad? The twenty-eight selections include tales from Scotland, Persia, England, France, Wales, Greece, New Zealand, and Africa, showing the different relationships between people and fairies. Sometimes fairies help, sometimes they hurt, and they're always unpredictable. They leave footprints in the butter, gold coins under trees, and also kidnap babies and blind midwives. Poems by Scott, Yeats, and Shakespeare have been included, some of which may be challenging for young readers. Richly colored oil paintings and gold-framed miniature portraits accurately represent the wide-ranging material and capture the mystery of the fairy folk. Source notes and a bibliography lend authenticity to this captivating anthology. (MNW)

22.39   Yolen, Jane, collector and reteller. **Not One Damsel in Distress: World Folktales for Strong Girls.** Illustrated by Susan Guevara. Harcourt Brace, 2000. ISBN 0-15-202047-0. 116 pp. (I).

This collection of thirteen folktales about courageous, strong women shouts, "You go, girl!" but invites boys to come along too. From a Grecian huntress, a medieval knight, and a pirate princess to a samurai maiden and a serpent slayer, there's a character and tale sure to thrill every reader. An excellent storytelling resource, these stories also work well when read aloud to children. The gray-scale interior illustrations evoke strength, sorrow, agility, bravery, and even mischief. The cover painting of a seafaring adventurer beckons readers to come along on a grand adventure. (JDA)

# 23 International Children's Literature

**Carl Tomlinson**

*Contributing reviewers included Carol Dunham, Tru Dee Griffin, Gayle Nelson, Stacy Slater, and Karen Wilson.*

---

### Criteria for Excellence

- Originally published in a country other than the United States
- An original concept or story that reveals how people in other countries live now or have lived in the past
- A theme concerned with the interests, problems, customs, and ways of thinking of people who live in countries other than the United States
- A story that both entertains and educates
- Excellent writing
- Original, evocative illustrations that help tell the story
- Concept and theme appropriate for children in grades K–6

---

## Primary Grades (K–2)

★ Erlbach, Arlene. **Happy New Year, Everywhere.** Illustrated by Sharon Lane Holm. Millbrook, 2000.

Godard, Alex. **Mama, Across the Sea.** Adapted from the French by George Wen. Holt, 2000.

Goodall, Jane. **The Eagle and the Wren.** Illustrated by Alexander Reichstein. Michael Neugebauer/North-South, 2000.

★ Highet, Alistair. **The Yellow Train.** Based on a story by Fred Bernard. Illustrated by François Roca. Pavilion, 2000.

Lester, Alison. **Ernie Dances to the Didgeridoo: For the Children of Gunbalanya.** Houghton Mifflin, 2001.

Lindenbaum, Pija. **Bridget and the Gray Wolves.** Translated from the Swedish by Kjersti Board. R & S Books, 2001.

★ Stark, Ulf. **Can You Whistle, Johanna? A Boy's Search for a Grandfather.** Illustrated by Anna Höglund. Translated from the Swedish by Ebba Segerberg. RDR Books, 1999.

Tibo, Giles. **Naomi and Mrs. Lumbago.** Illustrated by Louise-Andrée Laliberté. Translated from the French by Susan Ouriou. Tundra, 2001.

Vaugelade, Anaïs. **The War.** Translated from the French by Marie-Christine Rouffiac and Tom Streissguth. Carolrhoda, 2001.

Wheatley, Nadia. **Luke's Way of Looking.** Illustrated by Matt Ottley. Kane/Miller, 2001.

### Intermediate Grades (3–6)

Bjørk, Christina. **Vendela in Venice.** Illustrated by Inga-Karin Eriksson. Translated from the Swedish by Patricia Crampton. R & S Books, 1999.

★ Buchholz, Quint. **The Collector of Moments.** Translated from the German by Peter F. Neumeyer. Farrar, Straus & Giroux, 1999.

Carmi, Daniella. **Samir and Yonatan.** Translated from the Hebrew by Yael Lotan. Scholastic, 2000.

★ Dumas, Philippe. **A Farm: Reflections of Yesteryear.** Translated from the French by Mary Logue. Creative Editions, 1999.

Le Rochais, Marie-Ange. **Desert Trek: An Eye-Opening Journey through the World's Driest Places.** Translated from the French by George L. Newman. Walker, 2001.

★ Rodda, Emily. **Rowan of Rin.** Greenwillow, 2001.

Vos, Ida. **The Key Is Lost.** Translated from the German by Terese Edelstein. HarperCollins, 2000.

### All (K–6)

★ Sortland, Bjørn. **Anna's Art Adventure.** Illustrated by Lars Elling. Translated from the Norwegian by James Anderson. Lerner/Carolrhoda, 1999.

★ Vincent, Gabrielle. **A Day, a Dog.** Front Street, 1999.

★ Wild, Margaret. **Fox.** Illustrated by Ron Brooks. Kane/Miller, 2001.

---

To fulfill a commitment to write a book column for a journal, in the spring of 2001 I decided to find out what some of the recent award-winning children's books were in countries other than the United States. Networking from contacts made through the International Board on Books for Young People, the wonderful organization dedicated to promoting world peace through children's books, I soon found myself communicating over the Internet *in English* with interested, well-informed specialists in children's literature (librarians, publishers, authors, and illustrators) from countries as diverse as the Slovak Republic, Japan, Greece, Russia, and Colombia. Enticing book reviews and beautiful illustrations appeared on my computer screen just hours after I had made initial contacts. In accompanying notes, my correspondents expressed delight that someone in another country was interested in "their" books and that children in this country might someday read them. I realized from this experience how easily and closely connected we can be to our colleagues in other countries, if we want to be.

According to *The World through Children's Books* (Stan, 2002), international children's literature includes books originally published in other countries in a language of that country and later published in the United States. Some of these books are originally written in a language other than English and are then translated into English before being published in this country. Other international books are originally written in English but in a country other than the United States. Some international books are published in their original language (not English) in this country, but these are rare. Although we have always enjoyed international literature, from classics such as *Heidi* (Spyri, 1986/1880) to contemporary fiction such as *The Friends* (Yumoto, 1996) or *Amazing Grace* (Hoffman, 1991), the number of international books published annually in the United States is miniscule compared to the total number of children's books published annually in this country or compared to the number of international books published annually in other developed countries.

Organizations such as the United States Board on Books for Young People (USBBY), the American Library Association (ALA), the National Council of Teachers of English (NCTE), and the International Reading Association (IRA) regularly call attention to international children's literature. USBBY focuses solely on promoting international children's books in the United States, and the other organizations either have a special-interest group focused on global literature or regularly highlight international children's books in their publications. Particularly important are USBBY's biennial international children's literature conference and ALA/Association for Library Service to Children's Mildred L. Batchelder Award for the most outstanding translated book for children published in the previous year.

In addition to the international books reviewed in this chapter, good selections can be found in the aforementioned *The World through Children's Books* (Stan, 2002), *Children's Books from Other Countries* (Tomlinson, 1998), and *Global Perspectives in Children's Literature* (Freeman & Lehman, 2001). IBBY's quarterly journal *Bookbird: The Journal of International Children's Literature* and USBBY's *Bulletin* are other good sources. Some publishers and distributors such as Creative Editions; Farrar, Straus, & Giroux; Front Street; Holt; Kane/Miller; North-South Books; RDR Publishers; and Simon & Schuster consistently offer international titles, so their catalogs are invaluable resources.

Good international books can be springboards for student inquiry into the culture of a country. Use of the Internet can quickly lead students to information about any country and, perhaps, to pen pals. Teachers will find that many international titles lend themselves to reading aloud and then group discussion about similarities and differences between the lives of the book characters and the lives of the listeners. Often, works of historical fiction set in other countries and used as classroom read-alouds can lend authenticity and emotional interest to social studies and history units and classes. The main objective is to let these books help transcend political or cultural boundaries to show young people that they are more like their peers in other countries than they are different from them.

For a book to be included in this chapter, it had to be originally published in a country other than the United States or be written by a recent immigrant to the United States about the author's experiences in his or her native country. In addition, it had to have an original concept, the writing and illustration had to be of excellent quality, and the story had to be conceptually and thematically appropriate for children in grades K–6.

The limited number of international children's books published in the United States is reflected in the small number of books reviewed in this chapter. With so few books, our committee decided to organize reviews by intended grade level: primary, intermediate, and, in a few cases, K–6.

The committee members responsible for the selections in this chapter agreed that they wanted to look beyond the traditional focus on festivals, food, fashion, and folklore so often mistaken in classrooms for a real study of a different culture. Instead, most of the books in this chapter reveal how people in other countries live now or have lived in the past and are concerned with their interests, problems, customs, and ways of thinking. In all cases, the books both entertain and educate.

## References

Freeman, E., and Lehman, B. A. (2001). *Global perspectives in children's literature.* Boston: Allyn and Bacon.

Hoffman, M. (1991). *Amazing Grace.* Illustrated by C. Binch. New York: Dial.

Spyri, J. (1986). *Heidi.* New York: Crown. (Original work published 1880)

Stan, S. (Ed.). (2002). *The world through children's books.* Lanham, MD: Scarecrow Press.

Tomlinson, C. M. (Ed.). (1998). *Children's books from other countries.* Lanham, MD: Scarecrow Press.

Yumoto, K. (1996). *The Friends.* Translated by Cathy Hirano. New York: Farrar, Straus & Giroux.

## Primary Grades (K–2)

**23.1**   ★ Erlbach, Arlene. **Happy New Year, Everywhere.** Illustrated by Sharon Lane Holm. Millbrook, 2000. ISBN 0-761-31707-4. 48 pp. (P).

New Year festivities of twenty countries, spanning five continents, are showcased on vividly illustrated double-page spreads in this informational book. For each country, readers learn when the new year is celebrated, the name of the celebration, and a greeting for the new year in the language of that country. Illustrations provide brief glimpses into life in that country, such as clothing, architectural styles, and topography. Detailed instructions on how to make traditional crafts, foods, or music are also included. Smaller countries such as Belgium, Haiti, Iran, and Israel are among the twenty countries featured. (KW)

**23.2**   Godard, Alex. **Mama, Across the Sea.** Adapted from the French by George Wen. Holt, 2000. Originally published in France as *Maman-dlo* by Albin Michele Jeunesse in 1998. ISBN 0-8050-6161-4. Unpaged. (P).

Seven-year-old Cecile lives on an island in the West Indies with her grandparents while her mother is living and working on the mainland far away. How Cecile misses her mother! Day after day she stares out to sea hoping to see a boat bringing her mother back home. Instead, she gets a letter saying that it will be a full year before her mother can return for a visit. Sad but still hopeful, Cecile has much to do on the island, such as write and decorate a letter to her mother, listen to the storytellers at night, and teach her grandmother to read. Then, just as summer begins, a letter arrives. Cecile is to take the boat to the mainland and spend her school vacation with her mother! Godard's large, sunny, richly hued illustrations support the underlying message of family love and loyalty and provide a suitable Caribbean setting. (CT)

**23.3**   Goodall, Jane. **The Eagle and the Wren.** Illustrated by Alexander Reichstein. Michael Neugebauer/North-South, 2000. ISBN 0-735-81380-9. Unpaged. Simultaneously published in Switzerland by Nord-Süd Verlag AG as *Der Adler und der Zaunkönig* in 2000. (P).

Animal researcher Jane Goodall retells a favorite fable about friends helping one another realize their goals. Birds argue about who can fly the highest. A contest is called and, despite their braggadocio, each bird flies as high as nature intended, the eagle soaring above them all. Then a tiny wren emerges from the eagle's feathers and the contest is on again! This book would be a wonderful classroom discussion starter for fostering helpfulness and cooperation among students because it shows how individuality, diversity, and limitations can be combined for positive problem solving. Wonderfully rendered illustrations mirror the birds' differing perceptions of Earth. Goodall's illumination in an author's note is worth sharing after class discussion. (TDG/KW)

**23.4**   ★ Highet, Alistair. **The Yellow Train.** Based on a story by Fred Bernard. Illustrated by François Roca. Pavilion, 2000. ISBN 1-568-46128-3. 38 pp. Originally published in France by Éditions du Seuil as *Le Train Jaune* in 1998. (P).

Seven-year-old Theo and his grandfather embark on a magical journey aboard a yellow train, going back in time to revisit the wonderful, unspoiled places that Grandfather visited years before—places now despoiled by industrial civilization. It is ironic, Grandfather explains, that this wonderful train helped destroy the natural world by transporting the materials and workers who built the cities and factories. Theo, who is given the keys to the yellow train at the journey's end, is left to ponder how the world will change in his time. French artist Roca's bottom-up perspectives, use of shadow, and art deco style add mystery, a sense of foreboding, and overwhelming grandeur to landscapes and cityscapes alike. Fourth graders caught the rather subtle message of this work of modern fantasy: we often pay a terrible price for "progress." (CD)

**23.5**   Lester, Alison. **Ernie Dances to the Didgeridoo: For the Children of Gunbalanya.** Houghton Mifflin, 2001. ISBN 0-618-10442-9. Unpaged. Originally published by Hodder in Australia in 2000. (P).

Seven-year-old Ernie waves goodbye to his friends and sets off for Arnhem Land on the northernmost tip of Australia, where he will live with his parents for a year. There he makes friends with six Aboriginal children. He writes his friends at home during each of the six seasons, describing what his new friends do at that time of year. The seasons are Kudjewik, the monsoon season; Bangkerreng, harvest time; Yekke, the cool season; Wur-rkeng, the early dry season; Kurrung, the hot, dry season; and Kurnumeleng, the premonsoon season, which occurs around Christmastime. Lester's use of small, separate illustrations helps focus readers' attention on each child's activity, and her border illustrations show much of the native flora and fauna of Arnhem Land. Illustration cues and patterned language make this book easy to read despite the amount of information it contains. A glossary of Australian and Aboriginal terms is included. (CT)

23.6   Lindenbaum, Pija. **Bridget and the Gray Wolves.** Translated from the Swedish by Kjersti Board. R & S Books, 2001. ISBN 9-129653-95-9. Unpaged. Originally published in Sweden as *Gittan och gråvargarna* by Rabén & Sjögren Bokförlag in 2000. (P).

When overly careful five-year-old Bridget's nursery school is having a day out, she gets lost in the woods and left behind. Alone in the dusk, she is at first afraid when wolves' yellow eyes glimmer behind the trees. But Bridget suddenly becomes a tough girl who can speak up for herself (with the animals!) and decides to teach the wolves some games. The wolves are as anxious and timid as Bridget herself used to be, and she must help them climb down from trees and comfort them when they are afraid. In so doing, she overcomes her own fears. When morning arrives, strengthened by her adventure, Bridget finds her way back home. The last illustration shows her triumphantly standing on the roof of a playhouse. The watercolor illustrations use sprawling lines and beautiful, earthy colors to support the forest setting and Bridget's increasing self-confidence. The handwritten text adds personality to the story. Even primary students were able to grasp that the wolves represented Bridget's fears. (CT)

23.7   ★ Stark, Ulf. **Can You Whistle, Johanna? A Boy's Search for a Grandfather.** Illustrated by Anna Höglund. Translated from the Swedish by Ebba Segerberg. RDR Books, 1999. ISBN 1-571-43057-1. 48 pp. Originally published in Sweden as *Kan du vissla, Johanna?* by Bonnier Carlsen in 1994. (P).

Eight-year-olds Uffe and Berre have a happy visit with the latter's grandfather, but then Uffe feels sad that he has never known a grandfather. The boys find an elderly gentleman in the park and decide to make him Uffe's grandfather. The man lives in a retirement home and is fragile but quite feisty and full of fun, stories, and spunk. Uffe and his pretend grandfather both benefit greatly from their all-too-brief relationship. Second graders loved this work of realistic fiction as a read-aloud and could also handle its humorously illustrated twelve short chapters independently. The story naturally prompts children to want to share their own positive experiences with the elderly and hear other cross-generational stories. (GN)

23.8    Tibo, Giles. **Naomi and Mrs. Lumbago.** Illustrated by Louise-Andrée Laliberté. Translated from the French by Susan Ouriou. Tundra, 2001. ISBN 0-88776-551-3. 86 pp. Originally published as *Secret de Madame Lumbago* in Canada by Les Éditions Québec Amérique in 1996. (P).

Naomi is seven-and-three-quarter years old and in second grade. Her best friend is her elderly babysitter, Mrs. Lumbago, who lives with her ailing husband in the apartment above Naomi's. Because of Mrs. Lumbago's remark that "there's a treasure here," Naomi is convinced there is a secret hoard of money and jewels in the Lumbagos' apartment. Relentlessly she searches their apartment but always under the guise of doing something else, such as cleaning. When Mr. Lumbago dies, Naomi loses interest in the treasure until Mrs. Lumbago convinces her that life must go on. One day Naomi confesses that she has been searching for the treasure, and Mrs. Lumbago tells her that the treasure she had referred to was Naomi herself. Distraught, Naomi hits the wall, hears a clink, and dislodges a picture, revealing a slot cut into the wall. Knocking a hole in the wall, they watch amazed as an avalanche of coins rolls onto the floor. Mrs. Lumbago realizes that her husband had hidden his salary in the walls for years. The low-key mystery and theme of friendship and support make this transitional book good for reading aloud to first graders as well as for independent reading for second and third graders. (CT)

23.9    Vaugelade, Anaïs. **The War.** Translated from the French by Marie-Christine Rouffiac and Tom Streissguth. Carolrhoda, 2001. ISBN 1-57505-562-7. Unpaged. Originally published as *La guerre* in France by l'école des loisirs in 1998. (P).

In this tale about war and peace, a young pacifist prince tricks two warring kingdoms into joining forces against an imaginary common enemy long enough to prove that they can be friends. Meanwhile, he travels to another kingdom, is adopted by the king, and eventually rules without ever waging war. Primary students enjoyed comparing *The War* to another international book, the wordless *Why?* by Nikolai Popov (North-South, 1996). Both books make simple, easy-to-understand statements about the wastefulness of war, the politics of war, and the need to find alternative ways to settle our differences. Vaugelade's color-saturated illustrations help convey meaning through use of symbolic color (glowing red for war; cool blue for pacifism; sunny yellow for friendliness). (CT)

**23.10** Wheatley, Nadia. **Luke's Way of Looking.** Illustrated by Matt Ottley. Kane/Miller, 2001. ISBN 1-929132-18-2. Unpaged. Originally published in Australia by Hodder in 1999. (P).

Luke, about eight years old, attends a very conservative, strictly run school. He receives weekly lessons in art, which he loves, but his art teacher is also very conservative and strict and does not appreciate the fact that Luke sees things differently from most people and draws what he sees in brilliant color and a non-realistic style. Frustrated and upset by his teacher's ridicule, Luke runs away from school and wanders the streets until he happens upon a museum of modern art. What he sees there fills him with joy and validation: his way of looking at the world has been shared by many great artists. The illustrator's juxtaposition of Luke's two worlds—the drab, unhappy world of reality and the brilliant, joyous world of his imagination—makes a strong statement about the need for all teachers to accept children who see things differently. The book provides an excellent introduction to the world of modern art as well as a stimulus for students who are willing to try their hand at abstract style. (CT)

## Intermediate Grades (3–6)

**23.11** Bjørk, Christina. **Vendela in Venice.** Illustrated by Inga-Karin Eriksson. Translated from the Swedish by Patricia Crampton. R & S Books, 1999. ISBN 91-29-64559-X. 93 pp. Originally published in Sweden by Rabén & Sjögren as *Vendela i Venedig* in 1999. (I).

Ten-year-old Vendela writes in her journal about her preparation for and visit to beautiful Venice with her father. She researches the four golden horses in St. Mark's Basilica prior to her trip and then enjoys glassblowing, gondola construction, and good food when she arrives. Rich with actual photos of landmarks and artwork and laden with historical facts, this book is ideal for a social studies unit. Students will respond to Vendela's lively observations and experiences, and the Italian words interspersed throughout the book add to the feeling that this is a real trip. When used as a model for a class travel brochure, the book offers a multitude of experiences, sights, sounds, and even tastes for young children to modify for a brochure/journal of their own real or imaginary travels. As realistic fiction, *Vendela in Venice* also serves as a travel guide for readers who are planning a trip. (TDG)

23.12    ★ Buchholz, Quint. **The Collector of Moments.** Translated from the French by Peter F. Neumeyer. Farrar, Straus & Giroux, 1999. ISBN 0-374-31520-5. Unpaged. Originally published in Germany by Carl Hanser Verlag as *Sammler der Augenblicke* in 1997. (I).

Max is an artist who collects moments, such as the moment that rare snow elephants appear or the moment a circus wagon escapes from gravity, and captures them on canvas. Max's young neighbor, a bespectacled violinist who is teased at school, loves to watch Max work. Max always turns his paintings to the wall, however, saying, "One invisible and unique path leads into every picture. [The artist] can't show the picture too soon, or he might lose the path forever." When Max finally exhibits his paintings, their fantastic worlds fill the boy with joy and lead him to a greater acceptance of his own talents. Buchholz's elegant text and surrealistic illustrations provide the perfect springboard for students' self-expression. Sixth graders were intrigued by the odd juxtaposition of objects in the illustrations and enjoyed incorporating the captured moments into short stories. The text is more philosophical than that of most picture books, so students need careful guidance in exploring the themes of this beguiling, lyrical book. (SS)

23.13    Carmi, Daniella. **Samir and Yonatan.** Translated from the Hebrew by Yael Lotan. Scholastic, 2000. ISBN 0-439-13504-4. 183 pp. Originally published in Israel as *Samir ve-Yonatan 'al kokhav Ma'adim* in 1994. (I).

When his adored brother Fadi was killed by the Israelis, ten-year-old Palestinian Samir could not bear to go to the funeral.

Now Samir must travel to a Jewish hospital for an operation and stay in a ward filled with the children of those responsible for his brother's death. Haunted by memories of Fadi, Samir remains an outsider until Yonatan invites him on an imaginary mission to Mars. While on this otherworldly journey, Samir comes to terms with his brother's death and imagines a world free from conflict. The narrative shifts from present to past, between reality and dreams, and from realism to fantasy, which may be confusing for some readers. Those sophisticated enough to ponder the abstract themes of the book will find a delicately crafted story about overcoming differences and finding friendship. (SS)

23.14 ★ Dumas, Philippe. **A Farm: Reflections of Yesteryear.** Translated from the French by Mary Logue. Creative Editions, 1999. ISBN 1-56846-169-0. Unpaged. Originally published in France as *Une ferme* by l'école des loisirs in 1997. (I).

Charming double-spread watercolors in an oversize format transport the reader to pastoral Victorian England in this deceptively simple tale of a day in the life on a farm. Key messages of this peaceful, seemingly idyllic life—self-sufficiency and thrift—are established in the foreword and expertly woven into marginal annotations that add factual information about everything from the amount of milk the average cow gives each day to the mechanics of the garden gate lock. Students will develop an appreciation for the dawn-to-dusk labor involved in running a farm and the process by which food reaches the market. Dumas's introduction, decrying modern factory farms, could serve as a prompt for discussions comparing organic and traditional farming methods. Math connections include measuring in bushels and pecks. Social studies classes could trace the changes that have taken us from an agrarian society to an industrial one and the resulting effects on people's lives. (SS)

23.15 Le Rochais, Marie-Ange. **Desert Trek: An Eye-Opening Journey through the World's Driest Places.** Translated from the French by George L. Newman. Walker, 2001. ISBN 0-8027-8765-7. 37 pp. Originally published as *Vide, le désert* by l'école des loisirs in France in 1999. (I).

This informational book seeks to refute the misguided notion that the deserts of the world are empty, lifeless wastelands. Each double-spread presents a single column of text describing a different aspect of desert life and a large, beautifully rendered, information-rich painting of the desert feature. Saharan Tuaregs, or "blue people," oases, Kalahari bush hunters, various plants and animals, evidence of past civilizations, animal herds, cold, salt, oil, and water are aspects of the desert that will come as interesting surprises to most intermediate graders. Endpages filled with carefully captioned vignettes of desert animals and ancient desert rock paintings, interesting supplementary information about each picture, and a map of the world's deserts are bonuses. (CT)

23.16 ★ Rodda, Emily. **Rowan of Rin.** Greenwillow, 2001. ISBN 0-06029-707-7. 151 pp. Originally published by Omnibus Books/ Scholastic in Australia in 1993. (I).

When their water supply suddenly stops flowing down from the mysterious mountain behind their village, the people of Rin ask the advice of Sheba, the village wise woman. She gives them a map and tells them, in riddles, that they must climb the mountain and endure the dangers to be found there in order to unleash the waters again. The villagers select the strongest and bravest among them to climb the mountain, so no one is more surprised to be included than timid, ten-year-old Rowan, a shepherd boy, but he is the only one who can read Sheba's map. On their ascent, the group encounters one harrowing test after another, each revealing a weakness in one of the adults, until only Rowan is left to combat the dragon at the top of the mountain. Rowan's perseverance and intelligence prove to be more effective than great physical strength, and the village is saved. A likeable hero, well-paced action, suspense, and the theme of self-discovery make this work of modern fantasy an excellent read-aloud. This and the author's other books about Rowan are ideal for fourth- and fifth-grade readers. (CD)

Skármeta, Antonio. **The Composition.** Illustrated by Alfonso Ruano. Translated by Elisa Amado. Groundwood, 2000. ISBN 0-88899-390-0. Unpaged. Simultaneously published as *La composicion* by Ediciones Ekaré in Venezuela. (I). (See **24.25.**)

23.17 Vos, Ida. **The Key Is Lost.** Translated from the German by Terese Edelstein. HarperCollins, 2000. ISBN 0-688-16283-5. 271 pp. Originally published in Germany in 1996. (I).

Marie-Louise and Marie-Jeanne Dutour are not who they say they are. In reality they are Eva and Lisa Zilverstijn, Jewish children fleeing from the Nazis in occupied Holland. Smuggled from one safe house to another, the sisters encounter many who are willing to risk their own safety in order to thwart Hitler's extermination plan. Vos's semiautobiographical story raises many questions about cruelty and kindness and how it is sometimes impossible to have one without the other. *The Key Is Lost* would make an excellent precursor to *Anne Frank: The Diary of a Young Girl* because it has easier vocabulary and a happier ending. One twelve-year-old girl particularly liked the consistent use of present tense because "it makes you feel like you are right in the middle of everything." (SS)

## All (K–6)

**23.18** ★ Sortland, Bjørn. **Anna's Art Adventure.** Illustrated by Lars Elling. Translated from the Norwegian by James Anderson. Lerner/Carolrhoda, 1999. ISBN 1-575-05376-4. 39 pp. Originally published in Norway as *Raudt, Blått, og Litt Gult* by Det Norske Samlaget in 1993. (ALL).

*Anna's Art Adventure* is a delightful, fantastic romp through the world of art as young Anna, searching for a restroom in a museum, magically falls into internationally known pictures and interacts with their creators. As she enters each of the beautifully rendered classic works, Anna *becomes* the art. Older students will appreciate the humor, young children will enjoy Anna's antics, and everyone will close the book stimulated to learn more about the art world. Students will be eager to try their hand at various art styles and learn more about such featured artists as Rembrandt, Pablo Picasso, Jackson Pollack, and Andy Warhol. (TDG)

**23.19** ★ Vincent, Gabrielle. **A Day, a Dog.** Front Street, 1999. ISBN 1-886910-51-0. 64 pp. Originally published as *Un jour, un chien* by Éditions Duculot in 1982. (ALL).

With swift, deft strokes of her soft pencil, the artist-author tells a poignant, wordless story of a day in the life of an abandoned dog. Soon after being literally thrown out of its master's car, the dog inadvertently causes a serious roadway accident. Some might view this as unfortunate, but others might interpret it as a fateful justice upon humans for their mistreatment of animals. Vincent's ability to evoke emotion, from despair to suspicion to joy, with a minimum of line is evident as the dog moves through a stark, lonely landscape and then meets and befriends a child. Has the dog found a home? This book is a perfect vehicle to provoke discussion about pet care and animal abuse. As a wordless book, it also can be the basis of a variety of writing projects in grades 1 through 6. As an artistic tour de force, it can be used as a model for sketching, showing perspective, action, and composition. (SS/CT)

23.20 ★ Wild, Margaret. **Fox.** Illustrated by Ron Brooks. Kane/Miller, 2001. ISBN 1-929132-16-6. Unpaged. Originally published by Allen & Unwin in Australia in 2000. (ALL).

Set in the Australian bush, Dog is blind in one eye and Magpie has a burned wing and cannot fly, but together they make "a strange new creature," compensating for each other's disability. Then the beautiful but embittered Fox, jealous of Dog and Magpie's companionship, lures Magpie away to possible death in the desert. The eternal triangle, temptation in paradise, and fallen angels are three of many allusions that may occur to older readers of this fable. Hand-lettered text set askew requires readers to turn the book, while the use of symbolic colors (red for threat, cool greens, blues and browns for safety), add to the meaning. Themes include cooperation, coping with physical disabilities, friendship, jealousy, love, and loyalty. (CT)

# 24 Critical Literacy

**Christine H. Leland and Jerome C. Harste**

*Contributing reviewers included Beth Berghoff, Randy Bomer, Amy Seely Flint, Mitzi Lewison, and Karla Möller.*

---

**Criteria for Excellence**

- Stories that don't make difference invisible but rather explore *what differences make a difference*
- Stories that enrich our understanding of history and life by giving voice to those who traditionally have been silenced or marginalized—those we call "the indignant ones"
- Stories that show how people can begin to take action on important social issues
- Stories that explore dominant systems of meaning that operate in our society to position people and groups of people
- Stories that help us question why certain groups are positioned as "others"

---

## Understanding Differences That Make a Difference

★ Hesse, Karen. **Witness.** Scholastic, 2001.

Johnson, D. B. **Henry Hikes to Fitchburg.** Houghton Mifflin, 2000.

★ Lowry, Lois. **Gathering Blue.** Houghton Mifflin, 2000.

Roth, Susan L. **Happy Birthday, Mr. Kang.** National Geographic Society, 2001.

★ Spinelli, Jerry. **Stargirl.** Knopf, 2000.

Wiesner, David. **The Three Pigs.** Clarion, 2001.

## Giving Voice to "The Indignant Ones"

English, Karen. **Francie.** Farrar, Straus & Giroux, 1999.

Fradin, Dennis. **My Family Shall Be Free! The Life of Peter Still.** HarperCollins, 2001.

Grove, Vicki. **The Starplace.** Putnam, 1999.

Haskins, James, and Kathleen Benson. **Building a New Land: African Americans in Colonial America.** Illustrated by James E. Ransome. HarperCollins, 2001.

Meltzer, Milton. **There Comes a Time: The Struggle for Civil Rights.** Random House, 2001.

Noguchi, Rick, and Deneen Jenks. **Flowers from Mariko.** Illustrated by Michelle Reiko Kumata. Lee & Low, 2001.

Wiles, Deborah. **Freedom Summer.** Illustrated by Jerome Lagarrigue. Atheneum, 2001.

## Taking Social Action

Bartoletti, Susan Campbell. **Kids on Strike!** Illustrated with photographs. Houghton Mifflin, 1999.

Brumbeau, Jeff. **The Quiltmaker's Gift.** Illustrated by Gail de Marcken. Scholastic, 2000.

Fradin, Dennis, and Judith Fradin. **Ida B. Wells: Mother of the Civil Rights Movement.** Clarion, 2001.

Miller, William. **Rent Party Jazz.** Illustrated by Charlotte Riley-Webb. Lee & Low, 2001

Paladino, Catherine. **One Good Apple: Growing Our Food for the Sake of the Earth.** Houghton Mifflin, 1999.

★ Ringgold, Faith. **If a Bus Could Talk: The Story of Rosa Parks.** Simon & Schuster, 1999.

Wittlinger, Ellen. **Gracie's Girl.** Simon & Schuster, 2000.

## Understanding How Systems of Meaning in Society Position Us

Bunting, Eve. **Gleam and Glow.** Illustrated by Peter Sylvada. Harcourt, 2001.

★ Cronin, Doreen. **Click, Clack, Moo: Cows That Type.** Illustrated by Betsy Lewin. Simon & Schuster, 2000.

Konigsburg, E. L. **Silent to the Bone.** Atheneum, 2000.

★ Morrison, Toni, with Slade Morrison. **The Big Box.** Illustrated by Giselle Potter. Hyperion, 1999.

Skármeta, Antonio. **The Composition.** Illustrated by Alfonso Ruano. Translated by Elisa Amado. Groundwood, 2000.

Strasser, Todd. **Give a Boy a Gun.** Simon & Schuster, 2000.

Wittlinger, Ellen. **What's in a Name.** Simon & Schuster, 2000

## Examining Distance, Difference, and "Otherness"

Ancona, George. **Cuban Kids.** Marshall Cavendish, 2000.

Garden, Nancy. **Holly's Secret.** Farrar, Straus & Giroux, 2000.

Marx, Trish. **One Boy from Kosovo.** Photographs by Cindy Karp. HarperCollins, 2000.

Medina, Tony. **DeShawn Days.** Illustrated by R. Gregory Christie. Lee & Low, 2001.

★ Myers, Christopher. **Wings.** Scholastic, 2000.

Myers, Walter Dean. **Monster.** HarperCollins, 1999.

Smith, Frank Dabba. **My Secret Camera: Life in the Lodz Ghetto.**
    Photographs by Mendel Grossman. Harcourt, 2000.

★ Taylor, William. **Jerome.** Longacre, 1999.

Trueman, Terry. **Stuck in Neutral.** HarperCollins, 2000.

---

What's with all of this emphasis on *critical* stuff?" a friend asked recently. "You know that I read aloud to my class twice a day and introduce them to lots of great books. Isn't that enough?" This question is not an easy one to answer, since a simple yes or no belies the complexity of the issue. Of course, we would never suggest that reading lots of wonderful books to children isn't a good thing to do. At the same time, however, we also want to argue that reading aloud and even talking with children about books will not necessarily help them or us become critically literate. The way we talk about books and the kinds of questions we ask can make a big difference. Critical literacy isn't about books per se but about social practices that keep particular structures of knowing, believing, and being in place. It is about power relationships and how language positions others and us. It is about access and how language is used to welcome some children into "the literacy club" (Smith, 1988) while denying access to others. It is also about diversity—specifically, how issues of diversity force us to rethink our approach to how we share literature with children.

In response to the question of why we need to talk about *critical literacy* rather than just *literacy,* Gee (2001) offers the following explanation: "The forms of literacy learned in school usually do not lead to the urge or ability to think 'critically' in the sense of understanding how systems and institutions interrelate to help or harm people" (p. 2). Only when we read quality literature and then engage children in conversations about how systems of power are portrayed in books as helping or harming people do we begin to position children as critically literate beings. This role is further developed when these conversations lead children to make connections to their own lives and the part they might play in challenging inequities or supporting the status quo.

Within any given culture are many "different literacies associated with different domains of life" (Barton & Hamilton, 2000, p. 11). Similarly, any elementary school classroom has its own set of well-defined literacy practices and procedures. Providing time for reading aloud to children is a familiar literacy practice in many classrooms. This activity constitutes a distinct domain with its own set of rules and procedures. Children learn early on what to expect from their teacher during read-aloud time and what the teacher will expect from them during and after the experience. In many classrooms, the read-aloud domain is characterized by a focus on helping children enjoy books and make personal connections to them. Teachers frequently ask questions such as "What did you like about this story?" and "What was your favorite part?" Some teachers also see the read-aloud domain as an appropriate channel for assessing comprehension and for providing comprehension instruction.

But these aren't the only possibilities for the read-aloud domain. Teachers who want to reimagine it as an opportunity to engage children in critical conversations about power and social justice can help them begin to understand that every text is written from someone's perspective. Although authors often want readers to think they are neutral or unbiased, they can never separate themselves from the background of experiences and beliefs they bring to their texts. Asking questions such as "Whose story is this?" and "What would it be like if it had been written by a female [or male or young child or senior citizen] or an African American [or Hispanic or Asian] author" leads to conversations about perspective. Since critical literacy is about redesign, teachers might also ask children to identify other stories that need to be told about this subject in order to achieve a more equitable representation. Raising issues and moving on without taking the time to figure out what is going on and why is not productive in the long run. Although language always *means* something, it also always *does* something. Children should be invited to analyze texts and hypothesize about the work authors are doing and how they are using language to get this work done. Our belief is that in order to be truly literate for the twenty-first century, children need to do more than just read and respond superficially to text. They need to understand how language works, how to find and question the cultural story being told, and how to act on their new awareness.

One of the books we've included in our review is *Happy Birthday, Mr. Kang* (Roth, 2001). This is the story of Mr. Kang, a Chinese American who carries on the tradition of owning a caged *hua mei* bird. Every Sunday, Mr. Kang and his Chinese Americans friends meet with their birds at the Sara Delano Roosevelt Park in New York City. Tension arises when Sam, Mr. Kang's grandson, tells him that he shouldn't own a caged bird in the United States, the land of the free. Mr. Kang thinks about what Sam has said and, much to the surprise and horror of his fellow Chinese Americans, frees his *hua mei* bird. At one level, this book can be shared with children to build enjoyment for reading and increase comprehension; it is an interesting, beautifully illustrated story. Yet under the surface of the text is the unspoken question of who is an American and who gets to decide on the qualifications. Mr. Kang and his countrymen carry on their Chinese traditions, but Sam is becoming Americanized, and in this case, his attitude wins out. Should we be happy or sad? What social practices make immigrants feel that they must act like the dominant group in order to be seen as Americans? Why has Sam bought into these social practices? If we wanted to change things, what would we have to do? Rather than see diversity as a problem, we could see it as a strength. How might the diversity of our population lead to the betterment of our society?

From our perspective, even this set of conversations is not good enough. Children also need to be invited to think about how they are going to position themselves in the world. This often includes changing what they say as well as how they act. Critical literacy isn't something one takes up in sixth grade; it begins in kindergarten with books such as *Click, Clack, Moo: Cows That Type* (Cronin, 2000) and *The Big Box* (Morrison, 1999). These books, like the others included in this chapter, invite children to think about compelling social issues that might not be as obvious in other children's books. While any text can be (and should be) examined through a critical lens, the books described below lend themselves to the kind of conversations we have described. They all meet one or more of the criteria we developed for selecting books for our chapter in this edition of *Adventuring with Books*.

1. They don't make difference invisible but rather explore "what differences make a difference."

2. They enrich our understanding of history and life by giving voice to those who traditionally have been silenced or marginalized—those we call "the indignant ones."

3. They show how people can begin to take action on important social issues.

4. They explore dominant systems of meaning that operate in our society to position people and groups of people.

5. They help us question why certain groups are positioned as "others."

One new insight has evolved from our observation that most of the books meeting our criteria don't have neat or happy endings. They leave readers with a problem to think about long after the book has ended. But this lingering feeling of uneasiness is often what leads to social action. *Gracie's Girl* (Wittlinger, 2000), for example, leaves many unanswered questions about how to address the needs of homeless people. Is this an appropriate issue for children to consider? We think it's an issue for everyone—not only to consider, but also to try to solve.

Identifying books for critical discussions is a dangerous enterprise. On the one hand, if the books identified are not used in a critical fashion by teachers and children, then the whole business of building a critically literate consciousness is stopped in its tracks. On the other hand, some will think that using the books in the manner we suggest is equally dangerous. Using them in this way will change the social practice of how reading is taught and schooling is conducted. We, like other critical literacy educators, understand these concerns but believe that the issues raised by these books support conversations that are just too important not to have. But, in some ways, the critics are right. The books listed below are meant to support teachers in opening up space in their classrooms for the development of a very different literate being. Whether this being is "critically literate" depends on the social practices with which teachers surround these books, not just on the books themselves.

### References

Barton, D., & Hamilton, M. (2000). Literacy practices. In D. Barton, M. Hamilton, & R. Ivanic (Eds.), *Situated literacies: Reading and writing in context* (pp. 7–15). New York: Routledge.

Gee, J. (2001, April). *Critical literacy as critical discourse analysis.* In J. Harste & P. D. Pearson (Co-Chairs), (book of readings for) *Critical perspectives on literacy: Possibilities and practices,* preconvention institute conducted at the meeting of the International Reading Association, New Orleans.

Smith, F. (1988). *Joining the literacy club: Further essays into education.* Portsmouth, NH: Heinemann.

## Understanding Differences That Make a Difference

Clements, Andrew. **The Landry News.** Illustrated by Salvatore Murdocca. Simon & Schuster, 1999. ISBN 0-689-81817-3. 123 pp. (I) (See **19.2.**)

**24.1**   ★ Hesse, Karen. **Witness.** Scholastic, 2001. ISBN 0-439-27199-1. 161 pp. (ALL).

Fear and prejudice turn to violence in a small Vermont town in 1924 when the Ku Klux Klan moves in and successfully recruits members. The families of twelve-year-old Lenora, who is African American, and six-year-old Esther, who is Jewish, are targeted as many town members' racism and moral contradictions are revealed. Told in interconnecting first-person narratives from a cast of eleven townspeople, this story creates spaces for critical conversations about historical injustices, current prejudices, and the efficacy of neutrality in the face of racism. Rather than simplistically depicting good versus evil, Hesse encourages a deeper contemplation of the internal struggles that take place when people confront their own or others' hatred by developing relationships across barriers of prejudice. Forgoing either a happy or a tragic ending, Hesse skillfully gives readers room to examine horrific acts as well as consider the possibilities for change when hatred is replaced by humanity. (KM)

**24.2**  Johnson, D. B. **Henry Hikes to Fitchburg.** Houghton Mifflin, 2000. ISBN 0-395-96867-4. Unpaged. (ALL).

This book is critical only to the extent that teachers take time to consider the underlying issues it raises: Why is our society always on the go, thinking faster is better? What social practices keep this lifestyle in place? Who benefits? What do we as a society lose? How could we, like Henry (a.k.a. Thoreau), make a difference? The story line is simple: Two friends agree to go to Fitchburg to see the country. They choose different methods of travel based on their different approaches to life. It is, unfortunately, possible to reduce this charming little story to clichés such as "Take time to smell the roses," "Faster isn't necessarily better," and "Different strokes for different folks." The illustrations also don't provide a counterperspective. Nevertheless, in the hands of the right teacher, this book can rise above the level of "cute" to make a critical difference. One suggestion for doing this is to introduce the story with the explanatory note at the back of the book. (JCH)

Lester, Helen. **Hooway for Wodney Wat.** Illustrated by Lynn Munsinger. Houghton Mifflin, 1999. ISBN 0-395-92392-1. 32 pp. (P). (See **14.4.**)

**24.3**  ★ Lowry, Lois. **Gathering Blue.** Houghton Mifflin, 2000. ISBN 0-618-95581-9. 215 pp. (I).

Orphaned and physically flawed, Kira faces death in a futuristic society that shuns and discards the weak. When summoned to the Council of Guardians, Kira finds, much to her surprise, that the council has plans for her and her talent for weaving. While performing her new duties, Kira gathers "blue" (a metaphor for truth) and begins to question taken-for-granted notions of community, creativity, and values. Like her earlier book *The Giver* (Houghton Mifflin, 1993), *Gathering Blue* is a provocative tale that inspires contemplation long after the last page is turned. (JCH)

**24.4** Roth, Susan L. **Happy Birthday, Mr. Kang.** National Geographic Society, 2001. ISBN 0-7922-7723-6. Unpaged. (ALL).

Mr. Kang, a Chinese American, carries on the tradition of owning a caged *hua mei* bird. Every Sunday he and a group of his countrymen meet with their birds at the Sara Delano Roosevelt Park in New York City. Sam, Mr. Kang's grandson, doesn't believe that caged birds belong in the United States, the land of the free. Mr. Kang thinks about what Sam has said and, much to the surprise and horror of his fellow Chinese Americans, frees his *hua mei* bird. While on the surface this is a beautifully written and illustrated book, several critical issues just beg to be discussed: Who is an American? Who gets to decide who is an American? Sam has become Americanized, but should we be happy for him? What social practices make immigrants feel they must act like the dominant culture in order to be seen as American? How might our society benefit from the diversity that members from other cultures bring with them? (JCH)

**24.5** ★ Spinelli, Jerry. **Stargirl.** Knopf, 2000. ISBN 0-679-8837-0. 186 pp. (I).

"She was elusive. She was today. She was tomorrow. We did not know what to make of her. In our minds we tried to pin her to the corkboard like a butterfly, but the pin merely went through and away she flew" (p. 15). Who is she? Stargirl. Or at least that's what she calls herself today. She is new to town and new to Mica High. She is as strange as her pet rat and as mysterious as her name. The students are fascinated, but even the ones who love her urge her to become the very thing that can destroy her: normal. Fortunately, she manages to slip away as elusively as she arrived, the only difference being that lives have been touched and perspectives changed. This book is a celebration of identity, of nonconformity, and of differences that make a difference. *Stargirl* invites students to explore what our society means by "normal," as well as what life might be like if another definition of normal were commonplace; many students will want to explore the social practices operating in their own school. (JCH)

**24.6**  Wiesner, David. **The Three Pigs.** Clarion, 2001. ISBN 0-618-00701-6. Unpaged. (ALL).

In this delightful postmodern version of *The Three Little Pigs*, the story starts out traditionally, with the wolf discovering a house of straw and huffing and puffing and blowing the house down. The story takes an unexpected twist when the wolf also blows the first pig right off the page. Thus begins a refreshing tale of deconstruction, reconstruction, and liberation. When all three pigs get outside of the story, leaving the wolf trapped inside, they start a grand escapade by flying off on a paper airplane made from one of the folded pages of their story. On their adventure, they encounter other book characters, eventually bringing back a dragon they rescued along the way. This story presents an effective demonstration of how things don't have to be the way they've always been. (ML)

## Giving Voice to "The Indignant Ones"

★ Bridges, Ruby. **Through My Eyes.** Scholastic, 1999. ISBN 0-590-18923-9. 64 pp. (I). (See **2.4.**)

Corey, Shana. **You Forgot Your Skirt, Amelia Bloomer! A Very Improper Story.** Illustrated by Chesley McLaren. Scholastic, 2000. ISBN 0-439-07819-9. Unpaged. (P) (See **2.5.**)

**24.7**  English, Karen. **Francie.** Farrar, Straus & Giroux, 1999. ISBN 0-374-32456-5. 199 pp. (I).

English explores various levels of power and hope in this novel about twelve-year-old Francie, who endures social difficulty in a small Alabama town and longs for the day that she, her mother, and her brother will be able to join her father in Chicago. The story takes place during the Great Migration, and Francie's father has moved to Chicago for work. In his letters, however, he promises to find a way to bring his family to join him. Francie, who is good at school, begins tutoring an older boy who is then falsely accused of assaulting a white man. Through her compassion, Francie is drawn into a pervasively unjust social and judicial system. In the details of relationships, we see the ways in which unfairness and struggles for power are intricately complex, not simply matters of white over black, male over female. Well-crafted language makes this book valuable as a model for young writers as well. (RB)

**24.8**    Fradin, Dennis. **My Family Shall Be Free! The Life of Peter Still.** HarperCollins, 2001. ISBN 0-06-029328-4. 190 pp. (I).

This book recounts the life of Peter Still and his family. Born into slavery, Peter and his brother Levin are separated from their mother and sisters at the ages of six and seven, respectively. Deceived into believing they are being taken to their mother (who has escaped to freedom with their sisters), the two boys are sold to a plantation owner six hundred miles from their home. So begins the story of how Peter waits over half a century for his chance at freedom and to be reunited with his parents and sisters. Readers come to know Peter and Levin and how through years of backbreaking manual labor in cotton fields and brickyards, as well as abuse by slave owners, the two never give up the hope or ambition of being free. As they marry and have children of their own, their quest for freedom grows even stronger and more difficult. The accuracy of this text provides readers with useful information regarding the Underground Railroad and the work of abolitionists during the mid-1800s. (ASF)

Govenar, Alan, collector and editor. **Osceola: Memories of a Sharecropper's Daughter.** Illustrated by Shane W. Evans. Jump at the Sun/Hyperion, 2000. ISBN 0-7868-0407-6. 64 pp. (I). (See **2.24.**)

**24.9**    Grove, Vicki. **The Starplace.** Putnam, 1999. ISBN 0-399-23207-9. 224 pp. (I).

This novel for young adolescents is set in 1961 in Quiver, Oklahoma, where racial segregation has been an unquestioned way of life despite the 1954 *Brown v. Topeka* Supreme Court decision. Celeste is the first black student to enroll in Frannie's school, and the girls become friends. Without being heavy-handed, the narrative exposes the prejudice among the students, parents, and teachers at the school and recounts the story of the Klu Klux Klan's lynching of Celeste's grandfather. Discussions of this book may raise students' awareness that communities have a history that affects the present as well as ways of being that include and exclude certain people. Who do they accept into their social groups and who do they leave out? Why? Where did they learn their attitudes? Would other attitudes be more inclusive? (BB)

**24.10**    Haskins, James, and Kathleen Benson. **Building a New Land: African Americans in Colonial America.** Illustrated by James E. Ransome. HarperCollins, 2001. ISBN 0-06-029361-6. 44 pp. (I).

This book, part of the From African Beginnings series, describes the brutality of slave life in colonial America, including many uncelebrated aspects of slavery such as slave resistance, revolts, and rebellions. The slave economy is portrayed as it occurred in all of the colonies, not just in the South. Stories include those of individual slaves as well as lesser-known facts of the period, such as the existence of a thriving slave market on the spot that is now 60 Wall Street in New York City. *Building a New Land* strengthens the argument that this country could not have been built without forced black labor. *Bound for America: The Forced Migration of Africans to the New World* by James Haskins and Kathleen Benson (Lothrop, Lee & Shepard, 1999), another book in the same series, works well as a companion book. (ML)

Look, Lenore. **Love as Strong as Ginger.** Illustrated by Stephen T. Johnson. Atheneum, 1999. ISBN 0-689-81248-5. Unpaged. (ALL). (See **16.9.**)

**24.11**   Meltzer, Milton. **There Comes a Time: The Struggle for Civil Rights.** Random House, 2001. ISBN 0-375-80407-2. 180 pp. (I).

This historical account of the civil rights movement provides compelling stories and perspectives that will help older readers make sense of the need for social action. Meltzer traces the roots of racism back to slavery, describes the brutality of the segregated South in the first half of the 1900s, and chronicles the sit-ins, freedom rides, and other key events in the civil rights movement of the 1950s and 1960s. Children played an important role in this history, and Meltzer features them in the stories and black-and-white pictures. While he makes it clear that the civil rights movement was a partnership of blacks and whites, he also raises questions for readers to ponder. Why is power concentrated among the wealthiest members of society? Why do some people believe they can take the law into their own hands? How can a leader think racism is wrong but feel no moral passion to work for change? (BB)

Myers, Walter Dean. **Malcolm X: A Fire Burning Brightly.** Illustrated by Leonard Jenkins. HarperCollins, 2000. ISBN 0-06-027707-6. Unpaged. (P). (See **2.14.**)

**24.12**   Noguchi, Rick, and Deneen Jenks. **Flowers from Mariko.** Illustrated by Michelle Reiko Kumata. Lee & Low, 2001. ISBN 1-58430-032-9. Unpaged. (ALL).

After seeing the world through barbed wire for three years, Mariko's family eagerly awaits the end of World War II and the chance to leave the internment camp. Like hundreds of other families of Japanese origin, they were confined shortly after the attack on Pearl Harbor. "'Just because I look like the enemy doesn't mean I am,' Mariko told her mother angrily. 'I am American. I was born right here in Los Angeles.'" When they are finally allowed to leave, more challenges await this family. Mariko's father, who had owned a successful landscaping business, returns to find that his truck and tools have been stolen. He has to rummage through trashcans for broken tools that he can mend. This book provides a starting point for children to consider marginalization and what it means to be an American. In the wake of the tragedy of September 11, 2001, these conversations are needed more than ever. Pair *Flowers from Mariko* with *So Far from the Sea* by Eve Bunting (Clarion, 1998) for another perspective on Japanese internment camps. (CHL)

Pinkney, Andrea Davis. **Let It Shine: Stories of Black Women Freedom Fighters.** Illustrated by Stephen Alcorn. Harcourt, 2000. ISBN 0-15-201005-X. 107 pp. (I). (See **2.15.**)

Rockwell, Anne. **Only Passing Through: The Story of Sojourner Truth.** Illustrated by R. Gregory Christie. Knopf, 2000. ISBN 0-679-89186-2. Unpaged. (P). (See **2.17.**)

24.13   Wiles, Deborah. **Freedom Summer.** Illustrated by Jerome Lagarrigue. Atheneum, 2001. ISBN 0-689-83016-5. Unpaged. (ALL).

This is the heartfelt story of two young boys who discover that even though the Civil Rights Act was passed, attitudes and beliefs do not change overnight. Readers travel back to the summer of 1964 when, for the first time, the town swimming pool and other public places are open to all, regardless of skin color. As friends Joe and John Henry race to be the first to swim in water "so clear, you can jump to the bottom and open your eyes and still see," they are confronted head on with the power of discrimination: the swimming pool is being filled in with tar to prevent anyone from swimming. Illustrator Jerome Lagarrigue captures the anger and disappointment Joe and John Henry feel at this turn of events. Joe tries to comfort John Henry by suggesting that they go into town to buy ice pops at Mr. Mason's store.

Readers are left at the end of the story wondering whether John Henry will experience the same kind of discrimination in the store and why this type of incident was so common during this period of U.S. history. (ASF)

## Taking Social Action

**24.14**   Bartoletti, Susan Campbell. **Kids on Strike!** Illustrated with photographs. Houghton Mifflin, 1999. ISBN 0-395-88892-1. 208 pp. (I).

Are children being exploited today in ways similar to those during the industrial revolution in the United States? Bartoletti's historical account of children in the workforce is complemented by hundreds of authentic, gripping photographs of children at work on city streets, in coal mines, and in the garment industry. The images of the children and descriptions of their inhumane working conditions will raise questions about human nature, progress, and U.S. economic values. The author highlights the resiliency and collective power of children by recounting ways in which children have participated in acts of resistance and organized strikes, but she also asks readers to consider how effective their efforts were in changing their own lives. How does children's limited power compare to the power of others to silence and control them in the pursuit of wealth and progress? Who else gets "used" in our society? Pair this book with Russell Freedman's *Kids at Work* (Houghton Mifflin, 1994) for two perspectives on child labor. (BB)

**24.15**   Brumbeau, Jeff. **The Quiltmaker's Gift.** Illustrated by Gail de Marcken. Scholastic, 2000. ISBN 0-439-30910-7. Unpaged. (P).

A generous quiltmaker "with magic in her fingers" sews the most beautiful quilts in the world and then gives them away to the poor and needy. A greedy king, "his storehouse stuffed with treasures," yearns for something that will make him happy. Although he is sure a quilt will do it, the quiltmaker refuses, saying she will only make him a quilt if he gives away all of his treasures. In the end, the king does give away his treasures and in so doing learns several lessons from the quiltmaker, such as that true happiness comes not from hoarding material possessions but from letting them go in order to bring happiness to others. By taking social action to support others, the king finally finds his own happiness. Children might be asked to consider what might cause them to become greedy like the king. A question of this sort can help them begin to understand how they are being positioned as consumers by big corporations such as Nike, Coca Cola, Disney, and others. (JCH)

24.16    Fradin, Dennis, and Judith Fradin. **Ida B. Wells: Mother of the Civil Rights Movement.** Clarion, 2001. ISBN 0-395-89898-6. 178 pp. (I).

This book is a historical account of Ida B. Wells's life as she crusaded against the unlawful treatment of African Americans in the early part of the twentieth century. Through her writing and speaking, Ida championed voting rights for women, spoke out against lynching, and helped establish the National Association for the Advancement of Colored People (NAACP). She was outspoken in her beliefs, suggesting that those who did nothing to stop lynching and discriminatory practices were just as guilty as those who actually did them. By the time of her death in 1931, lynching had all but disappeared. The book includes striking photographs of Ida, her family, and her colleagues; pamphlets and other writings; and testaments to the horrors of lynching. Readers are invited to engage in important conversations about social action and how we all have the potential to make a difference. (ASF)

24.17    Miller, William. **Rent Party Jazz.** Illustrated by Charlotte Riley-Webb. Lee & Low, 2001. ISBN 1-58430-025-6. Unpaged. (ALL).

Rent parties originated in the South as a form of social action to help people in financial distress. They were most often held to protect African Americans from the harsh treatment of rent collectors who routinely changed the locks on doors and sold off people's belongings if they were even a day late paying the rent. Later, rent parties provided support for workers on strike and for people unjustly arrested. In this story, Sonny and his mother find themselves short on rent money after Mama is laid off from her job. While Sonny considers leaving school to get a job, a local musician helps him plan a rent party. As music spills out into the street, neighbors show up with food, coins, and hope for Sonny and his mother. The story emphasizes the power that is generated when community members come together to support one another. (CHL)

**24.18** Paladino, Catherine. **One Good Apple: Growing Our Food for the Sake of the Earth.** Houghton Mifflin, 1999. ISBN 0-395-85009-6. 48 pp. (I).

Despite the saying "What we don't know won't hurt us," this book points out how important it might be to know more about the foods we purchase and eat. *One Good Apple* explains how the pesticides and fertilizers used to grow perfect fruits and vegetables are toxic to our bodies and the balance of nature. The author's cogent, urgent argument for healthier agricultural practices raises many questions. Do the economic motivations of commercial farming justify the use of toxins? What are the alternatives? Whose needs are being met and whose are not? What can we do as consumers? Who is working on these issues? What other action is needed? (BB)

Polacco, Patrica. **The Butterfly.** Philomel, 2000. ISBN 0-399-23170-6. Unpaged. (I). (See **5.28.**)

**24.19** ★ Ringgold, Faith. **If a Bus Could Talk: The Story of Rosa Parks.** Simon & Schuster, 1999. ISBN 0-689-81892-0. Unpaged. (ALL).

Award-winning author Faith Ringgold uses brilliant acrylic illustrations and a simultaneously magical and realistic plot to tell the story of Rosa Parks. From the moment Marcie, a young African American girl, steps onto a strange, driverless bus, readers begin to learn about events in the life of Rosa Parks told in the voices of famous passengers, all of whom participated in the Montgomery Bus Boycott. Although criticized for its condensed form, this picture book contains a remarkable amount of information about Mrs. Parks. She is portrayed as a courageous political activist, and readers discover much about her life before and after the boycott. This book can open up conversations about the civil rights movement, segregation, and political activism. (ML)

Ryan, Pam Muñoz. **Esperanza Rising.** Scholastic, 2000. ISBN 0-439-12041-1. 262 pp. (I). (See **17.38.**)

**24.20** Wittlinger, Ellen. **Gracie's Girl.** Simon & Schuster, 2000. ISBN 0-689-82249-9. 186 pp. (I).

This is the story of an adolescent girl who learns that she is not the only person in the world who needs love and care. As Bess

Cunningham starts middle school, her main concerns are to become popular and to get more attention from her busy parents. Although she initially complains about her mother's commitment to a community soup kitchen and is reluctant to become a volunteer there, she becomes more involved after meeting and befriending Gracie, a homeless elderly woman. She finds a vacant building for Gracie to sleep in at night and enlists the help of her brother and friends in bringing her food. Instead of spending her time thinking of ways to be cool, Bess becomes more concerned with providing food and shelter for Gracie and others like her. Although the story doesn't have a happy ending, it provides many opportunities for starting conversations about how homeless people are positioned in society and what it means to take social action. (CHL)

## Understanding How Systems of Meaning in Society Position Us

24.21   Bunting, Eve. **Gleam and Glow.** Illustrated by Peter Sylvada. Harcourt, 2001. ISBN 0-15-202596-0. Unpaged. (P).

Set in a nonspecific country, Bunting's tale of wartime destruction and hope is narrated by eight-year-old Victor. With Papa in the Liberation Army, Victor describes the fears he and his sister share as they hear about burning villages from passing refugees. When Mama decides it's time for them to leave, Victor releases into the family pond two goldfish that a passing stranger had left with him, so that they can have a few more days of life. Reunited with Papa at the refugee camp, the family finally returns to find their home totally destroyed. Hope is renewed when they find their pond teeming with life, despite the destruction all around them. Accompanied by rich illustrations that depict both the joys of everyday life and the horrors of war, this book encourages discussion about topics that are common in the news but often not included as part of classroom discourse. (KM)

24.22   ★ Cronin, Doreen. **Click, Clack, Moo: Cows That Type.** Illustrated by Betsy Lewin. Simon & Schuster, 2000. ISBN 0-689-83213-3. Unpaged. (P).

Farmer Brown has a problem. His cows have found an old typewriter in the barn and are using it to make demands. They want electric blankets to keep them warm at night and are willing to withhold their milk until they get them. Even worse, the chickens have joined the cows in their strike. No more milk! No more eggs! The ducks are the not-so-neutral party. They carry the cows and chickens' message: a promise to turn over the typewriter in exchange for blankets. Once Farmer Brown capitulates, however, the ducks have a few demands of their own. The delightfully understated text and expressive illustrations add to the hilarity. This is a read-aloud must for teachers who wish to prompt conversations about literacy and power among even the youngest of readers. (JCH)

★ Fleischman, Paul. **Weslandia.** Illustrated by Kevin Hawkes. Candlewick, 1999. ISBN 0-763-60006-7. Unpaged. (ALL). (See **14.27.**)

★ Howard, Elizabeth Fitzgerald. **Virgie Goes to School with Us Boys.** Illustrated by E. B. Lewis. Simon & Schuster, 2000. ISBN 0-689-80076-2. Unpaged. (ALL). (See **6.9.**)

24.23   Konigsburg, E. L. **Silent to the Bone.** Atheneum, 2000. ISBN: 0-689-83601-5. 261 pp. (I).

*Silent to the Bone* involves readers in a mystery. Branwell, a thirteen-year-old boy, has been accused by a nanny of dropping his baby sister and putting her into a coma. He is being detained at the Clarion County Juvenile Behavioral Center and has been silent since the accident. Branwell's father, Dr. Z, asks his son's friend Conner to see if he can get Branwell to talk about what happened that fateful afternoon. Through the visits at the detention center, Conner and Branwell discover there are many ways to communicate without using speech. As clues are revealed, readers begin to see the many layers in the complex relationships between family members, friends, and peers. Students might be invited to consider why Branwell was unable to talk about what had happened that day. (ASF)

McGill, Alice. **Molly Bannaky.** Illustrated by Chris K. Soentpiet. Houghton Mifflin, 1999. ISBN 0-395-72287-X. Unpaged. (I). (See **19.22.**)

24.24   ★ Morrison, Toni, with Slade Morrison. **The Big Box.** Illustrated by Giselle Potter. Hyperion, 1999. ISBN 0-7868-0416-5. Unpaged. (P).

This outwardly humorous book has a haunting message about children who don't fit accepted definitions of what it means to be "normal." In poetic form, the authors tell the stories of Patty, Mickey, and Liza Sue, who live in a big brown box with doors that open "only one way." Because of the children's behavior, the adults who are responsible for them have concluded that they just can't handle their freedom and must be locked away. Although they are provided with lots of toys and "fun" items such as bean-bag chairs and Bubble Yum, the children are portrayed as prisoners who have been separated from their families and peers. The children's situation is reminiscent of students who are pulled out of regular education classes and segregated in special education classes because they don't meet the standard definition of what children at any specific age should be able to do. The story raises questions about the meaning of freedom and the fine line between maintaining order and destroying freedom. (CHL)

**24.25**  Skármeta, Antonio. **The Composition.** Illustrated by Alfonso Ruano. Translated by Elisa Amado. Groundwood, 2000. ISBN 0-88899-390-0. Unpaged. (I).

Chilean writer Skármeta, author of *Il Postino,* has created a children's book set in the dangerous environment of a dictatorship in an unidentified country. Pedro, a third grader, loves playing soccer with his friends. His parents listen to a "noisy" distant radio station every night to get news, which annoys Pedro. Although he's heard his parents talking about a dictatorship, the gravity of the situation he's living in doesn't touch Pedro until his friend Daniel's father is taken away by army troops. Soon after, a military captain comes to Pedro's classroom and has the students write on the topic "what my family does at night." Even though the book deals with a serious subject, Skármeta allows readers to experience tyranny from a child's perspective. This book can stimulate conversations about freedom, justice, and the double-edged power of writing to help and oppress in different situations. (ML)

**24.26**  Strasser, Todd. **Give a Boy a Gun.** Simon & Schuster, 2000. ISBN 0-689-81112-8. 128 pp. (I).

This multivoiced novel focuses squarely on gun violence and the social and personal issues facing adolescents. Two white middle-class students, Gary Searle and Brandon Lawlor, are both intelligent and exceptionally troubled. They move outside the circle of popular students at their high school. Gary's death by a self-inflicted bullet wound after he and Brandon terrorized the school with guns and homemade bombs is detailed in the opening pages. What follows is a story told by Gary's and Brandon's peers, teachers, and parents, as well as their own suicide notes, in interconnected interview segments. This is both a tragic story of the agony inflicted by students on peers and an indictment of gun availability and gun violence in the United States. This novel rings true. It can inspire important conversations about relationships and guns between adolescents and supportive adults. (KM)

24.27  Wittlinger, Ellen. **What's in a Name.** Simon & Schuster, 2000. ISBN 0-689-82551-X. 146 pp. (I).

"It's not just a name—it's an identity!" is more than simply the rallying cry of a group of wealthy citizens determined to change the name of the town of Scrub Harbor to the posh-sounding Folly Bay. This slogan also underlies the experiences of ten teens, each of whom narrates a chapter in this sophisticated novel. Through the backdrop of town politics, the characters struggle to understand their identities and how they are positioned both in school and in the community. The jock, the exchange student, the working-class kid, the immigrant, the brain—all are confronted with the realization of how much of who they are is constructed by others. This tale offers critical insights into how personal identity directly intersects larger social issues of class, language, sexual orientation, and race. (ML)

★ Woodson, Jacqueline. **Miracle's Boys.** Putnam, 2000. ISBN 0-399-23113-7. 133 pp. (I). (See **15.29.**)

## Examining Distance, Difference, and "Otherness"

24.28  Ancona, George. **Cuban Kids.** Marshall Cavendish, 2000. ISBN 0-7614-5077-7. 40 pp. (I).

*Cuban Kids* takes a sympathetic look at the lives of Cuban children, presenting an alternative to the typically negative image portrayed in the U.S. media. Snapshots from daily lives of children manage to make Cuba look both exotic and ordinary, so that students will notice differences while still recognizing that Cuban kids go to school, have friends and families, and like to have fun. These children, however, end their pledge of allegiance with *"Seremos como Che!—*We will be like Che!" A gentle mention of "American bosses" offers a window into U.S. complicity in Cuba's poverty, though the embargo is not discussed. It is impossible to look at Cuba without a political perspective, so examining this book alongside reports about Elian Gonzalez, for instance, provides an opportunity for critical reading. (JCH)

24.29   Garden, Nancy. **Holly's Secret.** Farrar, Straus & Giroux, 2000. ISBN 0-374-33273-8. 132 pp. (I).

Twelve-year-old Holly has a secret—her parents are gay. Rather than face a new round of painful jokes and secondhand gay bashing, she comes up with The Plan, a new identity for herself. She uses the opportunity of a family move to change into Yvette, the epitome of sophistication, normalcy, and grown-up femininity. But keeping her two moms a secret is no easy task and maybe not such a great idea in the first place. As the story unfolds, Holly becomes more enmeshed in the lies she tells her new friends, giving new credence to Shakespeare's admonition, "What a tangled web we weave when first we practice to deceive." Issues raised include identity, prejudice, homophobia, and the role that school plays in each. (JCH)

Grimes, Nikki. **My Man Blue: Poems.** Illustrated by Jerome Lagarrigue. Dial, 1999. ISBN 0-8037-2326-1. Unpaged. (P). (See **15.13.**)

24.30   Marx, Trish. **One Boy from Kosovo.** Photographs by Cindy Karp. HarperCollins, 2000. ISBN 0-688-17732-8. 24 pp. (I).

This book humanizes global conflicts and refugees by making them personal as well as political. Refugees are not "others" but people like us, complete with hopes and dreams. Global conflicts involve all of us, whether our response is to act or not. The story line focuses on Edi Fejzullahus, a twelve-year-old Albanian, and his family, who are driven from their home in Kosovo by Serbian soldiers. While the story ends with the family still in a refugee camp, their reunion with an uncle at the camp provides a note of hopefulness. An introductory chapter sets a historical and political context for questioning our society's practices and activities in the rest of the world. At issue are questions about the kind of people we wish to be, why we respond to some world crises and not others, what responsibilities we have to people in other nations, and how we might make a positive difference both locally and globally. (JCH)

**24.31**　Medina, Tony. **DeShawn Days.** Illustrated by R. Gregory Christie. Lee & Low, 2001. ISBN 1-58430-022-1. Unpaged. (P).

DeShawn Williams is a ten-year-old African American boy who shares his urban life in the "hood" with readers. Through the wonderful poetry and art of Tony Medina and R. Gregory Christie, we come to know DeShawn and his family. We meet his grandmother, who has "legs like an elephant's" and is in poor health. We meet his mother, "who's hardly ever home 'cause she works so hard and goes to college too," and his uncle Richie, who hugs DeShawn at night when bad dreams awaken him. DeShawn shares many aspects of his daily life with us. We learn that he is sometimes frightened by scary movies, graffiti, and watching the news on television. We share his grief when his beloved grandmother dies. Medina challenges stereotypical images of African American urban males and celebrates boys like DeShawn and the strong extended families that raise them. (CHL)

**24.32**　★ Myers, Christopher. **Wings.** Scholastic, 2000. ISBN 0-590-03377-8. Unpaged. (I).

Ikarus Johnson is a new kid in the neighborhood who is very different from everyone else—he has wings and flies. This Icarus-inspired character is relentlessly taunted and laughed at by other kids and ordered out of school by his teacher. The narrator, an extremely quiet girl who is also an outsider, feels a connection to Ikarus but remains silent for most of the book. After a policeman orders Ikarus off the top of a building, the girl wonders, "Could the policeman put him in jail for flying, for being too different?" This realization galvanizes her to action, and she finally shouts at the other kids to stop laughing at Ikarus and to leave him alone. The provocative collages of this award-winning author and illustrator augment the text and invite extended conversations about difference and diversity. (ML)

**24.33**　Myers, Walter Dean. **Monster.** HarperCollins, 1999. ISBN 0-06-028077-8. 288 pp. (I).

"The best time to cry is at night, when the lights are out and someone is being beaten up and screaming for help. That way even if you sniffle a little they won't hear you. If anybody knows that you are crying, they'll start talking about it and soon it'll be your turn to get beat up when the lights go out" (p. 1). Written in sixteen-year-old Steve Harmon's handwriting as he endures life in the Manhattan Detention Center, this powerful opening sets the stage for Steve's depiction of his life during his murder trial. Told with realistic intensity, Steve's story is personal and societal. Readers are forced to consider who Steve is and why he ended up where he is. Through flashbacks written as a movie script, readers share Steve's journey as he reveals his humanity in a narrative that parallels the prosecutor's depiction of him as a "monster." This book invites students to explore questions about justice and how it might be influenced by bias and notions of "otherness." (KM)

24.34    Smith, Frank Dabba. **My Secret Camera: Life in the Lodz Ghetto.** Photographs by Mendel Grossman. Harcourt, 2000. ISBN 0-15-20206-2. Unpaged. (I).

Mendel Grossman's life story is told in the afterword; the photographs he secretly took reveal the facts of life in the Lodz ghetto in Poland under Nazi rule. Teachers might want to begin with the afterword because Smith's fictionalized first-person narrative (presumably in Grossman's voice) almost takes away from the reality and historical significance of the document. The book serves as a painful reminder of the results of hate, prejudice, and, to some extent, our initial indifference and unwillingness to act to help others. While this story represents an extreme case of "othering," there are similar parallels in every classroom and playground that bear discussion with children. Students might be challenged to consider what kind of social action it will take to end the abusive treatment of other children that they witness or may participate in on a daily basis. (JCH)

24.35    ★ Taylor, William. **Jerome.** Longacre, 1999. ISBN 1-877-13529-1. 95 pp. (I/ Young Adult—graphic language).

Do you remember the Jenny Jones show on which a young man, on live television, named another young man he had a crush on? The result was that the young man he identified was so outraged that he hunted the first man down and killed him after the show. Should the first young man have kept his secret and killed himself instead? Is there any way to avoid such a violent ending? *Jerome* raises all of these issues as two friends, Marco and Katie, use e-mail, faxes, and online chats to come to grips with Jerome's suicide and his feelings for Marco. Given that as many as 33 percent of all teenage suicides are a result of adolescents failing to deal with issues of sexual identity, this book provides opportunities for conversation that teachers of upper elementary and middle school students cannot afford to overlook. Whether these discussions are seen as an exercise in preventing suicide or in helping adolescents develop critical literacy and emotional intelligence, they are crucial to the health and well-being of young people. (JCH)

**24.36**   Trueman, Terry. **Stuck in Neutral.** HarperCollins, 2000. ISBN 0-06-028519-2. 114 pp. (I).

*Stuck in Neutral* is the life history of a genius told from the perspective of the genius himself. Shawn is a fourteen-year-old with cerebral palsy. Since he cannot communicate, he has been diagnosed as profoundly developmentally disabled. As a result, he is at the mercy of everyone. His age-mates make fun of him, and his family members either resent the effect of his illness on the family or feel so sorry for him that they contemplate having him euthanized regardless of the cost to them personally. This story leaves both adults and children feeling rather stunned. Virtually anyone who experiences this book will interact with disabled people differently and change the language they use to describe them. Several critical issues are raised, including the definition of "normal" and who gets to decide what normal is. (JCH)

# Author Index

# Illustrator Index

# Subject Index

# Title Index

# Editors

**Amy A. McClure** is Rodefer Professor of Education and director of the early childhood program at Ohio Wesleyan University, where she teaches courses in children's literature and early literacy and supervises student teachers. She also coordinates the university's honors program. McClure is the coauthor or coeditor of several books, including *Sunrises and Songs: Reading and Writing Poetry in an Elementary Classroom; Books That Invite Talk, Wonder and Play with Literature; Inviting Children's Responses to Literature;* and *Through the Eyes of a Child.* She is also the author of numerous book chapters and articles and has presented at conferences throughout the United States and the world. She is past-president of the Children's Literature Assembly of NCTE, IRA's Children's Literature and Reading Special Interest Group, and the Ohio International Reading Association. She is currently co-chair of the selection committee for the NCTE Award for Excellence in Poetry for Children. McClure was selected NCTE's Promising Young Researcher, and her dissertation won Kappa Delta Pi's Outstanding Dissertation of the Year Award. She also received Ohio Wesleyan's Herbert Welch Meritorious Teaching Award. She lives in Dublin, Ohio, with her husband and two teenage daughters.

**Janice V. Kristo** is professor of education in literacy at the University of Maine. She received her master's degree from Teachers College at Columbia University and her Ph.D. from the University of Connecticut. Her areas of specialization are children's literature, reading, and integrated literacy learning, and she has extensive instructional experience in these areas at the preservice and graduate levels. Her current research interest is nonfiction literature and its use in the classroom. Kristo has served on NCTE's Children's Literature Assembly (CLA) advisory board and is past-president of IRA's Children's Literature and Reading Special Interest Group. She has also served as chair of CLA's Standing Committee on Notable Children's Trade Books in the Language Arts (K–8). Kristo currently serves on the selection committee of the NCTE Award for Excellence in Poetry for Children. In 2000 she was co-recipient with Rosemary A. Bamford of the University of Maine's Presidential Research and Creative Achievement Award. Kristo is coauthor or coeditor of several texts, including *Checking Out Nonfiction K–8: Good Choices for Best Learning,* as well as author of numerous articles and chapters on literacy learning. She currently serves on the editorial review board of the *Journal of Children's Literature.*

# Contributors

**Deborah Aizenstain,** upper-grade teacher at P.S. 24, Magnet School of Authors and Illustrators, New York, New York

**Evelyn Alessi,** kindergarten/second-grade multiage teacher, Belfast Central School, Belfast, New York

**Andrew H. Allen,** fifth-grade teacher, Horace Mann Laboratory School, Salem, Massachusetts

**Erin Allen,** fourth-grade teacher, Meroby Elementary School, Mexico, Maine

**Margaret Amberg,** kindergarten teacher, Dousman, Wisconsin

**Be Astengo,** librarian, Youth Services Department, Alachua County Library District, Gainesville, Florida

**Rosemary A. Bamford,** professor of literacy, University of Maine, Orono

**Beth Berghoff,** chair of undergraduate teacher education, Indiana University–Purdue University Indianapolis

**Margaret W. Bierden,** media specialist, Woonsocket, Rhode Island

**Randy Bomer,** assistant professor, University of Texas at Austin

**Jane Borden,** first-grade teacher, Tippecanoe School for the Arts and Humanities

**Jane A. LoBosco,** second-grade teacher, Queens, New York

**Joan C. Bownas,** retired third-grade teacher, Westerville, Ohio

**Donna E. Brady,** reading grant coordinator, Horace Mann Laboratory School, Salem, Massachusetts

**Darlene G. Bressler,** professor of language arts and literacy, Houghton College, Houghton, New York

**Jo Ann Brewer,** professor, University of Massachusetts Lowell

**Theda Buckley,** third-grade teacher, Myra Terwilliger Elementary School, Gainesville, Florida

**Diane E. Bushner,** associate professor of education, Salem State College, Salem, Massachusetts

**Linda Button,** assistant professor, University of Northern Colorado, Greeley

**E. Sharon Capobianco,** adjunct instructor, Salve Regina University, Newport, Rhode Island

**Colleen Clester,** fifth/sixth-grade looping teacher, Pioneer Middle School, Yorkshire, New York

**Jeri A. Clouston,** special education teacher, Happy Corner Elementary School, Ell-Saline #307 School District, Salina, Kansas

**Judith Cole,** children's librarian, teacher, freelance writer, and environmentalist, Milwaukee Public Schools

**Coralea Collins,** graduate, Otterbein College, Westerville, Ohio

**Jane Cook,** staff development specialist, EASTCONN, Willimantic, Connecticut

**Carol Cribbet-Bell,** teacher-librarian, Carrillo Magnet School, Tucson (Arizona) Unified School District

**Caryl Gottlieb Crowell,** bilingual primary grade teacher, Borton Primary Magnet School, Tucson (Arizona) Unified School District

**Ellen Crozier,** former classroom teacher, Milwaukee Public Schools, and program implementer, Golda Meir School for the Gifted and Talented, Milwaukee, Wisconsin

Culturally diverse three-, four-, five-, and six-year-olds, their parents, caregivers, and teachers who attend Thursday morning story hours at the Boulder Public Library, Boulder, Colorado

**Lisa Dapoz,** first-grade teacher, Emerson Elementary Magnet School, Westerville, Ohio

**Jane M. DeAngelis,** children's librarian, public library, southeastern Wisconsin

**Jodi Dodds Kinner,** doctoral student, Kent State University, and reading coordinator, Chicago Public Schools, Illinois

**Linda K. Duckstein,** special education and Title I teacher, Annie Vinton Elementary School, Mansfield, Connecticut

**Carol A. Dunham,** fourth-grade teacher, Gwendolyn Brooks Elementary School, DeKalb, Illinois

**Janice Elie,** Title I teacher, Webster School, Auburn, Maine

**Kelly Emerson,** fourth- and fifth-grade language arts teacher, Eastford Elementary School, Eastford, Connecticut

**Shirley B. Ernst,** professor of reading/language arts, Eastern Connecticut State University, Willimantic

**Mary Fusaro Evans,** fourth-grade teacher, Fairmount School, Bangor, Maine

**Pamela K. Evans,** third-grade teacher, Stewart Elementary School, Salina (Kansas) #305 School District

**Amy Seely Flint,** assistant professor, Indiana University, Bloomington

**Patricia Flint,** school librarian, Cascade Brook School, Farmington, Maine

**Barbara J. Franczyk,** eighth-grade English teacher, Maple Dale School, Fox Point, Wisconsin, and instructor, University of Wisconsin–Milwaukee

**Abby E. Franklin,** second-grade teacher, Bow Lake Elementary School, SeaTac, Washington

**Evelyn B. Freeman,** professor and director, School of Teaching and Learning, The Ohio State University, Columbus

**Marianne Fuscaldo,** first-grade teacher, P.S. 24, Flushing, New York

**Michelina M. Gannon,** sixth-grade teacher, Queens, New York

**Sabrina Gioieni,** fifth-grade teacher, P.S. 117, Briarwood, New York

**Cyndi Giorgis,** associate professor, School of Education, University of Nevada, Las Vegas

**Joan I. Glazer,** professor of education, Rhode Island College, Providence

**Melissa Gonzalez,** first-grade teacher, Brooklyn, New York

**Mary Lee Griffin,** assistant professor of education, Wheaton College, Norton, Massachusetts

**TruDee Griffin,** reading enrichment teacher, Roscoe Middle School, Roscoe, Illinois

**Danielle Grunenwald Gruhler,** doctoral student, Kent State University, and third-grade teacher, Solon, Ohio

**Teresa H. Gunn,** kindergarten teacher, Ansbach American Elementary School, Ansbach, Germany

**Kellie Hale,** former middle school language arts teacher, Arlington, Texas

**Katrina Willard Hall,** kindergarten teacher, Kimball Wiles Elementary School, Gainesville, Florida, and doctoral candidate, University of Florida

**Marjorie R. Hancock,** associate professor in the Department of Elementary Education, Kansas State University, Manhattan

**Carol W. Harris,** second-grade teacher, Wellsville Elementary School, Wellsville, New York

**Bud Harris,** fifth-grade teacher, Coal Creek Elementary, Louisville, Colorado

**Jerome C. Harste,** distinguished professor, Martha Lea and Bill Armstrong Chair in Teacher Education, Indiana University, Bloomington

**Mary Lynn Heimback,** professional development specialist, Tri-Rivers Educational Computer Association, Ohio

**Vicki Heisler,** fifth-grade teacher, Meeker Elementary, Greeley, Colorado

**Thomas H. Herman,** third-grade teacher, Delevan Elementary School, Delevan, New York

**Karen S. Hildebrand,** library media director, Dempsey Middle School, Delaware City Schools, Delaware, Ohio

**Nancy S. Hill,** primary teacher, Milwaukee (Wisconsin) Public Schools

**Kate Hunnicutt,** fifth-grade gifted and talented teacher, Grand Prairie, Texas

**Teresa Hurtares,** fourth-grade teacher, P.S. 214, Flushing, New York

**Jan Johnson,** Eastern Elementary School, Lexington, Ohio

**Nancy J. Johnson,** professor, Western Washington University, Bellingham

**Mary Ann Jordan,** Staffs the Teacher Center at JHS 185, District 25, Flushing, New York, and adjunct instructor, Queens College, CUNY

**Hye Sook Kang,** first-grade teacher, Heights School, Roslyn, New York

**Wendy C. Kasten,** professor of curriculum and instruction, Kent State University, Kent, Ohio

**Janet L. Kellogg,** first-grade teacher, Northview Elementary School, Manhattan-Ogden (Kansas) #383 School District

**Sue T. Kennedy,** Woodland Elementary School, Mansfield, Ohio

**Deise Kenny,** sixth-grade teacher, P.S. 164, Flushing, New York

**Rebecca Kerr,** second-grade teacher, Rumford Elementary, Rumford, Maine

**Janine A. King,** middle school language arts teacher, Brighton School, Lynnwood, Washington

**Traci A. Kozak-Krist,** second/third-grade teacher, Letchworth Central School, Gainesville, New York

**Linda Leonard Lamme,** professor of education, School of Teaching and Learning, University of Florida

**Elisa M. LaSota,** first-grade teacher, Horace Mann Laboratory School, Salem, Massachusetts

**Lola Lauri,** third-grade teacher, Queens, New York

**Yi-chuan Lee,** doctoral student, University of Northern Colorado, Greeley

**Barbara A. Lehman,** professor of teaching and learning, The Ohio State University, Mansfield

**Christine H. Leland,** associate dean for academic affairs, Indiana University–Purdue University Indianapolis

**Mitzi Lewison,** assistant professor, Indiana University, Bloomington

**Mary E. Lingenfelter,** third-grade reading and language arts teacher, Fillmore Central School, Fillmore, New York

**Kathy Lohse,** bilingual primary grade teacher, Borton Primary Magnet School, Tucson (Arizona) Unified School District

Evelyn Lolis, graduate student, Queens College, CUNY

Ruth McKoy Lowery, assistant professor of education, School of Teaching and Learning, University of Florida, Gainesville

Karen Moroney, fourth-grade teacher, Brooklyn, New York

Diane Masla, librarian, Youth Services Department, Alachua County Library District, Gainesville, Florida

Joan Masotti, multicultural music program teacher, kindergarten to fifth grade, Throgs Neck, Queens, New York

Susan J. Matthews, Royal Manor Elementary School, Gahanna, Ohio

MaryKate McDonald, second-grade teacher, Baldwin, Long Island, New York

Sarah McIntosh, fifth-grade teacher, Coal Creek Elementary, Louisville, Colorado

Carol McKinley, Hardin Central Elementary School, Kenton, Ohio

Heidi Mehringer-Macina, language arts consultant, Canterbury Public Schools, Canterbury, Connecticut

Judy Minger, fifth-grade teacher, Coal Creek Elementary, Louisville, Colorado

Karla J. Möller, assistant professor, Indiana University, Bloomington

Darice D. Mullen, third/fourth-grade multiage teacher, Belfast Central School, Belfast, New York

Patricia Munsch, fifth-grade teacher, Springfield Gardens, Queens, New York

Marcia F. Nash, professor of literacy education, University of Maine at Farmington

Mayra Sánchez Negrón, first-grade teacher, La Escuela Fratney, Milwaukee, Wisconsin

Gayle Nelson, second-grade teacher, Forest Glen Elementary School, Glen Ellyn, Illinois

Terry Nicki, fifth-grade teacher, Coal Creek Elementary, Louisville, Colorado

Madeline F. Nixon, professor, Department of Elementary Education, Rhode Island College, Providence

Helen A. O'Donnell, language arts and reading specialist, Ansbach Elementary School, Ansbach, Germany

William C. O'Donnell, second-grade teacher, Ansbach Elementary School, Ansbach Germany

Michael F. Opitz, professor of elementary education and reading, University of Northern Colorado, Greeley

Peggy S. Oxley, second-grade teacher, St. Paul's School, Westerville, Ohio

Michele A. Oxman, assistant principal, Luther Burbank Elementary School, Milwaukee, Wisconsin

Erika M. Padilla, sixth-grade teacher, P.S. 24, Flushing, New York

Lea Paliota, gifted and talented teacher, Maine School Administrative District #43

Laura E. Parkerson, media specialist, Henry Barnard Laboratory School, Providence, Rhode Island

Candis M. Penley, third-grade teacher, Weatherbee School, Hampden, Maine

Donna Peters, Elida Middle School, Elida, Ohio

Susan Pidhurney, multiage first- and second-grade teacher, Knowlton School, Ellsworth, Maine

Elizabeth M. Redondo, Safford Elementary School, Tucson (Arizona) Unified School District

**Rebecca A. Reid,** Granville Elementary School, Granville, Ohio

**Denise Richard,** fourth-grade teacher, Rumford Elementary, Rumford, Maine

**Mirella Rizzo,** fifth-grade teacher, P.S. 214, Flushing, New York

**Laurie Robilotto,** fourth-grade teacher, P.S. 166, District 20, Long Island City, New York

**Roseanne A. Russo,** manager of youth services, Alachua County Library District, Gainesville, Florida

**Debbie Savage,** kindergarten teacher, P. K. Yonge Developmental Research School, University of Florida, Gainesville

**Patricia L. Scharer,** associate professor in language, literacy, and culture, The Ohio State University, Columbus

**Elizabeth Schneider,** sixth-grade teacher, Forest Hills, New York

**Susan K. Semer,** Van Wert Middle School, Van Wert, Ohio

**Nancy Rankie Shelton,** fourth-grade teacher, Charles W. Duval Elementary School, Gainesville, Florida, and doctoral candidate, School of Teaching and Learning, University of Florida, Gainesville

**Patricia Shimchick,** language arts consultant, Windham Public Schools, Windham, Connecticut

**Yvonne Siu-Runyan,** professor emerita, University of Northern Colorado, Greeley

**Stacey R. Slater,** sixth-grade reading and language arts teacher, Hadley Junior High School, Glen Ellyn, Illinois

**Glenna Sloan,** professor, Queens College, CUNY

**Elizabeth Bridges Smith,** associate professor, Otterbein College, Westerville, Ohio

**Katrina Smits,** bilingual intermediate grade teacher, Carrillo Magnet School, Tucson (Arizona) Unified School District

**Anna Sperring,** multiage primary teacher, P. K. Yonge Developmental Research School, University of Florida, Gainesville, and doctoral student, University of Florida, Gainesville

**Andrew W. Stephenson,** sixth-grade teacher, Pemetic School, Southwest Harbor, Maine

**John Warren Stewig,** professor, Department of Curriculum and Instruction, University of Wisconsin–Milwaukee

**Anne Sylvan,** Columbus Public Schools, Columbus, Ohio

**Sylvia Tag,** librarian, Wilson Library, Western Washington University, Bellingham

**Lori L. Thompson,** Madison South Elementary School, Mansfield, Ohio

**Kathy Tomasino,** first-grade teacher, Oakwood Primary School, Huntington, New York, and adjunct instructor, Queens College, CUNY

**Carl M. Tomlinson,** professor of literacy education, Northern Illinois University, DeKalb

**Jennifer Tress,** reading teacher, Horace Mann Laboratory School, Salem, Massachusetts

**Maria Tsahalis,** first-grade teacher, P.S. 24, Flushing, New York

**Marcia H. Tyrrell,** library media specialist, Delevan Elementary School, Delevan, New York

**Sylvia M. Vardell,** professor of children's literature, Texas Woman's University, Denton

**Pat Villa,** third-grade teacher, Billie Martinez Elementary, Greeley, Colorado

**Judy Vole,** children's librarian, Boulder Public Library, Boulder, Colorado

**Scott Vonderheide,** school media specialist, Wellsville Elementary School, Wellsville, New York

**Nancy M. Walters,** first-grade teacher, Fillmore Central School, Fillmore, New York

**Marilyn J. Ward,** associate professor of education, Carthage College, Kenosha, Wisconsin

**Lillian Webb,** retired teacher of intermediate gifted children, Worthington Schools, Worthington, Ohio

**Peg Welch,** third-grade teacher, Downeast School, Bangor, Maine

**W. Quinn White,** Taylor University, Fort Wayne, Indiana

**Phyllis Whitin,** assistant professor of elementary education, Wayne State University, Detroit, Michigan

**David J. Whitin,** professor of elementary education, Wayne State University, Detroit, Michigan

**Karen S. Wilson,** fifth-grade teacher, Pleasant Prairie, Wisconsin

**Sandip L. Wilson,** curriculum coordinator, Machias, Maine

**Sherry L. Wilson,** sixth-grade teacher, Pioneer Middle School, Yorkshire, New York

**Shelby Wolf,** associate professor, University of Colorado at Boulder

**Linda Woolard,** third/fourth-grade teacher, William E. Miller Elementary, Newark City Schools, Newark, Ohio

**Daniel Woolsey,** professor of literature for children and adolescents, Houghton College, Houghton, New York

**Myra Zarnowski,** professor, Department of Elementary and Early Childhood Education, Queens College, CUNY